03/19.

Barney Hoskyns is the co-founder and editorial director of online music-journalism library Rock's Backpages (www.rocksbackpages.com). He is the author of several books, including *Across the Great Divide* (1993), *Waiting for the Sun* (1996) and *Hotel California* (2006). Between 1996 and 1999 he was the US correspondent for *Mojo*. He has contributed to *Uncut*, the *Guardian*, *GQ*, the *Independent* and other UK publications, and has written for *Rolling Stone*, *GQ*, *Spin* and *Harper's Bazaar* in the US. He lives in London.

@BarneyHoskyns

Further praise for *Lowside of the Road*:

'A comprehensive, engaging biography. Hoskyns gives us a more complete answer to the question "Who is Tom Waits?" than anyone has up to this point.' David Rubien, *San Francisco Chronicle*

'Hoskyns' superlative overview of one of America's major (though idiosyncratic) popular artists will likely stand as the best book on his life.' Bill Walker, *Library Journal*

'Mr Hoskyns' guile, dogged work and Nick Hornby-esque likeability place him a notch above the average rock biographer. His book lights up and whirls like one of the greasy carnival rides in Mr Waits' own sprawling oeuvre.' Dwight Garner, *New York Times*

'It's about time Tom Waits received biographical homage from a rock writer of Hoskyns' stature.' Stephen Poole, *Guardian*

'Wonderfully insightful the songs and their origins.' Tim

'The always awe-inspiring Hoskyns has performed a minor miracle
. . . *Lowside* pulls off the trick of providing an entirely fresh read . . .
As page-turningly compelling as any bestselling novel.' Jason Draper,
Record Collector

'Hoskyns builds his story from dozens of sources and archival interviews . . . [He] commendably shadow-boxes with the Waits
myth, revealing some real flesh underneath the artifice.' Erik
Himmelsbach, *Los Angeles Times*

---

by the same author

SAY IT ONE TIME FOR THE BROKENHEARTED: COUNTRY SOUL IN THE
AMERICAN SOUTH

PRINCE: IMP OF THE PERVERSE

JAMES DEAN: SHOOTING STAR

FROM A WHISPER TO A SCREAM: HEARING VOICES IN POPULAR MUSIC

MONTGOMERY CLIFT: BEAUTIFUL LOSER

ACROSS THE GREAT DIVIDE: THE BAND AND AMERICA

THE LONELY PLANET BOY: A POP ROMANCE

WAITING FOR THE SUN: STRANGE DAYS, WEIRD SCENES AND THE
SOUND OF LOS ANGELES

BENEATH THE DIAMOND SKY: HAIGHT-ASHBURY 1965–1970

GLAM! BOWIE, BOLAN AND THE GLITTER ROCK REVOLUTION

THE MULLET: HAIRSTYLE OF THE GODS (WITH MARK LARSON)

ARTHUR LEE: ALONE AGAIN, OR

THE SOUND AND THE FURY: A ROCK'S BACKPAGES READER (EDITOR)

RAGGED GLORIES: CITY LIGHTS, COUNTRY FUNK, AMERICAN MUSIC

OZZY OSBOURNE: A ROCK'S BACKPAGES READER (EDITOR)

HOTEL CALIFORNIA: SINGER-SONGWRITERS AND COCAINE

COWBOYS IN THE LA CANYONS

ROCK OF AGES: LED ZEPPELIN IV

TRAMPLED UNDER FOOT: THE POWER AND EXCESS OF LED ZEPPELIN

SMALL TOWN TALK: BOB DYLAN, THE BAND, VAN MORRISON, JANIS JOPLIN,
JIMI HENDRIX & FRIENDS IN THE WILD YEARS OF WOODSTOCK

NEVER ENOUGH: A WAY THROUGH ADDICTION

Lowside of the Road

A Life of Tom Waits

BARNEY HOSKYNS

FABER & FABER

First published in the UK in 2009
by Faber & Faber Limited
Bloomsbury House, 74–77 Great Russell Street
London WC1B 3DA
This paperback edition published in 2019

Typeset by Faber & Faber Ltd
Printed and bound by CPI Group (UK) Ltd, Croydon, CR0 4YY

The right of Barney Hoskyns to be identified as author of this work has
been asserted in accordance with Section 77 of the Copyright,
Designs and Patents Act 1988

A CIP record for this book
is available from the British Library

ISBN 978- 0–571–35133–6

For Tom Fry, who turned me on to Captain Beefheart – and so much more – at the tender age of twelve. Friends reunited by Brian Wilson after twenty-seven years.

And in fond memory of Rob Partridge.

Contents

Illustrations

"You can't really be too concerned with what people think of you. You're on your own adventure of growth and discovery. Like Charles Bukowski said, 'People think I'm down on Fifth and Main at the Blarney Stone, throwing back shooters and smoking a cigar, but really I'm on the top floor of the health club with a towel in my lap, watching Johnny Carson.' So it's not always good to be where people think you are, especially if you subscribe to it as well . . . which is easily done, because then you don't have to figure out who you are, you just ask somebody else."

(Tom Waits to the author, 24 April 1985)

Prologue

The Only Thing Worse than Being Misunderstood

> *"I do believe in the mysteries of things, about myself and the things I see. I enjoy being puzzled and arriving at my own incorrect conclusions."*
>
> (Tom Waits to Mark Rowland, *Musician*, October 1987)

I'm guessing the woman was a Jewish-American Princess, though I've no idea how cold she was on her honeymoon.* She certainly had a frosty look on her face as she did an about-turn and marched back towards me. Maybe not frosty, exactly; more plain scared. For she'd just let slip that Tom Waits had declined the chance to top one of the bills at California's Coachella Festival. The little nugget had popped out and, as she trotted away, it dawned on her what she'd done.

"Hey," she said in a palpably anxious voice as she returned, a clammy palm placed on my forearm. "Don't get me in trouble with that Coachella story, you hear?"

I beg your pardon? You'd think she'd whispered that Waits was cheating on his wife, not that he'd turned down the organizers of a frigging rock festival. What did it matter if people knew? To her, apparently, it mattered a lot. The mild panic on the woman's face told me something of what I was up against simply in *attempting* to write a book about Tom Waits.

* Cf. "Colder than a Jewish-American Princess on her honeymoon": an expression used frequently by Waits in his mid-seventies live shows.

A few weeks later, Keith Richards sent word from on high that he was happy to talk about working with Waits on *Rain Dogs* and *Bone Machine*. But the offer was summarily withdrawn because Tom – or more accurately, "Tom and Kathleen" (Brennan, Waits' wife) – had been apprised of my request. The apparent perversity of not wishing one of rock's undisputed greats to go on the record with his love and admiration confounded me. It also got me thinking about the Waitses' real agenda in stymieing biographers past, present, and future.

At various points during two years of researching Waits' life and work I had to stop and ask myself, "Do I actually have the right to write a book about Tom Waits?" It's tough not to personalize the rebuffs, not just from the Waits camp but from certain acquaintances and collaborators. Tough, too, not to see their polite requests that such people not consort with me as covert censorship.

"What do you think they're afraid of?" friends asked me. Generally what I said was something like: "I don't *know* what they're afraid of. I think they know I'm not Kitty Kelley or Albert Goldman or J. Randy Taraborrelli – or Nick Broomfield or A. J. Weberman or Rupert Pupkin. There's not a lot of dirt to dig up anyway. So Waits got loaded with Rickie Lee Jones and Chuck E. Weiss. So they defaced lawn jockeys in Bel Air and got into a spat with some cops at Duke's coffee shop. So what." Usually I paused before adding: "Actually I don't think they're afraid of *anything*. They just don't want a book out there that, in some cod-Freudian, *ad hominem* way, reduces Waits to the sum of his life experiences. And I have some sympathy with that; in fact, I have total respect for such a stance."

My friend Jeb Loy Nichols reminded me of how the artist Joseph Cornell (one of Waits' minor heroes) resisted all attempts at investigation of his life. For the eccentric Cornell – subject of Deborah Solomon's biography *Utopia Parkway* – the only thing worse than being misunderstood was . . . *being understood*. And as Bob Dylan – one of Waits' *major* heroes – once said, "What's so bad about being misunderstood?"

For decades Waits has played an elaborate game with the media, hiding behind the persona he projects. To the question "Will the real Tom Waits please stand up?" there is no real answer. "Tom Waits" is as much a character created for his fans as it is a real man behind the closed doors of family life. "Am I Frank Sinatra or am I Jimi Hendrix?" he said when I asked him if his persona had ever merged with his actual personality. "Or am I Jimi Sinatra? It's a ventriloquist act, everybody does one."

But, I countered, some artists are more honest about it being an act than others. We aren't supposed to think Neil Young is doing an act. "I don't know if honesty is an issue in show business," Waits retorted. "People don't care whether you're telling the truth or not, they just want to be told something they don't already know. Make me laugh or make me cry, it doesn't matter. If you're watching a really bad movie and somebody turns to you and says, 'You know, this is a true story,' does it improve the film in any way? Not really. It's still a bad movie."

Reading this quote again, I think that Waits a) should be right but b) is being disingenuous. He knows full well that fans and critics alike experience rock music as, in some sense, communing with an artist's soul. Robert Christgau, "dean of rock critics", called this "the idea that the artist's persona is their fundamental creation". Put another way, fans of auteur-artists such as Bob Dylan and Neil Young have long sought to establish a correspondence between their life and their work. Heritage rock mags are predicated on rooting out the "stories" behind albums such as *Blood on the Tracks* or *Tonight's the Night*. There's an inordinate amount of investment in the notion of the artist as suffering seer or tortured poet.

"I spend my entire time trying to explain to people that I'm a creative writer," P. J. Harvey – a hardcore Waits fan – told me. "People jump to conclusions, and I can understand it, because if

I'm very interested in an artist – whether it's Neil Young, Bob Dylan, whoever – I want to imagine that those stories are true. But I think also that when I listen to those writers I project my own stories into their songs. And I'd like people to be able to do that with mine."

Dylan and Young, of course, wrote the book on messing with the preconceptions of fans and critics – of not being the "Bob Dylan" or "Neil Young" that people want them to be. Not for nothing was Dylan the first singer-songwriter model for the young Tom Waits starting out in San Diego.

The games Waits plays with interviewers thwart all attempts to marry his music to his life: like Prince, an artist he loves, he's too protean to be so easily captured. Moreover, in our age of mass celebrity he refuses to sell himself as a rehab car-crash fuckup. He's the *anti-star* who declines to live according to the narrative of sin and redemption that celebrity culture requires. All of which puts a biographer in the invidious position of feeling like a parasite feeding on a resentful host. (In 1999, after years of following his career and writing at length about him, I finally had the opportunity to interview Prince. "Is it truth or is it conjecture?" he asked me about *Imp of the Perverse*, a book I'd written about him. "What gives you the right to write a book of conjecture about my life?" I had to think about that. I guess I'm still thinking about it.)

I've interviewed Waits in person twice, and spoken to him on the phone a number of times. Like most of the journalists who've talked to him, I (like to think I) have got along well with him. I've been regularly reduced to helpless laughter by his conversation. The first encounter was between albums in downtown New York, the interview a special concession to *New Musical Express*, who'd made *Swordfishtrombones* their Best Album of the Year. Not being on the interview treadmill, Waits was easy company, teasing waitresses and talking about the everyday madness of his adopted Manhattan.

The second time, fourteen years later in a diner near his northern California home, Waits was partway into a week of being grilled by the European press, and I got the distinct sense that he'd been ground down by the earnestness of his interlocutors. He loosened up some when we went for a backroads spin in his 1970 Coupe de Ville, but there was a wariness, a fatigue, about him that hadn't been there in 1985. The struggle to hold on to his privacy in the face of almost cultish fascination with his every move had, I thought, started to tell.

I first contemplated writing a book about him circa 1991. Somewhere in a drawer lies a thin proposal for a tome entitled *A Sucker on the Vine: Tom Waits in Tinseltown*. Fifteen years later came a phone call from an American editor and a conversation about possible biographical subjects. We stopped at Waits. I said that, as hard as it would be, a serious study of Waits as artist and man had to be attempted by *somebody*.

Yet nothing quite assuages the guilt a biographer feels in prying into the personal history of such a resistant subject. ("We have a right to know," Waits mutters with sinister invasiveness on 1999's hilarious "What's He Building?".) I've often tried to put myself in Waits' shoes during the process of researching this book, and try as I might to defend my right to write about a public figure I can understand his distaste for the idea of someone rooting about in his past. "The stories behind most songs are less interesting than the songs themselves," he said to me in Santa Rosa. "I mean, that's my opinion. So you tell somebody, 'Hey, this is about Jackie Kennedy.' And they go, 'Oh wow.' Then you say, 'No, I was just kidding, it's about Nancy Reagan.' Well, it's a different song now. In fact, all my songs are about Nancy Reagan."

Waits should be right when he says this. What difference should it make to our love of his music if we know that this song is about Rickie Lee Jones, or that one about Nancy Reagan? It shouldn't and ultimately doesn't. Yet Waits – the Waits of the

1970s, at least – uniquely invites conjecture about his "real" self, for the simple reason that he turned himself into a work of art at the very start of his career. The persona of the skid-row boho/hobo, a young man out of time and place, was an ongoing experiment in performance art that, by some accounts, nearly killed him. Or at least exhausted itself, running aground on its own limitations.

Any biographer of Waits is necessarily engaged in an impossible but irresistible quest to find the truth about a man who claims "truth" is overrated – or simply irrelevant in the context of "show business". But here's the rub: is it conceivable that actually we glean more about the "real" Tom Waits by, as it were, reading between the lines of his songs than we do about supposedly more "open" singer-songwriters?

"I'm not sure you can't tell more about *me* from what I've written than you can tell about purportedly confessional songwriters," Randy Newman, one of Waits' formative influences, once said to me. "When you meet them you're not so sure that's what they're writing about."

If Waits has always hidden behind his role as *unreliable entertainer*, the tension in his music is in the space between the mask and the emotion, the frame and the picture. We enjoy the artifice but are moved by the pain and compassion that seep through the tropes of the "Tom Waits" schtick. "Most readings of Tom see his work as either a direct reflection of his self or entirely a performance," says journalist Pete Silverton, who interviewed Waits a number of times over two decades. "I think it's a far more interesting and complex mixture than that."

Of course we have no "right to know" the real Tom Waits, any more than we have a right to know anyone who chooses to remove himself from everyday society. Yet artists unavoidably invite identification from the people who fall in love with their art: we all want to get closer to their greatness. "These American self-created men, like Woody [Guthrie] or Tom . . . I see them driving by sometimes," Rickie Lee Jones wrote memorably in 2000. "They create a language for themselves and stick everybody in a car and drive to where people can understand what they're saying. We feel fierce about these people. We want them to exist, we want them for ourselves, not just on magazine covers, but we want to live next door to them. We want them to be a part of the best of ourselves."* An unfortunate side-effect of this is the uneasy symbiosis between the artist's recalcitrance and our need to articulate the mystery of his art.

Interestingly, Waits has never gone down the Scott Walker route of refusing (almost) all interview requests. He is no rock-and-roll version of J. D. Salinger or Thomas Pynchon. He never hid out in the mountains like Dylan after his motorcycle accident, or like Bucky Wunderlick in Don DeLillo's novel *Great Jones Street*. He's never said, à la Melville's Bartleby (or Alex Chilton or Lewis Taylor†), "I would prefer not to." Generally he's been on hand to give good quote in support of the latest album. Yet for the better part of forty years he's managed to shield himself behind a smokescreen of humour and verbal dexterity. For all the "Gee, I dunno"s and "Aw shucks" that pepper his talk, he remains one of the most articulate interviewees in the business.

In "What's He Building?" a prying busybody tries to imagine

---

* But Jones also pointed out, in the same piece, that "there is no true telling in the selling of an artist – you won't find any truth in *Spin* or on VH1 . . . because they're selling it to you".

† I've had run-ins with both these obtuse geniuses. "I don't know anyone on earth that I really consider understands me as a human being whatsoever," Chilton, co-founder of the immortal Big Star, told me. "While I have nothing against you personally, for you to write about me would be the *best* way for me to begin to have something against you." As for Lewis Taylor, after I wrote a piece in June 2007 proclaiming his *Lost Album* one of the greatest ever made, I received at least two emails from the man ordering me to take it down. To quote Jeff Tweedy, "Is that the thanks I get for loving you?"

what his eccentric neighbour is up to in his uninviting abode. As the monologue unfolds, the conjecture becomes increasingly absurd. Vaguely sinister as the man sounds, it's clear that Waits' sympathies lie with him rather than with the nosy neighbour. Waits appears to lament the fact that America has become a country where any solitary activity spawns suspicions that there is a serial killer, or a Unabomber, living next door.

Cordoning off his own private life has made Waits prone to outbursts of fairly menacing temper. "Tom's a very contradictory character," his friend Jim Jarmusch pointed out. "He's potentially violent if he thinks someone is fucking with him, but he's gentle and kind too. It sounds schizophrenic but it makes perfect sense once you know him."

How badly am I fucking with Waits? Throughout my research I've been aware that he and Kathleen know what I'm doing, if only because of emails from people who've felt duty-bound to run my interview requests by them, their manager Stuart Ross, or their assistant Julianne Deery. I do appreciate that it must be a little like being stalked, or just being loved by someone you wish would go away.

I thought things couldn't get any worse when a veteran rock writer named "Uncle Ray" – pseudonym for a *Creem* contributor who'd met Waits in the mid-seventies – chose not to "interfere with Tom's privacy" by talking to me. (Jeez, I thought. If I can't even get ageing rock critics to talk to me, I really *am* screwed.) Things *could* have got worse, of course: one of Waits' previous biographers, Jay S. Jacobs, told me Bette Midler's response to his interview request was to threaten him with a lawsuit.

Fortunately there were many people from Waits' past who *were* prepared to talk about him, either because they had nothing to lose in doing so or because they weren't going to be told what to do, either by Waits, Brennan, Stuart Ross, or Julianne Deery.

"I think I have the right to tell you stuff about my days working with Tom," says saxophonist Ralph Carney, who played with Waits for fifteen years. "It's part of history now."

"I often think of Tom and wish him well," Bob Webb, one of his early mentors and sidemen, wrote me. "I mean him no disservice by answering your enquiry, though he apparently believes I'm doing just that. At heart I am too much of a biographer and historian myself to let these facts slip away unrecorded."

In Waits' defence I offer this email from Greg Cohen, for many years his virtual right-hand man (and indeed brother-in-law). "It has more to do with the fact that most people in the public eye have had a few bouts of having their privacy invaded," Greg wrote. "It's part of your job as an unauthorized biographer to deal with it, to find a way to either continue or let it go. Stuart isn't doing anything wrong. I have never spoken to him about you. I know him to be a good guy who just happens to help Tom with many things. I am sure *you* would love to have a Stuart Ross in *your* life."

I want to thank everybody who went on record with their (invariably glowing) recollections of working with Waits. I trust that by doing so they won't find themselves excommunicated from the Waits–Brennan "circle of trust". More than a few seem in any case to have been "dropped" by them years ago.

"I'm cut off," says Bones Howe, the man who produced seven of Waits' albums between 1974 and 1982. "There's no way I could pick up the phone and talk to Tom now. I would love to be able to just ask him what's going on. You know, what are his *kids* like? I mean, he came to my eldest daughter's wedding. He was kind of in our family."

One of the hardest things in the course of my research has been not taking umbrage at this intransigent duo – and particularly at the shadowy Kathleen, conceivably the architect of the wall of inaccessibility erected around her husband. At many points along the way I've had to stop and remind myself not to let their

Mr and Mrs Waits at a gala tribute to Nicolas Cage, San Francisco, April 1998.
(*Pamela Gentile*)

obstructions turn me against them: to reaffirm the reason for writing this book in the first place, which is to chart the growth of a remarkable artist – to look at where he came from, what he did with his experience, how he changed direction when he needed to – in the belief that people want to know more about it.

"I don't think Kathleen is alone in developing their approach," says *San Francisco Chronicle* critic Joel Selvin, who has met the Waitses informally and socially. "People love to see her as the power behind the throne, but my take is that they are very much a couple and highly collaborative. If she takes on a role that allows Tom to be more 'Who, me?', then I suspect that's part of the plan. They are fiercely private people who control the public's contact with Tom as much as they can. Once past that veil of privacy, they are the most charming, witty, intelligent and caring people."

Am I any more qualified to write a book about Waits than the many other writers who've followed his journey over the last four decades? I make no claims to be. Ten years his junior, I first noticed his name as a credit on Tim Buckley's *Sefronia*, which included a version of the beautiful "Martha". I remember thinking the jazzbo-beatnik posturing of *Nighthawks at the Diner* a little trite at the time. I'm not sure I grasped how great Waits really was until I lived for a long wet summer with Nick Cave, who often played *Small Change* and *Foreign Affairs* and *Blue Valentine* in the druggy crashpad we shared in Paddington.

And then came the miraculous metamorphosis of *Swordfishtrombones*, with its invoking of vanguard outsiders from Harry Partch to Howlin' Wolf and its heroic resistance to the synthetic banalities of eighties rock-pop. By the time I saw Waits play New York's Beacon Theater late in 1985, a few months after I'd first met him, it was plain that he was as important an American artist as anyone the twentieth century had produced.

The poet Rainer Maria Rilke famously stated that fame was simply "the sum of all the misunderstandings that gather about a name", and I can't see Waits taking issue with that little aperçu. But perhaps he also knows something that both Bob Dylan and Neil Young grasped early on in their careers, which is that the less information you give people, the more they want. Keep 'em hungry, keep 'em guessing.*

In 2004, Waits said it better than I or anyone else ever could: "You want to make sure that your demand is much higher than your supply. The public is a wild animal. It's better not to feed them too well."

Barney Hoskyns

London, August 2008

---

* Waits once wrote a poem on the subject. It consisted of two lines: "I want a sink and a drain/And a faucet for my fame."

Cast List

Bob Alcivar	Arranger on late Asylum albums and *One from the Heart*
Ray Bierl	San Diego folk singer and friend
Chris Blackwell	Founder of Island Records
Paul Body	Troubadour doorman and friend
Mathilde Bondo	Waltzing maiden of Copenhagen
Kathleen Brennan	Mrs Waits; partner and co-writer
Ralph Carney	Sax and other woodwinds player; sideman for fifteen years
Greg Cohen	Bass player; collaborator; ex-brother-in-law
Herb Cohen	Manager, 1971–81
Francis Ford Coppola	Director, *One from the Heart*, *Rumble Fish*, *The Outsiders*, *The Cotton Club*, *Bram Stoker's Dracula*
Sal Crivello	Co-owner of Napoleone's Pizza House; Tom's boss, 1963–9
Lou Curtiss	Mainstay of San Diego folk scene; owner of Folk Arts record store
Art Fein	Troubadour regular and friend
Michael C Ford	LA poet and friend
David Geffen	Asylum Records founder and early champion
Bill Goodwin	Waits' drummer, mid-1970s

Carlos Guitarlos	Rhythm Pig
Michael Hacker	Zoetrope employee, colleague of Kathleen Brennan
John Hammond	Blues singer and friend
Herb Hardesty	New Orleans saxophone legend, Waits sideman
Martin Henry	Veteran of San Diego folk circuit and friend
Stephen Hodges	Drummer on *Rain Dogs* and *Mule Variations*; touring musician, 1985–7
Bones Howe	Producer of Waits albums from *The Heart of Saturday Night* to *One from the Heart*
Jim Hughart	Studio bass player, 1974–9
Jim Jarmusch	Director of *Down by Law*, *Mystery Train*, and *Coffee and Cigarettes*
Rickie Lee Jones	Singer-songwriter; Waits' girlfriend, 1977–9
Bob LaBeau	San Diego folkie and friend
Louie Lista	Troubadour barman and blues harmonica player
Robert Marchese	Troubadour manager
David McGee	New York-based writer and friend
Mike Melvoin	Keyboard player and arranger, *The Heart of Saturday Night* and *Nighthawks at the Diner*
Bette Midler	Singer; Waits' friend/girlfriend, 1975–7
Jack Nicholson	Co-star, *Ironweed*
Bill Plummer	Bass player, *Closing Time*
Marc Ribot	Guitarist on Waits albums from *Rain Dogs* to present day
Keith Richards	Friend and musical accomplice, *Rain Dogs* and *Bone Machine*

Bill Schimmel	Accordionist, *Rain Dogs* and *Frank's Wild Years*
Joe Smith	President, Elektra-Asylum Records
Ron Stone	Manager with Geffen-Roberts, 1970s
Larry Taylor	Bass player with Waits, 1980 to present day
Jack Tempchin	San Diego songwriter and friend
Bobi Thomas	Waits' friend and girlfriend, early 1970s
Francis Thumm	San Diego friend and musical collaborator
Alma Waits	Mother
Casey Waits	Elder son
Frank Waits	Father
Kellesimone Waits	Daughter
Sullivan Waits	Younger son
Tom Waits	Himself
Bob Webb	Hootmaster, Heritage club; bass player on 1973–4 tours
Chuck E. Weiss	Friend and fellow musician
Chip White	Touring drummer, 1976–8
Hal Willner	Producer and compiler of tribute albums
Robert Wilson	Creator of *The Black Rider*, *Alice* and *Woyzeck*
Jerry Yester	Producer, *Closing Time*; arranger on *Small Change* and *Heartattack and Vine* tracks
Frank Zappa	Head Mother of Invention

Act One

Wasted and Wounded

"When he was asked in April 1952 for a biographic note, he felt as if someone had put to him that most inane of questions: 'Tell me about yourself.' He felt like writing back a parody of the author as a man of multiple occupations: He had worked as a towel boy in a Kalamazoo whorehouse, lavatory attendant, male whore, and part-time stool pigeon. He was currently living in a remodeled pissoir with a hermaphrodite and a succession of cats, which he took pleasure in torturing, favoring kerosene over gasoline because it burned slower."

(Ted Morgan, *Literary Outlaw: The Life and Times of William S. Burroughs*, 1991)

Northeastern Ohio Scene, December 1976. (*Courtesy of Pieter Hartmans*)

Chapter 1

Some Ways about Me that Just Aren't Right

"Take care of Tom. He needs a lot of love."
(Alma Waits to Ralph Carney, Chicago, 1986)

Tom Waits tends to bristle when interviewers probe him for the lowdown on his early years as a suburban oddball in the inland empire of Los Angeles. "I'm in therapy now?" he'll say with a mildly threatening laugh. "Should I lay down?"

But sometimes, if he's relaxed enough, Waits will drop his guard. When I asked him in 1999 if it was true he'd been alone a lot as a boy, he didn't answer the fairly innocuous question. But he did say this:

"I guess most entertainers are, on a certain level, part of the freak show. And most of them have some type of a wounding early on, either a death in the family or a breakup of the family unit, and it sends them off on some journey where they find themselves kneeling by a jukebox, praying to Ray Charles. Or you're out looking for your dad, who left the family when you were nine, and you know he drives a station wagon and that's all you've got to go on, and in some way you're going to become this big sensation and be on the cover of *Life* magazine and it'll somehow be this cathartic vindication or restitution."

On a simplistically Freudian level, here is the story of Tom Waits in capsule. His father *did* leave the family when his son was nine (or ten); and the teenage Tom *did*, literally, kneel before the sound of Brother Ray, dreaming of the "cathartic vindication" he

3

might experience if he too could become a voice coming out of the speaker.

In some ways, that's the story of all art, period. Extrinsic to human survival, art is nonetheless essential to those who wish to do more than survive – to, in fact, make stuff that'll enable them to stand out from the crowd. And often those people have, in Waits' words, "some type of a wounding" that "sends them off on some journey". Why, for example, are some of us driven to write when we could be doing perfectly normal jobs? Why am I writing this book?

Waits' great 1999 album *Mule Variations* featured a song called "Eyeball Kid", about a carnival freak whose head consists simply of a giant peeper. "Everybody in this business called show", he said of the song, "has something peculiar about them that they've been made fun of for or singled out in an unpleasant way or made to feel like they were not good enough to fit in. And at some point, you realize, 'Well, dammit, fine! Maybe I can make some dough off of it.'"

He put it more prosaically back in 1975. "I come from a good family and everything," he said. "But I've, over the years, developed some ways about me that just aren't right, so you just have to look for the kinks in your personality and it helps sometimes."

Tom Waits *did* come from a good family, or at least a family that from the outside looked conventional in the context of postwar American suburbia. "I had a pretty normal childhood," he admitted in 1976. "I learned to handle silverware and all of that stuff." He was the middle child of three siblings, a boy sandwiched between girls and born to schoolteachers who, at the time of his birth, resided at 318 North Pickering Avenue in Whittier, the same humdrum Los Angeles suburb that produced Richard Milhous Nixon. "He used to go to our church on occasion," Waits said of the American president in 1973. "That was a long time ago. He's come a long way since Whittier."

The main drag, Whittier, March 2007. (*Art Sperl*)

Founded by Quakers in the late nineteenth century, Whittier is twelve miles southeast of downtown LA and later achieved minor pop renown via the 1965 release of "Whittier Boulevard", a wildly pounding instrumental by Latino garage band Thee Midniters. ("*Let's take a trip down Whittier Boulevard!*" yells Little Willie G at the beginning, followed by Ronnie Figueroa's screamed "*Arriba! Arriba!*") But that was a very different Whittier – a Hispanic neighbourhood of low-rider *barrios* like Jimtown and Sunrise – from the middle-class suburb where Waits spent the first ten years of his life, one more akin to the setting for the film *Back to the Future*, which used Whittier High School as one of its locations. "Pat Nixon taught at Whittier High," says Pat DiPuccio, who founded the punk fanzine *Flipside* in the town in 1977. "High school was very big in Whittier. It was kind of like growing up in a Midwest suburb."

"Tom grew up very much in the way that I did, in the eastland suburban districts of Los Angeles," says poet Michael C Ford, a

Waits acquaintance in the 1970s. "Whittier in the fifties was untouched. The San Gabriel Valley had not been as poisoned as it is now – that grey poisonous ether that comes in now and lays against the San Gabriel mountains."

The circumstances of Waits' birth are shrouded in the mystery he prefers. Under duress he'll concede that he was born "at a very young age" but remains cagey about details beyond the actual date. Was his birthplace Park Avenue Hospital, as mentioned in the announcement of his birth in the *Pomona Progress-Bulletin*? Or was it Murphy Hospital, namechecked in a song intro on stage in New Jersey on 16 April 1976? And should we infer from Waits' regular references to being born in a taxi that either his parents didn't make it to the maternity ward in time or it was a mighty close shave?

Let us record the plain facts that Thomas Alan Waits was born on 7 December 1949, to "Mr. and Mrs. J. Frank Waits", and that he weighed in at a healthy 7 lb 10 oz. "All they ever wanted was a showbiz child," he would sing of Zenora Bariella and Coriander Pyle on "Eyeball Kid", "so on the seventh of December, 1949, they got what they'd been wishing for . . ."

Zenora and Coriander were Jesse Frank and Alma Waits. Frank, whose name would later be given to the protagonists of "Frank's Song" and "Frank's Wild Years", was the product of Scots–Irish ancestry and hailed from Sulphur Springs, Texas. His family had moved to La Verne, California, whose orange groves he worked in during the 1930s before becoming a radio technician in the Second World War. "He came west," said Waits. "In those days if you had any kind of bronchial problem they'd say, 'Aw, move to California!'" Alma Waits, too, was first-generation Californian, born of Norwegian stock and raised in Grant's Pass, Oregon.

Waits would later claim that he'd been "conceived one night in April 1949 at the Crossroads Motel in La Verne, amidst the broken bottle of Four Roses, the smoldering Lucky Strike, half a tuna salad sandwich, and the Old Spice across the railroad tracks . . ." If that fanciful scenario is even halfway accurate, it says more about Jesse Frank than it does about Alma. Named after legendary outlaw brothers Jesse and Frank James, Tom Waits' dad was a wild one – a boozer, a roving romantic, a lover of old sentimental Mexican songs. "He was really a tough one, always an outsider," Waits said in 2004.

Alma by comparison was a somewhat strait-laced 1950s hausfrau, and a regular churchgoer to boot. "Tom's mom was a very put-together suburban matron," says Bill Goodwin, drummer on Waits' *Nighthawks at the Diner*. "She was not what you'd imagine Tom Waits' mom would look like."

"The first time I met Tom's mother was the first time I ever heard his voice come up high," says another Waits drummer, Chip White. "He wasn't quite as gruff with her. We teased him about it. It was like, 'Oh hi, Mom, how you doing?' in a real high voice."

It's tempting to see the warring sides of Tom Waits' character in the unlikely pairing of his parents' marriage. "On my father's side we had all the psychopaths and alcoholics," he's said, "and on my mother's side we had all the evangelists." Throughout his life Waits has in some sense struggled to reconcile his father's impetuousness with his mother's domesticity. One pictures the marriage as somewhat akin to that of Nathan and Ruth Fisher in the LA-set *Six Feet Under* – Dad as louche bon viveur, Mom as fastidious domestic goddess.

"Tom and his sisters were very independent, avant-garde-type people, a little edgy," says Bob LaBeau, a folk singer and an early Waits champion. "Whereas his mother was this standard type of June Cleaver person. She was just a really neat lady, very pleasant and kind of pretty, a nice woman. I think they were all probably more like their father."

Waits had no brothers to play or compete with, perhaps explaining the comparative loneliness of his childhood. One has a sense of little Tom as an old soul, a playground introvert in the fifties idyll of the Eisenhower suburbs. "About the rest of his childhood he is fairly reticent," wrote Dave Lewis in 1979, "[. . .] admitting that he was often picked on at school for being skinny and 'funny-looking' then skimming swiftly over the rest of his background . . ." In 1999 Waits confessed that – in emulation of Popeye – he "ate spinach so I could get stronger [and] beat up the bullies".

Waits was small and peculiar, with wild hair that stood up and an odd pigeon-toed walk exacerbated by his "trick knee" – a knee joint that would lock in position, owing to longitudinal splitting of the medial meniscus. "What sort of a child was I?" he has said, clearly discomfited by the question. "I can't really answer that point-blank. But, you know, I liked trains and horses, birds and rocks, radios and bicycles." More recently, he said he "[grew] up in a drive-in, watching movies and eating popcorn out of a paper sack and falling asleep in the back seat and getting carried into bed by your dad".

If Waits did most of the things LA kids did in those innocent suburban days – delivering newspapers, going to Dodgers games, shoplifting, or just hanging around in Sav-On parking lots and trading baseball cards – one suspects he was rather more troubled than a lot of his peers. While Alma offered a measure of security and consistency, Frank was a more complex mixture of authority and nonconformity. On the one hand he taught Spanish in schools in Whittier, Pomona, La Verne, and Montebello; on the other he was a heavy drinker and regular patron of local alcoholic establishments. "I remember my father taking me into bars when I was very young," Waits said in 1979. "I remember climbing up a barstool like Jungle Jim, getting all the way up to the top and sitting there with my dad. He could tell stories in there forever."

Frank Waits and son, Santa Monica Civic Auditorium,
October 1975. (*Andy Kent*)

Frank Waits' family were a strange lot. For Tom and his sisters,
visits to his paternal grandmother's house amid La Verne's
orange groves usually involved encounters with uncles Vernon
and Robert, who both "had an effect on me very young and
shaped me in some way". Uncle Robert was blind and played the
organ, erratically, in a nearby Pentecostal church. When the
church in question was later torn down, Robert had the organ
disassembled and installed in his chaotically messy house, its
pipes running up through the ceiling. Vernon, meanwhile, spoke
in a deep, gruff voice that Waits claimed was the result of a childhood throat operation. Allegedly the doctors had forgotten to
remove a pair of scissors and gauze when they stitched him up.
Years later, during a Christmas dinner, Vernon choked and
coughed out the gauze and the scissors. "That's how [he] got his
voice, and that's how I got mine – from trying to sound just like
him," Waits said. "I always hated the sound of my voice when I
was a kid. I always wanted to sound more like my Uncle Vernon,
who had a raspy, gravelly voice."*

* It's interesting that, post-*Swordfishtrombones*, Waits should return to these
primal family memories to explain aspects of his own musical character. One

9

Years later, Waits inserted Uncle Vernon into "Cemetery Polka", third track on 1985's *Rain Dogs* and a first nod to the vagaries of family history. For Waits the song was an opportunity to round up as many of his eccentric relatives as possible and reunite them round the grave. "'Cemetery Polka' was, ah, discussing my family in a way that's difficult for me, to be honest," he explained. "The way we talk behind each other's backs: 'You know what happened to Uncle Vernon.' The kind of wickedness that nobody outside your family could say." Around Vernon was clustered the song's rather more fictionalized cast: Uncle Biltmore, for example, and Auntie Mame who's "gone insane" and "lives in the doorway of an old hotel".

La Verne represented more than the roots of Waits' extended family. It marked the beginning of his early love for the countryside he'd one day roam on *Bone Machine*, *Mule Variations*, and *Real Gone*. The journey from Whittier to his grandmother's house was then a long drive from the suburbs to the country, crossing railroad tracks as the landscape slowly changed. "We were always waiting for trains to pass," he said in 2006. "And the magic of that for a kid, hearing the bell – *ding ding* – and counting the cars as they go by . . . and I knew we were getting further out of town when I could smell horses . . . it was like perfume to me . . ." Now home to hip-hop icon Snoop Dogg, La Verne back then was just a long road, Foothill Boulevard, with orange groves all around and the sound of the Southern Pacific whistling through on the nearby railroad tracks.

On Alma's side were the Johnsons, who lived up in central

---

suspects that subconsciously he wanted to make more of his own ingrained experiences as a counter to critics' frequent allusions to such avant/outsider influences as Harry Partch and Captain Beefheart. Is it too po-faced to point out that if Uncle Vernon *had* been the influence on Waits' singing voice that he claimed, then we'd surely have heard ol' gravel-larynx a lot earlier than on 1976's *Small Change*?

northern California. Come summer, Waits and his sisters would visit their relatives in Gridley and Marysville, the latter name-checked in 1977's "Burma Shave". That song's inspiration was cousin Corinne, who couldn't wait to get out of the place. "[She] was always like, you know, 'Christ, man, I gotta get out of this fucking town,'" Waits recalled. "'I wanna go to LA.' She finally did. She hitchhiked out and stood by this Foster Freeze on Prom Night. Got in a car with a guy who was just some juvenile delinquent, and he took her all the way to LA, where she eventually cracked up."

Waits treasured happy memories of his Aunt Evelyn and Uncle Chalmer, who grew prunes and peaches in Gridley – and whose welcoming kitchen made an appearance on *Mule Variations'* "Pony". He also recalled visiting other relatives dotted about the Butte and Yuba County towns of Biggs, Oroville, Live Oak, and Chico.

Back in Whittier, the Waitses moved from North Pickering Avenue to a new build on Kentucky Avenue. On "Frank's Wild Years" Tom sang of their "thoroughly modern kitchen" with its "self-cleaning oven". Later the street was celebrated in one of his most emotional songs of childhood. "I had a little tree fort and everything," he said, introducing "Kentucky Avenue" on stage in 1981. "I had my first cigarette when I was about seven . . . it was such a thrill. I used to pick 'em up right out of the gutter after it was raining. My dad smoked Kents."

Waits liked to propel himself across the living-room floor in a large rocking chair. Rocking back and forth was a habit that stayed with Waits right into his adult life, and one sometimes associated with the repetitive "stimming" behaviour of autistics. Waits himself has voiced the possibility that he suffered a bout of autism, if such a thing is conceivable.

He liked to lose himself in books. At eight years old his favourite story was about a boy and a horse, and featured a risqué scene in which the boy lay down by a stream with a girl and "bees [were] buzzing all around". But his imagination was fecund enough without stories. At home was a set of drapes covered with water stains that resembled leaves and camels. "I made my own shapes out of them. And I still do that. When I'm looking at any kind of pattern, I'll find, say, noses or something." Years later, moreover, Waits realized he was colourblind. "I juggle with brown and green and blue and red," he told Elvis Costello. "Green looks brown, brown looks green, purple looks blue, blue looks purple."

A more disturbing memory of childhood was of a heightened aural sense Waits suffered for several months. As he lay in bed at night, the slightest sound became an almost deafening roar. "I'd put my hand on a sheet," he recalled, "and it would sound like a plane going by. Or like loud sandpaper." The experience was frightening enough for Waits to think that he was "mentally ill" or "emotionally disturbed". In later years he read that "certain artistic people" had had "periods where there was a distortion to the world that disturbed them".

By the time he was nine, Waits had made a name for himself as a kid who'd rescue cats from trees, and as "the little neighborhood mechanic" who repaired his friends' bikes while he observed the local characters: Joey Navinski, who played the trombone; Dickie Faulkner with his constantly running nose; and Mrs Storm, who had a twelve-gauge shotgun protruding ominously from her kitchen window. The latter made a cameo appearance in "Kentucky Avenue", Waits claiming she would "stab you with a steak knife" if you so much as stepped on her lawn. Also in the song were Joey, Dickie, Ronnie Arnold, Bobby Goodmanson, Eddie Grace's Buick (with "four bulletholes in its side") and Charley De Lisle, who could be found at the top of an avocado tree and who years later – as a journalist – interviewed Waits for the *Santa Barbara News*.

Not named in "Kentucky Avenue" was Waits' best friend Kipper, whose legs were in braces from polio and who would race Waits to the bus stop in his wheelchair. But it was Kipper's braces that Waits was offering to cut off and bury in the song's cornfield. "Childhood is very important to me as a writer," Waits would say in 1985. "I think the things that happen then, the way you perceive them and remember them in later life, have a very big effect on what you do later on." As an evocation of American childhood – furtive, inquisitive, reckless, aimless – "Kentucky Avenue" is unparalleled, bringing back all the tragicomic adventures of one's own youth.

By 1985, Waits evidently felt he'd gone too far with "Kentucky Avenue", describing it as "a little dramatic, a little puffed-up". Why he felt the need to slight this masterpiece of what Geoffrey O'Brien called "lovely grief" I cannot conceive. Call me sentimental, but I cannot get to the end of the song without crying.

Another Whittier acquaintance, redheaded Billy Swed, lived with his obese mother in a trailer on the blue-collar side of the town's railroad tracks. He also played guitar. "He taught me three chords – an A-minor blues progression – and I completely flipped," Waits told his friend Francis Thumm, claiming it was his clearest musical memory from childhood. "When he played, it was the first time I ever heard anybody play in a minor key. I really recognized it as minor and was attracted to it. I still am." In 1993 Waits claimed that "the secret knowledge of the chords" Swed taught him was to "outweigh all I learned in school and give me a foundation for all music".

When Waits went into Jordan Elementary School for show-and-tell one morning, he took a little guitar his father had given him and played his classmates the chord progression he'd learned from Swed. His friends looked abjectly at the marbles and rocks they'd brought. "That was a big moment for me," Waits told Thumm. It may have been his first live performance.

If there wasn't much blues in the Waits household, Frank and Alma's home was hardly unmusical. In their different ways both parents were passionately musical. Frank sang standards, Irish lullabies, and Mexican songs, accompanying himself on the guitar and teaching his son to play the ukulele; Alma sang in an Andrews Sisters-style family vocal group. "My mom came from a big family and they were all very musical," Waits has said. "She had three sisters and they all sang in four-part harmony." He has also recalled that his maternal grandfather "had a great low singing voice" and "was able to find all the roots of the chords".

"Tom has a background that he doesn't give himself credit for, a very old-fashioned music background where you're making music in the home," Francis Thumm has said. "He got a lot of that from his mom and church songs."

Meanwhile, the family gramophone blared out a mix of show tunes and *mariachi*, light jazz and Irish ballads, calypso and "country-western". Stacks of 78s included recordings by Bing Crosby and Perry Como; timeless songs like "I Get a Kick out of You" and "It's Been a Long, Long Time". Louis Armstrong followed Sinatra and Harry Belafonte and then gave way to Marty Robbins' "El Paso" (which Waits learned on the guitar, though he sang it in Spanish). In the family's Chevy station wagon, the radio was invariably tuned to Mexican music – *romantica* and *ranchera* songs broadcast from border stations. Frank, teaching Spanish in night school in nearby Montebello, even took Tom to see bolero kingpins Los Tres Aces – an archetypal "trio romantico" of the 1940s and 50s – at LA's Continental Club.

Frank, said his son, "didn't listen to jitterbug or anything like that"; he certainly had no time for the new teen craze that was rock and roll. One afternoon, at the height of Presleymania, father and son were driving along Whittier Boulevard when a souped-up automobile pulled alongside them at a stop light. In the driving seat was a delinquent with a greased-back ducktail, shades on and cigarette in the corner of his mouth. Fats Domino was pumping from the radio, and a girl sat in the passenger seat with black eye-makeup. Frank Waits looked down at the eight-year-old beside him. "You ever grow a ducktail," he said, "I'll kill you."

Doubtless southern California in the 1950s was full of father–son relationships like the one Frank Waits had with his son. On the one hand Dad railed against ducktailed Elvis clones; on the other he drank to excess, sang old Mexican songs, and refused to conform to suburban norms. For Tom it must have been confusing, making it difficult to rebel in the conventional sense. The fact that his father was a teacher made it doubly difficult. "My dad – I think it was a rebel raising a rebel," Waits said in 2004. "That's kind of what my kids are dealing with right now – when your mission is really to be immovable and filled with guidance and assurance and an ability to look over the hill and see what's coming? So somewhere in the conflict of all that is where I am."

From an early (or at least pre-adolescent) age, Tom seems to have wanted to be older – *much* older – than he was. Far from rejecting the values and tastes of his parents' generation, he seems in his own odd way to have emulated them. "I was real repressed," he's admitted. "I wanted to skip growing up and rush all the way to forty."

Waits went so far as to carry around a cane he'd acquired at a Salvation Army store, and into which he'd carved his initials. The stick set him apart, giving him a distinctive walk and identity. When he visited his friends' houses, he often stayed indoors talking to their dads about "real man stuff" like lawn mowing and life insurance. Plus he liked checking out their Frank Sinatra albums.

This sense of ten-year-old Waits as a Little Father Time is key to understanding him. Out of step with his own peers and dress-

In the wee small hours of Saturday night: Frank and Tom

rehearsing for adulthood, paradoxically he was rebelling by conforming. Musically he was drawn more to Gershwin and Jerome Kern than to Little Richard or Ricky Nelson, fascinated by "a lot of incongruous musical influences" from Harold Arlen and Hoagy Carmichael to Stravinsky and Mississippi John Hurt.

Instead of seeing himself as a renegade rocker, Waits had "an image of me in a dark sport coat and clean tie getting up and entertaining people". The jackets wouldn't be sport coats and the ties were rarely clean, but as a premonition it wasn't so far off the mark. The idea of being an entertainer set in early, if only because the alternatives – bricklaying, cab-driving, making shoes – looked dismal. "I knew what I *didn't* want to do," he once said.

There wasn't much encouragement at home. At elementary school Waits played the bugle – a silver Cleveland Greyhound he blew into as the Stars and Stripes was raised and lowered at the start and end of the school day. But the notion of going into show business was unthinkable. "There were a lot of preachers and teachers in my family," Waits has said. "In fact, my father was more than a little disappointed when he found out I was going to be neither. It was like, 'We aren't going to be able to help you, then'. Music wasn't the family business."

In 1959, when Waits was ten, Frank Waits left the family home. "The family kind of hit the wall and cracked up and it went by the wayside," Waits recalled later, "but I do remember the music." Did he perhaps try to recapture that music in the loungey arrangement for "Frank's Wild Years"? It was bold to use his father's name to tell the tale of a furniture salesman who – having "hung his wild years on a nail that he drove through his wife's forehead" – bought a gallon of gas and torched his suburban home. Metaphorically at least, Frank Waits did exactly that.

Long before "Frank's Wild Years", Waits wrote "Frank's Song", a curious outburst of misogyny that warned of women with "claws" and "laws", of women who'll "break you" and make you "lose your mind". Was it in some way an expression of sympathy for his father – sympathy mixed with reproach?

As any child of a broken home can attest, divorce feels like the two halves of one's soul have been wrenched apart. "It was an extreme loss of power, and totally unpredictable," Waits reflected later. "I was in turmoil over it for a long time." Divorce would have been rare at that time in a suburban community such as Whittier's, so Waits and his sisters may have felt as stigmatized as they were devastated. We know that whereas Frank would twice remarry, Alma remained single for some years.

Waits' mother made the decision to leave Los Angeles, taking the children to live in a suburb of San Diego near the Mexican border. Chula Vista was a middle-class neighbourhood – "definitely the upscale area of the whole south county", in the words of a future college classmate of Waits. Drive past its quiet rows of unpretentious bungalows today and it's much the same as it would have been circa 1960, when local kids shot along its streets on homemade plywood skateboards.

"We used to skate down this hill called Robert Avenue," Waits remembered. "It was a great curve and you dug up a lot of speed. It went by our neighbor Mr Sticha. He lived in the beauty of the curve, where all the momentum culminated in a beautiful slough of cement. It took you right past his house but as close as you could get to his porch." Namechecked years later in "What's He Building?", Mr Sticha would become so apoplectic at the skateboarders that his wife warned them they'd give him a heart attack. When eventually he *did* have a heart attack – on Halloween night, on his front porch – Mrs Sticha all but accused them of killing him.

For a boy to be separated from his father at ten years old is no small matter. With Frank remaining in LA, where for many years he would teach Spanish at Belmont High School, father and son would see each other only occasionally. At least in Chula Vista and nearby National City many of Waits' schoolfriends' fathers were at sea, making the absence of his own much less of an issue. "The military was the centre of life," Waits told me of San Diego. "My dad was gone for good, and their dads were gone in the Philippines for eight months at a time. So nobody had dads around." He told Patrick Humphries that he was "at home with these three women, my mother and two sisters, and although they were there I was on my own a lot . . ."

One of Waits' most treasured possessions was a broken Heathkit radio his father had built as a technician during the war. It represented a lost connection to Frank. "When you come from a broken home you'll always feel attracted to things that are also broken," he said in 1992. "You want to find something that's broken and then put it all together. You're going to feel sorry for that broken radio and that broken guitar."*

When, in 1963, Waits finally got the radio working with a broom-handle antenna on the roof of the house, the first song he heard was George Hamilton IV's hit "Abilene". "God, I loved it," Waits recalled in 2002. "When I heard that, it moved me. My

---

* "All this radio needs is a fuse . . ." ("Soldier's Things"). In the 1989 film *Bearskin*, Waits is seen repairing a radio.

folks had split up and I was sitting listening to a radio that my dad had given me."

Country songs, particularly those with place names in them, became a staple part of Waits' musical diet. "People have no idea how big country music was in southern California in the forties and fifties," says writer Todd Everett. "You had all these people coming out from Oklahoma or Arkansas to work in the defense plants or the oil fields, and they brought their music with them. Tom probably came in at sort of the tail end of that."

What had started with Marty Robbins' "El Paso" in 1958 continued with "Abilene" and then with Johnny Horton's "The Battle of New Orleans" and Bobby Bare's "Detroit City". The sense of America's immense landmass in these songs thrilled the budding poet in Waits. More haunting to him than even "Abilene" or "Detroit City" was the chillingly beautiful voice of Roy Orbison. When the two men met many years later, Waits asked the Texan singer where his operatic voice had come from. Orbison replied that "he used to hear a band playing miles away, across the plains, and by the time it reached him it sounded all watery like that . . . 'so I wanted to sound all watery when I sang.'"

When Frank Waits saw his kids, generally it involved collecting them – or sometimes just Tom – and driving down to Tijuana, the wild Mexican town just twenty miles south of Chula Vista across the border. "My dad taught Spanish all his life, so we went down to Mexico," Tom told me. "Used to go down there to get my hair cut a lot." Tijuana was very different from Chula Vista, with street scenes straight out of Buñuel's *Los Olvidados*. "That's when I started to develop the opinion that there was something Christ-like about beggars," Waits said. "You'd see a guy with no legs on a skateboard, mud streets, church bells going. These experiences are still with me at some level."

Invariably on these jaunts the Waitses wound up in some bar or restaurant where Frank would carouse into the early hours of the morning. "If you went to a restaurant in Mexico with my dad he would invite the mariachis to the table and give them two dollars for a song," his son reminisced in 2004. "Then he would wind up leaving with them and we would have to find our way back to the hotel on our own, and Dad would come home a day later, because he fell asleep on a hilltop somewhere looking down on the town."

Amusing as the story is, it reminds us that Tom and his sisters had an alcoholic father. "It's a very romantic [picture]," Waits conceded, "but it's in there with a lot of documentary footage where the lighting is not nearly as good." By 2006, Waits was more candid about Frank's drinking. "When I think back on it, my dad was an alcoholic then," he told writer Mick Brown. "He really left – this is getting a little personal – to go sit in a dark bar and drink whatever . . . Glenlivet. He was a binge drinker. There was no real *cognizance* of his drinking problem from my point of view." Waits added that Frank "removed himself – he was the bad tooth in the smile, and he kind of pulled himself out".*

On a trip to Baja California, Waits fell in with a band of local kids in the resort town of San Vicente. The boys would go out to the desert inland, bury themselves up to their necks in the sand, and wait for buzzards to arrive. "You stay as still as a corpse under the sand with just your head showing," Waits told Francis Thumm. "You wait for the vulture to land and walk over to you,

---

* Something of the hazardousness of being an ACOA (Adult Child Of an Alcoholic, in contemporary therapeutic parlance) can be inferred from a vivid dream Waits had at the ripe middle age of fifty-five. "I was on the back of a motorcycle and my dad was driving and we were going straight up the trunk of a tree," he told writer Richard Grant. "He had some special little hook device that he would throw up over a branch to increase our pull. I'm hanging on as best I can and finally I realise that we're gonna fall back on our backs, like a horse. And just at that moment I let go in terror and find that I'm only a foot off the ground."

and the first thing they do is try to peck your eyes out. And when they make that jab, you reach out from under the sand, grab them around the neck, and snap their head off." San Vicente was also where Waits witnessed an unforgettable sight: a woman with a tail at the local carnival. "She let me squeeze it," he remembered, "and she smiled at me with a rotting grin."

Waits claimed it was during these Mexican trips that he truly began to see music as a calling. The epiphany was simple enough – "probably [hearing] a *ranchera*, you know, on the car radio with my dad" – but it convinced the boy that music really was a route out of suburban conformity. "It was something I didn't completely understand," he said in 1985. "I thought, 'I'm going to ride this somewhere, it's going to take me somewhere.'"

Music was becoming ever more important to Waits, especially when he started to hear intoxicating new sounds – the Drifters, Solomon Burke, Bob Dylan, the Rolling Stones – on the radio. More thrilling than anything was disc jockey Bob "Wolfman Jack" Smith, who rasped and howled over the soul and R&B classics he broadcast from XERF across the border south of Del Rio, Texas. "The first station I got on [my] little two-dollar headphones was Wolfman," Tom told his friend Rip Rense. "And I thought I had discovered something that no one else had. I thought it was coming in from Kansas City or Omaha, that nobody was getting this station, and nobody knew who this guy was and nobody knew who these records were."

If Waits' fixation with the Great American Songbook was about rejecting the peer pressure to conform to California's bobby-sox teenage dream, now he found himself responding on an almost visceral level to the fevered syncopations of Ray Charles, James Brown, and Wilson Pickett. "I didn't have a lot of [musical] encouragement, to be honest," Waits said in 1983. "But sometimes that's good, you know? What you end up doing is a reaction to all that. So primarily, uh . . . black music, uh . . . New

Orleans music. Uh . . . James Brown I listened to in the sixties, uh, Wilson Pickett, the Four Tops, the Temptations, Ray Charles . . ." In 1976 he told *The New Yorker* that he'd attended "a predominantly black junior high school in San Diego where the only music was black hit parade".

O'Farrell Junior High School was located north of Chula Vista in nearby Encanto. Waits was there long enough for him to fall in with a group of classmates who dug the same R&B music he did. One night in 1962, he downed a bottle of cough syrup and jumped in the back of a powder-blue 1961 Lincoln Continental to go see James Brown and the Famous Flames perform an outdoor show in San Diego's Balboa Park. "We got in the back of the fence with some wire-cutters," he remembered of the gig. "I haven't had fun since then." For the thirteen-year-old Waits the experience was close to religious, as ceremonial in its ritual and pageantry as a St Patrick's Cathedral mass. "It was like you'd been dosed or taken a pill," he said in 2002. "It was like a revival meeting with an insane preacher at the pulpit talking in tongues." Years later Waits would perform a demented version of Brown's "Papa's Got a Brand New Bag" – title track of the first album he ever bought – as a homage to the Godfather's crazed showmanship.

Waits went so far as to join a school band, a "surf and soul" trio that played covers of R&B hits and rock instrumentals by the likes of Link Wray and the Ventures. "[We were] white kids trying to get that Motown sound," was how he later described the Systems. Assuming the role of frontman, teenage Tom sang and slashed away on rhythm guitar as a harelipped drummer stomped along behind him. There was no bassist, merely a lead guitarist who strangled a primitive instrument he'd built with his own hands.

As vital as this early immersion in black music was, it was offset by the influence of rock's first great poet. Bob Dylan's dense lyrics were a gateway for any aspiring singer-songwriter growing up in the early 1960s folk era, and Waits got the Dylan bug bad, plastering his bedroom walls with transcriptions of his songs. The complex chains of images in such masterpieces as *Highway 61 Revisited*'s epic "Desolation Row" would influence Waits for years to come. As seminal as seeing James Brown in Balboa Park was the Dylan show Waits saw two years later, on 4 December 1964. Held in the Peterson Gymnasium at San Diego State University, the concert set Waits reeling. "Here's a guy like Dylan on stage with a stool and a glass of water, and he comes out and tells these great stories in his songs," he recalled of the gig. "It helped unlock the mystery of performance." Four years away from writing his first song, the fifteen-year-old Waits was soon modelling his basic style and stance on Dylan.

Waits was not a well-adjusted adolescent. In fact, he was manifesting behaviour typical of kids from broken homes. Angry at being semi-abandoned by his father but stifled by his mother's starchy conservative values, he acted out his pain as only troubled teenagers can. "Too many teachers in my family," he growled in 1987. "Teachers and ministers. I wanted to break windows, smoke cigars and stay up late, you know?" Dragged along to the Friends Church every Sunday by Alma, Waits yearned to break out of Chula Vista. "I wore a tie that cut off the circulation to my head," he later recalled. "Then I discovered donuts, cigarettes and coffee when I was fourteen, and that was it for church. My mom said, 'Don't forget there's nothing the devil hates more than a singing Christian.'"

At his new school, Hilltop High in Chula Vista, Waits often found himself in trouble with the authorities, receiving little sympathy from his own teacher parents. He's described himself as "kind of an amateur juvenile delinquent" who was into "malicious mischief" and "enjoyed the thrill of breaking the law". Torn between the aesthetes on one hand and the car-club

Hilltop High, Chula Vista, March 2007. (*Art Sperl*)

hoodlums on the other, he threw in his lot with the latter "and watched my California Scholarship Federation plaque melt subsequently". Behind the delinquency lay a deeper confusion and melancholy. "I felt really peculiar when I was going through puberty," he remembered. "That was a very peculiar period for me."

What can't have been easy was Alma meeting and eventually marrying a man who worked both as a realtor and as a private investigator – and who, according to Waits, had once been employed by guitarist Duane Eddy. "He managed him for a while and had his guitar," Waits recalled of his stepfather Jim. "He was a strange guy . . . very interesting." Waits got along with Jim but felt less and less at home under his mother's roof.

Sometimes Waits lost himself in movies he watched at the local Globe theatre. Once he caught an unlikely double bill pairing *101 Dalmatians* with *The Pawnbroker*, starring Rod Steiger as a Holocaust survivor in the Bronx. "There in the darkness, it was like going to sleep with a whole bunch of people and dreaming your way into the film," he would recall. "It's an intimidating world out there and it was like finding your way to safety, like finding a rabbit hole where you could be warm and safe." Waits' adolescent love of cinema would carry all the way through to his own film career in the 1980s and 90s.

Waits also adored cult TV shows such as *The Alfred Hitchcock Hour* and Rod Serling's eerie *Twilight Zone.* "Serling had these great eyebrows and that indelible voice," Waits recalled in 2006. "There was something about the humanity of his *Twilight Zone* stories that was very appealing." One *Twilight Zone* episode in particular stayed in Waits' mind. Poignantly, "In Praise of Pip" (1963) starred Jack Klugman – the spitting image of Frank Waits, according to his son – as an alcoholic bookie who gets shot during a holdup. "As he's dying," Waits recalled, "he has a vision of his son as a child asking him for help, because he's now a soldier bleeding to death in a Vietnam field hospital. So he tries to make a deal with God to take him and let his son live."

Aside from music, movies, and television, Waits increasingly buried himself in books. His Dylan fixation led him indirectly to the Beat writers of the 1950s. High on his reading list were the movement's founding fathers Jack Kerouac and Allen Ginsberg. "I found [them] when I was a teenager and it saved me," he remembered. "Growing up without a dad, I was always looking for a father figure, and those guys sort of became my father figures. Reading [Kerouac's] *On the Road* added some interesting mythology to the ordinary and sent me off on the road myself with an investigative curiosity about the minutiae of life."[*]

In the company of his high-school pal Sam Jones – namechecked in the song "I Wish I Was in New Orleans" – Waits several times hitchhiked from southern California to neighbouring

[*] To Sean O'Hagan in 2006, Waits said that he was always looking for a father: "It was like, 'Are you my dad?'; 'Are you my dad?'; 'What about *you*? Are *you* my dad?' . . . I found a lot of these old salty guys along the way."

Hilltop High yearbook, 1966

Arizona.* "We would just see how far we could go in three days, on a weekend," he later recalled. "[We'd] see if we could get back by Monday." One New Year's Eve, the two teenagers were dropped off in a small town and ushered into the warm bosom of a Pentecostal church. "They were singing and they had a tambourine, an electric guitar and a drummer," Waits told Terry Gross. "They were talking in tongues and then they kept gesturing to me and Sam: 'These are our wayfaring strangers here.' So we felt kind of important. And they took up a collection, gave us some money and bought us a hotel room and a meal."

To Mick Brown, Waits said this was "probably the most pivotal religious experience I've had", perhaps explaining the regular forays into gospel scattered through his work of the past twenty-five years. "It was the first time I ever heard church music, with sexual innuendoes," he told Francis Thumm. "I'd heard the church in the street, but that's the first time I heard the street in the church."

Adventures such as these only made Waits the more eager to escape Chula Vista. Looking round at his classmates at Hilltop High, he saw a future that consisted either of joining the Navy or working at the nearby Lockheed plant before raising kids and heading to the beach at weekends. "I disavow any knowledge of

---

* Sam Jones is also mentioned in the booklet of *Nighthawks at the Diner*: "Special thanks to Sam (I'll pay you if I can and when I get it) Jones."

the world of surfing," he stressed on his first visit to the UK in 1976. "I don't know the first thing about surfboards. Which way you ride it, or what side is up, and I don't want to learn."

Waits knew his future lay outside – way beyond – San Diego. "My own background was very middle-class," he told Patrick Humphries on a UK visit in 1981. "I was desperately keen to get away."

But first it was time to get a job.

Chapter 2

Home I'll Never Be

"Never saw my home town, till I stayed away too long . . ."
("San Diego Serenade", 1974)

Forty years ago, Lou Curtiss looked like the novelist Richard Brautigan – all leftwing specs, long thinning hair, handlebar moustache. Today, wedged into the tiny office of his Folk Arts Rare Records store in the strangely named neighbourhood of Normal Heights, Lou could be Karl Marx crossed with Burl Ives, a throwback to the old San Diego hootenanny days when dungareed commies armed with banjos really thought they could change the world. The moustache has become the bushiest of beards, and Lou's tummy is a swollen drum barely covered by his ancient cheesecloth shirt.

Housed in a 1930s craftsman's cottage on Adams Avenue, Folk Arts is a tiny and all-but-forgotten institution in the musical history of San Diego. Despite a recent Grammy Foundation award to help Curtiss digitize the many recordings he made of the city's folk artists, there is the distinct whiff of Disappearing World about the cramped store. Now in its fourth or fifth location – nobody seems quite sure – Folk Arts is an inadvertent shrine to a lost subculture, with old blues and bluegrass vinyl squeezed into racks, and walls plastered with pictures of local folk legends and older icons. A familiar image of Robert Johnson jostles for space with a snapshot of dulcimer player Curt Bouterse; old Uncle Dave Macon sits alongside such stalwarts of the sixties San Diego

Lou Curtiss, San Diego, March 2007. (*Art Sperl*)

scene as Bob LaBeau, Ray Bierl, and Pam Ostergren. Oh, and over here's a pic from November 1973 of "Ole Bro Lou" with Tom Waits, who's just dropped by Folk Arts – then at 3743 Fifth Avenue – after the release of his debut album.

"Lou Curtiss is a heroic curmudgeon, entrepreneur and keeper of the flame," Waits says. "Folk Arts is a soul-food library and seed bank, much like the Library of Congress, where you go to light your torch. All the secrets of the universe are there, and if it closes the whole world will go dark."

Curtiss first spotted Waits in 1966, seated on the lawn at Hilltop High School, where the heroic curmudgeon was teaching occasional music classes. Struck by the wiry hipster sat cross-legged on the grass with a guitar, he walked back and forth past Waits several times, mainly to make sure his ears and eyes weren't deceiving him. "He was singing Bob Dylan songs," Curtiss says. "He was really affecting that little-boy look Dylan had on the first album. He even wore a little cap like Dylan did in the beginning."

Singer Bobi Thomas also recalls the first time she noticed Waits at Hilltop High. As she watched the "freewheeling strut" her fellow pupil affected as he sauntered along the school hallways, she thought to herself, "That guy's got music in him." It was, she says, "the easy way he moved, the way his shoulders swayed from side to side, his shoes clicking down the walkway".

Located in the more affluent eastern part of Chula Vista, Hilltop High was a respected school, primarily middle-class and white with a sprinkling of local Hispanic students. In his mind, though, Tom Waits had already dropped out, dreaming of the wide-open America beyond San Diego. "I was never voted 'Most Likely to Succeed' in school, but what the hell," he said in 1976. "I'm *glad* I wasn't."

Waits took his first part-time job when he was fourteen. "My parents split up when I was young," he recalled, "so I kind of took care of my mother and sisters." The idea that Alma Waits and her daughters were in any way financially dependent on the young man of the house was surely a conceit: Alma was herself still working as a teacher, and Frank Waits would have been making regular alimony payments. But clearly the feeling of responsibility appealed to Waits, even as he revisited a time in his life when he was struggling with his father's absence.

According to Waits, the succession of short-term jobs he undertook included bartending, working in a jewellery store, changing tyres at a gas station, driving taxis and ice-cream vans, and selling encyclopedias and vacuum cleaners. As a CV it smacks of mild embellishment, to say the least. What is certain is that an opening came up at a restaurant in downtown Chula Vista called La Bella Pizza Garden. "My brother-in-law . . . weighed about three hundred pounds," Waits recalled. "They decided there was no room for him in the kitchen. So they sacked him and I got the job." Waits began working at the restaurant, run by New Yorkers Tony and Kitty Raso at 373 Third Avenue.

Unfortunately he too failed to last the course. "I don't think he worked there very long, maybe two or three weeks," says Lou Curtiss. "I think he dropped too many things and got fired."

Waits had evidently got the pizza bug, though: it wasn't long before he was applying for a job at Napoleone's Pizza House at 619 National Avenue in nearby National City, a blue-collar suburb famous for the "Mile of Cars" strip of automobile outlets that dominates it to this day. This time he either dropped fewer plates or was lucky enough to have more tolerant employers. "He started when he was in high school, about sixteen years old," says Sal Crivello, co-owner of Napoleone's with his partner Joe Sardo. "He was shy at first, but I think that was just because he was young. He washed dishes, and then he became a cook. He was an excellent worker. He made good pizzas."

Crivello talks from behind the counter at which he's stood for nigh on fifty years. The jukebox is a different one but sits in the same spot as it did when the teenage Waits heard Ray Charles' "Crying Time" and "I Can't Stop Loving You" coming out of it. Above it hangs a picture of Sal seated in a booth with Tom on 23

Sal Crivello, National City, March 2007. (*Art Sperl*)

31

November 2002. "We're still friends," Crivello says. "He stops by and says hello once in a while."

"I thought high school was a joke," Waits told *Rolling Stone*. "I went to school at Napoleone's." How Waits managed to combine school attendance with his Napoleone's night shifts is something of a mystery. It's hard to imagine his mother rubber-stamping such a round-the-clock double life. Certainly Waits makes no bones about the resulting exhaustion he suffered. "I was wasted all day," he admitted in 1976. "I was dishwasher, waiter, cook, janitor, plumber – everything. They called me Speed O'Flash. Sundays I'd come in at 6 a.m. and wash, buff, and wax the floors." In a "Proust Questionnaire" for *Vanity Fair*, however, Waits stated that he was at his absolute happiest in "Nineteen sixty-three, one a.m., washing dishes on a Saturday night in the kitchen of Napoleone Pizza House, 619 National Avenue, National City, California."*

Napoleone's and National City offered Waits both release from his oestrogen-dominated home and a contrast to Chula Vista and the Whittier of his early childhood. "National City is this Naugahyde town in Southern California," was how he later put it, "and it's a sailor town, lots of vinyl-white-booted go-go dancers." The dancers – possibly Waits' euphemism for "late-night evening prostitutes", as he called them on one of his early songs – appeared around 4 a.m. on Saturday morning, together with clusters of marauding sailors in their cups. "Hookers would come in, grab and play with me," Waits remembered. Exposure to pool hustlers, gangsters, and older people in general meant that Waits "grew up real fast". It also peopled his imagination with characters he would later work into his songs.

Waits never forgot Napoleone's or the neighbouring stores, clubs, and diners where people searched for the elusive "heart of Saturday night": the Golden Barrel, Escelani's Liquor, Mario's

* The date looks slightly suspect: could Waits really have been working at Napoleone's at the age of fourteen?

Pizza; the Westerner, where Hank Williams had played; Phil's Porno and Iwo Jima Eddie's Tattoo Parlor. He got his first tattoos at Eddie's, which mainly catered to sailors on shore leave; one of the earliest was an elaborate design around the word "Nighthawk", a reference to a Chula Vista car club to which he briefly belonged.

Waits also remembered Sorenson's Triumph motorcycle shop, Burge Roberts' Mortuary, and a Shell gas station on the corner. Then there was Wong's, to which he was regularly despatched by Sal or Joe with pizzas he exchanged for chicken chow mein. As he sat there waiting, with Mr Wong yelling at his workers through the steam, the teenager felt like he'd been shanghaied.

Better than all of these was the Napoleone's jukebox. The sound of Ray Charles or Patsy Cline transported Waits from the pizza kitchen to some exalted sphere of emotion where he felt he belonged. Charles' grief-drenched, strings-saturated take on Don Gibson's "I Can't Stop Loving You" was ever-present on the jukebox. Hearing it made Waits – standing at the sink in his apron and paper hat – wonder how it felt to sing such a song, to be that heroically lonely figure at the keyboard, reaching for feelings of love and loss. "I worked on Saturday nights and I would take my break and I'd sit by the jukebox and I'd play my Ray Charles," he recalled. "He would kind of skate across country and sound like Floyd Cramer sometimes on the piano, and he brought that in there with the Jelly Roll Morton and he could play like Nat King Cole. It was just amazing what he absorbed and that voice; for years it was just *the genius of Ray Charles*."

In 1966, Waits bought the first of the many automobiles that would play such a vital and iconographic part in his life and art. Splashing out $125 in a GM showroom on the "Mile of Cars", he bought himself a 1955 Buick Roadmaster, a "pioneer GM product with the Dynaflow hydramatic transmission, a leviticously deuteronymous catastrophe sort of automobile" that lasted three

THOMAS WAITS
Art Guild
Red Cross Rep.

Hilltop High yearbook, 1968

years and sucked up more than three thousand of his hard-earned dollars. In this legendary vehicle – inspiration for his most famous early song – Waits got himself to and from home, school, and Napoleone's.

The freedom the Buick brought coincided with Waits' increasing curiosity about the rest of America – the sense of coast-to-coast possibility afforded by owning your own wheels. For the seventeen-year-old, the distances within the US were "exhilarating, especially when you set out in the morning in a late-model Ford, and you're leaving California, driving to New York". Knowing you could point your car east and drive nonstop for a week was for Waits the quintessence of the American dream.

Even so, Waits stayed put in San Diego, continuing the night shift at Napoleone's. In 1968, to his parents' displeasure and alarm, he took the plunge and dropped out of school. "I wanted to go into the world," he told Terry Gross. "Enough of this! I didn't like the ceilings in the rooms. I didn't like the holes in the ceiling, the little tiny holes in the cardboard and the long stick used for opening the windows." (In the Hilltop High yearbook, however, he is listed as being a member of the school's Art Guild and the Red Cross rep for his twelfth-grade class.)

Rather than grow his hair, smoke pot, and make the pilgrimage to San Francisco's Haight-Ashbury, Waits went back in time to the alcoholic Beat rebels of the 1950s. "I was a rebel against the rebels," he said in 2004. "I discovered alcohol at an early age and that guided me a lot." Waits was doing the same drug as his father, thereby making a statement about his refusal to conform to the hippie underground. Part of him still entertained the fantasy of being a nightclub entertainer, even applying at one point for a job playing piano in a lounge in a nearby golf club. "It was a little pathetic," he admitted. "I put on a suit. I didn't even know enough songs to pull it off, really, I learned some Frank Sinatra and Cole Porter. But it was interesting that that was the world I wanted to be part of, plaid pants and golf."

Preferring Bing Crosby to Blue Cheer, Waits "slept through the sixties", avoiding granola, incense, black lights, and Jimi Hendrix posters. "I'm just suspicious of large groups of people going anywhere together," he told me. "If there's thirty thousand people going to see some event, I'm suspicious of it." When he did finally make the trip to San Francisco, it was purely to seek out the North Beach Beat haven that was Lawrence Ferlinghetti's City Lights bookstore – and "the ghost of Jack Kerouac".

Reading *On the Road*, the bestselling 1957 novel that confirmed Kerouac's reputation as the champion of peripatetic beatitude, opened Waits' eyes wide to the choices he had in life. "Kerouac came roaring down each new highway hollering tokay haikus like a man possessed," wrote Lester Bangs, another San Diego misfit. "[He moved] on not from a sense of disenchantment but with a voracious and insatiable hunger for experience."

Alternatively, Kerouac just gave Waits a post-adolescent identity to use while he figured out how to express himself. "I guess everybody reads [him] at some point in their lives," he recalled. "Even though I was growing up in Southern California, he made a tremendous impression on me. I started wearing dark glasses and got myself a subscription to *Down Beat*." To me, Waits admitted his Kerouac infatuation was "just like when you buy a record and you hold it under your arm and make sure everyone can see the title of it".

By 1969 Kerouac himself was dead, another literary victim of chronic alcoholism. By then, too, the Beats had been replaced by the hippies. If Allen Ginsberg was present at the birth of the Haight-Ashbury scene in Golden Gate Park, and Neal Cassady – inspiration for *On the Road*'s Dean Moriarty and *Visions of Cody*'s Cody Pomeray – reborn as the totemic figurehead of Ken Kesey's Merry Pranksters, the work of Kerouac and company was seen as passé by those at the new frontier of psychedelia.

The Beats had come into being in the New York of the mid-1940s, a disparate group of writers throwing off the shackles of literary tradition in favour of an unfettered style akin to the improvisations of bebop iconoclasts like Charlie Parker. "Kerouac liked to consider himself a jazz poet, using words the same way Miles uses his horn," Waits said. "And it's a beautiful instrument. He had melody, a good sense of rhythm, structure, color, mood and intensity. I couldn't put [*On the Road*] down."

Damaged and narcissistic as they were, Kerouac and friends sought "100 per cent personal honesty" in the articulation of experience, cutting through received Western culture to raw truth and reality. Above all they were renouncing middle-class shibboleths, asserting brotherhood with the poor, the oppressed, and the black-skinned. In *On the Road*, Sal Paradise – Kerouac's own alter ego – wandered the "colored section" of Denver, "wishing I were a Negro, feeling that the best the white world had offered was not enough ecstasy for me, not enough life, joy, kicks, darkness, music, not enough night". The cult of the White Negro – the term famously coined by Norman Mailer – began with this shambling rebel restlessly searching for some spiritual answer to his inner turmoil.

The Beats expressed a post-war revolt against the American status quo – the suburban nuclear family unit of the Eisenhower years. For the disaffected middle classes, Kerouac's *On the Road*, Ferlinghetti's *A Coney Island of the Mind*, Gregory Corso's *Gasoline*, and Ginsberg's primal "Howl" of outrage against Mammon and Moloch had the same electrifying force as James Dean and Elvis Presley had for blue-collar teenagers. And in Waits' hero Bob Dylan the two strains would ineluctably come together.

For Kerouac, Neal Cassady was "the HOLY GOOF", an inverted saint or noble savage radiating Whitmanesque innocence. Even as *On the Road* revealed him to be little more than a glorified con-man, ruthlessly selfish to the end, Kerouac was compelled to forgive him, "to understand the impossible complexity of his life, how he had to leave me there, sick, to get on with his wives and woes".

It was Kerouac's America – a cityscape of displaced, marginalized street people – that hooked the teenage Waits as he scrubbed the cutlery at Napoleone's. "I enjoy [Kerouac's] impressions of America, certainly more than anything you'd find in *Reader's Digest*," he recalled. "The roar of the crowd in a bar after work; working for the railroad; living in cheap hotels; jazz." Kerouac was Waits' passport to the after-hours world, a place where a young nighthawk could pick up scraps of conversation and use them to piece together the lives of anonymous uncelebrated Americans.

Napoleone's wasn't the only place Waits eavesdropped on America's small talk. Rudford's, at the time San Diego's only twenty-four-hour diner, became a regular haunt for him in the late 1960s. Located on Adams Avenue, it was an eaterie of the kind Waits would celebrate in songs for years to come, a place where blowsy waitresses served dubious hamburgers to "ambulance drivers, cab drivers, street sweepers" getting through Sinatra's "wee small hours of the morning". Rudford's is still there, and the

Rudford's, San Diego, March 2007. (*Art Sperl*)

waitresses still offer free refills of authentically weak coffee once you've perched yourself at the counter or wedged your behind into one of the red-leather booths. Waits listened, observed, and absorbed; often he noted down phrases or snatches of dialogue on napkins.

Waits knew performing was his destiny but couldn't see how to translate that calling into practical action. All he knew was that a career in "showbiz" would almost certainly "beat the hell out of putting aluminum siding on recreational vehicles, or fixing radios – or writing for a magazine, you know". At least he was able to avoid being drafted for Vietnam, later explaining that he "went up for a physical and talked to the psychiatrist . . . I was 1-A for a long time and that's the last I heard of it." A quarter of a century later he said he "had a very low lottery number and . . . wound up being a fireman for three years – in the forestry service, way out in the sticks on the border between Mexico and California".

Waits was hedging his bets when he enrolled at Chula Vista's Southwestern Community College, taking a summer class in photography. "I think Tom and I were in that class together," says Carey Driscoll, now a promoter of acoustic music shows in San Diego. "He was noticeably a little bit different from the norm, the average student. He wasn't a total social outcast, either by society's standards or his own, but he was far from a social butterfly."

For a moment Waits seems to have been serious about photography, purchasing several cameras and trying to exhibit pictures where he could. "He told me he'd been really into it, and that he wanted to be a photographer," says songwriter Jack Tempchin. "He had all these cameras and he would go downtown and photograph the bums." Singer Bob LaBeau remembers buying a black-and-white print of a pair of folded hands. "They were real greasy, dirty work hands," he says. "It was a nice photo."

Waits' interest in lenses and light shutters waned as he became more serious about music. One by one the cameras were sold to pay for piano lessons he'd begun taking from a female classical teacher. "He took it pretty seriously," says folk legend Ray Bierl. "He said he was able to tell her the kind of thing he was interested in learning – which was not just your basic classical music. She was somebody who really saw what Tom was after and helped him on a lot of chord theory and the kind of thing that shows up in his early compositions on the piano."

Despite his early fantasies of becoming a saloon singer, Waits had rarely played the piano his mother kept in her house. When Alma and Jim finally decided to throw it out, however, Waits intervened to save its life. "I started sitting down, fooling around with it," he said. "After about a year or so I started writing on it." Waits never progressed much beyond proficiency as a piano player. What did come naturally was a gift for picking up and remembering chords. "I played and I learned songs," he told me, "and then I memorized songs and pretended to be reading the notes. I realized I was good at memorizing: if I heard a song I could play it. And I still pretty much can do that."

The chords Waits found on the keyboard had a distinctive feel that combined folk, country, Tin Pan Alley, and New Orleans. Inspiration came as much from Nashville session king Floyd Cramer as from Waits' early hero Ray Charles. It also came from the jazz mavericks he was learning about in *Down Beat* magazine. Exerting a particular influence on Waits the budding pianist was the sublimely eccentric Thelonious Monk. "Monk said, 'There is no wrong note, it has to do with how you resolve it,'" Waits said in 1999. "He almost sounded like a kid taking piano lessons."

In 1969, Waits befriended Francis Thumm, a classically trained pianist who would play a key collaborative role in Waits' music in the 1980s and 90s. The pair regularly sat at the piano together and played Gershwin songs, "like a couple of old men in the retirement home", as Thumm recalled. Another of the duo's pastimes was singing Doors songs in the style of Frank Sinatra. "My favorite", said Thumm, "was Tom singing 'Riders on the Storm.'"

Pianos weren't much in evidence on the San Diego folk circuit. The local scene was dominated by traditionalists like Lou Curtiss and his wife Virginia, the majority of them playing guitars, banjos, dobros, and other vintage stringed instruments. It was a small but fertile scene, cleaving hard to a purist vision of "old-timey" Americana. Out of the city's bluegrass scene had come the Byrds' Chris Hillman, who started out as a mandolin player in the Scottsville Squirrel Barkers.

The first San Diego coffeehouses had sprung up around 1958, several of them in the Mission Beach district. "It was a very bohemian area," says Randy Hoffman, a friend of Francis Thumm's. "Specifically *north* Mission Beach, which was more intellectual. A lot of musicians collected there, and at one time on the boardwalk was a very hip bookstore and theater run by a very leftist character." In 1962, in partnership with Englishman Stewart Glennan, banjo player Bill Nunn rented a single-storey cinder-block building on the beach at 3842 Mission Boulevard and opened the Heritage coffeehouse. The name made plain its leanings towards the traditional, a reaction to the pop-folk of acts like the Kingston Trio and Peter, Paul and Mary. In the mid-1960s, the Heritage became the most respected folk venue in San Diego, its only real rival being the End on Pacific Beach's Grand Avenue.

"The Heritage was like a little theater," says Jack Tempchin. "If somebody was performing and you talked to the person next to you, the waitress would come over and say there was no talking. And if you talked more they just kicked you out."

Tom Waits may have first wandered into the Heritage as early as 1965, possibly with his younger sister Cynthia in tow; though she didn't play an instrument, "Cinny" was as interested in music as her brother. As a coffeehouse without a liquor licence, the Heritage was open to local teenagers. Waits was just fifteen when he saw Texan blues legend Lightnin' Hopkins play there. "He was doing, I don't know, 'Black Snake Moan' or something, and I just thought, 'Wow, this is something I could do,'" Waits recalled. "I don't mean I could play guitar like him, I just mean that this could be a possible career opportunity for me."

Hopkins was the headliner on another seminal evening in Waits' musical education, this time at the Candy Company on El Cajon Boulevard. But it was support act Jack Tempchin, not Hopkins, who caught Waits' attention. Here was a local contemporary *singing his own songs* as opposed to covering Bob Dylan's. Tempchin, Waits recalled, was "the first real songwriter I really saw and really got enthused about . . . he was real casual and everything, [and] it was just something I wanted to try my hand at".

Jack Tempchin, Hollywood, March 2007. (*Art Sperl*)

Slowly Waits found himself drawn into the scene, a shy and unassuming presence at the Heritage, the Candy Company, Escondido's In the Alley, La Mesa's Bifrost Bridge, and – located on campus at San Diego State University – the Back Door. Soon he was meeting performers such as Tempchin, Ray Bierl, Bob Webb, Bob LaBeau, Grady Tuck, Martin Henry, and Ted Staak. "Tom was a pretty impressive guy from right off," says Bierl. "He just struck you as a guy who was a thoughtful person. There was some integrity to him. That reserve and shyness you saw as a positive thing, and I don't think that's inconsistent with being a performer." Bierl recalls Waits asking if he'd run into his *other* sister, then an active member of Students for a Democratic Society at San Diego State and later a Progressive Labor League activist in Philadelphia.

"Tom was always very friendly and easy-going," says Martin Henry. "He was wild-looking, though. He always looked like he'd been out partying late. I guess you create the world around you, and you go to the places that evoke that inner world."

In the fall of 1969, singer Bob Webb took over the Heritage from Bill Nunn, who wanted to retire to the coastal wilds of Big Sur. "Bill and I were both committed to preserving traditional music," says Webb, who'd become a fixture at the club after making his debut in March 1968. "We didn't stray much into the singer-songwriter bag but rather hired bluesmen like Sam Chatmon and Robert Shaw, old-time string bands such as the Highwoods String Band, and other folk musicians like the folk-song collector Sam Hinton." Occasionally, though, Webb hired "guitarist-singers who played songs with more contemporary or topical themes".

Webb turned out to be a big fan of the Beats. He lent Waits his copy of Kerouac's *The Dharma Bums*, and the two often talked about the Beats together. "Kerouac was the starting point of our friendship," says Webb. "We soon developed a friendly competition to see who could find unusual Beat titles. Together and separately we scouted all the secondhand bookstores around San Diego." After Webb found a first edition of Kerouac's *Tristessa*, Waits unearthed a first edition of *Visions of Gerard* and a rare signed edition of the abridged *Vanity of Duluoz*.

In 1969, an opening came up for someone to fill in for country-blues singer Steve Von Lutes as occasional doorman at the Heritage. "The only thing about the job that changed over the years", Von Lutes recalls, "was going from beating the crap out of drunken sailors to beating the crap out of drug-crazed hippies." When Bob LaBeau suggested him as a candidate, Waits jumped at the opportunity. "The reason I got the job was because I knew I was going to play there," he said in 1976. "I was sitting there incognito – like in the inner sanctum of this club, hobnobbing, doing some low-level social climbing . . . I was trying to soak up as much before I did so I wouldn't make an ass of myself."

"I remember Tom as a longish-haired but otherwise clean-shaven young man with a pleasant, plummy voice," says Von Lutes, who had been playing the Heritage since 1963. "I sold him one of his first guitars, an old Martin, probably for the price of a bag of pot." Bar the odd evening when some Hell's Angels dropped by or a group of rowdy conventioneers went slumming on Mission Beach, Waits earned his nightly $5 without too much aggravation. "I never thought of him as the bouncer," says Jack Tempchin, "but I guess he would have been the guy had some trouble started." More than anything, the job afforded Waits countless opportunities to gather scraps of conversation he heard from passers-by on the street. "I'd bring my books and my coffee and my cigarettes and put my feet up," he remembered. "And I'd read my Kerouac and watch the cars go by, and I just felt like I was on fire and I had a reason to live. Sitting there, my own ordinary life was just lifted out of that and I was all dusted with something sparkling."

Stories of Waits the bookworm soon made the rounds of the scene. "I heard about him working as the doorman, and he always had a book under his arm and was always reading and never said much," says Bill Goodwin. "And one day he appeared fully-formed with a guitar. That was what was related to me. 'He seemed like a quiet guy . . .' It was like the description of a serial killer."

As time passed, Waits turned his job into a showcase for the act he was developing. "On slow nights he'd sometimes have a bigger crowd out there than was inside listening to the music," says Ray Bierl. "Sometimes at the door he'd be practicing rhymes, pulling lines together, challenging himself." The verbal routines Bierl heard – prototypes for spoken-word raps like "Diamonds on My Windshield" – were inspired by recordings of Kerouac and other Beats reading over backing by small jazz combos. "Tom was influenced by the Beats' public performance of poetry," says Bob Webb. "It was an image we shared of Kerouac and his literary friends reciting poems in a smoky downtown jazz bar somewhere."

"Sometimes it was more fun standing outside gabbing with Tom than being inside the place," says Lou Curtiss. "He was great to talk to. He was reading everything he could get a hold of. He'd have books by Kierkegaard. He was getting into some pretty heavy philosophy along with Kerouac and all that stuff." Music, too, was the subject of much of the gabbing. "We'd stand out in front of the Heritage and talk about it," Curtiss says of a motley crew that included Ray Bierl, Wayne Stromberg, Tom Presley, Cathy Nichols, and others. "Anything from James Brown to Stax. I was into Eddie Floyd and Otis Redding. Tom would be talking about James Brown."

So popular was the Heritage's new doorman that Texan singer-songwriter Guy Clark later recalled him – "in a pork-pie hat and silver skates/juggling three collection plates" – in his song "Cold Dog Soup". Singer Suzanne Reed remembers frequent chats with the "gravely-voiced" ticket-taker. "I'd sit out there with my guitar and ask Tom about his music and tell him my dreams," she says. "He had that deadpan bad-boy delivery when he talked. He was really funny. He'd either give me long rambling answers to my questions or he'd be short and curt, depending on his moods."

When the Heritage had closed for the night, Waits accompanied Lou Curtiss and Ray Bierl down to Saska's, a steakhouse a few blocks along Mission Boulevard. "We'd have a hamburger and a beer and we'd tell jokes," Bierl recalls. "Somebody would say, 'Tom, tell that joke you always tell.' Everyone would have heard the joke three or four times already, but it was still funny."

"He was always a late-night guy," Curtiss says of Waits. "You'd get a call at two in the morning and he'd want to go shoot pool. I didn't do too much of that because I was a pretty good sleeper, but there were other people who would." Another establishment patronized by the Heritage crowd was Mr D's, a few blocks along Mission Beach from the club. "It was a cholesterol-loaded place where you could get deep-fried everything," says Steve Von Lutes. "Saska's closed at 2.30 a.m., so we'd get through with that, wake up after falling asleep on the beach, and go down to Mr D's as the sun came up."

Night owl though he was – and at this point he was still working occasional shifts at Napoleone's – Waits sometimes surfaced early enough to drop by Folk Arts, then in its original location on India Street. "I remember playing old 78s for Tom when the store first opened," says Lou Curtiss. "I'd play him everything from Billie Holiday to Cole Porter singing his own stuff."

When Waits finally summoned the courage to ask if he could sing a few songs at the Heritage hoot, he bowed to what was expected of the folk troubadour of the time. Certainly the influence of Porter or Gershwin was hard to detect in short sets that mixed Dylan with blues and country numbers. "I started with Bobby Dylan songs," Waits reminisced in 1974. "I was trying to learn some more tunes in a more traditional vein, to be able to sit in at the Heritage a little better, because it didn't seem as though songwriting was in vogue at the time."* Waits was so in thrall to the staple Dylan persona that he wore a harmonica around his neck without ever putting his lips to it.

Other early staples of Waits' open-mic slots included Ray

---

* One of Waits' favourite Dylan albums was the bootleg "basement tape" that began circulating in the late 1960s as *The Great White Wonder*. "I like my music with the rinds and the seeds and pulp left in," he later said of the 1967 recordings Dylan had made with the Hawks in Woodstock; "[. . .] the bootlegs I obtained in the sixties and seventies, where the noise and grit of the tapes became inseparable from the music, are essential to me."

Charles' "Hit the Road, Jack" and Elvis Presley's "Are You Lone-some Tonight", the latter delivered as a hokey impersonation. "He did the whole talking thing in the middle," says Ray Bierl. "He was a good mimic. He could do a pretty credible Ray Charles." Waits often ended his hoot sets with the old cowboy ballad "Happy Trails". He also began performing Red Sovine's country classic "Big Joe and Phantom 409" – taught to him by Bierl – about a truck driver who swerves to avoid a group of school kids and dies in the resulting crash.* "'Big Joe' was one of his set-pieces," says Bob Webb. "He enjoyed the dramatic story-telling and the supernatural material in that song."

"In the beginning Tom was just like the rest of us, finding his muse," says Bobi Thomas, then performing herself as half of old-timey duo Ostergren & Thomas. "He wasn't so unusual, other than being quite a bit more diamond-in-the-rough than the majority of people playing there at the time. He'd sing 'Phantom 409' or some old Dylan song, and always with the old guitar he had, a big old boxy blond thing. Sometimes he'd have his cigarette stuck in the strings of the tuning pegs, and in between singing he'd take a drag or two and chat-chat-chat."

Thomas and other Heritage regulars were struck by the ease of Waits' stage persona – what Ray Bierl calls his "slightly coy flirta-tiousness" – and the way he made his between-song patter so cen-tral to his act. "He had this comfortable-appearing façade," Thomas says. "He made us feel like we'd just stumbled into his liv-ing room." Interestingly, Ray Bierl believes Waits took "a lot of his

---

* Bierl revisited the song on his 2008 album *Any Place I Hang My Hat*, which carried the following encomium from the guy he'd taught it to all those years before. "I was nineteen in Mission Beach and barely old enough to shave," Waits recalled. "It was there, beneath a flood light in a coffee can, on a stage no bigger than a kitchen table, I used to hear Guy Clark, Rosalie Sorrels, Thomas Shaw, Guy Carawan, Utah Phillips and many nights I was lucky enough to hear the voice of the great Ray Bierl."

stage persona" from his father. According to Bob LaBeau, more-over, Waits talked often about Frank and had "a lot of respect" for him. "A lot of times people have trouble with their parents," LaBeau says, "but Tom was always very upbeat about his dad. He and I, underneath it all, were probably pretty conservative. He has a respect for people, for his elders, for taking care of business."

"He had a very unusual stage presence," confirms Martin Henry. "I would never have expected him, in all honesty, to go on and be a successful performer. His music was wonderful, but his bobbing and weaving and his voice were unusual." Henry says Jack Tempchin did something similar, communicating more obliquely with his audience: "Tom and Jack were different to the rest of us. They both were very inward-looking, self-contained entities who did their own thing."

For Suzanne Reed, Waits "wasn't really a singer *per se*, he was a story guy with attitude". But, she says, "you could hear a pin drop when he played . . . I thought he was a star." A big part of Waits' early act was his ribald comedy. "I asked him what kind of stuff he was doing," says Sal Crivello. "He said he sang and told jokes. I said, 'What kinda jokes?' He said, 'You know, the kinda jokes we tell here in the kitchen.' I said, 'Tom, you can't say those things in a *coffeehouse*!'"

Some of Waits' new fans felt that he was a singular enough talent to break free of his cover-version safety net and find his own voice. "He had a real nice bluesy sound and a nice sort of bluesy voice," says Bob LaBeau, "but he was doing all Bob Dylan songs and *everybody* was doing Bob Dylan songs. I said, 'Tom, you're good and you have a good stage presence and people like you. Why don't you start writing something of your own?'"

"The first times I saw him play I thought, 'He's just another Dylan guy,'" Lou Curtiss says. "The first song of his own I ever remember him doing was called 'Poncho's Lament.' I was stand-ing next to Bill Nunn and I said, 'That's a good song. He's got promise.'" One of Waits' earliest efforts, the song was a country waltz typical of the San Diego scene – an "I'm-glad-you're-gone-but-baby-please-come-home" pastiche sung in a tongue-in-cheek twang with spoken asides. "I don't know if they were really songs," Waits told me of such efforts. "Mostly they parodied existing songs with obscene lyrics. That's what most people do, or that's what I did."

"Parodies of country and western were quite common for people to do at the time," says Ray Bierl. "You know, like, '*I got tears in my ears from lyin' on my back cryin' over you . . .*' It took what was great about a lot of country music – specific references or metaphors – and twisted it." Another ironic homage to country music – "Looks Like I'm up Shit Creek Again" – was a song Gram Parsons might have tossed off in an idle moment. It was hardly surprising that Waits dabbled in country, given his constant exposure to bluegrass at the Heritage and other coffeehouses. Later he claimed he got "bluegrassed to death" at the Heritage, adding tersely that the only thing he hated more than bluegrass played badly was bluegrass played well.

Truer to Waits' muse were the songs he wrote at the turn of the decade. "Increasingly he performed his own material," says Bob Webb. "I think at one time or another he offered almost everything that later appeared on his first album." The first original Bob LaBeau recalls hearing was "Ice Cream Man", a jaunty sketch of one of his many part-time jobs replete with smutty double entendres. Singer Mary McCaslin, for whom he opened at the Heritage in April 1971, remembers "Had Me a Girl" (aka "The Doctor Says I'll Be Alright"), a song consisting of a list of former girlfriends from Chula Vista to North Dakota. But the songs that really stuck in people's minds were wry, bittersweet ballads like "Ol' '55" and "I Hope that I Don't Fall in Love with You". And the reason they stuck, most likely, was that they came from hard-won romantic experience.

One of Waits' first serious girlfriends was an attractive English redhead who waited tables at the Heritage. Pam Bowles was a few years Tom's senior and the mother of a young girl. "She lived next door to the Heritage," says Bob LaBeau. "She was a cute gal and Tom just was really stuck on her." Randy Hoffman recalls that before she clocked in at the Heritage, Bowles would drop her daughter off at the semi-communal Mission Beach house where he lived. When he returned home late at night, he would find the living room in disarray. Finally he asked Sherry – Bowles' baby-sitter and the co-owner of the house – what was going on. "Sherry said, 'Well, that's Tom, Pam's boyfriend,'" he remembers. "'They came over to pick up Pam's daughter and he was, like, laying over there.'"

Bowles was among the people who talked Bob Webb into giving Waits a chance as a paid performer at the Heritage. Webb admits he had to be "harangued" into letting Waits graduate beyond open-mic sets. "I was narrowly interested in traditional music," he says. "I was afraid of being overwhelmed by the large number of singer-songwriters who were beginning to emerge." Though impressed by Waits' hoot-night appearances, Webb felt his music wasn't right for the club. Finally he relented. Over the weekend of 20/21 November 1970, Waits appeared at the Heritage as "Thomas Waits", supporting a duo called Michael Claire. "I think I made more as a doorman than I did playing," he recalled. "Eight dollars a night on the door, six dollars a night on stage. A little strange."

Bob LaBeau thinks Waits' affair with Pam Bowles lasted no more than "a couple of months or so". Her ending of it gave him his first real taste of heartbreak. "They had, like, a torrid romance and then she dumped him," LaBeau says. "I know it really affected him. And it seemed like right after that he started writing a whole bunch of really pretty, sensitive songs. I think 'I Hope that I Don't Fall in Love with You' might have been about

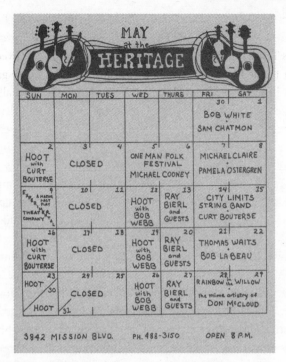

SUN	MON	TUES	WED	THURS	FRI	SAT
					30 BOB WHITE SAM CHATMON	1
2 HOOT with CURT BOUTERSE	3 CLOSED	4	5 ONE MAN FOLK FESTIVAL MICHAEL COONEY	6	7 MICHAEL CLAIRE • PAMELA OSTERGREN	8
9 A MAJOR HOLY PLAY THEATER COMPANY	10 CLOSED	11	12 HOOT with BOB WEBB	13 RAY BIERL and GUESTS	14 CITY LIMITS STRING BAND CURT BOUTERSE	15
16 HOOT with CURT BOUTERSE	17 CLOSED	18	19 HOOT with BOB WEBB	20 RAY BIERL and GUESTS	21 THOMAS WAITS • BOB LA BEAU	22
23 HOOT / 30 HOOT / 31	24 CLOSED	25	26 HOOT with BOB WEBB	27 RAY BIERL and GUESTS	28 RAINBOW in the WILLOW the mime artistry of DON McCLOUD	29

3842 MISSION BLVD.   PH. 488-3150   OPEN 8 P.M.

Heritage handbill, May 1971. (*Courtesy of Bob Webb*)

her. And I think he wrote 'Ol' '55' at the same time."

Waits' first great song, "Ol' '55" came out of the first flush of love rather than from its dissolution. A mumbly, countryish paean to his beat-up old Buick, it painted a vivid picture of a young man rising reluctantly from his girlfriend's bed at dawn to drive home on the freeway. He was pining for his girl, and the cars were flashing him to get out of the fast lane, but he felt "so holy" and "so alive" as the stars faded and the sun rose on the horizon. Historian Simon Schama would describe it as "the single most beautiful love song since Gershwin and Cole Porter shut their piano lids".

"I Hope that I Don't Fall in Love with You" was drier, more

"He was creating quite a buzz . . ." Waits onstage, circa 1972. (*Bobi Thomas*)

formal – a conversational prototype for such future pieces as "I Never Talk to Strangers" and "Picking up after You". Waits' shyness in the face of desire was delicately captured in a play of gestures – male and female staking each other out. On one level, the voice and its plucked acoustic accompaniment weren't so far from the singer-songwriter mood of a James Taylor. Yet this was the sound of a young man out of time, a lost soul hymning his own loneliness. "It wasn't until Tom began to write his own songs that the real sparks became apparent," says Bobi Thomas. "The songs he wrote in the beginning were just little gems. Little sparkly diamonds, lyrically *and* musically."

Thomas wasn't alone in her estimation of the doorman's talent. "We all recognized Tom's songwriting genius," says Martin Henry. "He was creating quite a buzz. I particularly remember 'Ol' '55' because I sang it for a while. Tom was looking for things, like we all were. You finally focus in on what your core entity is, which he did and which he refined."

"Almost all the local musicians were on the make," says Bob

Webb. "They were scrounging for any sort of thing – a gig, a drink, a lay, or a joint. Tom wasn't like that. He was polite, a little self-effacing, and in some real sense professional. I don't remember him having vices of the ordinary kind, though I suppose he smoked cigarettes. I never saw him do drugs, and he drank only moderately."

Waits increasingly began writing on the piano, to the point where an old upright was specially wheeled into the Heritage for him to play. The operation required hoisting the instrument onto a dolly, then pushing it down the sandy beachside alley on the south side of the Heritage. There they had to tip it across the threshold into the club, which was slightly below grade. From that time on, says Webb, Waits divided his sets between guitar and piano. "He would begin with guitar on stage, move over to the piano at the side of the room, and then return to the stage to close his set." To Heritage regulars, the sight of Waits at the keyboard was a revelation. Bobi Thomas remembers dropping by the club in the afternoon and finding Waits there "plunking on the old upright". He could also be found there after the evening's entertainment was over, lost in some old Broadway melody with a cigarette glued to his lips.

"You could tell right off that Tom had his ear on more mainstream and jazz things," says Ray Bierl. "What I heard, though I wouldn't have been able to identify it at the time, was more the Harold Arlen, Johnny Mercer thing – the best of the Tin Pan Alley tradition that Tom was channeling a whole lot more than folk music. And that's where Tom's music lessons paid off." For Bierl, the cover of *Closing Time* – Waits at the upright, illuminated by a lamp hanging over him – was "a total reference to the Heritage . . . a real conscious thank-you".

The Heritage wasn't the only place Waits played. As the reputation of this quirky new voice spread, he was booked for performances at all the other venues in and around San Diego.

Generally on these dates he would be supporting such venerable blues acts as Sonny Terry and Brownie McGhee – "a big thrill for me" – or sixties folk stars like Tim Buckley, with whom he played at In the Alley in August 1971. Sometimes, though, he'd play with local peers like Jack Tempchin. "I just hit it off with Tom for a while," Tempchin says. "He was a little bit of a character, but it wasn't a big change from anybody else. He didn't have the growly thing that came later, so it wasn't *that* acquired a taste. He was just a guy doing his songs, only they were better." Tempchin and Waits became close enough friends to collaborate on a song, the whimsical "(I Got Drunk on the Way Home from) Tijuana".

Most of the performers on the San Diego circuit were happy to stay put and develop a local following. Tempchin was one of the few to set his sights on success beyond the city. "As far as the music business went, it was never going to happen down there," he says. "There were no record companies, so anyone who really wanted to *do* something had to get off their butt and go to LA." Tempchin had for some time been making regular trips up to Los Angeles to play at Doug Weston's Troubadour club. The club's open-mic "hootenanny" night on Mondays was *the* showcase for any aspiring singer-songwriter in southern California – the stage where you hoped to make your mark and be heard by some passing manager or A&R man. Moreover, Tempchin had befriended some of the ambitious singers and musicians who were trying to make it in LA.

"A lot of them came down to San Diego," says Ray Bierl. "It seemed like we had something that they liked to come and connect with. It was just a more relaxed scene. I remember Glenn Frey and J. D. Souther and Chris Darrow coming down. One time I think I opened for Jackson Browne. These guys would just come down and hang out." Tempchin had first met Frey and Souther when they played the Candy Company as Longbranch Pennywhistle. Frey had come to LA from Detroit, Souther from

Hoot central: the Troubadour, West Hollywood, March 2007. (*Art Sperl*)

Amarillo in Texas. By 1971, Frey and Tempchin were good friends. When Tempchin was entrusted with the task of booking shows at San Diego State's Back Door, Frey helped him to haul carpet over to the campus. One of the more memorable Back Door shows was a double-header featuring Tempchin and Waits. "Tom just took the audience and, man, just kept playing and playing," Tempchin says. "I thought, 'This guy's got his thing happening.'"

Just as he'd been inspired by Tempchin's Candy Company show in 1968, so Waits now followed Jack's example in travelling up to the Troubadour hoot. "Jack and Tom both had their sights set on broader audiences than most of us in San Diego did," says Ray Bierl. "We had a little scene that we liked, and we were happy with that." When Bierl gave Waits a ride home one night, he heard about the younger man's plans. "Tom told me he was going to move to LA and really go for it," Bierl says. "And that was a big thing. LA was this huge behemoth. That's where people were on the make and competition was pretty fierce." Bob LaBeau, who'd played the Troubadour himself, remembers Waits coming into a Mission Beach bar one night with a magazine in his hand. "On the cover it said something about entertainment and how much money there was to be made in it," LaBeau says. "And Tom said, 'I don't know, I guess I really wanna make some money at this.'"

Playing the Troubadour hoot required dedication and discipline. Waits had to wake at 5 a.m., catching a Greyhound bus that left San Diego at six. At the terminal in downtown LA he would catch another bus that took him all the way up to West Hollywood. He'd then have to wait in line outside the Troubadour for hours until the club's "hootmaster" came out to decide who'd be given one of the handful of available slots. If Waits was *lucky* he'd get to sing three or four songs to the few remaining onlookers before racing to catch the early-morning bus back to San Diego. "[It] was like a slave market," Waits said. "People sell their souls to get up and play." The hoot, he said, was "the last resort . . . you see old vaudeville cats, bands that have hocked everything to come out here from the East Coast just to play one night".

A quarter of a century later, Waits spoke more affectionately of the club. "The hoot was the coolest thing," he told me. "They announced your name and picked you out with a spotlight at the cigarette machine. Then they'd walk you to the stage with the light. Doug Weston would go out on stage naked and recite 'The Love Song of J. Alfred Prufrock'. He'd have guys on acid who wanted to tell stories. It was like Ed Sullivan without Ed. Anyone could get up."

Waits' ambition surprised his San Diego friends as much as his talent had surprised them when he'd metamorphosed from the Heritage doorman into one of its most promising stars. "Clearly his music was wonderful, but having business acumen?" says Martin Henry. "I certainly never had the guts to go up to LA and break down those walls. It's a tough nut to crack, and he just went in there and did it."

The truth is that Waits had seen the writing on the wall in San Diego. Important as the Heritage in particular had been to him, the venue if anything represented the twilight of the city's coffeehouse scene. By 1971, Mission Beach had become a squalid neighbourhood of bikers, thieves, and junkies. "The gate at the Heritage had really started to decrease as Mission Beach deteriorated," says Steve Von Lutes. "I had people murdered out in front of me several times, or dying of drug overdoses. It was very depressing."

"Mission Beach became a little unseemly," Bob LaBeau concurs. "A lot of the people I knew and loved started doing drugs. People would say, 'This is great, this is the answer to everything,' and I'd say, 'I'll wait a couple of years and see what happens.' And many of them are dead." One of the early mainstays of the Heritage, guitarist and banjo player Grady Tuck, descended into such chronic alcoholism that Waits later namechecked him in the skid-row lullaby "On the Nickel".

An early Waits song from his San Diego years – a lightheartedly bluesy tune called "So Long I'll See Ya" that included a nod to "Blue Suede Shoes" – was a typical itchy-feet statement of the period. But it also spoke more intently of his desire to leave San Diego. "*Tom's gotta go,*" he sang. "*He's got them so-long-I'll-see-ya-'cause-my-Buick's-outside-waiting blues* . . ." He did have to go, and his old '55 Buick *was* waiting outside.

"San Diego musicians stay there and hope something is going to happen," Waits said in 1973. "But it never does. Nothing happens down there. You play in a rock band in high school and when you get out you end up playing in some swank club behind a girl singer or you stay in the rock band, play GI dances and get paid peanuts."

San Diegans who knew Waits seem split between those who

supported his move away and the ones who think he owes more to the city's music scene than he acknowledges. "I was never really part of that coffeehouse scene," he stated disingenuously in 1983. "I kind of missed that. I've always kind of been on the outside so I started doing this because I didn't fit."

"I think Tom plays down San Diego to take the pressure off his mother and sister, who still live here," says Lou Curtiss. "He doesn't want a bunch of people coming down and bothering them. I have an open invitation to him to come down and play the festival, but he's never taken it up. He's even played *up* the fact that he's originally from LA."

To this day Waits maintains a slightly strained relationship with the city where he spent his formative teenage years. "I don't want to make this one of those hometown-boys-make-good interviews," he said tersely to George Varga, music critic for the *San Diego Union-Tribune*. "I don't want to be the homecoming queen. I just want to talk about music."

Chapter 3

Understanding, Sympathy, and Encouragement

> *"You got to have a manager,*
> *That's what it's all about."*
> ("Eyeball Kid", 1999)

Herb Cohen is wedged behind a table at a restaurant on Beverly Boulevard, just around the corner from the office he retains despite having more or less retired from the music business. Imagine Dr John crossed with the Jack Nicholson of *The Departed*, a Jewish Godfather with small bored eyes set in a round flat face that bears the remnants of a beard. His hair is greased back, and his stomach juts out from under a loose cabana shirt.

You can take the man out of the South Bronx but you can't take the South Bronx out of the seventy-four-year-old Cohen, a living legend of the music business who first pitched up in southern California in the mid-1950s. You don't mess with this ageing street heavyweight. There is not a sentimental bone in the man's body, and any appeal to ordinary nostalgic impulses is quite futile. "Posterity?" Cohen says. "Kids on the street out there" – he waves a paw at the window – "they don't even know who *Stalin* was, for chrissakes."

Cohen's only passions these days seem to involve food. He's an avid consumer of cheeses and shows me his current stash, neatly wrapped in a plastic bag by his side. He's also keen on confectionery, only agreeing to meet me on condition I brought him a tube of chocolate Bath Olivers from London – a tube whose wrapping he proceeds to prise open with a vicious-looking knife he produces from his pocket. "They ain't how I remember them," he says after sampling one, recalling the days when he'd buy the thickly-coated plain chocolate biscuits on business trips to England.

Though he's seldom flatly rude, Cohen's conversation always borders on the ill-tempered. "I don't have time to be concerned with the reality of incidental bullshit," he says. "Artists think they're so important, but who really gives a fuck. People think Dylan changed the world, that he was a prophet. But he was just a reporter. The times would have been a-changin' with or without him."

I find myself feeling a begrudging admiration for Cohen's all-is-vanity cynicism – there really *isn't* any bullshit here – while remembering that said cynicism was what enabled him to help himself to money that technically belonged to the artists he represented. "People are obsessed with what goes on behind the scenes – the lives of artists, whether they fucked their mother or what have you," he says. "There are things I could tell you about Tom Waits or any of my artists that nobody knows, but why should I care if people want to know what an artist is really like? I always told my artists to lie about their lives anyway. I said, 'Who cares what the truth is? Feed the writers stuff that'll make the records sell.'"

Whether Tom Waits took that advice to heart we'll probably never know; what we do know is that Cohen was present at the Troubadour club on a Monday hoot night in June 1971, and that an unusual voice and style caught his ear from the stage. "I was on my way to the toilet when I heard Tom sing," he recalled matter-of-factly. "When I came out of the toilet I asked him what he was doing and he said, 'Nothing.' So I signed him up."

Waits remembered the encounter no less prosaically. "Herb came over to me, was very honest and upfront," he said. "And the next day I had a songwriting contract and $300 in my pocket." It was, Waits said wryly, "the big jump into showbiz" that he'd long hankered for.

Did Waits recognize the name of the stocky gentleman offering to make his Troubadour dreams come true? He might not have known that Cohen had opened the Unicorn, the first true coffeehouse in LA and a place dubbed "the headquarters of the Beat Generation" by banjo player Billy Faier. Nor, perhaps, would he have known of Cohen's Cosmo's Alley, which opened in 1957 and provided a regular stage for such cutting-edge comedians as Lord Buckley and Lenny Bruce. Waits probably wasn't aware that, with the help of his lawyer brother Martin (aka "Mutt"), Cohen had ruled the Hollywood folk scene of the late fifties.

"Herbie was a lot scarier than people would think," says Jerry Yester, one half of a fraternal folk duo that became the first act Cohen managed. "They'd think he was a kind of pudgy Jewish guy, but he was absolutely terrifying in conflict. I mean, he had a box of hand grenades in the trunk of his car." When Cohen disappeared in the early 1960s, rumours circulated in LA that he was fighting as a mercenary in South America or running guns for Castro. When he finally returned to America, he was scarier than ever. "He just kind of arrived back one day and he was a wild man," says Yester. "Mutt by contrast was very gentle and soft-spoken in comparison. He said he'd talk to Herbie, and Herbie did calm down a little."

Cohen also built up his management roster. Following Jim and Jerry, he took on singer-comedienne Judy Henske – Yester's future wife – and the Modern Folk Quartet. "A lot of managers were hitting on us," says the MFQ's Henry Diltz. "Herbie would say, 'Nah, that guy's fulla shit . . .' So we said, 'Well, why don't *you* manage us?' He had a way of looking after himself but he was a dear man. Whenever I see him I have to chuckle out loud. He cuts right to the point. Nobody to mess around with."

"He was like an adventurer soldier of fortune," says Joe Smith, then of Warner-Reprise Records. "For a little Jewish guy with a little beard, he was really something. I got a tremendous kick out of him. He was kind of shifty but he was a delightful rogue. And Mutt was a barracuda lawyer, so Herb could move through life doing his damage knowing he didn't have any legal fees."

Things got interesting when Cohen began managing a demented new act called the Mothers. A physically unprepossessing synthesis of theatre, satire, and avant-garde rock, the Mothers were led by maverick prankster Frank Zappa and had zero interest in becoming the new Beatles. It was Cohen – described by Zappa at the time as "a little Jewish man that nobody likes who always wears nylon shirts" – who persuaded producer Tom Wilson to catch a Mothers show at the Whisky a Go Go on Sunset. Impressed by the freaks coalescing around the group, Wilson convinced MGM Records that the Mothers were a blues band and set

"I wanted a big bruiser . . ." Herb Cohen (right) with client Frank Zappa at MIDEM, Cannes, in 1970.

to work producing their radical 1996 double-album debut *Freak Out!!*. Zappa loved to lampoon hippies, satirizing bandwagon-jumpers and the prevailing peace-and-love platitudes. 1967's *We're Only in It for the Money* was a prescient vision of the flower-power trip gone bad.

It was through Zappa that Cohen put together a stable of LA misfits which included Don Van Vliet (Captain Beefheart), super-groupies the GTOs (or Girls Together Outrageously), and the genuinely loopy Larry "Wild Man" Fischer. If there was also room on Cohen's management roster for jazz-folk bard Tim Buckley and country-rock princess Linda Ronstadt, as a lineup it begged the question whether Cohen really *was* only in it for the money. He himself claims he simply had more *fun* managing Zappa, Beefheart, and co. than he'd have had massaging the coked-out egos of, say, Crosby, Stills, and Nash. "Herb, I have to say, attached himself to some real interesting people," says Todd Everett. "You don't sign Frank Zappa and Captain Beefheart and Tim Buckley and Tom Waits because that's where you're going to become a multi-millionaire."

Cohen's taste in music didn't count for much in Waits' eyes. In April 1969, he'd seen the Mothers – or the Mothers of Invention, as they'd become – on a double bill with Country Joe and the Fish at San Diego's Convention Hall and walked out. "I hated it," he said in 1977. "I wasn't a snob or anything – I just thought it was a waste of time." For Waits, Cohen simply represented power and clout. "I wanted a big bruiser, the tough guy in the neigh-borhood," he said in 1999. "And I got it."[*]

"Waits knew you needed management, like Bob Dylan needed management," says Harvey Kubernik, LA correspondent for *Melody Maker* in the mid-seventies. "Guys like Dylan didn't go to the Post Office, they didn't go to Kinko's to photocopy. They

[*] "A knee-breaker?" the interviewer asks, to which Waits replies: "You said that, not me. I gotta be careful what I say about Herbie. I'll wind up in . . . court."

knew you must have a manager, an agent, and a major label. I remember Waits saying, 'I'm in the Herb Cohen program now.'" For Cohen it was Waits' songs, rather than his prospects as an artist, which made him attractive. While his roster of acts made it clear that he was partial to the Bizarre – the name of a label he launched with Zappa – his decision to offer Waits a publishing rather than a recording contract suggests he wasn't convinced by the twenty-one-year-old's chances as a singer-songwriter.

"They gave him a writing contract and he was getting some minimal amount," says Bob LaBeau of the deal Waits made with Cohen's Third Story company. "He had to turn in five songs a month or something like that, and they'd pay him a few hundred bucks. It wasn't a lot of dough but it seemed like a lot at the time."

The idea of being a writer-for-hire appealed to Waits, fascinated as he was by the great Tin Pan Alley writers and the classic Brill Building partnerships of the 1950s and 60s. Los Angeles had itself boasted stables of songwriters, many churning out disposable fluff for transient teen idols. One of Waits' new influences, Randy Newman, had started his professional life as a staffer at Metric Music, the song-publishing arm of Liberty Records. "Newman was always like a Brill Building guy," Waits said to me. "He was part of that whole tradition: you go sit down in a room and write songs all day. Then you get these runners and you get the songs out to Ray Charles or Dusty Springfield." In 2002, Waits told NPR's Terry Gross that he liked the concept of "writing at gunpoint", relishing the idea of being cooped up in a stuffy cubicle on Broadway with a major artist waiting on him to deliver a hit.

Waits was aware that the perception of the songwriter in American pop culture was changing. Los Angeles itself was the seedbed of a new kind of artist. Bob Dylan, the first modern troubadour, had opened the gates to a swath of solo performers graduating from folk music to a more personal mode of emotional reportage. Key artefacts of the so-called "confessional" school were the early albums by Canadian expats Neil Young and Joni Mitchell, as well as James Taylor's landmark second release *Sweet Baby James* (1970). "Taylor was immensely popular then," says Bob Webb. "I think we heard 'Sweet Baby James' from someone or other during just about every open-mic night we had."

"I caught that wave of songwriters garnering understanding, sympathy, and encouragement," Waits acknowledged to me. "Up until that point, who cared who wrote the songs? Just, you know, kill me with it. Nobody made a distinction between a song Elvis sang and a song Elvis wrote. Did he write it? Does it matter? No. And then everybody kind of wore that around. For a while there, anybody who wrote and performed their own songs could get a deal. *Anybody*. So I came in on that."

Back in San Diego, the news of Waits' good fortune was received with a mixture of envy and hometown pride. "I was very proud when Herb Cohen asked if he could manage Tom," says Bobi Thomas. "We'd all known that he was talented. We just never knew what the *big people* would think." Adds Ray Bierl, "It was interesting to me that Herb was taking Tom under his wing – in my mind Herb was just associated with the commercial business aspect of it, but this was telling me that here was a guy who really saw something artistically in Tom that he was able to relate to."

For the remainder of 1971, Waits focused on writing, commuting to LA to play the Troubadour hoot and using his slots there to air new songs. With his retainer coming in from Cohen, Waits finally quit the night shift at Napoleone's. "I felt I'd snuck in the back way," he said in 1981. "I had a songwriting contract. I'm sitting at a bus stop on Santa Monica Boulevard, it's pouring with rain, and I'm scared to death." Ray Bierl detected a new determination in Waits. "He said he was giving it all or nothing,"

Hooting at the Troub, spring 1973. (*Kim Gottlieb-Walker/www.lenswoman.com*)

Bierl recalls. "He said that if he hadn't gotten his foot on the ladder with that contract he probably would've gone nuts. Because he wasn't leaving himself any fallback. He put all his eggs in that basket." Waits confessed in 1976 that he was "as ambitious as hell". "I wasn't any good but I was ambitious. I thought I was better than anybody, and I sucked raw eggs. But you have to think that way. To let an audience intimidate you is musical suicide."

"One thing to learn from Tom is that he never bothered to play with anybody else," says sometime Waits sideman Stephen Hodges. "He had the balls and the inclination and the songs and the drive to just do it on his own from the very start, and I think there's a lot to be said for that whole spirit and the tack that he's taken."

For his new songs Waits drew as much on his memories as on his musical influences. With its echo of Ray Charles' "Lonely Avenue", the bluesy "Virginia Avenue" spoke of the smalltown ennui Waits felt in Chula Vista and National City, even if the song was putatively about Reno. The clubs have closed and the song's hero, trudging the streets at 1.45 a.m., has seen all the town's "highlights" anyway. It was also 1.45 a.m. in "Goin' Down Slow", a blithe hymn to cunnilingus that took us past "a quarter of three" and even "a quarter of four", when Waits was still "begging for more". In "I'm Your Late-Night Evening Prostitute", Waits put himself in the shoes of a hooker, equating her life with that of a professional entertainer.

Tom the tender lover could be heard on "Midnight Lullaby" and "Little Trip to Heaven", both written in the glow of love for Pam Bowles. If the first presaged the passing of time in a way unusual in such a young writer, Waits' ability to imagine old age came out even more distinctively in "Martha", wherein he presented himself as "old Tom Frost" telephoning the titular heroine, a girlfriend from forty years before. The song would become one of the standout tracks on *Closing Time*. "In early 1972, no one was doing stuff like that," says Jerry Yester, the album's producer. "Who the hell was doing songs like ['Martha'], except maybe Dave Van Ronk? And the way Tom played the piano, it was like Hoagy Carmichael, for Christ's sake."

The ragtimey New Orleans feel of "When You Ain't Got Nobody" betrayed the influence of Randy Newman's first two albums – as did the stark and rather lovely "Lonely", a kind of distillation of Newman's "I Think It's Going to Rain Today". Apart from sharing a title with one of his songs, "I Want You" was reminiscent of the limpid Dylan of 1970's *Self-Portrait*. With its dissonant piano figure, "Nobody" was a clear nod to the Great American Songbook as it drowsily evoked Cole Porter and company. "Grapefruit Moon" probed the synergy between music and heartbreak, the singer's romantic wounds continually being reopened by "that melody".

Waits gave vent to the influence of Beat writings and spoken-word jazz verse in an early version of "Diamonds on My Windshield" that he read at a poetry workshop in a little storefront on the main business street in Venice. "He showed up at a reading I was doing at the Beyond Baroque bookstore," says Michael C Ford, who edited the infrequently published magazine *Sunset Palms Hotel*. "My first impression was that this was a guy who would never compromise his art. He had an integrity that was immovable." When Waits came to Beyond Baroque to read "Diamonds", Ford was not the only poet to be impressed. "They loved the time signature," he says of such gurus of the Venice poetry

Sunset Palms Hotel, with cover by Charles Bukowski and poem by Tom Waits. (*Courtesy of Michael C Ford*)

scene as the gay mystery writer Joseph Hansen. "They said, 'This guy's coming out of the earth, he's the real deal.'" Ford published "Diamonds" as a poem in *Sunset Palms Hotel* and became friendly with Waits.

"Diamonds" was one of a number of songs and/or spoken-word pieces Waits recorded in demo form during the second half of 1971. Set up by Herb Cohen and using Tim Buckley's road manager Robert Duffey as an engineer, the demos featured minimal accompaniment: generally Waits alone on guitar or piano, sometimes fleshed out by acoustic bass and drums.

By early 1972, Waits knew it was time to move to Los Angeles permanently. He found a small one-bedroom apartment in Silver Lake, southeast of Hollywood, and moved himself in with his piano and his books and jazz albums and posters. With its vibrant Hispanic street life and lack of pretension, Waits loved the neighbourhood. "Silver Lake was both cheap and bohemian," says Jeff Walker, one of the first journalists to interview Waits. "You walked into Tom's apartment and you saw a kindred soul. There were stacks of records on the floor and lots of books and

At home in Silver Lake, spring 1973. (*Kim Gottlieb-Walker/www.lenswoman.com*)

69

there were posters on the wall. There was a little kitchen off to the side, but the bed was in the main room."

"It's a hovel," Waits said of his pad. "My landlord is about ninety. He's always coming over and asking if I live here. And my neighbor up front is a throwback to the fifties, an old harlot in pedal pushers and gold-flecked spiked heels and a big bouffant hairdo . . . and one of the worst mouths I've ever heard." The description might have come from the pages of *The Day of the Locust*, the Nathanael West novella that captured the scuzzy underside of Hollywood. But this was precisely the Los Angeles that Waits liked, as opposed to some quaint Laurel Canyon cabin where he might have rubbed shoulders with sensitive navel-gazers in denim jeans.

"People rarely understand Los Angeles," says Pat DiPuccio. "They focus on the West Side, but the San Gabriel Valley is where the city actually started, and the East Side is anything from east of downtown to the San Bernardino County Line. It's a different and oftentimes artistic world." Silver Lake was also close to where Frank Waits was living, having recently started teaching at Belmont High. "He stayed very tight with his father," recalls Michael C Ford. "I thought that was unusual for that kind of personality."

After a month of settling in, Waits began writing in earnest, setting off what he called a "chain reaction of tunes" with "Shiver Me Timbers", a hymn to the ageless pull of the sea that he would save for his second album. Mostly he wrote at an old upright piano, but he also kept a trumpet to hand for simpler melody lines.

Joining Waits in Silver Lake was Bobi Thomas, whose friendship with her old Hilltop High contemporary and Heritage peer had blossomed into a love affair. "We'd been best friends already for a long time, so we just happened to fall into it," she says. "It didn't really take long before we were out of the love part, but we never got out of the very strong friendship. And that best friendship continued for quite a few years after that too."

"The relationship between Tom and Bobi grew much more complex than dating," says Bob Webb, who'd sold the Heritage and moved into his parents' LA home with his wife Trudi. "They became something like comrades-in-arms, deep friends embarked on a quest to become successful songwriters and artists. They supported each other intellectually and emotionally." Bob and Trudi often had Tom and Bobi over to dinner in Culver City.

Thomas says she and Waits rarely listened to music together in the Silver Lake apartment. More often they simply sat together and read books or watched old movies on TV. "Tom would stay up till five or six in the morning reading," Thomas remembers. "He was voracious. He'd tell me how inspired he was by reading some short story or other, and I think that was the source of his muse. Some writers go to movies to get that emotional power, and then they write. I think Tom got a lot of it from books."

Waits also continued to draw on conversation overheard in diners – especially the Copper Penny in Hollywood, where Thomas held down a part-time waitressing job. "He'd come down to the restaurant and sit on the counter," Thomas recalls. "He'd have cup after cup of coffee and fill page after page of prose. He wrote a sheet of paper for me one day that ended '*and she serves it up hot and steaming and with a smile that would fix a flat tire.*' He'd take the stories or the lines he heard, or just the mood or ambience of the place, and incorporate them into his writing." When Thomas was out, Waits would "sit for hours at the old upright . . . trying to get the songs out". On her return he'd continue playing but wouldn't sing. "He didn't usually do more than play the music until the words were done," she says. "I think he was afraid that the magic of creation would be somehow broken if he played me an actual set of lyrics-in-progress."

A song Thomas remembers well was inspired by a row that led to her storming out of the apartment. "That night at the restaurant they needed me to stay until 6 a.m. to cover some-body's shift," she recalls. "Instead of calling Tom to let him know I'd be a little late, I just didn't call. I don't think I even thought about how he might be worried – that's how self-absorbed I was at the time." Two days later, Waits was tinkering with a bluesy melody on the upright. He told Thomas he was writing a song for her – a classic lover's-tiff plaint – but wouldn't play it through for her. "Please Call Me, Baby" would be one of the last songs Waits demoed for Herb Cohen.

Waits for the most part kept to himself in this period. "He kept everything tightly under his slouch cap," says Bob Webb. By mid-1972, however, the two men were friends again, regularly meeting to play pool and share their enduring love of Beat literature. "After we reconnected in LA he kept me more informed," Webb says. "I would visit him, and on some afternoons he would drop by my house and he'd pick up my guitar and play something he'd just written."

A new literary passion of Waits' was Charles Bukowski, alco-holic chronicler of Californian lowlife and a writer of prose that

With Bobi Thomas (front) and friends Doug Carnahan (left) and Bob Webb, Swenson's ice-cream parlor, West Hollywood, September 1973. (*Trudi Webb*)

was not only brutally sad and madly funny but as tight and direct as Kerouac's was florid and ramblingly expansive. Waits had discovered Bukowski through "Notes of a Dirty Old Man", his weekly column in the *LA Free Press*, and had instantly fallen for his piercing honesty. "I just thought this was remarkable," Waits recalled. "[I thought], 'This guy's the writer of the century and he's being published in this kind of street rag,' which seemed kind of poetic and perfect . . . and of course you felt much more like you had discovered him as well – that he wasn't being brought to you but you had to dig and find *him*."

Waits liked the fact that Bukowski was an LA native, ignored by the East Coast literary mafia. Indeed, Buk's upbringing in the city's West Adams district seemed a more extreme version of Waits' own background. Certainly Waits could relate to Bukowski as a kind of Californian aberration – a writer who shone a light on the less felicitous aspects of life in the Golden State. Many of his stories and poems were set in and around the area where Waits now lived. "An Alvarado Street bar", Bukowski wrote, "is about as close to getting to Skid Row as you can get."

"My dad spent a lot of time in the bars, so I was drawn to places like that – the dark places," Waits reminisced, though what really "hooked" him was "the fact that [Bukowski] seemed to be a writer of the common people and street people, looking in the dark corners where no one seems to want to go – and certainly not write about. So it seemed like he was the writer for the dispossessed and the people who didn't *have* a voice."

Bukowski had begun writing at thirteen, compelled to express the pain of his childhood and adolescence in notebooks. After being routinely and methodically beaten by his father for five years, his torment was compounded by the appalling acne that covered his body. "When you get the shit kicked out of you long enough and long enough and long enough," he said, "you will have a tendency to say what you really mean."

In the early 1940s Bukowski roamed the length and breadth of the USA, living in flophouses and drinking suicidally, churning out stories that were invariably rejected. He returned to LA in the late forties and, in 1952, began a soul-destroying job in the US Post Office that put the "stink" of the city in his bones and later inspired his first novel. An habitué of bars and racetracks, Bukowski was an avowed enemy of the Disneyfied American dream, his stories stripping away all the conceits of bourgeois existence.

Though Bukowski was never a Beat writer, he was as much a literary figurehead to Waits as Kerouac had been. "I guess everybody, when you're young and you enter the arts, you find father figures," Waits said of him. "For me it was more profound because I had no father – no operating father – so I found other men that supplied all that for me. I was looking for those guys all the time."*

Other "forefather" writers Waits discovered were Nelson Algren (*A Walk on the Wild Side*), John Rechy (*City of Night*), and Hubert Selby Jr. (*Last Exit to Brooklyn*). Though Algren's prose hasn't aged well, *A Walk on the Wild Side* (1956) was a novel populated by a raft of characters he called "the broken men and breaking ones; wingies, dingies, zanies and lop-sided kukes; cokies and queers and threadbare whores" – the "lonesome monsters" of America. Rechy's *City of Night* (1963), meanwhile, depicted an LA "nightworld" of fringe deviants who'd cut loose from the bright fantasyland of southern California. Selby's 1964 novel smashed through social taboos in its raw depiction of drugs, violence, and homosexuality in blue-collar Brooklyn.

Waits had also become heavily smitten with Richard "Lord" Buckley (1906–60), a California-based comedian whose "hip-

---

* Poignant in this context is Waits' later musical setting of Kerouac's "Home I'll Never Be". When he sings, "*Father, father, where you been/I've been in this world since I was only ten*," it's hard not to hear him calling out to his own errant pater.

semantic" routines about "flipsters and finger-popping daddies" were beloved of the Beats. "He was someone that I listened to for several years," Waits told a radio interviewer. "He was a real bebop prosody cat, certainly a real pioneer in the fifties along with Ken Nordine and Jack Kerouac, Lawrence Ferlinghetti and Gregory Corso, all those cats."

Waits was only ten when Lord Buckley was riffing and free-associating at Hollywood's Ivar Theater – a performance from February 1959 later issued as *So You Thought Hip Was New* and featuring such classic routines as "The Nazz" and "The Bap Rapping of the Marquis de Sade".

Throughout the first half of 1972, Waits continued to hoot at the Troubadour, honing the act he had developed in his San Diego shows. "Roger Perry, the hootmaster, would tell me about 'this real weird guy,'" says Todd Everett, one of Waits' earliest LA champions. "The idea was that Waits was really unlike anybody else. I mean, if you look at it another way he *was* like other people, but none of them was his age or showing up at hoot nights at the Troubadour. I was a little older than Tom but I was younger than Kerouac would have been, so here was this guy who was younger than me who was channeling all that stuff. I mean, he was never going to be the fourth member of Crosby, Stills and Nash."

"I was surprised to see somebody like that in the situation at that time," says Louie Lista, who worked as the Troubadour's barman but sang blues and R&B. "What Tom was doing was mostly acoustic, but the energy was very much akin to what *I* was doing. And the humor started making me like him."

"He really created a persona for himself on stage," says Bobi Thomas. "He never really was a big drinker when we hung out, but the persona he created had a flask of whiskey in his pocket at all times. I think he intuitively knew that the element of 'show' was more than half of the game."

Songs such as "Ol' '55", "I Hope that I Don't Fall in Love with You", and "Grapefruit Moon" caught the attention of the Troubadour cognoscenti, not least because a five-track tape of Waits' demos was busy making the rounds of the singer-songwriter community. Jerry Yester, who'd recently separated from Judy Henske after working with her in the short-lived Rosebud, heard about Waits from his old Lovin' Spoonful comrade Joe Butler. "Joe was living in California and trying to get some recordings going," Yester says. "He'd run into Waits and was doing one of his songs. It might have been 'Martha' or 'Grapefruit Moon'. Joe raved about 'this great writer.' He didn't speak of him as a performer."

Waits said Herb Cohen had "a lot of nips on the line" from interested record companies, though none bit. Almost a year on from the night Cohen had first heard him, another influential LA figure was stopped in his tracks by Waits at the Troubadour. Brooklyn-born David Geffen was the rising star of the West Coast music industry, cornering the market in singer-songwriters and denim-clad country rockers – first with his Geffen-Roberts management company and then with his recently launched Asylum label. The Troubadour was where Geffen and everybody else came to hear music and conduct business.

"I would check out the Troubadour relatively often," Geffen says. "I was always down on Mondays at the bar, which was a great place to hang out. Sometimes somebody would come in and say, 'Hey, there's somebody really good on,' and you'd go in and check them out." Geffen was standing in line for the men's room when he heard Waits' grainy tenor voice singing "Grapefruit Moon". "I thought, 'Wow,'" he remembers. "He was exactly what I wanted on Asylum. He didn't look like the kind of singer-songwriter performers of the day at all. He had his own voice, his own style, his own presentation, and his own seeming lack of interest in all of it, but I was blown away by the songs and I loved the way he sang."

David Geffen (right) with the Eagles' Don Henley and singer Rosemary Butler, Venice, April 1972. (*Henry Diltz*)

Geffen approached Waits as he came off stage. He said he was interested in signing him to Asylum, which had just launched with albums by Jackson Browne, David Blue, Judee Sill, and Jo Jo Gunne. When Waits said he was being managed by Herb Cohen, the young entrepreneur instantly backed off. "I said, 'Oh well, Herbie has his own label and he's a friend of mine, so please tell him I wasn't trying to poach you.'"

The next morning Cohen phoned Geffen at his office on Sunset Boulevard, catching the younger man off his guard. Knowing Cohen's reputation, Geffen apologized for the approach he'd made. "I said, 'Listen, I didn't know Tom was yours and I had no intention of doing anything wrong.'" Cohen reassured Geffen he hadn't, and that if he wanted to make a record with Waits he could. "I said, 'Herbie, what about *your* label?'" Geffen says. "And he said, 'Well, I'm really more interested in his songs.' I thought to myself at the time that if Frank Zappa and Captain Beefheart were the people Herbie was recording, and Tom Waits *wasn't*, I couldn't figure out exactly what he *was* interested in."

Had Geffen really never heard of – let alone actually heard – Tom Waits? According to Geffen's former business partner Elliot Roberts, David Blue had gotten hold of the Waits demos and played them at the company's offices. "David said, 'You have to hear this, it's unique,'" says Roberts. "At that point, unique was all we were looking for. Waits was so shy he would hardly look at you, but he took on a totally different persona on stage." Roberts told me in 1993 that "there were a lot of good writers we felt should have the chance to record, even though we knew they weren't going to be hugely successful". Waits, he said, "was a little different, because he'd reinvented himself as a beatnik", adding that he "had the luxury of doing that in LA because it was an empty white canvas".

Though Geffen is adamant that Waits was unknown to him before his Troubadour epiphany, the subsequent bad blood between him and Roberts leads one to wonder. "The first time Elliot heard Waits was from me, not from David Blue," he says tetchily. "Look, people's memories of these things are often wrong even though they think they remember them right. When Tom King's biography of me came out, there was something Elliot said in it and I said, 'Elliot, that's just not true.' And he said to me, 'Yes, it is.' I said, 'Elliot, let me remind you what happened with this particular thing,' and he said, 'Oh yeah, you're right. I've been telling this story for so long that I actually thought it was the truth.'"

Waits duly took his place among the elite group of artists that Geffen and Roberts were nurturing on the label. "I think Herbie knew we loved Tom and that we'd do a good job for him," Roberts says. "It was easier than to keep going to bed with the artists you managed." Created initially to provide a home for Jackson Browne, poster boy for the new Laurel Canyon introspection, Asylum prided itself on being artist-friendly. Geffen and Roberts had shrewdly intuited a shift in sensibility, away from heavy electric rock towards more contemplative music, as exemplified by the songs of Browne, Blue, Sill, and John David Souther. Just to cover themselves, Geffen and Roberts had also signed Jo Jo Gunne, partly made up of former members of LA hippies Spirit, and were in the process of adding a young country rock band called 'Eagles' to the roster.

"David Geffen does a lot for his artists," Waits said after he'd signed his deal. "He gets very excited about them. It's not just signing somebody's life away, he's personally interested in them. In the record industry most labels have a huge amount of artists – each has their biggies and their hopefuls. But Asylum is still small. Each artist is treated like one."

"The criterion at Asylum was artists of a unique nature," says Ron Stone, who assisted Elliot Roberts on the management side. "The vision was to commit to an artist and develop that artist over a long period. Clearly Tom fit that. He was unique, singular, and as a songwriter quite extraordinary." If Waits fitted the Asylum profile as an idiosyncratic voice, clearly he was at odds with the label's prevailing aesthetic. "Tom and Jackson Browne were both incredibly creative songwriters but their expression was radically different," says Stone. "Jackson was Prince Charming to Tom's Shrek."*

Waits' creative heart lay in the forties and fifties, not in the sixties and certainly not in the laid-back southern California of the early 1970s. For him, the James Taylor school of introspection was too effete. "Tom had the soul of a saloon singer, right from the ground up," says Michael C Ford. "There was a persona there, and it could have been a way of protecting himself from that sort of James Taylor/Jackson Browne sensibility. The persona was a kind of camouflage. A lot of his insecurity or shyness was probably a defense mechanism."

* Quoth Stone, "I'm sure that quote will turn up, and I'll be sorry I said it."

"I'm very glad I'm a departure for Asylum," Waits soon stated for the record. "I'm getting pretty sick of the country music thing. I went through it, wrote a lot of country songs and thought it was the answer to everything. Anyway, so much of it is really Los Angeles country music, which just isn't country, it's Laurel Canyon . . . it's very difficult to live a country frame of mind when you're living in LA, so I just identify more with the sounds of the city."

Waits had the Groucho Marx stance down pat: he wasn't going to join any club that wanted him as a member. "They always try to create scenes, just making connections so that they can create a circuitry," he told me with a hint of impatience. "It all has to do with demographics and who likes what: if you like that, you'll like this. If you like hairdryers, you'll like water-heaters."

"Tom may have interacted with Don Henley and Glenn Frey and Jackson Browne and whoever, but frankly I don't ever remember that happening," says Jack Tempchin, who'd also fallen in with the Asylum crowd and was pitching a song ("Peaceful Easy Feeling") to his friends the Eagles. "Tom was just on his own path, and he didn't really need the scene or anything."

"It wasn't like I was adopted into a family and was going to be *bathing* with these people," Waits told me. "The idea that you're on a label doesn't mean that we're breaking bread together every morning, and David Geffen's at the head of the table praying. I'm sure a lot of them were good friends, and if they weren't they probably thought it was good to have it *appear* that they were good friends." The latter insight is canny: Waits had sussed out that Asylum was all about marketing the incestuous community of the LA canyons, with strumming singer-songwriters who slept with each other, wrote songs about each other, and sat in on each other's sessions. It wasn't anything he wanted to be part of. In any case, the supposed cosiness of the Asylum "inner circle" was distinctly undermined by David Geffen's decision to sell out to Warner-

Reprise Records in late 1972. "Asylum was an artist-oriented label for about a minute, until the money showed up," the Eagles' Don Henley grouched. "Then my, how things changed."

While Geffen and Roberts had been quick to hook their artists up with each other – David Crosby and Graham Nash singing backup on Jackson Browne's "Doctor My Eyes", for instance, or Nash producing Judee Sill's "Jesus Was a Crossmaker" (about J. D. Souther) – they saw that Waits didn't fit easily into Asylum's extended family. In fact, Waits represented a unique link between Geffen's LA and the very different southern Californian scene that was the Herbie Cohen/Frank Zappa cluster of "freaks". Certainly he was more comfortable with the latter group. "Tom used to hang around our office at the Bizarre/Straight complex when he'd come see Herb," recalled Mark Volman, who – with fellow Turtle Howard Kaylan – had been absorbed into the Mothers as the Phlorescent Leech and Eddie. "He would just come in and sit down and smoke cigarettes and we would just crack him up . . . we would all just sit and laugh for hours."

Ultimately it made more sense for Waits to work with someone from Cohen's rather than Geffen's world. Jerry Yester, it turned out, was the right man at the right time. With the dissolution of Rosebud, the sometime producer of Tim Buckley was killing time and waiting for something good to happen. "There was a period of about six months where I didn't really do much except write, get drunk, and not mow my lawn," Yester says. "Rosebud broke up, literally on stage, in August of 1971. Shortly after that, Herbie called me about Waits."

Yester hadn't even had a chance to listen to the tape Cohen had mailed him when Waits showed up one afternoon on his Burbank doorstep. "We were right on the corner of Brighton and Clark Streets," Yester remembers. "Across the street was a store called Otto's Hungarian Imports. The phone rang and a voice said, 'Ah, Jerry, I'm lookin' for your house, man . . . I'm, uh, in

Jerry Yester, Hollywood Hills, circa 1971. (*Henry Diltz*)

Otto's Imports . . .'" A more fitting introduction to the goatee-sporting hipster in the slouch cap is hard to imagine. "He had longish hair down to his shoulders, but the first time you heard him talk or sing it was quaint because it really didn't fit," Yester recalls. "It didn't *not* fit, it was just odd. I had no idea how old he was, though I was pretty sure he was younger than me. He seemed right out of the fifties Beat Generation."

Yester never forgot the "absolutely magical afternoon" that ensued. He still has the tape of Waits running through the songs in his repertoire, complete with grunted introductions. "My girl-friend Marlene was scrubbing the bathtub," he recalls. "When she heard Tom she threw down her rag and came in and just sat and listened. I had a baby grand in the house and I just set up a microphone and he recorded everything he had." Waits was equally enthused about Yester. "Jerry was a great producer," he told me. "He was the first guy whose house I ever went to and found a pump organ."

A meeting to discuss the approach to Waits' first album was swiftly arranged. "We talked together about the instrumentation," Yester says of the conflab in David Geffen's office. "We wanted to keep it the same band and to keep it small. We wanted the musicians to have a versatile feel. And Tom made it absolutely clear he wanted a standup bass player." Yester lacked jazz contacts but was able to round up the perfect group of musicians for Waits' sessions. Drummer John Seiter had played with Spanky & Our Gang and the Turtles before joining Yester in Rosebud. Guitarist Peter Klimes was, says Yester, "just a wunderkind on the guitar, nineteen years old and absolutely phenomenal". Trumpeter Tony Terran had worked with Yester on, of all things, a Monkees session. Shep Cooke, who contributed guitar to "I Hope that I Don't Fall in Love with You" and the countrified "Old Shoes", had played with Linda Ronstadt and knew Waits from his San Diego days.

"Shep told me that Tom was much folkier down in San Diego," says Yester. "But the thing that Tom became really crystallized during and after the first album. The germ was there, and the stuff he was writing was so different from everybody, but it really crystallized afterward into the skid row character he became."

Through Seiter and Terran, Waits and Yester found their bass player. Bill Plummer had worked with a range of jazz artists from George Shearing to Al Jarreau before forming his own part-time group the Plumline. He had also played on the Rolling Stones' *Exile On Main St*, overdubbing acoustic bass parts on four tracks that included one of Waits' all-time favourite tracks, the spaced-out-gospel track "I Just Wanna See His Face".*

Yester booked Sunset Sound, the same Hollywood studio the Stones had used for the *Exile* overdubs in the spring of 1972. The sessions were completed in about ten days. For Waits, the

* The other *Exile* tracks Plummer played on were "Rip this Joint", "Turd on the Run", and "All down the Line".

experience was fraught with fear. He'd never seen inside of a recording studio before, nor worked with a full backing group. "It was kind of frightening," he admitted to Lou Curtiss. "You just realize how much you have at your disposal."

"Tom was very quiet," remembers Bill Plummer. "I later figured out that he was totally focused on what he was trying to do." Plummer recalls the "little upright piano" being set up for Tom in the studio. "He wanted that funky bar-room sound," he says. "It was nicely in tune but it had a flavor to it. I don't know if he had it shipped in specially but he knew it well and was very comfortable with it."

As the days went by, Waits became more assertive in his directions to the band. "He was absolutely communicative with all the musicians," Jerry Yester recalls. "He didn't talk to them a lot in musical terms, but he always got his point across and could tell them exactly what he wanted. He'd put things in terms of metaphors and they knew exactly what he was talking about." Waits commanded instant respect. "He was just so calm and relaxed about everything," Plummer says. "And he knew those songs backwards and forwards. There was a wonderful feeling that he was authentic about the whole thing. He had his cigarette there in the ashtray, and all that kind of stuff. Just his appearance and demeanor and everything felt very real."

Key to the feel of *Closing Time* was the fact that Plummer had been playing with drummer Seiter for over six months. When it came time to record "Ol' '55", Seiter so dug the song that he couldn't resist singing over Waits' voice in the chorus. Possessed of a strong tenor that Yester had already showcased with Rosebud, Seiter came up with a perfect harmony line that started faintly before the chorus even began.

The first sound heard on *Closing Time* was Waits counting "Ol' '55" in, followed by the song's gentle slipnote piano chords. In a way the young voice was unremarkable, but it was importantly different from James Taylor or Jackson Browne or Glenn Frey – immediately older, more lived-in. The song was sincere and believable and charming, full of youthful magic.

Listening to "I Hope that I Don't Fall in Love with You", which switched from piano to acoustic guitar, one could almost mistake Waits for someone who'd made a couple of inoffensive early-seventies singer-songwriter albums and then faded away like a hundred other young California hopefuls of the age. One certainly can't imagine him singing this quaint relic today.

"Virginia Avenue" was immediately bluesier. Waits' piano was pure Randy Newman, an influence so obvious on *Closing Time* that one sometimes misses it. Waits' voice was nothing like Newman's, however: on this song it was almost declamatory, reminiscent of singers such as Tim Buckley or David Ackles. More Asylum-esque was "Old Shoes (and Picture Postcards)", a country-rock waltz that picked up from the feel of "Ol' '55". Waits must have heard so many songs like this at the Troubadour that they eventually rubbed off on him. The song's voice belonged to a footloose young stud hitting the road and semi-sneering such cringey lines as "your tears cannot bind me anymore" and "my heart was not born to be tamed".

The sleepy and fairly ordinary "Midnight Lullaby" was an early instance of Waits borrowing from nursery rhymes and lullabies, in this case "Sing a Song of Sixpence" and "Hush Little Baby". Thus began a lifelong habit of assembling lyrics from fragments of oral tradition.

"Martha" only makes one realize how myopically narcissistic most singer-songwriters were in the early 1970s. Here was Waits, all of twenty-three, writing about an old man and the girl he'd loved forty years before. This was the kid who'd hung out with his friends' dads because they had more interesting stories to tell. "Martha" was also the first time any kind of orchestral lushness was heard on a Tom Waits album.

"Rosie" wasn't dissimilar to "Martha", just less special. Following on from "Martha" might have made sense in the days when one had to turn over a vinyl LP; on CD it is overshadowed, though it does echo the country feel of "Ol' '55", this time with a pedal steel thrown in. There was also another jejune line about "mell-oh-dee" to make the older Waits shudder.

The stark "Lonely" could have come from a musical – a poor man's *West Side Story*, perhaps. Things livened up with "Ice Cream Man", a more ribald version of John Brim's 1953 song of the same name and a spoof of countless double-entendre R&B songs of ladies-man swagger. "Little Trip to Heaven" was an anodyne declaration of affection, a second cousin to "Midnight Lullaby" with muted trumpet and space-travel metaphors. Marginally less trite was "Grapefruit Moon", which was very early-seventies "piano man" in feel. To say Waits hadn't found his voice yet is an understatement.

Recorded almost as an afterthought for *Closing Time* was the beautiful instrumental coda that shared its title. Cut on a Sunday at Western Recorders, "Closing Time" blended Waits' plangent piano chords with Tony Terran's wistful trumpet and the warm cello lines of Jesse Erlich. Unable to locate Bill Plummer, Yester had to rely on somebody's recommendation of Arni Egilsson, who tore himself away from a barbecue, threw his double bass in the car, and made it to the session just in time. "That was absolutely the most magical session I've ever been involved with," says Yester. "At the end of it, no one spoke for what felt like five minutes, either in the booth or out in the room. No one budged. Nobody wanted the moment to end."

"Closing Time" was "the capper of the experience" for Waits. Save for the string overdubs on "Martha" and "Grapefruit Moon", the album was complete. "I told him I wanted to put a string quartet on 'Grapefruit Moon'," says Yester. "He said, 'Ah, I don't know about that, man.' I said, 'Tell you what, let's do it and if you don't like it we won't use it.' We recorded it in the mixing studio at Wally Heider's and he loved it. In fact, he used strings a lot after that because he liked it so much. But he wasn't so crazy about the idea of Edgar Lustgarten playing cello on 'Martha'. He was very cautious about stuff."

Long after the fact, Waits seemed to take issue with Yester's production, perhaps because by then he'd so radically revised his view of his own musical persona. "We were pulling against each other," he said a little churlishly in 1977. "If [Jerry] had had his way he would have made it a more folk-based album, whereas I wanted to hear upright bass and muted trumpet." Had Waits really felt misgivings about Yester's production, it's unlikely he would have continued to hang out with him as frequently as he did after the album was finished. For the two men spent many hours together, often playing pool in cheap halls with Yester's friend Randy Benson. "There was a place in Burbank that was fifty cents an hour for a nine-foot table covered with cigarette burns," Yester recalled. "Tom really loved those kinds of places. It had that kind of funky atmosphere."

Sometimes Waits preferred simply to shoot the breeze over a beer or three, seated in a new 1952 Buick that was swamped with newspapers and candy wrappers. "He liked to buy a six-pack of Coors and go park somewhere and just *talk*," says Yester. "He'd talk about whatever was on his mind, and I'd talk about what was on *my* mind. I really liked that part of the relationship. He was real genuine, absolutely down to the nickel. He was the kind of person you felt you'd known for years." Even a budding attraction between Waits and Marlene failed to taint the friendship. "When I saw them getting close, I was like, 'Wait a minute,'" Jerry says. "It didn't really injure our relationship with Tom but everybody stood back and said, 'Oh, okay.'"

Those who come to early Waits via his post-*Swordfishtrombones* work may be nonplussed by *Closing Time*. "I think that first album could safely be called singer-songwriter and country-rock-ish," says Jeff Walker. "In terms of Elektra and Asylum they had plenty of those, from the Paul Siebels to the Tim Buckleys, so it never occurred to me that he was divorced from that. He wasn't that unusual, other than that here was this great singer-songwriter coming out of San Diego." Looking at the cover of *Closing Time*, one would have been forgiven in 1973 for tarring Waits with the Asylum brush. The very name "Tom" sounded folksy and approachable, like Tom Rush or Tom Paxton or Tom Jans.

Flecked with trademark traits and mannerisms – above all on "Martha", blueprint for so many of his lushly emotional ballads – *Closing Time* nonetheless sounded broadly in step with the singer-songwriter school of the early 1970s, reminding us that Waits was at least dwelling in the same musical hinterland as his labelmates. His singing on the album was reminiscent of David Ackles or even Billy Joel, who the following year would release an album with the Waitsian title *Streetlife Serenade*. Waits could even have been mistaken for one of the many "New Dylans" proliferating at the time. The strong Beat and jazz signatures of *The Heart of Saturday Night* and *Nighthawks at the Diner* were immanent in "Ice Cream Man" and "Closing Time" but not overt. "Tom stylized his voice a lot more in later years," says Jerry Yester, "but one fondness I have for *Closing Time* is that it *is* that early Tom."

Randy Hoffman, who'd crossed Waits' path in San Diego, recalls Francis Thumm playing him an advance tape of *Closing Time* some time in late 1972. "Franny said to me, 'Hey, this is Tom Waits, he's hanging around the Troubadour now and he's got this tape,'" Hoffman says. "So he gave it to me to listen to, and I wasn't knocked out by it. At this point we're sitting right squarely in the heyday of the singer-songwriter. A lot of San Diego people had gone to LA, and there was always this record deal that was imminent but never quite happened. So I thought, 'Here's another guy and it's great but it's probably never gonna happen.'"

When the album came out in March 1973, a few reviewers were hip enough to pick up on Waits' pre-rock references. "His voice is self-mocking, bordering on self-pity, and most of his songs could be described as all-purpose lounge music," wrote *Rolling Stone*'s Stephen Holden. For Holden, Waits' style evoked "an aura of crushed cigarettes in seedy bars and Sinatra singing 'One for My Baby'", his songs and piano playing parodying "the lounge music sub-genre so perfectly that we wonder if he's putting us on or if he's for real". For both Herb Cohen and Asylum Records, the challenge was how to sell Waits not simply to arena-boogie America but to people who liked their singer-songwriters a little smoother. Exactly who was going to fall for this hobo romantic with his heart in the past?

Thoughts turned to promoting *Closing Time* through live appearances – not easy, given that Waits had played only a handful of shows outside of the hoots at the Heritage and the Troubadour. Cohen was able to set up a number of support slots on the East Coast, with plans for Waits to be backed by a three-piece band. Trumpeter Rich Phelps was drafted in to play alongside guitarist John "Funky Fingers" Forscha, who doubled as tour manager. That left the vital role of standup bassist, with neither Bill Plummer nor Arni Egilsson able to free themselves of session commitments in LA.

Bob Webb, who'd been seeing a lot of him through the winter of 1972–3, was shooting pool with Waits one night when the subject of the tour came up. "He specifically wanted a jazz feel to his combo, which meant an acoustic stand-up bass, not an electric bass guitar," Webb remembers. "I'd played the bass in high school but had given it up. So I said, pretty nonchalantly, 'I play bass.' Tom's face lit up."

At the beginning of April 1973, with *Closing Time* in the stores for less than a month, Waits and Webb flew east with Phelps and Forscha, just ahead of their first dates at the Cellar Door in Washington, DC. "Phelps I recall as a tall, somewhat temperamental musician with long blond curls," says Webb. "He considered himself very handy with the girls and I suppose he was. In his defense, he played forcefully behind Tom's piano-playing. Forscha served as our road manager. He had a good sense of humor, a level attitude, and played effective guitar too."

The first week of April saw Waits and sidemen supporting Tom Rush at the Cellar Door, the club where Gram Parsons had first heard Emmylou Harris sing. The dates went well enough, giving Waits the opportunity to hone his patter while gelling with a band for the first time. Thrilled that his dream of "making it in music" was coming true, he was happier on the road than he would ever be again. "I was just happy to be [. . .] away from home, riding through the American night, you know, out of my mind," he reflected two decades later. "[I was] wild-eyed about everything."

"Tom never assumed the mantle of star or boss," Bob Webb says. "In fact, he tried to separate himself from the wrangles that inevitably attend getting four independent artists from one gig to another, one night to the next. He was an affable companion, understandably a little introverted."

From DC, the band travelled up the east coast to Massachusetts, where for the week of 11–15 April they supported Danny O'Keefe at Passim. The Cambridge club was of especial interest to both Waits and Webb, since owner Bob Donlin had been a drinking crony of Jack Kerouac's. (On one of the Passim nights, none other than Gregory Corso wandered into the club, Waits and Webb falling into conversation with him between sets.) When Donlin reminded them that Kerouac's grave was located in nearby Lowell, the two men made plans to visit the Beat shrine.

"We got the okay from Rich and John to take the car for the day," Webb says. "Lowell was an old dying mill town then, not the spruced-up urban national park it is today." Though Webb and Waits located two of his former residences, their search for Kerouac's grave was fruitless and they eventually gave up their quest. "Seeing Lowell and imagining Kerouac roaming the streets there was enough for both of us," Webb claims. "We really got a feel for the town as it must have been when he lived there as a young man."

Next stop was New York City, Waits' first exposure to the Big Apple. For the week of 18–23 April he was the support act for Charlie Rich, the bluesy Arkansas singer then restyling himself as the MOR-country hitmaker of "Behind Closed Doors" and "The Most Beautiful Girl in the World". Waits was a fan of Rich's blue-eyed soul baritone and thought he was "just cool as ice" at Max's Kansas City. "There was quite a hullabaloo around Rich's return to recording and performing," remembers Bob Webb. "We were advised that high-powered executives were coming around to hear Charlie, and some would be there to hear Tom too. We were all a little on edge on opening night."

The club itself was something of a shock to the Angelenos. Renowned for its Warholesque clientele, Max's made the Troubadour look positively homely. "The bar at Max's drew the strangest coterie I had ever seen," says Bob Webb. "There were a lot of glitter types, cross-dressers, wannabe transsexuals well over six feet tall in stiletto heels – the entire range of New York City underlife." In the event the flashbulbs were all on Rich, who played "Behind Closed Doors" alongside some of his older R&B material. "Some suits did take Tom aside," says Webb, "but neither John nor Rich [Phelps] nor I was included in those conversations. As I recall, Herb Cohen caught up with us at Max's. When anyone from the industry wanted to meet with Tom they took him aside, and Herb did likewise."

Bob Webb frequently had to accept that Waits was first and foremost on the road to promote his album and therefore unavailable for the kinds of adventure they'd once enjoyed together. "We'd make plans to peel away from the crowd to ramble round bookstores and coffeehouses," Webb says. "But his obligations often prevented him from doing that."

One of the more bizarre billings Waits endured on this first stretch was supporting children's entertainer "Buffalo Bob" Smith and his *Howdy Doody* revue at the Great South East Music Hall & Emporium, located in a shopping mall in Atlanta.* "That was a strange gig," Webb says. "Smith was doing a mixed-media retrospective of his career. It didn't seem like a perfect match, but the audience seemed to accept the intellectual disparity between our shows." For Waits, who'd watched *Howdy Doody* on TV as a kid, the experience was disturbing. "We did matinees at 10 a.m. for screaming children and women in curlers, and there was candy in the piano," he told Francis Thumm. "Show business was starting to look like a nightmare." Waits couldn't abide Smith referring to him as Tommy. "I couldn't stand it," he told Thumm. "I told him, 'Bob, please don't make me hurt you. I have a breaking point.'"

Almost as inappropriate was Waits supporting fading Motown stars Martha Reeves and the Vandellas in a converted stables in East Lansing, Michigan. "There was a small little postage stamp of a stage and they said they provided a piano so they put it way in the back, in the back row," Waits told Lou Curtiss. "They didn't say anything about putting it on stage."

If the week supporting John Hammond Jr in San Francisco (29

* Buffalo Bob, born Robert Schmidt on 27 November 1917, hosted one of the first American television shows for children. In 1947, NBC brought *The Howdy Doody Show* to television sets across the US. The show went off the air in 1960. From 1970 to 1976 Howdy Bob toured with his show and made hundreds of appearances across the US. Schmidt died in 1998 at the age of eighty.

May–3 June at the Boarding House) was a better fit – and the beginning of a lifelong friendship – it wasn't much of an appeasement. In early June, Waits returned to LA feeling utterly demoralized. "It was the old case of the one-size-fits-all industry-push on a new songwriter," he reflected four years on. "[They] throw you out there and see what you can do. I didn't know what the hell I was doing."

This early disillusion can't have been helped by the sale of Asylum to Warner Brothers. And when, in August 1973, Asylum was merged with Elektra Records – with David Geffen at the helm – the cold wind of corporatism crept into the idyllic milieu of Laurel Canyon and its singer-songwriters. Interestingly, Herb Cohen persuaded Waits to attend a picnic held to celebrate the merger of the labels. Somewhat peevishly, Waits showed up, relaxing for long enough to participate in a softball game with Tim Buckley, who'd taken a shine to "Martha" and recorded it on his *Sefronia* album – the first significant cover of a Waits song.* "It was a way for people from the company to meet Tom," recalls writer Tom Nolan. "He seemed kind of subdued – not tentative but not an aggressive personality. He told this long funny story with a punchline about the Shah of Iran – 'That's when the fit hit the shah,' or something. That was his mode of fitting into the social occasion, telling a story."†

That summer, Waits was interviewed by Jeff Walker for the free magazine *Music World*. "He was so open," Walker recalls. "We talked about music and jazz and Beat poetry. He picked up a trumpet and played a little riff on that. We loved him." Waits,

---

* Note, though, that the late Lee Hazlewood had first recorded "Martha" – as "Those Were Days of Roses (Martha)" – on his 1973 album *Poet, Fool or Bum*.
† Nolan, who knew Herb Cohen from hanging out at Frank Zappa's log cabin in Laurel Canyon, remembers that Cohen played well in the softball game. "He made a good catch and I think he got a good hit. I told him afterward that he was the MVP and he looked at me like I was trying to insult him."

Music World

Magazine : June 1973   FREE

American Graffiti
Billie Holliday
Gus Dudgeon
Doc Watson
David Blue
SLADE
Faust

Tom Waits

Cover star, *Music World*, June 1973. (*Courtesy of Kim Gottlieb-Walker/ www.lenswoman.com*)

says Walker, was smarting from a tattoo he'd just had done in a downtown parlour. "Thursday afternoon, sober as a judge," he said of the heart and flowers design. "And yes, it hurts."

As Jeff and his photographer girlfriend Kim Gottlieb drove home to Laurel Canyon, they decided to make Waits the cover star of the June issue. "Because we were a free magazine, we didn't have to put somebody well-known on the cover," says Gottlieb. "We could afford to take somebody that not too many people knew and put them on the cover." Adds Walker, "We went away and said to ourselves, 'This is going to be an important record and this guy's going to be an important artist.' You felt really privileged to be meeting him." Walker saw Waits' boho-beatnik act as a conscious assertion of identity. "It seemed to me this was all *very* deliberate, pushing the boundaries and genres that he had come out of," he says. "But he was fairly forthcoming. He wasn't holding back or mysterious."

Waits by now had broken up with Bobi Thomas. Tom Nolan recalls running into him at the Troubadour and hearing him mention it. "He was looking down and almost pawing the ground with his foot," Nolan says. "He said, quoting Muddy Waters, 'Ah, another mule kickin' in my stall . . .'" Waits wasn't heartbroken but he missed Thomas' company and kept in touch with her by mail. Letters to Bobi updated her on his career in prose that was as ingenuous as it was vivid. He wrote of moving to a larger apartment at 1309 North Coronado Street in Echo Park, not far from his former "cave" and this time boasting "a good-sized bedroom". He described his new neighbourhood as "Mexican-Oriental", adding that he spent most of his free time at "the Food House and the Casino Club, the Mohawk . . . I play a lot of craps."*

---

* In a *Los Angeles Times* piece published in March 1976, interviewer Richard Cromelin describes Waits' new cave as a "court cottage". By that time the place was so crammed with detritus – mainly books and albums but also parking tickets, discarded socks, ashtrays overflowing with Old Gold butts, and a neon "Cocktails" sign that Waits had yanked off the front of a downtown bar – that Cromelin wittily nicknamed it "the Waits Towers".

1309 North Coronado Street, Echo Park. (*Oscar Thompson*)

In one letter Waits mentioned the possibility of upcoming studio dates for his second album. Determined to be truer to his vision of himself as a jazz-centric Beat poet, he was busy writing songs that depicted the American street life he'd absorbed from Kerouac and others. Pride of place went to "(Looking for) The Heart of Saturday Night", a wistful slice of streetwise optimism born one Saturday afternoon as Waits and Bob Webb drove along Alvarado Street and then cruised Hollywood Boulevard in search of kicks and inspiration. The idea of "looking for the heart of Saturday night" came directly from *Visions of Cody*, in which Kerouac's eponymous hero was "hurrying for the big-traffic, ever-more-exciting, all-of-it-pouring-into-town-Saturday night". Waits claimed he'd written the song in five minutes.

"We struck on Kerouac's concept of wanting to be at 'the center of Saturday night in America,'" Bob Webb recalls. "We got caught up in that literary notion and decided that each of us would create something around the theme. I drove home and stayed up all night writing a short play about some denizens of a backstreet poolroom. Some time after I left, Tom picked up a guitar and wrote the lyrics and music for 'Heart of Saturday Night.' He had it the next day." Waits also wrote "Depot, Depot", a hymn to the downtown Los Angeles – and its Greyhound bus station – that he felt was neglected by the media and tourist fixation with the city's west side. "Not many people go to downtown LA," he said. "The *Free Press* did a big article called 'Downtown LA, Who Needs It?' I've been going there since I moved here. I live in Silver Lake so I'm about ten minutes from downtown. I go down there just to hang out."

Waits continued to attend the Venice Poetry Workshop, trying out new lyrics there and revamping old ones. In a 22 September letter to Bobi Thomas, he mentioned that he and Webb had attended the Venice workshop the night before, and that he'd read "The Heart of Saturday Night", "Semi Suite", and "Diamonds on My Windshield". He was now certain that a reworked "Diamonds on My Windshield" should feature on the next album, then taking shape in his mind as a sequence of songs about nightlife in America.

One night, Waits went for a ride with Jack Tempchin and talked of the new direction he wanted to take. He spoke about an album Jack Kerouac had made in 1959 with comedian-pianist Steve Allen, with the writer delivering his "beat prosody" over Allen's jazz chords. Waits said it was the kind of thing he wanted to explore, and that he wanted to move away from the more orthodox singer-songwriter style of *Closing Time*.

"I remember we were both into Kerouac and we were sitting in the car and he told me about the Kerouac–Allen album," Tempchin says. "He told me he was getting more and more into this Beat thing. I said I thought that was fabulous and he should go for it."

First, however, Waits had to undergo a major rite of passage.

Chapter 4

In Character

> "*Making fake biography, false history, concocting a half-imaginary existence out of the actual drama of my life is my life. There has to be some pleasure in this job, and that's it. To go around in disguise. To act a character. To pretend.*"
>
> (Philip Roth, 1984)

Counting on studio time before the end of 1973, Waits was sorely disappointed when Herb Cohen instead proposed that he take over the opening slot on a tour by Frank Zappa and the Mothers of Invention – the very band whose San Diego set he'd walked out on four years before.

The omens for the tour weren't good to start with: the original support act, Kathy Dalton, had just bailed out, citing the hostility of Zappa's fans. This time, moreover, there was no budget for a backing band: it would just be Waits and Bob Webb, thrown to the lions like meat.

The two men warmed up with low-key appearances in LA and San Diego. On 10 November, they were featured on KCRW's "Snap Sessions" in Santa Monica, performing "Ice Cream Man", "The Heart of Saturday Night", and "Big Joe and Phantom 309". Also featured on the session was Jack Tempchin, who joined Waits to duet with him on "Tijuana", the song they'd written together back in their old folkie days in San Diego.

A week later, Waits and Webb were in San Diego itself, booked to play at Lou Curtiss's Folk Arts on 16 and 17 November. "It was a cramped little store with record racks," remembers Carey Driscoll, who attended the homecoming show by San Diego's prodigal son. "People were literally sitting underneath the tables because there were so many crammed into the place." Driscoll was struck by the change in his former fellow student. "I think he created a character for himself and then became that character," he says. "I wouldn't even say it was a conscious creation of a character, more that every day you become a little further to the left of dead center and before you know it you've become the Tom Waits character that the public knows rather than the one that his classmates knew."

On 18 November, Waits and Webb boarded a stretch DC-8 from LAX to Toronto, arriving in time to hook up with the Mothers tour at the University of Waterloo in Ontario. Four days later they flew with Zappa's entourage from Buffalo to New York to play their first opening set. Greeted at La Guardia airport by a convoy of limousines that transported the party to the Waldorf

Waits tape reels at Folk Arts. (*Art Sperl*)

Astoria hotel, Waits and Webb were kept in the dark as to where the show was. "We went deep into an underground garage in midtown, maybe six floors down," Webb recalled. "[We] were swept up to a floor that included a giant room full of grand pianos and the most swank dressing rooms I ever saw – showers and fresh fruit and flowers." Only at that point were they informed they were in Avery Fisher Hall at the Lincoln Center, shortly to perform there for – in Webb's words – "some four thousand stoned and annoyed Zappa fans who didn't appreciate Tom's ballad style and told us so".

The gig was a complete shock, a baptism of fire. "We both got a quick education," says Webb. "Herb must have sent Tom out on that tour so he could learn how to deal with unfriendly audiences." Zappa's fans, primed for prankster satire and virtuoso noodling, were in no mood for this two-man throwback to a Beat subculture they hadn't even grown up with. Who *was* this weirdo in a hat and tie, stumbling on stage to sit at George Duke's electric piano? "We had to use Frank's gear," Webb remembers. "It meant that Tom had to climb into the middle of Zappa's set-up instead of standing separately on stage as his own man. And I don't think Tom had any prior stage experience on an electric keyboard." Nor had Webb any previous experience of playing electric bass.

The Avery Fisher Hall gig set the general tenor for the remainder of the tour. For three weeks, Waits and Webb suffered almost nightly at the hands of Zappa's fans. "The tour was not well thought-out," Waits told me. "It was like your dad saying, 'Why don't you go to the shooting range with your brother Earl?' And I was like, 'I don't really want to, I might get hurt.' And I *did* get hurt. I went out and subjected myself to all this really intimidating criticism from an audience that was not my own."

"We played two gigs in the Midwest where people received us

kindly," Webb says. "But the rest of the audiences had definitely come to see the Mothers and were audibly impatient." At Toronto's Massey Hall on 23 November, Waits' set degenerated into the slinging of expletives, one irate fan even setting off a firecracker from the balcony. At other shows, enough fruit was hurled at the stage for Waits to have made several salads.

The Mothers did their best to offer reassurance. "The cats in [Zappa's] band were easy to get along with, it wasn't their fault," Waits told *Down Beat*. "Tom Fowler was in Frank's band at the time . . . Bruce Fowler on trombone, Napoleon Murphy Brock, George Duke, Ruth Underwood . . . I went out every evening and proceeded to ruin my evening – and the audience's too, I guess." Zappa himself was more enigmatic, appearing to take a kind of smirking pleasure in the duo's distress. "Frank would just say, 'How were they out there?'" Waits told me. "He was using me to take the temperature, sticking me up the butt of the cow and pulling me out. Kind of funny in retrospect. I was always rather intimidated by him. He was like some type of a baron. There was so much mythology around him and he had such confidence."

Back in California on 3 December, Waits licked his wounds, spent Christmas with family and friends, and worked on the songs for his second album. He paid $135 a month for the Coronado Street apartment, cooked on a hot plate, and watched film noir classics on an old black-and-white Philco TV. Now completely at home in Los Angeles, he regularly cruised its streets and patronized its cheap diners on an almost daily basis. Interviewed by the *LA Free Press* in January 1974, he was *in situ* at Duke's, a coffee shop that sat in the shadow of a shabby establishment at 8585 Santa Monica Boulevard known as the Tropicana Motor Hotel.

"Tom Waits slouches on the corner stool, a shamble of newspapers at his feet," wrote the *Free Press*'s Marco Barla. "His place at the counter [is] cluttered with utensils, ashtrays and a package of bound volumes – a kind of spontaneous collage, he is, mirror to three months on the road, then home again on Santa Monica Boulevard, here underneath the Tropicana Motel – this bright, clattery, bustling, public dining room, his cap and vest and crumpled shirt, his eyes a little weary, bleary, wary – a sly grin rising from an empty coffee cup." Duke's was the perfect location for Waits, a rare rock hangout in a town with little discernible street life. "There were no hipster places in LA but Duke's always had a line," says filmmaker and editor Michael Hacker. "LA was a much smaller place then, and everyone went to Duke's. I went there on Sundays for breakfast for a couple of years and I saw Waits pretty much every time I went."

With no product to push as such, Waits talked off-guardedly to the *Free Press* about his life and his art. He bemoaned his lack of a decent automobile, stating that traffic was an environment he craved. If anyone doubted where his heart lay, he made it plain in this conversation, asserting his distance from LA's back-porch warblers and cowboy rockers alike. In a press release he declared that he was "a dedicated Angeleno" with "absolutely no intention of moving to a cabin in Colorado". Waits was staking his claim to an LA that had nothing to do with Laurel Canyon, let alone with the surf culture of the sixties. "He evoked those sort of grungy LA intersections like Hollywood and Western," points out Tom Nolan. "Also places that were important in Hollywood jazz history." Adjourning to the old Palms Bar on the other side of Santa Monica Boulevard, a lubricated Waits held forth to Barla on the subject of live performance. "I try to take myself up on stage and reach some level of spontaneity and just be as colorful and entertaining as I can without having to memorize it all," he said. "I want to avoid the unnaturalness of performing." Here was a man working out his stance as an entertainer, as someone in "show business".

On 11 January, after another set at the Folk Arts store – the last time Waits performed with Bob Webb – Lou Curtiss asked him if he'd ever thought of becoming a comedian. "It's hard sometimes to get up and just introduce a song as 'This one is called . . .'" Waits replied. "I guess it's important to make an audience feel at ease. At the same time I think it has to be a spectacle and entertaining as well. You can't get too loose. It's just kind of like sitting around your living room, but people don't have to pay in their living room and they want a spectacle."

In late April, Waits returned to San Diego to perform at the eighth annual State Folk Festival, taking part while there in a "Spicy Stories Workshop" led by Curtiss. "Tom was the world's greatest joke teller," Lou says. "He just reeled 'em off, and he wasn't shy about telling what you'd call the gaspers." Bierl thinks the workshop was Waits' idea, the intention being to "recapture the spirit of some of those late nights at Saska's". Waits also participated in the rather less bawdy Songwriting Workshop, playing and chatting with Jack Tempchin, Jim Ringer, and Bruce "Utah" Phillips, the hobo singer whose "Good Night Loving Trail" he was regularly playing live.[*]

Waits had ample opportunity to refine and polish his "act" through the early months of 1974. "He wasn't lazy and he worked," Harvey Kubernik says. "He got on the road and did residencies at places like Ebbet's Field in Denver."[†] At the latter establishment, a popular club founded by promoters Barry Fey and Chuck Morris, Waits supported Roger McGuinn and Jerry Jeff Walker during an icy week in mid-February. Interspersing

---

[*] Phillips, whose other songs included "Green Rolling Hills" and "Rock, Salt and Nails", died on 23 May 2008 aged seventy-three.

[†] Named after the famous Brooklyn Dodgers ballpark, Ebbet's Field was located beneath Brooks Towers at 15th Street and Curtis Street. It had a capacity of just 250 and hosted early-to-mid-seventies shows by everyone from Little Feat to Lynyrd Skynyrd. *Billboard* named it Club of the Year in 1975 and 1976.

Closing Time songs with those he was earmarking for the second album – including both "The Heart of Saturday Night" and "The Ghosts of Saturday Night" – Waits was also honing his between-songs patter. "At this point, to open a show is ideal for me," he told *The Colorado Daily*. "I don't feel that much pressure because no one's paid $4 to see me. I do feel a responsibility to make contact with the audience and I'm working hard on that. Being here is a lot easier than it was when I toured with Frank Zappa." Waits' onstage speaking voice at this time was still pointedly Dylanesque and a little phoney, the sound of a young man searching for his identity.

Denver was a city haunted by the ghosts of Kerouac and Cassady. A block away from Waits' hotel on 17th and Wazee was Larimer Street, slightly gentrified since Kerouac had written of its "bright huge glitter and swarming bums" but still sleazy enough to earn a namecheck in "Drunk on the Moon", a song Waits began in Denver and finished in time to include on *The Heart of Saturday Night*. It was outside Ebbet's Field, after one of his sets, that Waits ran into a striking local character who was destined to play a significant role in his life and career. Wearing a chinchilla coat and three-inch platform boots, Chuck E. Weiss was balancing precariously on the ice like some deranged Jewish glam rocker. Bonding in minutes, the two men repaired to the coffee shop next door to compare notes. "I thought he was just some bum folk singer," Weiss recalled.

Though hailing originally from Chicago, Weiss had been raised in Denver and was a music nut from his early teens. "When I arrived at the University of Colorado in 1965 I had a head full of oldies," writer Art Fein remembered. "There were few of us among the seventeen thousand campusites, and we gravitated to each other. One was Chuck Weiss, who had the enormous advantage of his dad owning a record store on the college hill." Blues-besotted, Weiss had hung out in clubs since his mid-teens. Sitting in on drums with Lightnin' Hopkins one night, "Chuckie" was soon buttonholing every blues legend who passed through the Rocky Mountains. He told Waits he'd met Muddy Waters, Howlin' Wolf, and Willie Dixon, adding that he'd recorded a 1970 session in Boulder with Dixon's band.

Waits was suitably impressed and talked of his own encounters with Hopkins and other blues heroes. He may even have told Weiss about the plans for his next album. In his interview with the *Colorado Daily*, he spoke of the frustrating delays he was experiencing, saying Asylum didn't want Jerry Yester to produce the next record. "As far as I'm concerned, Jerry's a great man and a great producer," he said. "I was expecting to record my second album with him but Asylum wants to find someone that can take my songs and make hits out of them."

As much as David Geffen had loved Waits' debut, he sensed something was missing in the record. Waits assumed this meant "hits", but actually Geffen's instinct was that he needed a more jazz-oriented producer to do justice to his sensibility. "I thought *Closing Time* was a great record and I still think it's a great record," Geffen says. "But it didn't sell very well and I suggested to Tom that perhaps he should get Bones Howe to produce him, because Bones had a background in jazz. Bones was a very close friend of mine and I thought he could make a more professional record with Tom."

Geffen's relationship with Dayton Burr "Bones" Howe dated back to the late 1960s. As a William Morris agent, Geffen had represented folk-pop group the Association, several of whose hits Howe produced. Bones had produced the Fifth Dimension's smash-hit versions of "Stoned Soul Picnic" and "Wedding Bell Blues" – songs written by Laura Nyro, the first artist Geffen managed – and served as musical director on Elvis Presley's 1968 "Comeback Special" on TV. But his CV also included engineering Ornette Coleman's milestone *The Shape*

Dayton "Bones" Howe, Wally Heider Studio 3, Hollywood, mid-seventies.
(*Courtesy of Bones Howe*)

of Jazz to Come (1959) and Frank Sinatra's *Swing Along with Me* (1961).

"David called me one day and said, 'You've had this great success in the pop world and you really should be doing records with an artist who's a little off the beaten path,'" says Howe, sitting in the airy living room of his idyllically located home in Montecito, south of Santa Barbara. "I went down to his office that afternoon and he played me several cuts off *Closing Time*. He said, 'I think I want a different producer for the next album.' He said he wanted someone to give Tom more guidance and make him feel more comfortable in the studio."

"Nobody would even think of sending you in the studio without a producer in those days," Waits told me. "They're not giving *you* thirty grand, they're giving it to this guy who plays tennis and wears sweaters and lives in a big house. Just show up on time and stay out of jail." Bones Howe did wear sweaters and he almost certainly played tennis. When the two men finally met, there was a cultural – and age – gap between them that would have been hard to bridge had Howe not casually mentioned that he'd once edited an album of Jack Kerouac recordings. "Tom said, 'Oh, that's wild,' and told me about the record Kerouac did with Steve Allen," Howe remembers. "I told him I'd made all these jazz records – mono first, and then live to two-track. He said he really wanted to make his next album live." Waits told Geffen he was happy to work with Howe.

In the event, *The Heart of Saturday Night* was multi-tracked in more orthodox style. "There were some things Tom wanted to do where he could put his voice in afterward, like recitation over the music," Howe says. "Also, I wasn't sure if we were going to need the horns on every track. Some of them he was going to play piano on, some he wasn't. So we elected to do it sixteen-track. It came out as a semi-produced studio record."

"You try to distinguish yourself in some way, find your little niche," Waits told me of the preparations for the album. "When you make your first record, you think, 'That's all I wanna do, is make a record.' Then you make a record and you realize, 'Now I'm one of a hundred thousand people who have records out. Now what? Maybe I ought to shave my head.'"

With the sessions booked at Wally Heider's Studio 3 on Cahuenga Boulevard, Howe handpicked a group of schooled musicians equally adept at jazz and pop. Foremost among them was pianist/organist/arranger Mike Melvoin, who'd played with Peggy Lee and other jazz greats but had also featured on the Beach Boys' *Pet Sounds* and on Howe's Fifth Dimension sessions. "I'd worked with Bones when I first got to town in late 1962," Melvoin told me in the kitchen of his North Hollywood home. "He looked to me as a jazz-informed resource. There were several other pianists who were purer pop or rock-and-roll piano players, but there was probably no one else who could do

Mike Melvoin (left) and Jim Hughart, Los Angeles, March 2007. (*Art Sperl*)

all of those things." Melvoin got Waits' attention with his recollections of backing poet Kenneth Rexroth while a student at Dartmouth College in New Hampshire. "In 1958 or 1959 you could barely get an English department to take a Beat poet seriously," Melvoin says. "The idea that Rexroth had been invited to read poetry at Dartmouth was unusual." Melvoin says the minute he met Waits – who'd read Rexroth – he knew he was in "a counterpart situation".

Joining Melvoin at Heider's were bassist Jim Hughart, guitarist Arthur Richards, drummer Jim Gordon, and hornmen Tom Scott and Oscar Brashear. All were somewhat flummoxed by the young man in the thrift-store duds to whom Bones introduced them. "I wasn't quite sure that Tom was even connected to what we were *doing*," laughs Hughart in his Granada Hills home. "He certainly didn't look like the usual people you ran into, with his Salvation Army clothes and scruffy beard and kind of a beat-up hat and talking in a voice that you could barely understand." Less fazed was Jim Gordon, a top-ranked session drummer who'd played with Eric Clapton's Derek and the

Dominos and Joe Cocker's Mad Dogs and Englishmen.*

For Hughart, who'd played with Frank Sinatra, Waits was a throwback to an era he assumed was over. "In Hollywood you get accustomed to seeing people in costume, projecting an image," he says. "I thought, 'Well, he's just another one of those.' It took a while for me to realize it wasn't costume but just the way he was. I figured he couldn't be broke, and had at least a father who was in academia. He seemed to live in self-imposed poverty."

Mike Melvoin saw Waits' persona not as a dissimulation but as round-the-clock performance art, the medium through which the twenty-three-year-old had chosen to express himself. "I thought of Tom as a professional poet who was in character," Melvoin says. "He needed to be thought of *as* the character. It's where you and your body and your personal experience are the artifact. The question was, 'How far are you willing to go with this jacket? How tight are you prepared to wear it?'" Melvoin draws parallels with Prince, whom he met several times when his daughter Wendy was a member of the Revolution in the eighties. "In Prince's case I think there's a pathological need not to lose character," he says. "Underneath the character he inhabits is a thoroughly acculturated guy from northern Minnesota with pencils in a pocket protector who goes home and fantasizes about being the Purple Master of the Universe. In Tom's case there was something a lot more organic about his love of his characters."

Part of the reason why Waits stayed in character was to mask

* Tragically, however, the drummer would go on to develop severe mental problems. In 1983, in a psychotic episode, he stabbed his mother to death after claiming he heard voices commanding him to do it. "Jimmy was quite a bit younger than the rest of us," says Jim Hughart. "He was a wonderful drummer who could play lots of different kinds of things but he was insane. It scared me when he stopped doing studio work to go out on the road with Mad Dogs & Englishmen. He was becoming very introverted, whereas before he was very outgoing. You'd have to drag words out of him."

his fear and inadequacy in the presence of such seasoned musicians. The *Heart of Saturday Night* sessions were a step up from *Closing Time*. He may not have known these men by name but their CVs were intimidating enough. He knew that as a piano player he couldn't hold a candle to Mike Melvoin. "One of the reasons Bones brought me in was that he thought I would have a way of translating what Tom was saying into concrete notes," Melvoin says. "It was about how to deal with somebody whose concept of song form was silly putty. Tom didn't care about technical ability, and that presented an interesting challenge to people who *had* to care about it."

For the most part, Waits kept his head down and let Howe do the talking. Though he wasn't exactly hip – was if anything sartorially and politically conservative – the forty-year-old producer seemed to function as yet another of the father figures Waits craved. "I definitely must have been in some ways," Howe says. "I was sixteen years older and very experienced in the record business. I understand enough about the psychology of the thing to know that that puts you in a different kind of place."

Jim Hughart watched the dynamic between Waits and Howe evolve over the course of the fortnight they worked on the record. "There seemed to be a little uneasiness between them, and that may go along with the surrogate father thing," Hughart recalls. "Kids frequently are uncomfortable with their parents. Tom seemed to depend on Bones to get us through a session, yet he was chafing at what Bones had to say to him. It was almost the kind of attitude that said, 'Okay, Bones, that's enough, go back to your little room and leave me alone.'"

Hughart recalls the notepads and scraps of paper that Waits worked from – and how he would frequently dip into his pockets to find a line for a song. "Material from one song could appear magically in another, so that the barriers even between songs were transgressed," adds Melvoin. "And you had to be ready somehow or other." It was Hughart who breathed new life into "Diamonds on My Windshield". As he remembers it, "Tom just looked at it, clicked his fingers, grunted 'Gimme something about *there* . . .'" He then proceeded to recite from the piece of paper he'd produced from his pocket. Recalled Waits, "Jim just started playing a modal bass line and I just started talking and Jim Gordon started playing a cool twelve-bar shuffle on brushes and we just winged it in one take . . ." To this day, Hughart is mildly aggrieved that he didn't get a co-credit for the track.

Asked about spoken-word tracks like "Diamonds", Waits told KPFK that poetry sometimes worked better than music in communicating images and other details. He talked of the influence of Jack Kerouac and Steve Allen.* "It frees you as a songwriter to be able to just throw down some color and not worry about any sort of meter at all," he said. "Lately I seem to be more concerned with that than writing real songs." Waits even contemplated a sideline career as a writer. He said he'd "read everything I can get my hands on" by Kerouac and hailed Bukowski as "one of the most colorful and most important writers of modern fiction, poetry and prose, in contemporary literature, right now".

Yet he also acknowledged the importance of craftsmanship in songwriting, citing the influence of Randy Newman, "someone who can evoke such a feeling from his listeners, and it comes from him really sweating over a song . . ." Mose Allison he

---

* The Kerouac/Allen album was *Poetry for the Beat Generation*, released by Hanover Records in 1959. Side One: "October in the Railroad Earth"; "Deadbelly"; "Charlie Parker"; "The Sounds of the Universe Coming in My Window"; "One Mother". Side Two: "Goofing at the Table"; "Bowery Blues"; "Abraham"; "Dave Brubeck"; "If I Had a Slouch Hat Too One Time"; "The Wheel of Quivering Meat Conception"; "MacDougal Street Blues"; "The Moon Her Majesty"; "I'd Rather Be Thin than Famous". The two men had met at the Village Vanguard at a reading Kerouac was giving. Allen sat in with him for the second show. Afterwards they decided to collaborate on the album, which was produced in one take.

described as "a very economical songwriter" who's "so damn stylized that you can't help but love him to death – he's like honey poured all over you".

"Diamonds" wasn't the only thing Waits resurrected for *The Heart of Saturday Night*. In January he'd told Lou Curtiss he wanted to record "some old things that I was writing when I was working at the Heritage" and even mentioned "being just dry as a bone and . . . faced with letting a record and a certain amount of popularity stifle me as a writer". As a result, he lined up "Shiver Me Timbers", "Please Call Me, Baby", and the song of sad hopefulness that was "Blue Skies" – all of which he'd demoed in 1971 – for inclusion on the album. "'Blue Skies' was very much like a Ray Charles song," says Bones Howe. "But then it just didn't sound like it fit the album at all, so we released it as a single instead."

Also dropped were "Better off without a Wife", an anthem for

"Blue Skies", Asylum Records, 1974. (*Courtesy of Bones Howe*)

lonesome bachelors the world over, and "On a Foggy Night", soundtrack for an imaginary film noir of the type Waits loved. "The film came out about 1947 and I wrote it just a couple of weeks ago," Waits joked in July. "It's about a foggy night on one of those 'triangle' films that you see on *The Late Show* and this is just about the eternal triangle – like George Raft and Fred Mac-Murray and Rosalind Russell." In all, fifteen songs were recorded for *The Heart of Saturday Night*, four of which bit the dust or resurfaced in live form on 1975's *Nighthawks at the Diner*. "It's . . . just like a fruit salad of all different kinds of songs and I'm real proud of it," he said. "I think it's gonna be a blockbuster, I don't know."

The sessions began tentatively on 22 April with "Better off without a Wife" and an early, discarded take of "Drunk on the Moon". They resumed three weeks later on 14 May, Waits recording "Semi Suite", "Diamonds on My Windshield", "Fumblin' with the Blues", "Blue Skies", and "On a Foggy Night". The next day produced "Depot, Depot" and the version of "Drunk on the Moon" that made it onto the album. Three further sessions the following week delivered "Shiver Me Timbers", "Please Call Me, Baby" (20 May), "San Diego Serenade", "(Looking for) The Heart of Saturday Night" (21 May), and "New Coat of Paint" and "The Ghosts of Saturday Night". (There was a late, unused recording of "Nobody", cut with Jim Hughart on 4 June. Furthermore, to Waits' considerable ire, strings and female backing vocals were added in his absence to "Blue Skies" in a session on 10 June. The track was eventually released as a single in December.)

The opening "New Coat of Paint" was immediately blacker and more authentically late-night-jazzy than anything on *Closing Time*. On this swinging Dr John jazz-blues, with Mike Melvoin on electric piano, Waits' white-negro timbre was pitched somewhere between the voice of *Closing Time* and the full-on baritone gravel to come, intoning a lyric that said, essentially, *Let's forget all the mess and stress of this relationship and just get royally wrecked.* "Tom had taken on some of the qualities of the black musicians I had worked with," Bones Howe reflects. "It was an affectation but he seemed comfortable in it. Where he picked it up I don't know. It just became part of his personality to me. People occasionally said to me, 'Is he really like that?' I would say to them, 'The one thing I can tell you is that he's not whacked-out all the time. He knows exactly what he is doing.'"

Covered by everyone from Eric Andersen to Nanci Griffith, "San Diego Serenade" returned us to the mood of *Closing Time*, but with looser, more Tim Buckleyesque vocals. This was Waits the sentimental nostalgist, looking back at his past and realizing he hadn't missed his water till his well ran dry. "Semi Suite", meanwhile, was Waits empathizing with a woman who accepted the neglect of her truck-driving boyfriend, before the mood switched back to the early-hours R&B feel of "New Coat of Paint". This was Ray Charles via Mac Rebennack – perhaps the two governing musical spirits on *The Heart of Saturday Night*. The album was back in San Diego mode for "Shiver Me Timbers", replacing the truck driver of "Semi Suite" with a sailor who invoked Herman Melville and *Martin Eden*. Like "Semi Suite" it was a rejection of domesticity, but a more romantic one. The song was neither blues nor jazz but the kind of Americana one associates with David Ackles' *American Gothic*. From that sea shanty it was back to jazz hipsterese again. "Diamonds on My Windshield" gave us Waits driving at night in the rain, overtaken by a Plymouth Duster as he drove the I-5 from San Diego to LA. The track's off-the-cuff quality would inspire Waits to expand the style for *Nighthawks at the Diner*.

The album's timeless title track lay somewhere between "New Coat of Paint" and "San Diego Serenade". The feel was jazz but there was a tender yearning in the song, with his pockets "jinglin'" and his arm around his girl in his Oldsmobile. "(Lookin' for) The Heart of Saturday Night" spoke of the hope and promise of romance and neon, the reward for the week's slog. Nor was it in any way sleazy: Kerouac-influenced, for sure, but more innocent than anything Jack ever wrote. For the track's sound effects, Waits and Howe wandered out into the traffic on Cahuenga Boulevard with a tape recorder.

"Fumblin' with the Blues" had a "St James' Infirmary"/"House of the Rising Sun" feel, with electric piano and a *42nd Street*-style clarinet. This was about men in dives and pool halls, drinking too much and being forsaken by "savage and cruel" women. It could have been Waits' Ice Cream Man after accepting an invitation to the blues. The ghosts of suave 1940s R&B balladeers on Modern or Imperial could be heard on "Please Call Me, Baby". Waits admitted he was no saint but most of the time he was just "blowing off steam".

"Depot, Depot" was cut from the same jazz-blues cloth as "Semi Suite" or "New Coat of Paint", giving us Waits in limbo at the downtown bus depot on Sixth Street. Waits joked that the depot was a great place to take a date on a Saturday night – with "plenty of quarters for the TV chairs" – but this was clearly a more downbeat experience than the one in the title track. Another underheralded song, "Drunk on the Moon" conjured nocturnal cityscapes, complete with a cigar-chewing news vendor. This was Denver's Larimer Street, the city of Jack and Neal, "teeming with that undulating beat" in the days when it was a twenty-five-block skid row. One could argue that the seed of *One from the Heart* was planted in this song.

Finishing up the album, "Ghosts of Saturday Night (After Hours at Napoleone's Pizza House)" was a snapshot of Waits' life in the employ of Joe Sardo and Sal Crivello, complete with sailors, town criers, waitresses, and gas-station attendants – an extended footnote to the title track, with a San Diego street cleaner sweeping up the remnants of the night's revels. With her "Maxwell House eyes" and "marmalade thighs", Irene the waitress seemed to be turning into breakfast before Waits' bloodshot eyes. She may have been part-based on Susan Michelson, who had recently become Waits' girlfriend – and to whom he dedicated "Fumblin' with the Blues" when he played it in a session on KPFK. "Susan worked at Denny's or some diner like that, out in the Valley somewhere," remembers Michael C Ford. "She was a really nice girl, and I don't know how that dissipated. Tom might have been in her company for a couple of years. Remembering Susan the way she was, she would be one who would keep very much out of the picture."

The cover of *The Heart of Saturday Night* – a painting by "Napoleon" – perfectly captured Waits' diffidence and bashfulness in the presence of women. As he played with his ear and gazed at his feet, was he responding to the curvaceous creature who approached or just minding his own business? The image couldn't have been less canyon-cowboy had it tried: what self-respecting musician in 1974 wore a *tie*?! The lurid neon sidewalk said LA noir, but the scene could have been Anywheresville, USA. It spoke of ordinary people, everyday alienation. On the back cover, meanwhile, a pair of black-and-white shots showed a tipsy-looking Tom leaning against a newsstand, very different from the waistcoated longhair on the cover of *Closing Time*.

"Here's this guy in the hat and the tie and the pointed shoes, and everyone else is wearing jeans or bellbottoms," says Paul Body, a Troubadour doorman who befriended Waits in late 1974. "I called Waits 'The Pointed Man' because of the shoes. He was really a fish out of water, because not only was the country rock thing happening but you had the big rock thing too. Plus he drove an old Cadillac. He was really like a man out of time." Harvey Kubernik concurs: "Waits was an oasis for us. See, I'm writing for *Melody Maker*, I like disco girls in spandex pants . . . and all of a sudden here's Tom Waits, a guy we *knew*. At least he was a solo guy and he wasn't doing phony country rock. When you went up to Elektra-Asylum on La Cienega Boulevard in 1974, you'd think, 'At least there's somebody here without a buckskin jacket.'"

Waits would look back on *The Heart of Saturday Night* with mixed feelings. "It was very ill-formed but I was trying," he said. "I don't know, in those days I think I really wanted to see my head on somebody else's body. It was that kind of deal. When I was writing, I kind of made up my own little Tin Pan Alley so I could sit at the piano, like a songwriter, with a bottle and an ashtray and come out of the room with a handful of songs, as they did."

When the album was done, Waits reluctantly agreed to rejoin Frank Zappa on the road. This time he didn't even have Bob Webb to support him. Instead he went out alone each night – into what he called "a chrome forest of equipment at rodeos and hockey arenas" – to brave the wrath of Frank's fans. "They figured [Frank] must have *wanted* them to abuse me," he said of the Mothers' audience. "I was a gift. I was the monkey." Years later he was able to see the experience as character-building. He also learned from Zappa, watching the way the head Mother commanded the respect of his musicians. But in the main the ordeal was relentlessly depressing. "Tom used to call me up periodically and he'd be kind of dejected," says Bob LaBeau. "We all learn a lot from our suffering, and he paid a lot of dues there." LaBeau also thinks that Waits, straining to be heard above the hecklers, damaged his voice on the Mothers tour. "He told me he was going to a doctor in New York that used to help Frank Sinatra," LaBeau recalls. "He did damage his voice, but then he created a character out of that voice. It added into what he was already doing."

Press pass for Zappa/Waits show, Ambassador Theater, St Louis, July 1974. (*Courtesy of Paul Yamada*)

"The crowd was most impatient during Waits' set," recalls
Paul Yamada, who caught the show at St Louis' Ambassador
Theater on 5 July and spoke to Waits afterwards. "Fortunately he
managed to get off stage without anything turning ugly." Afterwards, over a bottle of whiskey, the two men discussed literary
influences. "He was mainly into Beat fiction and narrative. I
asked him if he'd read Nathanael West. He hadn't and I urged
him to. I brought up William Faulkner but he wasn't into him
either. I'm sure I was a bit full of myself as a twenty-year-old, but
having this kind of discussion with Waits was invigorating. The
best moment came when he asked me, in a curious tone of
voice, 'Man, are you into Proust?' and I quickly replied, 'Fuck,
no!'"*

Twenty-five years later, Waits told me he still had nightmares
about the Zappa tour. "Frank shows up in my dreams, asking me
how the crowd was," he said. "I have dreams where the piano is
catching fire and the legs are falling off and the audience is com-

---

* Yamada's piece, which focused mainly on Zappa, was never published.
"Because it was so blisteringly honest about Zappa, who was beyond jerkdom
in the interview, the magazine would not run it," Yamada recalls. "The editor
told me it was 'drunken and effete.'"

ing at me with torches and dragging me away and beating me with sticks. So I think it was a good experience."

For those in the know, the response of Zappa's fans to Waits was beside the point. Supporting the Mothers gave him the Zappa imprimatur in the industry, and in the long run that could only help his career. "Herb Cohen was wise enough to channel Frank's particular taste," says Ron Stone. "Frank endorsed Waits, and that was what the tour was about. It didn't matter if anybody liked him. The larger creative community accepted him in that sphere of understanding."

Waits was finally put out of his misery when the tour wound up with a show at San Diego's Golden Hall on 11 August, followed by two nights at the Santa Monica Civic in LA. By the end of the first show on 16 August, he had had enough. "He was so heckled and so beleaguered by the rudeness of the audience that he didn't show up the next night," says Michael C Ford, who witnessed it. "He just lowered the lid on the piano and went home."

His hide thickened, Waits prepared for the release of *The Heart of Saturday Night*. At least he was able to console himself with the prospect of the royalties that would soon be rolling in from a cover of "Ol' '55". "I was in a bar one night and I ran into one of [the Eagles] and they said that they'd heard the record and they might want to do it on one of their records," Waits said. "And then I was on the road for three months and I never heard anything about it. And then it showed up on that album." The album was *On the Border*, the Eagles' third. "It put Tom on an entirely different level economically," says Louie Lista. "The younger we were back then, the more likely we were to say, 'Oh, that guy sold out.' But in reality that kind of prosperity makes certain things possible. 'Ol' '55' gave Tom a certain prosperity and power that I think he used wisely."

So delighted was David Geffen that Asylum's brightest hopes had given Waits a leg-up that he called Bones Howe to propose the band record a new version of "Ol' '55" with Waits singing. "David said to me, 'Put this all together and get these guys in the studio,'" Howe remembers. "One by one the Eagles became unavailable, so I assembled a group of the current hot studio players and we went in to Heider's to cut this one side live. We were there most of the night and never got a really good performance. I made a rough mix for David and took it to his office the next day. He agreed that we should forget it, and the tapes went into the Asylum vaults."

Given Waits' antipathy to everything the Eagles stood for, the only surprising thing is that he agreed to the idea in the first place. "In that group of people, Tom was the sort of turncoat," says Howe. "Even in a group that had its back turned to the commercial record business, he turned his back on *them*. In a lot of ways it was his way of becoming an individual away from individuals." Waits certainly believed he was different from Eric Andersen, a folk singer-songwriter on the periphery of the charmed Asylum circle. Waits loathed Andersen's rival cover of "Ol' '55" and later got in a scrap with him over a woman. "I wish he didn't like me," Waits said. "We had a fight once because he was messing about with my girl . . . it's really difficult to hit a guy who likes you, so I wish he didn't."

For Mike Melvoin, *The Heart of Saturday Night* was closer to Raymond Chandler's or Charles Bukowski's Los Angeles than to Don Henley's and Glenn Frey's. "I found it a lot easier to relate to Waits' view of LA than I did to the Eagles," Melvoin says. "The Eagles' milieu was the milieu of the record business itself." Waits was soon taking his own potshots at the Eagles, biting the Asylum hand that fed him. "I frankly was not that particularly crazy about their rendition of ['Ol' '55']," he told an interviewer on WAMU in Washington, DC. "I thought [it] was a little antiseptic." A year later, on his first visit to England, he was considerably more withering. The Eagles, he said, were "about as exciting as watching paint dry", adding that "they don't have cowshit on their boots, just dogshit from Laurel Canyon."*

The band's hackles quickly rose. "I still remember Tom saying listening to the Eagles was like watching paint dry," says Jack Tempchin, whose song "Already Gone" was *On the Border*'s euphoric opening track. "They read that and went, 'Well, okay, we ain't gonna record any more of *his* songs!'" Waits went even further in 1977, laying into the Eagles' peers and savaging lyrics by America and David Crosby. Not even Neil Young was spared. "[He's] another one who is embarrassing for displaying a third-grade mentality," Waits told *ZigZag*. "'*Old man take a look at my life . . .*' That's real good."

When, years later, I asked Waits about his comments, he seemed sincerely mortified. "I was a young kid," he sighed. "I was just corking off and being a prick. It was saying 'Notice me,' followed by 'Leave me the fuck alone,' sometimes in the same sentence." He added that he'd long since patched things up with Don Henley. But while one salutes the maturity of his regret, the young "prick" also deserves kudos for not playing along with the happy-family conspiracy fostered by Asylum (which, let's not forget, briefly had even Waits' beloved Bob Dylan on its roster). As much as it served his career well in the long run, Waits' lack of diplomacy about his musical dislikes was endearing.

The incidental extra exposure afforded by the Eagles' cover certainly didn't hurt: *The Heart of Saturday Night* was reviewed far more widely than *Closing Time* had been. "I'd tried to pitch stories on Waits because I had about a year and a half head start on everybody," recalls Harvey Kubernik. "Then the Eagles covered a song and all of a sudden it was 'Woah!'" Stephen Holden

* "Tom didn't really like our version of 'Ol' '55' when it first came out," Glenn Frey announced smarmily after the Eagles played the song at their Millennium show on New Year's Eve, 1999. "Then he got the check. And since then, Tom and I, we're really close."

again turned in an admiring piece for *Rolling Stone*, succinctly summarizing the record as "an evocation of ecstatic nighttime restlessness" and comparing Waits to his East Coast counterpart Bruce Springsteen. Closer to home, Michael C Ford reviewed his friend's album in the *LA Free Press*, remarking that Waits was "well on the way to becoming the poet of cool aloneness – his hard-rolling lines are emissaries to the bus terminals and the girl, the girl who put you there . . ."

Waits finally played his first date as a headlining act on 8 October 1974. ("Oh hush up now, I'm tryin' to sing this damn thing now," he snapped at the Ebbet's Field audience as they chatted over his introduction to a song. "I ain't *openin'* the show tonight . . .") A bootleg from the show, *The Dime-Store Novels, Vol. 1*, is one of the best early documents of Waits live as his inebriate-beatnik style started to crystallize. Switching back and forth between guitar and piano, Waits was wonderfully self-assured in this set, singing like a pickled Tim Buckley and telling jokes in a voice that still sounded like the mumbling Bob Dylan of a decade earlier.

It was on this trip to Denver that Waits began writing the long narrative piece that was "Nighthawk Postcards (from Easy Street)", an extension of what he called the "Metropolitan Doubletalk" style of "Diamonds on My Windshield". As the tour continued on the East Coast, he grabbed time in his hotel rooms to write and to record on a tape recorder he'd brought with him. As he worked, "Nighthawk Postcards" became a distillation of all his literary influences, from Kerouac to Runyon and even Mickey Spillane. (The "yellow biscuit of a buttery cue-ball moon" of the opening section came straight out of Bukowski.) He packed the piece with images from "the rhapsody of the pending evening", peopling it with conmen and cab drivers and the denizens of Chubb's Pool and Snooker, where he scoured the jukebox in vain for George Perkins' "High Blood Pressure".

On 19 November, Waits reached New York City in time for three dates at the Bottom Line. Holed up at the infamous Chelsea Hotel, he finished writing "Nighthawk Postcards", segueing from Chubb's to Manhattan's 23rd Street at dawn. "Tom was truly in his element at the Chelsea," says Danny Trifan, who later played bass with him. "He seemed to just fit in with the history of the place, with all the unusual poets, writers, and musicians who'd stayed or lived there." The Bottom Line shows attracted a smattering of pop VIPs, among them a ballsy diva then making waves in the music press. "He was singing 'The Heart of Saturday Night,'" Bette Midler remembered of her first live exposure to Waits; "I just fell in love with him on the spot." After the show Midler swanned into his dressing room to offer her congratulations. "You need some feathers, girls, hula skirts, and beaded curtains," she boomed at Waits. "Then you might have something." They became instant friends.

Back home in early December, Waits supported Little Feat for three nights at the Troubadour. For all his toughening-up on the road with Zappa and others, playing before his LA peers at the Troub was stressful. Opening each set boldly with "Diamonds on My Windshield" – "snapping his fingers on his right hand and waving his constant Old Gold in his left," *Rolling Stone* noted – he ran through a selection of songs from his two albums before finishing up with "Nighthawk Postcards", which already lasted well over seven minutes. "It was okay on the bill with Little Feat," he said in the New Year. "Opening night I was pretty inebriated. There was a lot of press there and everything and it just has the tendency to make you a little neurotic, I guess. On top of everything else I had never played there before. I'd hooted there several times so playing there, having a formal engagement there, was a little difficult somehow – but it went off okay."

"I thought he was very hip," says Paul Body, who watched from the side of the club. "He looked like he'd stepped out of a Chandler novel. Everybody else was doing the sensitive singer-songwriter thing and he was more like big-city. Don't forget he was happening at the same time that Springsteen was happening, so you had these two guys on opposite coasts doing more big-city stuff and not talking about moving to the country." Body approached Waits after his first show and got talking. "There was a restaurant called the Pantry, which was where all the Chandler types used to eat, and I suggested we check it out some time. Which we did." In due course Body would become an integral part of Waits' West Hollywood peer group.

Also present for at least one of the Troubadour shows was Frank Waits, who made a habit of catching his son's LA performances. "My old man likes me a lot," Waits said. "He sits right up front and tosses down Scotch on the rocks and gets snookered and enjoys himself thoroughly. He says, 'That's my son up there.'" Asked if he was close to his family, Waits said, "Yeah, we do okay. My family's pretty much split up. I live in LA, so does my dad. My mother lives in San Diego and I got a sister in San Diego and one in LA. I hang out with my father when I'm at home."

Doug Weston was delighted with Waits' Troubadour performances. "Doug was smart and knew that Tom was a unique talent," says Louie Lista. "He knew he was peculiar enough and yet not that problematic." According to Rich Wiseman in *Rolling Stone*, Weston complimented Waits in the Troubadour alley. With Doug's endorsement ringing in his ears, Waits – in "$2.50 used imitation alligator boots" – sauntered off into the night, taking Wiseman to a tired diner on Sunset called the Copper Skillet. Here, in the wee small hours, he reiterated his commitment to the nocturnal life, saying he'd always be a "night owl" and would never move to a cabin in Colorado. "The moon beats the hell out of the sun," Waits said. "There's something illusion-ary about the night . . . your imagination is working overtime . . . there's food for thought at our fingertips and it begs to be dealt with." Wiseman finally departed at 6.10 a.m., leaving Waits to catch a few hours' sleep at the Tropicana – even though "he's kept his one-bedroom house" – before leaving to play two nights at the University of Minnesota.

Asked whether the *Rolling Stone* feature, published on 30 January 1975, signified his commercial arrival on the American rock scene, Waits was sanguine. "Not really," he said. "I'm still an opening act." In the interview itself he acknowledged that releasing an album was merely a "diploma" that threw you out into "another arena with the thousands of other cats who have records just like you".

The new year found Waits working on songs for his next album. He said he would "probably go in the studio some time in maybe May" but had "quite a while to be at home now, so plenty of time to write songs". He even had the opportunity to write some songs for Barbra Streisand. He continued to hang out at the Troubadour and Duke's coffee shop, where he was frequently seen in the company of his new best friend from Denver. Chuck E. Weiss had just moved to LA with a view to making it as a singer himself, crashing for a while with Waits in Silver Lake. The two men collaborated on some songs Waits planned to record, and Weiss wanted to be present at the sessions.

"Chuckie was sort of Tom's road manager, and sort of his hanger-on," says Paul Body. "Well, not his hanger-on but . . . they were buddies, confidants. Chuckie was the wilder of the two, because Waits was still a kid. Weiss won't cop to it but he's a little older than us." Body often referred to Weiss as "Bighead" because that's what he once heard Muddy Waters call him. "Bighead was a mentor for all of us in a way," he says. "He was really the street-smart guy . . . he knew all these guys and we didn't."

Duke's coffee shop, summer 1975. (*Barry Schultz/Retna*)

Gradually a little gang began to coalesce around Waits. With the Troubadour as its unofficial HQ, the posse comprised Weiss, Body, Louie Lista, the club's manager Robert Marchese, and lighting man/songwriter Artie Leichter.* The glue that bonded them together was music. "Music was the main thing," says Body. "Tom would turn me on to something, and I'd turn *him* on to

---

* This, of course, was the roll call of cats "sharing a curbstone" in the long sub-title to Waits' 1976 song "Jitterbug Boy". Artie is often assumed wrongly to be Art Fein (aka "Fein Art").

something. See, he wasn't really a rock-and-roll guy. With him it was Al Cohn or other jazz guys. It was Lord Buckley." A common denominator was the sense of being profoundly out of step with the times. "I think we were all fish out of water to a great extent," Lista says of the crew. "We were all very strong performers, but that wasn't what was going on. What was going on was the Eagles."

Lista initially distrusted Waits' jazzbo routines, watching his "act" from behind the Troubadour bar. "Weiss was pretty likable, but I wasn't sure I liked Tom at all," he says. "I thought, 'Is this an act, this greasy-food-at-the-diner thing?' I was crazy enough and doped-up enough at the time to be suspicious, probably because he did it pretty well." As time wore on, Lista began to understand why Waits had developed the act in the first place. "I think Tom saw the humor element work, saw that he was able to get people to laugh and to break down their defenses with that kind of a character. It was, 'I'm an outsider, but I'll *revel* in being an outsider.'"

Marchese, a pugnacious Italian-American from Pittsburgh, was more sceptical. A man who'd strong-armed John Lennon out of the Troubadour the previous March – on the night the drunken ex-Beatle heckled the Smothers Brothers – Marchese was Doug Weston's right-hand-man and the owner of an A-grade bullshit detector. "I just thought Waits was fulla shit, which I always would tell him," Marchese snarls good-naturedly. "You know, the whole mystique of this real funky dude and all that Charles Bukowski crap. Because nobody was really like that. He was basically a middle-class, San-Diego-mom-and-pop-schoolteacher kid. And it was his impression of how funky poor folk really are." Harvey Kubernik recalls Marchese referring to Waits as "Ratzo", apparently believing the singer had based his shambling gait on Dustin Hoffman's character in *Midnight Cowboy*. "I'd see Waits with Marchese and

Louie and Body just hanging out at the Troubadour," Kubernik says. "Marchese really liked Tom but he would say to him, 'Hey, clear the aisle, Ratzo.' And Waits would say, 'Man, don't call me that.'"

Despite the derision, Waits warmed to Marchese; perhaps it was refreshing to encounter a bona fide street guy who didn't buy his act at face value. "For some odd reason Tom was very concerned about what I thought about his stuff," Marchese chuckles. "He gave me an acetate of one of his albums and said, 'I think I'm really takin' a chance with this one.' I said, 'I'll tell ya something, Tom. 1956 at the height of McCarthyism, Little Richard comes out in a silver suit singing "Tutti Frutti" . . . now *that's* somebody takin' a chance!' I would always say things like that, not out of belligerence but to keep everybody from getting bigheaded or losing perspective."*

Waits' contention that he was still just "an opening act" was confirmed by further support slots through the early months of 1975. Though he headlined at McCabe's Guitar Shop in Santa Monica at the end of January, he was the opening act for Bonnie Raitt, the Flying Burrito Brothers, former Byrd Gene Clark (back at Ebbet's Field), John Stewart (again), and Melissa Manchester, and (at Toronto's El Mocambo club) a Canadian country rock band called the Good Brothers. "I get tired of playing when I'm playing, like, at the El Mocambo club, like a steak house or a barbecue pit," he grouched. "When it's just a dragged week."

Did Waits complain to Herbie Cohen? Few of his friends

---

* Waits may have taken Marchese's putdown to heart. "[Some] songs just come out of you, like you're talking in tongues," he told Richard Grant thirty years later. "It's like 'Awop-bop-aloo-bop-awop-bam-boom!' Where did *that* come from? Incantation. It has great power and it scares the hell out of a lot of people, especially coming from a little black man with real high hair who looks a little effeminate and has a high voice and bug eyes and is completely out of his mind."

were privy to his true feelings about his manager, or the exact nature of their relationship. "Tom never really talked about Herb," says Paul Body. "Maybe that was because I didn't want to be privy to that kind of thing – I didn't want to know how the monster was built. Herb was sort of the West Coast version of Albert Grossman, and he was tough like Grossman. You need that sort of guy to sort of *get you in.* He wanted to do the things for you, but once you found out what he did it was like 'Uh-oh.'"

"Herb was a real street guy," says Bones Howe. "He pulled some things on me that I just called tuition. I thought, 'That's how you learn about this business. First time, you call it tuition. Let 'em do it to you again and you're a fool.' There were different layers of Herb Cohen. In some ways he was a sweetheart, and when my wife and I socialized with him and his wife Dee we always had a good time. But I didn't really feel like I wanted to get into business with him."

Others in the Troubadour posse thought Cohen possessive of Waits and threatened by the camaraderie he witnessed there. "Cohen would come and hang out in the Troubadour bar, but slowly I got this picture that there was jealousy," says Louie Lista. "Maybe it was just a case of someone who plays that heavier role becoming jealous when they see actual friendship or warmth between people."

Waits had another peer group in Bones Howe and the musicians he'd worked with on *The Heart of Saturday Night.* Their view of Cohen was much the same. "On one of his albums [*Nighthawks at the Diner*], Waits credited Herb Cohen with 'insistence,'" says Jim Hughart. "There was no diplomacy ever with Herbie. He was pushing, pushing, pushing, no matter who was around. He pushed on me and I don't even think he meant to, it was just the way he lived his life." Cohen meanwhile reminded Mike Melvoin of numerous Jewish uncles and cousins, "so it was impossible to intimidate me as a result of that". Cohen "would scare other people – seriously – but it never bothered me".

To Howe, Cohen was "almost like a big brother to Tom in a lot of ways", as well as being someone with a lot of input into how Waits presented himself. "It was Herb that helped him to get comfortable on stage," says Howe. "Tom was a natural performer but he needed help. Herb helped him organize his ideas so that they turned into a direction. He really coached Tom into this thing where his performances became not just a guy standing at the microphone." In March, Cohen floated the notion of making the next album a "live double" of the kind popular among seventies rock bands, except that this would be no *Live at the Fillmore East* affair, more an extended set from the ideal Waits venue, a dingy dive of a nightclub with cigarette smoke curling up to the cheap klieg lights. "Tom always wanted to make each record a little different from the one before," says Bones Howe. "He'd talked to Herbie about doing a live album but they just couldn't figure out where to do it. All they knew was they didn't want to do it at the Troubadour."

Howe happened to know that Barbra Streisand had recorded some tracks for her latest album *Lazy Afternoon* in a big room at the back of the Record Plant studio on Beverly Boulevard at Third Street: "I said we could clear the floor completely and put tables in there and you could have an invited audience and a nightclub atmosphere where you don't have to deal with Santa Monica Boulevard or whatever."

Reuniting the musicians who'd played on *The Heart of Saturday Night* but replacing Jim Gordon with drummer Bill Goodwin, Howe booked the Record Plant for two nights at the end of July and oversaw a week of rehearsals for the new songs Waits had written. The latter had met Goodwin – drummer with Mose Allison – the previous November at a Cambridge show where Allison was the support act for Bonnie Raitt. "I met this very interesting guy backstage wearing a rumpled suit and looking like a fifties beatnik," Goodwin says. "He said he really liked my playing, said I had this older approach." The next night, with no show to play, Goodwin was walking out of the band's hotel to catch a show in Boston when Raitt and her bassist Freebo buttonholed him and announced he was coming with them. "We went to see Tom play," Goodwin recalls. "He opened with 'Diamonds on My Windshield', just snapping his fingers, and it lasted about ten minutes. I was blown away, transfixed."

So wowed was Goodwin that he phoned Bones Howe and told him, "I'd be a really good drummer for Tom." Howe and Waits had already reached the same conclusion. With Jim Gordon on duty with the Souther Hillman Furay Band, Bill was a shoo-in. He flew to LA, a city he'd originally left in 1969, and slotted into the *Nighthawks* band alongside old friends Melvoin, Hughart, and the great tenor saxophonist Pete Christlieb. Waits quickly became tight with him. "Usually every night after rehearsal Tom and I would get into his Caddy – an old '55 Fleetwood four-door with fast-food wrappers and newspapers on the back seat – and literally just cruise around," Goodwin remembers. "I'd grown up in LA and we did what I'd done as a kid, which was cruise the Sunset Strip, and then we'd go over to the studio and see what Bonnie Raitt was doing." Raitt's 1975 album *Home Plate* featured Waits on inebriated backing vocals for the Nan O'Byrne song "Your Sweet and Shiny Eyes".

The two *Nighthawks* shows, on 30 and 31 July, were invitation-only, though a number of free tickets were distributed at the Troubadour. Along with friends such as Paul Body, Michael C Ford, and Chuck E. Weiss – who'd co-written "Spare Parts I (A Nocturnal Emission)" for the album – dozens of Elektra-Asylum employees poured into the Record Plant. "Looks like a bona fide,

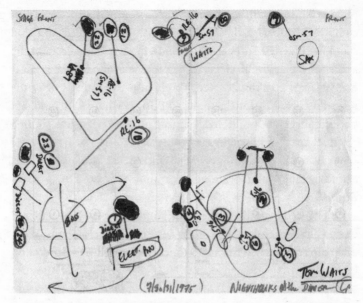

Nighthawks at the Diner stage setup, 30–31 July 1975. (*Courtesy of Bones Howe*)

high-voltage, decked-out-in-full-regalia Angeleno audience," Waits rapped as he introduced "On a Foggy Night".

"It was a pretty good-sized room," Jim Hughart recalled. "They set it up like a nightclub with big tables with checkerboard tablecloths and peanuts and pretzels and wine and beer . . . We did four shows each night and we changed the audience after each show. It was done like a nightclub thing." As a finishing touch Herb Cohen suggested opening the shows with a stripper named Dewanna, who twirled her tassels as the band played "Night Train" and the theme from *The Pink Panther*.

The recordings were a triumph, an authentic immersion in the hipster life that was also hysterically funny. Waits' delivery and timing on the extended intros to "Eggs and Sausage (in a Cadillac with Susan Michelson)", a verbal tour of such notable LA diners as Norm's on La Cienega Avenue, and "Better off without a Wife" (a bittersweet celebration of sad-sack bachelorhood, complete with masturbation references) were as sharp as any standup comedy. "You can hear on the record how ecstatic the audience was," says Bill Goodwin. "I was so mesmerized that I literally at one point came out of this state where I realized we were recording. We just hit this magical thing, this golden mean of performance."

After a three-minute intro that hinged on Jim Hughart's leathery, twisting bass and dipped the listener deep in Waits' new comic persona, the set took off with "Emotional Weather Report", a fixture of Waits' mid-seventies sets and the perfect vehicle for a self-portrait of shabby loneliness in the less salubrious neighbourhoods of Los Angeles. There were "gusty winds" at the intersection of Sunset and Alvarado (prime Bukowski country), ticket-takers at the Ivar Theater, and extended meteorological metaphors for Waits' "disconcerted precarious emotional situation".

"Gusty winds at times around the corner of Sunset and Alvarado . . ." (*Art Sperl*)

Waits switched to acoustic guitar for "On a Foggy Night", half singing and half rapping/scatting in a Louis Armstrong vibrato as he told of getting lost on an abandoned road. It was back to blue-note piano for "Eggs and Sausage", which could have segued straight out of "Ghosts of Saturday Night". This was Waits at large in Cholesterol City, voicing the hipster's love of junk food – of "strange-looking patty melts at Norm's" and "dangerous veal cutlets at the Copper Penny". The LA audience delighted in such parochial references. "Mike Melvoin called him the poet of the soft white underbelly," Bill Goodwin says. "Tom spoke for those people who had no voice – the guy in the next car on the freeway. It was very specific in a way and yet very universal."

The loser humour of the intro to "Better off without a Wife" was hilarious but poignant: there was real compassion for this man who was a version of Waits himself. "I've got a personality that an audience likes," he said in a 1976 interview. "I'm like the guy they knew – someone raggedy and irresponsible – who never really amounted to much but was always good for a few laughs. A victim, just a victim. But I don't mind the image."

The epic spoken-word "Nighthawk Postcards (from Easy Street)" asked a lot of the listener: it went on for eleven and a half minutes without developing musically in any very significant way. If the track was as close as some rock fans have ever come to "jazz" – to traps and brushes and muted trumpets and upright bass and squawking saxes – Waits was occasionally as guilty as the Beats themselves of over-writing.

"Warm Beer and Cold Women" was a blues ballad in the late-night, smoke-filled mode of Charles Brown. This was Waits the lachrymose boozer, listening to a country-and-western band play Tammy Wynette songs in a "last-ditch-attempt saloon". "Putnam County" was the ultimate backwater American location, the sort of place where Kerouac and Cassady would have searched for what Waits called "the dark warm narcotic American night". Again the milieu was country and western, with references to "the entire Hank Williams songbook", "the radio spittin' out Charlie Rich", and "Stratocasters slung over the Burghermeister beer guts".

"Spare Parts I (A Nocturnal Emission)" kicked off with rinky-dinky cocktail-hour muzak like the *Pink Panther* theme. From Putnam County we were straight back to the Los Angeles of the Tropicana and the Ivar, with a sky the colour of Pepto-Bismol. "Nobody" was the old Tin Pan Alley pastiche Waits had recorded in 1971, revisited as if by a drunken bum crooning to himself in the gutter. "It's story time again," Waits said as he switched back to acoustic guitar for "Big Joe and Phantom 309". For all its death-song kitsch, one suspects the cornball sentimentality of Tommy Faile's yarn genuinely appealed to Waits' sense of nobility.

Nighthawks wrapped up with a breezy reprise of "Spare Parts", over which Waits proffered outro thanks to the band. "They all come from good families," he grunted. "But over the years they just individually developed some ways about 'em that just aren't right . . ." It was a phrase that – three months earlier – he'd used about himself.

To this day, the *Nighthawks* musicians find themselves regularly being grilled about those two famous nights at the Record Plant. When people learn of their association with Tom Waits, the fact that they've played with innumerable jazz greats over the years apparently counts for nothing.

"People like Melvoin and Christlieb have traveled the world and played with *everybody*," laughs Bones Howe. "Yet the one thing people always ask them is, 'What was it like making *Nighthawks at the Diner*?'"

Chapter 5

Knee-deep in Grunge

> *"I have a lot of show folks staying here – you know,*
> *musicians and stuff. But don't get the wrong idea,*
> *you know . . . like, I run a respectable place."*
>
> (Pat Ast in *Andy Warhol's Heat*, 1972)

"There is a kidney-shaped swimming pool in the courtyard," William Burroughs wrote of the Tropicana Motor Hotel. "On the patio are rusty metal tables, deck chairs, palms and banana trees: a rundown Raymond Chandler set from the 1950s. One expects to find a dead man floating in the pool one morning . . ."

The Beat Generation's *éminence grise* was writing in 1980, reporting for *Rolling Stone* on the Jack Kerouac/Neal Cassady biopic *Heart Beat*, but the Tropicana hadn't changed greatly since Tom Waits first wandered into its seedy lobby. Nor did it change noticeably in the subsequent three years of its life. When I met up with Nick Cave there in 1983, the pool was still black. "It was black because it was all rusty from bands throwing lawn furniture in there," LA scenester Pleasant Gehman later explained to me. (In fact, the management had painted it black in order to avoid having to clean it.) Suffice to say it would have been unthinkable for Cave and his band the Birthday Party to stay anywhere in Los Angeles bar the motel Gehman knew fondly as "the Top Trop".

Opened by baseball player Sandy Koufax in the early 1960s, the Tropicana was a West Hollywood motel favoured by musicians, actors, artists, and assorted freaks. Jim Morrison crashed there when he wasn't dossing at the Alta Cienega up the road. Everybody from Alice Cooper to playwright Sam Shepard holed up at the Top Trop, which was as cheap as it was convenient. Used as the prime location for Paul Morrissey's 1972 film *Andy Warhol's Heat*, the Tropicana was the epitome of California gutter chic. The very name of the place, with its connotations of freshly squeezed health, was sublimely ironic. "It was like a Motel 6 with shag carpeting," film producer Mary Aloe told Jay Jacobs. "There was barely a good working TV . . . [and] there were old cigarette-butt holes burned in different things." But at the Trop, she said, you could mingle with "the famous and the infamous".

Among the LA denizens who loved the place was Warren Zevon, whose 1976 debut album on Asylum shared some of Waits' themes and sub-Hollywood locations. "Warren had this thing about the Tropicana because it fit into this image he had of what a rock star was supposed to look like and live like," said his photographer friend Richard Edlund. "He was all kind of Bukowski-esque . . . this was all in the 'too young to die old and too old to die young' era . . ." Waits was more prosaic about the place: "The Tropicana was really a businessmen's hotel and started out as a nine-dollar-a-night motel for, like, Fuller Brush men. It wasn't really very musical first time I came there. And slowly it got a reputation for bands."

"If it was your first gig in Los Angeles you'd stay at the Tropicana," says Todd Everett, who interviewed more than a few musicians there. "As you got a bit more successful you'd stay at the Continental Hyatt House. Then as you got *real* successful you'd be at the Chateau Marmont or the Beverly Hills Hotel. What attracted Tom to the Tropicana, God knows. Probably *not* because it was where all these musicians would stay."

What *really* attracted Waits to the Tropicana was Chuck E. Weiss, who'd moved into the motel early in 1975. "I was driving from Silver Lake to [Duke's] every day to eat," Weiss told Jay Jacobs, "and I thought, 'I'll just move there.'" Living full-time in a motel was the ultimate statement of anti-domesticity, and Weiss was nothing if not anti-domestic. "Chuckie was doing a lot of drugs then," says Robert Marchese. "All I had to say was 'Where?' and he'd be there with the drugs before I even arrived. I only ever did LSD and cocaine. Chuckie didn't drink but he did anything else he could get his hands on. Him and Louie Lista would sneak off and take downers and whatever. Chuckie, because he wasn't really working or anything, was kind of drifting. I gave him a job at the Troub and I think he lasted a month." Waits by contrast was faithful to alcohol and nicotine and certainly steered clear of heroin. "I never did any narcotics," he said in June 1976. "I've got more access to them now than I ever had, but I just ain't interested." Marchese confirms that Waits never did anything harder than cocaine. "He smoked like a chimney and once in a while he'd do a couple of lines, but Tom wasn't a druggie, I'll say that for him."

Marchese observed the Waits–Weiss double act with amusement, trying to figure out how it really operated. Despite bonding with Weiss over their shared love of Chicago blues, he couldn't help viewing the guy as a glorified male groupie. "I can't say anything negative about Waits and Chuckie," he says, "but I always got the impression that once Tom rolled, then Chuckie would roll with him." Bones Howe agrees: "Chuckie was a hanger. You'd meet a lot of actors that had walking-around people – they don't like to be alone. Tom liked having somebody to hang out with."

"When Chuck came into Tom's life, he and I stopped hanging out so exclusively together," says Bobi Thomas. "Little by little they became inseparable." Other observers were more cynical about Weiss. "I could never fathom what he was selling," says Mike Melvoin. "I didn't regard him as having any talent whatsoever except self-promotion – promoting his own celebrity. It was kind of saying, 'I am the street.' It was only two steps down to Wild Man Fischer as far as I was concerned."

Promoting *Nighthawks at the Diner* on its release in October 1975, Waits took stock of his commercial prospects. He told Todd Everett that Asylum still had "a lot of faith in me . . . with the idea that sooner or later I'll do something significant". Indeed, David Geffen himself couldn't understand why Tom wasn't breaking out and did everything possible to expose him to a broader audience. "I wasn't surprised by anything Tom did," the multi-billionaire says. "One only had to look at his car. I always liked the evolution of talented people and I always try to understand it. I'm not sure that making the fans happy was always a priority of Tom's, but I was always happy with whatever he did. He never got a single note from me."

Behind the scenes, Asylum *were* worrying about Waits' commercial potential. Having steered him towards a jazz-oriented producer, Geffen now thought Waits had gone too far the other way. "Geffen hated *Nighthawks*," claims Bill Goodwin. "He said it was too much of a jazz record. Bones told me Geffen's exact words were, 'This is a fucking *jazz* record!'" Perhaps Geffen was wondering why he couldn't have had a Bruce Springsteen for the money he'd spent on Waits. Stacking *Nighthawks* up against Springsteen's *Born to Run*, it was pretty clear where the bigger money lay. Had Waits taken a different turn, could he have sold as many records as Springsteen? "I don't know about that," Tom said in 2002. "If you're eccentric then you're eccentric. I don't think I ever got to a crossroads in my life when I could have done that."

Geffen's response to *Nighthawks* never reached Waits' ears. Certainly he wasn't looking to tone down the jazz elements in his music. On 14 and 15 August he played two more shows at the Troubadour, backed by Jim Hughart, Jim Gordon, and Mike

The Troubadour, August 1975, with Waits headlining. (*Barry Schultz/Retna*)

Melvoin, with the great LA tenor saxophonist Teddy Edwards depping for Pete Christlieb. The following month, as Waits prepared for the album's release, Herb Cohen asked Bill Goodwin to assemble a jazz trio for a week's residency in New York.

"Tom wanted some musicians to play some dates after *Nighthawks* came out," Goodwin remembers. "Herb got me to organize a little group for some dates at Reno Sweeney's. I got Al Cohn of Al and Zoot Sims fame. Tom was very excited and a little concerned. He idolized Al and Zoot because they'd played on Kerouac's *Blues and Haikus*. He said, 'That's one of my favorite records. I think Al plays too good for this gig.'"* Cohn, as it

---

* *Blues and Haikus* came out in 1960. "[They] played that one night in a storeroom of some club in New York, and it just killed me, man," Waits said. "It's such a low, moanin' lonesome, real tragic style."

turned out, had never heard of Waits. "He didn't know anything about Tom but I told him, 'Hey, we'll have fun with this guy,'" Goodwin says. "Al was the biggest *mensch* in the world and he loved Tom and dug playing with him and they got on really well."

Waits had a mild freakout at Reno Sweeney's when he formed the impression that the venue was a gay club. Unequivocally – some would say almost gruffly – heterosexual, Waits wanted to pull out of the engagement. "Tom wasn't homophobic but he thought it wasn't going to be his audience," Goodwin chuckles. "Herbie called me and said, 'You gotta talk to him.' So I called him and said we had to do the gig." It's unclear whether the sight of Barry Manilow and his mother in the front row one night allayed or confirmed Waits' fears about the club's orientation. Manilow had been urged to see Waits by Bette Midler, for whom he'd played piano in the heady days when she'd entertained the debauched patrons of Manhattan's Continental Baths.

Writer David McGee, who'd befriended Waits in New York the previous year – meeting up with him to hang out and play pool when he was in town – recalls his despondency over the Reno Sweeney's shows. "It was a true nightmare for Tom," McGee says. "And I think the decision he later took to break away from the status quo in the music business and in his career was forged in the misery of that nightmare."

For McGee, everything seemed to "darken" for Waits at this time: he was no longer the bashful charmer that McGee's wife Nikki had cooked for at the beginning of the year. "Tom seemed ambivalent about *Nighthawks at the Diner*, regarding it as a holding pattern and not the forward movement he felt his career needed," McGee says. "There was a decided change in him – a restlessness, an agitated energy, almost like he couldn't sit still even when he knew he needed to. He looked unhealthy, too, and when I inquired about his physical condition he admitted he needed to back off the drinking, which by now had become hard liquor instead of beer."

It was during this brief stay in New York that Waits and McGee witnessed a singularly shocking scene one night, just along 23rd Street from the Chelsea. The two men had left the hotel to eat at a nearby pizza parlour, only to find it blocked off with police tape. Inside, with his head at the foot of a gumball machine, was a black teenager, a puddle of blood fanning out from him as he lay dead on the floor. "Some guy had just shot him," Waits recalled. "He was sprawled right there against the wall. I was scared shitless." The two men speculated as to what had happened. "Tom said something like, 'Maybe he got rained on by the pizza man's .38,'" says McGee. Born in the conjecture of that conversation was the spoken-word masterpiece "Small Change".

On another evening at the Chelsea, Waits was just sitting down – in his underpants – to watch William Wellman's 1943 western *The Ox-Bow Incident* on TV when a key turned in the door and a couple entered the room. "It's okay, buddy, you can stay," the man told Waits. "We'll sleep over here." As his female companion used the bathroom, the man sat down beside Waits and started watching the film. Flabbergasted, Waits finally got rid of the pair by offering to pay for them to get their own room. "I went back to *The Ox-Bow Incident*," he remembered. "It was just wrapping up. The hanging had already taken place."

One beneficial effect of the Reno Sweeney's shows was an unlikely appearance on CBS chatfest *The Mike Douglas Show*. Don Ray King, the show's producer, caught one of the shows and was deeply impressed by Waits' "syncopated stutter-step of urban images and dark-side tales". Waiting for him to drop the mask, he eventually realized that Waits was going to stay in role. "[He played] the whole set as that derelict," King recalled. "A gutsy, shrewd act, I thought." The following year King booked Waits on to the Douglas show.

The fall of 1975 found Waits touring as support act to Bonnie Raitt, who liked to booze with the boys and adored Tom as much as she loved his music. For Raitt, a native Angeleno as much at ease with LA singer-songwriters like Jackson Browne and J. D. Souther as with venerable blues matrons like Sippie Wallace and Alberta Hunter, Waits offered something unique. "[He's] a real original," she told *Newsweek*. "He's a window on a scene we never

On the tour bus reading *Last Exit to Brooklyn*, 1975.
(*Michael Dobo*)

got close to. He's able to make all the double-knits both tragic and romantic at the same time."

Being on the road with Raitt can't have done Waits' drinking much good. Certainly he began to feel the strain of touring in a new way. "When you're on the road doing clubs, it's hard to stay out of the bars in the afternoons," he told *Down Beat*. "Then you hang around the club all night and you're up till dawn, so you hang around coffee shops. It stops being something you do – it becomes something you *are*." Talking to *Rolling Stone* at the end of 1976, he was still more candid about the pitfalls of life on the road. "I was sick through that whole period," he said. "I'd been traveling quite a bit, living in hotels, eating bad food, drinking a lot – too much. There's a lifestyle that's there before you arrive and you're introduced to it. It's unavoidable." He also bemoaned the lack of time and privacy in which to write.

On 9 November, Waits was back at the venue where he and Bob Webb had performed just two years before. Witnessing the show at Avery Fisher Hall, ironically, was a man who was about to turn Bruce Springsteen into a superstar. "He sings everything . . . in a rasp to end all rasps," Jon Landau wrote of Waits, "one filled with intimacy, energy and intensity." He noted that Waits had become a master storyteller. "[He] is different. He has no known history in the sixties. He didn't write an occasional album cut for anyone, the way Jackson and Joni did when they were starting out. He didn't play in some now obscure rock band the way Glenn Frey did."

Early in December, with the Raitt tour behind him, Waits used a radio interview on WMMS Cleveland to take further swipes at the Eagles. He also told Kid Leo that his next album would be called either *Pasties and a G-String*, *A Beer and a Cheap Shot*, or *Cheater Slicks and Baby Moons*. "Kid Leo really had an interest in Tom and would play his songs," says Fred Toedtman, who worked as a regional promo man for Elektra-Asylum. "He kind of had that same kind of deep gravelly voice as Tom, so they got on really well."*

Just before Christmas, Waits performed on the PBS concert show *Soundstage*, on which – to his considerable excitement – he shared the bill with his beloved Mose Allison. "He's great, right?" he said of Allison the following June. "But he just got dropped from his label because people couldn't put an easy tag on him. Well, he's not a blues singer, exactly. And he's not really progressive jazz, exactly, and he's not pop. So they get nervous and drop him." Perhaps Waits feared the same thing might happen to him.

In March 1976, Waits put together "a real high-voltage bebop trio" consisting of three New York players: tenor saxophonist Frank Vicari, a former mainstay of Woody Herman's and Maynard Ferguson's bands; drummer Alan "Chip" White, who'd played with Vicari in bands led by Dave Liebman and Steve Grossman; and a bassist with the memorable name Fitzgerald Huntington Jenkins III, who'd recently graduated from medical school.

"I didn't even know who he was," Chip White says of Waits. "Frank called me and said they wanted a New York jazz band and the guy was kind of a poet. We went down to SIR rehearsal studios and played with him for a couple of hours. I thought he was going to be a forty-year-old guy and he was a twenty-five-year-old kid. *Everybody* was older than him. But the chemistry between us was immediate." In time – after the subtitle to *Nighthawks'* "Spare Parts I" – the trio would become known as the Nocturnal Emissions. "I got a black bass player, a Sicilian tenor and a Cherokee and Afro-American drummer," Waits said of them. "We can go into any neighborhood in the world and hang out."

---

* Born Lawrence J. Travagliante, Kid Leo was an early and avid supporter of Bruce Springsteen on WMMS, which helped break many seventies rock acts in the Midwest and beyond.

Waits and his Emissions: (left to right) Fitz Jenkins, Frank Vicari, Chip White.
(*Courtesy of Chip White*)

One of the first dates Waits played with the new trio was the University of Pittsburgh, where they were supported by none other than Charles Bukowski. "Tom had given me a couple of his books," Chip White remembers. "Like, 'Check this out and you'll dig where I'm comin' from . . .' And I did." To White's astonishment, Bukowski brought a beer cooler on stage, downing one can after another without saying a word. Finally somebody yelled out, "Hey man, say something!" Bukowski burped in response and began reading.

By this point "Buk" had become a legend of the literary underground, his semi-autobiographical novels *Post Office* (1971) and *Factotum* (1975) bringing him a far larger audience than his early stories and poems while making his alter ego Hank Chinaski a cult hero. Waits thought *Factotum* "terrific . . . [it] talks about all the lousy jobs he had to take to be a poet". Despite his pitted face – "like a ravaged lion", he said of himself – Bukowski had become almost craggily handsome, with good hair and eyes that smiled. "He was like a big bear," Waits recalled of the writer. "He had this enormous head, as big as Frankenstein. He had a big presence and huge shoulders, and that face that looks like a mask, a scary mask. I was fascinated with him. He was like a . . . I don't know what you call it, a mentor."

Bashful in his presence, Waits refrained from grilling the fifty-five-year-old author. "I didn't want to be too cloying or inquisitive," he said. "He had his own world, his own life." What Bukowski made of his young fan is anyone's guess, though Jack Nitzsche allegedly overheard the writer opine of Waits that "the guy doesn't have an original bone in his body". It's not hard to imagine Bukowski the belligerent drunk muttering such a thing. Nor would it would have been so out of synch with a general suspicion that Waits was a fake. "Although Waits' integration of his stories into his show originally seemed promising," critic Dave Marsh had written of the Reno Sweeney's show, "it now seems, as an end in itself, a cul-de-sac. Without first-rate songs, his jive-talking, fingerpopping, his twitching mannerisms seem only affected – false in precisely the way all the guys at the truck stop would find transparently phony."

Would Waits have been hurt by such charges? Again we have to face the hoary issue of "authenticity" head-on. "All of a sudden it becomes your image," he told the *Los Angeles Times* in March 1976, "and it's hard to tell where the image stops and you begin, or where you stop and the image begins." He said he was a "caricature of myself" on stage, that his act had to be "choreographed and calculated . . . to make it look spontaneous". His self-awareness at this stage of his career was as remarkable as it was redeeming.

Waits stayed on the road through the rest of March into April.

"It was like a traveling party and it kind of went on that way for a couple of years," says Chip White. "It was the first time I'd done one of those tours where they took out all the seats on the bus so you could sleep in your bunk. They had videos and a kitchen and you could pick up fans and friends as you traveled along. We always kept a case of Heineken in the refrigerator." A frequent way of killing time was gambling. "We played a lot of cards," says White. "I'd come out of my bunk in the middle of the night and there'd be hundreds of dollars on the table. Tom gambled along with everyone else, including the bus driver. There was never any star shit with him."

One of the more notable nights on the tour was 7 April, when Waits and the Emissions played New York University's Loeb Student Center. Observing Waits as he "slithered" into the sound-check was the young Hal Willner, a man who would later oversee Tom's contributions to the Kurt Weill and Disney tribute albums *Lost in the Stars* and *Stay Awake*. To Willner, who ran shadow spotlight for the NYU show, Waits was out of sorts from the second he arrived in the theatre. ("If you've been a bad person," Waits liked to say, "you don't go to hell, you go to a sound-check.") Willner was instantly hit by the shock of Waits' voice. "Witnessing the big sound that came out of [his] small frame was absolutely frightening, like something from a Tex Avery/Max Fleischer cartoon," he wrote. "He seemed in pain, as if his body couldn't contain the sound." Willner himself came in for one of Waits' tongue-lashings during the gig. When he briefly screwed up with the lighting, "Waits stopped, glared up at me, and asked the audience if he was moving too fast . . ." After the set had finished, Willner wrote, Waits "literally ran off the stage in that slumped posture that suggests one's career is over and then sat rocking backstage, his head in his lap".

Interviewed in Ithaca – the upstate New York town that was home to Cornell University – Waits was beyond exhausted. "The eclectic singer/musician is sitting in the stale-aired dressing room," wrote the *New York Times*' Robert Ward, "and he can feel the whole damned room pressing in on him. He's tired and his mouth is dry, in spite of the Heineken brought to him by the nice waitress in the black tights. He's feeling spaced and dizzy, and he's coughing like a 70-year-old wino stevedore down for the last stroke."

An encounter in New York's Penn Station on 8 April made a powerful impression on Waits. A street character named Rocky – en route to bumhood but not quite there yet – struck up a rapport with Waits and proceeded to bend his ear in one of the station's bars. For every two drinks they had, Rocky would order a third for his pal Charlie Dutton. After a series of increasingly tall tales – and with twelve whiskies lined up for Charlie on the bar – Waits learned the latter had been dead for thirty long years. "Charlie had been this guy's best friend, they were in Iwo Jima together," Waits recounted. "Thirty years and this guy was still mourning him, man." Waits began writing the lyrics for a song called "One for Charlie Dutton", referring to it on occasion as a working title for his next album. In due course the song became *Small Change*'s "Jitterbug Boy".

Waits carried on through Detroit to the deep south till he reached New Orleans on 1 May. As much as he loved the Crescent City – the visit inspired *Small Change*'s "I Wish I Was in New Orleans" – his appearance at the city's Ballinjax Electric Bistro club convinced him once and for all that he was at odds with his own generation. For just as he was about to take the stage at Ballinjax, the Rolling Thunder Revue – a motley crew of semi-legends that had toured the previous year with Bob Dylan – commandeered the stage and began playing as though Waits didn't exist. "Nobody even asked me," Waits fumed to *Rolling Stone*. "Before I knew it, fucking Roger McGuinn was up there playing guitar and singing and Joan Baez and Kinky [Friedman] were singing. By the time I got on stage the audience was stoked. They were all looking around the room and shit. I don't need this crap – it was my show." Ballinjax proved to be a pivotal moment in Waits' growing antagonism towards the mid-seventies aristocracy of American rock. But Waits also admitted in the interview that he was "drinking too much on top of everything else". Alcohol was taking the toll it had taken on his father, fuelling a grouchiness that few friends witnessed at close quarters.

That spring, Herb Cohen set up Waits' first ever appearances in Europe. On 19 May, he flew to London with Vicari, White, and "Fitz", and the next day met the first of several journalists from the music press. All too aware of the reputation American tourists had in London, Waits told *ZigZag* he was afraid that "when the moon is high and my hotel room is dark . . . I'm going to start sprouting cameras round my neck and my trench coat is going to turn into a flowered shirt and my black slacks are going to turn into Bermuda shorts". In the event his customary attire remained in place, described by his first British interviewer – *Time Out*'s Mick Houghton – as "a battered Burton's-style suit, loosely-tied striped tie, and grubby beat cap".

Meeting Houghton at the Island Queen, an Islington pub renowned for the quality of its jukebox, Waits talked away the evening while downing pints of bitter and playing a steady flow of classic sixties hits by the likes of Them and the Animals. He said the music business was "too insulating", filling artists with confidence by "telling you you're the biggest thing since the invention of the indoor toilet". His main concern was "not compromising my integrity", which was why he wanted to stay close to the streets. "Right now," he said, "what I'm doing is no longer what I do, it's what I *am*."

Like other writers who spoke to him that week, Houghton had been primed for Waits by reviews and rumours in the American press. "I think he was almost being presented as the next singer-songwriter on the block," Houghton says. "Obviously he was signed to Asylum, so inevitably people were trying to roll him into the same bag as all the other singer-songwriters." Less steeped in the Beat heritage than their US counterparts, British writers were unsure how seriously to take this LA anomaly, who for all they knew was just another by-product of the 1970s nostalgia boom that had given the world the Manhattan Transfer, the revamped Pointer Sisters, and – dare one say it – Bette Midler. Waits himself was scornful of said boom. "The whole thing is rampant, you know," Waits told the *New Musical Express*'s Fred Dellar on 20 May. "Those people who go in and enjoy Manhattan Transfer don't know who the hell Lambert, Hendricks and Ross are. I don't see anything I do as being nostalgic – I feel very contemporary." He'd already told the *LA Times* that he hated all references to "beatniks", which made people think of "Maynard G. Krebs with some bongos". He said he wasn't "having a vicarious fifties thrill".

"Among the English press there was a feeling that he was acting something out and lacked authenticity," says Mick Brown, who spoke to Waits for *Sounds*. "I guess it was because he wasn't dressed in denim jeans and cowboy shirt, as if that were a mark of authenticity. Of course, the whole of rock and roll is a matter of self-invention anyway, so it never worried me or preoccupied me. What excited me was that he had immersed himself in this character to the point where it *wasn't* an act and had become an identity." Fred Dellar was even more hip to Waits' references. "Swapping story for story", the two men talked of Kerouac and Lord Buckley, of word-jazzer Ken Nordine, blind New York street musician Moondog, vocalese wizard King Pleasure, and jazz DJ Symphony Sid. "He really knew about jazz and Kerouac," Dellar remembers. "When we talked about Ken Nordine, he suddenly reeled off four titles of Nordine albums." Dellar found the young Californian "both easy and difficult" to interview – easy because he loved to spin yarns, difficult because Dellar couldn't be sure how tall those tales were.

On 27 May, Waits and band flew to Amsterdam, performing somewhat shakily in the cafe of the Hotel L'Americain. After a happier night in Brussels, they returned to London to begin a week-long residency at legendary Soho joint Ronnie Scott's. In a city on the cusp of punk, however, Waits' brand of LA noir wasn't the hot ticket Herb Cohen had hoped for. At least one hero of the new vanguard was a Waits fan, however. The late Joe Strummer, who'd only recently swapped the pub rock of the 101'ers for the sten-gun agitprop of the Clash, claimed he not only saw Waits at Ronnie's but spoke to him before the show.

On his first night at Ronnie's, Waits managed to get himself thrown out of the club after a row with its booker, Pete King. "We got in a big fight," Waits recalled years later. "We didn't see eye to eye. I was young and naive. I was new to everything and far from home." A lubricated Waits had befriended "two old spade cats" who'd wandered into Ronnie's long after he'd finished his last set. When one produced a battered trumpet from "an old brown paper sack" and started playing Louis Armstrong's "Muskrat Ramble", King – himself a saxophonist of some renown – walked over and requested that they leave. "I said, 'Wait a minute, man,'" Waits recalled. "'Forty years of playing, and you with your gut and your ink pens and your cash register are going to tell these guys they can't play? These aren't a bunch of drunk hippies with backpacks trying to play Neil Young songs and get to Big Sur. This is a magic moment!' We got into a big scuffle and all got thrown out."[*]

On the next night, when Fred Dellar saw the show, Waits was

* According to Chip White there was another scuffle at Ronnie's that week. During one of the sets, Waits and band became aware of a "commotion" at the bar. Turned out Peter O'Toole was in his cups and was being escorted off the premises.

battling with hecklers. "Your opinions are like assholes, buddy," Waits fired back in well-worn style. "Everybody's got one." When the unruliness continued, Waits flicked a lit cigarette in the direction of the offending voices. "Everybody holds their breath waiting for a fight to start," wrote Dellar. Fortunately there were no fisticuffs. Part of the problem Dellar identified was one of translation. Back in 1976, for all the typical rock fan's exposure to Americana through music and movies, Waits' language and references were still semi-obscure. And his delivery at times seemed deliberately opaque.

Melody Maker's Karl Dallas experienced Waits' testier side. "I just don't enjoy talking about it at length," Tom replied to a question about poetry. When Dallas used the word "manipulation", Waits was surly. "That's one of those ten-dollar words you get for like three-ninety-nine on sale," he said. "I try to avoid the three-syllable words because I dropped out of high school." (Rich coming from a guy who habitually peppered his lyrics – especially on *Nighthawks* – with words such as "precarious" and "provocative".) I asked Dallas if Waits had been as rude as he came across in the interview. "He was quite a daunting person," Dallas says. "You didn't feel like you wanted to waste his time." Shortly after finishing the interview at Ronnie Scott's, Dallas chanced upon Waits leaning against a wall at the corner of Dean and Old Compton Streets. "He stood there most of the day, just hanging out and observing. He seemed to be in his own scene. There was something very powerful and almost off-putting about him."

Mick Brown deemed Waits "probably the most delightful, original, outrageous and courageous manipulator of musical mesmerization [*sic*] you're likely to come across in a long time" and urged his readers to dismiss talk of Waits being "a 'cult performer' or, worse, the 'male version of Patti Smith'". Coincidentally, when Waits and Brown strolled down Notting Hill's famed Portobello Road, they passed Smith on the street. I saw Patti play

Comparing street fashions on the Portobello Road, London, May 1976.
(*Michael Putland/Retna*)

her thrilling first UK shows that week at the Roundhouse, so it's interesting to compare the two singers at this juncture in their careers. While Waits was perceived as a goatee-sporting LA throwback – the past – Smith was seen as the tomboy princess of New York punk, a harbinger of rock's future. Waits felt mildly threatened by her.*

To Brown, Waits was defensive about his better-off-without-a-wife love life ("I'm not going to change my environment and I don't plan on having it changed by anyone else"); unpleasantly hostile towards the Hollywood glitter-rock scene ("If I want to go to the fucking Rainbow Bar and Grill on Sunset Strip and beat up a transvestite, then I will"); and misanthropic about things in

---

* "What do you think of Patti Smith?" Waits asked *Downbeat* a week after returning to America. "Her band buries her, on record and on stage too. She's a merchandisable commodity and she's being marketed as a poet and it just seems that, under those circumstances, she should be a lot more concerned about her storytelling and the way she comes across lyrically."

general ("I just don't like the word 'fun' – it's like Volkswagen, or bell-bottoms, or patchouli-oil or bean-sprouts . . . it rubs me up the wrong way"). "Part of the persona seemed to be as cantankerous and difficult and obstructive as possible," Brown says of the interview. "I remember him being quite hostile towards me. It was about as uncomfortable as interviewing William Burroughs – the sense of him being on edge and you being made to feel a fool."

Waits' anger spilled out into his everyday life in London. When he requested a certain sandwich in a takeaway cafe, he was told they couldn't oblige. His response was to leap over the counter and start making the sandwich himself. "I grabbed the meat and grabbed the bread and the guy wanted to call a constable on me," he recalled. He also became impatient with the overly diligent maids at the President, the Holborn hotel where he and the band had put up. One morning, Chip White heard a scream and opened his door to see a girl tearing past him. When he looked back along the corridor, he saw Waits standing in his doorway stark naked. "He got pissed off at having to answer the door so often," says White. "He said the maids were obsessive."

Incidents like these would colour Waits' grumpy attitude towards touring for years to come. Yet it was also in London that he found a creative second wind and began writing new songs as he sat in his hotel room. Exactly which of the tracks on *Small Change* originated in London is a moot point.* "The Piano Has Been Drinking (Not Me)", a dementedly disingenuous apologia

---

* In his *NME* interview, Fred Dellar mentioned such song titles as "Bad Liver and a Broken Heart", "A Briefcase and the Blues", "Frank Is Here", and "Whitey Ford". The first of those, of course, made the cut on *Small Change*, while "A Briefcase and the Blues" was conceivably the working title for either "Tom Traubert's Blues" or "Invitation to the Blues". Baseball player Ford was namechecked in "A Sight for Sore Eyes", while "Frank Is Here" intrigues if for no other reason than that it sits on the Tom Waits timeline midway between "Frank's Song" and "Frank's Wild Years".

for alcoholism, came out of the Ronnie Scott's debacle and actually boasted the sub-subtitle "An Evening with Pete King". But tracks such as "Pasties and a G-String", "Jitterbug Boy", and "Small Change" itself began life earlier than June 1976.

Waits had been talking about "Pasties" since the beginning of the year, while "Small Change (Got Rained On with His Own .38)" was essentially the story of the shooting Waits had witnessed near the Chelsea Hotel. According to Bones Howe, "Tom Traubert's Blues" had started life on Fifth and Main (aka "the Nickel"), the skid-row area of downtown LA where the Doors had shot the cover of their 1970 album *Morrison Hotel*. "Tom told me one day that he really needed to spend some time there," Howe remembers of the song's genesis. "He said, 'Every one of those guys has a story.' And later he called me up and said, 'I took the bus down there, found a liquor store, bought a pint of rye in a brown paper bag, squatted down in the street and talked to everybody that came by. And then I went home, threw up, and wrote "Tom Traubert's Blues".'"*

Yet it was a short trip to Denmark that really brought "Tom Traubert's Blues" to life, leading Waits to append to it the subtitle "Four Sheets to the Wind in Copenhagen". While taping the TV show *Sange Efter Lukketid*, he was introduced to a pretty twenty-year-old singer named Mathilde Bondo, who offered to show Waits the sleazier side of Copenhagen. "I guess we were both very wild at that time, so I thought I would show him some of the shabby places in the city," Bondo remembers. "Tom thought that was a very funny idea, so we sort of dragged each other through Copenhagen visiting old bars and seeing some of my friends." Exactly how Bondo became fused with the "Waltzing Matilda" of

* I am not the only person to have double-checked this story with Bones, suggesting to him that the song's origins were more pertinent to *Heartattack and Vine*'s "On the Nickel". He remains adamant that "Traubert" was born after a visit to LA's skid row.

Australian legend is unclear, though she recalls playing the fiddle for Waits in one bar and says she knew several waltzes. Waits knew "Waltzing Matilda" itself from his father's copy of Harry Belafonte's 1963 album *Streets I Have Walked*.*

Departing London with most of the *Small Change* songs in his luggage, Waits flew to New York to work on them. To David McGee he looked bruised and battered; he said he'd "nearly died" in Europe. McGee recalls Waits writing some of "Tom Traubert's Blues" in his Hell's Kitchen apartment on West 56th Street. "He was noodling on the grand piano that my wife played," he says. "I remember him coming up with the phrase 'wasted and wounded' on one of those occasions – only that and nothing more, but obviously it came back to me when I heard *Small Change*."

From New York, Waits flew home to California and his Silver Lake apartment. Within a couple of weeks he'd made the decision to follow in Chuck E. Weiss' tracks and move into the Tropicana. "They were in two bungalows next to each other, at the rear of the motel," recalls Rick Dubov, another Troubadour employee. "It was like they became twins, totally inseparable." It was the beginning of a long residency that's become almost infamous in Waits' story, a very public place of privacy where he proceeded to live out his self-appointed role as the bard of the streets. At $9 a night it also provided bargain accommodation

---

* In its inspired use of the unofficial Australian national anthem, "Traubert" was another instance of Waits incorporating a popular folk melody into his music as a kind of quotation – see also "Here Comes the Bride" ("Better Off without a Wife"), "As Time Goes By" ("Bad Liver and a Broken Heart"), "Auld Lang Syne" ("A Sight for Sore Eyes"), "Silent Night" ("Christmas Card from a Hooker in Minneapolis"), and others. "I think it was 1903," Waits said of "Matilda". "Originally I believe it was a poem, and . . . it was put to music and became the unofficial national anthem of Australia, I believe. A Matilda is a backpack. So 'Waltzing Matilda' just means, really just to take off, you know? Like blow town, you know? And, you know, that's what the song means, maybe."

At home at the Tropicana, late 1977. (*Mitchell Rose*)

that enabled him to remain in a state of suspended adolescence.

Moving into the Tropicana was a conscious decision not to live in a Colorado cabin – or even a shack in nearby Laurel Canyon – and it would take Waits to some dark places. "Tom was a street guy, a hustler," says Henry Diltz, who visited the new digs with Jerry Yester. "Well, not a hustler but a *scuffler*. A guy closer to the street. Definitely not a folk-rock commercial songwriter. His career paralleled the whole canyon thing but was the exact antithesis of all that."

Waits' two-room apartment was emblematic of his state of mind. Ankle-deep in albums and ashtrays, books and beer cans – not to mention the porn mags scattered liberally across all surfaces – it was a space of creative chaos. "It was like a bungalow off in the back," says Paul Body, who was often found chez Waits. "You'd enter from the back, and it was like a little house. You couldn't see anything because it was filled up with junk that you could barely manoeuvre through." By the end of 1976, Waits had even managed to squeeze a Steinway upright into the apartment by sawing off a draining board and demolishing a broom closet. "I don't spend evenings around the piano with friends and hot toddies singing old Gershwin songs," he would joke the following spring. "Nobody comes over here much. Look around and figure it out."

When Waits began a sporadic affair with Bette Midler – whom he often saw when he was in New York – he was too embarrassed by the state of the Tropicana bungalow to invite her in. "Tom lives . . . sort of knee-deep in grunge," Midler said. "So he was reluctant for me to see his apartment. I grew up in lots of clutter myself and delicate I ain't, so I kept after him till he finally invited me over." The state of Waits' Tropicana apartment soon became a minor Los Angeles legend. "Though some myths have been perpetrated concerning Waits," his childhood friend Charley De Lisle wrote, "his apartment deserves everything it gets." Film-maker John Lamb recalled objects stacked up so high that one had to follow a path through the bungalow. Another friend, Charles Schwab, claimed he'd once opened Waits' fridge in search of a beer to find only "a claw hammer, a small jar of arti-choke hearts, an old parking ticket, and a can of roof cement . . ."

The Tropicana became a kind of stage, a backdrop to Waits' twenty-four-hours-a-day performance. It was a stage that also spilled out into Duke's and on to Santa Monica Boulevard. "I remember seeing him outside Duke's one morning about eleven o'clock," says Tom Nolan. "He had this long black car parked next to the curb, and he's got the hood up and his sleeves rolled up and he's, like, taking the carburetor apart. It was great but it twisted your mind that somebody like that could be fixing his car right there. To do it in this theatrically natural way. He was in his own movie and you wanted to buy a ticket!"

Without Waits so much as entering the club, the Troubadour afforded him a similar stage. "I remember him sitting on the sidewalk like a wino," says Michael Hacker. "He was full-on in his persona and I thought, 'Here's this minor rock figure and he's literally *sitting on the curb*, just *hanging out*.' And I thought, 'That's different.'" In hindsight, Waits' "hanging out" in West Hollywood could be seen as a kind of demystification, a refusal to put distance between himself and his audience. Even when he performed at the Troub, Waits declined to act the celebrity. "I'd go to Tom's dressing room and he'd sit there with his head down and not talk with anybody," says Joe Smith, who'd succeeded David Geffen at the helm of Elektra-Asylum Records. "People were flowing through and having drinks, and Tom was absolutely silent. He never even looked up. He was never obnoxious, but he was very shy. He didn't come to the office or hang out, and I don't know who his friends were."

Waits' cars were as notorious as the bungalow itself, their back seats littered with discarded books, newspapers, cans, and Styrofoam cups. When Jerry Yester helped Waits find a beautiful 1952 Buick, within two weeks it had been reduced to a trashmobile. "Every wrapper was still in the car, and he kind of reveled in that," Yester says. "He said, 'A car is like a suit. It's gotta fit real well.'"

Yet for all the chaos and the vampire hours he kept with Weiss and his Troubadour cronies, Waits retained a strong work ethic. "He was driven," says Paul Body. "And the reason he got in the position he got into was that he was a little bit more driven than everyone else. He wasn't messing around getting high." Robert Marchese agrees: "The image didn't mask the workaholic. Tom wrote constantly. He practiced a lot. He was on the scene and all that but he knew when it was time to work. For lack of a better word, Tom wanted to be a star. Chuckie was the farthest thing from that. He had no organizational skills and no direction."

Marchese had misgivings, however, about the way Waits slummed it at the Tropicana. Having grown up dirt-poor in Pittsburgh, he took umbrage at Tom's pastiche of poverty.

"Chuckie said to Waits once, 'I don't think Marchese likes comin' over here,'" Marchese says. "Waits asked why not, and Chuckie said, 'Well, he thinks what you're doing is kind of how you think poor people are supposed to be, and he's very offended by that because he was very poor and one of the things his mother constantly said was, 'They may say we're poor but they're never gonna say we're dirty.'" Waits defended himself by claiming it was essential to his art that he lived the part of the down-and-out. "You almost have to create situations in order to write about them," he explained to the *LA Times*, "so I live in a constant state of self-imposed poverty." He told *Rambler* that there were "different criteria for success – like the American credit card – but for me life in the streets is much more fascinating".

"Bones has a story about meeting up with Waits in New York," says LA jazz historian Kirk Silsbee. "From where Tom was staying it was about a five-minute cab ride. Well, the cab pulls up and as Waits is paying the fare he's saying to the driver, 'Man, I hope your wife's operation turns out all right, and maybe your kid will come around and straighten out.' In that short period of time, Waits had gotten into that cab driver's life." Howe says that "that's how Tom's mind worked . . . he snagged every piece of information, and it kind of rattled around in his brain till it became a title or a piece of verse or whatever."

Installed at the Tropicana, Waits settled into the rituals that would define his working relationship with Howe. "He would call me and say, 'I'm going into the studio to do some demos,'" Howe says. "And he'd go in with his lyrics strewn all over the floor and the songs would come together." Working closely with Biff Dawes, who'd been Howe's second engineer at Heider's, Waits would emerge with a collection of what Howe called "fragments and bits and pieces". He would then send Howe the tapes and book the first of a series of "pre-production meetings" at either Duke's or Ben Frank's. "We'd sit for hours in one of those dumpy restaurants," Howe says. "We'd talk about what the album was going to be, just in general. Most of our relationship was talk." By this point, Howe feels, "we had played in the sandbox enough that I felt like I really got to know him . . . and I really liked him as a human being."

Waits told Bones about the spoken-word pieces he'd begun in London. He said he wanted to do something akin to "Diamonds on My Windshield" but wanted it more fleshed-out. "Tom said, 'I've got some lyrics but they don't feel like a song to me,'" Howe recalls. "He said, 'I don't wanna sing 'em, I wanna *recite* 'em.' So I asked him to read them to me and then I said, 'It would be great if we could *score* that with an orchestra.' We talked about movies and underscoring and sort of moved away from the idea of *songs*."

Upping the ante, Howe suggested they do what they'd always promised themselves, which was record the album live to two-track. Talk of recording in the 1950s led to Howe reminiscing about the great bop drummer Shelly Manne, who'd been responsible for his moving to California in the first place. A huge Manne fan, Waits was suitably awed. "Tom was incredibly curious about jazz musicians," Howe says. "He was like, '*You know Shelly Manne?!*'" When Howe suggested they ask Manne to play on the album, Waits flipped out.

Waits also told Howe that he wanted to play all the piano on the record. Thus Mike Melvoin, who'd done so much to help Waits on both *The Heart of Saturday Night* and *Nighthawks at the Diner*, was dropped as both keyboard player and arranger. "There was no actual end," says Melvoin, who was stung by the decision. "He just didn't call me for the record. Whatever I could have handled differently, I wished that I had. But you cannot be on board forever for anything, no matter how well you do it." Melvoin believes the main issue was that Waits felt in some way cramped as an instrumentalist. "Tom liked the way he played for himself," he says. "It was easier for him, and more satisfying too, not to have some jazz pianist with a character of his own on board."

Perhaps it was an earlier guilt that made Waits hire Jerry Yester to write the string arrangements for *Small Change*. It was the first time the two men had worked together since *Closing Time*, and Yester was impressed by how far Waits had come as an artist. "He didn't change that much personally," he says, "but by *Small Change* he'd learned so much more and been influenced by the world a lot more."

With Pete Christlieb unavailable – he was replaced by Lew Tabackin – the only survivor from the *Nighthawks* group was Jim Hughart. Encouraged by the latter, Shelly Manne came on board for the sessions, which started in Studio 4 at Heider's on 15 July. Manne took to Waits instantly. After the very first take he said to the other musicians, "Who *is* this guy? He's the oldest young guy – or the youngest old guy – I ever met!" Manne's presence eased the usual studio tensions for Waits. "Shelly was so outgoing and Tom was the complete opposite of that, but there was a symbiosis there," says Hughart. "Shelly was not only the most efficient drummer-percussionist you could hire, he was one of the best people you could ever imagine being around. He had all kinds of wonderful suggestions, some of them accepted, some of them not."*

The *Small Change* sessions took up five days over the course of two weeks. "Step Right Up" was recorded on 15 July, as were the

---

* Note the acknowledgement on the sleeve of *Small Change*: "Special thanks to Shelly Manne for his drumistikly pasteurized conktribution and the 8x10 glossy and the neck tie." Says Kirk Silsbee, "With all these guys – Melvoin, Hughart, Vicari, Manne – Tom didn't just do a Van Morrison and sit in the control booth while they played. He was hanging with them and talking to them and listening to them." Silsbee's reference is to Morrison's classic *Astral Weeks* album, on which such jazz giants as drummer Connie Kay and bassist Richard Davis played.

unused "Stray Dog" and "What Else Is New?" and a full-band version of "Jitterbug Boy". Four days later, Waits cut "Pasties and a G-String", "The Piano Has Been Drinking", and "I Can't Wait to Get off Work". On 20 July, he recorded "Tom Traubert's Blues" (in nine takes) and "I Wish I Was in New Orleans"; the following day it was the turn of "Invitation to the Blues". The title track and "The One that Got Away" were recorded on 29 July, as were a full-band "Bad Liver and a Broken Heart" and the unused "A Sight for Sore Eyes". On the final date, 30 July, Waits redid "Bad Liver" and "Jitterbug Boy" as solo performances. "When we went in to assemble the album that day, Tom decided he wanted to do them over by himself just with the piano," says Bones Howe. "I went out in the studio and hung a couple of mics and he re-recorded them with just voice and piano."

Howe points out that Waits' albums were "nickel-and-dime productions" that rarely came in over $15,000. "We weren't deliberately economizing," he adds. "We were making the records we wanted to make. Plus we were making them as I promised Tom I would, the same way I'd made jazz records – getting the best performances and not fooling with them."

By the last date, Waits had taken a giant step forward with his art. Twelve years later he told Francis Thumm he hadn't felt "completely confident in the craft" until he made *Small Change*. "I felt I was learning and getting the confidence to keep doing it," he said. "'Tom Traubert's Blues', 'Small Change', and 'I Wish I Was in New Orleans' gave me some confidence." His tune hadn't changed when I interviewed him in 1999. "I'd say there's probably more songs off *Small Change* that I continued to play on the road, and that endured," he said. "Some songs you may write and record but you may never sing them again. Others you sing every night and try and figure out what they mean. 'Tom Traubert's Blues' was certainly one of the songs I continued to sing and in fact close my show with."

Everything changed with "Tom Traubert's Blues". Nothing on the earlier albums prepares us for the depths, the wounded ravages, of the new voice on the song. Just how *did* Waits stumble on what was an exaggeration of an already exaggerated vocal style? "On one of the tours his voice changed," Paul Body contends. "I think when he went to Europe something happened. When he came back it was different. He caught a cold or something, and after that the voice was forever gravelly. The sweet voice that's on *Closing Time* and *Heart of Saturday Night* was gone."

"Traubert" was all about the contrast between the groaning pain of the voice and the aching beauty of the music. The template for all Waits' great late-seventies ballads from "Kentucky Avenue" to "Ruby's Arms", "Traubert" took his skid-row experience, transposed it to a place where "no one speaks English and everything's broken", and turned the song into something far more rich and complex than a sketch about meths-swilling winos. (As with the old man in "Martha", Waits gave his own name to the song's protagonist; meanwhile, the guy he wants to borrow a couple of bucks from is called Frank.) The great weight of an individual man's tragedy fills "Traubert". The way Waits shapes his words, bearing down on them, pressing them out, gives the song endless solemnity and pathos. This is where Waits becomes the patron saint of the Pogues and all alcoholic romantics the world over: without "Traubert" no "Fairytale of New York".

There couldn't be a more defined mood switch than that from "Traubert" to "Step Right Up". *Small Change*'s second track was Waits in the role of a conman flogging a miracle product that could do almost anything required of it – an American archetype that went all the way back to snake-oil salesmen and drew on everything from fairground carnies to Waits' memories of Wolfman Jack selling baby chicks over the airwaves. He had the delivery down pat, the language so rhythmically musical it sounded like Lord Buckley reborn as a rapper. "All that jargon we hear in the music business is just like what you hear in the restaurant or casket business," Waits said of the track's genesis. "So instead of spouting my views in *Scientific American* on the vulnerability of the American public to our product-oriented society, I wrote 'Step Right Up'." The track was the first of four spoken-word pieces to appear on *Small Change*.

"Jitterbug Boy", born in New York the previous April, was Waits playing another American archetype: the buttonholing boozer with a bagful of implausible stories. Waits' "Boy" – the jitterbug had been named after swing dancers whose movements resembled alcoholic jitters – had fought with Rocky Marciano, drunk with Louis Armstrong, and taught Mickey Mantle everything he knew. With its lyric finished, Waits hung the song on a wistful piano lick extruded from Gershwin's "I Got Plenty o' Nuthin'", rounded it off with some prime *zoobah-zee* Satchmo scatting, and added the wonderfully unwieldy subtitle "Sharing a Curbstone with Chuck E. Weiss, Robert Marchese, Paul Body and the Mug* and Artie." The song thus became an inebriated tribute to Tom's Troubadour pals and their frequent yarn-spinning confabulations outside the club – Weiss above all.

"Chuckie was the king of the one-up," laughs Body. "'Oh, you know this guy? Well, I know *this* guy!' I mean, Chuckie never even had a *job*. The only job he ever had was working at the Troubadour." Live, "Jitterbug Boy" became a glorious vehicle not only for comedic introductions but for medleyized incorporations of such standards as "When I Fall in Love", "Take Me Out to the Ball Game", "Can't Help Falling in Love", "Enjoy Yourself (It's

---

* "The Mug came from Marchese, I think," Louie Lista says of his nickname. "Among Bogart's earlier movies there's one [1932's *Three on a Match*] where he plays an underworld character known as 'The Mug.' That scene at the Troubadour is gone with the wind, by the way. Do not look for it now. There was a lot of closeness and that song reveals that."

Sharing a curbstone outside the Troub with Paul Body (second left, in Waits' fedora), Robert Marchese (in Waits' Cadillac), and Chuck E. Weiss, circa 1976. (*Courtesy of Robert Marchese*)

Later than You Think)", Cole Porter's "Friendship", and Irving Berlin's "The Girl that I Marry" and "I Got the Sun in the Morning".

"I Wish I Was in New Orleans (in the Ninth Ward)" hankered nostalgically for the "old haunts" of a city Waits barely knew. The album's second namecheck for Weiss acknowledged that ol' Bighead had spent far more time in the Big Easy than Waits had. There was a hint of Randy Newman's "Louisiana 1927" in the piano chords and Jerry Yester's elegiac strings; Waits may have known that Newman had spent chunks of his childhood in and around the city. Naturally there was also a nod to Dr John, the pre-eminent rock figure to come out of New Orleans in the 1970s and already a huge influence – instrumentally *and* vocally – on Waits.

A souvenir from his London visit, "The Piano Has Been Drinking (Not Me)" was Waits at the ivories, plinking away unsteadily and grunting out a surreal lyric about his unhappy experience at Ronnie Scott's. The lighting man was blind in one eye, the piano tuner had a hearing aid, and "the owner" was "a mental midget with the IQ of a fence post". The song was the slightest thing on *Small Change* but brought the original first side to a neat conclusion.

"Invitation to the Blues" was a self-consciously Tin Pan Alley "blues" in the vein of, say, "Blues in the Night". It was also Hollywood noir set to music, with a femme fatale of a divorced waitress who looked like Rita Hayworth and a sense of dread in the melody that Nic Roeg clearly intuited when he used the track in the opening sequence of his 1979 film *Bad Timing*.

Small Change's second spoken-word track, "Pasties and a G-String (at the Two O'Clock Club)" was a homage to the Great American Strip Joint and a soundtrack to the album's cover photo, which depicted a seedy-looking Waits in a bored stripper's dressing room, its table covered with makeup, pill bottles, and dildos. The weakest piece on the record, it sounded as though it had been designed principally to showcase Shelly Manne, whose martial fills supplied punctuation and commentary for the lascivious sleaze of Waits' scatted "slanguage".

"Bad Liver and a Broken Heart" – its subtitle "In Lowell" being a clear reference to the booze-ravaged Jack Kerouac – faced the grim realities of alcoholism in a way that was new for Waits. Opening with the famous refrain from *Casablanca*'s "As Time Goes By", the song was really a kind of check on himself. "I was really starting to believe that there was something amusing and wonderfully American about a drunk," Waits admitted after recording the song. "I ended up telling myself to cut that shit out. On top of everything else, talking about boozing substantiates the rumors that people hear about you, and people hear that I'm a drunk."

"The One that Got Away", a third helping of bop poetry, was a slice of crime-scene noir complete with allusions to such LA landmarks as Ben Frank's and burlesque hotspot the Ivar Theater. Built on a walking Jim Hughart bass line, with squawks and breathy interjections from Lew Tabackin, the track's playful menace paraded various lowlifes before us, all of them ruing lost opportunities that might have put them on Easy Street.*

"The One" set us up for the album's spoken-word *pièce de résistance*, "Small Change (Got Rained On with His Own .38)", arguably *the* jewel in Waits' Beat-verse crown. Backed by a lonesome Tabackin sax line that sounded like a bugle lament, Waits turned a seventies street shooting in New York into a forties scene from a Weegee photograph. He hadn't forgotten his shock at the sight of the kid bleeding to death on 23rd Street, nor his disbelief at how blasé the NYPD on the scene were. In his way he wanted to pay tribute to an anonymous black life destined to become just another statistic. Detail was everything in "Small Change": the blood by the jukebox on "an old linoleum floor"; the kid's trousers that were "cold" and "twisted"; the racing form in his pocket with "Blue Boots" circled in the third race; the whores' mouths that "cut like razorblades".

Both "Small Change" and "The One that Got Away" betrayed the clear influence of hardboiled crime fiction while also drawing on Damon Runyon and Nelson Algren. This was Waits paying homage to the gritty vernacular of Dashiell Hammett and John D. MacDonald, invoking the urban underbelly of the 1940s and 50s as he addressed the sleaze and violence of the 1970s.

Winding up the album on a happier note was "I Can't Wait to

* Three years before the launch of MTV, "The One that Got Away" became the subject of an animation directed by John Lamb, the head animator being none other than *The Simpsons'* David Silberman. It has some claim to being the first true music video.

Get Off Work (and See My Baby on Montgomery Avenue)",* a song that took us back to Waits' youth at Napoleone's. Conjuring the years Waits slaved in the restaurant with only the prospect of heading home to his girl to keep his spirits up, "I Can't Wait . . ." was "Ol' '55" in reverse, Waits hurrying to "get off before the dawn's early light".

Released in October, *Small Change* was not only a hit with the critics but actually crept into *Billboard*'s Top 100 albums chart – a first for Waits. Though the ever-sceptical *Rolling Stone* contended that his "purview remains stringently narrow", Waits found himself profiled in such prestigious publications as *Time*, *Newsweek*, *Vogue*, and *The New Yorker*. (Alma finally believed her son was legit when she saw his picture in *Time*.) Not that the success made much difference to the folks at Elektra-Asylum. "I feel at times I'm residually in jeopardy with my record company," Waits sighed in December. "I don't pull in a lot of dividends. Most of the money I make is from personal appearances and I spend most of that on the band and the bus. I made it to 169 on the record charts and figured if we could only get to 200 it would be great. But I found out it goes the other way."

The first leg of the *Small Change* tour lasted three months. Backed again by the Nocturnal Emissions, who had feelings about not being used on the album, Waits kicked off on the East Coast in early October, swung through the south, and then headed back east and into the Midwest in November. Among the headliners he supported was Ry Cooder, then touring with the Tejano accordionist Flaco Jiménez. "We had a bus together," Cooder recalls. "It was interesting to pick up on this character. In those days he was very committed. He stayed only in flophouse hotels. He insisted on putting his band up in nice hotels while *he* stayed in *bad* hotels. I asked him why he did that and he said, 'Well, then

* There's no Montgomery Avenue in San Diego, but there is one about twenty miles up the coast just south of Encinitas.

Four eggs for a buck: Chicago, November 1976. (*Herb Nolan*)

nobody can complain.' I thought, 'Wow, that's really smart.'"

By the end of the month Waits was back in California, playing a homecoming show in San Diego on the 30th. "It didn't start till two in the morning," recalls Randy Hoffman of the gig at San Diego State's Back Door, where Waits had once jammed with Jack Tempchin. "And man, I'm telling you, he delivered one of the most amazing live performances I have ever seen." Hoffman, who'd seen Waits play in his Heritage days, was stunned by the reinvention he witnessed. "I remember thinking, 'God, this guy made a serious left-turn!' He'd developed into a whole thing that I could never have imagined, and I was just knocked out."

By the time Waits pulled into Cleveland in early December he was close to exhausted. "He came in on a promotional tour but I felt like he didn't want to do very much," Fred Toedtman remembers. "He was kind of a loner. He'd talk if he was spoken to but he wouldn't initiate any conversation." That was putting it mildly. Waits was in a foul mood in Cleveland, bellyaching about the room Toedtman had booked for him at the Keg & Quarter Hotel and angry at learning that his show at the Agora Ballroom would be taped.

When Jim Gerard arrived to interview Waits for Northeastern Ohio's *Scene*, the singer was downright rude. "Boy, you're long-winded," Tom snapped when Gerard waffled. Later, shivering with cold, he said he'd "been gone so long and I don't get any time to myself . . . I just want to go home." Gerard formed "the impression that Tom Waits would rather be left alone", adding that "when he has to deal with a lot of people he hunches up and withdraws".

Tickled by *Small Change*'s "Pasties and a G-String", Toedtman decided it might cheer Waits up if a stripper came out on stage during the performance of that song. A girl named Bunny O'Hara was swiftly located. "She came down and I set it up with the band that she was going to come on stage when they started 'Pasties'," says Toedtman. "The drummer says, 'I'll start a tango beat, so send her out on stage at that point.' So she came on stage fully clothed and I had put pasties on her, one of them saying 'Tom' and the other 'Waits.' She walked out to him and just dropped her whole outfit. And he started to tango around the stage with her." When Bunny walked off the stage, Waits didn't miss a beat. "Gee, that was great," he barked. "I haven't seen my mother in years." From hereon in, road manager John Forscha

Onstage with stripper, Theatre del Mar, Santa Cruz, December 1977. (*Greg Arrufat*)

ensured that a stripper came on stage for "Pasties" during almost every show Waits played.

Three nights after Cleveland, Waits returned to New York for the first of three shows at the Bottom Line. He was in phenomenal form as he growled his way through extended versions of songs from every album bar *Closing Time*: a ten-minute "Small Change"; a thirteen-minute "Heart of Saturday Night" that commenced with a truncated take on Sam Cooke's "Cupid"; "Jitterbug Boy" reframed as a tribute to Charlie Dutton and "San Diego Serenade" as "Escondido Serenade". Supporting him at the club was comedienne Elayne Boosler, with whom he was about to become briefly involved. "Tom had this thing for Elayne, who I also saw for a little bit," says Robert Marchese. "It was weird because a Jewish girl comedian was not my idea of the ideal woman, but I liked her a lot. Waits was messing around with her. It didn't last very long."

When David McGee interviewed Waits for *Rolling Stone* in an "ill-lit, vomit-green" room at the Chelsea, he found the singer surrounded by copies of *Penthouse*, *Screw*, and *PleaZure* strewn among the Viceroy cigarette butts. Looking back on what McGee called "his hellish year", Waits pondered his career and his goals. McGee was struck by the seriousness of his tone. "I'm not money-oriented except to the point that I have bills to pay and I have to support a trio," Waits told him. "I want to be respected by my peers and I want my old man to think that what I'm doing is good."

Asked if the glowing reviews for *Small Change* had made him more "present-minded", Waits demurred. "No, not really," he said. "I've got to cinch something before we get out of the seventies. I've got a lot invested in this whole thing – just in confidence, in my development as a writer and all that. I don't want to be a has-been before I've even arrived. I don't want to think about it, man."

By Christmas, Waits was back home at the Tropicana.

Chapter 6

Real Romantic Dreamers Stuck in the Wrong Time Zone

> *"Shall we weigh along these streets,*
> *Young lions on the lam?"*
>
> (Rickie Lee Jones, "We Belong Together", 1980)

When Dave Bates first came to Los Angeles in December 1978 to bone up on the city's music scene, he asked Harvey Kubernik where he should stay. Naturally the *Melody Maker* man recommended the Tropicana Motor Hotel. Where else would an aspiring English A&R scout – Bates later signed Def Leppard, Tears for Fears, and many more – wish to hole up in LA?

"$22 a night gets you a room on the perimeter of the Tropicana's swimming pool," fellow Brit Mark Williams wrote that very month. "If you check in a little early, say at three in the afternoon, you might see the more determined of LA's groupies slinking and blinking out into the daylight, looking considerably less made-up than they were the previous evening at the Roxy."

What Bates remembers best about the Tropicana was the double daily encounter with Tom Waits. "Every day I'd be leaving in the morning and Tom would be coming in," he laughs. "And then at night when I came back he'd just have woken up and he'd be heading out to the Troubadour." Elvis Costello, later a friend of Waits', recalled staying at the motel in the same period and being a "nodding acquaintance, literally, as [Tom] would be passing by with his groceries".

Tickling the ivories at the Tropicana, late 1977. (*Mitchell Rose*)

The first time I met Waits I took a risk and asked him – as though it were some revelatory insight that had never occurred to him – if his nightfly existence at the Tropicana motel had ever been . . . well, a pose. "Oh, gosh," he said, because he usually prefaced any answer with "Oh, gosh," or "Uh, gee." "When I moved into that place it was, like, nine dollars a night. But it became a . . . a stage, because I became associated with it and people came looking for me and calling me in the middle of the night. I think I really wanted to kind of get lost in it all . . . so I did." For Waits, "getting lost" in the role he'd written for himself was partly about avoiding the bigger questions of identity – of who he was and what he really wanted from life. The alternating rituals of touring and then of hanging out at the Tropicana and the Troubadour slowly blurred the distinction between Tom Waits and "Tom Waits".

To some local onlookers, though, the Waits act was as valid as any comparable mask. Tom Nolan figured that if you were going to strike a pose on the LA scene – one populated by cocaine cowboys in jeans and aviator shades – the Waits stance was more appealing than the alternatives. "Of course there was a persona that he affected," Nolan says. "And of course you would tussle with that and think, 'Well, obviously he's *not* a 1950s jazzbo beat-nik.' But the quality was there. He made *me* feel personally more creative."

"If I was going to decide to be a cowboy, I'd get *real damn cowboy*," adds Nolan's fellow writer Todd Everett. "Personally I never thought of Waits as someone who went home and took off his Tom Waits suit and put on an Aloha shirt and flip-flops in order to go down to the beach." Waits didn't see himself like that either. "I don't normally wear Bermuda shorts and white socks and wingtips and read Kahlil Gibran," he quipped. "I'm the closest thing to myself that I know." He had also begun to resent the way the media pigeonholed him as a kind of latterday Maynard G. Krebs. "It's usually journalists . . . who create a period of music and eventually destroy it as well," he remarked sourly. When people asked him about Kerouac, they seemed to insinuate that he was "trying to recreate the beat scene or some bullshit", thus revealing nothing but "their own stupidity . . . [and] limited experience".

Waits' "act" was really a self-protective device, a screen to deflect attention. "The fact is that everybody who starts doing this to a certain extent develops some kind of a persona or image in order to survive," he argued in hindsight. "It's much safer to approach this with some kind of persona, because if it's not a ventriloquist act, if it's just you, then it's really scary." The prob-lem was, Waits' twilight life at the Tropicana was becoming pretty scary anyway. Much as he made light of the place, even he knew it was becoming a little heavy. "I saw Tom on one or two occasions where I thought, 'This is getting a little too serious,'" recalls Jerry Yester. "I didn't say it and I'm not sure anybody did, but I felt like saying, 'Tom, you better get your shit together.' Maybe Herbie said it, I don't know."

Waits later reflected that his life in this period was like going to a fancy-dress party and waking up the next morning in the same outfit. "I really became a character in my own story," he said. "I'd go out at night, get drunk, fall asleep underneath a car. Come home with leaves in my hair, grease on the side of my face, stumble into the kitchen, bang my head on the piano and somehow chronicle my own demise and the parade of horribles that lived next door."

Like the Tropicana, the Troubadour was unravelling by 1977. Struggling to come to terms with the changing musical climate – the punk winds blowing in from New York and London – the former folk sanctuary was now rife with drugs. "The bartenders there were all fucked up on pills and coke," says Robert Marchese. "It became an ugly scene, and Doug Weston was fading." Adds Louie Lista, "Things were getting so out of hand that I'd look back at what happened on a given Saturday night and think, 'This is too out in the open, this is getting dangerous.'"

If Herb Cohen had turned a blind eye to the drink-fuelled scrapes Waits was getting into, an incident in late May made them harder to ignore. Waits already harboured a belligerent attitude towards cops when three plainclothes policemen came into the coffee shop on the night of the 27th. "I remember this one African-American cop asking Tom if he'd ever been arrested," Louie Lista remembers of an earlier incident. "Tom grunted, 'Nothin' to write home about.' And there was something in the chemistry with this guy that struck a little bit of a spark. I said afterwards, 'Waits, you got a bad attitude, man.' He was like, 'No, I don't! That guy was tryin' to screw with me!'" On another occasion, when an LAPD funeral procession was wending past the Tropicana, Waits and Chuck E. Weiss broke into a raucous rendition of Bob Marley's "I Shot the Sheriff".

Waits and Bobi Thomas were supping with Weiss at Duke's when one of the coffeeshop regulars pushed in front of the plainclothes deputies. Watching as the men became physically aggressive with the guy, Waits and Weiss leapt to his defence. "They'd taken over the tables of some people we knew at the restaurant," Waits claimed. "They'd bullied their way into a table. We let them know we didn't think it was the kind of thing that we do around here, and they didn't like that." The police report stated that "suspects Weiss and Waits . . . yelled to the unknown male, 'Hey man, I got these dudes covered . . .' then told the deputies 'You guys wanna fight? Come on.'"

Thomas recalls that Waits shouted for her to "call Herb!" Waits and Weiss then followed her out of the coffee shop, only to have the cops pursue them. In Herb Cohen's words the deputies "pulled their guns, threw them down on the ground and hand-cuffed them . . . [and] told Chuck they were arresting them for homosexual soliciting and being drunk and disorderly". Eyewit-ness Mike Ruiz, drummer with a band called Milk'n'Cookies, watched as one cop got Waits in a headlock and began pounding his head on the side of a phone booth. "[They] threw us into the back of a Toyota pickup with guns to our temples," Waits remembered. "Guy says, 'Do you know what one of these things does to your head when you fire it at close range?' He said, 'Your head will explode like a cantaloupe.' I thought about that. I was very still."

Three months later Waits and Weiss were found not guilty on two charges of disturbing the peace. The verdict concluded a three-day trial in which the pair's lawyer, Terry Steinhart, a part-ner in the firm founded by Mutt Cohen, presented eight wit-nesses who disputed the report of the original arresting officers and presented testimony of "extreme abuse" to Waits and Weiss. In a sign of legal things to come, Waits decided to sue for mone-tary damages from the LAPD. "It dragged on for five years before I got my day in court with a little arbitration hearing," Waits recalled. He eventually pocketed the modest sum of $7,500.

1977 kicked off with Waits' first tour of Japan. Shows in Tokyo, Osaka, Kyoto, and other cities proved a welcome antidote to his usual experience on the road. He told friends that Japanese audiences and promoters alike treated American performers like kings, even if he suspected that they viewed him as a two-dimensional jazzbo caricature. "The people were so quiet and respectful," recalls Chip White. "We walked out on stage in front of two thousand people and Tom said, 'This is as quiet as it was at soundcheck!' They were like samurai listeners – they listened with a deadly intent!"

Among Waits' Japanese fans was a woman who befriended him after a show and mistook a casual remark to be a proposal of marriage. Five months and a European tour later, she tracked him down to LA. On 19 May, supported by bluesman Jimmy Witherspoon, Waits was making his debut at the Roxy on Sunset when a car smashed into a telephone pole outside, causing a blackout on the entire block of Sunset Boulevard. Just at that moment the lovestruck Japanese girl appeared. As the Strip became the scene of a candle-lit block party, a mumbling Waits tried to explain that she'd misunderstood what he'd said in Japan.

Some of Waits' female admirers were more persistent, not to mention more alarming. One girl who'd escaped from an institution in Illinois hitchhiked all the way to LA to meet him. Dressed head to toe in black, she would sit on the porch of the bungalow and await his early-hours return. Rebuffed, she took to calling him in hotel rooms, announcing that she was going to kill him before putting the phone down. Though Waits accepted this was the price he had to pay not only for living in a motel but for being *famous* for living in a motel, he was understandably jittery after the experience. The pimps next door didn't help matters either; nor did the "maniac, misfit unemployed actor" who lived on the other side and once broke into Waits' bungalow to be discovered, high as a kite, playing his piano at three in the morning by a spooked Chuck E. Weiss.

Among other fellow guests at the Tropicana were members of certain punk and rockabilly bands. "The Dead Boys were living there," Weiss recalled. "Levi and the Rockats were living there. Pretty soon Blondie would stay there. I'm sure this was because of Tom. As soon as he moved in, the place started to get an international reputation." Though he dug local band the Zeros, admiring "these nutty Mexican kids with their pointy shoes", Waits felt ambivalent about punk. Caught in a no-man's-land somewhere between Fleetwood Mac and the Sex Pistols, he apparently had no home at either extreme. On the one hand, punk gave the middle finger to much of the music he loved, whether that was Johnny Mercer or Randy Newman; on the other it represented a breath of fresh air he welcomed with open arms.

"It may be revolting to a lot of people, but at least it's an alternative to the garbage that's been around for ten years," he declared. "I've had it up to here with Crosby Steals the Cash. I'd rather listen to some young kid in a leather jacket singing 'I want to eat out my mother' than to hear some of these insipid guys with their cowboy boots and embroidered shirts doing 'Six Days on the Road'."

"When people like Crosby were bad-rapping Devo and treating punk rockers like vermin, Waits wasn't," says Harvey Kubernik, who saw the emerging punk scene in local clubs like Brendan Mullen's Masque. "Why? Because he might have been at Duke's sitting next to Joey Ramone." Ironically, Waits adopted the same position on punk as Neil Young, who in his 1974 song "Revolution Blues" had declared war on the smugness of his peers and might well have shared Waits' characterization of Crosby and co. as "the assholes who live in Resting On My Laurels Canyon".

More to Waits' taste than the Sex Pistols – or LA bands like the Germs and the Weirdos – were the New York group Mink de Ville, whose musical and sartorial inclinations (streetcorner R&B roots, pointed shoes) roughly paralleled his own. "I was on the Bowery in New York and stood out in front of CBGB's one night," he said. "There were all these cats in small lapels and pointed shoes smoking Pall Malls and bullshitting with the winos. It was good."

For now, Waits stuck to his own musical vision as he worked on songs for his fifth Asylum album. As he'd done a year earlier, he set up a series of pre-production meetings with Bones Howe. Having spent much of his down time on tour watching forgotten masterpieces of Hollywood film noir on TV, he told Bones he wanted to go one step further than *Small Change* and create musical settings that were quasi-cinematic. "I once asked Waits what touring was like," Harvey Kubernik says. "He said, 'Man, you're gonna watch a lotta late-night movies.' We would talk about Dan Duryea and Lee Marvin. A lot of black-and-white films in motel rooms." According to Chip White, Waits knew the script of Billy Wilder's *Double Indemnity* off by heart: "The whole *band* knew it. One of us would take Fred MacMurray's character and another would take Barbara Stanwyck's. It was like learning the lines to a song."

As Waits outlined his vision for the album, Bones Howe had an idea. Arranger Bob Alcivar had written vocal charts and rhythm tracks for him – notably on such Fifth Dimension hits as "Stoned Soul Picnic" – before graduating to full orchestral charts. "Bones was looking for somebody who could do orchestra and function with Tom," Alcivar says in his home in the Valley suburb of Northridge. "I don't know if I was a likely candidate for that job and I don't know if Tom thought so, but Bones arranged a meeting with Tom and he seemed to like what I was saying."

Bob Alcivar, Los Angeles, March 2007. (*Art Sperl*)

Like Howe, Alcivar was a fairly straight character. For Waits, the clincher was an item on Bob's career résumé: he had once worked with Lord Buckley. "Tom was just floored and started asked me questions. Eventually he just said, 'Well, if you knew *him*, we can work together.'" Waits was keen for Alcivar to score "Potter's Field", a long and dense spoken-word piece inspired by Sam Fuller's 1953 film *Pickup on South Street*. On first exposure to the Waits larynx, Alcivar went into mild shock. "But then because of the songs and the material it became beautiful to me," he says. "I immediately liked him and admired him. He was a very intelligent guy and he knew much more about jazz musicians and history than I did."

Preparing for the album that became *Foreign Affairs*, Waits often visited Alcivar in North Hollywood. "We'd sit around the piano and play songs," Alcivar recalls. "He wanted to know how to score and he said, 'Maybe you can teach me.' He wrote some beautiful ballads and they were very conducive to strings, so it was a joy to orchestrate a lot of those songs. He said the trouble with most strings was they made everyone sound like Perry Como."

The sessions for *Foreign Affairs* – Waits' working titles for the album included *Stolen Cars* and *Ten Dollars* – began at Filmways/ Heider Recording (as it was now known) on 26 July and were fraught with indecision and revision. The first day produced versions of "Potter's Field" and "Burma Shave" that Waits rejected. Versions of "Barber Shop" and "Foreign Affair" recorded the following day were also junked when he later revisited them. The first recording to stick was "Muriel", recorded on 28 July, the same day Waits cut a discarded version of the "Jack and Neal"/ "California, Here I Come" medley.

An acceptable version of "Barber Shop" was delivered on 1 August. The following day Waits recorded "A Sight for Sore Eyes", which had originally been recorded for *Small Change*, and successfully revisited "Jack and Neal"/"California, Here I Come". (He also cut the unused "Playin' Hooky" and "Saving All My Love for You".) "I Never Talk to Strangers" was recorded once on 8 August and then again on the 12th. "Cinny's Waltz" and a reworked "Foreign Affair" were done on the 11th, and a re-orchestrated "Potter's Field" on the 12th. "Burma Shave" was more of a struggle, recorded on 15 August and then again the following day, with Jack Sheldon's trumpet cadenza from the 15th tacked on to the end. (Another *Foreign Affairs* outtake, "Tie Undone", was subsequently re-recorded during the *Heartattack and Vine* sessions as "Mr Henry". A beautifully woozy ballad about a hungover, henpecked alcoholic, it was the only previously unreleased track on Waits' 1981 compilation *Bounced Checks*.)

The rhythm section for *Foreign Affairs* once again comprised Jim Hughart and Shelly Manne, with Edgar Lustgarten serving as orchestra manager. West Coast jazz veteran Sheldon played trumpet, while the tenor solos this time came courtesy of the wiry, silver-haired Frank Vicari – "my right-hand man", as Waits dubbed him despite his continuing heroin use. "Frank was a bad junkie," says Hughart. "He'd get so out of it he'd defy the laws of gravity. At one session he was either unconscious or had left the room, and I said to Shelly, 'This guy's about to flame out.' He quoted that I don't know how many times." Counters Chip White, "Frank was a pro – he kept his shit to himself. Him and Tom never had a problem."

Waits found the recording process no easier to bear, describing it as "excruciating, like going to the dentist". The orchestral sessions alone sent him spiralling into self-doubt. "They were done over two nights because the first night didn't really work out the way Tom wanted it," Bones Howe remembers. "Bob took it back and worked on the score for 'Potter's Field', and he made it tighter and made it better." But that wasn't all. Overnight, without telling Howe or Alcivar, Waits rewrote the song. "He changed a lot of lyrics, and I didn't know about it," Alcivar says. "It threw everything off a few frames here and there – things weren't hitting right." Concerned, Alcivar asked Waits if he was still happy with the orchestration. "He said, 'I don't care, it's perfect the way it is.' Really, again, it was Waits' feeling of being a little off the wall, not quite being absolutely on the money. I was too exact and mathematical, and it wasn't the way to think with him."

"Potter's Field" turned out to be the album's centrepiece. Opening with a scene-setting orchestral intro that tipped a hat at Waits' love of Gershwin and was dominated by Gene Cipriano's blithe clarinet, the near-nine-minute track led the listener into a sinister film-noir world that used the Big Apple – from the Bronx to St Mark's Place – as its menacing monochrome backdrop. Waits was Nickels, the blind stool-pigeon narrator offering cryptic clues to the whereabouts of the pickpocket Nightsticks. As he spun a web of rhymes from the tongue of his treacherous informer, the track's eerie mood was gradually built by horns, vibes, eerie strings, even tubular bells. In Runyonesque slang Nickels described how Nightsticks came by his half-million-dollar haul before locating him in Potter's Field, the cemetery where unidentified corpses were buried. ("If I was to be buried in Potter's Field," Thelma Ritter had protested in *Pickup on South Street*, "it'd just about kill me.") So pleased was Waits with "Potter's Field" that he gave Alcivar a co-credit for the track.

Equally cinematic was the instrumental overture that opened *Foreign Affairs*. Anticipating the music Waits and Alcivar created for *One from the Heart*, "Cinny's Waltz" – a nod to his kid sister – was pure Hollywood soundtrack, dreamy strings floating over pining piano chords before the belated entrance of Jack Sheldon's gorgeously warm trumpet. Waits stayed in *One from the Heart* mode for "Muriel", one of his loveliest late-night/bluenote melodies and a song inspired by Edie Adams, beautiful wife of comedian Ernie Kovacs and a 1960s model for Muriel Cigars. Alcivar sat out this track, which consisted simply of Waits' piano, Hughart's beautifully economical bass, and the wistful tenor of Frank Vicari in the wings, sighing of better times.

"I Never Talk to Strangers" was born one night when Bones and his wife Melodie took Waits and Bette Midler to dinner at the venerable Hollywood Boulevard restaurant Musso and Frank's. "Tom had been dating Bette," Howe remembers. "It kind of was off and on for years and years. At dinner he said he wanted to do a version of 'Baby, It's Cold Outside' with her." Howe thought the Ray Charles/Betty Carter classic too obvious a choice. "I said it would be great but it would stick out like a sore thumb. I said, 'What you need to do is go home and write a duet for you and Bette.' So he wrote 'Strangers', which is so much more fun."

Bones was right. As if taking "I Hope that I Don't Fall in Love with You" a stage further, Waits set up a time-honoured chat-up scenario in a bar as he regaled Midler with what she waved away as his "sad repartee". Inevitably these veterans of heartbreak overcame their cynicism as they got to the first base of flirtation. "Bette was in the middle of making *Broken Blossom*," Howe recalls. "But she came to the studio and we put two mics at the piano and she went out and sat next to Tom on the piano bench and we probably did six takes before we got it."

The song was slightly below Midler's range, forcing her to sing more conversationally. "When you write for a duet," says Bob Alcivar, "you've got to kind of psych out the two singers and decide what the key's going to be. In this case it was Tom's key, so Bette had to kind of fake it and go up and down and change the registers." Vocal-jazz connoisseurs would surely have something to say about Midler as canary, but her turn here as a kind of white Betty Carter worked *because* of its imperfection. "She drove me crazy for three months," says Howe. "She kept saying, 'I was sharp on that note, I was flat on that one.' I said, 'It doesn't get any better than that, it could be a stage performance.'"

On the semi-rapped "Jack and Neal", Waits paid belated homage to his literary mainman and the crazed, chaotic buddy who'd served as his muse. In the song, Cassady bragged of screwing a redheaded nurse as he motored through Nebraska; Kerouac nodded off in the back seat and dreamed of Charlie Parker; the nurse stuck her "fat ass" out the window and mooned the traffic; and Waits slipped into Al Jolson's "California, Here I Come" as the track neared its end. Musically throwaway, "Jack and Neal" perfectly replicated the loose flow of Kerouac's prose. Asked if the myth of Jack the beatific holy man hadn't been punctured of late – notably in a biography by Ann Charters – Waits was honest in his assessment. "I actually would prefer to see the other side," he said. "He wasn't a hero who could do no wrong. He saw a lot, got around. He wasn't nearly as mad and impetuous as Neal Cassady."

It's interesting to consider here how the Kerouac–Cassady dynamic was paralleled by the friendship between Waits and Chuck E. Weiss. For Waits, Weiss embodied the same recklessness Cassady did for Kerouac. "[He] had become . . . the great Idiot of us all," Kerouac wrote in *Visions of Cody,* his almost homoerotic paean to Cassady, "[. . .] entirely irresponsible to the point of wild example and purgation for us to learn and not to have to go through." While Weiss and Cassady harboured aspirations to being artists themselves, really they functioned as Ids to the Egos of the men who observed them and had the discipline to make art of their observations. For Waits to note that Kerouac wasn't "nearly as mad and impetuous" as the damaged Cassady may have been an interesting admission of his own relative cautiousness.

"A Sight for Sore Eyes", opening with a snatch of "Auld Lang Syne", was the archetypal Waits lullaby and a kind of benign reworking of "Tom Traubert's Blues". Sung in a gargled alcoholic voice, the song consisted of little more than two drunks sitting round in a bar and reminiscing about old friends and baseball players. Francis Thumm got a namecheck, but "Nash" was killed in a crash and "Sid" was in the slammer for armed robbery. "Tom would often greet you by saying, 'You're a sight for sore eyes!'" remembers Michael C Ford. "A lot of what he said came out of what I call the folk graveyard. He said to me once, 'You ever heard the expression "walking Spanish"?' He latched on to those things and used them."

Foreign Affairs' finest track followed "Potter's Field" on the second side of the vinyl album. Six and a half minutes long, "Burma Shave" remains one of Waits' great accounts of flight and escape. Inspired by Nick Ray's doomed-romance classic *They Live by Night*, the lyric tapped into the great American dream of a Better Place lying over the horizon. On the heels of "Potter's Field" it was another dose of film noir, but this time we were in the back of beyond, fleeing the "wide spot in the road" that was Marysville. Recalling his cousin Corinne and her longing to get out of the California town of that name, Waits imagined a girl thumbing a ride from a delinquent Farley Granger lookalike in a cowboy hat and heading for Burma Shave. Waits' imaginary town – the first of several such destinations in his work – was actually named after a 1950s shaving cream whose billboards he recalled from his childhood. The song took the form of dialogue between this wannabe Bonnie and Clyde doomed to die when the boy's car crashes. He's only stopping to buy gas; she's jumping her parole. He asks her to change the station; she dares him to overtake a car. "I used Burma Shave as a dream, a mythical community, a place two people are trying to get to," Waits said. "They don't make it."

One of the striking things about "Burma Shave" was Waits' voice, which dropped the Traubert growl in favour of something airier and breathier. "I was trying to sing instead of just growling and grunting, which by the time I get off the road is all I can muster up," he said. With minimal instrumentation – the mini-epic featured nothing except Waits, his piano, and a short trumpet solo – "Burma Shave" remains one of Waits' most haunting performances, a song of timeless suspense and dread.

Out of its violent ending came the light relief of "Barber Shop", a minor slice of bop banter and a showcase for Jim Hughart and Shelly Manne. A wiseass kid wanders into a barbershop and semi-taunts the two old gents who cut hair there. The kid says he can get his hair cut cheaper in Mexico; they tell him to put out his cigarette. He says he has tickets for the circus; they remind him that he owes for his previous haircut. Imagine the missing link between "Diamonds on My Windshield" and "Step Right Up" and you're not far off. Imagine Waits as a cocky juvenile in Chula Vista and you're closer still.

The last track was the album's title song: Tom in expansive

Satchmode, pastiching Cole Porter sophistication to wordily comic effect as though Tom Traubert had suddenly been transported into a city where nothing was broken after all. It was also a dissertation on touring and related issues of separation and infidelity.

For the album cover Waits wanted to convey the film-noir mood that coloured so many of the songs. Veteran Hollywood portraitist George Hurrell was hired to shoot Waits, both alone and in a clutch with a shadowy female whose ring-encrusted right hand clamped a passport to his chest. The back-cover shot of Tom was particularly good, casting him as a slicked-back hoodlum – half matinee idol, half hair-trigger psychopath. The inner sleeve depicted the soused singer clawing at the keys of his Tropicana upright.

Foreign Affairs is a grievously underrated album that suffers primarily from the reputation of its predecessor. I'll stick my neck out further still: it actually has more great Waits music on it ("Muriel", "I Never Talk to Strangers", "A Sight for Sore Eyes", "Potter's Field", "Burma Shave") than *Small Change*. Unfortunately too few critics were convinced, perceiving Waits as stuck in a boho-Beat rut. Even Fred Schruers in an otherwise positive *Rolling Stone* review wrote that the "chief sin [Waits] can't shake is an overabundance of the facile, researched-and-rehearsed jive talk that is meant to dazzle but in fact fatigues the listener".

Unlike *Small Change*, *Foreign Affairs* failed to dent the Top 100 albums chart and left a dismayed Waits wondering if he wasn't now a spent force. Nor was there much support at Elektra-Asylum. "When Tom came out with a record, nobody at the label had been part of the process of making it," says Joe Smith. "He just delivered a tape. I'd listen to his records and think, 'Jeez, this guy does clever stuff but how do we market him?' No disc jockeys wanted to play his records."

As he geared up to promote the record with yet another

debilitating tour, Waits spent the remainder of the summer sequestered at the Tropicana or hanging with Chuck E. Weiss and the Troubadour crew. Often joining them was Art Fein (aka "Fein Art"), who was doing his best to push Waits in his day job in Elektra-Asylum's press department. "Me and Weiss and Waits used to hang around in front of the Troub every Monday night in 1977," Fein told me. He said the "gang" consisted of Weiss, Waits, Paul Body, Rick Dubov, and himself – two Troub employees and two hangers-on. "Tom was really funnier casually, just hanging out," says Dubov, who took tickets at the door. "It was like having a standup comedian on call. I was having a drink with him one night and we saw some Beverly Hills girl with this rich guy. Tom lent over to me and said what he imagined the girl was saying to the guy: 'Put your stiff throbbing C-note into my juicy bank account.' Chuckie was the same: he hit on this chick and when she asked him what music he listened to, he said, 'Oh, mostly I just listen to old nigger music.'"

Neither Waits nor Weiss could abide spoiled LA brats. Asked by Flo and Eddie to define a typical Hollywood princess, Waits said, "Oh you know, they cross their sevens and say 'Ciao' . . . they drive Porsches with tennis rackets in the backseat, you know?" Upper-middle-class American teenagers in general appalled him. "I'd rather play a club with vomit all around me," he told *Time*, "than a clean little college with sassy little girls and guys with razor-cut hair and coke spoons around their necks."

The streetcorner posse mostly stood around talking about roots music. Paul Body recalls Art Fein pulling up outside the club in a car even more beat-up than Waits' and regaling everyone with the latest obscure rockabilly classics he'd acquired. After the Troub hoot was over, says Body, the gang would adjourn to Canter's, the twenty-four-hour Jewish deli on Fairfax Avenue that for years had welcomed music scenesters in the small hours. "People would come up and talk to Tom there," Body says. "He'd say, 'Aw man, I don't like this.' Somebody said to him once, 'What about when they *don't* do it?'"

Waits' love life was somewhat fitful in this period. While his relationship with Bette Midler was never an entirely serious affair, he continued to see her during the summer. "My idea of a good time in LA is to go to the Fatburger with Tom Waits," she announced in one interview. Waits in turn described her as "the only girl I know who'll come over and sit in my kitchen and not make fun of me". When he played a benefit for the Troubadour in mid-September, he asked Midler to join him on stage to sing a duet. "It was one of the greatest shows I've ever seen," says Michael Hacker. "Bette came out and they did 'Never Talk to Strangers'. The place was packed. People were shoulder to shoulder."

The following night, to return the favour, Midler persuaded Waits to perform at a gay rights show at the Hollywood Bowl. It turned out to be an event neither would forget. After a wired Richard Pryor lurched on to the stage and let loose a stream of homophobic expletives, Waits was left holding the baby. "After ten minutes, someone gave [Tom] the signal to get on with it," remembered Art Fein, who'd witnessed Pryor's outburst. "With people shouting 'Kill him!' and 'Fuck Richard Pryor!' the spotlight hit Tom Waits sitting on top of the wall. He was virtually unknown to this crowd and decided it wasn't time to get acquainted. He just sat there smoking a cigarette for five long minutes."

When Waits wasn't seeing Midler, he spent time with another Troubadour employee – in Louie Lista's words, "a pretty girl with dark brown hair and a funny sense of humor" who worked in the club's box office. Marchiela, the girl featured on the cover of *Foreign Affairs*, was by all accounts keen on Waits. "She was a girl who was . . . not a girlfriend but she *thought* she was a girlfriend," says Paul Body. "And there were other girls that were hitting on

Tom. There was a girl working in the Troubadour bar who had a crush on him. But I didn't know any of his girlfriends because he kept that all separate. That was like a separate thing. Chuckie was always the one who had the girls." Recalls Chip White, "He had a girlfriend in Philadelphia, a nice-looking Italian lady with dark hair. Every time we got to Philly he had to straighten up."

It was Chuck E. Weiss who first alerted Waits to a young singer who'd begun showing up at the Troubadour hoot nights. Rickie Lee Jones was a wild child of twenty-three, a free spirit with her own boho baggage and a way with language that made people think of, well, Tom Waits. "I remember Louie Lista telling me, 'Man, you oughta see the scene this broad is staging on Santa Monica Boulevard to try and get a label deal,'" says Harvey Kubernik. "'This chick is doing a whole canary scene down there. I don't know if she has any talent but she knows how to make a scene.'"

Jones' back-story would have made her hot poop in the age of Amy Winehouse; the name alone smacked of trailer-trash romance. Born in 1954 in Chicago, Rickie Lee was a renegade from a rootless vaudeville family that moved round the country as employment opportunities dictated. "Maybe my family were outlaws to an extent," she reflected. "The atmosphere at home was not one of *Father Knows Best*, which is how I saw the rest of the world. My parents were pretty wild – they passed the misfit thing on to us."

The second of four kids born to Richard and Bettye Jones, Rickie Lee classified her folks as "lower-middle-class-hillbilly-hipster". Her hobo dad supplemented his income from performing with work as a waiter, gardener, and furniture removals man; Bettye was a waitress who sometimes moonlighted as a nurse. Though close to older brother Danny, the only boy out of the four siblings, Rickie Lee was an essentially solitary child, living in a world of make-believe friends.

Settling for a period in Phoenix, Arizona, the family was devastated when sixteen-year-old Danny lost a leg in a motorcycle accident. When Richard and Bettye split up, little Rickie Lee began acting out, running away from home as she went in search of hippie kicks. Mom sent her to live with Dad, who tried without success to tame the girl. "I never knew when I was going to leave," Jones recalled of her teenage truancies. "I might be walking over to a kid's house, then all of a sudden I would just stick out my thumb and hitchhike across three states." At fourteen Jones ran off to a rock festival in California, freaking out on acid as she beheld the satanic apparition that was Jethro Tull's flute-toting frontman Ian Anderson. She learned to play songs on an acoustic guitar. The first was Jefferson Airplane's "Comin' Back to Me", later recorded on her album *Pop Pop*. At sixteen she was expelled from Timberline High in the logging town of Olympia, Washington, where Bettye now lived. Two years later, she packed up her life in an orange Vega and followed a boyfriend down to southern California. "I knew this was where I wanted to be," she said of southern California. "It just didn't seem like anywhere else was real life."

By 1975 she was living on Westminster Avenue in the old beatnik neighbourhood of Venice, waitressing and writing and playing the local coffeehouse, Suzanne's, when she could swing a gig. The area had become as rundown as Mission Beach in San Diego, but the "bikers, degenerates, drunken men, and toothless women" offered ample material for early songs whose themes weren't a million miles from Waits'. "I never did hang out, I just wrote about it," she later admitted. "I've always been a very private person. When I was twenty-one and very lonely, I hung out in bars for about a year."

Appearances at the Comeback Inn – and at the A La Carte and Ivar Theater in Hollywood – bolstered Jones' modest reputation. Rumours spread that she was so broke she sometimes slept under the Hollywood sign. Songs she'd written or co-written made people's ears prick up. But it was the Troubadour hoot that really got her noticed. One night in the summer of 1977, Chuck E. Weiss was washing dishes in the club's kitchen when through the doors he heard the sound of a girl singer. Weiss watched Jones sing two numbers, her own "Easy Money" and fellow aspirant Ivan Ulz's "You Almost Look Chinese", and was knocked out. Ulz introduced them after she'd performed.

"She didn't appear to be driven at all," Weiss remembered. "She appeared to be a real freeform spirit that wasn't interested in any of the hoopla that went around in Hollywood." But he added that he'd later stumbled on a diary that made clear how ambitious Jones actually was. "I found out a lot of the things she did were very planned and contrived," he said. "It was quite surprising. It was planned as to who she would want to meet to get along. As soon as she got some recognition, she knew exactly what to do – what lawyer to approach, what manager to approach. She had it all worked out." Paul Body recalls how Jones would sit outside the Troubadour and busk on the street: "There's nothing guys who are musicians like more than a girl who can play. That just drives us nuts."

Waits first spoke to Jones outside the club on a late summer evening. The circumstances of their meeting were pure Rickie Lee. "It was warm and everyone was sitting out front on the street," Louie Lista remembers. "I had a fondness for her from the start, because I'd always liked women who added a theatrical touch to the usual war-of-the-sexes stuff. She had a young lady with her, and there was nothing real overt about it, but they were doing a little performance to make it look as though they were a romantic couple. But it was very tastefully handled. And this was driving Tom *nuts*. Chuckie said, 'We've been waiting *years* for something like this!'" When Waits said he wanted to buy Jones a drink, Lista reminded him he couldn't take alcohol out on the street. Instead Tom brought out a cup of coffee and handed it to her on the kerb. "That I recall as his first overture to her," Lista says. "I have no idea how it went down."

"The first time I saw Rickie Lee she reminded me of Jayne Mansfield," Waits said in 1979. "I thought she was extremely attractive, which is to say that my first reactions were rather primitive – primeval even." When he finally saw her perform, he was even more turned on. "Her style on stage was appealing and arousing," he said. "Sorta like that of a sexy white spade." The coffee seems to have done the trick: by the end of the year, Waits and Jones were an item. Lubricated by booze and a shared love of jazz, the Beats, and *West Side Story*, the relationship quickly became passionate. "She was drinking a lot then and I was too, so we drank together," Waits said, à la Bukowski. "You can learn a lot about a woman by getting smashed with her." Waits and Jones not only drank together, they drank (and drugged) with Chuck E. Weiss. As though re-enacting the fabled *ménage à trois* between Jack Kerouac and Neal and Carolyn Cassady, the three friends ran amok in West Hollywood, gatecrashing parties and stumbling along the street with their arms interlocked. "I remember her getting her first pair of high heels . . . and coming by one night to holler in my window to take her out celebrating," Waits said. "There she was, walking down Santa Monica Boulevard, drunk and falling off her shoes."

"She's all woman and seems tough . . . but she's also real soft and playful," Weiss remarked in 1979 as he reminisced about the high jinks and antics the trio got up to. For Jones, Weiss and Waits provided a surrogate family, a gang of three united against both the straight world and the phoney world of 1970s LA. "All the people come out at night," Jones reflected years later. "It's a world that isn't available during the day. To be a part of other people's lives, you have to go to where they are at night. Those people weren't the types to be at Denny's at ten in the morning."

All for one and one for all: Waits, Chuck E. Weiss, and Rickie Lee Jones at Shangri-La, Zuma Beach, June 1979. (*Jenny Lens*)

Cocooned in their own bubble of hipster (be)attitude, the trio ignored their peers and dropped out of the Hollywood rock scene in order to create a parallel world that was equal parts Bukowski and Lord Buckley. "It seems sometimes like we're real romantic dreamers who got stuck in the wrong time zone," Jones told *Rolling Stone*. "So we cling, we love each other very much."

If there was any concession to the present, it lay in a partiality to artists such as Elvis Costello, whose "Mystery Dance" was ever-present on Jones' turntable. Her own songs seemed to combine the influences of Laura Nyro and Van Morrison with that of Waits himself. When he heard her "Easy Money", Waits must have known it was part-mimicry of his own street portraiture. "I always tend to become whomever I am involved with," Jones admitted in 2004, "and so I think I took on his swaggering masculinity. It was a good coat to wear, a good thing to hide behind: myself being so very vulnerable, that big persona seemed safe."

"Rickie Lee arguably cadged her entire characterization from Waits whole," reflects Mike Melvoin. "I wondered later about how he would allow himself to get involved with her after she had lifted her very existence from him." Would Jones have made it without the Waits connection? Would she even have assembled her boho look, with the trademark beret, without his influence? Well, so what if she did. Rock and roll wouldn't exist without such borrowings. Rickie Lee was living out a sexy fantasy of walking on LA's wild side with a man she hugely admired and – as it turned out – deeply loved. "We walk around the same streets and I guess it's primarily a jazz-motivated situation for both of us," she said. "We're living on the jazz side of life."

By early 1978, it was clear that Jones was a genuine talent – a writer arguably as good as Waits, boasting a voice combining funky eroticism with childlike vulnerability. "What's amazing . . . is that Rickie could make people cry quicker than Laura Nyro could," Chuck E. Weiss recalled. "At her shows I used to watch people in the audience just crying their eyes out when she sang." In March 1978, when she showcased at the Troubadour, Jones sensed she was on the cusp of success. For half an hour afterwards everybody in the club wanted to shake her hand. The record companies perked up and came sniffing round; A&M bankrolled demos. One night, Little Feat's Lowell George heard Jones sing in Topanga, flipped over "Easy Money" and said he wanted to cut the song on his solo album *Thanks, I'll Eat It Here*.

At night Jones would swim in the Tropicana pool. "I'd [. . .] look up at the moon and imagine, 'So this is what it's like to be a movie star, to own the moon and the palms and the night air, to be beautiful and have the whole history of your life still approaching,'" she recalled. She said she preferred night to day in

LA because the city was "very quiet and empty at night", making it easier to "fill in the darkness" with her imagination.

Jones had time to herself when, early in October 1977, Waits headed back out on the road. The Nocturnal Emissions were again along for the ride, though after a row in Hartford, Connecticut, on the fourth, Fitz Jenkins was given his marching orders. "Something happened that was weird," Chip White recalls of the firing. "I think Tom had promised Fitz he could do some recording and then it didn't happen. I wasn't on the inside of it, but I was sorry it happened." Jenkins' replacement was sometime Blood, Sweat and Tears bassist Danny Trifan, an old jazz comrade of Frank Vicari's.

Keen to inject something new into his act, Waits for the first

time employed onstage props to enhance the theatricality of his performances. Foremost among them was a street lamp that he alternately clung to and crooned under. Audiences and critics alike responded well to Waits taking his act beyond the tried and tested drunk-at-the-piano ritual.

Though reserved on first acquaintance, Waits slowly opened up to Danny Trifan as the tour wore on. "You always got the feeling there was much more to him than he let you see," Trifan says. "He once came into the dressing room, folded himself into a chair, and sat there rocking with his eyes closed. We all kept talking and a few minutes later he opened his eyes, made a

Waits and street lamp, Theatre del Mar, Santa Cruz, December 1977. (*Greg Arrufat*)

brief comment that clearly indicated he'd heard every word, and left."

The road proved as taxing as ever, and Waits was now missing Ms Jones into the bargain. "Tom may be a bit . . . cranky," John Forscha warned interviewer Bart Bull before an encounter in Scottsdale, Arizona. "I'm not a lush," Waits snapped, bristling at one of Bull's questions. "I work real hard all year. If I was a drunk I don't think I'd have five albums out. I don't think I'd be able to stay on the road eight months out of the year." When Forscha attempted to lighten the mood, Waits resumed his aggressive tack. "I don't know what you want from me," he griped. "I'm not a geek, I'm not a drunk, I'm a regular guy . . . I take shits, I've got a girlfriend, I live in a hotel . . ." With Bull on the point of walking out, Waits attempted contrition by way of explaining his crankiness. "You know, I'm tired," he said. "I've been on the bus. I don't sleep. I haven't had a night off in three weeks. I've been entertaining and talking to journalists and getting my picture taken and playing in nightclubs and it gets to be a little too much."

For all the aggravations of touring, Waits held fast to the belief that his music was important. "There's something about what I'm doing," he told *Circus* magazine. "I'm kind of obsessed . . . not in the sense [of being] psychotic, it's just I've got a lot of miles under my belt [and] . . . I can't go back . . . it's very difficult for me to go home." It was as if Waits felt he had started something he had to finish – that on this particular creative journey there was no turning back.

Reunited with Rickie Lee, Chuck E. Weiss, and the Tropicana–Troubadour troupe, Waits spent a suitably crazed Christmas in California. A new song he was working on, "Red Shoes by the Drugstore", hinted at their Yuletide capers. Jones was surely the "little bluejay/in a red dress" wearing the shoes Waits was so taken with. The "ski room" that Santa Claus is drunk in was a bar at 5851 Sunset – a stone's throw from Herb Cohen's office – that Waits, Weiss, and Jones regularly frequented.

Among the trio's favourite pastimes was cruising Beverly Hills or Bel Air in search of lawn jockeys whose faces had been painted white by guilt-ridden millionaires and movie stars. "Once upon a time they'd been black," Weiss recalled. "But instead of taking them down they'd painted them white. So Rickie and Tom and I would go around painting them black again." From there they progressed to actually stealing the jockeys. "I still have a couple in my back yard," Weiss admitted almost thirty years later.*

It was in a similarly plush neighbourhood that Weiss, Waits, and Jones once turned up to attend a party thrown by Herb Cohen's brother Mutt. Making a beeline for the refreshments, Jones grabbed an avocado pear, sat down in a chair, and inserted it between her legs. Cohen's industry friends were appalled. "Tom was embarrassed but got a great kick out of it," Weiss claimed. "Nobody would talk to us after that, so we spent the evening going up to people with cocktail dip hidden in our palms and shaking hands with them." To Weiss, "as absurd as it may sound", the trio's mindset was "kind of like us against the suits", a refusal to play the entertainment game. "Tom absolutely despised phonies," Danny Trifan remembers. "I remember one time a record company official came into the dressing room and greeted him with a loud 'Hey, babe!' Waits just turned on his heel and left, leaving the guy standing there asking me, 'What I do?' I told him he had to be real with Waits and never call him 'babe' again."

It was ironic that the film industry, which had an even higher quota of phonies, now came knocking at Waits' door. Nobody seems quite sure how Sylvester Stallone, star of *Rocky*, befriended Tom Waits. "Maybe Sly saw him at the Troubadour or met him

* The credits on the sleeve of *Blue Valentine* give thanks not only to Weiss and Louie Lista but to "Diane 'Steal That Black Jockey Off The Lawn' Quinn".

through somebody," Bones Howe told Jay S. Jacobs. "He was suddenly there. But it wasn't unusual, because Tom had a way of
accumulating people." Stallone was in pre-production for his
period piece *Paradise Alley* and decided Waits was ideal for a
cameo role as – what else? – a down-at-heel saloon pianist
named Mumbles. "Stallone said, 'Be a drunk piano player in an
Irish bar . . . that should be easy,'" Waits told *Playgirl*. "I'd like to
have played an axe-murderer but this is a start."

Stallone also asked Waits and Howe to provide songs for the
movie's soundtrack. "(Meet Me in) Paradise Alley" was a typically pretty ballad, while the wistful "Annie's Back in Town"
could have come straight from the Broadway songbooks of Cole
Porter and Irving Berlin. None of the remaining tracks – a version of *Small Change*'s "Bad Liver and a Broken Heart" and two
very different versions of "With a Suitcase" – made the cut,
though a "street band" version of the latter was a sign of things to
come, with Howe and others dragooned into banging on a selection of drums and other percussive instruments. *Paradise Alley*
gave Waits a first taste of life in front of a movie camera. He sum-
marized the experience tersely – "I went and sat in front of a
piano for three weeks and then I went home" – but was fascinated by watching Stallone at work in his dual roles as director
and star. He confessed he was "real timid" about acting, claiming
he was "walking on eggshells" in his scenes, most of which were
cut anyway. Years later, when he finally got to see the critically
mauled *Paradise Alley* on television, he blinked and all but
missed himself.

A string of West Coast dates kept Waits busy through February 1978. Street life, in and around the Tropicana, continued in its
haphazard way. "We want to say hello to you all from the Tropicana Hotel, some would say one of the sleaziest places in Hollywood," blared Flo and Eddie when they came to interview Waits
in April. "It's twelve dollars a night, the pool has little things

swimming in it . . . [we] can smell the onions at Duke's cafe next door." With punk rock and new wave increasingly taking hold of the LA scene, Waits often found himself at Duke's sitting next to bands from New York and London. Even Doug Weston took a punt on punk, booking young bands at the Troubadour. When local band the Bags played the club one Sunday night in February, Waits and Chuck E. Weiss showed up to witness the changing of the guard in a club formerly reserved for mellow singer-songwriters and country rockers out of Laurel Canyon. However, as if to illustrate that some gulfs aren't bridged that easily, Waits and Weiss got into a fracas with the band after hitting on their female singer Alice Bag.

"Nicky Beat [Bags' drummer] gets up on stage and says, 'There's a famous asshole in the audience tonight – Tom Waits,'" recalls Paul Body. "Then he jumps out into the audience and it's *on*, in the middle of everybody! Everybody has a different take on it, it's like *Rashomon*. Alice has *her* take on it, Chuckie has *his* take on it, and Brendan Mullen has *his*." Mullen, a pioneer punk impresario in Hollywood, saw the Waits/Weiss flirtation with punk as calculated opportunism. "Waits wanted that open-minded punk/new wave audience badly," he says cynically. "He had none of his own yet beyond the Troubadour. The *Nighthawks* faux-jazzbo schtick had run its course, and now punk was ablaze, something he didn't get. Or couldn't get, since it unseated the rock status quo he'd beat his brains out trying to get in with."

"The Trashing of the Troub", as Mullen terms it, was a significant moment in the trajectory of Waits' reinvention. As much as he may have welcomed its snotty iconoclasm, he couldn't help regarding punk as a kind of barbarism, with little or no redeeming musical merit. In his cups he often dismissed the music as "a buncha shit". Yet increasingly he knew something had to change in the way his music was formulated.

A turning point may have been a second tour of Japan in

With punk scenester Trixie at the Tropicana, summer 1979. (*Jenny Lens*)

March. While on the one hand it gave Waits the chance to experiment further with what he saw as the more "pantomime" aspects of his stage act, on the other he felt more boxed in than ever by the "faux-jazzbo schtick" and wanted to find a way out of it. Visiting Louie Lista on his return from the tour, Waits voiced his frustration. "Tom said to me, 'In Japan I thought, "This is really great and it could get a lot better,"'" Lista remembers. "'But I kind of feel like an old prizefighter who's just going through the motions. I keep doing this character – the down-and-out but amusing and interesting Bowery character. And it's the same routine that I've been going through for so long as a live performer.'"

Struck by Waits' desire to get out of his rut, Lista urged him to pursue the parallel acting career he'd begun with *Paradise Alley*. "I said, 'Tom, I think you could do really well with acting,'" he recalls. "With him there were a lot of different mediums involved. There was singing, there was instrument playing, but there was also comedic acting and there was dancing and there

were all kinds of theatrical things involved. I think he was starting to see them as all akin."

In addition to acting, there was another string Waits wanted to
add to his bow: writing. In April, he flew to Paris to talk with the
Belgian illustrator Guy Peellaert about providing the text for a
book. In 1974, Peellaert had published *Rock Dreams*, a collaboration with writer Nik Cohn that imagined notable pop and rock
stars in striking tableaux that drew thematically on the myths
surrounding them. Now he wanted to pay tribute to a number of
pre-rock entertainers and associated figures, most of them connected to Las Vegas. "It's about American heroes from Jimmy
Durante to Jimmy Hoffa," Waits explained. "It's got . . . uh . . .
Marlene Dietrich and Jack Benny and Mario Lanza and Elvis
Presley and Milton Berle and Lenny Bruce and . . . stories to
accompany each painting . . . my own perspective, not a biography." On the pretext of research, Waits and Chuck E. Weiss made
a field trip to Vegas and wound up being thrown out of the
MGM Grand. "They threw us out for hanging around the eleva-
tors looking for drunk cheerleaders," Waits told *Playgirl*. "They
thought we looked like bad security risks."

Waits was simultaneously at work on a movie musical with
lyricist Paul Hampton, a sometime partner of Burt Bacharach's.
With the working title *Why Is the Dream Always So Much Sweeter
than the Taste?*, the "opera" (as Waits referred to it) was about two
old friends reunited on a New Year's Eve in the Orange County
town of Torrance. Jack Farley Fairchild ("a used-car dealer") and
Donald Fedore ("his partner and side-kick") were another per-
mutation of the Kerouac–Cassady and Waits–Weiss double acts.
Though the project never got off the ground, either as a film or
as a musical, *Why Is the Dream . . .?* produced the concept of the
"Used Carlotta" sequence in *One from the Heart* and almost certainly sowed the seeds for *Frank's Wild Years* and Waits' work
with director Robert Wilson in the 1980s and 90s. Waits and

Hampton were still apparently working on their "opera" in early 1979, when Waits said he'd "never tried anything like this before" and that it was "the hardest thing I've ever done . . . well, the most challenging anyway".

But it was in his music itself that Waits made the biggest changes. "If I have to write one more song about booze and being drunk and all that, I'm going to throw up!" he said. Renting a little room on Sunset at Van Ness, a stone's throw from the "Rock'n'Roll Denny's" beloved of bands and music scenesters alike, Waits threw out his rulebook and wrote a dozen new songs on the guitar. "I think for a while I had a certain romance with Tin Pan Alley," he told me in 1985. "But it was actually rather rigid for me. I wrote primarily at the piano and you write a certain kind of song at the piano." Getting away from the Tropicana was liberating in itself. "I live in a neighborhood that far from insulates me from life out there," he told Charley De Lisle. "I feed off it. But at some point you really have to stop and go away and sit down and collect all of the things you've been through. You have to be away to let your imagination work along with your memory."

When the *Blue Valentine* sessions began at Filmways/Heider Recording on 24 July, the musicians were surprised to find Waits standing in the studio with an electric guitar. "I'm playing [it] for the first time," he told *Rolling Stone* a little disingenuously, "and shit, I know three chords just like every other guitar player." Among the sidemen was Jim Hughart, last man standing from the core of jazz players on *Small Change*. "Maybe Tom felt a bit more at ease around me," Hughart says. "Drummers and saxophone players changed, but I was the one consistent member of the recording unit from beginning to end." Yet even Jim would only appear on two of the album's tracks. After using Chip White and Frank Vicari on "Wrong Side of the Road", "Romeo Is Bleeding", and a discarded version of "$29.00", Waits decided it was time for a change and called a halt to the sessions. "[I needed] something different," he said. "I've got to keep it fresh. God, it was tough letting those guys go."

"I think he flew us out to LA because he wanted to put us on a record," Chip White says. "He didn't know how much longer this situation was going to last. He said he was just trying out new blood, and I understood that. There were no hard feelings." Tiring of the jazz-trio basis of his sound, Waits wanted an altogether blacker feel for the album. After brainstorming with Bones Howe and Herbie Cohen, he booked drummer Ricky Lawson, guitarist Roland Bautista, and fellow Cohen client George Duke, who guested on the record as "Da Willie Gonga" to avoid detection by the Musicians' Union. "They're all Negroes," Waits quipped. "I'm the only spot in the group."

Jim Hughart's place, meanwhile, was taken by Byron Miller and Scott Edwards, electric bass players from R&B and funk backgrounds. It was ironic that Duke played Yamaha electric piano on three tracks, since Waits had always detested the instrument and carried painful memories of playing Duke's keyboard during his support slots on the Zappa tours. The new ensemble went into the studio with Waits on 8 August, recording "$29.00" that day, followed by "Red Shoes by the Drugstore" and "Christmas Card from a Hooker in Minneapolis" two days later.

But that wasn't all. Long a devotee of New Orleans R&B, Waits had of late saturated himself in music by Dr John, Allen Toussaint, Professor Longhair, Huey "Piano" Smith, and other Crescent City legends. "*Blue Valentine* really started because Tom was fascinated by second-line New Orleans R&B," says Bones Howe, who knew Los Angeles was home to a number of displaced "N'awlins" musicians. In one of the pair's coffeeshop meetings, Howe suggested Waits record some tracks with the likes of drummer Earl Palmer, guitarist Alvin "Shine" Robinson, tenor saxophonist Herb Hardesty, and keyboard player Harold Battiste. All had played on classic New Orleans sides of the 1950s and 60s. Hardesty had been a linchpin of Fats Domino's band, and Palmer had played on Little Richard's explosive "Tutti Frutti" before becoming one of LA's premier session drummers. Battiste had made a similar move to California and wound up arranging pop hits for the likes of Sonny and Cher.

For Hardesty, the Waits dates in late August were a revelation. "I didn't know Tom until Earl Palmer called me to LA," he said the following year. "He specializes in musical freedom. If you feel like jazz you put it in, if you want to get a little bluesy you put that in too. There's complete freedom – it's one of the most interesting groups I've ever worked with." Reminiscing almost thirty years later, Hardesty told me Waits was "a very pleasant human being, a very nice person who projected himself through his work and had his own style of doing things".

After big orchestrated sessions for "Somewhere" and "Kentucky Avenue" on 21 August, Waits went back into Heider's with the New Orleans veterans the next day and banged out "Whistlin' Past the Graveyard" and "A Sweet Little Bullet from a Pretty Blue Gun". Hardesty, Palmer, and co. gave Waits the vintage R&B feel he wanted for songs that were closer to the present-day reality of the streets than anything he'd written before. "There's more blood in this record, probably more detective-type stories," Waits said. "It just comes from living in Los Angeles, hanging out where I hang out. I kind of feel like a private eye sometimes. I'm just trying to give some dignity to some of the things I see without being patronizing or maudlin about it."

Waits told *Circus* that most of the "stories" on *Blue Valentine* "took place in Los Angeles in the last few months". That was certainly true of "Romeo Is Bleeding", his account of a Mexican gang slaying in an East LA movie house. The track instantly sounded new for Waits. With its sauntering bass line, rimshot beat, and sleazy wheezing organ, "Romeo" was supper-club

R&B-jazz with a Jimmy Smith feel. Waits played muted guitar alongside Ray Crawford, and Bobbye Hall Porter bopped along on congas. "Romeo" was also Waits' first foray into Hispanic LA, surprising when you consider his early experiences in Mexico. This was low-rider country, the lyrics semi-rapped as Waits laid out his fatal tale of *pachuco* machismo.

Romeo was one of several characters to die on *Blue Valentine*. Violent death seemed to have become an unavoidable subject for Waits. "I'm not optimistic about things," he said. "I know this girl who had her arms cut off. It's getting very sick out there." Vulnerable young women were a particular preoccupation on the album. Both "$29.00" and "A Sweet Little Bullet from a Pretty Blue Gun" concerned girls who headed to LA with their heads full of movie-star dreams, only to be lured into prostitution by pimps in souped-up automobiles. "I've just developed a more and more grim attitude," Waits said. "I can't write about '*Dear baby I love you and everything's gonna be alright 'cause we're gonna get married*.' It's presented problems in my personal life as well." "Sweet Little Bullet", a Dr John-esque strut powered by Earl Palmer and his New Orleans brethren, was based on the suicide of a fifteen-year-old who'd leapt to her death from a seventeenth-floor window on Hollywood Boulevard.

"$29.00" was eight minutes of urban blues, with George Duke and sidemen sounding like the house band in a dingy South Central club. The result was a masterpiece of early-hours sleaze, born one night at the Tropicana when Waits' pimp neighbour was being harangued by one of his girls. "[She'd] had her dress ripped by a trick and she wanted him to reimburse her for the dress and the dress cost $29," Waits recalled. "So I heard '$29' for an hour and I was trying to watch *Twilight Zone*."

Featuring the Hughart/Vicari/White group, with Charles Kynard on organ and Ray Crawford on guitar, "Wrong Side of the Road" took another leaf out of the Dr John manual. Half hoodoo instruction manual, half an account of Waits' wild romance with Rickie Lee, "Wrong Side" was sleazy blues-funk that picked up from "$29.00" without missing a beat. "Whistlin' Past the Graveyard" was closer to the Robins' "Riot in Cell Block No. 9" than to Professor Longhair. More radical musically was "Red Shoes by the Drugstore". With its electric bass, guitar flicks, shimmering electric piano, and rolling toms, it was more urban and contemporary than anything we'd heard from Waits before. The lyrics were magnificent, moreover, as if the new genre setting had focused and tightened his writing.

Waits didn't entirely abandon piano and strings on *Blue Valentine*. For the third album in a row he kicked off with a glorious schmaltzfest, this time in the form of *West Side Story*'s immortal "Somewhere". A favourite of Rickie Lee Jones', the Bernstein–Sondheim ballad was street-corner *liebestod*, the ultimate song of longing for a better place in the midst of stress and violence. "Tom said, 'I've always wanted to sing that song,'" remembers Bob Alcivar, whose sweeping strings on the track would melt the stoniest heart. "I said, 'How are we going to do it?' He said, 'Why don't you pretend I'm Frank Sinatra and write what Nelson Riddle would write?' And it was perfect." Waits used at least two voices for the song. One moment he gave us an airy, wistful tenor reaching for bel canto, the next he was Louis Armstrong. This was the yin and yang of Waits' music, with "Somewhere" the syrup to the salt of "Red Shoes" and "Romeo Is Bleeding".

Still more lushly sentimental was "Kentucky Avenue", the great song of Waits' childhood. One of his most unashamedly emotional outpourings, it mourned lost innocence with a compassion few other songwriters have ever attempted, let alone achieved. This wasn't *The Waltons* – the lyric was full of wanton violence and vandalism – but as the song reached its climax, the love in Waits' voice, heaved from his memory, was almost too much to bear. "It still brings tears to my eyes," says Bones Howe. "I fought him for the cellos, and in the end he relented. There's another version of him doing it just sitting at a piano, but it just doesn't have the power or the emotional feel."

Waits later felt he'd given away too much in the song, letting the mask slip too far. Indeed, he became increasingly uneasy about anything too cloying. "Once I left town and they'd added strings and chick singers and all this," he told me. "I was like, 'I don't like that. Let's just do it so it's done.' Bones had a background in jazz, and he'd done a lot of records like that anyway, but it was like MSG – enough already, enough with the corn starch."

Two other tracks on *Blue Valentine* served as bridges between the twin poles of the sentimental and the hard-edged Waits. "Christmas Card from a Hooker in Minneapolis" found him back at the keyboard but with George Duke for company, tinkling bluesily away on a Yamaha electric grand. The song was one of Waits' great inhabitations: he really got inside the battered soul of this woman who'd stumbled from the pages of Bukowski. The epistolary self-deception was a kind of unreliable narration, redeemed by such touching details as the reference to "that record of Little Anthony and the Imperials". This was no lush life, this was heroin and jail time. Under the surface sentimentality we heard the hard edge of self-destruction. And we never even found out if Charlie got the letter.

The last song, the not-quite-title track that was "Blue Valentines", was a throwback to Waits in late-night blue-note mode. "Muriel" *sans* piano – with Waits accompanying himself on guitar – the track could be another dry run for the music from *One from the Heart*.

After the last session on 26 August, Waits felt he'd finally laid his own stereotype to rest. "I'm really getting a little tired of being referred to as Wino Man," he said. "It was okay for a while, but I'd like to be a little more three-dimensional." He said the typecasting had been both a blessing and a curse. "It's important to have an image and a signature and all that," he remarked. "But from there I want to build and show some other sides of me."

No one could have guessed just how many sides Tom Waits would turn out to have.

Chapter 7

Ready to Scream

> *"The road ain't what it used to be, kid . . . bad*
> *food and everything looks the same."*
>
> (Waits as Al Silk in *Candy Mountain*, 1987)

Suffering from a bad cold, Rickie Lee Jones sits in a darkened suite in London's plush Connaught Hotel. Suddenly she lets rip with a piercing little-girl shriek: "*I don't wanna talk any-more!!!*" Then she laughs to let me know it's nothing personal. It's just that she's barely set foot outside the hotel in three days.

Jones is in town to tout *Pop Pop*, a 1991 album of cover versions. Mainly the songs are old Tin Pan Alley selections – "My One and Only Love", "Bye Bye Blackbird", "The Second Time Around" – that make the interpretations of Jimi Hendrix's "Up from the Skies" and Jefferson Airplane's "Comin' back to Me" stick out like psychedelic sore thumbs. Unlike *Girl at Her Volcano*, the stunning live mini-album she made in 1983, *Pop Pop* is not a vehicle for the kind of bravura treatments Jones accorded "Lush Life", "My Funny Valentine", and Tom Waits' tender "Rainbow Sleeves". Accompanied for the most part by acoustic nylon-string guitar and standup bass, the songs are performed in a decidedly low-key, even occasionally *off*-key style that's clearly disconcerted many of the album's reviewers. "I picked songs that were less dramatic, less suicidal in their texts," she tells me. "And then I sang them in a more remote style, a style that was more sensual than emotional. The overall theme was tenderness instead of sadness, and it made it all a little new for me."

Sniffling in the darkness, Jones is endearingly direct. "What's your name?" she asks suddenly. When she sees me chewing a fingernail, I receive a swift admonishment. "Don't bite your nails," she counsels. "Don't bite your skin." We talk for a while about the highs and lows of her career; of her friendships (or otherwise) with fellow musicians. "You have to go out to make friends," she says, "and I'm not comfortable enough with people to sit with them for very long." On the matter of her career Jones is equally sanguine. "When you're really successful in pop music, disaster is always around the corner," she states cheerily. "How long can you maintain that, and what will it mean if you don't? You make enough money to keep going, and you're famous among people you'd like to know you. The negative side is that sometimes you feel misunderstood; you feel the record company doesn't even *think* of trying to sell you to people outside the core of those who already like you."

At the end of the interview I choose my moment and inform Jones that I'm planning a book about her old beau. A frosty look crosses her face as she matter-of-factly declares it's her policy never to talk about Tom Waits or their relationship. It's a stance she's pretty much stuck to since we spoke that day. "It's like, 'Isn't there anything else here you want to know?'" she said crossly in 2003. "I knew that guy for a year twenty-four years ago, and they're still asking me about it." On the one hand it's insulting for a female artist to find herself appraised only in the context of her relationships with men; on the other it's in any case a relationship where the myths have long outstripped any reality. "[Waits] said something nice," Jones told the *Guardian*. "[He said] maybe the reason people are so obsessed with this . . . maybe it wasn't a great love affair, maybe it's just all mythology, just part of their pop thing. I guess I would only have my heart hurt if I thought

"Maybe it's just all mythology . . ." With Rickie Lee at Shangri-La, June 1979. (*Jenny Lens*)

they're asking me but they're not asking him. Because then it feels disrespectful. Then I thought, he's so scary they wouldn't dare ask him!"

When Jones showed up for Waits' *Blue Valentine* cover shoot in early September 1978, she was flying high on the news that she'd just been signed to Warner Brothers Records by the label's head of A&R, Lenny Waronker. "I remember I went to the shoot and Tom introduced me to her," says Bones Howe. "She said, 'I just got a contract with Warner Brothers!' I said, 'That's wonderful. Lenny's a great guy and you'll have a good time.' And I thought to myself, 'There's another singer-songwriter shot through the breeze.'" How wrong he was.

Using photographer Elliot Gilbert, Waits staged the shoot in a twenty-four-hour gas station. Jones vamped it up in a red jacket, Waits pinning her against the bonnet of the customized 1964 Thunderbird he'd bought to replace his beloved black Cadillac. The pictures of the couple, with Chuck E. Weiss hovering in the background, were as theatrical as they were sexy: Waits as Clyde to Jones' Bonnie, curly locks piled high over his unshaven face, arms skinny and tattooed; Jones clinging to her bad-boy lover, shooting a look at Gilbert's camera that said, "Hands off, he's mine."

With the album completed, Waits prepared once again to hit the road. Interviewed at the Tropicana, he described how he'd just had four years of clutter cleared from his kitchen so he could get to his refrigerator. The prospect of touring again was clearly depressing him. "To go on the road for eight months and lean on a lamppost and play the town drunk . . . well, it's limiting," he sighed. To promote *Blue Valentine* he assembled a new touring group. Replacing Frank Vicari was Herb Hardesty, who, in addition to playing tenor sax, was a dab hand on the trumpet and flugelhorn. There was a fellow New Orleans import in the form of John Evans "Big John" Thomassie, a bearded hulk recommended by Paul Body. "Big fat guy," Body says. "Heck of a drummer." Body also alerted Waits to twenty-five-year-old bassist Greg Cohen, native Angeleno and graduate of the California School of the Arts. "Waits auditioned us all at once, so he couldn't really tell how well each of us played individually," Cohen recalled. "He ended up hiring the whole band. At the time I was playing with a lounge band in Los Angeles, doing the schlocky pop tunes of the day, so Tom rescued me from all that." Completing the lineup was Arthur Richards, the bluesy guitarist who'd played on *The Heart of Saturday Night*.

Determined to heighten the sense of theatre in his live performances, Waits had an entire gas-station stage set – complete with spare tyres and a Super 76 petrol pump straight out of Edward Hopper's 1940 painting *Gas* – built for the tour. The Tom Waits Experience had turned into a miniature Broadway show. "We had a good time on the road," says Herb Hardesty. "All the musicians got along well, and we played to our very best standard every night. When Tom started telling his stories and singing on stage, the audience got very quiet. As soon as he finished the song, the crowd broke out in applause. It was one of the highlights of my life."

Supported by Leon Redbone, Waits once again started in the Pacific Northwest in early October before zigzagging down through northern California and then heading east to Chicago via Boulder. The road quickly took its usual toll. When he arrived in Minneapolis on 22 October, he was livid to learn that *Blue Valentine* hadn't yet made it to local record stores. "It's supposed to be coming out a week before I come into a town," he grumbled to an interviewer. "If I do a new song now, you see, no one's familiar with it, so I have to set it up."

Waits suspected the bean-counters at Elektra-Asylum now viewed him as a bad bet. On a roster that included the Eagles and Linda Ronstadt – not to mention Queen and Carly Simon – he had officially been demoted to the dubious category of Prestige Artist. "It bothers me that I work so hard at something and nobody hears it," he said in Minneapolis. His hostility towards his labelmates hadn't abated either. "I don't like them people," he said. "I don't hang out in the same places that they do. There is an inner sanctum of pathetic sort of groups out here that I find very tiresome and tedious." Increasingly jaundiced towards his LA peers, he was contemplating a move to New York. "My music is very urban," he said during a promotional stop in Manhattan. "I like LA but I enjoy going to New York, I feel very at home here . . . just hanging around."

Waits bemoaned the fact that he could no longer write when he was on tour. "I used to, because I traveled alone," he said. "Now I got the whole catastrophe – I've got a truck, bus, van and a road manager . . . and an agent and a crew, a prop man and a light man. The entire disaster." This is not the sound of a man embracing the hurly-burly of life on the road. "[There's] somebody pulling on my coat all the time," he grouched. "[I] get no sleep; different town every night. I'm a real scatterbrain out there – now I just come home to write."

Waits' spirits hardly improved when, in Valparaiso, Indiana, a man leapt on to the stage of the Bridge-Vu Theater and made off with his jacket. In its pockets were cash, credit cards, letters, and the driving licence he'd only just got back from the City of Los Angeles. But the real nadir was reached after Waits played Miami's Gusman Cultural Center on 10 November. Attempting to score cocaine in the early hours of the next morning, he found himself in a rundown apartment with a dealer who'd just been shot in the chest. "Black guy with suspenders and a terrible wound," he recalled of the "hellish" scene. "He was bleeding through the bandage . . . and we were counting out the money on a glass table . . . real gangster stuff."

The jaunt on Miami's wild side made Waits think hard about his drinking and drug use. "I'm off the sauce," he announced in New York at the end of the month. "Touring sixty cities, I gotta stay healthy." The idea of Waits not drinking – and even not smoking, which he attempted less successfully – was unfathomable to his fans. But Waits had been playing the part of "Wino Man" for so long it was starting to catch up with him.*

It was ironic, therefore, when he agreed to write a theme song for a documentary film about LA's skid row down on Fifth Street, where he'd done his early research for "Tom Traubert's Blues". Approached by Ralph Waite of *The Waltons*, he delivered "On the Nickel", one of his great lullaby-ballads. A namecheck for tragic

---

* The notion of Waits as "Wino Man" evokes something Lou Reed said to me in 1996: "I ducked behind [my] image for so long that after a while there was a real danger of it becoming just a parody thing. Even if I was trying to be serious, you didn't know whether to take it seriously or not. There'd been so much posturing that there was a real confusion between that life and real life. I was doing a tightrope act that was pretty scary no matter *where* you were viewing it from."

Grady Tuck, an eccentric and much-loved figure on the San Diego folk scene, made the song still more poignant for those in the know.

The *Blue Valentine* tour ground on into December. "This has been one long experiment in terror these last two weeks," Waits said in Dallas on 8 December. "The hardest part is no sleep and a lot of traveling." It was striking that Waits used the exact same phrase – "experiment in terror" – that he'd used of his live experiences with Frank Zappa. More often Waits was less terrified than simply irritated, especially when fans and critics complained that his live repertoire stemmed mainly from *Foreign Affairs* and *Blue Valentine*. "I decide what I'm going to play," he snapped. "I don't ask the audience. I don't have any hits. Helen Keller gets more airplay than I do . . . when I get on stage it's my radio show and I'll do whatever I want." He said that what he really wanted was to stay in one place for two months – to "do it, like, in New York, in a theater, on Broadway". He was tired of playing "beer bars . . . with bad plumbing, termites and junk all over the carpet".

Waits wound up the first leg of the tour with a homecoming show at San Diego's California Theater. Aired on KGB-FM, it gave at least *some* of his fans what they wanted in the form of songs from *Small Change* ("Jitterbug Boy", "The One that Got Away") and even *The Heart of Saturday Night* ("Depot, Depot", "New Coat of Paint"). After four sellouts at the Hartford Theater in Huntington Beach, he crawled back to the Tropicana.

At home he was restless, lamenting the fact that his natural instinct after coming off a tour was to lie around drinking beer and watching *Bonanza* or *I Love Lucy* on TV. He even made noises about quitting the motel that had been home for two and a half years. "I like it because I'm very accessible there, but sometimes that's annoying," he confessed. "I've thought about moving out but I never seem to get around to it. Where would I go? Probably another motel somewhere."

Waits' inamorata hadn't slowed down any during the three months he was away on tour. But at least Rickie Lee Jones was now at work on her debut album for Warners, who were putting all their guns behind her. Bones Howe may have figured Rickie was "just another singer-songwriter shot through the breeze", but Lenny Waronker was convinced of her talent. "She came in with massive attitude, to the point where you were kind of intimidated," he says. "She was such a unique individual." Lenny recalls her talking very little about Waits. "She was very private about the relationship," he says. "If she referred to him, it was in a very minimal way. But one thing she got from him really struck home with me. It had to do with imagination and the importance of using it. It was one of those small statements that says a lot. Something like, 'Never let anybody mess with your imagination.'"

For all that he liked to portray the relationship as an outlaw romance, Waits was himself intimidated by Jones. "I love her madly in my own way – you'll gather that our relationship wasn't exactly like Mike Todd and Elizabeth Taylor – but she scares me to death," he said. "She is much older than I am in terms of street wisdom. Sometimes she seems as ancient as dirt, and yet other times she's so like a little girl." If that sounded like an outtake

For the attention of Mr Waits: Rickie Lee writes . . .

219

from Dylan's "Just Like a Woman", Jones' streetwise recklessness certainly masked a deeper insecurity. "I think she was a lot more special than I ever knew, because I didn't think she was very pretty or smart," she said of herself in 1984. "She was real scared of everybody and everything, every staircase she walked down, every move she made, every word she said." Waits, she felt, had a confidence she would always lack. "He was always, I thought – and maybe this is because I was in love with him – much more charming than me. He could charm the socks off you. And he seemed to really be able to make friends with big wheels and do it gracefully on their level."

The songs for *Rickie Lee Jones* had come together slowly. "Easy Money" had, as planned, appeared on Lowell George's solo album, while "The Last Chance Texaco" was heard on her 1978 demo tape by a knocked-out Emmylou Harris. "Company", "After Hours", and "On Saturday Afternoons in 1963" were as delicately beautiful as any of Waits' great ballads. For Waronker the obvious choice as lead single was a song called "Chuck E's in Love", inspired by a phone call Waits had received as he and Jones slobbed around one night at the Tropicana. It was Weiss calling from Denver to say he'd been smitten by a distant cousin. When Waits uttered the immortal line, Jones instantly seized on it. (The sassy boho classic concealed a deeper grief for a friendship Jones thought she might be about to lose, revealing at the end that Weiss was in love with *her*. If that was true, it must have been a factor in the gradual dissolution of the Waits–Jones–Weiss triad.)

Recording sessions for *Rickie Lee Jones* had begun in late 1978, with Waronker and co-producer Russ Titelman recruiting a slew of studio personnel that rivalled the average Steely Dan album. Steve Gadd and Jeff Porcaro drummed, Dr John and Randy Newman guested, and Michael McDonald sang backup on "Young Blood". The only conspicuous absentee was Waits him-

self, who felt peeved as his girlfriend got the big-budget treatment at a time when Elektra-Asylum was losing interest in him.
The production – Waronker's fabled "Burbank sound" – was far
slicker than Waits' had ever been. "Rickie Lee was fairly wild,"
Titelman told me of the recordings. "But you knew you were in
the presence of something special. The sessions were spontaneous, explosive. She'd never done this before, she was just a kid
with a guitar, but she knew exactly what she wanted. At the end
of the session, we played through the album and she sat there
and asked, 'Is that *me*?'"

Lenny's hunch had been dead-on. By May, after an appearance
on *Saturday Night Live*, "Chuck E's in Love" was in the charts. By
early July it was at No. 4 and the beret-sporting, cigarillo-toting
Jones – who'd only dared to dream of the cult acclaim accorded
her boyfriend – was almost a household name. Success changed
everything, as it invariably does. On one hand it made Jones
manic; on the other it made her feel inadequate and undeserving. In a long *Rolling Stone* cover story that included an Annie
Leibovitz shot of Jones and Chuck E. Weiss at Duke's, Rickie Lee
spilled all her beans while paradoxically voicing the belief that "if
you talk to magazines . . . then you're vulnerable and it'll fuck you
every time". Jones boasted that she liked "taking *any* kind of risk"
and had "done every kind of drug you can do – STP, pot, cocaine,
everything but junk . . ." She also took interviewer Timothy
White to the Tropicana and showed him Waits' bungalow, with
the piano where he let her write. "I just thought you'd like to see
this nice, crazy little place," she giggled. "Now you've seen just
about everything in my world."

In fact, Jones was being subtly undermined by Waits. "I started
feeling more insecure as my career began," she said. "Maybe it's
the influence of other people who were more dominant, without
naming names . . ." For Waits, Rickie's "overnight success" was an
uncomfortable remake of *A Star Is Born* on the sleazier streets of

West Hollywood. Eclipsed by the attention she was getting, he was unsure how to deal with it. And as he withdrew emotionally from her, she fell into the consoling arms of heroin. "Tom didn't have as much recognition as Rickie Lee had, and he'd been around much longer," Chuck E. Weiss said. "It was the same with me. I had a bit of envy for what she achieved too. But she couldn't handle it, man."

For Weiss, "Chuck E's in Love" became more of a curse than a blessing. Being namechecked on "Jitterbug Boy" and "I Wish I Was in New Orleans" was one thing; being on America's lips was quite another level of fame. "I was honored that a friend of mine would write a song about me," he said. "But when it became such a huge hit, I wasn't as honored as before. It became less personal. I imagine it's the same for Rickie as it is for me. She's known for the song and so am I." Like Jones, Weiss felt the sadness of the change in the friendship. "It affected all three of us in a very strange way," he said. "There was a lot of emotional stuff going on with all three of us. It had to do with her success and we were all taking drugs and getting high. And that intensified the drama of it, for sure. So it was all mixed up. And we were very young. Things were never really normal again after that."*

In mid-April, Waits and band flew to Holland for a short

* Attempting to capitalize on Weiss' sudden fame, Art Fein dangled a $5,000 deal with Mercury in front of him. "Chuckie was a sometime singer but I didn't know him as a *songwriter*," Fein told me. "He would sing R&B stuff, and to no effect. He wasn't playing anywhere, it was just something he did. So when 'Chuck E's' came out, I said, 'So Chuck, are you gonna put a record out?' And he said yes, but he was doing whatever drugs he was doing and generally not being together. He said, 'I wanna do my own material,' and he went into a studio in Malibu with Dr John. They were both about equally coherent at the time." Fein recalled Weiss being carried unconscious out of Canter's Deli the night before the sessions began. *The Other Side of Town* eventually appeared in 1981 and featured "Sidekick", a duet with Rickie Lee. Said Fein, "It came out in France and it came out here too, but needless to say nobody heard it and it was too late."

European tour that took in Rotterdam, Copenhagen, Vienna, London, Dublin, Brussels, and Paris. Performances were interspersed with TV appearances and press interviews. "I'm trying to cut down on the road because everything gets run down," Waits said in Copenhagen. "Lot of traveling. No sleep. Bad food. Get tired of myself, usually want to get twelve hours of sleep and some twelve-year-old Scotch. Huh-huh. Trying to get healthy. Doing push-ups now. In the hotel room. All by myself. Feel kinda stupid. Have to do *something*."* If the bellyaching was becoming monotonous, few rock stars of the era were as honest about how debilitating it was to play nightly shows in different cities and countries. Evidently Herb Cohen had clocked his boy's state of mind, because he decided to tag along for the ride.

In Vienna on 19 April, Waits was filmed by Rudi Dolezal and Hannes Rossacher for a short documentary that incorporated live performances of "Sweet Little Bullet", "Christmas Card", and a loose-limbed take on "Shake, Rattle and Roll". "He came in from Amsterdam saying he hadn't slept all night, but he agreed on the spot to let us film him," says Rossacher. "He said he didn't want to do a proper interview but instead he wanted to tell stories." Rossacher and Dolezal drove Waits to a gas station, where he reminisced about working for Spotco's Self-Service in National City – "*One day, Spotco, I'll be leaning against a gas pump in Vienna, Austria . . .*" – before adjourning to a Greek cafe where he told a long joke about a saxophonist who moves to Rome to rekindle his musical fire, miming a horn solo in his

* The "twelve-year-old Scotch" quip almost became the title of Waits' next album. "He would call me from the road," remembers Bones Howe. "He'd wake me up in the middle of the night to make me laugh. My wife handed me the phone once and Tom said, 'I just figured out the name of the next album. *Twelve-Year-Old Scotch and Twelve-Year-Old Girls*.' And he hung up the phone."

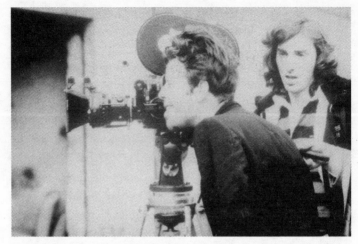

Scoping the scene with Rudi Dolezal, Vienna, April 1979. (*Hannes Rossacher*)

phlegmiest scat voice. Early the next morning they wound up in a bar where a soused Waits danced with a Thai prostitute.

At the Konzerthaus that night, Waits was out front as a showman, freed from the refuge of the piano stool as he slashed at his guitar and pulled off a jerky fusion of Mick Jagger and James Brown at the microphone. Backstage, as he prepared to encore, he paced between hangers-on, grinning like a cheeky urchin before firing up "When the Saints Go Marching In", the Dixieland anthem he was tacking on to the end of "I Wish I Was in New Orleans". Skinny and shuffling compulsively, a tie round his collarless neck, he resembled a penniless pub rocker. The can in his hand gave the lie to his claims that he'd forsaken booze. "I've been trying to give up drinking," he said in London, "but every time I stop it makes me so nervous I have to take a drink." It was a cavalier bon mot that masked the deeper reality of his alcoholism. Years later he would reflect on his drinking in this period. "When you begin, it's a man takes a drink," he said. "When you end up, it's a drink takes a man. Keeping my balance during that period was tricky. When I was in my twenties I thought I was invincible, made out of rubber. You skate along the straight razor and flirt with it all the time."

The more Waits divorced himself from the Beat verse/jazz-trio platform of his core sound, the more he dreamed of junking it altogether. "I'm trying to do an R&B album when I get home," he said in Copenhagen. "Trying to do something a little more, uh, mix-it-up." He said he had two months to write an album and "no idea of what I'm going to come up with". In London to play the Palladium, he told the *New Musical Express* he planned to do something "harder" than he'd ever attempted before, something *Blue Valentine* had only hinted at. "I think my voice is ready for it now," he stated. "I'm ready to scream . . . yeah, I really feel like screaming."*

On stage in that European fortnight you could hear Waits tapping into a hard-blues mode that suggested Howlin' Wolf via Captain Beefheart, harnessing his bourbon-soaked growl in the service of a music that rocked. "I was trying to find some new channel or breakthrough for myself," he told me. "I was still in the rhythm of making a record, going out on the road for eight months, coming home and making another record, living in hotels. And I was still with Herbie Cohen in this tight little world."

After two shows at the Palace Theatre in Paris, Waits and

---

* According to Paolo Hewitt, then of *Melody Maker*, the London Palladium show was particularly memorable for Waits' encore. The curtain closed after the set and when it reopened it had been done up like a sitting room, with Waits seated on the sofa in a white dressing gown, smoking and reading a newspaper with the TV on. "He finally looked up and asked the audience if they wanted to watch anything," Hewitt says. "It being Saturday night, the reply was '*Match of the Day*'. Of course, Waits had no idea what was being asked for, until someone shouted, 'The football!' He tried to change channels but couldn't tune in to the BBC. So instead he ambled over to the piano in his dressing gown and played the encore."

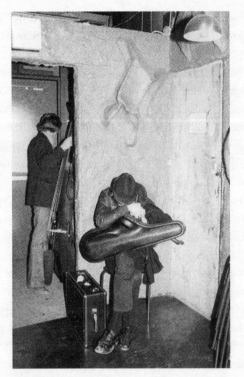

Road burnout: backstage with Greg Cohen, Copenhagen,
April 1979. (*Tom Sheehan*)

entourage flew twenty-two hours to the land of "Waltzing
Matilda". His appearance on Don Lane's chat show was a memorable introduction to the Antipodes. All itchy shuffling and bony
angles, with his pork-pie hat and cigarettes as failsafe props,
Waits happily played up to his image as showbiz hobo. Paradoxically Waits never seemed more comfortable than on chat shows,
teasing interrogators as he kept them guessing as to how real his
"act" was.

Taking in Melbourne, Sydney, Canberra, Adelaide, Brisbane,
and Perth, Waits' first Australian tour was a triumph. He would

kick off with the swingingest "Romeo Is Bleeding", cool down with "Annie's Back in Town" and a medley of "Jitterbug Boy"/ "Better Off without a Wife", and – halfway through "I Wish I Was in New Orleans" – go full-pelt into "When the Saints Go Marching In", Herb Hardesty blowing up a storm on second-line trumpet as Waits' voice resembled a blend of Dr John and Joe Cocker. A lachrymose rendition of the blues ballad "Since I Fell for You" would give way to the sinister "Red Shoes", introduced as "a little Christmas carol". He'd come out of the applause and segue into "Silent Night", itself a preface to "Christmas Card from a Hooker in Minneapolis". Romping it up again, the band would kick into a "Pasties and a G-String" ingeniously reframed as "Do the Hokey Cokey", Waits deconstructing the piece in his most demented, syllable-eliding, meta-Satchmo gurgle of a voice.

"Burma Shave" was sublime, Hardesty riffing on Gershwin's "Summertime" as Arthur Richards laid bittersweet chords over Greg Cohen's ambling bass line. Waits turned the song into a theatre piece, slouching between the petrol pumps in a smalltown-punk leather jacket and prefacing the song with the back-story of his Marysville cousin before delivering the song in a conspiratorial spoken-word whisper. Waits' stage act was now a virtual mime show of contorted gestures, with one arm raised over his head while the other's long double-jointed fingers crawled on his shoulders like a tarantula. Bent over with his eyes closed, his tousled head was lost in a shroud of cigarette smoke. The voice sounded blacker than ever.

At the piano, Waits' head lolled every which way and his chin bobbed around the microphone. Naturally in Australia he had to play "Tom Traubert's Blues", announcing that he'd "kind of borrowed your unofficial national anthem on this little thing" and tearing the guts out of its alcoholic tragicomedy. For an encore Waits delivered a long and chilling "Small Change", Hardesty wheezing around him as Tom spat out the words and even broke into a lurchingly inebriated "Hey, Big Spender". As a seventy-five-minute set it was magnificent.

Returning to LA in May, Waits glanced around his glorified Tropicana crash pad and knew it was time for a change of scenery. The fact that the Tropicana management had just painted the pool black seemed to augur ill. "That's when I said this has gone too far," he told me. "It was a pretty heavy place at times. I had a good seat at the bar and I could see everyone in the room, but I think there are other things to write about."

The scale of Rickie Lee Jones' heroin problem wasn't helping matters. Though he continued to hare around with her and Weiss, their drug use kept him at one remove. "For all the craziness he projects, Tom's a fairly normal guy," Paul Body says. "That whole sort of jazz-junkie life was never his thing and I think it might have freaked him out." In amongst the jockey-stealing escapades there were moments of danger that terrified the middle-class boy from Whittier and Chula Vista. "I found myself in some places I can't believe I made it out of alive," he confessed years later. "People with guns. People with gunshot wounds. People with heavy drug problems. People who carried guns everywhere they went, always had a gun. You live like that, you attract lower company."

The fact that Rickie Lee was now a star made little difference to her drug intake. "The record company were making such a fuss over her," Chuck E. Weiss said. "They more or less chose to ignore some of the heavy drug use that was going on. I thought that was bullshit at the time, that they wouldn't pay attention to that. As long as she kept producing the songs, it didn't matter to them. It was a harsh lesson for all of us to learn at that point." Weiss' words are themselves harsh. Both Lenny Waronker and Russ Titelman did their best to help Jones and certainly didn't ignore her problems. But there was far less understanding of addiction than there is today, when rehab has become a virtual career move.

Jones has said she was a heroin addict for two years, though it was a subsequent six months of cocaine use that ultimately brought her to her knees. Being with Waits, a man all too familiar with the effects of drugs on jazz musicians, would only have made her shame greater. "Rickie Lee's heroin problem was being gossiped about," says Louie Lista. "Chuckie was having a lot of trouble with that at the time as well. The party started becoming a little too costly. In that pre-Betty Ford era a lot of us started taking falls behind all the excess."

Waits' experiences with Jones and Weiss impacted directly on the new songs he was writing. The harsh and unforgiving world of junkies and prostitutes flowed into his music at the precise time when it was becoming harder, blacker, more grittily bluesy. *Blue Valentine* had taken Waits halfway there, but now he wanted to up the ante with a sound that spared no one. It was Howlin' Wolf in Hollywood Babylon, a brutal blues that cranked up guitar and drums and unleashed Waits' voice at its most savage and inflamed.

Exerting an influence on Waits at this time was a new and exciting wave of LA roots-rock bands emerging from the city's punk scene. In amongst such bands as the Blasters and Los Lobos, a group Waits particularly loved was Top Jimmy and the Rhythm Pigs, who held down a chaotic Monday night residency at Hollywood's Cathay de Grande club. "The Pigs were a soulful bunch," says Stephen Hodges, who drummed in Long Beach rivals the James Harman Band. "You'd go to the gig and then by the end it's going really bad because Jimmy's getting drunker and drunker. But he was a really intelligent guy and we all had some really brilliant moments with him."

Pigs guitarist Carlos "Guitarlos" Ayala recalls Waits checking out the band at the Cathay de Grande, and later hanging out and

Benefit for Top Jimmy and wife Luci, busted for possession in
Oklahoma, December 1981. (*Courtesy of Carlos Guitarlos*)

drinking with Jimmy Koncek. "He hit it off with Jimmy because
nobody else could understand him," Guitarlos says. "Jimmy had
that loser's vibe, that James Dean charisma, and I think Tom
wanted to cultivate that too." Stephen Hodges says the Pigs' style
and attitude was as important to Waits as their sound. "It was the
whole thing, because that was how *Waits* dressed," he says. "It was
the whole bowling shirt and hairspray thing." The band eventually became enough of a local legend to inspire a song on Van
Halen's 1984 album *Jump*.

One night Waits was slouched in the Ski Room when a woman
stumbled in off Sunset Boulevard, collapsed on the floor, and
cried out that she was having a heart attack. As Waits looked on
in disbelief, the bartender took one look at the distraught creature and told her to take it outside. This was a new low in Californian cold-bloodedness. Waits went back to the Tropicana and
sketched out a stark piece called "Heartattack and Vine" – "Sweet
Little Bullet" with added rage and cynicism.

Waits planned to call the new album *Lucky Streak* and have it ready for a fall release. But he was also continuing work on Guy Peellaert's Las Vegas book and on *Why Is the Dream So Much Sweeter than the Taste?* with Paul Hampton, projects that may have eaten into time he'd normally have channelled into his music. Further delaying recording was Waits' surprise decision to accompany Jones on part of her first European tour. Flying with her to London in late August, Waits was by her side as she played dates in Edinburgh, Amsterdam, Manchester, Birmingham, and London. Photographed before a show at the capital's Dominion Theatre, the couple were all over each other, Jones clinging to Waits like a little girl on her dad's lap. But Waits knew the relationship wasn't right, wasn't healthy: within weeks of returning home he had broken up with her.

"I think one of the reasons Tom backed off Rickie Lee was the heroin factor," says Robert Marchese. But it wasn't only heroin that made him pull back from her. Jones' underlying dependency was not ultimately what Waits needed in a woman, and years later Jones came to understand that. "I think Tom had his feet on the ground much more than me," she said. "He was making himself up, but he didn't have so much trouble in his background as I did."

The loss of Waits devastated Jones, who holed up with her habit in a suite at the swanky Chateau Marmont and began a six-month slide into cocaine psychosis. "It's an evil, evil drug," she said. "It's the best argument for the idea of a devil, because it opens the door to the worst parts of the human spirit and mind." Gradually Jones pulled herself together, pouring her pain into one of pop's great breakup albums. Musically a fusion of Steely Dan's *Aja* and Joni Mitchell's majestic *Court and Spark*, 1981's *Pirates* was a testament to overpowering grief, perfectly described by *Rolling Stone*'s Stephen Holden as "explosively passionate and exhilaratingly eccentric". "*I think you picked this up in Mexico from your dad*," she sang on "We Belong Together", dispelling any doubt as to who she was singing about. In "A Lucky Guy" she foolishly told Waits she loved him, her girlish soprano only underscoring the sense of unrequited adoration. "Living It Up" told the tale of the Waits–Weiss–Jones triad, casting them as Louie, Eddie, and Zero. On the sublime "Traces of the Western Slopes" she sang of the extremes of grief.

"The western slopes was a phrase my friend from Denver used to use to refer to whacked-out people," Jones said in 2001. "'She's off on the western slope,' he might say. So did I ever find the western slopes? I came back with maps. I left a trail of bread. I made a poster for the tourist board." When Jones came to Britain to promote *Pirates*, she was "somewhat worse for wear", according to interviewer Paolo Hewitt. "About five minutes into the interview, in a room on the fourteenth floor, she pointed at the window and said people kept walking past and looking in at her." If that isn't cocaine psychosis I don't know what it is.

Jones still hadn't gotten over Waits in 1983, when she released the part-live mini-album *Girl at Her Volcano*, complete with versions of Rodgers and Hart's "My Funny Valentine", Billy Strayhorn's "Lush Life", and June Christy's signature ballad "Something Cool" that were as agonizingly vulnerable as Billie Holiday at her most broken. The choice of "Rainbow Sleeves", an exquisite if shamelessly sentimental ballad Waits had written for Bette Midler, seemed almost masochistic.

Waits' breakup with Jones was symptomatic of a more general desire for change on his part. He was tired of playing "Tom Waits" for people who couldn't see the true depths of his music, who wanted jokes from a performing seal. In late September, shortly before setting off on tour, he finally moved out of his Tropicana bungalow and into a quiet East Hollywood neighbourhood close to his father. "It got a little too aggravating for me," he said of the Trop. "So I left and I now live on Crenshaw Boulevard. No one will ever find me, it's a long street."

By the end of October, Waits felt he was "poised on the threshold of some sort of a new direction". He said he was "getting a little tired of growling and scratching the back of my neck". His deepest dread was of sinking into a rut. When I first met him in 1985, he looked back on this watershed period of his career and compared the compromises he'd made to those made by politicians. "Something compels you to be popular," he said. "Seems like the politics of music do to a lot of musicians the same thing as politics do to a guy when he finally gets into office – he sells all his ideas to get there." For Waits, creative stagnation was bound up with everything else negative in his life, not least his drinking. On some level he understood that alcohol was part of his act, trapping him in a role he no longer wanted to play. "Most of us expect artists to do irresponsible things, to be out of control," he said in 1999. "Somehow we believe that if you're way down there, you're going to bring something back up for us, and we won't have to make the trip." Sadly, as the example of Amy Winehouse can attest, this seems to be a lesson each musical generation has to learn for itself.

As Waits approached thirty that December, he was concerned enough about his health to quit smoking (again) and "ration" his drinking (again). "As I turn the corner on 30 I'm fastly becoming concerned about personal hygiene," he said. "Drinking and smoking and smoking and drinking started slowing me down." He even alluded for the first time to the possibility of one day starting a family. He said he hadn't found Ms. Right but would "take a white girl, about five-two with big tits and bad teeth". He pointedly refused to answer questions about Rickie Lee Jones.

David McGee became aware of Waits' desire for a family when he played New York's Beacon Theater again at the beginning of November. Visiting McGee and his wife, Waits took a great shine to their one-year-old son Travis, dandling him on his knee as he played the piano in their Hell's Kitchen apartment. "Looking back on those years I can see the metamorphosis in Tom taking shape," McGee reflects. "I can only surmise that in my stable home, with a wife and a young son, he found a sanctuary he didn't have anywhere else in New York and dearly wanted in his own life."

For the first time since his 1973 debut, Waits hadn't released a new album for over a year. The Paul Hampton project was fizzling out and the Peellaert book looked to be heading the same way. (In the end Peellaert gave up on Waits, instead commissioning Michael Herr to write the text. It eventually appeared, as *The Big Room*, in 1986.) Stallone's *Paradise Alley* had opened in September with most of Waits' cameo cut out of it. The relationship with Rickie Lee had failed, or had proved to be a kind of *amour fou*. He'd moved out of the Tropicana, effectively putting a distance between himself and his best friend Chuck E. Weiss – a man who very obviously *was* stuck in a rut. Waits was so disillusioned that he was close to jacking music in altogether.

Asked in 1992 whether he'd ever contemplated suicide, Waits admitted he'd thought about it. "For people who are very depressed, thoughts about suicide are like erotic thoughts," he said. "These are the thoughts you toy with that make you very excited. But . . . if I had really been thinking about it, it already would have happened." As Christmas loomed, Waits felt a deeper loneliness than he'd ever known. "I've tried all kinds and nothing works," he'd joked of women the previous year. "I may have to settle for livestock, like my first meaningful experience." He added that he generally ended up "making the scene with a magazine", a phrase he'd used three years before on *Nighthawks at the Diner*. "I've got a subscription to the Frederick's of Hollywood's catalogue," he said. "I used to jack off to *Vogue*, but now it takes a little more. I occasionally read *Hustler*. They show photographs of the ovaries themselves."

The onanistic jokes masked Waits' longing for love. While

facetiously he claimed he wanted to "adopt a bunch of Mexicans and live out in Pico Rivera and watch a black and white TV set with a T-shirt on and a beer in one hand and dogshit on the lawn", like many a child of divorced parents he wanted to heal the wound inside by recreating the family. "As much as he surrounded himself with people, Tom in some ways was a lonely guy," maintains Bones Howe. "He spent a lot of time alone, writing. He did value the fact that he could be off by himself and write and explore people and all of that that he was very good at, but also I think that he was a guy who longed for closer friendships and family."

With the approach of the eighties, Waits made the decision to move to New York. As a personal sendoff to La-la Land he agreed to accompany Chuck E. Weiss to a New Year's Eve party at the Troupers' Hall on La Brea Avenue. It was the second annual event promoted by Pumpin' Piano Productions, spearheaded by Art Fein, and featured R&B legend Roy Brown, Pee Wee Crayton, and sax legend Lee Allen. "Each year they'd resurrect some relic from the fifties," remembers Paul Body. "It was the hippest party around, man."

Waits and Weiss rolled up at the hall, bought tickets, and proceeded to get royally wrecked. To Waits' mild amusement, part of the evening's entertainment was a "Beatnik Poetry Contest", with people reading to the accompaniment of a female bongo player. "I was moved to participate by reading a poem about the death of Louis Armstrong," recalls writer Tom Nolan. "I didn't win the audience applause contest but Waits came up afterwards and hugged me. And I thought, 'Well, I think I'm gonna retire as a poet now.'"

Waits saw old faces at the party and took the opportunity to say goodbye to friends. Joking that he was moving to New York "for the shoes", he told Paul Body and others that he'd stay in touch. As Art Fein strolled on stage to announce the raffle-ticket winner of a 1962 Cadillac bought that afternoon for $200, Waits was suddenly introduced to a pretty blonde dressed all in black. "It was love at first sight, no question of it," he recalled. "I was leaving town the next day going to New York, never to return. But never say never." Barely catching more than the girl's name – Kathleen – Waits slunk off into the bowels of the party, listened to Roy Brown belting out "Good Rockin' Tonight", and at some point left the party with a female friend on whose floor he crashed as the new decade commenced. "On New Year's morning I woke up and my best friend had puked in my kitchen," says Michael Hacker, who lived across the hall from the woman in question. "I was standing in my doorway and the first voice I heard in the new decade was Waits."

That night, three thousand miles away, Waits checked into the Chelsea, which he intended to be his temporary base in Manhattan. "I just needed a new urban landscape," he said on 28 January. "I've always wanted to live here. It's a good working atmosphere for me. So I packed up three suitcases and took off. Once I get located I'll go back to LA and get the rest of my stuff." Within a month he had found a $600-a-month apartment on West 26th Street with windows that overlooked Eighth Avenue. A stone's throw from Macy's department store, Waits was right in the noisy heart of what he called "a fascinating urban landscape".

Anyone au fait with recovery from alcoholism or addiction will have worked out that Waits' city-swap was essentially a "geographical", defined as the fantasy of removing oneself from Place A in the hope of feeling different in Place B. For four months he made a valiant effort to start again in a city that in some ways seemed a more appropriate environment for him than Los Angeles. He even went to the unprecedented lengths of seeing a psychiatrist, a Dr David Feuer, and joining a fitness class at the McBurney YMCA. One morning, however, he found himself running down the street to work out, a drink in one hand and a cigarette in the other. "The glass . . . [had] some aluminum foil over it so it wouldn't spill," he recalled in 1999. "I realized I was kind of coming apart." His drinking seemed to increase in proportion to his frustration at not being able to find a new channel. "You're like a wound-up toy car who's hit a wall and you just keep hitting it," he said in 2004. "I was very self-destructive. Drinking and smoking and staying out all night long, and it wasn't good for me so I sounded like I'd been screaming into a pillow. You know, I needed to shift gears – I knew that I wanted to change but I didn't really know how to do it."

Among the new projects Waits contemplated was an idea for a Broadway musical based on Thornton Wilder's *Our Town*, to be written with David McGee. The concept, according to McGee, was "to take stock of New York in the seventies", with Waits suggesting they replace Wilder's Stage Manager with a grizzled newsstand vendor who comments on the action as it unfolds but also hides a dark secret – a murder – of his own. Hardened as he was to urban street life, Waits nonetheless felt like a fish out of water in Manhattan. "It's a hard city, you know?" he told me. "You have to be on your toes. When I arrived, I actually had a cab driver say to me, 'If you can make it here, you can make it anywhere, just like Frank said . . .' You have to be a little off-center because it's overwhelming."

As Waits braved the vicious winter, he thought long and hard about changes he wanted to make. Tempted to throw the baby out with the bathwater, he considered making a clean sweep of things. Rumours reached Bones Howe that Waits was recording demos with Jack Nitzsche, the irascible arranger and producer who'd worked with everyone from Phil Spector and Neil Young to Graham Parker and who was about to start work on a new album by Mink de Ville. Asked about it later in the year, Waits didn't deny that he'd met with Nitzsche. "I had some plans to explore new producers," he said. "I'd moved to New York for about five–six months, wanting to challenge myself with an entirely new environment." But he told Stephen Peeples that in the end his "very close and personal" relationship with Howe had won out over other considerations. "I decided that the change was something that had to take place inside of me and with my own musical growth," he said. "I wanted to take some dangerous chances, and I felt Bones could best accommodate me."

This was slightly disingenuous. What actually drew Waits back to California was a phone call from film director Francis Ford Coppola, then recovering from the drama and hype of his Vietnam epic *Apocalypse Now*. For his follow-up project Coppola was making a film set in Las Vegas, itself a subject Waits had thought a lot about. *One from the Heart* was intended to be an intensely stylized look at a group of intertwined love affairs in the garish desert city of neon and slot machines.

Wanting the film to be built around music, Coppola had asked his son to recommend contemporary singer-songwriters who wrote in the Tin Pan Alley idiom. When Gian-Carlo Coppola played his father his Tom Waits albums, the director flipped. "I Never Talk to Strangers", the *Foreign Affairs* duet with Bette Midler, was *exactly* how he heard the music for *One from the Heart* in his mind. "He liked the relationship between the singers, a conversation between a guy and a girl in a bar," Waits recalled. "That was the impetus for him contacting me and asking me if I was interested in writing music for his film."

Still stoked about plans for *Our Town*, David McGee took the news in his stride when Waits called to tell him about Coppola. "I don't know what to do," he told McGee plaintively. "Are you crazy?" McGee replied. "You have to go. Francis Ford Coppola called you. Go. Get out of here as fast as you can." "You think?" "And never look back. We can pick up our thing when you finish. Go. Tom, *Francis Ford Coppola* called." McGee says he can still hear how blasé Waits sounded, "though I don't think he was that way at all . . . he knew how big this was".

When Coppola flew to New York to oversee auditions for the film, he scheduled a meeting with Waits. Though Waits instantly responded to Coppola's vision and enthusiasm, he felt conflicted about the idea of the film. It was as if he was at the biggest cross-roads of his life with no idea which way to turn. On one hand he was exhilarated at the prospect of writing a movie soundtrack; on the other the film entailed revisiting a whole genre of music he'd already decided to leave behind. It was, he later admitted, a "step backwards" to return to his old milieu of "mortuary piano" and "cocktail hairdos" at the precise time he was trying to slam the door on it.

"By the time Francis asked me to write those songs, I had really decided I was going to move away from that whole lounge thing," he told me. "He said he wanted a 'lounge operetta,' and I was thinking, 'Well, you're about a couple of years too late.' All that was coming to a close for me, so I had to kind of go and bring it all back. It was like growing up and hitting the roof."

Still, Waits wasn't having much fun in New York. With wind-chill temperatures some days dropping to thirty below and con-stant fears that his tiny apartment was being burgled, his sojourn in the City That Never Slept was turning into what he remem-bered as a "prison sentence". The narrowness of Manhattan, with its giant buildings bearing down on him, made him feel claus-trophobic. Flying back to the sprawl of Los Angeles on 30 April, he was relieved to be home. "Tom was always just an LA guy to me," says Paul Body. "There was nothing New York about him. I didn't get any East Coast vibe off of him anytime."

The *One from the Heart* assignment was almost scuppered when Herb Cohen refused to yield publishing rights to Coppola. Fortunately Bones Howe, whom Coppola had hired to oversee the music, intervened to work out a compromise. "One of the things Francis wanted was to own all the music in the film," Howe says. "I had a meeting with Francis and told him I had a conflict of interest. He said, 'Well, think of someone else to do the music.' I read the script and said, 'Francis, I think you should make a deal with Tom because I think he would be perfect for this movie.' Between Herb and Francis' lawyers, they managed to make it work." In the end publishing rights were split between Cohen and Zoetrope.

By May, Waits was installed in his own wood-panelled office on the Zoetrope lot. Complete with a grand piano, a battered couch, and the usual Waits detritus of books, papers, ashtrays, and beer cans, it was little more than a tony version of his old Tropicana bungalow. But for the first time in his life Waits felt like those for-hire songwriters who'd worked to order on Tin Pan Alley. He was living in the songwriting fantasy he'd had when he'd first showed up in Los Angeles eight years before.

And then one afternoon came a soft knock at the door. Tom Waits' life was about to change for ever.

Chapter 8

Lucky Guy

> *"I will leave behind all of my clothes*
> *I wore when I was with you . . ."*
> ("Ruby's Arms", 1980)

Francis Ford Coppola was a bearded maverick of a movie director who, in Tom Waits' words, was "distrusted by all the cigar-smoking moguls" in Hollywood. He was also the latest in a long line of surrogate fathers to surface in Waits' life.

Like fellow Italian-American filmmakers Martin Scorsese and Brian De Palma, Coppola had snuck into the cinematic mainstream via the back door that was B-movies. Against the odds his mob masterpiece *The Godfather* became a defining film of the 1970s and led to the crazed psychodrama of his Vietnam epic *Apocalypse Now*. Even *that* wasn't enough for Coppola, who in 1979 decided he needed a studio of his own to realize his vision of cinema. In September of that year, he paid $6.7 million for the vacant Hollywood General studios at 1040 Las Palmas Avenue. Built in 1919, Hollywood General had produced movies featuring stars such as Mary Pickford and Mae West.

Founded by Coppola as "a studio that is civilized, pro-artistic, makes money and makes sense", Zoetrope was launched with the aim of making four films a year. Coppola's idol, the British veteran Michael Powell – who had made *The Thief of Baghdad* at Hollywood General decades before – was brought in as a senior adviser. Jean-Luc Godard, *enfant terrible* of the French *nouvelle vague,* flew in from Paris to talk about adapting Kerouac's *On the Road* – a project that naturally caught the ear of Tom Waits. "The atmosphere at Zoetrope was fantastic," says Michael Hacker, hired as a production assistant at the company's inception a year earlier. "I'd walk into the building and Gene Kelly would be walking down the hallway. And then I'd say hello to Michael Powell. And this was every morning."

Yet Zoetrope had huge problems. Saddled with debts from the swollen budget on *Apocalypse Now*, Coppola was undercapitalized from the minute he took possession of the lot. Wim Wenders' biopic of crime writer Dashiell Hammett had the plug pulled on it after ten weeks and $7 million, with Coppola ordering the German director to fire his own wife Ronee Blakely, the film's female lead. (*Hammett* was later finished without Blakely in it.)

Coppola wanted his own next film to be the antithesis of *Apocalypse Now*. *One from the Heart* was to be a light love story, set at first in Chicago and then moved to Las Vegas for added neon garishness. "I tried to tell a love story in a city that was like love itself," Coppola said. "A city of glitter one second and depression the next." He decided he wanted to make the film as a kind of musical, with a male and a female voice representing the thoughts and feelings of his characters – like Zeus and Hera looking down on the romantic struggles of foolish mortals. When the film's co-producer Fred Roos asked Michael Hacker which singers might work for the music, the young assistant suggested Van Morrison and – somewhat ironically – Rickie Lee Jones. Morrison even took a meeting with Coppola but said he loathed Las Vegas and wouldn't in any case be able to write to order. And then Gian-Carlo Coppola walked into his pop's office one afternoon with his copy of *Foreign Affairs*. Enter Tom Waits.

"Suddenly here was my old street-homey figure from Duke's on the lot," says Michael Hacker. "But nobody was making a big deal about Waits. They set him up in an office with an upright piano and he would come in and noodle around." Waits took to his new surroundings with a mixture of excitement and trepidation. "I'd never really written in an office before with wood paneling and all that," he said in 1992. Nor had he written much without alcohol in his system. The pressure to write to order – to be a craftsman who was part of a bigger team – caused minor palpitations as Waits sat at the piano staring out at the Gulf service station through his slatted blinds. "I went aaaagh, I can't do this, Jesus *Christ*," he said. "I'd sit at the piano with no ideas . . ." Recalls Henry Diltz, who photographed Waits in the office in September, "It was a little room with a grand piano and a couch and papers strewn over the floor and cigarette butts . . . it felt like the guy was just locked in there week after week." For Diltz, the room wasn't so different from the Tropicana bungalow, for all that Waits joked about its "David Niven feel".

Coppola's original concept, explained to Waits and Howe in a convivial meeting at his Napa Valley home, was to have all the music written and recorded before filming began. "I originally told [them], 'What I really want you guys to do is make an album called *One from the Heart* and then I'll make a movie that goes with it,'" he recalled in 2003. But the director kept changing his

"I'd sit at the piano with no ideas . . ." Zoetrope Studios, 1980. (*Henry Diltz*)

mind about how he wanted to intertwine the story and the music. Joe Smith, who'd put together a soundtrack for *Apocalypse Now*, claims Coppola was "the most indecisive man I have ever met". Says Michael Hacker, "Tom loved Francis but he found it all a bit chaotic and freeform. His attitude was a little bit like, 'What the hell's going *on* here?' Not caustically. Humorously. He was bemused."

In an adjoining office, thankfully, sat Bones Howe, whom Coppola hoped would become Zoetrope's head of music. "He certainly keeps my confidence up in myself, which I need a lot," Waits said of Bones. "I was so insecure when I started, I had no idea that I would be capable of writing an entire score for a major motion picture . . . I was sweating bullets." Both men observed a regular daily ritual at Zoetrope. "I'd come in at ten o'clock in the morning and there would be paperwork and budgets to deal with," Howe says. "And then Tom would come in at noon. Later he'd come back from a meeting with Francis and say he didn't think Francis really knew what he wanted for the movie."

"The Coppola mindset was always, 'Do one more,'" recalls Bob Alcivar, brought in by Bones to orchestrate the songs. "Tom got a little upset once in a while. I remember him saying, 'Well, this is a perfect song, "Candy Apple Red",' and Francis said, 'Try another one.' Tom would get a little irritated by the constant changes." Working closely with Waits, Howe, and Alcivar was Richard Beggs, a "sound sculptor" who'd been part of Coppola's setup for over a decade. "[Richard] would sit in a little room, around the clock, with a catalog of musical cues," Waits said of Beggs. "[He] was the one most responsible for getting all the music to mesh with the film."

In another office, meanwhile, sat a young Irish-American girl who'd been hired as an assistant story editor. Though Waits was ignorant of her proximity, Kathleen Patricia Brennan was the ethereal blonde he'd met at the New Year's Eve party just a few months before. "She was pretty and smart and shy," says Michael Hacker, who took Brennan to lunch one afternoon. "Sort of a nice American version of an Irish girl who wore diaphanous blouses and was very shy but extremely well-read." Brennan hadn't been in Los Angeles long; she was also the furthest thing imaginable from an LA rock chick. "I think she'd been a poetry major," he says. "My take was that she'd never been to a gig in her life." Hacker and Brennan hit it off and had further lunches together. "I remember I had Flann O'Brien's *The Third Policeman* with me and she had read or had even just read it," he recalls. "There was no music talk." In early June, Hacker was sufficiently taken with Brennan to propose a date: "She said yes but she was going up to Napa that weekend to help Francis with a reading for *One from the Heart*." When she returned a few days later, she was engaged to Tom Waits.

Hacker was astonished. Someone had suggested Brennan knock on the door of the crusty-looking character who was working on the music for *One from the Heart*. Had she seen Waits shuffling around the Zoetrope lot? Did she recall him from the party at Troupers' Hall? Did she even know who Tom Waits was? All we really know is that she knocked at the door and that, on the spot, Waits fell in love with her. "I opened the door and there she was and that was it," he said. "That was it for me. Love at first sight. Love at second sight."

"Tom came into my office the next morning," Bones Howe remembers. "He said, 'The most amazing thing happened last night. I was sitting here playing the piano and there was a knock on the door, and I opened it and there was this beautiful girl standing there. And she said, "What are you doing?" And I said, "I'm writing songs for *One from the Heart*. Who are *you*?"' He was obviously knocked off his feet."

The relationship took off like a wildfire. Several years Waits' junior, Brennan had a poise and maturity that stopped him in his tracks. But she was also capable of mischievous spontaneity. "We used to play a game called 'Let's Go Get Lost,'" Waits remembered of their early courtship. "We'd drive into a town and I would say, 'But, baby – I know this place like the back of my hand, I can't get lost.' And she'd say, 'Oh, hell you can't, turn here, now turn here. Now go back, now turn left, now go right again.' And we'd do that all night until we got lost, and she'd say, 'See, I thought you knew this town? Now you're getting somewhere, now you're lost.'" Sometimes they'd end up in the scariest parts of south-central LA, or further out in Native American neighbourhoods – places, Waits joked, where you could get shot just for wearing corduroy. "We were going into these bars – I don't know what was protecting us – but we were loaded," he recalled. "God protects drunks and fools and little children. And dogs. Jesus, we had so much fun." As a metaphor for the course their relationship would take, the story is perfect. "In the beginning, when he was still talking to me about her, I would listen and I thought it was very, very interesting," says Bones Howe. "But the relationship quickly became more and more private."

Waits had found the stabilizing, nurturing companion he'd always wanted. A kind of anti-Rickie Lee, Brennan was the product of a big Irish-American family whose warmth and closeness contrasted markedly with his – and Rickie Lee's – more fractured experience. "[Kathleen's] most important formative musical experiences took place within the Catholic church," Waits said in 2006. "Then standing at the barstool next to her father while he listened to Jim Reeves and George Jones. They were the only Irish family in an all-German town."

Waits has always paradoxically depicted Brennan as the wilder half of their relationship, possibly recognizing that his alcoholism belied not recklessness but fear. "I think I'm the conservative one of both of us," he said in 2002. "She's much more adventurous. I keep her from floating off." He is deadly serious when he claims that Kathleen Brennan saved his life. "In a good way I'm alive because of her," he told Mick Brown. "I was a mess. I was addicted. I wouldn't have made it. I really was saved at the last minute, like *deus ex machina*."

For Waits, the experience of being loved by an emotionally healthy woman was like a rebirth. With an alcoholic for a father and a church-going hausfrau for a mom, Waits' internalized parents were less than unconditionally nurturing. Brennan brought him a sense of emotional security he had never known. Meeting and falling in love with her, he said, was "really the end of a certain long period of my life".

Engaged within a week of meeting Brennan, Waits by the early summer of 1980 was deliriously happy. But he was also exasperated by *One from the Heart*, never really knowing what Coppola wanted for the movie. "I got in a humbug over my whole thing with the picture there," he admitted. "For a brief spell I moved out of my office at Zoetrope and went and wrote a record."

The record in question was the hard-hitting album – tentatively titled *Lucky Streak* and then (with a nod to Chuck E. Weiss and Rickie Lee Jones) *White Spades* – he'd planned to make the previous summer. It was a collection that would include "On the Nickel", the blistering "Heartattack and Vine", the soppy *Foreign Affairs* holdover "Saving All My Love for You", and an instrumental track ("Breakfast in Jail") that he'd played on his late 1979 tour. (Other song titles mentioned were "Drinkin' Whiskey in Church", "Whose Sportcoat Is That?", and "Pomona Lisa".) Elektra-Asylum was owed an album and it was time to deliver it.

To flesh out the record, Waits set himself the task of writing a song a day – or rather a night. Moving into the old RCA building on Sunset and Ivar, spitting distance from his beloved Ivar Theater, he took fragments of works in progress and ground out gritty R&B-based numbers ("Downtown", "Mr Siegal", "'Til the

Money Runs Out") and deathless love songs ("Jersey Girl", "Ruby's Arms"). "I just wanted to stay there because I was writing about one tune ahead of Bones every day," he said. "I was writing each night and every day so when the band got there, I'd have something new for everybody." Forgoing both alcohol and nicotine, Waits "tried to arrive at some level of personal hygiene . . . to clean myself up a little". How much that had to do with Kathleen we can only guess.

Commencing on 16 June, Waits went into Filmways/Heider Recording with a core rhythm section of Big John Thomassie (drums) and Canned Heat veteran Larry "The Mole" Taylor (bass), augmented by *Blue Valentine* guitarist Roland Bautista and New Orleans legend Ronnie Barron on greasy Hammond organ. This unit bashed out the five R&B tracks – with "Breakfast in Jail" retitled "In Shades" and credited to "The Tom Waits Band" – and outtakes "Cad-Mag" and "Baby It's Wrong". On 23

Heartattack and Vine sessions, Filmways/Heider Recording, July 1980. (*Geoff Howe*)

June, he returned to Heider's with a slightly reshuffled ensemble – and an orchestra – to cut the quieter pieces.

Bones Howe offered unconditional support. "I know Tom wanted to change," he says. "Every time he did something he wanted it to be a little different from what he'd done before." With Waits champing at the bit, Bones took more of a backseat role in the sessions. "I remember coming back from Francis' winery when we were doing pre-production on *One from the Heart* and doing *Heartattack*," he says. "I said, 'Hey, my job is to suggest but you have the last call on these things.'" Yet Waits also said that on both *Heartattack and Vine* and *Blue Valentine* he was "kind of rebelling against this established way of recording that I'd developed with Bones".

Whenever I hear "Heartattack and Vine" – one of Waits' indisputable masterpieces – I'm reminded of arriving for the first time in downtown LA and then being dumped by a bus at the intersection of Hollywood and Cahuenga Boulevards. It was June 1978 and I alighted with my friend Christian in this scuzzy 'hood that didn't resemble any Hollywood *I'd* ever imagined, knowing no better than to wander up Cahuenga and check into the first motel we could find: the lovely Hollywood 8, where we were swiftly befriended by a crew of feral street creatures who sold us mind-shredding grass and later relieved us of our traveller's cheques before absconding, the lot of them, into the dark warm narcotic American night.

Cahuenga Boulevard got a namecheck on "Heartattack", Waits advising us it was better to stay in Iowa than to wind up "crawling down" said thoroughfare on broken legs. The song picked up where he left off on "Sweet Little Bullet from a Pretty Blue Gun", but this time Waits went for the jugular. "The subject matter I was dealing with was caustic enough to require an ensemble that perhaps sounded a little more jagged," Waits said. "It's not Mahogany Rush, but it's the best I can do." From the distorted chords that open the track it was clear we weren't looking for the heart of Saturday night anymore. There was no Philip Marlowe noir romanticism here, no friendly ladies of the night. The voice of the song was that of a sociopathic predator who bet the little girl from New Jersey was still a virgin but it was only 8.35 p.m. The singing was bestial as only Howlin' Wolf knew how to snarl – a corrosive yowl, the sound of a man slurping Sterno and inhaling dimestore cigars. The instrumentation was South Side minimalist: the guitar savage, Wolf's Memphis mainman Willie Johnson via Keith Richards, the bass notes hard and stubby, and the snare brutally thudding. This was the Wolf Man via Beefheart, haunting the junkie side-streets of Hollywood Babylon. For Waits there was no devil, just God on a bender. As a personal theology it didn't get much more nihilistic.*

"It was me trying to avoid using a knife and a fork and a spoon," Waits said. "It wasn't 100 per cent successful but it's usually the small breakthroughs that give you a tunnel to laterally make some kind of transition. The title track was a breakthrough for me, using that kind of Yardbirds fuzz guitar, having the drummer use sticks instead of brushes, and small things like that. More or less putting on a different costume."

"In Shades" was how we came down from "Heartattack", a chance to catch the breath and digest the visceral shock of that opening salvo. A sleazy lounge-blues instrumental that revisited the ambience of "$29.00", it was little more than half-assedly funky background music to order drinks to – you could even

---

* Of the line ". . . God when he's drunk", Waits told Ian Penman of the following inspiration: "I was just sitting on the toilet, and there was this spider web in the corner, and I lit a match and a cigarette, and I held the match up to the spider and the spider started crawling up the web. So I got the match closer. I opened up a can of beer, drank the beer, tried to decide whether I should burn the spider off his web or let him go on his way . . . I figured there must be somebody like that up there: has a couple of cocktails every now and then and there's trouble on Times Square."

hear the patrons chatting and clinking glasses. The one real high spot in the track was Ronnie Barron (no stranger to addiction himself) taking off on the organ. Right at the end, after two fake endings, we heard the tentative debut of Waits' gospel scream, as utilized on such future outings as "Jesus Gonna Be Here".

It was back to sentimental basics for "Saving All My Love for You", with the tubular bells of "Potter's Field" making a re-appearance courtesy of sessionman Victor Feldman. Bob Alcivar orchestrated and Jim Hughart took a final bow as a Waits side-man on upright bass. Though Waits later pooh-poohed this song – Kathleen apparently thought it corny – it was one of his heavenliest melodies. You could really see/feel/smell the empty pre-dawn street he described on what was effectively a reworking of Randy Newman's "Marie" – a song that broadly said, "I may be a whoring slob and loser but I do genuinely love you."

There is no other Waits album on which his musical personal-ity is more split than *Heartattack and Vine*. We come straight out of "Saving . . ." into the thump and noxious swirl of "Downtown", a slice of noir that drags us down to LA's Temple Street amidst the lowlife detritus of stolen-goods fencers and sexual deviants. Arguably the album's least distinguished R&B track, once again it is a showcase for the whirring organ of Mr Barron.

If "Jersey Girl" wasn't written as a Bruce Springsteen pastiche, it should have been. It was certainly a self-conscious homage to the East Coast pop tradition that Springsteen drew on – the her-itage of doo-wop and street-corner vocal groups like Dion and the Belmonts. "I never thought I would catch myself saying 'sha-la-la' in a song," Waits confessed. "This is my first experiment with 'sha-la-la.' It has one of them kind of Drifters feels. Lyrically I tried to do it straight ahead, a guy walking down the street to see his girl." Musically a slow-dance mix of Ben E. King's "Span-ish Harlem", Bang-period Van Morrison, and Springsteen's blue-collar Asbury Park rock, the song was a pure effusion of love for

Kathleen, whose family had moved from Johnsburg, Illinois, to Morristown, New Jersey, when she was a teenager.* The following summer, a terrified Waits joined Springsteen on stage at LA's vast Sports Arena and sang the song with him. "I've done all I can for him," Waits said in 1985. "He's on his own now."

For the song's string arrangement, Waits decided to recruit an old friend. Jerry Yester hadn't worked with – had in fact barely *seen* – Waits since *Small Change* and was amazed by the changed man he found in the studio that July. "Overnight, the skid-row guy was gone and he became his new character," Yester says. "It wasn't like he was a schizophrenic or multiple personality – he just *was his art* at the time. And his art became a lot healthier. One day he said, 'This is gonna kill me,' so he stopped it on a dime. He was no longer the scruffy guy, he was almost dapper. But very hip. And everybody breathed a sigh of relief."

When Waits heard Yester's arrangement for "Jersey Girl", however, he hated it. "He wanted it to sound like but not be obviously influenced by Springsteen," Jerry recalls. "He was doing it live with the strings and the band. And there was glockenspiel, which was my little nod to Bruce and Phil Spector, but it didn't become the grand thing Tom wanted it to be. And when it didn't become that, he was just very frustrated. He said, 'Ah, I don't like it at all, man. It sucks.' And that was the end of the evening for me." The next day, Waits came by Yester's house and apologized.

Turning the original vinyl album over, we were straight back in Sleaze City with the pimps and dealers of "'Til the Money Runs Out". The "pointed man" of the last verse was Waits himself – the moniker Paul Body bestowed on Tom when he acquired his first pair of cool shoes. A funky R&B mambo with a *Blues Brothers* groove and a doubled bass/guitar riff right out of "Peter

---

* "All the great things that came out of New Jersey don't hold a candle to Kathleen Brennan, at least not in Tom's eyes . . ." (Bob Dylan, Theme Time Radio Hour, first broadcast 13 September 2006).

Gunn" or "Brand New Cadillac", "'Til the Money" was close kin to "Downtown" but a pale echo of "Heartattack and Vine".

The yin-and-yang continued with "On the Nickel", the song Waits had written for Ralph Waite's 1979 film of that name. Brimful of compassion for the drunks of downtown LA, the track was as tender as "Kentucky Avenue". With Michael Lang's piano and Bob Alcivar's heartbreak strings, the song stands as one of Waits' last great lullabies and close in mood to what he was writing for *One from the Heart*.*

With "Mr Siegal" we were once again propelled out of tenderness and back into the amoral dog-eat-dog world of "Heartattack and Vine". Though (Bugsy) Siegal was an infamous Vegas mobster, the album's penultimate track was the most consciously New Orleans-infused song Waits ever wrote, with Ronnie Barron's piano straight from the Allen Toussaint/Dr John school and almost Randy Newman-ish in its loping funk. For all the stylistic distance Waits had long kept from his Warner-Reprise/Elektra-Asylum contemporaries, here he finally got to sound like some kind of composite of Newman/Cooder/Raitt and Dr John/Lowell George, the track's thuddy rhythm section closer to Lenny Waronker's "Burbank Sound" than anything Waits had done or would do again.

To sign off on *Heartattack* – and effectively to wrap up his eight-year stint on Asylum Records – Waits opted to close with an extraordinarily moving ballad. Whether he intended it as such or not, "Ruby's Arms" was a song of closure and healing – at the very least a gesture of concern for Rickie Lee Jones. Starting

---

* Interestingly, "On the Nickel" echoed Cindy Williams' tender remarks about an unconscious park-bench bum in Coppola's conspiracy thriller *The Conversation* (1974): "I always think that he was once somebody's baby boy, and he had a mother and a father who loved him. And now, there he is, half-dead on a park bench and where is his mother or his father or his uncles now? Anyway, that's what I always think."

out with Jerry Yester's mournful horns – imagine the Grime-thorpe Colliery Band playing "The Night They Drove Old Dixie Down" – the song said goodbye not just to the girl whose heart he'd broken but arguably to the whole persona and lifestyle of the decade just passed. Like the protagonist of Jimmy Webb's "By the Time I Get to Phoenix" – and almost like a reverse version of the callow youth in "Ol' '55" – the Waits of "Ruby's Arms" stole out into the dawn, grabbing only his jacket and boots (and "the scarf off of your clothesline") as he left forever. "*You'll find another soldier*," he promised in a voice that was almost oratorical. The Australian group Frente!, who covered it in 1995, called it "the saddest song ever written".

On the soiled newspaper that was *Heartattack*'s cover, Waits resembled nothing so much as a feverish James Chance, whose postpunk-funk band the Contortions he said Kathleen had introduced him to. Scrawled at the top with a fake Manhattan phone number was the name of "David 'Doc' Feuer", the psychiatrist Waits had visited during his four bleak months in the Big Apple.*

Released in September, *Heartattack and Vine* repeated the feat of *Small Change* by sneaking into the Top 100 album chart. It bettered *Foreign Affairs* and *Blue Valentine* but not enough to impress the bean-counters at Elektra-Asylum. Waits' old *Rolling Stone* champion Stephen Holden gave it three and a half stars, noting that the singer's "woozy, far-out optimism" had "never seemed fresher". For me, *Heartattack* remains one of Waits' pinnacle achievements, a magnificent blend of bitter and sweet, savage and soothing, and as good as any album he would make in the ensuing twenty-five years.

Waits now felt a whole lot better about going back to work on *One from the Heart*. For one thing, he didn't immediately have to

---

* Years later, Feuer contributed an essay titled "Confessions of a Middle-Aged Ecstasy Eater" to *Granta* magazine.

hit the road to promote a new album. "I came right off of the album back into this office," he said on 4 September. "This is a whole other world for me."

First, though, there was something he needed to take care of. At midnight on 10 August he paged the Right Reverend Donald W. Washington, pastor of the twenty-four-hour "Always Forever Yours Wedding Chapel" on Manchester Boulevard in Watts; an hour later, he and Kathleen were married. "My wife had fifty bucks on her and I had twenty," Waits recalled of the service. "She thought this was not a good way to start. But you know, it worked out. Sometimes really expensive weddings only last a couple of weeks."*

The following weekend Tom and Kathleen celebrated their nuptials with a raucous gathering at Molly Malone's on Fairfax Avenue. Everybody from Bones Howe and Herb Cohen to Jerry Yester and Michael Hacker to Bobi Thomas and Francis Thumm showed up. Greg Cohen got talking with Kathleen's sister Marguerite, an artist and potter, and two years later they too would marry. Waits, says Yester, was "just the happiest I'd ever seen him". The marriage reminded him of "a good version" of the ending to *Sunset Boulevard*: "Kathleen was kind of like the girl in that movie working in the script department." But it was also the first and last time Yester ever met Brennan. "It was kind of the end of an era in terms of Tom and me," he says.

Marital matters continued in a Celtic vein when Waits and wife flew to Ireland for their honeymoon. Here they spent two weeks in a cottage in Tralee, County Kerry – all "dogs, children, blackbirds, and clothesline", as Tom described it – in the beautiful southwest of the country. "We get over there every now and then," Waits said of Ireland in 2004. "She comes from a big wild

---

* As a souvenir the chapel presented the Waitses with a bag containing a novel (*The Vanishing Bride*), a Tampax, two prophylactics, and some bleach – "to wash out, so you start clean as a couple", Waits explained to Jim Jarmusch.

loud Irish family, you know? There was a lot of noise at the dinner table and carrying-on and [. . .] I fell in love with the whole clan . . ." Interestingly, he found time to squeeze in an interview with Dublin's *Hot Press*, whose Dermot Stokes was struck by the couple's inseparability. "Apart from the interview and photographs," Stokes wrote, "Tom and Kathleen never seemed more than an inch apart." Waits claimed in the interview that he'd had "a hellish ten years" and was "trying to get some normalcy" into his life. As a harbinger of things to come he added that he and Kathleen had been writing "these black sonnets" together in Tralee.* "If you trust somebody creatively and they trust you," he said, "wonderful things can come out of it."

Waits' optimism was less well-founded when he breezily informed Stokes that *One from the Heart* would be finished by the time he and Kathleen returned to California, ready for him to "do all the post-scoring". In fact, the couple clocked in at Zoetrope in early September to find the production in a state of chaos. Thanks to the decision to recreate Las Vegas on the lot rather than shoot it on location, the budget was escalating daily. By the time Coppola began filming the following February, costs on art director Dean Tavoularis' vast neon-dominated sets had climbed to a staggering $10 million. What had started as a small, contained picture was swelling into an overblown spectacle of *Heaven's Gate* dimensions, with the production taking over the entire studio.

While not oblivious to the pressures and tensions at Zoetrope, Waits decided simply to focus on the job in hand. Tough as it was to return to what he called Coppola's "cocktail landscape" – "music that wasn't a little gnarled and driving" – he got to work

---

* Tralee later made an appearance in "Rain Dogs", which namechecked the nineteenth-century ballad "The Rose of Tralee". Tom and Kathleen may have been in Ireland for the annual "Rose of Tralee" competition inspired by the song.

with a new sense of discipline. "I put on a suit and tie, shaved, read the paper, had a cup of coffee and went to work along with millions of other Americans," he recalled in 1983. "[It] was good for me, it disciplined me, it made me . . . I had to sit in a little room and they'd ring me up on the phone and put memos under my door . . . it was like working in an office."

At night Tom and Kathleen drove home to their new apartment on Union Avenue, between downtown LA and MacArthur Park. "It's mainly for all the churches, dogs, and children," he said when asked why he'd chosen to live in the neighbourhood. "We live in the upstairs of an old home, and it's quiet. Now I'm feeling more that I want to . . . have a little more privacy. And, uh, being married and trying to create somehow a life for myself . . . I am trying to, uh, build more order in my life in that sense." Recalls former resident Hunter Drohojowska-Philp, "The complex of Victorian houses was owned by Planaria Plante and stood about a hundred yards north of Beverly Boulevard on the west side of Union, between a convenience store and a Filipino church that eventually bought the properties and leveled them to make a parking lot." Running parallel to Alvarado Street, Union Avenue was also adjacent to Waits' old stomping grounds of Echo Park and Silver Lake, a long way from the music community in West Hollywood and Laurel Canyon. It was an unpretentious part of LA where he had long felt comfortable.

As the pieces of the film's musical jigsaw began to fit together, Waits surrendered to the process. "Francis had this mobile home with feeds from all the cameras, and Tom just liked being around all that," says Bones Howe. "It was part of that period in his life when I think he was really caught up in the idea of the magic of the picture business." As Waits relaxed and accepted the chaos, his old notions of life as a Tin Pan Alley songsmith seemed to be coming true. Increasingly he overcame the daunting nature of the job and wrote on pure instinct, turning on

In the neighbourhood: Union Avenue. (*Art Sperl*)

streams of musical consciousness from which he could pull melodic ideas or snatches of lyrics.

Using a bulletin board on which he moved lyrics and melodic fragments around, Waits worked from his impressions of the scenes and relationships in Armyan Bernstein's original story. "The songs were supposed to be a subtext, an interior dialogue, creating a kind of lounge operetta," he said. "It was a new experience for me, because in the past I had always written songs by framing the ordinary, the commonplace and the parade of characters that I came in contact with."

As he had done three years earlier while working on *Foreign Affairs*, Waits paid regular visits to the home of Bob Alcivar.

"Tom would come over to the house, put his hands on the keyboard, and say, 'Now that's it,'" Alcivar says. "He'd say, 'I don't know what the chords are but that's the beginning of the song.' I learned a lot from this, because Tom was doing things that were out of school and had nothing to do with education or music theory. He was just doing it from the heart and soul." Alcivar worked closely with Waits on arrangements of the *One from the Heart* songs, scoring them for jazz trio or quintet, for a Basie-esque big-band sound, or symphonically for orchestra. He estimates that over the course of the following months they recorded as much as six hours of music.

The earliest material for the *One from the Heart* soundtrack was recorded in October, six months after Waits began work on the film. "Little Boy Blue" was born after Ronnie Barron and Big John Thomassie flew in from New Orleans to lay down a greasy R&B instrumental in the vein of *Heartattack and Vine*. Waits took the tape home and, stuck for a lyric, turned to a book of nursery rhymes that was lying around the house. The resulting track, motored by Greg Cohen's walking bass, lifted and adapted the famous rhyme to Waits' suitably loungey purposes. In the process its smoky Hammond feel anticipated *Swordfishtrombones*' timeless "Frank's Wild Years", which also featured Barron.

For the film's core group, however, Waits and Bones Howe assembled a team of veteran players from the glory years of West Coast jazz. An awestruck Greg Cohen, the baby of the band, found himself surrounded by such leading lights of the California "cool jazz" era as pianist Pete Jolly and (returning to the Waits fold) drummer Shelly Manne and trumpeter Jack Sheldon. Tenor-sax legend Teddy Edwards, who'd played with Waits back in 1975, had been a leading light of Central Avenue bebop in the 1940s before joining Howard Rumsey's Lighthouse All-Stars in Hermosa Beach in the following decade. "The house group was Jack and Teddy," says Bob Alcivar. "Tom said that was the sound of this movie. No matter what else was going on, there was always Jack or Teddy."

Using this group, Waits began demoing further instrumental pieces such as the "montage" of "The Tango" and "Circus Girl", the latter being his first real foray into waltz-time. "That was where this Bertolt Brecht quality of his work began to emerge, and where he began to see how much he liked that dissonant quality," says Bones Howe. "And it got more and more that way through the picture. *One from the Heart* was that magic door opening up. Francis just wanted him to be Tom Waits, and Tom was already jumping ahead a generation." Yet "Circus Girl" was essentially a deviation from the film's main musical thrust, for Coppola was still fixated with the "I Never Talk to Strangers" blueprint and clung to the hope Bette Midler would play Hera to Waits' Zeus. Midler even came into the studio to hear the early songs Waits and Alcivar had worked up. "There were a lot of early contenders for that role, like Rickie Lee Jones and Sarah Vaughan," Alcivar says. "Bette was a contender and would have been perfect for it. I realized what a perfectionist she was – she had to go over everything a thousand times. Then she announced that she couldn't do it because she was contracted to do another film."

It was Kathleen, of all people, who first floated the notion of Crystal Gayle as Waits' female counterpart on the soundtrack. On paper the idea seemed wildly off the mark. Gayle was a country-pop canary whose middle-of-the-road hits "Don't It Make My Brown Eyes Blue" and "Talking in Your Sleep" had put her high in the charts in the late seventies but certainly didn't suggest she'd be capable of torchy jazz emoting. However, Gayle's version of the Julie London classic "Cry Me a River" told a different story about the pretty girl with chestnut hair down to her waist – who happened to be the baby sister of country icon Loretta Lynn. And when Gayle flew to LA to try out for Waits,

Howe, and Alcivar, her timbre immediately sounded perfect. Where a Midler or a Rickie Lee Jones had if anything too much character in their voices, Gayle's was pretty while retaining a certain neutrality that perfectly complemented Waits' grainier tone. Gayle was also more pliant than Midler would have been, following Waits' every direction and suggestion to the letter.

"Crystal seemed to enjoy every moment," Alcivar says. "She was a very happy, upbeat person and just did everything beautifully." If Waits initially found it hard writing for a woman, he was soon projecting himself into the minds of the film's female characters. "Is There Any Way out of This Dream?" and "Take Me Home" were written specifically for Gayle to sing. The magnificently morose "Old Boyfriends" was transformed first into a duet and then into another of Gayle's solo spots. "This One's from the Heart" and "Picking Up after You" – the latter a kind of sequel to

With Bones and Crystal Gayle, *One from the Heart* soundtrack sessions, early 1981. (*Courtesy of Bones Howe*)

"I Never Talk to Strangers" – were composed as duets and saved for the last session Gayle recorded.

With pre-production on Coppola's movie dragging on indefinitely, Waits decided to promote *Heartattack and Vine* with a tour. "It was necessary at times to take a little sabbatical from my work on *One from the Heart*," he said in 1982. "I needed to get a little distance from the film periodically." Backed this time by Greg Cohen, Teddy Edwards, and Ronnie Barron – and with Kathleen by his side for most of the dates – Waits spent three weeks on the road in North America in November, following up with a month in Europe the following spring.*

By the time he reached London in early March, Waits was tired of trotting out old favourites for fans who had scant idea of the changes taking place inside him. Though he dropped the occasional *One from the Heart* song into the mix, he still felt obliged to perform evergreens like "Eggs and Sausage". He was bored of the piano and even of the lamp-post prop. Assuming perhaps rightly that they still had him typecast as the poet laureate of bars and prostitutes, he treated interviewers with wariness and occasionally disdain. "He was brittle and unbudging, not in the mood at all," says Ian Penman, who spoke to him for the *NME* prior to his 20 March show at the Apollo Victoria. Waits told Penman he enjoyed talking to people "but not at gunpoint", adding that it was "just raining magazines right now . . . so I just do it, then I go home". He was no less surly on stage. Penman, who counted himself "a huge slavering obsessional fan", felt let down by the Apollo show. "He played solo at the piano and his heart obviously was *so* not in it," Penman says. "He was in the process of shucking off Old Tom – and old label, and old girlfriend, and old

---

* Back in LA in December, Waits went to see Warren Zevon record his 1981 live album *Stand in the Fire* at the Roxy. According to songwriter Jimmy Wachtel – brother of guitarist Waddy – Waits got into a "wrestling" match with John Belushi in the club's bathroom. "Over what, I don't know," Jimmy said.

mythic aura, and old habits – but here he was having to project the Drunken Bard schtick, to re-run it one more time. I actually walked out, I found it so sapping."*

Waits was only too conscious of his predicament. Trapped in the role he'd written for himself in 1974–5, he understood that this was nonetheless the product he was peddling. "I've grown a little," he told Mick Brown, who'd met him four years earlier. "I think it's important now to be able to separate yourself as a performer and writer from whom you actually are." Waits said he'd come to the realization that "a guy who writes murder mysteries doesn't have to be a murderer".

The one real positive from the tour, which wrapped up in Belgium and Holland at the end of the month, was the blossoming friendship between Waits and Teddy Edwards. "Teddy was very proud of that tour of Europe," says Kirk Silsbee. "He told me, 'We were having such a good time.' Somewhere in the middle of the tour, Tom told the other guys to go home and he and Teddy finished it out together. Teddy said they had a ball."

Waits' "sabbaticals" from *One from the Heart* meant things had changed when he reported back to Zoetrope. With the American leg of the *Heartattack* tour ending in late November 1980, he returned to Las Palmas Avenue to find the soundtrack had taken new directions. "While Tom was gone I'd be writing stuff for Francis," says Bob Alcivar. "And Tom would be like, 'Oh, did *you* write this?' It didn't sit well with him, but he couldn't be involved with everything. I always kept that same Waits feeling but I know that it upset him a bit. He felt uninvolved."

One from the Heart finally started shooting in February 1981,

* Another of the UK journalists who interviewed Waits on this trip, Johnny Black, claims he spent several hours with him, during which time he "didn't see Tom drink anything in the whole period". When Waits went on stage at the Apollo, however, he appeared to be drunk. "I decided then", says Black, "that the whole drunk thing was probably an act. I'm still not sure if it is or isn't."

rescued from the jaws of financial catastrophe by flamboyant Canadian oil tycoon Jack Singer. Though much of the film had been shot by the time Waits returned from Europe in early April, there was still work to be done throughout the summer. For a moment it looked as though one of the prettiest songs, the forlorn "Broken Bicycles", wouldn't make it into the movie at all. "[It] was an orphan for a while," Waits said, "until Francis shot a separate scene with Freddie [Forrest] in the junkyard, despondent." A piece entitled "It's Raining Cuban Cigars" was completed by none other than Gene Kelly but didn't make the cut. Still another, "Empty Pockets", had been intended for the opening of the film but was subsequently replaced by "The Wages of Love".

As post-production neared its end, Coppola decided the film needed a spot of optimism after all the desolation. Waits obliged by turning in "Take Me Home", a solo vehicle for Crystal Gayle. "I tried to sing it and it sounded real soppy, so I gave it to Crystal," Waits said. "She was in town for just this one day. I sat down at the piano, played it three or four times for her, then she cut it. I liked the way she did it." The very last session saw the recording of the sardonic "Picking Up after You" and the tremulous "This One's from the Heart". Gayle's mother had fallen ill and she was worried and upset. "I thought she sounded really vulnerable and figured if I could get her to the studio now I might really get something," Bones Howe said. "She came into the studio, and she and Tom . . . sat at the piano together and sang those duets. It was such a wonderful, wonderful day." That didn't stop Waits, at the eleventh hour, getting cold feet about Gayle's involvement. "Toward the end Tom started . . . saying, 'Well, you know, [Crystal's] really vanilla and all,'" recalled Howe, who urged him to keep her vocals and told him how important it was to have "somebody who really sings those melodies so you can hear them". Thankfully sense prevailed.

With all the music written and recorded by early September, Coppola and Richard Beggs spent weeks trying out different songs in different places, moving the pieces around to match the mood of each scene. "Richard would work up in his studio in San Francisco and weave these pieces in and out of the film," says Bob Alcivar. "He had all this tape, and he could take two different pieces and blend them together." By Christmas, after nearly nine months of post-production and an astonishing outlay of $26 million, *One from the Heart* was complete. But Paramount, set to distribute it, was increasingly jittery about Coppola's extravagant folly. Ever since a "blind bid" print had been shown to exhibitors in August, word had leaked out to the media that *Heart* was a turkey. In January 1982, after Paramount threatened to pull out of its deal with Zoetrope, Coppola – in an act of magnificent hubris – announced he was screening the film at New York's Radio City Music Hall so the public could decide for themselves. The screening backfired horribly. The audience was bemused at best, hostile at worst. "I thought it was a beautiful-looking movie," one of the more charitable vox-pop interviewees remarked, "but it lacked emotional impact."

Although Columbia took over the film's distribution and opened it in forty-one theatres on 11 February, *One from the Heart* was doomed. After grossing a pitiful $800,000, Coppola pulled his Vegas fantasia from the screens. It was the beginning of the end for Zoetrope, the studio that itself had been a giant, heart-fluttering gamble. Jack Singer got control of the Hollywood General real estate; two years later he held a fire sale of what was left of Zoetrope's assets. Coppola, having learned to be more frugal, spent the remainder of the decade paying off his debts, interspersing hackwork like *Peggy Sue Got Married* with artier projects like *Rumble Fish*.

Waits would stay loyal to Coppola, travelling with him on his cinematic journey through the eighties. But even Waits must have looked back on *One from the Heart* as a cautionary tale. Coppola's mistake was allowing himself to become more consumed by the grandiose plans for his studio than with whether his current project was any good. With all his highfalutin ideas about synthesizing cinema, theatre, and music, at the end of the day he was just a moviemaker and couldn't make this stuff work on screen. As a cinematic experience, *One from the Heart* was unengaging, the characters mere ciphers for what looked like an overblown music video. Teri Garr was likable enough in the picture, and Raul Julia swarthily sexy, but Frederic Forrest and Nastassja Kinski were puppets incapable of carrying their scenes. What was alarming was that no one thought to point any of this out to Coppola, a naked emperor who'd gotten far too big for his boots.

It's no wonder, frankly, that Waits' music for *One from the Heart* has long outlived the film itself. The soundtrack album that originally came out in 1982 – long after the film died its ignominious death – was one of Waits' best, a big-budget musical version of all his early themes and scenes: "The Heart of Saturday Night" on Broadway, one might say. It was also a sublime tribute to the era of the jazz torch song, a personal homage to the great writers, singers, and arrangers of the 1940s and 50s.

The album's "Opening Montage" started with a snatch of "I Beg Your Pardon" that suggested Dooley Wilson at the piano in *Casablanca*. The sound of a coin dropping to the floor and spinning to a stop took us into "Once upon a Town", with a breezy-voiced Waits followed by Crystal Gayle's more pellucid tones. A lonesome street-corner saxophone gave way to the smoky "Wages of Love", complete with Basie-esque horn charts by Bob Alcivar. The track faded into ambient audio of Vegas slot machines.

The first song proper was "Is There Any Way out of This Dream?" A solo vehicle for Gayle, the piece was at once weary and yearning, with elegantly witty wordcraft that might have been plucked from a great Cole Porter musical. Jack Sheldon's woozy trumpet introduced "Picking Up after You" and provided sarcastically flatulent asides through the song as Waits and Gayle bickered and scored points. The mood shifted radically with the beautiful "Old Boyfriends", whose early-hours blue-note guitar recalled "Blue Valentines". There was nostalgic longing and loss in Gayle's Julie London delivery, while the image of keeping old flames in a drawer like keepsakes was wonderfully touching. The solo Waits piece "Broken Bicycles" was really another way of telling the same story, a song that touched on old, broken, disused things and explicitly connected them to the theme of orphanhood that emerges so often in Waits' later work. It was as if he felt actual compassion for inanimate objects that once mattered but that no one wanted anymore. He almost crooned here, phrasing the lyric like some elegant *flâneur*. And the trickling piano line, played by Pete Jolly, may be the loveliest melody Waits ever wrote.

"I Beg Your Pardon" – Waits alone again – was another exquisite ballad. "I was listening to a lot of Ellington when I wrote that song," he told me. "In fact, there's a quote from 'Sophisticated Lady' in it." The song, garnished with Jack Sheldon's Herb Alpert-esque trumpet, found Waits dropping lower in his vocal register than ever, then floating up into an airy head voice. It's one of the great songs of contrition, à la "Marie" or "Saving All My Love for You". The couple are playing Monopoly and he'll give her Boardwalk and Park Place and all his hotels to make up for the tiff they've had. "Little Boy Blue" – the missing link between "In Shades" and "Frank's Wild Years" – offered an instant contrast, Waits clicking his fingers to Greg Cohen's stepping bass line as Ronnie Barron whirred around the mutated nursery-rhyme lyric.

Written to provide a Latin dance showcase for Raul Julia, "The

Tango" was the first half of an "instrumental montage" that unfurled into "Circus Girl", a wheezing Sousa-style waltz featuring lugubrious woodwind and accordion that wouldn't have been out of place on Waits' 1993 album *The Black Rider*. For Bones Howe it was "a clue as to where Tom wanted to go . . . [and] I couldn't go with him". With its sparse, spooky instrumentation – just Greg Cohen's bass and Victor Feldman's rolling tympani – the same could be said of "You Can't Unring a Bell". If one can't quite imagine it on *Bone Machine* or *Mule Variations*, its sinister Leonard Cohen-ish delivery anticipated tracks such as "Black Wings". "There was a lot of banging on tire irons," Bones said of demos for the piece. "What I call Tom's junkyard music was really coming."

"This One's from the Heart" started out with Jack Sheldon parping over piano, strings, and harp. Waits came in rueful but floaty, a few drinks into a protracted drunk. Alcivar's strings swelled as Gayle's pining voice entered the scene. "Take Me Home", a touchingly tender song of rapprochement, was ninety seconds of Gayle accompanied by Waits at the piano. The closing "Presents" was simply "Take Me Home" arranged for celeste, glockenspiel, harp, and bass. Two bonus tracks appeared on the 2004 CD release *One from the Heart: Music from the Motion Picture*. "Candy Apple Red" was just Waits at piano with Cohen and Sheldon, and didn't stand up well against the songs that made the cut. The second was a moody reprise of "Once upon a Town" introduced by a baleful Teddy Edwards tenor line and folding into "Empty Pockets", another deflated ballad.

We almost never got to hear the *One from the Heart* album as we know it. Bones Howe had already delivered the album to Columbia Records – "with a pretty sizeable advance and a pretty good promotion plan", he says – when Waits called to say he didn't want to release the recordings as they were heard in the movie. "I'm not going to allow it to come out," he told Bones. "I want to go in and redo all the songs, just voice and piano."

Howe couldn't believe what he was hearing. "Tom, they paid an advance for this," he said. "They've got the record they wanted and they're very excited about it." Waits countered by saying it wasn't him, that the album was too produced. "I said, 'Well, if that's what you want to do, you've got to convince Francis,'" Howe recalls. "We butted heads about it and the lawyers got involved. The next thing I knew, the release of the album had been suspended, and the picture came out without the album."

The following year, Howe read in *Variety* that *One from the Heart* was being given a belated release in three European countries, including Britain. He got on the phone to CBS in London and urged them to put out the soundtrack album. "I said to them, 'If the people there find out that you've got a record with Tom Waits that goes with this picture, they'll go crazy,'" Howe recalls. "What happened was that it started the wires buzzing and they decided they would do it." The record came out in the UK to almost unanimously glowing reviews, and to this day retains a special place in the affections of all Waits fans.

Waits' misgivings about the *One from the Heart* soundtrack were symptomatic of his deeper need to change tack. As appreciative as he'd been of the chance Coppola had given him, the movie's setting of his music felt regressive to Waits. With *One from the Heart* behind him, he took stock of every aspect of his career, re-examining his working relationship with Bones Howe and asking himself if he could only move forward by cutting his ties to the producer who'd nurtured and protected him for so long.

"Bones is a gentleman," Waits said to me. "He loves the mythology of the music scene. He'll say, 'I stood right here with Elvis Presley.' A lot of stories. See, I was not really able to articulate what I wanted to do. We ended up putting strings on everything. My voice has this cracked quality, so let's put strings behind it. It was kind of like taking a painting that's made out of mud and putting a real expensive frame around it."

One afternoon the phone rang in Howe's office. It was Waits, asking if they could meet for a drink at Martoni's, the famous Hollywood watering hole. A few evenings later they sat down, ordered two glasses of wine, and began talking. When Waits said he wanted to do his next album by himself, Howe took the news in his stride. "I said, 'Tom, that's always been your choice at any point that you wanted.'" He said that if Waits wanted to pursue the directions he'd hinted at on "Circus Girl" and "You Can't Unring a Bell", it probably wasn't going to work anyway. "If you're going to be banging on tire irons and out-of-tune guitars," he told Waits, "I'm not the right guy for the job. But understand one thing: if you ever want to make a record with me again, I'll be very happy to do it and I'll look forward to doing it." Waits mumbled something about never wanting to play the piano again and they drank another glass of wine. Then they shook hands and didn't see each other again for ten years. "I just needed to make a clean break," was how Waits put it to me. "I was at the end of a cycle."

Discussing plans for his next album in an interview in late February of 1982, Waits said he wanted to "be responsible for all facets of conceiving, producing and putting together the entire package". He was just then in the process of firing Herb Cohen, saying he'd "gotten rid of my ex-manager and a lot of the flesh-peddlers and professional vermin I'd thrown in with". He added that "my wife and I are taking care of all my affairs now". The strong language reflected the fact that Waits would soon be in court with Cohen, alleging fraudulent accounting practices that had robbed Waits of royalties for years. Kathleen Brennan, it so happened, came with a useful asset: according to Bones Howe, her father was an accountant. "I thought I was a millionaire and it turned out I had, like, twenty bucks," Waits told me in 1999.

"And what followed was a lot of court battles, and it was a difficult ride for both of us, particularly being newly-weds."

"Kathleen told me Herbie had nicked a lot of money from Tom," says Jerry Yester. "She was the one who woke him up to what Herbie was doing. She was very smart and just had a lot of really good input." To the likes of Yester, the news hardly came as a surprise. Cohen had already been taken to court by Frank Zappa several years before, and was fired as his manager in May 1976. "What was so distressing was that Herbie had always been part of the family," Yester says. "It was like your father or your brother doing it to you. And he and Waits were inseparable for a long time. Everywhere he went in Europe, they were together. Waits absolutely trusted Herbie to his core, and it devastated him when he found out that he had grabbed a lot of the royalties."

To Bones Howe, Kathleen Brennan saved her husband, not just emotionally but financially. "She provided emotional security *and* financial security," Howe says. "She was able to bring about these things that put the money back in his pocket. Because of her they sued Herb and Tom got a lot of money and got control of his copyrights. And when you get older those things become really important, because the big advances and big bucks aren't there – particularly for a guy that's as much a hermit as he is."

"Basically, Kathleen saved Tom," Paul Body agrees. "I can't say anything better than that. If he'd kept going the other way, it would have just been sort of a dead end. It would have fizzled out and nobody would have cared. But he somehow managed to re-invent himself, and Kathleen had a lot to do with that." Yet Brennan's new role as Waits' protector was felt not only by Bones Howe but by almost everybody who'd been involved with Tom over the preceding decade. "He cut himself off from his old life," Howe says. "It was like he was saying, 'That was a different person and now I'm a new person.' I began to see this happening and quite frankly I wasn't surprised." Adds Bob Alcivar, "Everyone was gone except Greg Cohen – we all went, Bones, me, all the guys."

"Kathleen changed his life radically," says Jim Hughart. "In some ways you might say she saved his life. He was getting out of control. But the perception I had was that *she* wanted to make the changes. It was like if he was going to go through with his marriage he'd better change, because she'd kick his ass otherwise. She was the warden, and you couldn't get through to him without going through her first." Hughart even felt that Waits and Brennan began turning into each other, or at least meeting at some midway point between their personalities. "She started wearing his wardrobe," he says, "and he started dressing more conservatively."

Waits began giving his wife a degree of power unusual in rock and roll. Some might see that as the only way to make a show-business marriage work. More curious were the claims Waits made for Kathleen's influence on his music. Where Michael Hacker assured me that she was completely ignorant about rock music, Waits claimed his wife's record collection was "much better" – and certainly much more eclectic – than his own. "Most of my records were all scratched and had cheese on them," he said in 2004. "[Kathleen] had a lot of real cool stuff." Among the albums she owned, he said, were cult classics by Captain Beefheart, Gavin Bryars, Harry Partch, Mabel Mercer, and the Wild Tchoupitoulas.

Where does the truth lie here, and does it ultimately matter? Michael Hacker thinks not. "She showed him a way out," he says of his old Zoetrope colleague. "She's very smart, and she was kind of a muse figure, a lovely person. To me, in thinking about him, that was really Waits making a move from this minor figure. He really stepped up to become a world figure."

Few people would disagree, given the extraordinary music he was about to make.

Act Two

Behind the Mule

"Perhaps this yarn's the only thing that holds this man together.
Some say he was never here at all."

("Swordfish Trombone", 1983)

Straight No Chaser, spring 1993.

Chapter 1

Trying to Arrive at Some Type of Cathartic Epiphany in Terms of My Bifocals

> *"Be regular and orderly in your life like a bourgeois, that you may be violent and original in your work."*
>
> (Gustave Flaubert)

It came to Tom Waits in a terrible dream. In amongst the old clothes and shoes in the Salvation Army store was a stack of old vinyl albums. As he flipped through them he chanced upon one of his own. The sleeve stared at him almost reproachfully, and he knew something had to change. He didn't want to be a has-been, a seventies bargain-bin relic. He had to create something unique, "something you'd want to keep".

Like the most uncompromising singer-songwriters of the decade just past – Dylan, Young, Bowie, and others – Waits decided it was time to reinvent himself, to shake off everything he'd stood for. It was make or break, a bloodless coup that would dispense with all and any safety nets: Herb Cohen, Bones Howe, Chuck E. Weiss, and the old Tropicana/Troubadour crew, maybe even Elektra-Asylum Records. The baby might get thrown out with the bathwater, but it was that or rest on what scant laurels he could claim.

Having Kathleen at his side was the only green light Waits needed. Thinking back to his first albums, he realized he'd lived his life in reverse, starting out as a cautious old man before entering a radical middle age. By the time he was physically old, he figured, he might regain the innocence and intuitiveness of childhood. "I hatched out of the egg I was living in," he said, looking back on this time. "I'd nailed one foot to the floor and kept going in circles, making the same record."

Those who love Waits' seventies albums as much as I do will take issue with this statement, yet the fact remains that up to this point Waits had borrowed a bunch of styles and mannerisms – from music, movies, books – and jumbled together his voice and style. However great the songs were, to his ears they were derivative, unoriginal. He hadn't staked out a musical terrain he could sincerely call his own. "For a long time I heard everything with an upright bass and a tenor saxophone," he said. "I was very prejudiced and Republican in terms of my opinions. Now I'm starting to hear more. It's very hard to stop doing things you're used to doing. You almost have to dismantle yourself and scatter it all around and then put a blindfold on and put it back together so that you avoid old habits."

Talking to the *New York Times* a decade later, Waits half-joked that he had assembled his "character" out of three building blocks: his father; Frank Fontaine's idiot-grinning Crazy Guggenheim in Jackie Gleason's *American Scene Magazine*; and the immortal Mexican comedian Cantinflas.* "I found after a while that I was limiting myself," he said of this "Tom Waits". "It was too much like I had my own TV show and it was *The Red Skelton Show*. I was doing sketches."

Waits has given a lot of credit to Kathleen for exposing him to sounds that lay outside the commercial pop-rock spectrum. "She was the one that started playing bizarre music," he later claimed.

---

* Born Mario Moreno Reyes (1911–93), Cantinflas was a Mexican actor, circus performer, and comedian whose characters, such as El Barrendero, struck up conversations with people that left them confused and bewildered. This became known as Cantinfleada, with the expression "*Estas cantinfleando!*" ("You're pulling a Cantinflas!") becoming common in Mexico.

"She said, 'You can take this and this and put all this together. There's a place where all these things overlap. Field recordings and Caruso and tribal music and Lithuanian language records and Leadbelly. You can put that in a pot.'" The process that had tentatively begun with the harder-edged R&B of *Blue Valentine* and *Heartattack and Vine*, then taken a twist with the aberrations on the *One from the Heart* soundtrack ("Circus Girl" and "You Can't Unring a Bell"), now paved the way for a music that fell completely outside Waits' old vocabulary. Most importantly, Kathleen urged her husband to push his polarities – to widen the gap between beautiful and ugly, tender and abrasive, melodic and dissonant. Music, she said, should reflect the fact that life can be strange and grotesque.

Waits has even claimed he'd never really listened to Captain Beefheart before meeting Kathleen – that, despite being signed by Beefheart's manager and supporting his mentor Frank Zappa on tour, he was oblivious to the gruff-voiced Dadaist genius born Don Van Vliet. "I was such a one-man show," he has said; "very isolated in what I allowed myself to be exposed to." Where "Heartattack and Vine" hinted at Beefheart's influence – or at least the influence of Howlin' Wolf via Beefheart, blended with the debauched snarl of Orson Welles in *Touch of Evil* – Waits' new songs ("16 Shells from a Thirty-Ought Six", "Gin Soaked Boy") made the debt clearer still. "Once you've heard Beefheart it's hard to wash him out of your clothes," he would later state. "It stains, like coffee or blood."

Whether or not it was Kathleen who turned her husband on to Captain Beefheart matters less than the fact that she was the catalyst for change. "It was certainly not the first time that a relationship with a strong and well-organized woman has had that kind of effect on an artist's life," says Mike Melvoin. "Over the long haul I think it's been constructive, in that it's spread Tom into a variety of different media." But Melvoin also believes

Brennan "put a stake through the heart of various things" in order to free Waits from his past. "It's very easy for a woman to say, 'I love you so much, it's hard for me to see you put up with that,'" he says. "Then you begin to look at what *that* is in a different way. You didn't even realize you were putting up with it, but now you feel it must diminish you in the eyes of others."

"I don't blame Tom for it, I blame Kathleen," adds Bones Howe. "She really separated him from everybody. I don't know if it was her personal jealousy or what. I don't harbor any bad feelings towards her, because I really believe she saved his life. She came along at a time when his relationship with Herb was getting strained. She's a very strong woman and she found Tom's soft points. She provided him with strength when he needed strength. I have no idea what would have happened to him without somebody to really kind of take charge of his life."

For the few who saw Brennan as a Yoko Ono implanting herself in Waits' career, many more saw the galvanizing effect she had on his work. "You can't really overestimate how much she brought positively to the table in a creative sense," says Michael Hacker. "As great as his early stuff is, his new music was so revolutionary." In retrospect, Brennan was more like Neil Young's wife Pegi, following in wild Rickie Lee Jones' footsteps as Pegi had followed in those of emotionally unstable actress Carrie Snodgress.* "Kathleen was very concerned and very motherly and very protective of Tom," says Joe Smith, who was still at the helm of Elektra-Asylum. "To get to Tom now you had to go through her. And even when you *got* to him, what did you get? He was non-communicative, which was odd considering the roster I had at Elektra-Asylum, where they were all big talkers. Tom always had his head down mumbling."

---

* Another long-term creative partnership that bears comparison with Waits and Brennan is that between Robert Wyatt and Alfie Benge. "Everyone should have an Alfie," Wyatt told the *Guardian*.

The new Waits music, which began taking shape in 1982, was fashioned out of diverse and disparate ingredients. Written substantially in a feverish two-week spurt on a second visit to Ireland, the tracks that came to make up *Swordfishtrombones* followed a rough narrative trajectory. "The songs have a relationship," Waits explained. "I tried to get them to knit. It's not entirely successful as far as a libretto goes, it's just one guy who leaves the old neighborhood and joins the Merchant Marines, gets in a little trouble in Hong Kong, comes home, marries the girl, burns his house down, and takes off on an adventure, that kind of a story."

For his new work Waits used images rather than moods or characters as starting points for songs. The almost cinematic approach to writing seemed to crank open a place in his creative brain that he hadn't previously accessed. "I think the whole experience of working with images and music works a muscle somewhere in you," he said. "With this stuff I tried to run little things in my head, feed them first." He was, he said, "trying to arrive at some type of cathartic epiphany in terms of my bifocals".

Along with Beefheart, a major influence on Waits' new sound was the eccentric Harry Partch, hobo composer, homosexual, and inventor not only of a forty-three-tone scale but of such bizarre instruments as the Gourd Tree and the Cloud Chamber Bowls. Though Partch had spent his final years in San Diego – with Francis Thumm playing the so-called "Chromelodeon" in his ensemble – Waits had only recently begun to understand how much there was to learn from such ambitious works as *Revelation in the Courthouse Park* (1960) and *Delusion of the Fury* (1969). "I could make some very good guesses as to why Tom was attracted to Harry's music," says Partch percussionist Randy Hoffman, who recalls Waits coming to a show by the ensemble at LA's Royce Hall. "Partch had spent a good part of his life as a hobo and he had that kind of ultra-bohemianism built into him

The man who went outside: Harry Partch with "adapted guitar", mid-fifties.
(*Courtesy of Randy Hoffman/Harry Partch Foundation*)

in the way Waits did. Partch was a rebel and a revolutionary. He confronted people with this new thing, and it was very theatrical. Tom probably said to himself, as Partch did, 'I'm going to do it my way, I'm going to get things done in ways that have not been done before.'"

"Like most innovators he became gravel on the road that most people drive on," Waits said of Partch. "Nobody has done anything like that since. The idea of designing your own instruments, playing them and then designing your own scale, your own system of music . . . that's dramatic, and particularly for the time that he was doing it." Waits was enthralled by a remark of Partch's that he often quoted: "Once upon a time there was a little boy who went outside, and that boy was me – I went outside in music."

A central concern of Partch's was the concept of corporeality –

of sound grounded in the body. Randy Hoffman recalls Waits coming to a Partch Ensemble concert and quizzing him about the Cloud Chamber Bowls, a series of Pyrex bowls suspended in a frame. "I remember Tom pounding on my chest," Hoffman says. "He said, 'That just gets you right *here*!'" Waits was equally fascinated by the many kinds of marimba Partch devised and built for his music. The vibraphonic sounds of these percussive/melodic instruments – beloved also of Beefheart and played on *Lick My Decals Off, Baby* (1970) and *The Spotlight Kid* (1972) by one Ed Marimba, no less – suggested something at once exotic and strange, a world away from the jazz/R&B instrumentation he'd relied on for so long.

Two of the musicians who'd played on *One from the Heart*, Emil Richards and Victor Feldman, had introduced Waits to a range of percussive instruments that he now wanted to incorporate into his sound. Along with Francis Thumm, Feldman became a crucial participant in Waits' new experiments, "suggesting instruments I wouldn't have considered – squeeze drums, Balinese percussion, calliopes, glass harmonica, marimba". The forty-eight-year-old had been a child prodigy in his native England, playing drums on a Glenn Miller show at the ripe young age of ten, then moving to America when he was twenty-three and playing piano, vibes, and percussion with everyone from Woody Herman to Steely Dan.

Feldman's marimbas – the standard *and* the bass kind – were the prevailing musical texture on "Shore Leave", a song demoed to illustrate Waits' new sound. Also featured on the track were the still more obscure metal aunglongs played by Thumm, which blended with the marimbas to provide a murky undertow that offset the jagged interjections of Fred Tackett's guitar and banjo – not to mention the high-pitched sound of a chair. ("Someone was fixing a mic and dragging a chair across the floor," Waits recalled. "It made the most beautiful sound like, [in a high pitch]

LOWSIDE OF THE ROAD

'*eeeeeehhh*'. And I was thinking, jeez, that's as musical as anything I heard all day and I'm here to make music.") Along with
"Frank's Wild Years", whipped up with the aid of Ronnie Barron
and Larry Taylor, and the mighty "16 Shells from a Thirty-Ought
Six" – dominated by the pounding thwack of Feldman's brake
drum and bell plate – "Shore Leave" was what Waits played for
Elektra-Asylum's Joe Smith one afternoon in April 1982, only to
watch the blood drain from the veteran music man's face as he
listened.

Smith, who in the late sixties had signed the Grateful Dead
and Van Morrison to Warner Brothers, was now running a company whose flagship artists were the Eagles, Queen, and Carly
Simon. Where the pre-merged Elektra and Asylum labels had
focused on prestige acts from Judy Collins to Jackson Browne,
Smith's brief now was to expand and build the brand within the
Warner Music Group. Waits felt ever more out of place in this
corporate environment. "I think they thought I was a drunk," he
said. "And I was really non-communicative. I scratched the back
of my neck . . . and I looked down at my shoes a lot, you know,

Joe Smith, West Hollywood, March
2007. (*Courtesy of Joe Smith*)

and I wore old suits. They were nervous about me. But it's understandable."

"You have to understand that my eye wasn't on Tom," Smith says in his defence. "I was trying to keep Freddie Mercury from falling apart. I was trying to get Don Henley and Glenn Frey into a studio together. Or I was trying to sign new acts like the Cars. My promotion and marketing staff would roll their eyes when I announced we had a new Tom Waits record. I'm playing Queen and Jackson Browne, and we have a meeting and we play Waits and that's when everybody goes to the bathroom. There were a couple of aficionados at the company but they were swamped with the more commercial artists."

With the three sample tracks sounding like some wilfully primitivist experiment, Smith baulked. Though he doesn't recall his exact wording, he admits he "would have said something like, 'Your audience expects something from you, so if you're going to go away from that, then wean yourself off of it.'" When Joni Mitchell had informed Smith of her plan to record a jazz album about Charles Mingus, he figured she would do something more commercial next time around. But Waits "didn't *have* any audience . . . whatever audience he had, there was no point in trying to alienate them".

After some discussion, Smith decided to let Waits finish the album, hoping there might be friendlier music on it. "Tom and Kathleen decided they could make it better themselves," he says. "There was no point in battling that out because I didn't think another producer was going to up him to three hundred thousand sales. I thought he'd made a mistake in leaving Bones anyway."

"It wasn't like I was at a crossroads and asked myself, 'Am I going to go down AM Boulevard or Eccentric Avenue?'" Waits later reflected. "It wasn't that simple." With hindsight it probably *was* that simple: either Waits went out on a limb now or he would stay in his seventies rut forever. The nightmare of the Salvation Army bargain bins haunted him. On the other hand, simply going into the studio without Bones Howe made him nervous. "The idea of [...] doing your own record is a little scary, you know," Waits admitted. "Pick the engineer, pick all the musicians, write some kind of mission statement for yourself where you want it to be and sound like and feel like and take responsibility for everything that goes on tape. That's a lot to do."

At each step of the way – at each moment of self-doubt – Kathleen urged him on, telling him they didn't need to give up six points on an album to a producer. "It was really Kathleen that said, 'Look, you can do this,'" Waits told me. "You know, I'd broken off with Herbie and we were managing my career at that point and there were a lot of decisions to make. At the same time it was exciting, because I had never been in a studio without a producer. You know, 'They know more than I do, I don't know anything about the board...' I was really old-fashioned that way."

After a short spring tour – with Teddy Edwards playing alongside Greg Cohen and guitarist Jim Nichols – Waits went into Sunset Sound with engineer Biff Dawes and the core session group that was Victor Feldman, Larry Taylor, Fred Tackett, and Stephen Hodges, whom he'd met playing with the James Harman Band. They proceeded to turn Studio A into a kind of sonic junk shop. "It was like a big old California studio, like a high-school gym or something," says Hodges. "We tried to create kind of a hollowness. Rather than going out after the people with all this volume, you go after them with truer dynamics."

For the musicians, *Swordfishtrombones* was as much about *un*learning as about taking on new information. Attempting to undo or deconstruct his own sound, Waits banished not only saxophones but even cymbals from the instrumental setup. "I wasn't exactly clued in," says Hodges. "We can know all this in retrospect. But Francis Thumm was always around, and Tom was *sans* Bones Howe, so there were no strings. Tom definitely took a grip and pulled his music into another place, though you could tell all of this was coming if you look back at 'Red Shoes by the Drugstore'." Part of the reason for the reconfiguration of rhythm and melodics was the prominent role in the mix of the marimbas. "The marimba takes over a part that is not only melodic but is rhythmic," says Hodges. "It's about the way it positions itself in the mix."

Hodges remembers Waits as "kind of quiet but really personable". He loved the way Waits went round the musicians in a circle, humming what he wanted to hear from each of them. Waits was strong on spontaneity, flying by the seat of his pants. "I learned from Tom that if you don't get it in the first two or three takes you just move on," Hodges says. "You keep going till you catch some of the *innocence* you have when you know that you know but you *don't* quite know." With Feldman as "the grand poobah" and Thumm as the Partch-affiliated adviser, Waits fashioned a kind of personal World Music out of these disparate exotic rhythms. "We were re-voicing things," says Hodges. "Like we put in a mambo rhythm where I would play maybe a big giant bass drum with a pedal, or a talking drum. The reference cassette he played for 'Trouble's Braids' was this African bootleg thing that I'd had for like twenty years prior to that."

Often present at the sessions was Kathleen Brennan, whose literary background came to the fore in comments about lyrics and phrasing. "Kathleen was way into words and how the story was coming across," Hodges says. "She's so into that shit, it's scary how she can break it all down." Brennan, Waits told me, "really co-produced that record with me, though she didn't get credit ... she was the spark and the feed". Waits has claimed he "kind of plumbed more the depths of myself" after he started working with Brennan, and we can hear this in verse that's more physical and visceral than anything he wrote before.

If the opening track, "Underground", was ostensibly about mutant dwarves, it was also a metaphor for the subterranean musical realm Waits had discovered. This was the world Waits now wanted to delve into. A short Seven Dwarves stomp with more than a hint of Brecht–Weill in it, the song's martial Pere Ubu cabaret boasted the building blocks of Waits' wild new sound: Feldman's clonky, windchimey marimba; Randy Aldcroft's flatulent trombone; Fred Tackett's proto-Marc Ribot Telecaster spitting out staccato notes; the dull thud of Hodges' beat. "I broke every stick in my bag trying to do 'Underground'," the drummer says. "Finally I just went and found these parade drumsticks that were like big old logs, and I shoved cymbal felts on top of them so they were like a big felt mallet."

To anyone coming fresh from *One from the Heart*, "Underground" was either a bold proclamation of change or an inspired joke. With the next track, moreover, Waits pulled us into the strange new aural world on which he'd just parted the curtains. "Shore Leave" was music from a parallel universe of warped exotica. The song was nothing more than a minor-chord blues, and even the theme – a bedraggled, bewildered sailor "in bad need of a shave", pining for his Illinois sweetheart – was vintage Waits. But the melee of sounds was wonderfully unorthodox: multiple Feldman marimbas; Franny Thumm's metal aunglongs; Aldcroft's trombone sounding like a rubbed balloon; Tackett's no-wave guitar (played with a car key) and a banjo that sounded like busted bedsprings; plus the chair being dragged – in tune – along the studio floor. The song's setting was ambient to the point of being environmental: what we heard was not music as such but *what the character himself heard* in this nightmare version of Hong Kong. "I was trying to find music that felt more like the people that were in the songs, rather than everybody being kind of dressed up in the same outfit," Waits told me. "It just felt more honest."

Most of "Shore Leave" was spoken-word – the latest adventure in a series that had begun over a decade earlier with "Diamonds on My Windshield" – but on the chorus Waits switched to his most wistful singing voice ("kind of an oriental Bobby 'Blue' Bland approach", he said) as Feldman grooved behind him on marimba. As the song climaxed Waits began howling like some devil-possessed fishwife – a kind of female impersonation, born on "In Shades", that he'd borrowed from the Mick Jagger of "I Just Wanna See His Face".

Next, Waits dared us to go one step further with him on the road to strangeness. "Dave the Butcher" was a dissonant instrumental performed by a lunatic: Nino Rota scoring *Eraserhead*, perhaps, or a fiendish *Carnival of Souls* outtake performed by a retarded Garth Hudson. Perhaps it was also Tom's homage to his wacky Uncle Robert back in La Verne. The actual inspiration for Dave, however, was a slaughterhouse worker back in Ireland. "He wore two different shoes, an Oxford and a boot," Waits said of him. "His house was filled with religious items and crucifixes and he worked at a butcher shop. I tried to imagine what was going on in his head while he was cutting up a little pork loin."

Though "Johnsburg, Illinois" threw a lifeline to anyone struggling at this point, in some ways it was striking that Waits reverted to tender type as he hymned the woman who'd been pushing him to change his sound. The ninety-second piano ballad – named after the town, fifty miles northwest of Chicago, where Kathleen Brennan had spent the early years of her life – reassured us that our old friend hadn't gone completely AWOL. Sung in his softest *One from the Heart* tones rather than his schmaltzy Satchmo growl, it nonetheless featured – lest anyone got too comfortable – an eerily discordant middle eight. "I guess they're different facets of things I'm drawn to," Waits said when I asked him about the hard/soft dialectic within his albums. "Or maybe it's just that you put your fist through the wall and then you apologize – the alcoholic cycle!"

"16 Shells from a Thirty-Ought Six", which had started life as a fragment of a *Foreign Affairs* outtake called "Scarecrow", took its cue from "Heartattack and Vine". The voice was raw and gargled, the beat as brutal as industrial Beefheart or chain-gang Chester Burnett. It was also a new landscape for Waits, a primordial America that connected Carson McCullers to Cormac McCarthy. Like the bizarrely gothic image of a crow trapped behind the "bars" of a guitar's strings, the song's lyrics might have come from Nick Cave's novel *And the Ass Saw the Angel*. All mules and deep-blues rage, "16 Shells" was the true progenitor of future Waits opuses *Bone Machine* and *Mule Variations*.

Trailed by Anthony Clark-Barnett's bagpipes – "[he] looked like he was strangling a goose", Waits said – the often-overlooked "Town with No Cheer" was inspired by a newspaper story Tom had chanced upon during his most recent Australian tour. Trains no longer stopped at Serviceton, a boozeless hamlet whose sheer dismalness was conveyed by a wheezy accordion, a plinky toy keyboard, and even a ghostly synthesizer. "When my wife heard that for the first time she said, 'Oh gee, you must have loved her very much,'" Waits said. "So I said, 'Wait a minute. This is not a love song, this is about a guy who can't get a drink!'"

A very different waltz, "In the Neighborhood" was the last track on the album's original first side. Resurrecting the Salvation Army brass band of "Ruby's Arms", the track was essentially a march through the Waitses' LA neighbourhood, with a pair of giggling Filipino girls and a jackhammer digging up the sidewalks. "I was trying to bring the music outdoors with tuba, trombone, trumpets, snare, cymbals, accordion," Waits said of the arrangement. "So it had that feeling of a Fellini-esque marching band going down the dirt road."

"Just Another Sucker on the Vine" was the second of *Swordfishtrombones*' instrumentals, with Waits on harmonium and Joe Romano on trumpet. The feel was sleepy and whimsical, Sunday afternoon in a Roman suburb. "I tried to give a little Nino Rota feel to it," Waits explained. "Kind of like a car running out of gas, you know, just before it makes the crest of a hill and it starts to roll back down."

"Frank's Wild Years" was at once the album's most famous and least typical track. Ronnie Barron's cheesy Jimmy Smith pastiche was an anomaly amidst the organic instrumentation that otherwise dominated the record. This was Waits back in *Heartattack* mode – "In Shades" meets "Little Boy Blue" with Ken Nordine narration – as he told the story of his father walking out on the suburban dream of fifties family life. "I may have been telling some of that story," he admitted. "It was probably a reaction to that. I was rewriting the story and putting it in my own language."

Frank sells used office furniture in the San Fernando Valley and comes home every night to his wife's kitchen, Chihuahua, and Bloody Marys. One day he flips, torches the fifties dream home, and hits the Hollywood Freeway going north. "Bukowski had a story that essentially was saying that it's the little things that drive men mad," Waits said of the song. "It's the broken shoelace when there's no time left that sends men completely out their minds." To another interviewer Waits said Frank was "a little bit of that American dream gone straight to hell", thus planting the seed of the "musical" that would become *Frank's Wild Years*. But the song, like "Underground", could also be read as another metaphor for Waits' self-reinvention: like Frank, he was torching his past and starting over.

Marimbas were to the fore again on "Swordfish Trombone", which sounded like Mexican lounge king Esquivel reworking Donald Fagen's "The Goodbye Look". The fusion of "swordfish" and "trombone" was pure surrealism, like the Comte de Lautréamont's erotic conjunction of the sewing machine and the umbrella. The flavour of the song was louche-Cuban, though it took several rearrangements to get it right. Like "Shore Leave", it signalled Waits' increasing interest in such old Latin dance forms as the rumba, mambo, tango, tarantella, and barcarole.

"Down, Down, Down" was another reprise of *Heartattack*'s R&B, this time with a tambourine-driven Pentecostal edge. Alongside Barron, Taylor, and Feldman, Carlos Guitarlos supplied feverish bar-band guitar. "Tom called me up and said, 'I'm in the studio, can you come by?'" recalls the former Rhythm Pig. "There was no vocal on it yet, but they were really jumping. I kept playing and playing, and Waits said, 'It doesn't seem quite right.' So we tuned one string down a little bit so it was a little bit flat." Drawing on Waits' memories of his adolescent exposure to the black church in Arizona, the song was the first of several gospel pastiches he would write.

After that "Pentecostal reprimand", Waits reached out to diehard fans again with the delicate "Soldier's Things". A second outing for slow, trickling piano, with Greg Cohen on subtly tasteful bass, the song was inspired by memories of Waits' National City days. Like "Broken Bicycles", the song expressed sadness over what people left behind: relics and knick-knacks in yard sales, the itemization of a man's assets. "Sometimes you go to a garage sale or a pawn shop . . . and [you] look through other people's things," Waits said. "Shoes in particular, that have walked around with somebody else inside them for a long time, seem to have . . . [they] seem to be able to almost talk."

On "Gin Soaked Boy" the pendulum again swung back the other way. With its menacingly jealous vocal and lazy shuffle of a beat, there couldn't be a more overt homage to Howlin' Wolf. The star of the show was Fred Tackett, whose slide/pick combo fused Willie Johnson and Hubert Sumlin in a single awesome performance. "That fucking thing is off the hook," says Stephen Hodges of Tackett's playing. "When Fred goes into that contorted seventh or whatever it is, it was like a perfectly placed nugget of some kind of crazy answer. It's some bitchin'-ass shit, like a classic blues thing where he almost made a separate hook in there."

Penultimate track "Trouble's Braids" was a world-music extrapolation from Waits' Beat-verse style. An exhilarating mix of clattering African percussion and fiddly, frenetic bass, full of urgent dread, the piece inhabited the mythical America of "16 Shells" while implicitly invoking *Blue Valentine*'s "Red Shoes". Stephen Hodges remembers the session as a blast: "I played this standing talking drum with my knees and my hands while Victor played that fucking crackerjack drum, whacking it every time Tom said 'Trouble's Braids.' Victor was pretty dry. I just got in his face, all happy about that track, and he cracked a smile."

"Rainbirds", the last track and final instrumental, started out with Francis Thumm's glass harmonica before giving way to a beautiful piano/bass duet between Waits and Greg Cohen. "Greg was the jazz player and Larry Taylor the blues player," says Hodges. "They both traded off some qualities, but Greg was the leader at playing a ballad. He was really the first one to really get in behind that thing, whereas Larry was always a little bit more like Willie Dixon."

When the sessions were done, a feeling of depression fell over the musicians. Though Waits was keen not to tour, there was a reluctance to break up the band. "I don't think we were expecting to tour after *Swordfish*," says Hodges. "I mean, we really weren't a *band* per se anyway. But I remember looking at Tom and Kathleen and going, 'Well, I guess I gotta go home and clean my garage now.' We were all kinda long-faced." Before he could even get to his garage, Hodges was hit by a hammer blow. "Tom came in and said, 'We've been dropped by Asylum.' For a second we were wondering if the record was even coming out."

Waits had taken an acetate of *Swordfishtrombones* to Elektra-Asylum, played the album for Joe Smith, and been greeted with a look of stunned disbelief. Though Smith had been part of the pioneering Warner-Reprise A&R staff that took chances on such poor commercial prospects as the Fugs and Van Dyke Parks, tracks such as "Shore Leave" and "Town with No Cheer" left him utterly bemused. "He hated it," Waits recalled in 2006. "I mean, this is a guy who looked like a sports announcer, so I didn't really have much of a rapport with him. I felt like I was talking to an insurance agent. He fancied himself as something of a mob boss but he also had a little bit of a fraternity feel to him."

Waits' words were unnecessarily harsh, but there's no disputing that Smith was old-school music business and a man in any case with far bigger fish to fry. "I didn't have enough revenue coming in to spend any money with Tom," he says. "When you're putting out too many records and you don't have the resources to do it and you've got an artist like Tom where there's not any payday . . . I mean, it wasn't like with Randy Newman at Warners, where Randy attracted other artists to the label. Springsteen didn't come to me and say, 'I wanna sign with Elektra-Asylum because you took a shot with Tom Waits.'"

Uneasy about entrusting the album to a company that no longer believed in him, Waits wanted off the label. "They liked dropping my name in terms of me being a 'prestige' artist," he said after the fact, "but when it came down to it they didn't invest a whole lot in me in terms of faith . . . their identity was always more aligned with that California rock thing." Spotting a once-in-a-lifetime chance to bolt, Waits grabbed his moment. "Amidst all the broken glass and barbed wire I crawled out between the legs of the presidents," he said. "It was the big shakedown at Gimble's."

Happily, rescue came fast. Chris Blackwell, founder of Island Records, got wind of Waits' predicament through Lionel Conway, head of his music division. Though Island was now home to acts such as U2, Blackwell had long prided himself on taking risks with eccentric artists. "I didn't know Tom's albums well, though I'd always loved 'Tom Traubert's Blues,'" he says. "I loved the aura he projected – his presence, his extraordinary intelligence, and his musical originality." Flying to LA in early 1983, Blackwell and Conway met with Tom and Kathleen in a cafe in Los Feliz and offered to release *Swordfishtrombones*. A monosyllabic Waits left most of the talking to his wife, who greatly impressed the Island boss. "Tom didn't speak much," Blackwell says. "Most of the conversation was with Kathleen. Frankly, she played a big part in my decision to sign him."

Blackwell remembers *Swordfishtrombones* as "a genius production, totally original". Though Blackwell's playboy charm concealed a ruthless streak – Joe Smith referred to him as "the blond assassin" – he was a genuine music man, a guy who'd signed all manner of maverick artists, from Roxy Music to the Wailers. "I'm happier to be on a small label," Waits said. "Blackwell is artistic, a philanthropist. You can sit and talk with him and you don't feel you're at Texaco or Heineken or Budweiser. There's something operating here that has a brain, curiosity, and imagination."

I can still recall the astonishment that greeted the UK release of *Swordfishtrombones* in the offices of *New Musical Express*, where I was working in late 1983. For one man to have released albums as different as the *One from the Heart* soundtrack and *Swordfishtrombones* in the space of a year was hard to believe. Even those who loved the lush Waits of the soundtrack album hailed *Swordfish* as the most exciting record of the year. To hear music that sounded so raw and organic at a time when ninety per cent of Anglo-American rock – not excluding albums by such sixties/seventies icons as Bob Dylan, Neil Young, and Joni Mitchell – was so "cooked" (to use Claude Lévi-Strauss' formulation) was a shot in the arm for all true musical believers. Every Captain Beefheart fanatic on *NME* came spilling out of the closet, hailing this eccentric collection from a man who'd looked in danger of becoming a stereotype. Musicians, too, sat up in awe. "I think I was envious," said Elvis Costello, who would later employ some of Waits' sidemen on his *Spike* and *Mighty like a Rose* albums. "Not so much of the music but of [Waits'] ability to rewrite himself out of the corner he appeared to have backed himself into."

More than anything, *NME*'s writers applauded the sheer bravery of making music so apparently devoid of commercial prospects. "I would rather be a failure on my own terms than a success on someone else's," Waits said on the album's release. "That's a difficult statement to live up to, but then I've always believed the way you affect your audience is more important than how many of them there are." When all was said and done, however, what endured in *Swordfishtrombones* was the sheer quality of the songs – the tunes and the words. "I think the main contribution is that Tom has had great, great songs," Stephen Hodges says. "Not just jive little bits or snippets but giant handfuls of all kinds of great melodies and chord progressions."

"The music on *Swordfish* might have been different from the music he made before but it wasn't different from his whole outlook," says Carlos Guitarlos. "You could say it was like a World Music album, but it wasn't. You could say it was a new direction, but Tom was always capable of seeing all those things. It was more like something he just *did* finally, like he was stepping out of his own shadows."

Waits' decision not to tour – "the uncontrollable urge to play Iowa has finally left me," he said – had more than a little to do with a big change in his circumstances: Kathleen was pregnant. As a result the couple spent the summer of 1983 quietly together on Union Avenue, Waits taking breaks only to do interviews and shoot the video for "In the Neighborhood" in and around the neighbourhood itself. The video – his first real concession to the new MTV era – was co-directed by veteran documentary maker Haskell (*Medium Cool*) Wexler and artist Michael Andreas Russ, who'd designed the *Swordfishtrombones* sleeve. Waits' languorous pose on the cover, complete with touched-up blush and eye shadow, said much about the sloughing off of his skid-row image. "He said he needed a new image," Russ recalled. "We met over coffee and cigarettes and Vietnamese food and touched base." This was Tom at large in a Tod Browning universe, hanging backstage with strongman Lee Kolima and bootlace-tie-wearing midget Angelo Rossito.

Waits was ambivalent about the new video phenomenon. "It's unbelievable how many people watch them," he said in a downtown diner on 1 October. "It's not just people with tight pants. I don't see them too often, but I don't think they're the savior in any way, and a lot of them are real cheap. It's arcade shit." Yet the "In the Neighborhood" video was fun, with Waits leading a

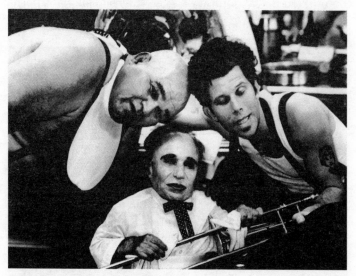

With Lee Kolima (left) and Angelo Rossito, *Swordfishtrombones* cover sessions, 1983. (*Michael Russ*)

295

motley band of musicians and assorted local eccentrics along Union Avenue and surrounding streets.

The summer also found Waits in front of another camera, appearing in not one but two films by Francis Ford Coppola. Adapted from the novels by S. E. Hinton, *Rumble Fish* and *The Outsiders* gave Waits his first break as an actor since *Paradise Alley*. "I think Tom was fascinated with the idea that he might actually be an actor," says Bones Howe. "I'd really got the feeling that he had this idea that he could be Humphrey Bogart, and I didn't disagree with him. I thought he really had a shot at this." From Elvis Presley to Debbie Harry, other musicians had tried their hands at film acting. It wasn't an easy adjustment, and most had failed dismally along the way. "Enjoy yourself," actor Anthony Zerbe counselled Kris Kristofferson before Dennis Hopper's 1971 fiasco *The Last Movie*. "Ignore the camera." But Kristofferson was one of the few who'd succeeded.

Waits was the second character we saw in *Rumble Fish*, a movie about teen violence and heartbreak in a small Midwestern town.

As Benny in Francis Ford Coppola's *Rumble Fish*, 1983. (*Kobal*)

Sporting taped-up glasses and a heinous sub-*Superfly* shirt, Tom played Benny of Benny's Billboards, an idiot savant muttering to himself behind his counter as delinquent pretty boy Matt Dillon and friends psyched themselves up for fights. An extended monochrome pop video, *Rumble Fish* was as mannered as *One from the Heart*, but it gave Waits the taste he needed to pursue this sideline career. "That was a good moment, really cool," he remembered twenty years later. "Francis just said, 'Write your own dialogue.' He says, 'I'm not even going to tell you what to say – man, this is your diner, this is your apron, your spatula. I'm not going to give you any lines. You just make it all up.' So it was fun." In *The Outsiders* he was Buck Merrill, dubbed "The Prince of Melancholy" by Coppola. "I had one line," Waits recalled. "'What is it you boys want?' I still have it down if they need me to go back and recreate the scene for any reason."

In late September, Kathleen gave birth to a daughter whom Waits wanted to name Wilder, captivated by an image of her in "a red convertible going down the Pacific Coast Highway, blowing smoke up America's ass . . ." (She sounded a bit like Rickie Lee Jones, ironically.) Instead she was given the Franco-Irish name Kellesimone, and was instantly adored by both mother and father. Waits was determined to be a good dad, to put family first and not fuck it up like ninety per cent of entertainers did. Waits wanted to change the script of his own childhood, to be present and attentive and responsible in the ways his own errant father hadn't managed. "In a sense I come from a family of runners," he admitted in 2006. "And if I'd followed in my father's footsteps I'd be a runner myself, and so would my kids." He said there was a "path" that Frank Waits had left for him, "and you get to a cross-roads eventually and you see his path and there's a magnetic quality to it . . . so yeah, I was pulled".

Kellesimone's arrival coincided with a firm decision on Waits' part to keep his family life separate from the public face of his art. "A lot of the problems connected with fame are perpetuated by the performers more than the public," he said. "Many performers use the press as if it's a priest. They tell journalists very private details of their lives and you have to be careful about that because it can be dangerous and damaging." He was also keen to emphasize that his Tropicana persona was behind him for good. "I think you can continue to write about certain things without staying overnight there," he said. "Hubert Selby Jr has a nice family and . . . he writes about the dark side."

With all the acclaim greeting *Swordfishtrombones* in Europe, Waits agreed to make a promotional visit to London in late October. While there his usual jetlag-fuelled grumpiness erupted in a cringe-inducing interview on Channel 4's woeful pop-culture show *Loose Talk*. Grilled by host Steve Taylor, who seemed intent on pigeonholing Waits as precisely the clichéd Beat-bum he no longer was, Waits deftly parried the questions in ways that made Taylor look foolish. "You mean like a farming community?" he asked when Taylor suggested he was an habitué of "the seedier parts of Los Angeles". Worse was to come: when *Private Eye*'s smug young editor Ian Hislop suggested he promote his album more effectively by speaking clearly, Waits rounded on him and snapped that he'd "promote it in my own damn way". In those pre-reality-TV days it was almost shocking.

Back in America, Waits had a third Coppola cameo to get his teeth into as 1983 drew to a close. In *The Cotton Club*, a big-budget film about the Harlem nightclub where well-to-do whiteys did their darktown slumming in the 1940s, Waits played manager Irving Stark. This time, however, there was a lot more waiting around – "I was in a tuxedo for, like, two and a half months" – and only conversations with Fred (*The Munsters*) Gwynne to offer respite from the tedium. "We used to talk all the time, very deep guy," Waits said of Gwynne. "We rode to work every day in a van. We'd hang out for hours and hours. Sweet guy. Head bigger than a horse." With creative time flying by, Waits had to ask himself if there weren't more fulfilling ways to fill the hours between cradle and grave. It would prove an ongoing dilemma as, over the coming years, he juggled music and movies.

As 1983 ended, Waits could look back over a watershed year, the most pivotal of his life. He'd recorded and produced his most ambitious album, and he'd taken his first meaningful steps as a screen actor. With Kathleen he was now hatching plans to write a musical – an operatic/theatrical piece – about the further adventures of the pyromaniac hero of "Frank's Wild Years". Money wasn't rolling in but creatively the world was his oyster.

Most precious of all to Waits was the birth of Kellesimone. After years of restless loneliness, he had – literally *and* metaphorically – come home. "I love the way things are, I love having a family," he told me two years later. "Family's real important, you know. If you don't have one you invent one. Even Hell's Angels have a sense of family."

Chapter 2

Wreck Collections

> *"I'll make a splash on the Hudson*
> *That's how I will arrive . . ."*
>
> ("I'll Take New York", 1986)

I remember it as a bright spring day, the Big Apple stretching as it came out of its winter hibernation. I'd arrived on the train from Philadelphia after spending two days with Chris Blackwell's new favourite sons U2. Though Tom Waits had no new product to push, Island's Rob Partridge had shoehorned an interview with him into my itinerary, keen to sustain the media momentum fomented in the UK by *Swordfishtrombones*. I would talk to Tom, and Anton Corbijn would follow up a photo session he'd done with Waits in LA eighteen months before.

The man I met at the Ear bar on SoHo's Spring Street couldn't have been more engaging.* I instantly loved this bright, shy, wonderfully funny thirty-five-year-old father as he sat cradling a beer and talking hyperbolically of the city he and his wife – pregnant again and expecting in the fall – had adopted the previous year. "This lady came up to me at a newsstand and said, ''Scuse me, sir, is this the place where the clocks are?' I said, 'Uh, yeah, this is the place where the clocks are.' She asked me who I was, so I said, 'I'm

---

* Coincidentally, it was in a SoHo loft at 147 Spring Street that Robert Wilson – the avant-garde theatre director with whom Waits would work so fruitfully from the nineties onwards – had rehearsed his late-sixties company the Byrd Hoffman School of Byrds.

Father Time.' And she opened her arms and said, '*Dad!*'"

We talked for some time about New York, a city Waits had been playing since 1973 and where he'd initially attempted to put down roots early in 1980. "There are times when New York becomes like a nightmare," he told me. "There's no logic." Compared to the infinite horizontal sprawl of his native LA, the predominantly vertical Manhattan felt to Waits like a vast ship. "There's no real indication that this is actually on the earth itself," he said. "Anything outside Manhattan becomes the ocean." It was an environment, he said, that made people desperate, even psychotic. "You have to be a little off-center here. If you don't bend with it, it'll snap you. You could go out on the street

Taking New York: Times Square, early 1985.
(*George Dubose*)

and drop your trousers and start singing 'Fly Me to the Moon' and no one would notice."

For Waits, New York was a place where overlapping worlds were thrust together, creating hybrid individuals. "You get a taxi driver who's playing Romanian music full blast in his cab and he has a picture of Malcolm X on the dashboard and he's wearing a Budweiser hat, you know, and he has two different shoes, a tennis shoe and an Oxford, you know, and he's telling you about a club in Queens."

The madness of Manhattan proved a potent environment. Like many of the artists and musicians based in the city, Waits found the chaos of its street life as freeing as it was intimidating. "The garbage in New York is unbelievable," he told me. "I mean, it's just ... *thrilling*, you know? As a matter of fact, I furnished my entire apartment with things I found on the street." Just as artists assembled sculptures out of garbage, so for Waits music too could be built out of disparate objects. "The way I'm constructing songs is different now from the way I used to," he said. "It's more like ... collage or something. I want to make a record called *Wreck Collections*."

The Waitses first discussed the idea of moving to New York in early 1984. Three factors contributed to the decision. First, Tom was now signed to a label whose US offices were located on the East Coast. Second, the "Frank's Wild Years" musical stood a significantly greater chance of getting off the ground as an off-Broadway production than it did of seeing the light in Los Angeles. And third, Jersey girl Kathleen's parents lived just half an hour outside Manhattan.

In LA, Waits' decision to move to New York was perceived by some as an abandonment, by others as merely opportunistic. "I had one of the last meals with him at the Pantry," recalls Harvey Kubernik, whose 1983 spoken-word anthology *English as a Second Language* featured a blurb from Waits. "All of a sudden it was, 'Hey, we're moving to New York.'" Among those who made cynical noises was producer/manager Denny Bruce. "Take a look at your wristwatch," Bruce told Kubernik. "He needs about a year in New York for credibility." For the local scenesters, Waits was perceived to be dumping the likes of Louie Lista and Paul Body and replacing them with producers and casting directors. "I'm not saying that's bad but it was different in terms of the scene," Kubernik says. "I thought, 'This is a long way from the Troubadour.' But Waits always had the apparatus around him. For everybody who gives him the salute of indie cred, he is still a by-product of the machinery." Adds a cynical Brendan Mullen, "It was time to get professionally weird – Waits' term – and to go for Satchmo, Weill, Dr John, and Van Vliet." The ambition of Kathleen Brennan was perceived by some as the real catalyst behind the move.

With baby Kellesimone in tow, Waits and wife installed themselves in a loft in "Little Spain", just off West 14th Street near Union Square. The neighbourhood was hip and happening, with an array of unassuming establishments – Courmey's, the Ricky Ricardo Lounge, the Salvation Army Diner, the Babalu Bar and Grill – to hold court in. "That's what we want here, that kind of diner ambience," Waits told an interviewer from London as he strolled into Fanelli's in SoHo on a snowy day in early 1984. That morning, he said, he'd been at the piano working on songs for the "Frank's Wild Years" musical.

The demented energy of Manhattan took its toll on Waits, who never quite adjusted to the city's feverish pace and missed the inviolable space provided in California by automobiles. For a while he drove a Cadillac bequeathed him by Kathleen's dad, but "I was towed three or four times, just crazy . . . $1,500-worth of tickets." Waits relished the basic acceptance of rage in New York – "being able to confront people without feeling conspicuous" – but confessed that Kathleen was upset by his short fuse. "My wife says, 'Well, you yelled at the guy at the hardware store so you can't go back there,'" he said. "'You lost your temper at the cafe so now we can't eat there. You screamed at the guy at the cleaners so we have to find a new one.' I've become forced to forage for the things I need and must travel to increasingly distant neighborhoods for supplies."

As angry as Manhattan made him, the city introduced Waits to numerous fellow musicians and artists. Among those he met in his first months in New York was saxophonist and actor John Lurie, leader of avant-jazz band the Lounge Lizards. Tall and droll, Lurie hit it off with Waits and suggested they share a room in the famous Westbeth artist-community building in Greenwich Village. Working on music in the loft with a baby just a few months old was proving difficult, so this was just the creative refuge he needed. Situated by the Hudson, the Westbeth was like an alternative Brill Building, crammed with musicians whose sounds echoed along the building's hallways.

"There were tiny little rooms and each one had a piano in it and you could sit in a little room and . . . hear all the music in the whole building," Waits recalled. "You could hear opera, you could hear show tunes, you could hear jazz guys, you could hear hip-hop guys. And it all filtered in through the wall, through the window." The building was quieter at night, when Waits often returned with Lurie and his brother Evan. "We'd go down there at night and write songs," he told me. "The thing when you have kids is that you can stay up till five in the morning, but you're still going to have to get up and feed them." To his credit, Waits did exactly that, becoming a hands-on New Man dad. "I guess you could say I rose to the occasion," he said in 1999.

Lurie turned out to be Waits' passport to New York's downtown art/music scene, where chic and bohemianism intersected and everyone was terminally cool. Waits certainly got around on the scene, going to parties and networking with anyone who was happening. When artist Jean-Michel Basquiat threw a pre-tour going-away party for Lurie, Waits found himself in the thick of Andy Warhol's Manhattan, surrounded by glamorous figures – Bianca Jagger, Steve Rubell, Julian Schnabel, Francesco Clemente, Warhol himself – he would probably have shunned in LA. "This party was just a great party," Lurie recalled. "Warhol writes in his diaries that this party was *the best party* he's been to in, like, five or ten years and he was going to stop hanging out with faggots and start hanging out with artists because they are just so much more elegant and interesting."*

Also present at the Lurie party was filmmaker Jim Jarmusch, who'd played keyboards in downtown postpunk band the Del-Byzanteens before becoming an assistant to Wim Wenders on the Nick Ray documentary *Lightning over Water*. Lurie, who would shortly star in Jarmusch's acclaimed debut feature *Stranger than Paradise*, introduced the prematurely greying director to Waits. "I don't really much enjoy that kind of thing, with celebrities hanging around," Jarmusch recalled of the bash. "I'm still kind of shy, and Tom seemed to be sort of in a corner also. He was sort of shy and guarded, yet he had an incredible sense of humor." After talking for a while, the two misfits split from the party and embarked on a downtown bar crawl. They would soon become fast friends, Jarmusch often dropping by the loft to see Tom and Kathleen.

Another rising star of the downtown scene was Hal Willner, the man who'd been abused by Waits for his erratic spotlighting at an NYU show nearly a decade earlier. Willner and Waits both attended a regular songwriting workshop hosted by Brill Building legend Jerome "Doc" Pomus in his apartment on West 72nd Street. "One night Tom sat at the piano, played a few songs, and

---

* In Warhol's *Diaries*, Lurie and Waits hilariously merge into "John Waite" – the ex-Baby of "Missing You" fame – thanks to sloppy fact-checking by editor Pat Hackett.

talked about songwriting," Willner recalled. "[*Swordfishtrombones*] had been out a number of months, and upon hearing three seconds of it one knew that a whole new world had opened up. The voice, the attitude, sound and instrumentation brought time to a stop." An instant connection sparked between Waits and Willner, who moonlighted from his day job as music supervisor on *Saturday Night Live* by putting together unusual tribute albums, the first being a 1981 salute to Nino Rota's music for the great Federico Fellini films. "I remember how excited I felt after hearing the Nino Rota album," says musician/arranger Kate St John, who would later work with both Willner and Waits. "I thought, 'I want to be involved in this type of project. This is my world. It's not classical, it's not pop, it's this fantastic land that does exist between the two.' Hal's one of the generators or kings of this interesting eclectic world that doesn't fall into any pre-defined categories."

Waits was precisely the kind of uncategorizable maverick Willner favoured for his offbeat compilations. A fan of both Rota and Thelonious Monk – the subject of Willner's second tribute album – Waits soon got talking with the producer, whose next tribute project proposed Kurt Weill as its subject. Willner couldn't have dangled a more intriguing name under Waits' nose. The German-Jewish composer had become something of an obsession for Waits in recent months, though he'd only explored the great operas of the late 1920s and 30s after a friend pointed out parallels with songs such as "Underground" and "Circus Girl". "I didn't really know that much about [him] until people started saying, 'Hey, he must be listening to a lot of Kurt Weill,'" Waits told me. "[I like] that macabre, dissonant style. I hear a lot of anger in those songs. I started listening to *Happy End* and *The Threepenny Opera* and *Mahagonny* and all that really expressionistic music."

On *Lost in the Stars*, Willner's Weill album, Waits was lined up alongside such luminaries as Lou Reed and Carla Bley, recording a superb version of *The Threepenny Opera*'s "What Keeps Mankind Alive?". Also featured on *Lost in the Stars* was Marianne Faithfull, fresh out of rehab and recruited by Willner to sing "The Ballad of the Soldier's Wife". Waits loved the ravaged, Dietrich-esque quality of Faithfull's smoky contralto and viewed her as a kindred spirit. When the Island labelmates became friends, Willner suggested Waits as the producer of Faithfull's next album. Grieving the loss of lover Howard Tose, the former Swinging London siren wanted to "take the classic jazz and blues love songs of loss and yearning, and filter them through the devastation I was feeling about Howie's death, a sort of exorcism". In the end, Waits' contribution to *Strange Weather* amounted to providing her with its title track. Written with Kathleen, the song was loosely a song about English melancholia, though its real inspiration was the Dietrich of *Der Blaue Engel*.*

Most likely Waits elected not to produce Faithfull's album because he knew it was time to knuckle down to his own next record. Having broken such radical new ground with *Swordfishtrombones*, there was a certain trepidation in following it up. "I don't write year round," he told me as he started work on the album. "For me, a lot of it's like going back to a place where you go a lot but the season changed and the vines grew over the entrance . . . and you get back there and you say, 'Well, I'm standing right where I was, how come I can't get back in?'"

Waits wrote most of the album in a basement room at the corner of Washington and Horatio Streets – "kind of a rough area,

* Waits' concept for the album was somewhat at odds with Faithfull's. He wanted to record it in New Orleans, its theme the story of an ageing whore's revenge. The album would be called *Storyville* after the city's notorious red-light district. "In Tom's view of it I would be bawling out raunchy songs in a pair of fishnet stockings and a suspender belt," Faithfull wrote. "It's curious the way people see me in a much more sexual light than I see myself . . ."

Lower Manhattan between Canal and 14th Street, just about a block in from the river". The two-month writing jag, distinct from the work on *Frank's Wild Years*, took place in the fall of 1984. "[A] Siamese cat would go by sounding like a crying baby every night," he recalled. "It was a good place for me to work. Very quiet, except for the water coming through the pipes every now and then. Sort of like being in a vault."

Waits told me he'd been recording street sounds and other ambient noises on a cassette recorder. "How that'll integrate itself into what I'm doing I'm not certain," he said. "I play it back at night because you miss it when it gets quiet." Some of the songs for the album he now planned to call *Evening Train Wrecks* – "Union Square", "Walking Spanish", "Downtown Train", "Rain Dogs", the instrumental "Midtown" – betrayed the obvious influence of the city where they were born. "Any place you move is going to have some effect," Waits told me later. "I was exposed to a kind of melange of sounds [in New York], because I went out to clubs more. It's rather oppressive, I think." Everything from the steam rising out of the city's manholes to the ceaseless human commotion at the Port Authority Bus Terminal filtered through to the songs. "You drag these things home from your day," he said. "[You] put them somewhere and you have three weeks to make something out of it."*

The album's general theme was that of the urban dispossessed – life's losers, adrift in the shadow of Mammon. "Most of the stories", Waits said, "have to do with people in New York who are experiencing a considerable amount of pain and discomfort." But a few of the songs could have been written anywhere in the

---

* When Chris Roberts of *Sounds* flew to New York in late September to interview him, Waits offered a personal guided tour of downtown Manhattan. With the city recovering from a pummelling by Hurricane Gloria, Waits supplied "articulate, prose-poetic, boho anecdotes about every corner, street, bar, diner, full of quirky Runyonesque characters . . ."

US, or indeed the world. "Gun Street Girl" suggested the country-blues America Waits would explore in greater depth on *Bone Machine* and *Mule Variations*. The spooky spoken-word piece "9th and Hennepin" could have been set in any faintly desolate Midwestern city. In "Time" we were "east of East St Louis"; in "Tango till They're Sore" Waits wished, for the second time, that he was in New Orleans. "Singapore" spoke for itself; the sheets in "Jockey Full of Bourbon" were on "a Hong Kong bed".

Asked to explain the album's eventual title, Waits said that *Rain Dogs* were "people who sleep in doorways . . . people who don't have credit cards [. . .] who don't go to church [. . .] who don't have, you know, a mortgage . . . who fly in this whole plane by the seat of their pants". Later he classified such characters as "hobos, prostitutes, people in trouble . . . the negative machinery I create to motivate myself".*

The "rain dogs" theme was inspired partly by a documentary to which Waits had been asked to contribute music. Martin Bell's *Streetwise* concerned the desperate lives of nine homeless teenagers in Seattle. With a child of his own now, Waits was touched enough by the kids' plight to write the moving gospel song "Take Care of All My Children". When the time came to record the song in late 1984, Waits wanted to replicate the Salvation Army horns he'd used on "Ruby's Arms" and "In the Neighborhood". Hal Willner knew of an eccentric New York street band featuring Akron-born reedsman Ralph Carney and set up a meeting.

"I'd never met Tom before and was never even really a huge

---

* Two such were the stars of the album's cover. Habitués of Hamburg's infamous Reeperbahn district, Rose and Lily had been photographed by Swedish photographer Anders Petersen for his celebrated 1978 book *Café Lehmitz*. Like Waits, who bore a striking resemblance to "Rose", Petersen had fled his middle-class upbringing to – in his own words – "try and get rid of this rucksack of bourgeois thinking and behaving, the lies and so on". Waits liked to joke that *Rain Dogs*' cover stars were "me and Liza Minnelli right after she got out of the Betty Ford Center".

fan or anything," Carney says. "I just thought, 'Well, he uses a lot of good tenor players!'" Waits so liked Carney's style that, six months later, he asked him to play on *Rain Dogs*. On a sweltering Fourth of July weekend, Carney rushed over to RCA Studios in midtown to overdub bass sax on "Union Square" and "Jockey Full of Bourbon".

Also playing on *Rain Dogs* were Stephen Hodges and Larry Taylor, whom Waits had flown in from LA. Hodges was struck by how acclimatized Waits had become in his adopted city. "He seemed like the frigging Pope of New York," he laughs. "He was taking care of business. He was all *over* the place." The sessions, more labour-intensive than those on *Swordfishtrombones*, stretched over two and a half months through the simmering summer of 1985. "At first all the songs just seemed like one big song," Hodges recalls. "Little by little they all sort of swirled around and found homes for themselves." As with *Swordfish*, Waits' main aim in the recordings was to ensure the arrangements never resembled orthodox rock music. "It's more rhythmic [than *Swordfish*]," he told me before the sessions started, "but maybe even more oddball . . . well, oddball for *me*. One man's ceiling is another man's floor."

Through John Lurie, Waits befriended Lounge Lizards guitarist Marc Ribot, whose jagged, uneasy style – a mix of Beefheart's Magic Band and James Chance's Contortions – took Fred Tackett's work on the previous album a significant step further. "He prepares his guitar with alligator clips," Waits said of Ribot. "[He] has this whole apparatus made out of tin foil and transistors that he kinda sticks on the guitar." Replacing Victor Feldman, meanwhile, was multi-instrumentalist Michael Blair, whose primary responsibility on *Rain Dogs* was to maintain Waits' marimba quota. Blair's contributions were all over the album's first five tracks, which followed on from its predecessor's more uncompromising experiments.

All but absent from *Rain Dogs* was the piano. Instead Waits played guitar and banjo and rented a pump organ and harmonium. "Tom told me he wanted to use instruments nobody liked anymore," says Bill Schimmel, who played accordion on three tracks. "Somebody once said that every high-tech era is followed by a *high-touch* era, and nothing was more high-touch than the accordion. Tom was a proud Luddite." Confronted by engineers trying to persuade him to sample drum sounds, Waits would reply that he preferred to bash doors with bits of two-by-four. "I got pushed into a lot of really uncomfortable positions, but we just made it work," says Stephen Hodges. "We banged our hands bloody fucking around with sounds, till we finally learned how to suss out sounds and metals to the point where it was . . . not exactly a science but kind of."

Opener "Singapore" instantly announced we were in Kurt Weill country while simultaneously revisiting the far-flung exotica of "Shore Leave". The marimba, accompanied by a puffing trombone, was again the signature sound in the mix, while the percussion consisted of Michael Blair whacking at a chest of drawers. "On the last bar of the song the whole piece of furniture collapsed and there was nothing left of it," Waits reminisced fondly in 1998. "That's what I think of when I hear the song. I see the pile of wood and it excites me."

As on *Swordfish*, there was no easy respite with the second track. "Clap Hands" was even more jarringly percussive and tuneless, its clanky loping rhythm disrupted only by a wiry solo from Ribot. There was precious little melodic flesh on the bones of a song like this, which functioned as an extreme counterpoint to the lush passion of Waits' discarded ballad style. "I just tried to imagine all these [. . .] guys going up on the A-train," Waits said of the oblique lyric about Manhattan's upper crust slumming it in "places that are downbeat, that aren't so chi-chi". (Did the song's subversion of an old nursery rhyme – a trick repeated on

"Jockey Full of Bourbon" – have anything to do with parent-hood? And what on earth did little Kellesimone think of these songs if she heard them?)

"Cemetery Polka" was more uncompromising still, a mutant stomp offset by the unholy blend of Waits' Farfisa organ and Bill Schimmel's accordion. There was no softening on this barkingly dissonant round-up of eccentric Waits and Johnson relatives. Precisely why Waits chose this moment to chronicle his distant kith and kin we can't know. "There are times when you totally disregard things in your memory and your experience," he said to me. "You just have to wait till they can be used . . . and you hope somebody's still listening by the time you get there." In time he came to regret "Cemetery Polka". "Never talk about your family in public," he said. "I learned my lesson, but I keep putting my foot in my mouth." Uncle Vernon – "independent as a hog on ice" – was the gruff-voiced man who'd once coughed up a pair of scissors.

Less grating was "Jockey Full of Bourbon", the crazed song of a hopeless drunk, set to the swaying sexiness of a rumba beat. "*Rain Dogs* wasn't only little mutant ensembles," Stephen Hodges says. "Some of the songs seemed more produced. 'Jockey Full of Bourbon' was kind of cinematic." While saxophones had been banished from *Swordfishtrombones*, on *Rain Dogs* they returned as squalling, almost ugly-sounding beasts, closer to the post-bop free jazz of Albert Ayler or Rahsaan Roland Kirk than to the languid sound of Al Cohn or Teddy Edwards.

"Tango till They're Sore" dragged us still deeper into the musical past. One of only two piano outings for Waits on *Rain Dogs*, the song was underpinned by Greg Cohen's spare bass, the vocal dovetailing with Bob Funk's palm-court trombone. The lyric was no less deranged than "Jockey"'s. It was hard to pinpoint what was going on in these songs, other than that they involved colourful drunken souls in sundry exotic locations.

One could argue that *Rain Dogs* was polarized between the abstruse weirdness of "Polka"/"Jockey"/"Tango" and a clutch of more accessible songs, three featuring a man who literally embodied the meaning and spirit of "rock and roll". Waits had always been a Rolling Stones nut, even if he'd sometimes kept schtum about it. "He was a *huge* fan," says Paul Body. "The Stones was the one rock-and-roll thing we had in common." Body recalls Waits showing him a letter that said, simply, "Let's get the dance started." It was a note Waits had received from Keith Richards after enquiring – in a "what've-I-gotta-lose" spirit – if the guitarist might be available to play on *Rain Dogs*. "Somebody said, 'Who do you want to play on the record?' And I said, 'Ah, Keith Richards . . .' They said, 'Call him right now.' I was like, 'Jesus, please don't do that, I was just kiddin' around.'"

Richards got the dance started by showing up at New York's RCA Studios, arriving at nine at night with a guitar tech and an arsenal of axes and amps. Waits claimed he was "entirely shy" in Keith's presence. "He had these old shoes . . . [that] looked like a dog chewed 'em up. And, uh, he was drinking this Rebel Yell sour mash whiskey and . . . he looks like a pirate." The two men worked till four in the morning, Richards overdubbing sublime *Exile on Main St* riffs on "Big Black Mariah" and "Union Square" – plus country-soul twang on the cornpoke "Blind Love" – and leaning at perilous angles to the floor.*

"Keith came in on his own, so we never got to lay eyes on him,"

---

* Was Waits on or off the wagon at this point? If the latter, he wisely made no attempt to match Richards' alcohol intake. "You really can't keep up with Keith," he noted. "He's from a different stock." Asked about his drinking in general in this period, Waits would deflect the question with characteristic wit. "You know, you have a little glass of sherry before bed, read a little Balzac, hit the light about 8.30 . . . before you know it they've got you with a case of Cutty Sark in a cheap room with a dirty magazine." When *NME*'s Gavin Martin met him on a Sunday morning in October, however, Waits was "bleary-eyed, unshaven, breakfasting on dark beer and cigarettes . . ."

says Stephen Hodges of the session. "Tom was very cool about it, though. He just, like, hunkered down and did this dance to show us what Keith was doing when he heard 'Big Black Mariah' coming at him." When Hodges asked how he'd lured Richards in, Waits said the Rolling Stone owed him money.

"Big Black Mariah" dragged the listener unceremoniously back to the raucous menace and R&B energy of "Heartattack and Vine". You immediately knew Richards was having fun; that this was what he'd really like to have been doing in the Stones. When three years later he finally made his first solo album, Richards acknowledged Waits' encouragement in the credits. "There were two turning points in the making of *Talk Is Cheap*," says the album's drummer and co-writer Steve Jordan. "One of them was sitting down with Tom one evening in LA and listening to an acetate of *Frank's Wild Years*. Virgin were trying to figure out what sort of record Keith should make, which just struck me as absurd, and hearing *Frank's Wild Years* set us all free about the integrity of the project." If the Rolling Stones had made music as unslick as "Big Black Mariah" in the 1980s, there might have been some hope for them as a creative force. Not for nothing did they call their 1995 live album *Stripped*.

It was back to Marimbaville for "Diamonds and Gold", a Weill-esque waltz of a song that obliquely counselled against greed. Coming after "Big Black Mariah", this low-key track has long been overlooked and may be the least loved number on *Rain Dogs*. In comparison "Hang Down Your Head" was an oddly conventional guitar song, with faint pump organ and clumpy, awkward drums. Born of a melody Waits heard Kathleen whistling – close cousin to the Kingston Trio's "Tom Dooley", one surmises – it became the first official Waits/Brennan composition. "Kathleen was there all the time when we did most everything," says Stephen Hodges. "She and Tom worked out more and more resources between the two of them, to where it became sort of a tag team. She's been through all kinds of phases and is such a gorgeous person." In contrast, Bill Schimmel only remembers meeting Kathleen – "quite heavily pregnant" – in the loft on West 14th Street.

Concluding Side One of the original vinyl album, "Time" was an acoustic throwback to *Closing Time* and *The Heart of Saturday Night*, with Waits picking "Ol' '55" guitar, backed only by upright bass and accordion. The spare, tired ballad gathered some of the album's themes: the waning of memory, the remorselessness of time's passing, the street people who "all pretend they're orphans". The Napoleon who'd shattered his knees in "Diamonds and Gold" was now "weeping in the Carnival saloon", his fiancée Matilda sticking around "until the bandages come off". There was no need to underscore the resonance of *those* names.

Beginning with the flourish of Bill Schimmel's mittel-European accordion, "Rain Dogs" soon settled into another helping of gruff Kurt Weill expressionism. Marc Ribot spat out staccato notes as Stephen Hodges thumped another cymbal-free rhythm and Michael Blair clonked away on the marimba. On its heels, the instrumental "Midtown" was crazed jazz from Ralph Carney and the Uptown Horns – a Mingus troupe romping through rush-hour Manhattan. "'Midtown' is . . . kind of what it's like to get stuck behind a van when you thought you had a brilliant idea," Waits explained.

"9th and Hennepin" was the missing link between "Shore Leave" and subsequent spoken-word pieces like "The Ocean Doesn't Want Me", "What's He Building?", and "Circus". Part Lord Buckley, part Ken Nordine, it was an astounding portrait of human detritus on the streets of America, people who "started out with bad directions" and were now "full of rag water and bitters and blue ruin". The creepy soundscape was made up of Waits' dark piano notes, a percussive mix of metals and marimba, and a caterwauling mix of clarinet and bowed saw.

"Gun Street Girl" took us somewhere very different. This was *Bone Machine/Mule Variations* country, something like an acoustic "16 Shells from a Thirty-Ought Six". As if digging up memories of Lightnin' Hopkins on the San Diego coffeehouse circuit, the "he-went-thattaway" song was Waits' take on Appalachian blues, the Dock Boggs seedpod for "Get Behind the Mule" and others. Waits played metallic banjo as Greg Cohen's bass anchored the track and Michael Blair clattered away on tin-cup percussion. "[It's] about a guy who's having trouble with the law," Waits said. "And he traces all these events back to this girl he met on Gun Street right there on Center Market in Little Italy."

Keith Richards popped up again on the next two tracks. Waits' Stones jones screamed from every bar of "Union Square", whose Richards guitar part channelled Chuck Berry and whose Ralph Carney sax phrases were pure Bobby Keys. "Blind Love", meanwhile, was Keef in Gram Parsons country-soul mode, the wasted cowboy-dandy of *Let It Bleed*'s "You Got the Silver". Waits claimed he'd been on the point of dropping the song when guitarist Robert Quine stopped by and put "a little bit of Jimmy Reed in there". The clipped rimshot beat, twangy intertwining guitars, keening fiddle and bleating Richards backing vocal make the track a proto-alternative-country classic.

"Walking Spanish", one of *Rain Dogs*' most immediately likable tracks, took us back to the greasy R&B groove of *Blue Valentine* and *Heartattack*. The vocal was Beefheart, the sax – courtesy of John Lurie – sleazily louche. "Walking Spanish is an expression you use when you don't want to go somewhere," Waits said of the phrase his old friend Michael C Ford had heard him use. "It's 5:30 in the morning and the baby just woke you up screaming and you drag yourself out of bed, you're walking Spanish." It was a measure of Waits' enduring hipness that – over twenty years later – the phrase became a *leitmotif* in Joshua Ferris' brilliant office novel *Then We Came to the End*.

Ironically the most shocking track on *Rain Dogs* was "Downtown Train". If Tom Waits had consciously set out to write a stadium-pop Top 40 hit as an intellectual exercise, he couldn't have done a better job. "That's kind of a pop song," he confessed. "Or an *attempt* at a pop song." With the chuggy new wave/AOR guitar chords that fuelled so much pop-rock in the early-to-mideighties, the song brazenly crossed the tracks that divided Waitsville from Springstown. By the time Rod Stewart had turned it into a Top 5 pop hit in 1990, "Downtown Train" was something that might have been churned out by almost any hack rock songwriter. What made it even more anomalous was that Waits junked the initial versions of the track he recorded with the core *Rain Dogs* band, replacing Hodges, Taylor, and co. with a one-off lineup of more mainstream New York sessionmen: guitarist G. E. Smith, bassist Tony Levin, organist Robert Kilgore, drummer Mickey Curry.

"I liked *our* versions of 'Downtown Train,'" says Hodges. "I knew where he was going, but we were trying *not* to do that rock thing. But then he just went ahead and did it anyway. Some people accuse Waits of salting his records with songs that people will stumble into and make him buckets of money with, and you can hear that here." Certain friends of Waits' believe this had much to do with his finally owning his own publishing. "Guys take that real serious," says Paul Body. "Some of the earlier songs might be tainted because of how it ended with Herbie Cohen." Waits boasted that he wasn't "gonna work on Maggie's farm no more". Instead he'd "send my songs out there . . . tell 'em to stick together and look out for their brothers". If "Downtown Train" demonstrated that Waits could have held his own as a mainstream songwriter, it nonetheless left him uneasy. "I like things that are unfinished," he said, apropos the song. "That's the thing that bothers me about radio. I end up laughing at myself when I try to do it. It seems very unnatural for me."

As if to underline what an aberration "Downtown Train" was, Waits followed it with a highly discordant reprise of the title track, "Bride of Rain Dogs", featuring gasping Ralph Carney sax and Waits himself on asthmatic harmonium. "Anywhere I Lay My Head", finally, was the defiant cry of a drunk forsaken by life. As a coda, the Salvation Army horns turned into a drunken Dixieland troupe – the last sounds heard on this dazzlingly diverse nineteen-track album.[*]

Thanks to "Downtown Train" and the presence of Keith Richards, *Rain Dogs* has acquired an unwarranted reputation for being more commercial than its predecessor. It isn't at all. For the most part it's a museum or freak show of immigrant music styles, archaic dance forms that Waits shapes to his own studied ends. If in the end the album doesn't entirely hang together as a collection – pulling in a few too many directions – it remains an eighties landmark.

With *Rain Dogs* set for a fall release, Waits busied himself in preparation – not just for his first tour in over three years but for the birth of his second child and the shooting of a new Jim Jarmusch film in New Orleans. As he gave interviews and began rehearsals for the tour, Kathleen and Kellesimone moved in with her parents in New Jersey. Casey Xavier Waits finally arrived on 30 September, by which time his father had satisfactorily drilled a road band consisting of Greg Cohen, Stephen Hodges, Marc Ribot, Michael Blair, and Ralph Carney. "That's when I met all those guys and we bonded real good," Carney says. "It was like, 'Hey, this is a cool band!' We'd jam for, like, half an hour and then Tom would show up with his clipboard, kind of like David Frost. And he'd just start playing and we'd follow him. It wasn't like, 'Play a G7th here.' Greg was the guy to do that if it was

---

[*] Among the songs Waits dropped for lack of room were "Skeleton Bones", "Dressed Up in Rags", and "Bethlehem, PA", about a Chevy salesman named Bob Christ.

needed. Tom would give you a riff and you'd just fall along with it."

The intense Ribot initially "scared the shit" out of Carney. "I was just kind of a nerdy kid, you know," Ralph says. "It was like, 'Woah, he's got such dark eyes, he's looking right *through* me!'" Ribot, said Waits, "gets himself whipped up into a voodoo frenzy ... [he] gets the look in his eye that makes you want to back off". Carney and Ribot eventually hit it off, "and once we went on the road he and I were the ones that really hung out".

The tour started in Scotland on 12 October. TV appearances on *The Tube* and *The Old Grey Whistle Test* were followed by a phenomenal run of seven sold-out nights at London's Dominion Theatre, testament to Waits' ballooning cult following in the UK. The tour continued through Scandinavia, Germany, the Netherlands, and France before he returned to America for dates in New York and LA. "On that first tour, Tom brought his family along and there'd be times when he would travel with them," Ralph Carney remembers. "Casey had just been born. I think they made camp in, like, Amsterdam or someplace and he'd go visit them."

The shows were magnificent. With set lists primarily made up of songs from the two Island albums, there was still room for a sprinkling of older favourites, drawn from a pool that included "Tom Traubert's Blues", "I Beg Your Pardon", "Ruby's Arms", "Red Shoes", "$29.00", "'Til the Money Runs Out", "Step Right Up", "Christmas Card from a Hooker in Minneapolis", "Invitation to the Blues", "Annie's back in Town", and "I Wish I Was in New Orleans". "Tom would do his piano songs and I literally would sit there sometimes almost crying," says Carney. "He never did 'The Piano Has Been Drinking' or any of that stuff, but he sometimes did the ballads." Few of the older songs were free of doctoring. "'Til the Money Runs Out", for instance, wound up with a brilliantly nutty coda that was more in tune with the *Swordfish/Rain Dogs* aesthetic. "They're more attuned to the stuff I'm doing now," Waits said of the band, "but they're also capable of doing some pre-*Swordfish* stuff but I hope with a different slant to it."

Waits occasionally proved a hard taskmaster, throwing curveballs at the band. "There'd be moments where you weren't ready," says Carney. "You might be playing another instrument and you'd get a look from Tom and it would be like, 'I'm sorry . . . I can't switch instruments that quickly.'" Carney also got grief from Waits for the white socks and navy uniform he wore. "We had band uniforms," Waits would inform audiences. "Five of them were lost in a fire, and Ralph has the only one left . . ."

Carney recalls Waits being especially hard on Stephen Hodges, who was already in shock from his wife's announcing that she wanted a divorce. On one of the last shows in Europe, an infuriated Hodges began beating the hell out of the drums. Waits' response was to say that that was what he'd wanted all along. Hodges says Carney overstates the friction between him and Waits. "That's just sort of what stuck out in Ralph's mind," he responds. "It isn't exactly right and it isn't exactly wrong. There was a fair amount of trial and error. We would change things around a lot, every night. Tom presented one of the most challenging monitor mixes on the face of the globe, with all these marimbas and pump organs. So you had to be on your toes."

"The first tour was really brilliant . . . and intensely creative, but [it] also drove us crazy," Marc Ribot confirmed. "Tom never had a set list. Normally if you're playing in a small club you can get by without a set list, but Tom changed it every single night. He was playing these fairly large theaters like he was playing in a tiny bar. We would rehearse intensely every day rather than soundcheck. He didn't really know whether people would like his new direction, so he was really driving himself very hard, putting a lot of pressure on himself . . ."*

By the time I snagged a ticket for the first of two shows at New York's Beacon Theater, Waits and band were definitely on the same page. Jetlagged as he must have been after arriving from Paris the previous day, clearly he was relieved to be home and it showed. In my journal I wrote that the show was "a joyous affair", with Waits "so funny and lovable" and "the 'demented little parade' version of the Magic Band especially good on the hard Howlin' Wolf beat of '16 Shells'". I still recall the gig as one of the best I've ever witnessed.

"When Tom came out, there was so much love in the air it was like we were kids or something," Stephen Hodges says of the shows on the 1985 tour. "It was like he was the Principal of some global arts high school and everyone wanted the Principal to come out of his office and play some songs at the assembly. Like, 'Come on, Mr Waits! Play some songs, sir!'" The tour climaxed with two awesome appearances at LA's Beverly Theater on 23 November. "We had the set where Tom came down the stairway and glitter fell on him," Hodges recalls. "But then in this show they got the yellow moon for '9th and Hennepin' and the shit went off . . . I mean, nobody *breathed* after that song was over and everybody knew it. My friends still talk about it to this day. There was a lot of cool shit that went down on that tour."

The Waits family had barely caught its collective breath when they had to fly on to New Orleans for Tom to start rehearsals for the Jim Jarmusch film. Earlier in the year Waits had asked Jarmusch to direct *Frank's Wild Years*. Instead he was offered the part of a luckless musician in a deadpan black-and-white comedy about three men escaping from a Louisiana prison. "Tom

* "The new band is all midgets," Waits joked. "They all have a basic persecution complex and they want me to punish them for things that have happened in their past life and I have agreed."

With Jim Jarmusch, New York City, 1985. (*Deborah Feingold*)

and I have a kindred aesthetic," Jarmusch claimed. "An interest in unambitious people, marginal people." The thirty-three-year-old director – who looked more like a rock star than Waits – had written *Down by Law* specifically with Waits and John Lurie in mind, the latter playing a languorously cool New Orleans pimp. Assuming it would be a modest part, Waits was shocked to discover that Zack was one of the three main characters, the third being an itinerant Italian played by Roberto Benigni.

With Kathleen, Kellesimone, and baby Casey installed in a New Orleans motel, a month of rehearsals and location-scouting led up to Christmas. The budget was low and the crew small, with Wim Wenders stalwart Robby Muller in place as director of photography. The chemistry between Waits, Lurie, and Benigni –

a star in his native country – was instant. Zack and Jack (Lurie) were two sides of the same retro-hipster coin, rubbing each other up the wrong way. Roberto, or "Bob" (Benigni), was the Chaplinesque holy fool whose comedic innocence helped the other two to bond for long enough to get out of Orleans Parish Prison and survive a desperate trek through the swamps.

Though essentially playing himself in *Down by Law*, Waits was smart enough to suggest to Jarmusch that Zack be a disc jockey rather than a musician. We don't see Lee "Baby" Sims – Zack's on-air alter ego – in the studio, but we see him do his schtick at the wheel of a Jaguar and we also watch him perform for the amusement of Jack. Basing the character on his early memories of American radio jocks, Waits explained that he saw DJs as "faceless nomads" with a hint of the conman about them. "Zack's very sullen and doesn't want to talk, and yet as a DJ he's someone who talks for a living," Jarmusch said of the role. "And I think that's sort of about Tom too, in a way." It was Waits' idea that Zack should wear plaid pants with his trademark pointed alligator shoes. ("*Not the shoes, babe, not the shoes!*" he protests as Ellen Barkin prepares to hurl them out of a window.) Neither Waits nor Jarmusch, however, took credit for the unforgettable hairnet Waits wore in his jail cell.*

Down by Law couldn't have been more perfect for Waits. It was a movie out of time about the very street creatures that peopled his songs, observed with wry care and affection. Waits was playing second fiddle to the superb Lurie and he knew it. His body language was hunched, almost simian, as he loped through the

* Lonely Lee "Baby" Sims actually existed – he was a DJ Waits had heard circa 1970 on KCBQ in San Diego. Sims was none too thrilled about Waits' supposed depiction of him in the film. "He didn't like being portrayed as a ne'er-do-well," Waits said. "There was no offense made or intended, honestly . . . No offense, Lee Baby – it's all done with love and affection . . . don't sue me." A little rich coming from a man who almost certainly would have brought out the big legal guns had such a thing happened to *him*.

strangely empty streets of the city – the musical wellspring of New Orleans – he so loved. His best moments came with his amusement at Benigni, whose character spoke in cod-American phrases he'd jotted down in a notebook and who quoted Walt Whitman and Robert Frost. "Benigni is filled with hope," Waits said of the Italian. "He takes off his hat and all the birds fly out of his head. He still believes in songs and things he saw in movies. He walks between the raindrops. So all things come to him, he's a force of nature . . ."

Excited but nervous at the responsibility Jarmusch had given him, Waits sought constant guidance. "[He] worked in a very precise way," Jarmusch said. "[He stuck] close to the text of the script, asking a lot of questions and wanting . . . direction very specifically." Amazed by the respect Jarmusch showed his actors, Waits gradually allowed himself to have fun. "Mostly I just tried to relax and be natural," he reflected later. "As far as developing a detailed character filled with all the geography of the imagination, I don't think I covered a real deep tree. But I had never really done anything that intensive." Only the pre-dawn starts for the swamp scenes, and the occasional long waits for Robby Muller's camera setup, taxed Tom's stress levels. "You feel like a candle," he said. "You've been lit and you want to make sure you do your scene before you burn down."

One quickly senses the bonhomie and camaraderie behind the camera: Jarmusch himself claimed his "fondest memories" as a filmmaker were bound up with shooting *Down by Law*. In that era of slick big-budget action, the film's meditative pace and understated tone made it stick out in the same way *Swordfishtrombones* and *Rain Dogs* stuck out in music. (The film opened with "Jockey Full of Bourbon" playing and closed with "Tango till They're Sore".) "It's like a Russian neo-fugitive episode of *The Honeymooners*," Waits remarked in 2002. "It's an odd ride . . . a funhouse ride but the car's going real slow."

The friendship between Waits and Jarmusch would endure for decades to come. Four years Waits' junior, Jarmusch earned sufficient respect to make them equals. While Waits referred to Jarmusch as "Dr Sullen", Jarmusch borrowed a phrase Coppola had once coined for Waits: "The Prince of Melancholy". Benigni, meanwhile, was "Bob Angeles" and Lurie "the Great Complainer". Few fellow artists have come to know Waits as well as Dr Sullen has. In the weeks they worked together on *Down by Law*, Jarmusch had ample opportunity to see Tom at close quarters and grasp the apparent contradictions in his personality. Waits, he said, was "somebody who's very tough and very gentle at the same time. He doesn't really stop between those two poles. He's always shifting back and forth between them. It makes me like him a lot."

Four years later, Jarmusch experienced the tough side of Tom Waits when he directed a quirky video for the latter's warped version of Cole Porter's "It's All Right with Me". "[He] said, 'Look, it's not your film, it's a promo for my song,'" Jarmusch recalled. "It was about the editing. But he was right. And it wasn't a fight. It wasn't anything that disturbed. It was an argument, just one night. I remember I locked him outside in the parking lot, and he's hammering at the door and he's shouting through, 'Jim! I'm gonna glue your head to the wall!'"

Waits never forgot the break Jarmusch gave him. "Thanks for giving me a chance, Jim," he said in 2002. "I was green, and wet behind the ears." As a result of *Down by Law*, Waits sustained a sideline movie career for years to come.

Chapter 3

Something for All the Family

> *"That's why people make up these little stories, in*
> *order to escape into them sometimes. You become*
> *impatient with your life and so you find these*
> *little places where you can move people around . . ."*
>
> (Tom Waits to Bill Forman, *New Musical Express*, 10 January 1987)

The first thing I asked Tom Waits when I met him in April 1985 was whether the "spent piece of used jet trash" in *Swordfishtrombones'* "Frank's Wild Years" had survived her husband's torching of their San Fernando Valley bungalow.

Waits said Frank's missus had been at the beauty parlour that evening but admitted that Carlos – her blind Chihuahua – might just have gone up in the "Hallowe'en orange and chimney red" smoke of the conflagration. He went on to explain that the song had mushroomed into a two-act musical that turned Frank's micro-narrative into a far bigger "story about failed dreams". The eponymous hero was now an accordion player from the tiny California town of Rainville, a man who'd gone off to seek fame and fortune in Las Vegas and beyond. "I would describe it as a cross between *Eraserhead* and *It's a Wonderful Life*," Waits said. "It's bent and misshapen, tawdry and warm . . . something for all the family."*

* Waits is a master of the descriptive X-meets-Y simile. On *Late Night with David Letterman* in February 1986 he told his host that *Frank's Wild Years* was "kind of a cross between *The Love Machine* and the New Testament". To *Rolling*

326

Waits ran down the plot for me, sketching out a potted biography for Frank Leroux, who would later – in a Cajun/Irish switch – become Frank O'Brien. "When he was a kid, Frank's parents ran a funeral parlor," Tom told me. "While his mother did hair and makeup for the passengers, Frank played accordion. So he'd already started a career in showbiz as a child." Waits described how Leroux went to Vegas and became a spokesman for an all-night clothing store; how he won a lot of money on the craps tables but was rolled by a treacherous cigarette girl; and how – despondent and penniless – he chanced upon an accordion in a trashcan.

At that time I had no idea that Waits' father was called Frank, or that *Frank's Wild Years* would partly be Waits' attempt to make sense of his father's artistic frustrations and dereliction of paternal duty. I assumed Frank was just Waits' all-purpose dreamer-loser, an American archetype that he and Kathleen saw as the ideal cipher for their parable about "the business of show".

Ever since his work on the unfinished *Why Is the Dream So Much Sweeter than the Taste?* and then on *One from the Heart*, Waits had wanted to produce something more substantial than a standard rock album. With Brennan by his side, the impetus to distance himself from his pop-rock/singer-songwriter contemporaries only grew stronger. Being hailed as *Rolling Stone*'s Songwriter of the Year for 1985 was gratifying, but Waits was determined to create something like a novel or a movie or an opera. Already Kathleen was introducing him to the work of avant-garde theatre director Robert Wilson.

But Waits and Brennan drew blanks as they touted *Frank's Wild Years* round the New York theatre world. "The ritual around here is very well-established," he told me. "If you're coming in from some other place, well, you wait for a table." Waits was also

Stone's Merle Ginsberg he described it as "a little bit *The Lady and the Tramp*, a little bit *The Pawnbroker*".

contending with a deeper prejudice, one stipulating that rock musicians should stay in their places. "Most people don't want you to be able to do two things at once," he said. "Either you're a plumber or you play the violin." Those words were spoken a year after my interview, as Waits and family prepared to leave for Chicago to start rehearsals for the Steppenwolf Theater Company production of *Frank's Wild Years*.

Founded in 1974 by Gary Sinise, Terry Kinney, and Jeff Perry, Steppenwolf had launched the careers of such actors as John Malkovich, Joan Allen, John Mahoney, Martha Plimpton, and Laurie Metcalf – not to mention Sinise himself. After the company used a number of his songs in the Malkovich-directed 1984 production of Lanford Wilson's *Balm in Gilead*, Waits met with Sinise, Kinney, and Malkovich in New York. In late 1985, the company green-lighted a three-month summer run for *Frank's Wild Years* at Chicago's Briar Street Theater. Kinney was set to direct, with Waits himself playing Frank. "We really landed in the right place after a lot of dead ends," Waits said. "Kind of a garage-band-style theater, three chords and turn it up real loud."

For the pit musicians, Waits booked the core of the *Rain Dogs* group minus Marc Ribot (who couldn't commit to being away from New York) and Stephen Hodges (who never found out why he didn't get the call). Joining Greg Cohen (bass, occasional horns), Ralph Carney (saxes), and Michael Blair (drums, marimba, glockenspiel) were Bill Schimmel (accordion and other keyboards) and – in Ribot's stead – sometime Captain Beefheart guitarist (Jef) Morris Tepper.

Schimmel had been approached directly by Steppenwolf after accompanying Waits on the David Letterman show in February. "We had an elaborate rehearsal process for about six weeks, working it out together in a workshop situation," he remembers. "We were doing the whole Brechtian thing and then breaking in the Vegas thing as well. We had to be ready to do fifteen bars of something that could have been right out of Vegas." Fortunately the *Frank's Wild Years* songs were, in the main, harmonically simple: to allow room for Kathleen's dialogue to work over them, they had to be. "She was around a lot during the rehearsals, when it was on its feet," Schimmel says. "A lot of those words were her words and she wanted to make sure they were mounted properly."

For the Juilliard-trained Schimmel, about to turn forty, *Frank's Wild Years* was the most rock-and-roll experience he'd ever had. "In many ways we were very unlikely rock stars," he admits. "None of us looked like rock stars and none of us *acted* like rock stars. But all of a sudden we're in this band and sort of *becoming* rock stars." Schimmel says Waits was inspirational throughout the rehearsals. When the band had worked up and taped an arrangement, Greg Cohen would hand a cassette to Waits, who'd come in after rehearsing with the Steppenwolf actors. Concerned that the music might stagnate through nightly repetition, Waits urged the musicians to make deliberate mistakes. "He'd want more funny notes and he'd want tricky little train wrecks in the textures," says Schimmel. "If we were getting a little too tight, he would be a little bit wary about that. He always wanted a bit of a *rub* in everything, and when we got that right he seemed to be relatively satisfied."

Schimmel has never forgotten a nightly ritual enacted by his employer. Before each performance of *Frank's Wild Years*, Waits would show up outside the theatre, park his yellow Chevy Citation on the opposite side of the street, and walk straight past the people lining up for tickets. Nobody, says Schimmel, ever recognized him. "He'd have his blues hat on and an old school bag that he carried," Schimmel says. "He'd get out of the car very slowly, close the door, and walk past the crowd into the door . . . *and they wouldn't see him*. He could do the Rasputin thing. Tom could make himself invisible, and that blew me away." For Schimmel it was part of the mystery of Waits that he could somehow act his way into *not being Tom Waits*.

Schimmel also witnessed Waits unwind after his performances as Frank. "He would sometimes drive me home from the theater in the Citation," Bill recalls. "And in the car he would start to free-associate. He was coming down after the performance, and he would start to free-associate poetically. I really enjoyed that."

No theatrical production is complete without its share of friction and conflict. "You have to be a little foolish to do something like this," Waits told me. "A play takes a lot of energy – emotionally, financially." Just a few weeks before it was set to open, Terry Kinney resigned and handed the directorial reins over to Gary Sinise. Though no one ever explained the reasons for Kinney's departure, clearly there was friction between him and Waits. Stepping into the breach, Sinise kept the show on track. "Gary has been great," Waits said in a Chicago radio interview on 11 July. "He whipped it into shape and it's been a lot of work, it's been a great collaboration."

Among those who came to see *Frank's Wild Years* was Bill Goodwin, Waits' drummer on *Nighthawks at the Diner*. "Tom was terrific in it," Goodwin recalls. "He did this thing where he was supposed to be tap-dancing but he really just *imitated* a guy tap-dancing, and it was really effective. After the show I went backstage to see him and he wasn't keeping the late hours anymore. His mom was there and his wife was there. He really looked well-rested and well-fed, and Kathleen seemed really nice."

Reviews of *Frank's Wild Years* were polite but not ecstatic. "The play, nearly three hours in length, could use some pruning," wrote *Rolling Stone*'s Moira McCormick. In the *New York Times*, John Rockwell opined that "the writing is not sure enough to redeem the inherent clichés, as [Waits'] best concerts have done". For all the keenness to break moulds, the production was "decent but conventional". A "slightly awkward, actorish quality" persisted in the performances, "caught between cinematic realism and low-life stylization".

Plans to rework the show with a view to a New York run were quickly shelved. "I just didn't have the time to do the work the play would have needed," Waits said. Instead, believing the songs were as strong as those on the two previous albums and seeing the opportunity to complete a kind of "Frank trilogy", he decided to get *Frank's Wild Years* on tape as soon as the Steppenwolf run ended. "Once the play was over, Tom said, 'Well, why don't we just record?'" Ralph Carney remembers. "So we ended up staying in Chicago a couple more weeks and recording the album."

Waits being Waits, almost every song changed shape as he worked with the band at Universal Recording studios. Surviving demos of the songs make clear the radical metamorphoses that pieces such as "Temptation", "Blow Wind Blow", and "Yesterday Is Here" underwent. "In the stage play the music was a little more conventional," Waits said. "I got a chance to work on it and push

Ralph Carney, Oakland, 1991. (*Kristina Perry*)

it around and stretch it and take it out of focus [. . .] to flatten things out and push them to their limit . . ." Ralph Carney recalls Bill Schimmel being thrown by the rearrangements, unused as he was to such change-for-change's-sake. In fact, Schimmel quickly intuited that recordings and live performances were different phenomena for Waits. "Tom knew that a record is a record and a show is a show," he says. "The way he works, a recording has to be a mystical experience. And the songs had to be done differently to make a conceptual-sounding thing work properly."

Keen to instill freshness into the proceedings, Waits pushed the musicians out of their comfort zones. "He'd try things like giving me a marimba," Ralph Carney remembers. "Greg Cohen went out and bought an alto horn, I bought a baritone horn, and Morris Tepper bought a cornet." On the "bar-room" version of "Innocent when You Dream", Carney played a barely detectable violin. "You never knew who was playing drums," Bill Schimmel adds. "We all got a chance. And a lot of times when you listen to the textures, you don't know who's playing what."*

A couple of weeks into the sessions, Waits called Marc Ribot and asked him to come to Chicago. He also flew Francis Thumm and Larry Taylor in from LA to work on certain tracks. "Francis showed up and offered suggestions," says Schimmel. "Not only did he have good ears for what he was doing but he knew his rock and roll." For Morris Tepper, Ribot's arrival was humiliating; Carney remembers the Beefheart alumnus waiting in his hotel room to be called while Ribot added typically gnarly fills to "Hang On St Christopher" and "Way Down in the Hole". In the

* Supplying many of those textures was a keyboard known as the Optical Organ, or "Optigan" for short. Made between 1968 and 1972 and marketed by Penney's stores, the Optigan featured a library of pre-recorded sounds, Waits' favourites being Polynesian Village – "complete with birds and waterfall" – and Romantic Strings. Also featured on *Frank's Wild Years* was the Mellotron, a keyboard produced by Streetly Electronics from the early 1960s and a favourite of such English bands as the Moody Blues and King Crimson.

end Tepper appeared on four tracks, playing alongside Ribot on both "Temptation" and "Telephone Call from Istanbul".*

Given that we can't see the Steppenwolf production of *Frank's Wild Years* – some of the early performances were videotaped but have never been commercially available – we have no choice but to take the album for what it is: a collection of discrete tracks that either hang together or don't. Since we lack the theatrical context of their onstage deployment, striving to make sense of the songs as a narrative thread is, frankly, unrewarding. "[Frank] dreams his way back home and then kind of relives these things," Waits said by way of explication. "He went out on the road with an idea that kind of unraveled for him and became kind of a nightmare, so that's kind of the gist of it." But he conceded that *Frank's Wild Years* wasn't "complete[ly] linear . . . it left-turns and then it shifts around a little bit".

If the album had a central theme, it was that of dream and fantasy. Just how much of Frank O'Brien's experience was real and how much imagined? Was he just fantasizing, as in the braggadocio of "Straight to the Top", or were these events actually happening? "Everything is made from dreams." "You're innocent when you dream." "Please wake me up in my dreams." "All our dreams come true/Baby up ahead." On "I'll Take New York" Frank was going to "ride this dream to the end of the line". "Frank's Theme" counselled us to "dream away the tears in [our] eyes". On the penultimate "Cold Cold Ground", "Times Square is a dream . . ."

Frank's Wild Years started with one of its most accessible tracks, and one of only two songs on the album with an identifiably R&B feel to it. "Hang On St Christopher" featured Bill Schimmel pounding a Hammond organ's bass pedals with his

---

* Tepper, who initially agreed to talk to me about Waits, withdrew the offer after months of my chasing him. When asked why, he replied cryptically that he "knew more about the situation now".

fists, the effect creating a murky bass line that anchored the song's twisted R&B groove. "It was the right percussive sound," Schimmel says. "You almost didn't need drums on the track." Essentially a song of escape – Frank fleeing Rainville in a precarious junkheap and hoping to reach Reno in one piece – "Hang On" rode the 4/4 groove as Waits barked his bullhorn vocal over squawking horns and Ribot's glassy vibrato guitar. "I think it moves along rather well," Waits reflected. "Kind of mutant James Brown." Waits had started using bullhorns – crowd-controlling megaphones – after Biff Dawes bought him one from Radio Shack as a birthday present. Mainly, he said, it was just to "get my voice to sound like it sounded at the bottom of a pool [. . .] to tamper with the qualities it already has". He said he was "sick and tired of the way I sound" and wanted to make his voice "skinnier" so it would fit in the song and allow more room for nonvocal sounds. To this day the bullhorn remains an ever-present in Waits' musical toolbox.

Hot on the heels of "Hang On", the locomotive groove of "Straight to the Top (Rhumba)" faded in with Michael Blair's rumbling congas and Larry Taylor's thumping, Bill Black-style bass. Blowing over them like a train-whistle was Ralph Carney, blasting two saxes simultaneously à la Rahsaan Roland Kirk. "I loved Kirk and what he did was amazing stuff, but what I was doing was nothing compared to that," Carney says. "I was just messing around and put two horns in my mouth, and Tom said, 'Hey, what's that? *Do that!*'" Consciously or unconsciously, the song referenced *One from the Heart* with its Vegas/Rat Pack bravado.

"Blow Wind Blow" told a more honest story, Frank consigning himself to the gales of fate after a dalliance with a married woman. The surreal lyric and creepy fairground instrumentation (banjo, pump organ, glockenspiel) only enhanced the sense of disorientation. The track was also an early instance of Waits switching voices mid-song, ascending from his standard grainy growl to a strangely moving sub-Caruso timbre that conveyed Frank's genuine distress. "You always work on your voice," Waits said. "You want to be able to make turns and fly upside down – but not by mistake. You want it to be a conscious decision, and to do it well."

Waits also tried new voices for "Temptation", flipping from falsetto to an impassioned bel canto yodel as our hero succumbed to the charms of the cigarette girl. From its inauspicious demo start, the song had been transformed into a slinky dance number, with vocal lines wonderfully reworked by Kathleen Brennan. "That one started out real tame," Waits admitted. "I added a bunch of stuff to it, and it started to swing a little bit. Now it sounds practically danceable to me." Complete with sleepy Cuban horns, it is one of Waits' greatest tracks, at once sexy and harrowing.

With the "bar-room" version of "Innocent when You Dream", Waits pulled us into the smoky snug of an Irish pub. Coming out of "Temptation", the song touched on the pain of loss and wallowed in the sort of sentimental bellowing he might have heard in County Kerry or on the John McCormack records his father-in-law played. The chorus posited the intriguing idea that in waking consciousness we're somehow guilty or furtively dishonest – that only in our unconscious are we truly innocent.

With its stiff Schimmel accordion and intermittent baritone-horn farts, the gruff polka of "I'll Be Gone" recalled "Rain Dogs". Frank's resolve was back up and running as a cock crew and a new dawn beckoned. The marimba appeared for the first and only time on the album as Morris Tepper supplied single-string Beefheart guitar lines. "[It's] kind of a Taras Bulba number," Waits explained. "Almost like a tarantella. Halloween music . . . from Torrance."

"Yesterday Is Here" had begun life as a Tin Pan Alley ballad that would have been a shoo-in for *One from the Heart*. With Kathleen's help, Waits transformed it into something like a spaghetti-western "House of the Rising Sun", playing doomy Morricone guitar with only Larry Taylor's sparse bass for company. Once again Frank was gloomy as he bid farewell to a woman. The road was "out before me" as he split for New York City.

Waits used Optigan *and* Mellotron on the spectral lullaby that was "Please Wake Me Up", the third consecutive Waits/Brennan composition on *Frank's Wild Years*. He sang the wistful lyrics in an airy Rudy Vallée tenor, sounding like a 78 rpm ghost on a cobwebbed Victrola, and the Optigan returned for a waltz-time coda.

Side One of the original vinyl release finished with "Frank's Theme", the most overt statement yet of our hero's feckless escapism. Waits urged us to dream away our tears and sorrows and goodbyes, accompanying himself on a wheezy pump organ. "The pump organ really has lungs," Waits said. "It actually breathes. I think I like the physical action of playing it, the sound it makes. It's always a little sour, always a little off."

The feel of "More than Rain", at the start of Side Two, was more Montmartre than Manhattan. Frank was truly in the dumps on this *chanson* of alcoholic remorse. Though it featured Michael Blair on orchestra bells and Francis Thumm on prepared piano, it was Bill Schimmel's swirling accordion that dominated the track. "He plugged me into a Leslie Twin-Cat, which is not an easy thing to do," Schimmel says. "We worked half a day to get that sound, and he wouldn't stop until we got it. We had to wire me up. I had wires between my knees. It looked like an execution."

"Way Down in the Hole", with Frank stumbling on a ranting preacher at a revivalist meeting, was minimalist gospel-blues: shakers, upright bass, and double-tracked horns, plus a brilliantly flinty solo by Marc Ribot. Waits' fascination with rabid Bible-belt evangelists was like a missing link between John Huston's 1979 movie of Flannery O'Connor's *Wise Blood* and Nick Cave's 1989 novel *And the Ass Saw the Angel*. Later used as the title song for cult TV series *The Wire*, it gave voice to the scary fundamentalist idea that the best we can do is repress evil rather than free ourselves from it. "We wrote that one real fast," Waits said. "It was practically written in the studio. Checkerboard Lounge gospel."*

Following "Way Down" with the pub-singer reprise of "Straight to the Top" was a minor stroke of genius. Frank had become a down-at-heel sub-Sinatra, a supper-club hack; the idea of this man being anywhere "where the air is fresh and clean" was faintly absurd. Redeeming the track were Schimmel's sublime cocktail piano and Carney's fluid tenor solo. "Waits was definitely anti-jazz by this point," Carney says.† "But I got to be a little more jazzy on this one. I did a Johnny Hodges kind of thing." And, of course, one could detect a sincere admiration for Sinatra's phrasing in Waits' vocal. "It's a secret dream to work the big rooms," he quipped to Rip Rense. "To get in there and work the Stardust, you know? Make it stick."

From the "Straight" reprise, the album slid seamlessly into the drunken Buddy Greco nightmare that was "I'll Take New York". Inspired by the declamatory drunks he'd witnessed in and around Times Square, Waits became a demonic Ethel Merman,

---

* Waits went so far as to approach a guitarist at said lounge, a South Side blues institution. "The guy was probably in his late fifties," remembers Ralph Carney. "He was kind of shabbily dressed with a CAT hat, and he seemed to have an attitude from the git-go. Eventually Tom came out and thanked him and gave him a check for a couple of hundred bucks. The guy looked at it scornfully and said something like, 'Ah thought you was a *rock star*!'"

† In a 1987 interview with *Music & Sound Output*, Waits claimed that with the exception of "maybe Monk and Mingus, Bud Powell, Miles", most jazz conjured up "nylon socks and swimming pools and little hurricane lanterns and, you know, clean bathrooms and new suits".

backed by seasick sax and pump organ. "[It] frightened me a little bit, especially toward the end when the ground starts to move a little bit," Waits confessed. "[It's a] guy standing in Times Square with tuberculosis and no money; his last postcard to New York." The song eventually petered out amidst a welter of coughs.

Of all the songs on *Frank's Wild Years*, "Telephone Call from Istanbul" sounded the most like an outtake from *Rain Dogs*. Again the track was minimal, built simply out of drums, banjo, and muted grunge guitar. With its bizarre lyrics, it begged the question whether it was really part of Frank's story or merely slotted in to make up the numbers. Waits' slashing Farfisa organ took us into the fade in fine style.

The album's last two songs were recorded not in Chicago but some weeks later at LA's Sunset Sound. Playing mariachi-style accordion on both "Cold Cold Ground" and "Train Song" was David Hidalgo of the great Mex-Angeleno band Los Lobos, a favourite of Waits'. "I'm looking toward that part of music that comes from my memories," Waits said of the songs' Spanish flavour. "Hearing Los Tres Aces at the Continental Club with my dad when I was a kid." "Cold Cold Ground" hadn't featured in the Steppenwolf show and was written as an afterthought in LA. A song of retirement and resignation, the simple strummed ballad had Frank heading home with Times Square behind him and only death ahead. In some ways, though, the song was Waits' trailer-trash picture of the rural haven he would eventually seek in northern California.

"Train Song" was *Frank's Wild Years*' very own "Anywhere I Lay My Head", sung with the same ravaged emotion as that epilogue to *Rain Dogs*. Did Frank perhaps never get any further than East St Louis? On this song of awful remorse, which opened with a faint melodic echo of "Ruby's Arms", it was hard not to think so. "[It's] kind of a gospel number," Waits said. "Frank is on the bench, really on his knees and can't go any further. At the end of his rope on a park bench with an advertisement that says 'Palladin Funeral Home.'" As if he couldn't bear to end the record on such a bleak note, Waits stuck a second reprise at the end of the record – essentially the bar-room "Innocent when You Dream" with the drunken singalong removed and Waits' voice once again a ghostly noise emanating from an ancient 78.

Frank's Wild Years wouldn't see the light of day until almost a year after the Chicago recordings. When it did appear, it instantly asked a lot of Waits' fans. The sound of a man radically out of step with eighties rock, the album signed off on the adventures of Frank Leroux/O'Brien while clothing them in Waits' most extreme music to date. "Somehow the three [albums] seem to go together," Waits said. "Frank took off in *Swordfish*, had a good time in *Rain Dogs*, and he's all grown up in *Frank's Wild Years*. They seem to be related – maybe not so much in content but at least in terms of being a marked departure from the albums that came before." Most strikingly, perhaps, the songs Waits and Brennan had written about this archetypal American Quixote were mostly Latin and/or European in feel: there was no rock and roll here and precious little R&B.

Perhaps the real point about *Frank's Wild Years* was its theatricality. "[These] are really songs *about* performance," I wrote in my *NME* review of the album. "From the pulpit declamations of the preacher via the drinking-song roar of 'Innocent when You Dream' to the louche Sinatra hallucinating Las Vegas, they make up a rogues' gallery of performing *alter egos*." Indeed, Waits made clear the connection between his new music and his burgeoning sideline career as an actor, telling Rip Rense his movie experience had helped him "to write and record and play different characters in songs without feeling like it compromises my own personality . . ." Where formerly he'd felt compelled to inhabit his own music, Waits knew he could now separate himself from his own songs. "Before, I felt like this song is *me*," he said. "I'm trying to get away from feeling that way, and to let the songs have their own anatomy, their own itinerary, their own outfits."

Fittingly, Waits deferred the release of *Frank's Wild Years* in order to undertake another film role. One of his Beat-era heroes, photographer and filmmaker Robert Frank, had collaborated with writer Rudy Wurlitzer on a screenplay about a young New York musician who sets out to find – in the words of David Johansen's character – "the best goddamn acoustic guitar maker in the country". Both men wanted Waits in the film, which was to be called *Candy Mountain*. The Swiss-born Frank had made his name with *The Americans*, a book of black-and-white photographs taken on a coast-to-coast road trip in the mid-1950s. An attempt to "see" America for what it really was – to see it as the Beats saw it – the eighty-three images subverted the country's self-satisfaction, stripping away the Norman Rockwell veneer of the Eisenhower era. Looking at the photographs today is tantamount to looking at Tom Waits' America: a place of pathos and inequality, Edward Hopper's smalltown diners and gas stations bled of colour. "I think he changed the face of photography forever with that little Leica he used," Waits said of the book.

After the 1959 publication of *The Americans*, Frank had all but given up photography to make films, starting with his short Beat documentary *Pull My Daisy*. Shot on a handheld 16-mm camera in a New York loft, with manic narration by Jack Kerouac, the film captured Allen Ginsberg, Gregory Corso, and friends riffing and sparring for the benefit of a young Swiss bishop and his wife and sister. By 1972, when the Rolling Stones hired him to make a documentary about their debauched American tour of that year, Frank was a cult figure in the art world of downtown New York. "He takes a really romantic position," Rudy Wurlitzer said. "The old-fashioned artist who worships at the altar of total self-expression. And he protects his myth at any cost."

An altogether more diffuse and murky portrait of the Stones' milieu than the Maysles brothers' 1970 film *Gimme Shelter*, Frank's *Cocksucker Blues* – with its scenes of fellatio and shooting up – riled the group enough for them to veto its release. For years the film was shown only five times a year, and then only when Frank himself was present. Waits' love of the Stones helped him bond with Frank when the two men first met in New York in 1984. Frank subsequently shot Waits for the back cover of *Rain Dogs* and thought of him for the small part of Al Silk in *Candy Mountain*. "It's an odyssey about someone in New York searching for someone," Waits said of the film. "I hesitate to say what it's really about, I doubt if it would be . . . you know, it's Robert's film. I'm just in it."

Shot in Manhattan, upstate New York, and Canada in the late fall of 1986, *Candy Mountain* was, by Frank's standards, a big-budget production at $1.3 million. Wurlitzer, who'd written the screenplays for Sam Peckinpah's *Pat Garrett and Billy the Kid* and Monte Hellman's *Two-Lane Blacktop* (both featuring rock stars), had scripted this strange road movie with one eye on involving as many musicians as could be funnelled into a two-hour picture.* Alongside Waits there were cameo roles for Dr John, David Johansen, Leon Redbone, and Joe Strummer, as well as for such obscure figures as Arto Lindsay and Mary Margaret O'Hara. There was even a role for Jim Jarmusch, while Hal Willner oversaw the music and hired both Michael Blair and Ralph Carney to perform it.

Though Waits was only in *Candy Mountain* for a few minutes, he made the most of his scenes as a character who was

---

* Waits would almost certainly have seen *Two-Lane Blacktop* (1970), in which Warren Oates (GTO) raced James Taylor (The Driver) and Dennis Wilson (The Mechanic) across America in a sunflower-coloured Pontiac while growling lines like "That'll give you a set of emotions that'll stay with you!" GTO was an American out of time, a counterpoint to the longhair cool of Taylor and Wilson. According to producer L. Dean Jones, Oates once saw Waits on TV and blurted the words, "That guy stole my act!"

temperamentally his own antithesis. A self-made, golf-playing millionaire, Al Silk refuses to divulge the whereabouts of his reclusive guitar-maker brother and urges his young visitor (Kevin O'Connor) to abandon his quest. "You should be playing golf," he counsels as he brandishes an absurdly long cigar. Smashed on Jack Daniels, Waits bawls the old Irish ballad "Once More before I Go" before adjourning to an upright piano and singing through cupped hands. Later he reappears in a comically florid dressing gown and entrusts an old Pontiac T-Bird to Julius, who heads on towards Niagara Falls in it.

Candy Mountain was creaky and laboured; neither Frank nor Wurlitzer appeared to know what they were trying to say in this unconvincing anti-grail film. Julius was an unsympathetic hero, and none of the characters he encountered – barring the bizarre father-and-son duo of Roberts Blossom and Leon Redbone – was remotely compelling. "Robert sabotages himself a lot, and out of that comes his aesthetic," Wurlitzer said in Frank's defence. "He purposefully creates a sense of chaos, and that creates a lot of stress in the people around him."

There was less chaos in Waits' subsequent movie project, which – like much of *Candy Mountain* – was shot in upstate New York. This time, moreover, the budget was Big Hollywood, with starring roles for Jack Nicholson and Meryl Streep. *Cotton Club* screenwriter William Kennedy had adapted *Ironweed*, his own Pulitzer-winning novel about alcoholic bums in 1930s Albany, for Argentinian director Hector Babenco, then flush with the success of 1985's *Kiss of the Spiderwoman*. Filming in the late winter and spring of 1987, Waits was given the sizeable role of Rudy the Kraut, a gangling simpleton we encounter at the very start of the film. "It's all about [. . .] alcohol, baptism, and redemption," Waits said of *Ironweed*. "It was a good experience for me."

For Babenco, *Ironweed* was about "a collective soul, anonymous vagabonds . . . the courage and beauty of people we don't usually think of as having deep and complex emotions". For Waits it was almost as if Babenco had transposed "On the Nickel" or "Tom Traubert's Blues" to the big screen. Nicholson was Francis Phelan, an ex-baseball player haunted by the deaths of his infant son and of a strike-breaker he'd accidentally killed as a young man; Streep played his companion Helen Archer, a sometime concert pianist fallen on hard times. Waits' Rudy was by turns a goofy sidekick to Phelan and a kind of surrogate son to the couple. "The character for me was more like a little kid, you know," Waits reflected. "[But] he was like a middle-aged man, you know."

"He looked like any moment he might break at the waist or his head fall off his shoulders on to the floor," Nicholson said of Waits' Rudy. "I once saw a smalltown idiot walking across the park, totally drunk, but he was holding an ice cream, staggering but also concentrating on not allowing the ice cream to fall. I felt there was something similar in Tom."

If Rudy was close to typecasting, Waits had figured he was no more than "a dark horse" for *Ironweed*. Bit parts in Coppola's films and a co-lead in Jarmusch's indie pic had hardly made him a household name. Preparing for the audition in New York, he had the sudden bright idea to stick a piece of toast and an old toothbrush in his shirt pocket: details he was convinced bagged him the role, especially since he was competing for it with both Dennis Hopper and Harry Dean Stanton.

Waits' initial appearance in *Ironweed* was a defining one. The first thing Phelan saw was the pair of spats on Rudy's feet; as his gaze rose he took in Waits in a grey pinstripe suit, topped off with a fancy yellow check waistcoat. "I-I got the whole outfit!" Rudy cackled with boyish glee. But there was a stinger in his tale: he'd just come from being diagnosed with cancer at the hospital ("first thing I ever got!"). Shuffling and shambling and sticking out his arms, Waits' body language as Rudy was superb. Yet he was never entirely comfortable in the role, his nervousness in Nicholson's presence almost palpable. "I have somebody that helps me out privately a little bit," he admitted. "You know, I was very nervous about it and I thought I needed a shot in the arm."

Neither Nicholson nor Streep made Waits feel uncomfortable for a second. He instantly admired these very different actors, Nicholson for his mischievous humour, Streep for her focused intensity. "Jack makes you look good when you're with him," he said. "He's not picking your pocket, never grandstanding, not trying to eclipse the people he's with. He's trying to make himself small." Streep's "preparation and commitment and concentration within the characters" were, Waits said, "devastating". He paid close attention to the way the two stars put together their characters. It was, he said, "like they build a doll from Grandmother's mouth and Aunt Betty's walk and Ethel Merman's posture, then they push their own truthful feelings through that exterior".

Waits learned as much from Nicholson offscreen as he did from watching him on camera. If anybody could teach you how to survive fame, he thought, Joker Jack could. He was the Keith Richards of actors. "People get frightened that success is going to take them out of life," Waits said. "Life will only be something you can get through the mail. But Jack . . . just stays in there, being himself. He's a good ad for success." It helped that Nicholson was a music buff, regularly regaling cast and crew with mix tapes of songs by Billie Holiday and Robert Johnson.

If *Ironweed* was firmly in the tradition of middlebrow Hollywood compassion, the performances brought Kennedy's compellingly bleak vision of poverty to life. "Until now I'd always thought that being a hobo was like running away from home," Waits confessed. "[It was] letting your beard grow, eating out of cans in hobo jungles under a railroad bridge . . ." The reality – especially of alcoholism – was somewhat different. Indeed,

Waits' own drinking went unremarked amidst the general imbibing that took place on set. He was, he claimed, "forced to drink against my will . . . everybody was told, "Cause it's part of the story.'"

Wrapping *Ironweed* in late May, Waits could look back with some satisfaction on a growing movie CV. Despite its commercial failure, Babenco's film was a bigger break for him than *Down by Law*, putting him on the mainstream Hollywood map as a character actor. "I think any artist who knows himself knows he functions best within his own parameters," says Bill Schimmel. "Tom seemed to have the right balance between art and rock and roll, and he was the actor who was one step away from it – the fourth wall. On one level he seemed totally immersed in the part, but on another level there was a part that was a little disassociated from it."

The extreme cold of *Ironweed*'s location shoot in Albany may have had something to do with Tom's and Kathleen's decision to return to California as soon as the film was finished. The climate alone did not explain the decision, however. "I wasn't well-suited [to] the temperament of that town," Waits said of New York in 2006. "I need something that's a little more . . . not as volatile." The city, he said, made him develop Tourette's Syndrome: "I was blurting out obscenities in the middle of Eighth Avenue." Waits told David Letterman that he was "treated better" in California. "I think Tom had got New York out of his system," says Bill Schimmel. "I think he'd got what he needed. I just sort of imagine him on the open road like Harry Partch, with his thumb out. I don't see him as a subway person. He just struck me as a person who functions better with space around him."

In the late fall of 1987, Waits and wife returned to the area of Los Angeles in which he – and they – had formerly lived. Moving back to Union Avenue, they were once again living near his father, who was still teaching at Belmont High. For Waits it was a genuine community, a world away from the white middle classes on the West Side. "I'm more interested in these types of things . . . these people, I guess, in these neighborhoods," he told *Snowblind* author Robert Sabbag, adding that he sometimes got recognized in the area as "Frank's boy". Memories of travelling through Mexico as a kid were triggered by the area in question. "The music down there was never an event, it was always a condiment," Frank's boy reminisced to Francis Thumm. "Where I live in LA I go down to the liquor store and there's a guy standing on the street corner with an accordion and a guy with an upright bass."

Back on his home turf, Waits' family life became ever more important. "I'm beginning to create a world for myself that I can live in," he said, before adding quickly that "I'm not happy or anything like that . . . I mean, I'm happy for a minute and then most of us are manic-depressive." Behind the scenes Waits continued his on-off affair with alcohol, never quite able to shake it

"Beginning to create a world for myself that I can live in": return to Union Avenue, late 1987. (*Art Sperl*)

off. "Am I still a drunk?" he said to *NME*'s Sean O'Hagan. "I have a little sherry before retiring, sure. When I'm writing I'm usually pretty clean. I don't think it's alcohol that makes the music come out. It's hard to tell. Sometimes alcohol massages the beast, sometimes it doesn't."*

As happy as he was to be home in LA, Waits already had one eye on getting away from it all. A long-harboured fantasy of sitting on a porch in the back of beyond continued to hold sway for him. Used to "a certain gypsy quality", he was "moving towards needing a compound" while "operating out of a storefront here in the Los Angeles area". As if quoting from "Cold, Cold Ground", Waits pictured himself beside a "briar patch" in Missouri, "a place where everything I drag home I can leave in the yard". He was still two years shy of forty.

Come the summer, Waits geared up for the belated release of *Frank's Wild Years* and for his first tour in two years. With Kathleen's urging, furthermore, plans were made to shoot certain dates for a concert film. "I'd get home from the road and I wouldn't have any pictures of the band or anything," Waits reflected. "We'd talk about it like something that didn't really happen. It was the first time we pursued pulling it together." Chris Blackwell agreed to bankroll the project, installing Nic Roeg's son Luc as the film's producer. Ironically it was a noted TV-ad director, Chris Blum, whom Tom and Kathleen approached to direct the film. Blum had shot several TV spots for Levi-Strauss and helped develop the company's memorable campaign for 501 jeans. Blum quickly agreed that it was imperative they

* "He'd just moved house and was a bit irascible," Sean O'Hagan recalls of this interview. "Did the whole thing in character, which was entertaining but not altogether revealing. I felt like he could have done that schtick in his sleep, but I was a fan and in awe. He gave Lawrence Watson two minutes to take pictures: 'You got two minutes, bud.' It was unfair given that Lawrence had journeyed from London via New York with a bunch of cameras and lights."

conceive something quirkier than the standard in-concert document, working in a subplot about a ticket-usher who falls asleep
in a theatre and dreams that he's hit the *Big Time* (the film's eventual title).

The release of *Frank's Wild Years* necessitated a splurge of
interviews, a ritual Waits was starting to find as taxing as touring.
"I've been asked all these things before," he told one interrogator
as he sat in his beloved local diner the Traveler's Café in January
1988. "If I sound a little like I'm watching the clock, it's because
I've been asked every one of those questions. I'm just being honest with you." Behind the fatigue lay a deepening mistrust of the
media. "I see the way a lot of people talk to the press," he said. "To
me it's a bit like talking to a cop." To Waits, the relationship
between artists and the media had become unhealthy, with journalists reducing art to something knowable and commodifiable
and artists obliging by fitting in with the media's precepts. In his
own way, Waits was holding fast to Beat ideals of bohemian
purity, of not being defined and pigeonholed for painless con-
sumption. Linked to his unease was Waits' belief that the connection between an artist's life and his work should never be
presupposed; that any sane songwriter should refrain from representing his life in his music and instead conceal it. For him,
Frank's Wild Years was itself a kind of masquerade of personae
that refused to reveal the "truth" about their creator. "Usually you
hide what everything represents," he stated. "You're the only one
who really knows."

Waits particularly resented the way his old seventies persona
was still hauled out by the media as a gauge of who he was. For
all that he'd successfully deconstructed the "Beat wino" persona
of his seventies albums, not everybody chose to notice. He
bemoaned the fact that America hadn't caught up with Europe's
embrace of his changes. "Here I have a lot of people who've been
listening to me since 1972," he sighed. "They want me to come

out unshaven, drink whiskey, and tell stories about broken-down hotels." He explained that he was trying to return to the freedom and primitivism of the child's imagination – to unlearn the stylistic tropes of his act and the reflex actions of his hands at the piano. He cited Kathleen as someone who was "very unself-conscious, like the way kids will sing things just as they occur to them".

Waits told *NME* that he'd got more "angry" and "fractured" with *Swordfishtrombones*, the subsequent records following suit and building on the risks he'd taken with it. What he particularly relished about his post-Asylum sound was its brokenness, the fact that it sounded unfinished. "If it's too beautiful, too pro-duced, I back off a little, start getting intimidated," he said, citing the Pogues, the Replacements, and Alex Chilton as kindred cre-ative souls. "Keith Richards had an expression for it that's very a propos," he said. "He called it 'the hair in the gate'. It's like when you hear music 'wrong' or when you hear it coming through a wall and it mixes in – I pay attention to those things." (Richards' expression derives from a movie term referring to hairs or other objects getting into the "gate" of a film projector and thus appearing on screen.)

Asked what he might do next, Waits said he wanted to "try and do something with a much harder edge, something with more abandon". He planned to unleash his pent-up rage at the world and call the album *The World I Hate to Live In.* "I get angry about some of the things I see ... but I never say anything about it," he grunted. "I think next time I will." (Little did anyone know almost five years would elapse before his next album appeared.) Waits claimed he'd even been listening to "a lot of this rap stuff", not least because it was unavoidable in a neighbourhood where souped-up jeeps blasted it from ginormous woofers. Like Neil Young, Waits resisted the impulse to be reactionary, embracing the threat from the upcoming generation and the "vitality" of this new urban form. The recent release of NWA's incendiary *Straight Outta Compton* had shifted hip hop's axis to the West Coast, and Waits loved it.

Though his music was a million miles from NWA, Roy Orbison had long been an idol of Waits'. When T-Bone Burnett asked if he would take part in a "Black and White Night" to celebrate Orbison's life and music, Waits put aside his usual disdain for Live Aid-style cronyism and agreed to join Bruce Springsteen, Elvis Costello, Jackson Browne, Bonnie Raitt, k. d. lang, J. D. Souther, and others at the Coconut Grove in LA's legendary Ambassador Hotel. Waits' soft spot for Orbison dated back to the almost spooky effect of hearing the Texan's freakishly beautiful voice through the airwaves as a teenager. At the Coconut Grove on 30 September, Waits remained for the most part in the shadows, supplying low-key guitar and organ as Springsteen and friends flanked Orbison. When the latter died just a year later, Waits wrote that his dreamy songs were "more like dreams themselves, like arias . . . he was a rockabilly Rigoletto, as important as Caruso . . ."

"It was definitely an evening where every ounce of ego was checked at the door," k. d. lang told me. "And it was amazing, because you had really diverse people there. We were like disciples in a way. We were all very quiet and very focused on doing our jobs."

A week after the Black and White Night, Waits kicked off his fall/winter tour. With ever-presents Cohen, Carney, and Blair augmented by Marc Ribot and new accordionist Willy "The Squeeze" Schwarz, the itinerary began in Canada with three consecutive nights at Toronto's Massey Hall. Waits approached the tour with his usual antsiness. He detested the conventional stage setup for rock shows, the way the instruments and amplifiers were arranged, the wires winding round everything like the band was in a hospital ward. "I'm trying to put together the right way

Big Time band and crew, November 1987, including Willy Schwarz (bow tie), Michael Blair (frizzy hair), Ralph Carney (leaning, demented grin), tour manager Stuart Ross (top, beard), Greg Cohen (with megaphone), and Marc Ribot (in front of Waits, intense stare). (*Courtesy of Ralph Carney*)

of seeing the music," he said. "I worry about these things. If I didn't it would be easier."

To ensure that the "concert film" – working title *Crooked Time* – bore no resemblance to any earlier example of the genre, Chris Blum worked with lighting designer Darryl Palagi on a stage concept based around a series of light boxes. "The original stage set started out as a junkyard," he explained. "We had an idea for these huge plexiglass signs, like the ones you see in LA's Koreatown – back-lit, primary-colored." Palagi simplified this idea, giving each band member a different box. "Even though they're supplemented by other sources, we wanted to give the impression that they were the only light sources," Blum said. "The attempt was . . . to have things look non-art-directed."

Drawing predictably on a pool of songs from "the Frank trilogy" but intermittently dropping in such old chestnuts as "Tom Traubert", "Christmas Card", "Jersey Girl", "Jitterbug Boy", and "I Wish I Was in New Orleans" – plus a crazed version of James Brown's "Papa's Got a Brand New Bag" – Waits pulled out all the stops in an effort to stimulate, provoke, and entertain. Flipping from one persona (slimy cabaret MC in sunglasses/tux/pencil moustache) to another (folk troubadour in waistcoat and porkpie hat), he drew on his Steppenwolf experience to turn the in-concert rock experience into something meta-theatrical.

The US leg of the tour continued down the East Coast – including six nights at New York's Eugene O'Neill Theater – then headed into the Midwest before climaxing in California in early November with two shows at San Francisco's Fox Warfield Theater and three at the Wiltern in LA. It was from the West Coast dates that *Big Time* was drawn, the hope being that all kinks would have been ironed out of the show by that point. "We did it in only two nights of concerts," Waits told Francis Thumm. "Six cameras the first and two the next." Subtitled "*Un Operachi Romantico*"* – as *Frank's Wild Years* had been – *Big Time* consisted of straight live footage interspersed with more staged sequences and narrative links starring Waits as the usher dreaming of stardom. "A musicotheatrical experience played in dreamtime," in the words of the blurb for the video release, the disjointed film desperately wanted to be Robert Wilson meets Robert Frank. Some of the uptempo material translated well enough, with Waits doing what by now was a well-honed hands-

---

* The term "operachi" was coined by Kathleen as a hybrid of opera and mariachi. "We were just looking for a word that had something to do with what this is all about," Waits said. "I don't want this music to intimidate people, make them think they have to take a course or something to be able to enjoy it."

on-hips Mick Jagger impersonation. "16 Shells" and "Hang On St Christopher" rocked, "Telephone Call from Istanbul" was an exultant jump blues, and "Rain Dogs" climaxed with a hilarious cod-Hebrew dance by Waits. But the more diffuse numbers – "Shore Leave", "9th and Hennepin" – were uninvolving and the non-musical links stilted.

At times recalling the clunky artiness of Neil Young's *Rust Never Sleeps*, at others resembling nothing more than a bad eighties promo video, *Big Time* failed to snare the experience of Waits live. "It's difficult to retain what happened at that moment and preserve it," Waits acknowledged. "You don't want to kill the beast while you're trying to capture it." As he said to Franny Thumm, "Even when it's great you think, 'It's great, but shouldn't we have been there?'"

From LA, Waits and his motley entourage flew to Europe for three weeks of dates in the UK, Scandinavia, France, and Germany. Deliriously received shows in Dublin, London, Stockholm, Paris, and Berlin confirmed that Waits was better known across the Atlantic for *Swordfishtrombones* than for *Small Change*. Again the sets were made up almost exclusively of songs from the Island albums, though a smattering of occasional pre-Frank numbers (including "Red Shoes", "Burma Shave", "Blue Valentines", and "I Beg Your Pardon") appeased the diehards. (On the final date, at Berlin's Freie Volksbuehne, Waits played "Muriel", "Ruby's Arms", "Step Right Up", "$29.00", "Christmas Card", "I Can't Wait to Get off Work", "On the Nickel", *and* "Tom Traubert's Blues".)

Asked about his fan base when the tour was over, Waits replied that "the kind of thing I'm working on now, I would hope in some cases – I don't want this to sound pretentious – but it may earn me a bit of youth . . ."

Waits had been so much older then. He was younger than that now.

Chapter 4

In a Suit When You Dream

> *"Here's the deal, folks. You do a commercial, you're*
> *off the artistic roll call for ever. End of story, okay?"*
> (Bill Hicks, *Arizona Bay*)

It all started with Tex Avery, genius creator of Bugs Bunny and animator of a pistol-packin' bandit who held up ordinary hard-working Americans and relieved them of their scrumptious Frito Corn Chips. "*Aye, yi, yi, yi, I am the Frito Bandito!*" the little guy chirped in a Mel Blanc voiceover.

> *I like Frito's Corn Chips, I love them I do*
> *I want Frito's Corn Chips, I'll get them from you!*

In 1971, following four years of repeated complaints from the

Step Right Up for the Frito Bandito!

National Mexican-American Anti-Defamation Committee, Avery's Speedy Gonzales stereotype was rightly put out to pasture and Frito-Lay, makers of said chips, were forced to figure out alternative ways to hawk their product to ordinary hard-working Americans.

Years passed. In 1988, ad agency Tracy-Locke hit on the inspired idea of adapting the Tom Waits track "Step Right Up" to flog a new Frito-

Lay product called SalsaRio Doritos. The garrulous parody of a salesman hyping a mysterious product that solved all life's problems in an instant went down a storm at Frito-Lay. Session singer Stephen Carter was duly roped in to ape Waits' gruff hipster delivery and, in September 1988, the ads were aired on some 250 US radio stations. "*It's buffo, boffo, bravo, gung ho, tallyho, but never mellow,*" Carter barked. "*Try 'em, buy 'em, get 'em, got 'em!*"

The first Waits knew of the SalsaRio Doritos ad was when a DJ happened to play it on the morning of 3 October 1988. For the next week he did little but call friends and acquaintances to set them straight. Frito-Lay was messing with the wrong guy. Waits had already expressed strong opposition to artists letting their work be hijacked for commercial purposes. The irony of customizing the very track that lampooned the hyperbole of America's hucksters clearly bypassed the suits at the company. A lawsuit was brought against Frito-Lay, and against Tracy-Locke, in November 1988 and came to court in LA in April 1990.

True, Waits had once succumbed to the lure of the advertising dollar himself. In August 1981, he'd done the voice-over for a commercial advertising Butcher's Blend dry dog food.* "As Dog travels through the envied and often tempting world of Man," Waits growled as a Dalmatian padded hungrily past neon signs flashing "Beef", "Liver", and "Bacon", "there's one thing above all that tempts him most – the taste of meat! And that's why Purina makes Butcher's Blend. Butcher's Blend is the first dry dog food with three tempting meaty tastes: beef, liver, and bacon. All in one bag. So c'mon, deliver your dog from the world of temptation. The world of Butcher's Blend. The first dry dog food with three meaty tastes."

Waits had certainly left himself open to charges of hypocrisy. But his real bone of contention was artists who allowed their

* "I was down on my luck," Waits said in his defence. "And I've always liked dogs."

songs to be repurposed as advertising slogans. Two such were Lou Reed, pictured astride a Honda motorcycle, and Waits' old influence Dr John, whose talents were enlisted to help shift toilet rolls. "You know, when a guy is singing to me about toilet paper . . . you may need the money but I mean, rob a 7-11!" Waits fulminated. "Do something with dignity and save us all the trouble of peeing on your grave."

Fifteen years later, in a letter to *The Nation*, he put it more thoughtfully. "Songs carry emotional information, and some transport us back to a poignant time, place or event in our lives," he wrote. "It's no wonder a corporation would want to hitch a ride on the spell these songs cast and encourage you to buy soft drinks, underwear or automobiles while you're in the trance. Artists who take money for ads poison and pervert their songs."

On this issue Waits was with Bill Hicks, the taboo-busting comedian whose raging routines he had come to revere. After comedian Jay Leno did an ad for – guess what – Doritos, Hicks had stated that endorsing such products made you "another corporate fucking shill, another whore at the capitalist gangbang", rendering "everything you say" suspect and "every word that comes out of your mouth" like "a turd falling into my drink". Waits also claimed he'd had an epiphany upon hearing Jimmie Rodgers – not the Singing Brakeman but the late-fifties folk-pop singer of "Honeycomb" and "Kisses Sweeter than Wine" fame – adapt one of his songs into a TV jingle for Carpeteria. Disturbed by the experience, he'd worked it into *Frank's Wild Years*, contorting "Innocent when You Dream" into "You're in a Suit of Your Dreams" for the scene in which his hero took a job in an all-night Las Vegas haberdashery.

In 1992, Waits won his David-and-Goliath case against Frito-Lay and Tracy-Locke, earning more money (a handy $2.6 million) from the settlement than he'd made from all his albums to date. Bizarrely, the award failed to deter others from using Waits' music to market their wares. When Herb Cohen licensed Screamin' Jay Hawkins' version of "Heartattack and Vine" to Levi-Strauss, the singer again went to war. This time he couldn't sue on the grounds that Levi-Strauss had committed "the Midler tort" – misappropriating Waits' vocal style and thus implying that he himself endorsed the product – but he still won the case and an apology in *Billboard*.

Waits knew that Levi-Strauss had used soul classics such as Marvin Gaye's "I Heard It through the Grapevine" to sell their 501 jeans. For him the pernicious influence of music videos had filtered through to television commercials. Now immortal songs like "Grapevine" and "Revolution" and "Good Vibrations" were being attached to products whose taint they would never escape. Songs, he believed, should be non-visual, magical experiences that inspired the listener to supply his own accompanying images. At a time when nothing apparently had inherent value anymore – when the value of a copyrighted intellectual property lay solely in its ability to sell something *else* – Waits' stand against selling out to Mammon was (and remains) heartwarmingly stubborn.

Aside from post-production work on *Big Time* – and preparing the music for CD release – Waits took it easy for much of 1988. The film, he explained, was supposed to "go out on the road" while he stayed home and enjoyed quality time with Kellesimone and Casey. "They don't think I have a job," he said of his kids. "They think I'm just like them." Family life in Los Angeles was, he said, "a happy ending . . . to a terrible story", though bringing up children was "like living with a bunch of drunks . . . you really have to be on your toes all the time". Tom and Kathleen sometimes held parties on Union Avenue, gatherings such as the one that inspired the bizarre-sounding "Filipino Box Spring Hog". "We sawed the floorboards out of the living room," Waits explained of the indoor barbecue in the song. "We took the bed, the box spring, and first dug out the hole and filled it with wood, poured gasoline on it, and lit a fire. And the box spring over the top . . . was the grill. We brought in a pig and cooked it right there."

Among the friends who showed up at the parties was Chuck E. Weiss, who'd cleaned up his act and now held down a Monday night residency at an unglamorous Sunset Strip club called the Central. "I've known Chuck for about a hundred years," Waits said. "I go down there to the Central and [. . .] that's a damn good show, a good place to be on Monday nights." Weiss and his band the Goddamn Liars played the Central almost every week for eleven years. The place was on the point of closing when he called actor pal Johnny Depp and suggested they renovate the place and change its name to the Viper Room. Overnight it became *the* place for decadent young movie stars to mingle, achieving a certain infamy in 1993 when River Phoenix collapsed and died on the street outside.

The late summer found Waits decamping to the Gallatin National Forest, halfway between Butte and Billings in Montana, to play a hit man in Austrian director Robert Dornhelm's caper comedy *Cold Feet*. Co-starring with Sally Kirkland and Robert Altman regular Keith Carradine – with cameos from Jeff Bridges and a pre-*Larry Sanders* Rip Torn – Waits once again found himself living in a state of suspended animation as he waited to be called for scenes. "Movies are done in such small segments that you have to be very careful about preparation in order to stay in character," he said. "You can't really sit around and watch the world news." Scripted by Montana-based novelists Thomas McGuane and Jim Harrison, *Cold Feet* was a likable if insubstantial comedy about a trio of smalltime crooks who smuggle emeralds into the US inside a thoroughbred horse. Double-crossed by Monte (Carradine), his ditzy girlfriend Maureen (Kirkland) motors north to Montana in a camper van with the deranged

As Kenny in Robert Dornhelm's *Cold Feet* (1989), with Sally Kirkland as Maureen. (*Kobal*)

Kenny Prewitt (Waits) in order to track down her errant lover and the horse. Much of the movie was taken up with the relationship between Maureen and Kenny, whose dynamic suggested a pair of dysfunctional siblings. Waits drew on both the Zack of *Down by Law* and the Rudy of *Ironweed* to create Kenny, a kind of sulky brother to Kirkland's oversexed bombshell.

With his bleached eighties hair, fingerless leather gloves, and predilection for Turkish figs, Kenny was about as unsinister as any comedy psychopath in American cinema. Waits used his oddly loping, pigeon-toed gait to good effect and was the beneficiary of a few good McGuane/Harrison lines. "Actually I think of myself as executive material," he confided in Kirkland as they sat round a campfire. "I don't wanna grow old as just another murderer." If *Cold Feet* was received less warmly than Dornhelm's earlier *Echo Park*, Waits' Kenny was generally liked. "Waits' advantage is that he's a character actor, which allows him a lot of range," *Premiere*'s Christopher Connelly noted, adding that unlike the critically panned Madonna he didn't have "a mass following" and wasn't "used up as a cultural icon".

As tedious as the filmmaking process was, Waits relished the chance to spend time with his family in the wilds of Montana. "This is the best summer I've had in a long, long time," he told Franny Thumm, describing the afternoon he'd just enjoyed in a nearby swimming hole. He said he'd been out collecting rocks with Kellesimone, who told him that pretty stones were good people that had died, whereas "all the little ones you're not interested in are bad people". He said the mountains and "wide open spaces" were so beautiful "it takes the top of your head off".

Montana made Tom and Kathleen think hard about where they wanted to live and what they wanted for their children. "[We've] been gridlocked in LA for so long," Waits told Thumm. "I would like to exchange the dynamic so that going into town would be what going into the country is now." Both Waits and Brennan wanted to distance themselves from what LA represented. "They've always lived simply and sensibly and seem really grounded," Chris Blackwell says of the couple.

For Blackwell, too, the marriage only became stronger as it evolved. "As long as I've known them I have seen them as a team, as partners," he says. Waits told Franny Thumm that no one made him laugh like Kathleen. "She's great in emergencies and she's brutally honest." He added that she continued to challenge him as a songwriter, helping him to "feel safe in my uncertainty". Brennan had helped Waits to demystify music, dissolving the artificial barriers that separated the creative process from the life that nurtured it. "After a while you realize that music – the writing and enjoying of it – is not off the coast of anything," he said. "It's not sovereign, it's well-woven, a fabric of everything else: sunglasses, a great martini, Turkish figs, grand pianos." It was a beautiful insight that changed the whole way he looked at his work.

Waits kept his toes in the musical waters with a splendidly irascible version of "Heigh Ho" for *Stay Awake*, Hal Willner's 1988 album of Disney songs, while also providing an offscreen cameo as the voice of a DJ in Jim Jarmusch's Memphis-set narrative triptych *Mystery Train*. But his main focus as 1989 commenced was on two projects: a role in the LA production of cult playwright Thomas Babe's *Demon Wine*, and a collaboration on a "cowboy opera" called *The Black Rider: The Casting of the Magic Bullets* with Robert Wilson.

In the world premiere of Babe's play, which opened on 1 December at the Los Angeles Theater Center, Waits played Curly, son of a mobster (Philip Baker Hall) and pal of Jimmie (Bill Pullman, who'd played Buck in *Cold Feet*). "I feel a little intimidated," he said of his first stage role since *Frank's Wild Years*. The schedule was punishing for Waits, who wasn't used to rehearsing eight hours before driving home to learn lines and prepare for the following day's work. He felt sometimes "like an ant hanging onto a cracker in the middle of a storm". But he enjoyed the freedom from musical responsibilities and saw parallels between *Demon Wine* and his own writing. "Both my songs and [Babe's] play are about 'the gravel of the earth,' as he puts it," he said. "He's written this comedy that really slams into the American idea of success, the Horatio Alger myth that you can get what you want." Director David Schweizer, he added, was "like a conductor, and we're his orchestra, and he brings out something new in us every day".

Robert Wilson was already a towering figure in avant-garde theatre when Kathleen Brennan took her husband to see the four-and-a-half-hour opera *Einstein on the Beach* at the Brooklyn Academy of Music. The tall, gay son of an overbearing civic leader and an emotionally remote mother, Wilson had grown up in Texas with a chronic speech impediment that only improved when dance teacher Byrd Hoffman urged him to "take more time to speak". Frustrated by smalltown Baptist life, Wilson moved to

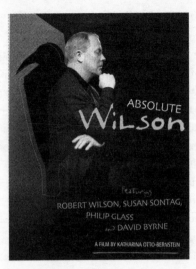

Absolute Robert Wilson (2006).

New York in 1962 to study architecture at Brooklyn's Pratt Institute. What really liberated him was New York itself, along with the discovery of the avant-garde dance/performance art scene in downtown Manhattan. "Being awkward and shy, and not comfortable with my body, dance was a liberation," he has said. "If you know your body, then you know yourself and you can relate." He also became actively involved in movement and speech therapy with brain-damaged children, a fascination that runs through his subsequent career. For him, the secret to communicating with such kids was to relate to them *as a child*.

Returning to Texas in 1965 was a mistake: enmeshed once again with his toxic family, Wilson attempted suicide and was briefly committed to a mental institution. The day he was released, he left Waco once and for all, moving back to New York and the brave new world of its experimental theatre. After founding the experimental Byrd Hoffman School of Byrds company, Wilson's early productions included *The Life and Times of*

Sigmund Freud, the twelve-hour *Life and Times of Joseph Stalin*, and the seven-day *KA MOUNTain and GUARDenia Terrace*, staged on a mountaintop in Iran. This was radical sixties theatre as communal art, with Wilson as the charismatic leader of what was a virtual cult. The extraordinary *Deafman Glance*, featuring a deaf African-American boy Wilson had adopted, was (said *The New Yorker*) "almost impossible to describe . . . [containing] elements of dance, mime, 'happening,' tableau vivant, farce, and medieval mystery play". In France, Wilson was anointed by Louis Aragon and others as a natural heir to Surrealism. "It was not coming out of what the popular theatre was, which were the psychological, naturalistic theatre groups coming from a more artistic background," Wilson said in 2000. "I think without John Cage, Alan Kaprow, Robert Morris, and [Robert] Rauschenberg, I probably couldn't have been doing what I was doing, but I took it and went somewhere else with it."

After *A Letter for Queen Victoria* flopped on Broadway in 1974, Wilson disbanded the Byrd Hoffman school, recognizing that many of its actors had become overly dependent on him. 1976's *Einstein on the Beach* – originally staged at New York's Metropolitan Opera House on 21 November 1976 – featured a brilliant minimalist score by Philip Glass and marked Wilson's entry into the world of opera. The acclaim notwithstanding, he made the decision to focus on working in Europe, where grants and subsidies for such forbidding work were easier to come by. If he'd had any doubts about America's hostility towards the avant-garde, those were dispelled when *the CIVIL wars*, a vast performance commissioned for the 1984 Olympic Games, was cancelled at the last minute after the Olympic committee refused to cough up the final $200,000 to stage the work.

Wilson's work was a full-scale imagistic assault on traditional theatre: stark but monumental, slow and dreamlike. His productions broke language down, forcing audiences to question the use of – and even the need for – words. For him, the movement of the human body was at least as important as verbal language as a code of communication. In his work, moreover, they were often in opposition to each other. Waits was entranced by the spectacle of Wilson's theatre; its use of lighting and props profoundly affected his ideas for *Big Time*. "[*Einstein*] was real long, but it's the closest thing to film I've ever seen in the theater because of what he does with the light," he said. "It felt like waking up on an airplane in the middle of the night [. . .] you look out the window and you don't know where you are."

Wilson in turn was captivated by the unorthodoxies of Waits' music and expressed interest in collaborating when they first met in New York. "Tom and I are very different men," he said in 1993. "He and I dress differently, have different styles. I tend to be cooler, more formal. But nevertheless I think we're emotionally tied somehow. In my work the emotion is sometimes hidden or buried, and Tom's music has a very deep emotional centre for me. I immediately liked it when I first heard it."

"When I met him I felt I was with an inventor, Alexander Graham Bell or one of those guys," Waits recalled of their first encounter. "He's a deep thinker, a man who chooses his words very carefully and is not to be trifled with. We found out we were very different, but there was something we both understood about each other, which was a good thing." The two very different men – described by writer Paul Schmidt as "America's greatest minimalist" (Wilson) and its "greatest maximalist" – stayed in touch through the late eighties. "What I like about Robert", Waits said, "is [that] he'll go through his calendar when you're talking about doing something, and he'll say very seriously, 'Well, I have a little time in 1998.' And he's not joking. And in 1998 you'll get a call." It didn't take quite that long. When he did finally call, Wilson told Waits about the old German folk tale on which Carl Maria von Weber had based the 1821 opera *Der Freischütz*.

"I read this strange story in a library in Stuttgart," the director said. "And I immediately thought it was something you might want to do." In the story – "a sad little tale with a brutal ending", said Waits – a file clerk falls for a forester's daughter but to win her hand has to prove to her father that he is as good with a gun as he is with a pen. Offered magic bullets by the devil, the clerk enters into a classic Faustian pact that concludes tragically with the death of his new bride.

Waits agreed to write the songs for the play, which Wilson wanted to call *The Black Rider*, but said he wasn't qualified to write the text. It was Allen Ginsberg who suggested Wilson turn instead to William Burroughs, whose own experience of accidentally shooting his wife dead in a drunken game of "William Tell" was eerily recalled by the play. Over a long meeting with Waits and Brennan at Hollywood's Roosevelt Hotel, Wilson proposed that Tom spend several weeks in Hamburg writing the music for a production at the city's Thalia Theatre. Waits was simultaneously "intrigued, flattered, and scared". The old fears he'd had about scoring *One from the Heart* flared up again, as did anxieties about being away from his family for long stretches of time. But Kathleen, a huge Wilson fan, urged Waits to seize the opportunity to work not only with the director but with seventy-five-year-old Burroughs, the model for Old Bull Lee in *On the Road*. "He was the [Beat writer] that I guess was more like Mark Twain with an edge," Waits said when I asked about the author of *Naked Lunch*. "He was more suited [than Kerouac] to the whole notion of the country having some type of alter ego. He seemed to have an overview, one of maturity and cynicism. He had a strongly developed sense of irony, and I guess that's really at the heart of the American experience."

With Wilson and Greg Cohen, Waits flew to Kansas to meet Burroughs at his home in Lawrence. In Waits' eyes, Burroughs had always been the scary old man of the Beat Generation, and in person he didn't disappoint. Waits liked the fact that Burroughs had retired to the flat, featureless Midwest, living "like the crooked sheriff in a bad town". Like some warped retake of the Napa Valley brainstorms on *One from the Heart*, the visit was a kind of literary summit, though the self-doubting Waits felt like a pygmy amidst avant-garde giants. "It was very exciting, really," he told me. "Around three o'clock Burroughs started fondling his watch as we got closer to cocktail hour. He was very learned and serious. Obviously an authority on a wide variety of topics. Knew a lot about snakes, insects, firearms."

At one point the cadaverous Burroughs, cocktail in hand, commenced "a little jig" and broke into the macabre 1930s ballroom-dance song "T'aint No Sin". For all present it was a moment of sublime inspiration, the song later being included in *The Black Rider*. "When Tom was here in Lawrence, he had some very good ideas," Burroughs testified. "I had the idea of comparing the magic bullet in the original German story to heroin. Once you use one, you'll use another. Tom said, 'Yeah, and the first one's always free,' and of course that went right in." After the summit, Burroughs began mailing texts to Waits, "piles of material" that dramaturge Wolfgang Wiens then cut and paste into the narrative. "[Burroughs] was just coughing up all this stuff, not writing in any linear way," Waits explained. "Sometimes I would take something he wrote and turn it into a lyric. Sometimes we'd collaborate, like in 'Just the Right Bullets'."

In May 1989, Waits and Cohen departed the spring sunshine of LA for "the rainy streets, church bells, and train station" of Hamburg, the city where – in dives on the infamous Reeperbahn – British R&B bands had plied their trade and Anders Petersen shot the photograph used on the cover of *Rain Dogs*. Kathleen and the kids would once have accompanied him on such a trip, but Kellesimone was now in elementary school and Casey in kindergarten. Waits flew with heavy heart, not to mention the unvoiced fear that *The Black Rider* would somehow take him out of his depth. As with *One from the Heart*, however, the creative process quickly took shape.

Working by night with Thalia veteran Gerd Bessler at his nearby Music Factory studio, Waits and Cohen wrote and demoed songs that were then brought to Bob Wilson the next morning. "Long hours, cold coffee, hard rolls, and no place to lie down" made for fittingly Spartan conditions in which to create the harsh, discordant music.* "Gerd and Greg and I were the core of the music department in the early stages," Waits wrote in his liner notes for the 1993 *Black Rider* album. "We fashioned together tapes in this crude fashion, never imagining they would be released, which gave us all an innocence and a freedom to abandon conventional recording techniques and work under the gun to have something finished to bring to Wilson's carnival each morning."

Eight years Waits' senior, Wilson was the latest father (or at least older-brother) figure in his life, and the younger man was as anxious for "Bob's" approval as he'd been eager to please Francis Ford Coppola. "For me, in all my years in school [there was] nothing like Wilson," Waits said in 2004. "Like you'll always remember a particular teacher? I'd say Wilson is my teacher. There's nobody that's affected me that much as an artist." In turn, Wilson was deeply affected the first time he heard Waits play the piano. "Somehow he touched me, he got me," the director recalled. "From the beginning there was this attraction. I can't explain it because it's so complicated ... it's funny, it's sad, it's touching, it's noble, it's elegant. It's his signature, it's something personal."

---

* Offering some respite from the austerity was Harry's Hafen Basar (or Harry's Harbour Bazaar), a junk shop on the Hamburg waterfront that became a regular stopoff for Waits. "Sailors from all over the world, when they land in Hamburg, that's where they sell their $2 guitars, stuffed snakes, zebra jackets," he said.

Joining Wilson and Waits in Hamburg was Burroughs himself – less a father figure than a formative ancestor. Burroughs continued to ply Waits with cut-up texts that, in the latter's words, "became a river of words for me to draw from in the lyrics for the songs". Like Waits, Burroughs wrote at night and brought his texts to rehearsals the following morning. "[He] was as solid as a metal desk," Waits wrote, "and his text was the branch this bundle would swing from." (On the *Black Rider* album, three tracks – "That's the Way", "Flash Pan Hunter", and "Crossroads" – were credited to Waits/Burroughs.)

If *Frank's Wild Years* had made few concessions to conventional rock instrumentation, the *Black Rider* music veered still closer to the organic sound of a 1930s pit band playing songs by Kurt Weill and Hanns Eisler. "[Greg] uses oboe, bass clarinet, low brass, low reeds," Waits told Franny Thumm, who would work on the *Black Rider* recordings in California four years later. "It's real wooden, he uses almost no percussion, but all his percussion is handled by the attack of the low reeds: *Cha chung, chung, chung, chung*. I love that." Waits added that Robert Wilson was "right into the Eisler stuff and loves the German composers". Undoubtedly the Weill/Eisler influence was more marked than usual because Waits and Cohen were actually working in Germany. Certainly it seeped from "Flash Pan Hunter" and the songs the pair fashioned for Pegleg to sing: both "The Black Rider" and "Just the Right Bullets" were rendered by Waits in a sardonically evil accent that recalled the Joel Grey of *Cabaret*.

Other songs were less Germanic but no less sombre. The bleak "November" was sung in the quavering voice of the ageing forester Bertram. "Gospel Train" was "Way Down in the Hole" arranged by Hieronymous Bosch, "Chase the Clouds" a demented hymn sung by a pastor so zealous his stentorian baritone gave way to a shrieking falsetto. "The Briar and the Rose", with Waits on pump organ, was a love song to Kathleen disguised as a folk ballad. "I'll Shoot the Moon" was a Tin Pan Alley pastiche delivered in a woozy croon, "Crossroads" a spaghetti-western cowboy song featuring hysterical yodelling from Waits and searing electric viola by Gerd Bessler. "We were trying", Waits wrote of the songs, "to find a music that could dream its way into the forest of Wilson's images and be absurd, terrifying, and fragile." They succeeded. "I think that was a great test for Tom," Wilson said later. "That he came in as a composer and could find a voice for other people whose voices are very different to his. In that sense he's a real composer."

Working with Wilson was unlike anything Waits had experienced, either in theatre or in film. The feeling of being thrown into the unknown, of having to trust methods that made no rational sense, amazed Waits. It necessitated letting go of the superego and entering a kind of dream state without maps or signs or cultural reference points of any kind. What made *The Black Rider* work was how the actors – "fearless, tireless, insane", in Waits' words – completely gave themselves up to Wilson's vision and instincts for the play. During one rehearsal, Waits himself had to stand in for a member of the company who was off sick. "It was like, '[Bob's] using these people like clay,'" he said of the experience. "And this particular group of actors were thrilled, they'd melt themselves down, pour themselves into any mold." By the end, Waits said, everybody was transformed.

While Wilson continued work on *The Black Rider* – the play would only premiere at the Thalia on 30 March 1990 – Waits flew to London in late June to start filming on Ann Guedes' *Bearskin: An Urban Fairytale*. He got top billing in this odd little film, playing half of a Punch-and-Judy act who employ a seventeen-year-old boy on the run from vengeful casino operators. British-financed and shot in London and Portugal, *Bearskin* was a stilted affair, devoid of credible characters or a remotely gripping plot. Waits had a lot of time on screen – including two brief scenes with Ian Dury* – but aside from the occasional fun he had with the voices for Punch and co. he seemed unengaged on screen, bemused to be carrying a film as lead actor. "I don't like coming out front," his character Silva says of the Punch-and-Judy act. "You don't know me. Maybe I got my own reasons for staying in the box." Maybe he did.

In the fall, Waits and family made another trip to Ireland, visiting Brennan relatives in and around Tralee and attending the Thirty-fourth Cork Film Festival – where *Big Time* got a screening – in October. Two months later he turned forty, an often unwelcome landmark in any man's life and certainly a turning point for anyone operating in the ageist world of western entertainment. Marking the onset of the traditional mid-life crisis, the forties were when the proverbial shit hit the fan – when you either sorted through your emotional baggage or drowned in it. Perhaps it was significant that Waits now commenced a run of seven movie appearances in four years, as though making up for lost time.

First up was *The Two Jakes* (1990), an underwhelming sequel to Roman Polanski's timeless 1974 corruption picture *Chinatown*. Waits was given a one-minute walk-on as a plainclothes cop by his *Ironweed* co-star Jack Nicholson, who in the brief scene found himself on the receiving end of one of Waits' boots. In Terry Gilliam's *The Fisher King* (1991) he played to type as a disabled Viet-vet panhandler dispensing street sagacity to homeless Jeff Bridges in a brief scene in New York's Grand Central Station. "[Tom] was a friend of [Jeff's], basically," Gilliam said. "It's

* Dury was another middle-class teacher's son who'd made himself over as a chronicler of the proletariat – to the point where his "Mockney" act took over from his class reality. "It was all part of inhabiting a persona," said writer and broadcaster Charlie Gillett, who managed Dury's early band Kilburn & the High Roads. "But that persona eventually became intertwined with Ian himself. In that way he's more like Tom Waits – someone inseparable from the persona he's created."

funny, because when I met him, and even in the course of making the film, I'd never heard a Tom Waits record. I just met him and liked him immediately." Columbia Pictures complained that Waits' character did nothing to advance Gilliam's modern-day-*Parsifal* plot, but the Monty Python veteran insisted on keeping his scene.

Steve Rash's *Queens Logic* (1991) gave us another Waits cameo as Monte, a garishly dressed loner who semi-socializes with a *Big Chill*-ish group of overwrought New Yorkers. With a high-calibre ensemble that included Joe Mantegna, Kevin Bacon, Chloe Webb, Linda Fiorentino, and John Malkovich, the film was a stilted example of the *Thirtysomething* genre, full of big female hair, men in vests, and people who spoke like characters in movies. As so often, Waits was a marginal presence in the drama, a man who couldn't quite be placed in its peer group. In his one notable scene, sporting an unspeakable leather vest and an unconvincing Queens brogue, he toasted Webb and Fiorentino in a bar, lamenting the fact that – with one of them married and the other about to be – there were "no more fish in the sea" for him. Interestingly, Waits was also the last person we saw in the film, arriving alone at Webb's wedding in a tux and ruffled shirt.

In the epic *At Play in the Fields of the Lord* (1991), Waits was reunited with *Ironweed*'s Hector Babenco, who cast him as a bearded pilot-for-hire at large in the Amazon jungle. Waits' Morty Wolf was a grizzled cynic, a Jew "without a country" and partner of the brooding, half-Cheyenne Lewis Moon (Tom Berenger). In his vest and Bermuda shorts, Wolf was as dissolute as he was mercenary. To him the Amazon rain forest – its mountains and stunning waterfalls shot as if for a travel brochure – was just a "green hell" that "gives me the fucking creeps". Like Kenny in *Cold Feet*, Waits seemed to have been cast in this ponderous story of missionaries and native Indians more for his tantrums than anything else; certainly he didn't have to dig far to channel his rage. But one wonders whether Wolf wasn't also a sly – or just unconscious – portrayal of Herb Cohen in his gun-running days.

Next up was Waits' turn as the insane insect-eater R. M. Renfield in Coppola's 1992 film *Bram Stoker's Dracula*, starring Keanu Reeves, Gary Oldman, and Winona Ryder. "I told [Francis] I was Renfield and you gotta get me in there," Waits said. "He hadn't cast [it] yet – he'd cast all the other parts – and I really came at it like a kid . . . 'Make me Renfield!'" The part, Waits said, was "a masochist's nirvana", requiring him to wear a straitjacket and sinister finger manacles for long stretches of time. Worst of all was the zoophagy: in one scene Waits was obliged to put real bugs in his mouth. His singular vocal talents also came in handy when Oldman failed to make Dracula sound menacing enough. Overdubbing the Count's lustful grunts was, Waits said, "like porno radio". Renfield afforded Waits the chance to explore the truly lurid side of his personality – to go, as he put it, into "your own dark rooms". But the film was schlock, with Waits acting as hammily as everyone else involved and affecting a shocking English accent (spiced up with a little Romanian). How one longed for the austerity of Murnau's *Nosferatu* or Dreyer's *Vampyr* as Coppola overegged his pudding to a degree that would surely have appalled Robert Wilson.

Dracula at least provided a welcome excuse to work once again with Coppola, especially when the shoot entailed a two-week stay in the director's idyllic Napa Valley retreat. "It was great to be in that environment," Keanu Reeves recalled. "Going for a run in the morning, looking at the stars at night, going into Francis's research library, spending time with him." Among Reeves' treasured memories of the stay was Waits serenading Winona Ryder at the piano with a rendition of "Tom Traubert's Blues" that made her cry. British actress Sadie Frost, making her Hollywood debut in *Dracula* as Lucy, remembers Waits as "shy and brooding" around the more extrovert young stars Coppola had cast in the film. "Francis was playing little games with us to try and get us into character," she says. "Tom seemed slightly pained and uncomfortable in the groups and, as I recall, was quite a heavy drinker. He was warm and friendly but seemed lacking in self-confidence and was missing his wife and kids – they were clearly his stability. In the end, I think, Francis had his hands so full with Gary Oldman and the others that he left Tom alone."

Shooting with Coppola at Sony Pictures in Culver City in the summer of 1992 led to another reunion, this time an unforeseen one. Bones Howe, then heading up the studio's music department, got wind that Waits was on the lot and stopped by to say hello. The two men hadn't spoken in almost a decade. "It was like we hadn't seen each other since last Thursday," Howe says. "We talked about his production ideas for the next record, about how less was more and how you could get a bigger sound for each instrument . . . and we had this wonderful conversation. And then I had to go back to my office and he had to go back on set. And we haven't seen each other since."

More rewarding than either Wolf or Renfield was Earl Piggot in *Short Cuts*, based on the short stories of the great minimalist Raymond Carver but shifting them from the writer's Pacific Northwest to an unglamorous part of Los Angeles – suburban Downey – that wasn't far removed from the Whittier of Waits' childhood. In this sprawling ensemble film directed by the veteran Robert Altman in the late summer of 1992, Waits played an alcoholic limo driver married to waitress Doreen (Lily Tomlin). The Piggot story was just one of a number of narrative threads woven together by Altman and co-writer Frank Barhydt, bringing into contact characters played by Andie MacDowell, Tim Robbins, Julianne Moore, Jennifer Jason Leigh, Robert Downey Jr, Frances McDormand, Lyle Lovett, and Jack Lemmon. Following up Altman's return to form *The Player*, *Short Cuts* was critically lauded, won a

As Earl in Robert Altman's *Short Cuts* (1992), with Lily Tomlin as Doreen. (*Kobal*)

special Golden Globe award, and spawned a virtual sub-genre of LA-based ensemble films that included *Pulp Fiction*, *Magnolia*, and *Crash*. "Altman was great to work with," Waits stated. "He's like a good sheriff in a bad town."

Piggot may be the best performance Waits ever gave as an actor. "Tom is unique, completely his own person," Altman said later. "He's bent, but in the right way. It's a good bend." The first of the film's characters we see on the screen (unless one counts anchor man Howard Finnigan on the limo's TV), Piggot was astutely caught by Waits as a man at once abusive and sentimental. Waits drew on his own alcoholism as he gave us a man more rounded and likable than the "drunken stupid pig" he is in his daughter's estimation. For obvious reasons he was at home in the scenes shot in Johnnie's Coffee Shop, as well as in a cocktail bar with the very Waitsian name the Low Note (whose house band included Greg Cohen). The Earl/Doreen storyline ended happily with the couple drinking cocktails and shaking maracas as a 7.4

quake hit LA. "*This is it, baby!*" Waits yelled. "*We're going out together!*" (It wasn't it and they weren't, but it made for a great climax.)

Glancing back over his cinematic CV in late 1993, Waits sounded far from convinced that this was really what he was meant to be doing. "I don't really consider myself an actor," he told the *New York Times*. "I do some acting. I don't have the confidence I'd like to have as an actor at this point. But I've learned that the acting and the music and the other projects all serve each other." Six years later he piped the same tune to me. "I don't know if I really think of myself as an actor," he said. "I like doing it, but there's a difference between being an actor and doing some acting." What continued to grate with Waits was the fact that movie actors were paid less for their thespian skills than for the sheer boredom of waiting around in trailers. He also saw most actors as inherently immature. "I find myself usually having more in common with the directors than maybe sometimes the actors," he admitted to Jim Jarmusch. "A lot of directors look at actors as insecurities with arms and legs – they're just children, and they need to be constantly reassured and directed and given rewards and discipline."

Waits' gruffly impatient, almost macho side came strongly to the fore with his film acting. "Somebody told me acting makes a woman more of a woman and a man less of a man," he grumbled. "Fussing around with your hair. Getting up at six in the morning and having all these people fussing around."* Compared to theatre – whether that was *Demon Wine* or *The Black Rider* – film was "so broken up . . . a mosaic". In theatre you might actually "leave the ground", where some films were "like you

---

* For an interesting academic discussion of "the extent to which Waits' music represents a theatrics of masculinity", see Gabriel Solis, "Workin' Hard, Hardly Workin'/Hey Man, You Know Me", *Journal of Popular Music Studies*, Vol. 19, Issue 1, April 2007.

bought the last ticket on a death ship". Waits would not appear in another mainstream film for six years.

By late 1992, in any case, Waits had made more than a few major changes in his life. Getting off the Hollywood merry-go-round was, in hindsight, the least of them.

Chapter 5

Bones, Cemeteries, and Dirty Blood

> *"I'm better off here in the sticks where I can't hurt myself."*
> (Tom Waits to Amanda Petrusich, Pitchfork.com, 27 November 2006)

Bob Seger was driving through Westwood in the summer of 1988 when he spotted a familiar figure walking in the eighty-five-degree sunshine. Ambling along in his ungainly way, dressed head to toe in black, was Tom Waits.

Seger pulled over to the kerb to offer Waits a ride, and the two men rode around the well-heeled LA neighbourhood conversing somewhat awkwardly. Waits sat in the passenger seat wondering what on earth he had in common with the Michigan-born singer of "Still the Same" and "Shame on the Moon" – a man who, into the bargain, was wearing shorts and a Hawaiian shirt. "Hey, can I drop you somewhere?" Seger asked after fifteen uncomfortable minutes. Waits pondered the offer for a second. "Uh, just drop me back where you picked me up, Bob," he replied finally. "I wasn't done walking."

It turned out that Waits was one of Seger's favourite songwriters. The following year, Seger recorded a version of "Downtown Train", a song he'd fallen in love with. Somewhat rashly, though, he mentioned it to Rod Stewart on a summer visit to London. The next thing he knew, Stewart had cut his *own* version of "Downtown Train". The track soared to No. 3 on the US singles chart. Seger was livid, calling Stewart a "nonperson" for stealing the idea of covering the song. (Former Scandal singer Patty

Smyth had actually got there first, recording "Downtown Train" in 1987.) Stewart in turn claimed he'd already recorded the song in London and only then decided to redo it in LA. "It's most disappointing to hear something like this, since the geezer knows very well the full truth," Stewart said. "It sounds like sour grapes to me."

Stewart's success with the song in early 1990 certainly made up for Waits' own lack of chart success. Moreover, the former Faces singer went on to record "Tom Traubert's Blues" on his 1993 album *Unplugged . . . and Seated*, while over the years Seger himself has cut at least three other Waits songs ("New Coat of Paint", "16 Shells from a Thirty-Ought Six", and "Blind Love"). Royalties from Stewart's covers in particular would keep Waits and family comfortable through the nineties. "Tom's brilliant," Rod said. "[He] said he put a swimming pool for his kids in his back garden and I paid for it!"

1990 also brought an award of $2.6 million – $375,000 in actual compensatory damages, $2 million in punitive damages, $100,000 in damages for violating the Lanham Act, and $125,000 in attorney fees – against Frito-Lay and Tracy-Locke. The defendants appealed but to no avail: Waits finally saw a payout of $2.5 million in August 1992. "I spent it all on candy," he said. "My mom told me I was foolish." Fighting the battle against Frito-Lay had been gruelling, but it sent out a message that Tom and Kathleen were tireless adversaries. "Never get involved in litigation," Waits said just a couple of months before the cheque came. "Your hair will fall out, your bones will turn to sand." But, he added, "when you have to, you have to . . . if somebody burned your house down, you'd have to do something about it".

On another copyright issue, Waits was powerless to act. 1991 saw the release of *The Early Years*, a selection of the demo recordings Waits had made for Herb Cohen in 1971. Waits was furious that these callow sketches from his musical youth were being made available. Listening to the voice of "Virginia Avenue" or "I'm Your Late Night Evening Prostitute" was for Waits as mortifying as Stephen Carter's soundalike on the Frito-Lay ad. "My early records, I can barely listen to them," he said. "I sound like a kid. I said, 'Boy, what are they doing recording a guy that sounds like that?'" Rubbing salt in the wound was the countenancing of the album's UK release by Demon-Edsel's co-owner Elvis Costello, with whom Waits had become friendly. "Waits gave Elvis a real hard time about it," says a former Demon-Edsel employee. "It caused quite a bit of friction between them." Costello can't have helped his cause by subsequently okaying the UK release of Screamin' Jay Hawkins' Bizarre/Straight album *Black Music for White People*, with the version of "Heartattack and Vine" that Herb Cohen licensed to Levi-Strauss.*

While Waits concentrated on films and fatherhood in 1990–1, he contributed to a number of albums by people he admired. There were two tracks on *Devout Catalyst*, an album by his "word-jazz" hero Ken Nordine. "We did a little kind of word duet," Waits said of "The Movie", which also featured the Grateful Dead's Jerry Garcia. "I did a little story and he talked in the pauses, and I talked in his pauses, and it was kind of a little woven duet." There was also a brace of songs on *Mississippi Lad*, a twilight release by Waits' tenor-saxophone idol – and sometime sideman – Teddy Edwards, whose PolyGram deal the younger man had helped to arrange. "[Tom is] America's best lyricist since Johnny Mercer," Edwards said. "He came down to the studio . . . and he sang two of my songs, wouldn't accept any money, just trying to give me the best boost that he could." "I'm Not Your

* This time the lawsuit did not drag on *ad infinitum*. Levi-Strauss dropped the ad and publicly apologized to Waits. Muddying matters somewhat was the fact that Hawkins – godfather of horror rock and most famous for the immortal "I Put a Spell on You" – had had a prominent role as a hotel night clerk in Jim Jarmusch's *Mystery Train*.

Fool Anymore" and the exquisite "Little Man" were recorded at Sunset Sound in mid-March 1991.

It wasn't only the old guard that Waits helped out, however. He'd become a fan of alterna-metal funksters Primus, an exuberant and eclectic band that spliced the influences of Frank Zappa and the Red Hot Chili Peppers, and agreed to guest on their song "Tommy the Cat" on the loopily-named 1991 album *Sailing the Seas of Cheese*. The band's bassist Les Claypool – and, later, its drummer Bryan Mantia, aka "Brain" – would become regular Waits collaborators over the next fifteen years. Waits had met the band while fishing in northern California. "I was over at Bodega Bay and I wasn't catching a thing," he recalled of the encounter. "I flagged these guys down and asked them if they'd sell me one of their fish to put on my line and have my picture taken with it so I wouldn't feel humiliated when I got home."

Primus turned out to be natives of an area where Tom and Kathleen were now thinking of putting down roots of their own. Having come to know the area well through their visits to Francis Ford Coppola's estate in the Napa Valley, they'd decided that somewhere north of the Bay Area was the ideal setting for their new life – a region that combined beautiful scenery with civilized and liberal people. "It just seemed a good place to go – north," Waits reflected in 1999. "You live in LA, you go south, there's just more LA."

The first place Waits bought, on the outskirts of Sonoma, proved a dud. Though it was love at first sight – a house with a porch and a view of nearby railroad tracks – the trains stopped running soon after the Waitses moved in and a bypass road was built to handle the resulting automobile traffic. Tom and Kathleen wasted little time in selling up, and this time they *really* got away from it all. "Now I live out," he said. "*Way* out." They found their second home near the small town of Valley Ford, located in the Two Rock area midway between Santa Rosa and the Pacific

Ocean, and have lived there ever since: not bad for a man whose idea of hell on earth had once been a cabin in Colorado.

Though he felt like "an unplugged appliance" for the first few months – "it gets really dark and really, really quiet," he observed – Waits loved being in the back of beyond. "I live in a little town out in the sticks," he said in October 1992. "The radio is terrible where I am. The food's terrible and everyone's got gun racks. There's a lot of roadkill out there too." A visitor to the Waits compound that very month was none other than Jim Jarmusch. "Tom lives with his family in a big, strange house hidden away somewhere in California," Jarmusch reported. "I think of it as the Tom Waits version of a gangster hideout – a world in and of itself." He added that – "for reasons I am very respectful of" – its location would remain anonymous. Those close to Waits religiously observe the same etiquette. While journalists are never permitted near the place, Waits is wary even of allowing music-business acquaintances to visit the house. "I'm trying to learn how to be invisible," he told Jarmusch. "I haven't been pulled over since I moved out of LA. I think it's possible to be invisible, certainly more in an area like this than it is in Los Angeles or New York City."*

1992 saw another dramatic change in Waits' life: he quit drinking. "My wife said, 'You drank enough,'" he told Mick Brown. "It comes from love, you know? 'I want you to stick around, God-damn it.'" It took a few months of slipping and sliding – clambering onto and then falling off the wagon – before his recovery began in earnest. Waits was still drinking the night he stopped by a recording session for John Hammond, the blues singer he'd first met in 1973. After hanging out with Hammond, producer J. J. Cale, and a guesting John Lee Hooker, he had to be driven

---

* "Are you a cop?" Waits half-seriously demanded of one interviewer who asked where he lived. "Are you from the census bureau? Is this a deposition? Are you in real estate? I'm not talking!"

home to Valley Ford from San Francisco. It must have been a night like this that finally pushed him to his rock bottom. "Some day you just have to quit being a vagabond and being drunk every day," he said in October. "One day you just wake up and realize there's an empty space in your soul. It's not cool, just weird." Many years later he came clean and – breaking his anonymity – admitted he was in AA. "I'm in the program," he stated. "I'm clean and sober. Hooray. But you know, it was a struggle."*

It didn't take long for Waits to figure out that recovery and ongoing twelve-step sobriety meant growing up. If he was really going to be the father he wanted to be, he knew he had to change. Perhaps Kathleen, too, had had enough of enabling him. "Because I utterly adore my wife and kids I had no choice but to grow up fast," Waits said. "You can't bring kids up if you're still one yourself." That summer, he wrote the brilliantly bratty "I Don't Wanna Grow Up", about the ingrained aversion to maturity. Rebutting Cyril Connolly's famous line that there was "no more sombre enemy of good art than the pram in the hall", he willed himself to believe that "life starts with the family unit and [doesn't end] with it". Holding a baby in your arms, he said, made you realize "how strong life is".

As other musicians have done, Waits worried that sobriety would stop the creative juices flowing. But he maintained that "all the big questions" came only when one finally forsook the bottle. "You know, 'What am I made of? What's left when you drain the pool?'" In time, recovery entailed coming to terms with himself and his past. "I never got along with myself," he admitted. Though Waits has never been one for soul-baring confession, he has in recent years been more open about the specific

* It's not inconceivable that Chuck E. Weiss had a hand in Waits' recovery, and may even have "twelfth-stepped" his friend into AA. Chuckie had cleaned up in "the program" nine years earlier.

dysfunction of his childhood and the effects of his father's own alcoholism. "[With] popular music there aren't very many real serious qualifications to enter that field," he said in 1992. "A lot of broken people find their way into it because nobody belongs near them." Broken people, like broken bicycles and broken shoes, had long been a fixation of Waits'. "I like things that are kind of falling apart," he admitted to another interviewer. "[Because] I come from a broken home, I guess. I like things that have been ignored or need to be put back together."

April 1992 saw the release of Waits' first new album in almost five years. Recorded as the soundtrack to an episodic Jim Jarmusch film about nocturnal taxi drivers and their passengers in LA, New York, Rome, and Helsinki, *Night on Earth* was mainly instrumental, consisting of variations on a theme interspersed with three vocal pieces ("Good Old World", "Back in the Good Old World", "On the Other Side of the World") that Waits had co-written with Kathleen. Though Jarmusch had originally put in a modest order for two themes, when Waits played the waltz-time "Good Old World" over the phone the director flipped and asked him to underscore the whole film. Jarmusch was so enthused he flew to California to sit in some of the recordings.

Jarmusch found Waits holed up in a funky recording studio that he'd discovered in the small town of Cotati – a converted chicken ranch called Prairie Sun. With Biff Dawes engineering and Francis Thumm serving as keyboardist and co-arranger, Waits worked on the *Night on Earth* music with a new group of Bay Area musicians that included guitarist Joe Gore, cellist Matt Brubeck, bassist Clark Suprynowicz, accordionist Josef Brinck-mann, and pianist/percussionist Mule Patterson.* The session

---

* Patterson was a humorous alias for Waits himself, an allusion to the stub-bornness Kathleen often accused him of. In the long conversation Jim Jar-musch recorded with him in October 1992, Waits invented an entire persona for Patterson, complete with a loaded .38 stuffed in a gym bag.

group also included Ralph Carney, who'd recently moved to Oakland from Brooklyn and knew Jarmusch from his native Ohio. Carney's saxes and other woodwinds were all over *Night on Earth*; on certain tracks he even experimented with flute and pan pipes. "There were a couple of things I did that were too hippie for Tom," he says. "He was like, 'I hate flute!' Jim would say he liked something and I could see Tom champing at the bit."

"It was a fairly egalitarian situation, though Tom was definitely leading things," recalls Clark Suprynowicz. "I really think I learned something from the experience, because Tom's way of directing the ensemble was very much as a theatre person. He would go into the recording booth and listen back to a take we'd done of something. Then he'd come out and look at Ralph and say, 'It just sounds too friendly! Can't we make it more anti-social?!'" After an early take of "Good Old World (Waltz)", Waits emerged from the booth and began dragging himself around the studio like he had a club foot. "Boys, boys!" he implored the musicians. "It's gotta limp a little bit!" Suprynowicz, co-founder of the Bay Area Jazz Composers' Orchestra, says he found Waits' methodology educational: "Sometimes to get the result you want from music, that's the only way to get it. There are things that just aren't captured by terms like crescendo or diminuendo."

Anybody assuming *Night on Earth* was a bona fide follow-up to *Frank's Wild Years* would have been scratching his head a quarter of the way into the record. Though "Back in the Good Old World (Gypsy)" kicked things off in a *Swordfish/Rain Dogs* vein, with Waits growling a lyric of regretful nostalgia over an unsettling fusion of cello, harmonium, guitar, baritone horn and *Flintstones* percussion, the soundtrack's ensuing "mood" pieces all followed the same eerily suspenseful, slightly monotonous pattern. For "Los Angeles Theme (Another Private Dick)", played as Winona Ryder ferried Gena Rowlands through LA, Waits drew on his own Hollywood-noir roots. But this wasn't "Heart of Saturday Night" or even "Heartattack and Vine": rather it was a dark city of lonely souls floating through empty streets. "New York Theme" (subtitled "Hey You Can Have That Heartattack Outside, Buddy") took the same riff and made it slightly swingier in feel. The Paris and Helsinki moods offered minor variations on the main motif.

Markedly different were the instrumental "Good Old World (Waltz)", a front-parlour recital complete with tentative, quaintly amateurish strings. "Carnival (Brunello Del Montalcino)" – heard as sheep-loving Roberto Benigni drove through Rome – was a reprise of "Back in the Good Old World" that might have been scored by Nino Rota. "Dragging a Dead Priest" sounded like a pit band from hell warming up for a version of "Shore Leave", all scraping sounds and tinkling bottles. "It was five minutes of really spooky, meandering music," says Clark Suprynowicz. "When we finished it I said to Tom, 'Hey, we could get a *grant* with this!' He was hip enough to the art world to get a laugh out of that."

"On the Other Side of the World" was a prototype nineties Waits ballad featuring sparse accordion/piano/banjo/clarinet instrumentation and a line about a white horse lost in his wife's hair. The stiff, slightly formal *chanson* nature of the song, like the references to "roses" and "crows", was fast becoming Waits' new orthodoxy. This was music like rock had never happened, with zero concession to youth's need for amplified angst and anger.

Night on Earth was barely in stores – and being greeted quizzically by critics – when Waits figured it was time to make a *real* new album. Sobriety seemed to energize him as he set to work on a record that forsook the *cabaret noir* tendencies of *The Black Rider* in favour of something more primordially American. Waits wanted to get back to basics, strip things to the bone, whether on gritty blues/gospel songs or sparse piano ballads. Thematically, too, the album would get down to the irreducible core of human existence. "Blood and death, those are my pet subjects," Waits said with a leery grin. "It really *is* all about bones, cemeteries, and dirty blood."

Eight of the songs on *Bone Machine* were co-written with Kathleen, clear evidence of her growing role in Waits' music. "[We] went into a room for about a month and banged them out," Waits said. "It's a different kind of thing, writing songs with someone. But hey, we got kids together – we can make songs together." Most of the songs were on the quiet side; a few were loud and pounding. None came easy. "I get real cranky about the songs," he admitted. "I get mad at [them]. 'Oh, you little sissy, you little wimp, you're not gonna go on my fucking record, y'little bastard!'" Waits estimated that altogether there were "about sixty ideas for songs" for *Bone Machine*, most demoed at home on a cheap Sony tape recorder. In the late spring of '92, with a pared-down shortlist of twenty or so, Waits went back into Prairie Sun with Biff Dawes and the redoubtable Larry Taylor. Seven years Waits' senior, Taylor had become part of his musical furniture, as trusted a sidekick as his fellow bassist Greg Cohen had been for so long. In his trademark baseball cap and ZZ Top beard, Taylor would be an ever-present in Waits' setup for years to come.

This time, the main Prairie Sun studio felt too sterile for the music; Waits sensed that nothing would "grow" in it. Instead he set up camp in an old storage room whose acoustics he instantly preferred. "I said, 'What about this room over here, I bet this room sounds good,' and everybody laughed," he recalled. "I said, 'No, really, what's wrong with this room here? Get all these crates out of here and let's do it right here, just run the wires down the hill.'" Waits dug the fact that the room wasn't soundproofed – that ambient sounds from the outside world entered the normally hermetic chamber of recording. "We had airplanes to deal with and cars," he said. "So – 'Oh, we'd better stop, wait for that train to pass.' I like dealing with that, it puts you in correct perspective on what you're doing."

With rain pouring down around them, Waits, Taylor, and Dawes quickly laid the foundations for the album's sixteen tracks, Waits variously supplying vocals, guitar, piano, and primitive percussion. There were almost no drums per se on the finished record. "You can go crazy trying to communicate certain details of what you want to a drummer," Waits said, "so I started hitting them myself." The very title of the album was as much a reflection of the sound Waits wanted for it as a metaphor for the human body and its inevitable demise. "I wanted to explore more machinery sounds," he explained. "I'm exploring more and more things that make a sound but are not traditional instruments. It's a good time to do it, too, because there's a lot of garbage in the world that I can use that is just sitting out there rusting." The more technologically disembodied modern life seemed, the more stubbornly Luddite Waits became. Bashing away at various metal objects that dangled off the Conundrum – a "kind of perverted giant Spanish iron cross" built by his friend Serge Etienne – also helped Waits discharge some of the rage that could no longer be defused by alcohol. "Drumming is therapeutic," he testified. "I wish I'd found it when I was younger."

Though three tracks consisted simply of Waits and Taylor, a handful of supplementary musicians came to Cotati to flesh out *Bone Machine*. Along with old reliable Ralph Carney, there were Les Claypool of Primus, and Brain, then of the Limbomaniacs. Joe Gore returned on guitar, David Phillips sweetened three songs with pining pedal steel, and David Hidalgo played fiddle and accordion on "Whistle down the Wind". Second engineer Joe Marquez added banjo to "Murder in the Red Barn", and was – along with Waits and wife – one of the stick-banging percussionists christened "the Boners" on "Earth Died Screaming". Also present for the sessions was Francis Thumm, though this time employed in the curious capacity of "security guard".

Sobriety seems to have changed Waits' recording routine, for the *Bone Machine* sessions started promptly at 10 a.m. each morning. "Everybody hates it but me," Waits admitted. "But I think this is the best time 'cause everyone's clean and everyone is empty." The recordings were also done fast, with minimum fuss. "I thought I was going to be up there for longer and it turned out to be just one day," Ralph Carney recalls. To Waits' consternation, halfway through the sessions he had to put *Bone Machine* on hold. Francis Ford Coppola needed him in LA for *Bram Stoker's Dracula*. "I just thought, 'Oh God, I have to stop recording and go get a bad haircut and eat bugs,'" Waits recalled. "And then come back home again."

Fittingly, *Bone Machine* began with the sound of "the Boners" approaching as if over the brow of a hill – a ramshackle percussion unit bashing away like cannibals. Switching from the menacing spoken word of the verses to the unholy howl of its choruses, "Earth Died Screaming" was the scariest opening track of Waits' career to date, a brutal distillation of the apocalypse. Though Waits joked that the biblical influence was the result of Kathleen's lapsed Catholicism, like the Dylan of *John Wesley Harding* he had dipped into the Book of Revelation, drawing also on memories of fire-and-brimstone street preachers he'd known in downtown LA. The song concluded with a strange, sad coda that Waits played on the Chamberlin, an electro-mechanical instrument first developed in 1946, with tapes of recorded sounds activated by a keyboard.

Heaven was still "full" on "Dirt in the Ground", a mournful dirge improbably inspired by a pickup line of Teddy Edwards'. "[Teddy] used to tell girls that in hotel lobbies," Waits recalled. "He'd say, 'Listen darling, we all gon' be dirt in the ground.' So I always thought that would be a good song title." Like most western men in their forties, Waits had woken up to his own mortality – to what death really meant as you hit the middle of your life. Though he denied the subject was morbid, his ulterior motive in writing about it seemed to be to disarm it – to face the terror of the end and thus vanquish it. "Dirt" consisted of Waits at the piano, Taylor on bass, and Ralph Carney doing little more than exhaling through a bass clarinet and alto and tenor saxes. The vocal was a raspy falsetto – what Waits called his "Prince voice" – that he claimed he could "only do . . . once or twice and then it's gone".

"Such a Scream" came as light relief – an explosion of sexual energy – after "Earth" and "Dirt". A love-call to Kathleen, "Scream" was as ecstatic as it was frenetic, all machine-gun drums and saxophone-yapping as Waits hymned his wife and muse. The track got even more combustive as Waits' grinding rhythm guitar gatecrashed the second verse like a poor man's Keith Richards. One of *Bone Machine*'s indisputable highlights, "Scream" remains the most exhilaratingly funky track Waits ever recorded.

A splurge of percussion and distorted vocals guided the listener into the home-recorded "All Stripped Down", a vision of apocalypse-as-party that took its cue from Burroughs' "T'ain't No Sin". Vocally the track sounded like Captain Beefheart duetting with Prince, flipping between villainous growl and distressed-chicken falsetto. "What I like to try and do with my voice is get kind of schizophrenic with it," Waits said.

By contrast, "Who Are You" was the most traditional song Waits had recorded in an age, with strummed guitars and Springsteen-esque vocal lines. It was also startlingly vituperative: a classic putdown song in the mode of Dylan's "Positively Fourth Street" and reminiscent of his swipes at the likes of Edie Sedgwick. So acerbic was the Waits/Brennan lyric that it was difficult not to infer a real-life object of their contempt.

"The Ocean Doesn't Want Me" gave us another new Waits voice, one clearly influenced by Ken Nordine. A failed-suicide note as whimsical as it was creepy, the spoken-word lyric posited a curious metaphysic: the desire to die, it suggested, was not enough for suicide to occur – nature had to be ready to receive you. Accompanying himself on Chamberlin and percussion, Waits sang of "strangels" and "braingels", marine creatures who would assist in the drowning. The former was a word Kellesi-mone had coined, a hybrid of "strange" and "angels".

Waits' falsetto got yet another airing on "Jesus Gonna Be Here", his most overt gospel pastiche to date. This was Waits in black-face, singing with a lisp as he parodied – or paid homage to – the country-blues preachers of yesteryear. In an inspired switch, Waits took over the "bull fiddle" while Larry Taylor played greasy Ry Cooder slide, staying in the same key when Waits changed to fit the standard twelve-bar progression. As the song ended, the drone of a helicopter could be heard over the studio.

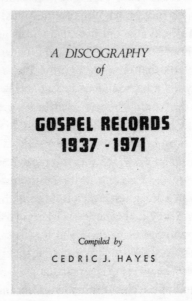

A DISCOGRAPHY
of

GOSPEL RECORDS 1937 - 1971

Compiled by
CEDRIC J. HAYES

Jesus gonna be here: Waits preaches the gospel

Kathleen Brennan collaborated on "A Little Rain", prototype for a new kind of ballad we'd hear more of on *Mule Variations*. No Steinways for Waits anymore: here was the humble, almost domesticated sound of the upright piano, bringing him full circle from *Closing Time*. He said he liked to "go back and forth" between rage and soppiness. While he loved hearing "family heirlooms thrown against the wall", he still had "the other side of me, the old drunk in the corner who had too much wine starting to get a little sentimental". "A Little Rain" stemmed primarily from protective feelings towards his children, the third verse prompted by the murder of a local fifteen-year-old girl who'd climbed into a stranger's car. Having lived most of his life in big cities, Waits was fascinated by the local news in and around Sonoma County. Where murder was commonplace in LA or New York, "here, where you see the golden fields or whatever, it's in greater relief". Reports of teenagers losing their lives in car wrecks naturally affected Tom and Kathleen. Did his mind also go back to "Burma Shave" and the memory of his own cousin hightailing it out of Marysville? Or even to his own memories of being trapped in Chula Vista? "People see the world through MTV and movies and they don't see much of the world where they live," he reflected. "So they go screaming out of these little towns looking for a piece of that, so they can jump into that river somewhere."

"In the Colosseum" brought an instant change of mood. With Waits hammering the Conundrum as Brain bashed out a 4/4 stomp of a beat, the track was the closest thing on the album to *The Black Rider*. Yet even here, as Waits welcomed us to the horrorshow of Roman barbarity, there was less of the Weill/Eisler imprint in the music. For Waits, with the presidential elections just months away, the song was a first stab at a political statement. "I just kind of imagine this modern *Caligula* that government has become," he said. "[We're] all kind of marooned in this place where information and ideas become very abstract, yet the hyena is still tearing at the flesh."

Bone Machine's standout track was "Goin' out West", a throwback to the demonic R&B of "Heartattack and Vine" and "16 Shells from a Thirty-Ought Six". Over possibly the greatest drum sound ever – Waits whacking what sounds like a metal door – Joe Gore and Larry Taylor created an infernal Cramps-ish racket that put the likes of the Jon Spencer Blues Explosion utterly in the shade. Waits raged away in the guise of a wannabe actor en route to California, a deluded ex-con who claimed he looked good with his shirt off and planned to call himself Hannibal or Rex. The song was Elmore Leonard's *Be Cool* distilled into three frenzied minutes, a capsule snapshot of a dumb Everglades hunk with a head full of celluloid fantasies. Waits had seen dolts like this swarming into LA for years. "I figured, 'Let's do a rocker,'" Waits said of the song. "'We'll just slam it and scream.'" It was Brennan who argued it should be more specific; should in fact be about people who come to California with "a phone number somebody gave them, you know, for a psychic who used to work with Ann-Margret". As a native Angeleno, Waits understood how outsiders coming to LA had "this golden image that everything will be all right when you get here, no matter how twisted your imagination . . . orange trees, bikinis, sunglasses".

"Murder in the Red Barn" offered an immediate contrast. With its loping rhythm and twangy banjo, the minimal, backwoodsy arrangement recalled *Rain Dogs*' "Gun Street Girl". This was Waits and Brennan taking in their new surroundings and the murky things going on behind the scenes. "I buy the local papers every day," Waits told me. "They're full of car wrecks and . . . I guess it all depends on what it is in the paper that attracts you. I'm always drawn to these terrible stories, I don't know why. 'Murder in the Red Barn' is just one of those stories, like an old Flannery O'Connor story." The song – and *Bone Machine* in general – also reflected the influence of Cormac McCarthy, whose primordial, brutally beautiful *All the Pretty Horses* he had recently finished.*

The sinister "Black Wings" was another departure for Waits. The spoken-word portrait of a shadowy protean figure, the voice suggested a demonic Leonard Cohen, the music spaghetti-western guitar noir. "I like that place with my voice," Waits said of what was really a kind of acting turn. "[A] little of that Marconi feeling." Nobody admits to knowing this furtive entity, who may be a CIA agent out of a Burroughs novel – or may be Death itself.

Tom Jans was a Californian singer-songwriter, a melancholy folkie whose country-soul ballad "Lovin' Arms" had been covered by dozens of artists from Dobie Gray and Millie Jackson to Elvis Presley. The pathos of Jans' 1984 death prompted Tom to dedicate *Bone Machine*'s "Whistle down the Wind" to him. "[He was] from the central coast of California, kind of a Steinbeck upbringing in a small town," Waits said. "It was written about another friend, but it was the kind of song Tom would have written." Close in feel to "A Little Rain", the track again featured simple upright piano and discreet pedal steel, along this time with David Hidalgo's overdubbed fiddle and accordion. It remains one of Waits' most tender ballads, the sad song of a man who's lost all hope. The writing is exquisite, full of poetic detail and touching regret.†

* On "Murder in the Red Barn", Waits could almost be Nick Cave – or, rather, Nick Cave impersonating Tom Waits. Like Waits, Cave was a middle-class boy with a schoolteacher father; like Waits, too, he was obsessed by the Bible and the Southern Gothic strain in American literature, pastiching both in *And the Ass Saw the Angel*.

† The cause and circumstances of Jans' death in Santa Monica remain mysterious to this day. Though he'd been involved in a motorcycle accident not long before, rumours abound that his death was drug-related. Certainly he was depressed that his 1982 album *Champion* – whose sleeve thanked Tom and Kathleen – failed even to secure a US release.

The album's mood again switched dramatically with the intemperate strum-along of "I Don't Wanna Grow Up". This howl of indignation at the pressures of mid-life responsibility was almost certainly a side-effect of Waits sobering up. "Everybody wants to grow up until they grow up," he commented. "You ever been to a party and you look around and everybody around you is real grown up and you feel like, 'Oh, Jesus'?" But the song was also a child's honest (and rather moving) perception of the adult world, and a cry of alarm at how quickly life was zipping by. Waits had been on the point of binning the song when Kathleen – its co-author – came to its rescue. Waits' response was to "put it through a Marshall and [turn] it up real loud, and then it felt better".

Recorded on a tape recorder at home, "Let Me Get Up on It" was an experiment in unabashed lo-fi – and maybe how Waits would have liked the whole of *Bone Machine* to sound. "I ended up liking it better than anything we got in the studio for a while," Waits confessed. DIY percussion and chain-link clanking met bullhorn snarl in a minute-long track that anticipated "Top of the Hill" and other raucous examples of Waitsian neo-primitivism.

Bone Machine's last song, "That Feel", was a capsule manifesto, a testament to the endurance of the spirit and the indestructible worth of one's humanity. Like *Hair*'s "Ain't Got No . . . I Got Life", it said that while you can strip everything to the bone – reduce life to calcium – nothing can kill the soul. In a sense it was Waits' homage to everything that shouldn't be anaesthetized by alcohol and drugs – to *the very fact of feeling* – which made it ironic that the song's co-author and singer was Keith Richards, overdubbed at his Studio 900 in New York's Flatiron district after the basic track was done at Prairie Sun with Larry Taylor and David Phillips.

Though Waits spent "several weeks" earlier in the year writing with Richards – ostensibly for the latter's *Main Offender* album –

this was the only song to see the light of day. "It wasn't *for* anything," Richards claimed of the sessions. "We enjoy doing it, just kicking it around, having some fun. Maybe when we've got a few more songs we might think about doing it for something." Waddy Wachtel, then a member of Richards' X-pensive Winos, recalls the session for "That Feel" as "kind of mellow", adding that "it wasn't a long night at all . . . weird, I know". How Waits survived the session without drinking was an AA miracle. "You can't drink with [Keith], but you can write with him," Waits claimed of an experience he remembered as "a total joy". Howling along on backing vocals, Richards helped turn the song into something almost religious. For Waits, Richards was a holy innocent, a piratical gypsy who literally lived for music. "I felt like I've known him a long time," he said of the Stone. "He loves those shadows in music. And he's totally mystified by music, like a kid. He finds great joy in it, and madness and abandon."

When *Bone Machine* was released in August 1992, Waits' mother was appalled by the title. "She said it sounds so degrading," Waits laughed. "Sounds like something hellish or devilish." What Alma thought of the album's cover – conceived by Waits with Bob Dylan's photographer son Jesse – is anyone's guess. In his glacier goggles and a "devil's-horns" skull cup borrowed from Casey, Waits resembled the cadaverous Bruce Spence in *Mad Max 3*, his expression somewhere between triumphant glee and a Francis Bacon scream of agony.

Island set up a slew of interviews to publicize the record, flying Waits to Paris in July to talk to the European press. As ever, he alternated in interviews between grouchiness, leg-pulling, and disarming candour. "He was staying at a chic hotel in the Place des Vosges," says Pete Silverton, who talked to him for the UK magazine *Vox*. "After we'd finished we walked across the square and had coffee with Kathleen. She and I chatted about this and that and Paris and art. Then I said, 'How about talking about

Tom?' She looked at me as if to say, 'You know better than that,' and we went back to talking about Paris and art. To me it was clear she was his salvation, the Zimmer frame for his genius. She was smart and bright and fun and interesting and amused by Tom's shtick, seeing it for what it was – a clever performance that refracted parts of Tom and left other parts untouched and private."

In America, where American journalists invariably met him in such establishments as the Limbo Diner in San Francisco or Rinehart's Truck Stop in Petaluma, Waits complained that he was still being pigeonholed as some booze-addled Beat throwback. "A lot of people seem to have bought one record . . . a long time ago and got me down," he sighed. "'Oh, that guy. The one with the deep voice without a shave? Know him. Sings about eggs and sausage? Yeah, got it.'"

When Jim Jarmusch came to Sonoma County to shoot the video for "I Don't Wanna Grow Up" – a be-goggled, devil-horned Waits scooting about the local hills on Casey's bicycle – he found his friend in a state of near-exhaustion. He began to regret asking Waits to appear in *Coffee and Cigarettes*, a series of semi-staged conversations between people the director admired. Certainly Waits was in a surly mood when Jarmusch arrived late in the morning to film him with Iggy Pop. "You said this was going to be funny, Jim," Waits barked. "Maybe you better just circle the jokes 'cause I don't see 'em." He glanced at Iggy and asked what *he* thought. Iggy replied diplomatically that he was going to get some coffee. Jarmusch calmed Waits down. "I knew it was just early in the morning and Tom was in a bad mood," he said. "His attitude changed completely, but I wanted him to keep some of that paranoid surliness in the script." One suspects the "paranoid surliness" was the result of being asked to tread such a slender line between fact and fiction: Jarmusch wanted him to play a version of himself for the camera.

In the Waits/Pop segment of *Coffee and Cigarettes*, filmed in the booth of a diner near Waits' house, Waits was clearly the alpha male of the encounter. Iggy ("call me Jim") was all sweetness and light as Waits talked. With a pedal steel whining on the jukebox in the background, Waits and Pop agreed that life was so much better without smoking, then tempted each other into a nicotine relapse. "The beauty of quitting is that now I've quit, I can have one," Waits rationalized. "'Cause I've quit." The conversation meandered on. Pop noted the lack of Waits records on the jukebox; Waits asked if Pop preferred Taco Bell or the International House of Pancakes; Pop recommended a drummer to Waits; Waits took offence. When Pop could stand the tension no longer and split, Waits checked the jukebox and – with a grunt of satisfaction – remarked that "*he's* not on here either." Then, furtively, he sparked up another cigarette.

No wonder Waits was exhausted: he'd bitten off more than he could chew in 1992. Like many alcoholics in early recovery, he wanted to make up for what he perceived as lost time by working overtime. Barely had he finished *Bone Machine* when he decided he wanted to make a lasting document of the *Black Rider* music he and Greg Cohen had demoed in Hamburg.

Bringing the *Black Rider* tapes to Prairie Sun, Waits sorted the usable material from the tracks he wanted to redo with a new ensemble of Bay Area musicians. Retained from Hamburg were "The Black Rider", "T'Ain't No Sin", "Flash Pan Hunter (Intro)", "That's the Way", "The Briar and the Rose", "Crossroads", Greg Cohen's "Interlude", "The Last Rose of Summer", and "Carnival". "November" hailed from Hamburg but overdubbed Don Neely's saw. The vocal "Gospel Train" was from Hamburg, but with Ralph Carney and Bill Douglass overdubbed. Where the Hamburg musicians had been christened "the Devil's Rhubato Band", Waits referred to the new California group as "Rhubato West". (*Rubato* is a musical term meaning rhythmic flexibility within a phrase or measure.) Alongside a core of players who'd worked on *Night on Earth* and/or *Bone Machine* – Ralph Carney, Francis Thumm, Joe Gore, Matt Brubeck – came a troupe of versatile jazz/classical/experimental musicians based in the Bay Area. This slightly more schooled edition of the "demented ensembles" Waits had employed since *Swordfishtrombones* comprised Don Neely (bowed saw), Bill Douglass (bass), Nik Phelps (French horn), Larry Rhodes (bassoon, contra bassoon), Kenny Wollesen (percussion, marimba), Linda Deluca (viola), and Kevin Porter (trombone). From this pool of musicians came the performances on "Just the Right Bullets", "Black Box Theme", "Russian Dance", "Gospel Train (Orchestra)", "I'll Shoot the Moon", "Flash Pan Hunter", "Oily Night", and "Lucky Day".

"Tom had a lot of different horn players on *The Black Rider*, and of course my insecurity came up," says Ralph Carney. "I'm a player that, like, if I get someone I really like to play with, I'll play with them for fifty years. It's that Duke Ellington thing. *The Black Rider* was the last thing I did for a while. It was kind of like, 'Okay, this is real sporadic. It's not a sure thing anymore.'"

Starting out with charts for the songs, Waits realized the music required a cruder, more intuitive tack. He used the expression "going out to the meadow" to connote this departure from the script or score. However, the risks entailed in going out to the meadow were great: all it took was one player not being on board and a piece of music could fall apart irreversibly. "Blood is all over the walls and the fucking thing will never breathe again," Waits said melodramatically. "And you point to one of the musicians and you accuse him of murder." Waits was only half-kidding; sometimes there was a mere hair's breadth between saving a great track and losing it for ever. His frustration in the studio could sometimes boil over into rage.

On *The Black Rider*'s opening track, "Lucky Day (Overture)", Waits enacted the long-harboured fantasy of being a Big Top

With new toys at Prairie Sun, Cotati, August 1993. (*Jay Blakesberg*)

MC, introducing an assortment of "human oddities" he'd learned about in Daniel P. Mannix's cult book *Freaks: We Who Are Not as Others* (1976). Waits namechecked Harry's Harbour Bazaar, the junk shop he'd found in Hamburg, and invited us to view a three-headed baby, a dog-faced boy and a monkey woman, Johnny Eck ("the man born without a body"), and even Hitler's brain. Recreating the demi-monde of the Reeperbahn in rural northern California, Waits transferred all the fascination and empathy he'd once felt for hobos and drunks to the kinds of deformed creature who'd appeared in Tod Browning's classic 1932 film *Freaks*.

"The Black Rider" itself was another excuse for Waits to play MC, this time in the form of Pegleg's macabre invitation to a kind of death trip. The demonic cabaret of the piece, recording grainily in Hamburg, was pure Brecht/Weill. The forlorn "November" also hailed from Hamburg but began with the eerie sound of Don Neely's bowed saw and replaced Waits' frail septuagenarian vocal with a more recognizable croak. Weill was back with a bang on the menacing "Just the Right Bullets", Pegleg offering Wilhelm the magic bullets that would enable him to win the hand of Katchen. A highlight of the track was Joe Gore's Morricone guitar playing off Kenny Wollesen's Looney Tunes percussion.

The instrumental "Black Box Theme" began with gamelan-style tinkling before settling into an eerie mix of Chamberlin, banjo, and woodwind. Burroughs' creepy cameo "T'ain't No Sin", with Waits playing marimba, was followed by the short bassoon/bass/clarinet instrumental "Flash Pan Hunter (Intro)". Set to Hans-Jorn Braudenberg's funereal pump organ, "That's the Way" flowed seamlessly into a less hymnal version of "The Briar and the Rose", sung – cracked notes and all – as a tender love song to Kathleen.

The new "Russian Dance" was an ominous instrumental with a succession of false endings, arranged for cello, viola, synthesized strings, and the stomping Cossack-style boots of Waits, Brennan, Francis Thumm, Joe Marquez, and ranch foreman Clive Butters. The stiff, lurching rhythm of "Gospel Train (Orchestra)", with its grinding bass/cello underpinning and dissonant woodwind, was almost industrial.

There was some light relief in "I'll Shoot the Moon", the album's sole concession to Tin Pan Americana. The ghost of Hoagy Carmichael inhabited Waits' vocal, wafting over a palm-court blend of sax and pump organ, marimba, and trombone. Then we were back in Weill time for "Flash Pan Hunter", Waits snarling Burroughs' mocking lyric before reviving the hysterical yodel-sob of *Frank's Wild Years'* "Temptation".

On "Crossroads" – the tragic denouement of the "magic bullets" story – Waits affected a cowboy burr somewhere between Johnny Cash and Waylon Jennings. He also played guitar and Chamberlin before loosing his throatiest yodel at the end of the track. "Gospel Train" was yet another MC exhortation, except that here it was a revivalist preacher – a variation on "Way Down in the Hole" and "Jesus Gonna Be Here" – urging us to turn away from Satan and board the locomotive to heaven.

Greg Cohen's half-minute "Interlude" – a little trio piece for bassoon, French horn, and clarinet – fed directly into the deranged "Oily Night", whose pizzicato viola and cello were augmented by the Boners, making their first appearance since "Earth Died Screaming" and sounding like a hundred ticking clocks. A melee of brass, woodwind, and percussion then entered the fray, followed by Waits' fiendishly slowed-down voice. This was the music of nightmares, finally relieved by the album's penultimate song. Like a reprise of "Innocent when You Dream", "Lucky Day" was all pump organ, Salvation Army horns, and bellowing sentimentality.

"The Last Rose of Summer", with Waits on pump organ and Chamberlin and Cohen on bass, lamented the loss of summer as the year moved inexorably towards decay and death. "Carnival", finally, brought the album's carousel madness full circle, all staccato Emax strings, Chamberlin effects . . . and one last train whistle.

Waits had intended *The Black Rider* to come out in the spring of 1993 but delayed the album's release until the fall, presumably to leave enough of a gap between releases. For reasons not entirely clear, he decided to mix the record not at Prairie Sun but at an old haunt of his in LA. Working obsessively at the twenty-three-year-old studio now known as the Sunset Sound Factory, Waits spent three weeks trying to capture the sound he heard in his head. When in doubt, he and Biff Dawes would leave the studio with a cassette tape and listen intently to a track in the 1964 gold Sedan de Ville he kept in the parking lot. He trusted the car's acoustics more than the speakers at Sunset Sound.

When the album did finally appear, a year after *Bone Machine*, it sorted the men from the boys among Waits' fans. If *Night on Earth* had mystified people, *The Black Rider* perplexed and alienated in about equal measure. "[Island] didn't do much with it," Waits said in 2000. "But you know, people don't know what to do with recordings from theatre experiences. They wonder, 'Should I have seen the show? And if I haven't will it make sense?'" Anyone open to demanding, avant-garde sounds was with Waits all the way. "I remember I had the same feeling with the album that I'd had with the Hal Willner albums," says Kate St John, who would be part of the group that performed *The Black Rider* in London in 2004. "I was kind of disenchanted with music at the time and I thought, 'There are great things going on musically after all, and thank God for people like Tom Waits, who's older and clever and interesting.'"

The *Black Rider* sessions had barely finished when Waits turned his attention to another enticing commission from Robert Wilson. "Make hay while the sun shines," he told Jim Jarmusch. This time Wilson's proposal was an operatic treatment of the relationship between Charles Lutwidge Dodgson (Lewis Carroll) and Alice Pleasance Liddell, the enchanting girl who'd inspired *Alice's Adventures in Wonderland*. Though William Burroughs was too ill to get involved, Wilson once again chose to work with the Thalia company, not least because *The Black Rider* had been a success and would continue to tour the world profitably in a variety of productions. He had first discussed the opera with writer Paul Schmidt and dramaturge Wolfgang Wiens in August 1991. As with nearly all his work, *Alice* would be a complex narrative mixing fact and fiction, blending the story of the Carroll/Liddell relationship with fantastical scenes from *Alice's Adventures in Wonderland* and its sequel *Through the*

Looking Glass. Central to the text would be Dodgson the photographer of children – and specifically of young girls. Relishing the theatrical possibilities of Carroll's hallucinatory dreamscapes, Waits was quick to join the team. He remained in awe of Wilson, describing him as the "sighted giant" on whose shoulders he himself – a "blind crippled midget" – perched. Once again there was the prospect of being apart from Kathleen and the kids, but once again she begged him not to pass up the chance to work with a man she regarded as a genius.

The first tryouts for *Alice* were held in Hamburg in the early spring of 1992, at which time Paul Schmidt incorporated the texts he'd adapted from Carroll. So busy was Waits during the spring and summer that he could only mull over the material Schmidt was sending him. By the time he was preparing to leave for Hamburg at the start of November, he and Kathleen had sketched out fifteen songs for Wilson. "I'm still not packed," Waits said on the eve of his departure. "But I'll never be ready for this trip till I get home from it." Along with his clothes were a number of strange instruments he'd been gathering, the creations of a group of Bay Area eccentrics bored of conventional sounds and textures. Most of these men were influenced by Harry Partch – who'd lived for a period in Petaluma – and most were contributors to the quarterly publication *Experimental Musical Instruments.* Among the contraptions Waits liked were Darrell DeVore's Wind Wands, Bart Hopkin's PVC Membrane saxophone, and Qubias Reed Ghazala's photon clarinet, played by beams of light bouncing off light-sensitive keys. Richard A. Waters' Waterphone was a polytonal metal instrument, complete with a pipe into which one poured water; Tom Nunn's T-Rodimba was assembled out of plywood and hardware and fitted with a violin pickup.

With just six weeks to complete the *Alice* music, Waits was under intense pressure in Hamburg. This time, too, he was working more or less alone, demoing the songs at Gerd Bessler's studio without Greg Cohen at his side. "It was a pretty fraught time for Tom," recalled the BBC's Mark Cooper, who came to Hamburg to film a piece about the production for the *Late Show* arts programme. "When we arrived he was involved in all the fine-tuning, and the sheer stress was obviously getting to him." Waits "threw a complete paddy" when he saw the grand piano Cooper had set up for his interview. Instead he demanded to be filmed at a dilapidated upright piano in the corner of the room.

In the *Late Show* piece, Robert Wilson again stated that the deep differences between him and Waits were key to their collaboration. "We're very different men," he said. "Different lifestyles, different aesthetics. We dress differently. Even our ideas about art are quite different. I'm a little more formal and cooler and he's a little freer. But somehow it works together." Wilson, who'd divided *Alice* into two acts of seven scenes and seven of his "knee plays",* told Waits he wanted to use the songs as "intersections" with Schmidt's text. To a degree this meant that Waits was given carte blanche with the songs. "Once you go down the rabbit hole, anybody can say anything they want," he said. "You could have songs about convenience stores. And you're far from home, which is a bit like falling down the rabbit hole, in a way. So it's conducive, Hamburg." The influence of the city itself was manifest in songs such as "Kommienezuspadt" (a piece of cod-German gibberish that Waits invented) and "Down There in the Reeperbahn", a hysterical portrait of the street deviants and androgynous flotsam that flocked to Hamburg's wildest thoroughfare.

If Waits took liberties with the brief Wilson and Schmidt had set him, they were mainly to do with his ongoing immersion in the literature of carnivals and "freaks". The phantasmagoria of

---

* Wilson coined the term "knee play" to indicate an interlude between scenes – the connective tissue in the "meat" of a performance.

Alice's experience in Carroll's novels found equivalence in the aberrations of American freak shows and amusement parks. "It seemed to me it was kind of a natural connection," Schmidt observed. "The other interesting thing that Tom really found was sort of the underside of Victorian life ... and that's where a lot of [his] images plug in beautifully." Several references were made in the *Alice* songs to Dreamland, the Coney Island park that operated in the early years of the twentieth century, while "Table Top Joe" and "Chained Together for Life" (aka "Poor Edward") were specifically about Johnny Eck – who'd appeared in *Freaks* – and Edward Mordrake, an English aristocrat born with a woman's face on the back of his head. "Obviously I'm making light of something and I hope it's not at anybody's expense," Waits would later say of such songs. "[There] are people with physical deformities and I'm not poking fun at that at all. I'm just taking the idea of show business to a ridiculous place."

Most of the *Alice* music was more approachable than *The Black Rider*, pointing forward to the parlour ballads of *Mule Variations* and *Orphans* while drawing on Waits' Tin Pan Alley style of old. Later, Waits characterized it as "adult songs for children, or children's songs for adults ... an odyssey in dream logic and nonsense". As with *The Black Rider* and *Night on Earth*, his primary choice of instrumentation – woodwinds, viola, pump organ, upright piano – suggested an amateur chamber group playing in a church hall.

"Alice" itself was something of a throwback, a tender blend of Kurt Weill and *One from the Heart*. Performed by the White Rabbit in Scene One and positing Alice as a kind of frozen surface that Dodgson/Carroll falls through, it hinted at the suspect nature of Dodgson's feelings for Liddell but carried a more universal meaning: Waits would later describe Kathleen as "my Alice".

Performed by the Caterpillar in Scene Two, "Table Top Joe"

was sung by Waits in a strange languid croon accompanied by a rickety xylophonic instrument that most likely was Tom Nunn's Bug. For "Down There in the Reeperbahn", Waits came up with another new voice, sobbing like a hysterical drag queen as he sang of "little Hans" who ran off with a man. For "Hang Me in the Bottle" (aka "We're All Mad Here"), Waits reverted to the evil-Beefheart voice of Pegleg in a song that revisited the *Black Rider*-esque subject of death and putrefaction. The same sardonic timbre was used for the White Knight's "Everything You Can Think of Is True", the song in which he most clearly celebrated the loss of co-ordinates in Carroll's work. The frantic "Kommienezuspadt", driven by ticking clocks and percussion that sounded like a cash-register opening and shutting, was the closest thing in *Alice* to the feel of *The Black Rider*. Performed by a chorus of Victorian vicars, "One, Two, and Through" was Waits' setting of Carroll's famous Jabberwocky poem from *Through the Looking Glass*.

"But There's Never a Rose" (aka "Lost in the Harbor") was a melancholy pump-organ dirge with political overtones – specifically, references to the collapse of the Berlin Wall. "Whatever Became of Old Father Craft?" was a hysterical pisstake of Catholicism, with Waits corpsing in the studio as he drawled morosely of being abused by a priest. "Chained Together for Life" was a song of grave compassion for the unfortunate Mordrake, Gerd Bessler's viola soaring tragically over Waits' disconsolate pump organ.

Exactly how the *Alice* songs sounded in Wilson's production is hard to say with any certainty. We do know that the Bay Area instruments were utilized in the production, most of them played by Ali Husseini. Bessler himself occasionally switched from his Stroh-viola to the PVC Membrane saxophone. We have a rough idea of what Waits intended for the individual pieces only because a tape of his demo recordings from Bessler's Music

Factory studio was stolen from the back of a car outside Harry's Harbour Bazaar – while Waits was purchasing a stuffed anaconda – and subsequently bootlegged. To recover the tapes, Waits was obliged to pay a ransom of $3,000, a sum he found vaguely insulting. "Not a lot of money, was it," he remarked. "I was a little insulted. I think they wanted fast cash and no arguments."

Waits remained in Hamburg long enough to see the premiere of *Alice* on 19 December, taking the stage after the final curtain to declaim a version of "Down There in the Reeperbahn" that thrilled the audience. The production, however, met with mixed reviews, critics praising the first act but carping about the second. Waits was too exhausted to be overly concerned. By Christmas he was home with Kathleen and the children, relieved to have survived the busiest year of his life and the first tenuous months of his sobriety. Having contemplated a tour to promote *Bone Machine* just a few months earlier, he now decided that he needed a break for his sanity. "Sometimes when I think about touring, I would rather be attacked by a school of hagfish," he said. "Hagfish eat another fish from the inside out. That's sometimes what touring does to you."

As 1993 began, there was an even more compelling reason for Waits to take his foot off the accelerator. Kathleen was pregnant with their third child.

Chapter 6

The Crooked Tree and the Straight Tree

> *"The boggy wasteland of the American spirit, as it*
> *exists here and now, is more fluorescent than ever."*
>
> (Beck to the author, 14 October 1998)

Tom Waits squats on the fender of his blue 1970 Coupe de Ville and tells me a joke.

Two old guys, he says, are sitting on a bench in Central Park and talking about retirement.

"I got this new hobby," says one. "I took up beekeeping."

"That's nice," says the other man.

"Yeah, I got two thousand bees in my apartment."

"Two thousand bees, huh? Where you keep 'em?"

"I keep 'em in a shoebox."

"A shoebox? Isn't that a little uncomfortable for the bees?"

"Ah, fuck 'em. It's just a hobby."

Tom Waits says that Eddie Izzard – with whom he'd recently appeared in the movie *Mystery Men* – didn't get the joke either. He concedes that you probably have to have lived in New York City to appreciate it fully.

Watching him on this sun-dappled afternoon in January 1999, kicking back on a country road on the outskirts of Santa Rosa, it's hard to imagine Waits living in New York or any *other* city. With his feet planted in a pair of old boots and a nest of russet hair dancing atop his creased, kindly face, he looks like he's just wandered in from his backyard after a long afternoon wrestling with some farm equipment. His strong, gnarled fingers – several adorned with chunky silver rings – are grey-brown and calloused. He is nine months shy of his fiftieth birthday and is starting to resemble some weatherbeaten drifter out of Richard Avedon's *In the American West*.

When he's finished the joke, Waits climbs into the Coupe de Ville, a replacement for the 1967 model he totalled last year. ("I'm not hurt," he protested when his son Casey saw him staunching a head wound with a McDonald's takeout bag.) He drives me back to Santa Rosa, decrying the way people move up here from San Francisco, tear down trees, and build gated communities called Twin Oaks or Pine Bluffs. "You ever notice when they're building a new housing development," he says, "they always name it after the thing they destroyed?"

Casey wasn't even born the last time I met Waits. Fourteen years on, a second son – Sullivan – has been added to the Waits brood. "You know," their father muses as he drives, "I didn't want to be the guy who woke up when he was sixty-five and said, 'Gee, I forgot to have kids.' I mean, somebody took the time to have *us*,

Our hero's Coupe de Ville and trumpet, Santa Rosa, January 1999. (*Art Sperl*)

409

right?" Being a proper dad is clearly high on Waits' priority list. Though he and Kathleen write together, he says there's little overlap between work and domesticity in the house. "Mostly my kids are just looking for any way I can come in handy," he says ruefully. "Clothes, rides and money . . . that's about all I'm good for. But I think it's the way it's supposed to be."

Parenthood was generally the reason Waits gave at this time for the seven-year gap between *Bone Machine* and *Mule Variations*. Other times he merely grunted that he'd got stuck in traffic. Predictably, rumours of ill-health – including one that he had throat cancer – circulated as he stayed out of view. The same thing had happened to Bob Dylan after his motorcycle accident.*

Pressed on the idea of being a contented paterfamilias, Waits wriggled his way out of such a stereotype. "It sounds like a loaded question," he said to me. "If I say no, I'll be in trouble with my family. If I say yes, I get in trouble with everybody else." He paused before adding, "I live in a house with my wife and a lot of kids and dogs and I have to fight for every piece of ground I get." What Waits didn't say was that he'd spent several years growing up. To quote the kind of old-timers he'd have heard in AA meetings around Santa Rosa and Petaluma, he'd "put the cork back in the bottle", accepted that – a day at a time – he couldn't drink again, and embarked on a journey of profound spiritual change. Responsibility to his family was a core part of that change.

---

* According to Robert Christgau in a *Village Voice* review of *Mule Variations*, there was also a rumour making the rounds that Waits had "split with his wife". Christgau says he doesn't recall the origin of the rumour, "but I can tell you I didn't fabricate it – I must have read something, or somebody must have said something to me. Gossip means too little to me as a writer for me to make shit up. If it was merely my own speculation, I would have felt free to put it that way." Christgau's claim of said rumour is all the more surprising given that no one else has ever commented on it (though David Smay, who quoted Christgau's *Village Voice* reference, explored the possibility of marital problems in his 2008 book on *Swordfishtrombones*).

Asked for the "toughest thing" he'd ever had to deal with, Waits replied that it was "raising kids, being a grown-up, living in the real world, paying the bills, bringing home the groceries, having responsibilities". He said American culture had a "codependent relationship" with artists that enabled many of them to behave irresponsibly and that he himself had once subscribed to that tacit collusion. "There's a notion that artists are kind of impetuous and eccentric and irresponsible and unreliable," he said. "But I don't think you have to be."

For three years, Waits changed a lot of diapers and made a lot of school runs in a humungous and environmentally unfriendly Chevy Suburban. He played no gigs and turned down all movie offers. "I wanted to pull myself out of the limelight for a while," he said. It helped that money had come in from the Frito-Lay award and from cover versions of his songs. Rod Stewart followed up "Downtown Train" and "Tom Traubert's Blues" with "Hang On St Christopher". Johnny Cash sang "Down There by the Train" on the first of his *American Recordings* albums. Canadian singer Holly Cole recorded an album of idiosyncratic covers, 1995's *Temptation*, that spanned Waits' twenty-year *oeuvre* from "I Want You" to "The Briar and the Rose". And a clutch of Waits songs showed up in movies such as *Twelve Monkeys* (1995), *Things to Do in Denver when You're Dead* (1995), and *The End of Violence* (1997).

Less pleasing to him was the 1995 tribute album assembled by Herb Cohen's son Evan. Though *Step Right Up* comprised versions of Asylum-era Waits songs by such respected indie acts as Tindersticks ("Mockin' Bird"), 10,000 Maniacs ("I Hope that I Don't Fall in Love with You"), and Violent Femmes ("Step Right Up"), few of the treatments bar Jeffrey Lee Pierce's take on "Pasties and a G-String" and Tim Buckley's original 1973 cover of "Martha" were very distinguished. Few of the contributors, however, would have known that *Step Right Up* was being put together without Waits' blessing, and most were paying sincere tribute to him. As former Blaster Dave Alvin noted after recording "Ol' '55", "When I was eighteen years old working in a warehouse in Whittier, I heard Tom Waits on the radio playing and it inspired me to become a songwriter."

When Waits *did* work, family life was never far away. "He sits at the mixing board, a little preoccupied and unable to get comfortable in his chair, until he discovers he is sitting on a bottle of baby formula he'd forgotten was tucked in a back pocket," wrote a journalist who watched Waits mixing *The Black Rider* at Sunset Sound. "He will not talk about his wife Kathleen or his three children, but their pictures always seem to be close by, newborn photos on the Chamberlin keyboard, photos tucked in a visor, or edging out of a bedside book."

One afternoon, Casey came home from school and said he'd been in a fight with a kid who claimed his father sang better than Waits. Like most kids, Casey and Kellesimone were embarrassed to be seen at school with their father. "Hey dad, your pants are halfway down around your knees," Kellesimone would tut. "And do something with your hair! Kids are starting to talk!" When the children asked why he didn't have a regular job like the other dads, Waits' response was to tell the story of the crooked tree and the straight tree. "Every day the straight tree would say to the crooked tree, 'Look at me, I'm tall and I'm straight and I'm handsome. You're all crooked and bent over. No one wants to look at you.' One day the loggers came and saw the crooked tree and the straight tree, and they said, 'Just cut down the straight trees and leave the rest.' The loggers turned all the straight trees into lumber and toothpicks and paper. But the crooked tree is still there, growing stronger and stranger every day." As time went on, Kellesimone and Casey decided it was actually pretty cool to have a crooked tree for a dad, even if his pants did hang down around his knees.

Resisting his workaholic urges didn't mean that Waits kept his powder entirely dry. In addition to promoting the *Black Rider* album in the fall of 1993, he kept semi-busy with a series of cameos and guest appearances on albums by people he'd long admired. Among these was his contribution to a remarkable orchestral work by the British composer Gavin Bryars.

Twenty years earlier, Bryars had taped a tramp singing a religious song in southeast London and then looped the recording for an orchestral work called *Jesus' Blood Never Failed Me Yet.* "Although he died before he could hear what I had done with his singing," Bryars later wrote, "the piece remains as an eloquent but understated testimony to his spirit and optimism." Released in 1975 on Brian Eno's Obscure label, *Jesus' Blood* happened to be playing on the radio chez Waits one night. "[All] of a sudden this song kind of drifted into the room and it just put such a nice dust on everything," Waits said. "I taped it and then I played it hundreds of times in the car and then I found myself singing it as well . . . there's something about it that's so naive and something that rarely happens when you're recording in a formal environment." After Waits wrote Bryars to ask for a copy of the recording, the two men discussed the idea of redoing *Jesus' Blood* with Waits singing alongside the tramp's vocal. Bryars duly flew out to California and spent an afternoon at Prairie Sun – "probably one of the most sublime experiences of my life", as he recalled. The result was as entrancing as it was heartbreaking, Waits drawing on all his old compassion for tramps and alcoholics.

A very different musical experience was a 1993 gathering of the Bay Area luminaries who'd built the experimental instruments for *Alice.* Bart Hopkin and Richard Waters had invited him to bring along an instrument of his choice and participate in an improvisatory evening of "democratic music" at a Sebastopol studio operated by Gary "Gatmo" Knowlton. When Waits arrived, he found Hopkin, Waters, Tom Nunn, Darrell DeVore, and others all blowing or banging on their own personal creations.

Hopkin played a reed instrument made from a dried piece of seaweed, Waters played his Waterphone, DeVore the Wind Wands. A guy named Bob Hobbes made a lot of noise on a variety of percussive objects. "I'm not sure what happened, but we 'went out to the meadow,' that's for sure," Waits later wrote of the evening. "Everything was permitted, suspending all logic and direction. The sound was more insect ritual than human." On the three Gatmo Sessions albums released so far, Waits can be heard howling away on such unhinged *Black Rider*-esque pieces as "Keep the Change", the hilarious "In Your Underwear", and a version on "Kommienezuspadt" called "White Rabbit's Lament".

For Waits, the improvisations of the Experimental Musical Instruments group were an antidote to the soulless mechanization of modern rock. (Waits abhorred the internet and claimed he didn't even own a computer.) "With the digital revolution wound up and rattling," he wrote in an introduction to Hopkin's 1996 book *Gravikords, Whirlies & Pyrophones*, "the deconstructionists are combing the wreckage of our age. They are cannibalizing the marooned shuttle to send us on to a place that will sound like a roaring player piano left burning on the beach."

As the 1990s unfolded, events at home and abroad began to prick Waits' social conscience. Though the gestural hypocrisy of so much rock-and-roll do-gooding had long kept him from taking part in anything like Live Aid, he now lent his name to good causes – starting with his contribution to the 1990 AIDS benefit album *Red Hot + Blue,* the version of Cole Porter's "It's All Right with Me" for which Jim Jarmusch shot a distorted video. At a fundraising show for victims of the 1992 LA riots at the Wiltern Theater, he performed alongside Fishbone, Los Lobos, and his old buddy Chuck E. Weiss. He also contributed a track to the 1992 album *Brother, Can You Spare a Dime?*, in aid of the National Fundraising Day of Action. And in late 1995 he recorded two tracks, "The Fall of Troy" and "Walk Away", for the album released to coincide with Tim Robbins' anti-death-penalty film *Dead Man Walking*, the proceeds going to Hope House and Murder Victims' Families for Reconciliation.

It was another good cause that temporarily brought Waits out of his four-year retirement from live performance. When his friend Don Hyde, proprietor of the Raven Film Center in nearby Healdsburg, was charged with distributing LSD, Waits offered to stage a concert at Oakland's Paramount Theater to raise money for his legal defence. The show, on 4 February 1996, was an instant sellout, raising $35,000 and giving the fortunate few a much-needed fix of live Waits. Backed by Greg Cohen, Ralph Carney, Joe Gore, and percussionist Kenny Wollesen, the show was a triumph, its set list inevitably weighted towards *Bone Machine* songs but finding room for "Singapore", "Cemetery Polka", "Gun Street Girl", "Innocent when You Dream", and even "Big Joe and Phantom 309". The gig also included a ballad-heavy section of older, piano-based material that suggested Waits was making peace with his pre-Island self. Included in what was a virtual interlude were "Broken Bicycles", "Invitation to the Blues", "On the Nickel", and "Christmas Card from a Hooker in Minneapolis". Bay Area blues-harmonica legend Charlie Musselwhite turned "Heartattack and Vine" into a loose juke-joint blues before blowing up a storm on the swampy funk of "Filipino Box Spring Hog". After playing both "Walk Away" and "The Fall of Troy", Waits gave the people what they wanted and finished up the night by encoring with a magnificently tender "Tom Traubert's Blues".*

Waits gave his time to other causes that weren't necessarily charitable. An old hero of his, Ramblin' Jack Elliott, came to

---

* Waits played a second benefit for Hyde, this time at the Raven Theater itself. The seventy-five-minute set saw Waits not just dusting down "Jitterbug Boy", "I Wish I Was in New Orleans", "Burma Shave", and even "Ol' '55" but also covering "Fever" and "Goodnight, Irene" and – for the first and only time to date – singing "Down There by the Train".

Cotati in May 1996 to record the Waits/Brennan song "Louise" at Prairie Sun. Starting life in Brooklyn as the son of a Jewish doctor, Elliott had reinvented himself as a teenage rodeo cowboy in the 1940s, later becoming the missing musical hobo link between Woody Guthrie and Bob Dylan. Jack had been everywhere: LA, San Francisco, even London, where Kenneth Williams parodied him on radio's *Round the Horne* as "Rambling Syd Rumpo". Waits first met him at the Heritage, a regular stop on Jack's endless rambles through the US, and remembered his 1967 album *Young Brigham* being a fixture on the club's turntable. When Elliott leaked word that he was planning an album of duets with such longtime fans and disciples as Guy Clark and Jerry Jeff Walker, Waits sent a tape of the bereft, crestfallen "Louise". At Prairie Sun, Waits duetted with Elliott on the song and sang with another Heritage-era friend – Guy Clark – on "Old Time Feelin'", the final track on the 1998 album *Friends of Mine*.

Another reinvented Jew, Chuck E. Weiss, was the beneficiary of Waits' aid in late 1998. A belated follow-up to Weiss' disposable 1981 album *The Other Side of Town* – featuring "Sidekick", a duet with Rickie Lee Jones – *Extremely Cool* was the favour Waits had always wanted to do his old pal. "Tom was always trying to get me to go into the studio," Weiss said. "I'd go in . . . and then the tapes would just kind of sit there, because I didn't have a manager [and] didn't want to hustle them." In the event, Waits and Brennan not only produced *Extremely Cool* but funded it, with Waits guesting on the gospelly "It Rains on Me" and the humorous sub-rap novelty "Do You Know What I Idi Amin". The first – musically a dry run for *Mule Variations*' "Cold Water" – was a junkie's song of Job-like self-pity, with Weiss recapping on his drug years and namechecking the old Troubadour troupe of Robert Marchese, Louie Lista, and Paul Body. Other tracks included the Cajun-flavoured "Oh Marcy" and the self-explanatory "Rocking in the Kibbitz Room". "It was really a labor of love," Waits said. "Chuckie did most of the work, you know. We put up the money and my wife shopped it around and got a lot of interest. I'm glad it came out. Everybody seemed to love it." Most of the record sounded like a poor man's Buster Poindexter, but then Poindexter [aka David Johansen] had often sounded like a poor man's Tom Waits. "[Tom] was really a mentor, telling me what I needed to do to get it done," Weiss said in gratitude. "It was kinda like Snoop and Dr Dre!"

Waits was now gearing up for the release of his *own* new album. Two years earlier, Chris Blackwell had invited him to stay at Goldeneye, Ian Fleming's former residence in Jamaica where he now spent much of his time. There they'd discussed ideas for the follow-up to *Bone Machine* while Waits enjoyed the luxurious surroundings. Six months later, Blackwell resigned as head of Island Entertainment, leaving Waits feeling as he had when he and Kathleen had gone to see Joe Smith at Elektra-Asylum. "Tom's contract expired," says Blackwell, "and I think he felt that as Island was now owned by a conglomerate he would get less attention."

As Waits and Brennan contemplated alternative homes for his music, they began writing for the album that would become *Mule Variations*. On 31 March 1998, Waits appeared on KCRW's *Morning Becomes Eclectic* and told host Chris Douridas that the album would not be coming out on Island. "We're writing it now," he said. "Maybe we'll record in May, some time in May . . . I don't know what it's called yet. I wanted to call it *The Eyeball Kid*." Waits and Brennan already had a number of songs, some dating back to a two-month family vacation in Ireland the previous summer. The feel of the material was markedly American, picking up from the more rural-sounding moments on *Bone Machine*.

Waits had been listening to a lot of early blues, particularly the Library of Congress field recordings made between 1936 and 1942 by archivist Alan Lomax. He'd always loved the music but was now immersing himself in the music of Leadbelly, Memphis Minnie, and Charley Patton. Something about living out in the middle of nowhere – a place he would jokingly refer to as "the Sacramento Delta" – made primitive, scratchy recordings like Son House's "John the Revelator" and Skip James' "Look at the People" more vital than ever. Waits had also noticed a general drift towards older blues and country in the burgeoning Americana or "alt.country" sound. For artists such as Beck, whose poll-topping *Odelay* (1996) suggested the influence of *Swordfishtrombones*, Waits was himself a godfather to this new/old music. "Tom's someone I see at the airport," Beck had said to me in 1997. "He'll be going through the security machine and I'll be coming out of it, and we'll just pull over and talk about welding for a couple of minutes. He's definitely one of the luminaries, and one of those rare products of Los Angeles who has an interest in the history and background of the place."

Beck's admiration was reciprocated. "I like him very much," Waits told me. "I saw him in concert a couple of times and it really moved me. It was funny, I heard him talking about Sonny Terry and Brownie McGhee, and I used to open shows for them in the old days. It was nice to hear a kid as young as he is talking

Delta blues ancestors: Charley Patton and Son House.

about them, because I loved those guys. There's a really rich cultural heritage there, and it's nice to see that living on in someone as well-rounded and as good a spokesman as Beck seems to be."

As Waits and Brennan worked on songs such as "Cold Water", "Lowside of the Road", and "Get Behind the Mule", they coined a witty term to describe a sound that yoked traditional country-blues forms to their own weird warp factors. "We call it *surrural*," Waits said. "That's what these songs are. There's an element of something old about them and yet it's kind of disorienting, because it's not an old record by an old guy." Waits was nonetheless very taken with a batch of raw blues recordings – by old guys like R. L. Burnside and T-Model Ford – on Mississippi's Fat Possum label.

Part of what made the new songs so fresh was the attention Brennan in particular paid to local and global events – stories she was constantly harvesting from newspapers and magazines. "She writes down in journals all the time, just a constant log going of all things happening in the world," Waits said. By the time work began on the album in early June, Waits and Brennan had twenty-five songs ready for recording. Moving their own Fischer upright piano into Prairie Sun's little storage room, they used the studio's own engineers Oz Fritz and Jacquire King to help capture the sound. As with *Bone Machine*, the emphasis was on raw, lo-fi ambience, to the extent that a couple of tracks were actually recorded outdoors using directional mics. "If it's right for it, then it works," Waits said. "Most blues people like the texture on a record. And the grit that's there through time and the limitations of that particular time become part of the charm of the record."

The musicians were a motley crew drawn from different eras of Waits' music. While the core unit consisted once more of Waits on keyboards/rhythm guitar and Larry Taylor on bass, lead guitar parts were variously played by Joe Gore, a returning Marc Ribot, and Smokey Hormel, whom Waits had first heard playing in Beck's band. "There's this little room with a barn door," Hormel recalled of the setup. "You could hear the dogs in the background and see the people walking by on the road below. It was very rustic and homey." Fellow newcomers to Waitsworld included trumpeter Chris Grady, drummers Andrew Borger and Christopher Marvin, and turntablist DJ Ill Media (aka Mark Reitman of San Francisco's Go Go Market). Woodwind players Nik Phelps and Larry Rhodes were graduates of the 1992 *Black Rider* sessions. Veterans Charlie Musselwhite and John Hammond came in at different times to play harmonica. Other musicians returning to the Waits fold were Greg Cohen, Ralph Carney, and even drummer Stephen Hodges. "Nearly all the people that were on *Swordfish* and *Rain Dogs* had gone through the whole thing and – *pshew!* – out the other end," Hodges says with a laugh. "It was like, 'Where'd they all go?!'"

The scene that greeted Hodges was music to his eyes and ears. "It was a great studio to work in, because the rooms were so varied," he says. "There was a really big room where it was just like *total echo*, and that room was where a lot of the really ringy percussion stuff got done. Then you had the little teeny room where Tom had his piano and organ, and that was usually where he would sing. It was really cool, the way the different textures were available."

Hodges was also struck by the change in Waits since they'd last been in a studio together. "He's always been a heartfelt guy, but the way the sessions go down has changed," he says. "Like, they even have a chef that comes and makes lunch now. Kids make all of us grow up and then change, but I think it's only made Tom more punk. He's as out there as ever." For Hodges, the key to everything was Kathleen Brennan's involvement, not just in the songs but in the production. "She was usually there," he says. "They sang stuff together and she commented on his phrasing, helped with the enunciations. They definitely worked together at sculpting this thing, and they were really honest about how much they needed each other. It's a fucking beautiful thing they have. Who wouldn't think it's pretty cool that these guys can relate on stuff and work together? Tom is a Renaissance man of a sort. To be so powerful without being macho is . . . very cool."

While several songs on the album were tried a number of different ways – with nine subsequently being cast aside – the simpler tracks invariably started life in the storage room with Tom on piano or guitar and Larry Taylor or Greg Cohen playing bass. "We were usually tracking him with at least one other person, most of the time an upright bass player, sometimes a drummer," recalled Jacquire King of the sessions. "His vocal performance and his piano or guitar, plus the bass, are the basic take. What you hear on the album are often first takes."

Mule Variations started with its least typical song. Prefaced by an old tape-recorded loop of Waits bashing away on a chest of drawers in a Mexican hotel room, "Big in Japan" was a Brennan-generated commentary on fame and its absurdities, an extension of the self-delusion in *Bone Machine*'s "Goin' out West". It was also rather mainstream, in a poundingly alternative-rock kind of way – a beefed-up "In the Colosseum" featuring most of Primus (Brain, Les Claypool, and guitarist Larry LaLonde), along with Ralph Carney supplying spurts of sax and trumpet. The sound of Waits flaunting his stardom was inherently comical: was the character in the song actually big *anywhere*, let alone in Tokyo and Osaka?

Waits had already sung of the "Wrong Side of the Road" on *Blue Valentine*. On *Mule Variations* he turned his attention to its *low* side, a metaphor for hard times and tough luck rooted in the blues experience. With its swampy textures and weirdly dragging on-beat groove, "Lowside of the Road" was one of the album's best tracks: *Down by Law* meets Beck's "Hotwax" on a kind of field recording. A unique mix of guitar, Optigan percussion, and

African stringed instruments brought to the session by Smokey Hormel, "Lowside" was strewn with spooky images of depression, murder, and apocalypse.

There was a striking shift in mood as the third track eased in. A sequel of sorts to "Jersey Girl", "Hold On" was a conscious or unconscious Springsteen pastiche/homage, with Waits singing over a minimal arrangement of strummed guitars, bass, and shaker. Here was another archetypal Waits moll, another variation on the cousin who'd split from Marysville all those years before. Except that this woman had a man who stood by her, who held on like Waits and Brennan had held on. "We're all holding onto something," Waits said. "None of us wants to come out of the ground." For Waits, "Hold On" was "two people who are in love, writing a song . . . about being in love".

Kathleen has reputedly stated that she didn't marry a man, she "married a mule". On the overtly bluesy "Get Behind the Mule", Waits was less a mule than a man who needed to get off his behind. Supposedly the phrase came from Robert Johnson's father, despairing of his drifting genius of a son. "There've been plenty of days when I've gotten up too late in the morning and the mule is gone," Waits further elucidated. "Or somebody else is behind the mule, and I have to get behind the guy who's behind the mule." The song was attempted in so many different arrangements that the phrase "mule variations" came into play and replaced *The Eyeball Kid* as the album's title. The sparsely funky track was long and almost trancelike, meat and potatoes to blues veterans Larry Taylor and Charlie Musselwhite (who knew each other from the rock ballroom circuit in 1960s California). Musselwhite blew harmonica lines that curled round Smokey Hormel's fluid slide licks, his tone taut as Miles Davis'. The song was a feast of place names – Atchison, Placerville, Weaverville – and proper names. Waits claimed that Molly Be Damned, Jimmy the Harp, Big Jack Earl, Jack the Cutter, the Pock-Marked Kid, and Birdie Joe Hoaks were all real people. "They're just folks, just plain folks," he smokescreened. Big Jack Earl had been the eight-foot-one giant in Barnum and Bailey's Circus, Birdie Joe Hoaks a girl who'd swindled the Greyhound bus company.

There were four tracks on *Mule Variations* that Waits had written on his own. One of them, significantly, was "House where Nobody Lives", a plaintive country-soul ballad prompted by memories of an abandoned home Waits had passed every day on the way to school. I say significantly because it makes sense that Waits was alone when he wrote about what for him was a nightmare: the memory of a place where a family had lived, and from which love had vanished. As he relived his memories of staring at the broken windows and overgrown weeds, the song pondered what had happened there, the Fischer upright fleshed out by perfect Marc Ribot guitar fills that mimicked the voicings of such Memphis/Nashville session greats as Reggie Young.*

"Cold Water" was a hobo bellow of a song with chunky Keef-style riffing that bridged the gap between Howlin' Wolf and "Honky Tonk Women". (Ribot, playing alongside Waits, soloed with the greatest Richards imitation you could ever want to hear.) A song of poverty, petty crime, and *Ironweed* redemption, "Cold Water" returned us to the basic Waits/Larry Taylor R&B grind and featured Lee Marvin's son Christopher on drums. Asked if the America of songs like "Cold Water" had faded away, Waits replied that "this stuff is all over the place . . . if by evening

---

* Between 1979 and 1983, Ribot had played in a New York pickup soul band called the Realtones, backing the likes of Solomon Burke and Wilson Pickett when they were booked into such Manhattan venues as the Lone Star Road-house. In this connection, Waits' long-serving UK publicist Rob Partridge told me his client was a huge fan of Southern soul and suggested I send him a copy of my *Say It One Time for the Brokenhearted: Country Soul in the American South* (1987). Naturally it made no difference to my cause, but I like to think Waits dipped into it. When Jim Christy of *The Georgia Straight* spoke to him in 2004, he was engrossed in Peter Guralnick's *Sweet Soul Music*.

tomorrow you wanted to be by a campfire by a railroad track, you could do so". Part of him still dreamed of living that way.

The pining "Pony" took the ebullience of "Cold Water" and offered its deflated, defeated flipside. A sad résumé of a tattered life stretching from Mississippi to Chicago, the song yearned for home – specifically the memory Waits held of his Aunt Evelyn's kitchen in Gridley. The beautifully spartan arrangement, with Smokey Hormel's dobro and John Hammond's harmonica winding round Waits' guitar and faint pump organ, recalled the feel of The Band's "Rockin' Chair". It was another song rife with place names (the Mississippi towns of Murfreesboro, Natchez, Belzoni, and, best of all, Hushpuckena) and itinerant characters (old blind Darby, Ida Jane, Tallulah, Burnt-Face Jake) who could have stepped straight out of *Ironweed*.

"What's He Building?", another solo composition, took on its Ken Nordine flavour after Waits failed to make it work as a song. Similar in feel to *Bone Machine*'s "The Ocean Doesn't Want Me", it was one of Waits' great comic cameos, the sound of a man's fevered imagination as he spied on the apparently furtive activities of his mysterious bachelor neighbour. "They're really stories . . . little *Twilight Zone*s from the dark recesses of his brain," Waits said of Nordine's recordings. Sonically a combination of eccentric percussion, creepy Ralph Carney reeds, and stray samples assembled by Mark Reitman, the piece was a brilliantly funny commentary on middle-America's witch-hunt suspicion of anything solitary or even merely different. "We seem to be compelled to perceive our neighbors through the keyhole," Waits told me when we discussed the track. "There's always someone in the neighborhood – the Boo Radley, the village idiot – and you see that he drives this yellow station wagon without a windshield, and he has chickens in the backyard and doesn't get home till 3 a.m., and he says he's from Florida but the license plate says Indiana . . . so, you know, 'I don't trust him.' It's really a disturbed creative process."

"Black Market Baby" was one of the few tracks that would not be out of place on *The Black Rider* or *Alice* or *Blood Money*. Substantially the work of Kathleen Brennan, this Tin Pan Alley outing concerned a miniature femme fatale partly inspired by actress Patricia Arquette. With its sleepy Leon Redbone feel and grainy Pro Tools loop of needle noise, the track could have been an ancient 78 from the 1930s – at least until Marc Ribot's painstakingly primitive guitar solo commenced three minutes into the song.

Waits seemed surprised when I mentioned that the Eyeball Kid had appeared in his work as early as 1992's "Such a Scream". Clearly this unfortunate creature meant a lot to him. For Waits, "the Eyeball Kid" was a metaphor for show business itself, hence his decision to give the Kid his own birth date and to make the song in part a parable about the artist/manager relationship. "I'll always be here to protect you/And to cut down on the glare," he barked in a couplet that said P. T. Barnum but implicitly hinted at Herb Cohen. A raucous collage of clanky percussion, low-frequency reeds, and gamelan and gospel samples, the track could have been Pere Ubu attempting hip hop: in one line towards the end of the track, Waits actually seemed to be doing an impersonation of Ubu singer David Thomas. The showbiz metaphors aside, Waits' "freak" songs were at least more honest than people who pretended severely handicapped people weren't different at all. Waits looked head-on at such people, exploring what disabled actor Mat Fraser saw as "the need to stare and ask questions about disabled people, instead of the pretence of PC's awful politeness".

The Fischer upright took centre stage on "Picture in a Frame", a simple courtship ballad that was almost Victorian in its Sunday-best formality. Unadorned by anything save Greg Cohen's bass and a pair of wheezy saxophones, the track was a perfect instance of Waits' "hair-in-the-gate" aesthetic, retaining the incidental ambient sounds of "the Waits room". "We were always going for a mood and never concerned with cleaning things up," Jacquire King said. "We happily left all the creaking of the piano stool and pedals . . . what you're listening to is not all overdubbed and clinical but a real performance that happened in a very small and intimate environment."

The blues returned on "Chocolate Jesus", whose banjo/harmonica instrumentation took "Gun Street Girl" and "Murder in the Red Barn" as its cues but whose vocal lines derived from Little Willie John's "Fever". Charlie Musselwhite had a starring role on the track. "He's great," Waits told *Blues Revue*. "He brings about three hundred harmonicas and microphones. And he's up for anything." A surrural and somewhat bathetic variation on "Jesus Gonna Be Here", the song conjoined consumerism and zealotry in a way that was faithful to both those American traditions. "Someone might think it's blasphemous," Waits conceded, "but it's actually kind of a grassroots spirituality."

Georgia Lee Moses was a twelve-year-old Santa Rosa girl whose dead body had been found in 1997 near Highway 101 in Petaluma. When Tom and Kathleen read about her murder, they were moved to write a heartrending ballad that confronted man's relationship with a senselessly cruel universe. Asking why God wasn't "watching" was tantamount to asking if God even existed. "Georgia Lee" tapped into Waits' abiding concern for runaways and kids in danger – a lineage of songs running from "Burma Shave" through "Heartattack and Vine" to "Take Care of All My Children". It also, of course, articulated anxieties about his own children and the deep dread every parent lives with.

Originally attempted on *Bone Machine*, "Filipino Box Spring Hog" was a thunderously funky song about the Saturday night barbecues in the Waitses' old downtown LA neighbourhood. With its thumping beat and raw guitar/harmonica combo, the track was a typically Waitsian gathering of inebriates and amputees, not to mention Mr and Mrs Waits themselves. To her slight chagrin, Kathleen was pictured in her underwear in Red's Recovery Room, a famously atmospheric bar on Highway 116 in Cotati. "Thanks a lot," Brennan allegedly protested. "You finally stick me in a song and I'm sitting in a bar in my bra."

Debatably the best track on *Mule Variations* – if not the loveliest song Tom Waits and Kathleen Brennan have ever written together – "Take It with Me" was simply Waits at the upright with discreet Greg Cohen accompaniment on the double bass. "We checked into a hotel room and moved a piano in there and wrote it," Waits said of its composition. "We both like Elmer Bernstein a lot. It's like an old Tin Pan Alley song."[*]

A simple statement of tenderness and contentment, "Take It with Me" was the testimony of a man who continued to adore his wife almost twenty years after they'd first met. More than even that, it was a song of great spirituality, boasting one of the most moving couplets in all of American pop:

> *It's got to be more than flesh and bone*
> *All that you've loved is all that you own . . .*

"Maybe I feel more at peace with myself, more able to talk about these things without being afraid of what people are going to say," Waits told the *Los Angeles Times*. Predictably he then pulled back, anxious at giving too much away. "I don't know where we're going with all this," he says. "We in therapy or something?"

To *Rolling Stone* Waits admitted that he still went "back and forth between deeply sentimental, then very mad and decapitated . . . I live with a bipolar disorder." Kathleen claimed her husband broadly wrote two kinds of song, "the grand weeper" and "the grim reaper". To Waits they were "two dogs fighting all the

---

[*] In the third line of each verse, curiously, there was a melodic echo – presumably unconscious – of *Closing Time*'s "Grapefruit Moon".

time". The title "Take It with Me" can, of course, be taken two ways. "It" could be a matrimonial/familial joy that lasts beyond death, or it could be a secret that you take to the grave. And in that ambiguity, perhaps, lies the real essence of Tom Waits: on one hand a man of great emotional warmth, on the other an artist fiercely protective not only of his private life but of the mystery of his own gifts.

Mule Variations should really have ended on this sunset note. Instead Waits wrapped up the album with something altogether more gregarious. As if moving into the deserted "House where Nobody Lives" and turning it back into a loving home, "Come On up to the House" was really a gospel song of community, inviting wounded souls to come together in a kind of secular church. "Does life seem nasty, brutish and short?" Waits almost yelped. "Come on up to the house!" One could almost read the lyric as a song of AA fellowship, counselling the listener – in twelve-step parlance that was either conscious or unconscious – to "surrender" and "let go".

Of the outtakes from *Mule Variations*, the three most well-known were "Buzz Fledderjohn", "Fish in the Jailhouse", and "2:19", all dropped to make way for the likes of "Picture in a Frame" and "House where Nobody Lives". (Curiously, it was Kathleen – averse to such pre-Island slushfests as "Saving All My Love for You" – who lobbied hardest for the ballads on *Mule Variations*.) The eponymous Fledderjohn, all six feet nine of her, had been Waits' scary neighbour as a kid. The song he wrote about her all those years later was a "Lowside"-style back-porch blues, recorded out of doors with a barking hound for company. "2:19" was a more understated "Filipino Box Spring Hog", a funk-blues train song featuring floods, hellfire preachers, and the looped sound of a log sawn in half. A raucous prison song inspired by a dream of Kathleen's, "Fish in the Jailhouse" offered not just a colourful array of place and proper names but a list of fish that included salmon, carp, and shark . . . not to mention the endangered totuava.

It was probably a good thing Waits dropped these tracks, which later appeared on *Orphans*. For *Mule Variations* was too long as it was. "I thought it was a really good record, but there were too many cuts," says Bones Howe. "There were at least three that could have gone, because that's what Tom and I always did. The problem with him and Kathleen producing their own records is they can't step back to look at their work." I have to say I agree with Howe and would argue that dropping any three of the following six tracks – "Big in Japan", "Black Market Baby", "Eyeball Kid", "Chocolate Jesus", "Filipino Box Spring Hog", or "Come On up to the House" – would by some distance make *Mule Variations* Waits' best post-Asylum album.

Accompanying the effusive praise for the album when it came out in March 1999 was widespread discussion of the fact that it had been released on Anti, a brand-new offshoot of the independent LA punk label Epitaph. With Chris Blackwell gone from Island in late 1997, Waits and Kathleen inked a deal with Epitaph president Andy Caulkin in June 1998. "They're pro-artist, they're forward-thinking, and I like their taste in music, barbecue, and cars," Waits said of the label, which was home to such tattooed acts as Rancid and Offspring. "It's a friendly place, independent label. It's surprising how many people at the label are musicians, and are still playing gigs."

As a last order of business at Island, Waits had to select twenty-three tracks for the 1998 compilation *Beautiful Maladies*. The album comprised five tracks apiece from *Swordfishtrombones*, *Rain Dogs*, and *Frank's Wild Years*, plus three from *Bone Machine*, two each from *Big Time* and *The Black Rider*, and just the one from *Night on Earth*. "We'd already started writing *Mule Variations*, so we had to kind of stop and put that together," Waits said. "That was a little hard, because we had some forward momentum and then had to slam on the brakes."

Another thing interviewers asked Waits about on the eve of *Mule Variations'* release was his first movie role in six years. "I don't know why I agreed to do this," he said of the part in superhero spoof *Mystery Men*, directed by Tim Burton using the pseudonym Kinka Usher. "Except [Burton] made the whole thing sound like a softball game." Appearing alongside Ben Stiller, Janeane Garofalo, William H. Macy, Paul Rubens, Greg Kinnear, Geoffrey Rush, and a disco-infatuated Eddie Izzard, Waits had big fun in what was a moderately amusing send-up of the genre – as well as of *Blade Runner*, *The Warriors*, and several other films. Some would say Dr A. Heller was another case of typecasting. Waits himself must have seen the parallels between himself and the eccentric, unshaven designer of such "non-lethal" weapons as the Blamethrower and the Psycho-Fraculator, holed up in an abandoned amusement park in the desert with some chickens for company.

On 20 March, at Austin's South by Southwest conference, Waits played his first live show in three years at the city's Paramount Theater. Backed by Larry Taylor, Stephen Hodges, and Smokey Hormel, his appearance was both the talk of SXSW '99 and its biggest hit. Every music-biz mover and shaker fought to watch Waits play three songs from the imminent *Mule Variations* ("House where Nobody Lives", "Hold On", and "Filipino Box Spring Hog") and even dust off such pre-Island crowd-pleasers as "I Can't Wait to Get off Work", "Heartattack and Vine", and "Heart of Saturday Night". "I get requests for things from the early records," he told the *Austin Chronicle*. "It's hard. Pretty much you've got to do whatever you feel like doing. I'm not a jukebox, you know."

There was a sour note struck towards the end of the show, when a female heckler loudly upbraided Waits for allowing so many tickets to go to industry liggers rather than to genuine fans. He seemed stung by the remarks: favouring A&R and marketing men was the last thing he would have chosen to do. Even more upsettingly, Don Hyde – the friend for whom Waits had played two benefit shows three years earlier – was savagely beaten by bouncers after an SXSW show by Alejandro Escovedo at La Zona Rosa the following night.

The general feel of Waits' SXSW set may be gauged by his appearance in VH1's *Storytellers* series that spring. Taped on April Fool's Day at Burbank's Soundstage One, Waits was backed only by Smokey Hormel and Larry Taylor.* Nine of the Austin numbers were included in the set, though only "Downtown Train" and "House where Nobody Lives" made it to the show's airing in May. Understandably, producer Bill Flanagan honed the broadcast down to the better-known songs, but the fact that Waits was even happy to include "Downtown Train", "Ol' '55", and "Jersey Girl" among the eighteen songs said something about his willingness to meet commercial imperatives halfway.

Waits certainly took the show's brief at face value, regaling the audience with such vintage yarns as the legendary *Ox-Bow Incident* story while plinking discordantly away at his upright piano. "Some of these, I don't remember where they came from," he admitted. "But I'll make something up that might be better." A convoluted story about a friend knocking on his door at the Tropicana motel and asking to borrow gas money so he could drive his sixteen-year-old date back to Pasadena – in reverse – was cited as the inspiration behind "Ol' '55". The song, of course, was written long before Waits had even *heard* of the Tropicana. More heartfelt was the introduction to "Jersey Girl", dedicated to Kathleen and New Jersey. Even Waits couldn't deny this was a song with autobiographical roots. During the VH1 taping, however, he talked

---

* Anxiety about his voice had prompted Waits to get a cortisone shot in Austin and then to call Warren Zevon, with whom he shared the managerial services of Stuart Ross. "Stu told [Tom] I knew vocal exercises that help hoarseness," Zevon wrote in his journal on 29 March.

about the sort of person who leans over to a companion during a movie and whispers that it's based on a true story. "Does it really improve the film?" Waits asked rhetorically.

It was a pet peeve that recurred in many interviews Waits gave to promote *Mule Variations*, including mine. When asked if we were supposed to know who "Who Are You" was about, he told me it was better if people didn't. "It's a song," he said, "and the stories behind most songs are less interesting than the songs themselves." He was right, but I still want to know who "Who Are You" is about, and Waits certainly isn't saying. (Perhaps it is about Nancy Reagan.)

Sitting in the old Driskill Hotel in Austin, Waits talked to the *Dallas Observer* about the preconceptions of fans who button-holed him when he came through the lobby. What he said made it still clearer that "What's He Building?" was an allegory about America's growing celebrity fixation. "You use the word 'I' or 'me' in a song," he said, "and [people go], 'My God, is that autobiographical?' We have this thing about onstage and backstage. It's that keyhole mentality." As I did, other journalists got the well-honed riff about a performer's persona. "It's a ventriloquist act," he would invariably say. "Everybody does one." To Robert Hilburn, Waits pointed out that even Bob Dylan had an act. "I guess it's a question of who's the dummy. Where do you leave off and where does a character begin?"

Exhausting as the media treadmill was, promoting *Mule Variations* paid off. The album even entered the *Billboard* 200 at No. 30, the highest position any Waits album had attained. Asked if he intended to tour, Waits joked that he planned instead to open his own theatre in Branford, Missouri, the town where ageing has-beens set up shop in their own theatres and audiences were bussed in for the night. He savoured the image of a Tom Waits Theater next to Trini Lopez's.

Waits had thought about consulting Robert Wilson on how to

shake up the conventional experience of live music. "I really want to create a stage environment for me that [gives me] confidence," he said to Jim Jarmusch. "And not use all this stuff that is thrust upon me . . ." What had shaken him up the most was playing on the same bill as ska-funk-metal fusioneers Fishbone at the LA Riots benefit in May 1992. "The show they did just changed me," he told Jarmusch. "Really, it combed my hair and gave me a sunburn. That's when you realize that music, it does something physically to you. It can actually lift you and throw you around." Seven years on, Waits recalled Fishbone's impact as he agreed to four gruelling months of touring North America and Europe.

Augmenting Larry Taylor and Smokey Hormel with drummer Andrew Borger and keyboard player Danny McGough, Waits kicked off with shows on 9 and 10 June at Oakland's Paramount, the venue where he'd played the first Don Hyde benefit three and a half years before. Conspicuous by his absence was the long-serving Ralph Carney. "Everyone was like, 'Let's tour, let's tour,'" Carney remembers. "And then he went out with Smokey, who I knew from the early nineties when he was playing with John Doe. It was Smokey and Larry and him, and that was the first real heartbreak." Stops on the tour included three nights at LA's Wiltern, two at Stockholm's Cirkus, three at Berlin's Metropol, three at Boston's Orpheum, and four at New York's Beacon. The exhausting jaunt finished up with two nights at Seattle's Fifth Avenue Theater in mid-October.

Mule Variations accounted for roughly half the songs on the tour, the other half drawn from the Island albums. At the Paramount, Waits began boldly with "Lucky Day (Overture)", "The Black Rider", and "Singapore", before easing into a more surrural mood with songs from *Mule Variations* and *Bone Machine*. The sole concessions to the seventies in the opening shows were "I Can't Wait to Get off Work" and "Heart of Saturday Night". Generally Waits slowed things down with two or three songs from a pool that included "A Little Rain", "Picture in a Frame", "Johnsburg, Illinois", "Pony", and "Take It with Me". Other old songs to receive periodic airings on the tour were "Ol' '55", "Step Right Up", "Jersey Girl", "Invitation to the Blues", "Christmas Card", "A Sight for Sore Eyes", "Burma Shave", "I Beg Your Pardon", "Broken Bicycles", "Heartattack and Vine", "Muriel", "Blue Valentines", and even "Eggs and Sausage".

On 7 December, Tom Waits reached the venerable rock-and-roll age of fifty. He had attained a status that made him the envy of his contemporaries and peers. Like Neil Young, at whose annual Bridge School benefit he performed on 30 October (playing "Tom Traubert's Blues"), Waits was an iconic alternative figure, not just to the fans who'd grown up with him but to subsequent generations of music geeks. "To the postboomer generation, he's more Dylan than Dylan himself," Karen Schoemer wrote in *Newsweek*. "[His] melting-pot approach to Americana, his brilliant narratives and his hardiness against commercial trends have made him the ultimate icon for the alternative-minded." Like Young, too, Waits had sustained a marriage that continued to nurture him and support his work.

When I spent my afternoon with Waits in Santa Rosa, I remarked on the irony of a forty-nine-year-old man making grittier music than he'd made at half that age. "I always start at the wrong end of everything," he said. "I don't know, maybe I'm raging against the dying light. What do they say? Youth is wasted on the young?"

He stopped and for a second became more philosophical. What he said made it clear that, for him, midlife had been far from a crisis. "Time is not a line, or a road where you get further away from things," he said. "It's all exponential. Everything that you experienced when you were eighteen is still with you."

434

Chapter 7

Rust Never Sleeps

> *"We all die kind of a toe at a time, but . . .*
> *some old fruit trees put out the best stuff."*
> (Tom Waits to Sylvie Simmons, *Mojo*, 2004)

Tom Waits fumed after *Bone Machine* won a Grammy for Best Alternative Album. "Alternative to *what*?!" he huffed to Jim Jarmusch. He was marginally less irked when *Mule Variations* instead won a Grammy for Best Contemporary Folk Album. (Beck's beautiful *Mutations* scooped Best Alternative Album this time.) "That's not a bad thing to be called if you've got to be in some kind of category," he said. "I have a kind of miscellaneous quality to myself, but I'll take folk. I started when I was a teenager playing folk clubs."

Still, Waits would have preferred to be classified as a blues singer, and argued that in any case Grammy awards were like Food and Drug Administration stickers. "It's safer," he said. "It's kind of people formulating their tastes for what they like." Giving Waits a second Grammy seemed a faintly desperate attempt to drag him into the musical mainstream, to make this truculent cult figure *fit*. To go from "alternative" to "folk" in seven years was absurd. Shoehorning Waits into "folk" smacked of Grammy apparatchiks soliciting brownie points for hipness.

The next best thing to being deemed a "blues" artist was producing an album by John Hammond, son of the A&R legend who'd signed Billie Holiday, Bob Dylan, and Bruce Springsteen to Columbia Records. Waits had been friendly with Hammond ever since opening for him in San Francisco in 1973. One of the finest white bluesmen to emerge from the 1960s, Hammond had blown mean harmonica on *Mule Variations*, whose bluesier tracks had given Waits a new appetite for black American roots music. "John's particular dialect in music is that of Charley Patton's shoe size and Skip James' watch chain," Waits said in tribute. "He has a blacksmith's rhythm and the kind of soul and precision it takes to cut diamonds or to handle snakes."

Still, donning the producer's cap was daunting. Aside from keeping a watchful eye on Chuck E. Weiss' *Extremely Cool*, Waits had never produced another artist. (Among the other artists who'd requested his services were Morphine and – via Keith Richards – the Neville Brothers.) "[Hammond] asked me to produce the record and I said to myself, 'Jesus, how could I say no?'" Waits recalled. "Except I don't know what that means, to produce a record. 'You mean stand around and drink coffee while you play?'" Doubtless it was Hammond's suggestion that *Wicked Grin* consist almost entirely of Waits songs that clinched his friend's involvement. Soon Waits was stoked for the sessions, enlisting Larry Taylor and Stephen Hodges as the rhythm section, former Sir Douglas Quintet mainstay Augie Meyers as the keyboardist, and Charlie Musselwhite as the specialist harmonica player. He himself opted to play rhythm guitar throughout the album.

"Tom played guitar a lot better than he played it back in 1982," says Hodges, who had drummed on the original *Swordfishtrombones* version of "16 Shells from a Thirty-Ought Six". "I mean, he never played it *badly*, but he'd gotten into playing really cool bass lines and rhythms – R. L. Burnsidey, Howlin' Wolfey things. He played ninety-eight per cent of the rhythm guitar on *Wicked Grin*, and that is one bitchin'-ass rhythm-guitar record. He knows where to hit the holes. He could set the mood pretty much on his own."

Wicked grins: with blues veterans John Hammond (centre) and Charlie Musselwhite, San Francisco, May 2001. (*Jay Blakesberg*)

Though Hammond had played with everyone from The Band to Duane Allman, bluesifying Waits' songs – "the most evocative, imagistic, incredible material I've ever recorded" – was a whole new ballgame. "With the arrival of the musicians, a new shape took form," he said of the sessions. "There was magic involved. And with Tom on hand and in the band, the songs just came together. I was inspired. Another side of me emerged."

Of the album's thirteen tracks, some made more blues sense than others. "2:19" and "Buzz Fledderjohn" were *Mule Variations* outtakes tailor-made for Hammond. "16 Shells" and "Get Behind the Mule" were no-brainers, as were "Gin Soaked Boy" and "Lowside of the Road" (both left off *Wicked Grin* but snuck on to Hammond's 2001 album *Ready for Love*). "Heartattack and Vine" and "'Til the Money Runs Out" were pre-Island relics into which new life was breathed. "Fannin Street", a country-folk parable about forsaking love for the bright lights of Houston, was a Waits/Brennan song written specially for the sessions. "I Know I've Been Changed" was a traditional spiritual and the sole track to feature Waits' voice. The producer's personal favourite, however, was a spooky reworking of *Bone Machine*'s "Murder in the Red Barn".

Somehow it was typical of Waits to lurch straight from the mutant blues of *Wicked Grin* into the milieu of nineteenth-century Germany. But then it wasn't every day that Robert Wilson came a-calling, and Waits had got the Americana bug out of his system for long enough to contemplate the notion of writing songs for Wilson's version of Georg Büchner's *Woyzeck*, to be staged in Copenhagen in November 2000. Adapted from Büchner by Ann-Christin Rommen and Wolfgang Wiens, *Woyzeck* – left unfinished and fragmentary when the twenty-three-year-old playwright died of typhus in 1837 – told the story of a young working-class soldier who supports his mistress and illegitimate son by performing menial tasks for a condescending captain and submitting to medical experiments by a doctor in a small town. When his mistress, Marie, is unfaithful to him with a handsome drum major, Woyzeck seeks drunken solace in the arms of another woman but wakes to find a bloody knife in his hand and Marie's lifeless body before him.

"It's a story that continues to surface in Europe," said Waits, who'd first heard it in a Boston coffee shop. "He slits her throat and throws his knife in the lake, goes in after it and drowns, and then his child is raised by the village idiot. I said, 'OK, I'm in. You had me at "He slits her throat."'" But the increasingly politicized Waits also liked the fact that *Woyzeck* – based on a real murder in Leipzig in 1821 – was "a proletariat story . . . about a poor soldier who is manipulated by the government". In a sense Woyzeck was a typical Waits (anti)hero, a man who'd been dealt a tough hand and couldn't make sense of his life. First performed in 1913, the play had long been recognized as one of the great proto-expressionist works of German theatre, as well as a play that refused to shirk the determinism of class and exploitation. "It's much more contemporary than most modern plays," Wilson said. "Five hundred years from now this'll still be interesting because there's no shit, there's no garbage." Turned into a famous opera by Alban Berg (*Wozzeck*, 1925) and a 1979 film by Werner Herzog, its stark anti-naturalism greatly appealed to Robert Wilson, who had most recently been working with Lou Reed on 1997's *Time Rocker* and 2000's *POEtry*.

In turn, Wilson's obsessiveness continued to appeal to Waits, who flew to Copenhagen in early February 2000 for preliminary discussions. "I must have recognized aspects of myself in him," Waits said of Wilson. "He seems almost autistic as he's compelled to communicate, but has the limits of certain known forms of communication, and he's gone far beyond in developing others." He added that, "for a sober person like myself", working with Wilson was "the closest thing to a drug experience" available.

As intoxicating as the prospect of working with Wilson again was, self-doubt quickly set in as Waits and Brennan began work on the *Woyzeck* songs. But then Wilson had never been interested in formal technique anyway. "[It] is not important," he argued. "Emotional telegraphing and truth is what is important." As with *Alice* seven years before, Waits again mined his fascination with carnivals and freaks, watching Hitchcock's *Strangers on a Train* "to get some inspiration" from the film's sinister fairground scenes. Sure enough, *Woyzeck* started with a carnival announcer inviting the audience to view "the astronomical horse and the two little canary birds", together with a monkey puppet that spoke in a voice remarkably similar to Waits'. As the announcer paraded these creatures, he and the entire cast sang the opening

"Misery Is the River of the World", a gruff trudge of a song that could have been the bastard child of "Heigh Ho" and "Underground".

Juggling writing and parenthood as they'd now done for some years, Waits and Brennan worked hard on the songs through the summer of 2000 before he once again flew solo to Europe. Joining Robert Wilson at the Betty Nansen Theatre, Waits found memories of *The Black Rider* and *Alice* flooding back as full musical rehearsals began in October. The insomniac hothouse atmosphere of Wilson's productions was "kind of like being an astronaut for a few months . . . sitting out there in the dark at a little table with these little lamps like you're at Cape Canaveral". As with the Thalia company in Hamburg, the Danish actors were enthusiastic participants, submitting their egos to Wilson's vision of Büchner. Waits himself felt more confident than he had on *Alice* or *The Black Rider*. Working closely with actors was an intricately intuitive business. "You really have to give it away and at the same time you really are kind of spotting somebody who's on the trapeze," Waits said of the process. "You can't tell them to get down and let you up there so you can show them how to do it."

Four years later, when an acclaimed British production of *The Black Rider* – with Marianne Faithfull as Pegleg – came to San Francisco's American Conservatory Theater, multi-instrumentalist Kate St John had an opportunity to observe exactly how Waits "directed" performers. "He was really, really interesting and inspiring," she remembers. "He had a bit of a problem with 'Gospel Train' and wanted to deconstruct what we'd done. So he got us to play and just sort of paced around listening really hard and thinking intently about what he wanted. We stopped and he said, 'What this piece needs is a short-back-and-sides.' And that was great, because we all knew what he meant. I was playing a rhythmic thing on the accordion, and he said, 'Just do it really straight like a train.' It was completely changed and so much better."

Waits raced against the clock to get the songs right for *Woyzeck*'s premiere on 21 November. Panic stations seemed to be the normal course of events for Wilson's productions. "A week before they open, most plays or operas are just dreck, complete pandemonium," Waits said. "You want to shoot yourself and then quit, or quit and then shoot yourself." But somehow, against all odds, things fell into place just before opening night.*

As he had done after *Alice*, Waits spent Christmas and the New Year recovering at home with Kathleen and the children. For the first half of 2001 he kept his head down in Valley Ford, though he did join John Hammond on stage in San Francisco on 21 March for three numbers from *Wicked Grin*. There were occasional visits to Prairie Sun to record songs for soundtracks and other projects – tracks that would later appear on the *Orphans* box set – but for the most part he focused on life as a family man. Waits was often sighted locally, not least at Kellesimone's soccer games. "Any regular at Sebastopol's Food for Thought or Lucy's Cafe or Incredible Records has probably seen the hapless drifter wander through," wrote local reporter John Beck. "Adding another volume to West County folklore, Tom Waits stories abound. Like the time he paced the sideline at his daughter's soccer game, wearing a low-brow porkpie hat, cigarette hanging from his lip, yelling 'Kick the ball!'"

Nine months after *Woyzeck* began its Copenhagen run, however, Waits decided to repeat what he'd done with *The Black Rider* and record his own versions of the songs he'd written for

---

* In the audience for the *Woyzeck* premiere was none other than Mathilde Bondo. When she approached Waits afterwards to say hello, he got away from her as quickly as possible, treating her as if she were just another fan rather than the woman who'd part-inspired the most famous song he ever wrote. Perhaps he simply didn't recognize her after all those years.

both *Woyzeck* and *Alice*. The plan was to release the two sets of songs simultaneously as separate albums – a feat attempted with varying degrees of success by artists as unalike as Bruce Springsteen (*Human Touch/Lucky Town*) and Guns N' Roses (*Use Your Illusion 1* and *2*). They would be released as *Alice* and *Blood Money*. "We were going to call [it] *Woyzeck* but it was thought nobody knew who he was," Waits said. "Kathleen said, 'Let's call it *Blood Money*,' and that made sense. The guy's a lowly soldier who's offered money for medical experiments which contribute to his loss of balance and sanity."*

Brennan had been badgering Waits for some years to revisit *Alice*, and now seemed the right time to pull its songs out of the vault. Among other things, this required Waits to locate the demos that had been stolen and then sold back to the Thalia Theatre in Hamburg. (He claimed he had to buy the bootleg on eBay, but an avid Dutch fan is said to have sent him a copy.) "It's like giving away a box of clothes and then you get them back, you know," he said. "'Hey, those pants, I like those pants, that shirt. I always liked that shirt.'"

Recording the *Alice* and *Woyzeck* music together – in parallel – was draining. "The reason no one does two records at the same time is that it's just too damn much work," Waits told Terry Gilliam, adding he went "back and forth" between the two works "depending on how I was feeling". Even on productive days Waits felt as if he'd "been in the foxhole all day". On bad ones, "when the right sound won't reveal itself", he would pace the studio in circles or rock himself back and forth on a chair in his customary way.

The contrast with *Mule Variations* was marked, Waits assembling a large pool of musicians from the jazz and avant-garde cir-

---

* Originally, with a nod to Stanley Kubrick's *The Shining*, *Blood Money* was to be called *Redrum*.

cuits in San Francisco. Alongside Larry Taylor came more recent collaborators (Joe Gore, Matt Brubeck, Andrew Borger, Nik Phelps, Charlie Musselwhite) and debutants Eric Perney (bass), Colin Stetson (woodwinds), Gino Robair (drums), Ara Anderson (horns), Tim Allen (scraper [*sic*]), Matthew Sperry (bass), Dawn Harms (Stroh violin and viola), Myles Boisen (banjo, guitar), Carla Kihlstedt (violin), and Don Plonsey (clarinet). In addition, the two principal arrangers in the Copenhagen production of *Woyzeck* – keyboardist Bent Clausen and violinist/multi-instrumentalist Bebe Risenfors – were flown to California for the sessions, which took place not at Prairie Sun but in a studio called In the Pocket, in nearby Forestville. Rounding out the eclectic musical company – on a couple of tracks – were two percussionists: former Police man Stewart Copeland and a sixteen-year-old named Casey Waits. "If you grow up in the mortuary business, you're probably going to be an undertaker," Waits said of his son's appearance on *Blood Money*'s sinister "Knife Chase". "I told him, 'If you want to be an astronaut I can't help you.'"

Pointedly *not* called for the sessions was Ralph Carney, who was hurt and let it be known among fellow Bay Area musicians. Peeved, Waits called Carney and vented his anger. "He explained that he needed to have new people around to shake things up," Carney remembers. "It was such a heavy call that I kind of blocked it out."

Just as with *Bone Machine* and *Mule Variations*, Waits demanded a certain discipline from the *Alice/Woyzeck* players. "Most of the musicians drove up from San Francisco, and I wanted them there by 10 a.m. so they were clean," he said. "I instructed them that they were not allowed to listen to any music in the car on the way up." It was as if Waits was "directing" the recording sessions like Robert Wilson – and the musicians responded as actors responded to Wilson. The basic arrangements and textures in the *Alice/Blood Money* recordings were comparable to those on *The*

443

Black Rider. Just as *One from the Heart* had forced him to resurrect the Gin Pan Alley style of the seventies, working with Wilson on *Woyzeck* drew Waits back into a style he'd almost outgrown by *Mule Variations*. Small chamber groups of strings and woodwinds performed alongside piano and/or pump organ and other favoured Waits keyboards (Mellotron, Chamberlin, etc.). Guitars were conspicuous by their near-absence. "The electric guitar thing is so overused," Waits said. "They show up on everything, it almost seems like it's the guiding force of popular music. Without it I wonder what people's music would sound like. So it was like tying one hand behind your back just for the hell of it."

Oddly, few of the Gatmo contraptions showed up on the recordings, though the Stroh violin – an old hybrid instrument with a metal cone attached to the bridge for amplification – was ubiquitous on *Alice*'s nocturnes, played by either Bebe Risenfors or Dawn Harms. There was also a four-foot-long Indonesian "seed pod" that Waits himself played on "Kommienezuspadt".

Though *Blood Money* had its hushed moments ("All the World Is Green", "Lullaby", "The Part You Throw Away", "Woe"), in the main it was *Alice* that featured the softer, dreamier music. "I guess *Alice* is probably more metaphysical or something, maybe more water, more feminine maybe," Waits said. "It's like taking a pill . . . or a mushroom or something." By contrast, Waits saw *Blood Money* as "more earthbound, more carnival, more the slaving meat-wheel that we're all on". The key to distinguishing the two works, Waits said, was "making sure both of them had diverse textures and subject matter". Both sets of songs also had to work sequentially, irrespective of their context in the plays. "You try to create some sort of counterpoint for this story," he noted, "but you're still dealing with song logic."

On *Alice*'s opening "Alice", Colin Stetson's languid tenor phrases recalled Teddy Edwards and Frank Vicari as they danced round piano chords that wouldn't have been out of place on *One from the Heart.* "It's like a private moment," Waits said of the song. "It's like sitting in a chair . . . by yourself . . . thinking about someone." Next up, "Everything You Can Think" pulled us into Lewis Carroll's hallucinatory universe, Waits growling at us in his gruffest "Underground" voice while Mellotron chords meshed with Matt Brubeck's uneasy cello in a kind of fever-waltz. "Flower's Grave" was a spare piano ballad in the "Briar and the Rose" mode, Waits' weary growl backed by a clarinet and a small chamber string section. The chamber feel continued on the sombre "No One Knows I'm Gone", originally sung by Alice at the start of the Wilson/Paul Schmidt play and similar to the demo version of the song from Hamburg. Sung as if by a corpse lying six feet under, "No One Knows" was Waits' idea of what it was like for Alice disappearing down the rabbit hole.

"Kommienezuspadt" was less berserk than Waits' Hamburg demo, more of a frisky gallop this time, with Waits spewing out his cod-Kraut gibberish and bashing away on the seed pod while Colin Stetson blew R&B baritone sax behind him. Topped off with an anguished viola solo by Bebe Risenfors, "Poor Edward" came close to the mordant Tod Browning melodrama of its demo version. "Table Top Joe", however, was almost lounge-jazz in feel. *This* Joe was a "Straight to the Top" swinger, Waits scatting like he'd done in his *Nighthawks* days as Bent Clausen fooled around on the piano and Stewart Copeland shuffled along on a little trap kit. In stark contrast, "Lost in the Harbor" returned us to the deep melancholia of "No One Knows I'm Gone", Waits wheezing away on the pump organ and warbling like an old man. "That's the Humpty Dumpty situation," he said of the song, "looking over one side of the wall and the other – 'over here, over there,'" Waits says. "It's East Berlin–West Berlin, Palestine and Israel, Northern Ireland. That [enemies] are really kind of neighbors as well."

"We're All Mad Here" was slower and less leering than the

"Hang Me in a Bottle" demo, its pizzicato violin/marimba/bass clarinet blend recalling "Shore Leave". "Watch Her Disappear", not included in the original demos, was a poem of voyeuristic love recited in the almost prurient voice of "What's He Building?" Kurt Weill was revived on a version of "Reeperbahn" that was much less hysterical than its demo version, while "I'm Still Here" was Waits in "Picture in a Frame"/"Take It with Me" mode, alone at the piano as he imagined Alice in old age. Where once Waits felt he'd been drowned in strings, now he elected to use no more than a cello and a pair of violins to create the same orchestral drapes. It's hard not to hear this exquisite ballad as a song for Kathleen.

Another *Mule Variations* song, "Georgia Lee", came to mind with "Fish & Bird", a muted waltz featuring a small ensemble of piano, pump organ, violins, trumpet, and clarinet. The plea of a sailor asking his beloved to wait for him, the song was another coded articulation of Carroll's love for Alice. "I'm imagining a whole Victorian atmosphere and someone like himself, who had this obsession and compulsion," Waits said of Carroll. "I'm trying to explore the nature of obsession, not just in his frame of mind but also as it applies to any love affair."

The penultimate "Barcarolle" took its name from the musical term for a sailors' waltz. Sailors, Waits explained, were "always waltzing . . . moving from one side to the next". The song in question was a recap of the *Alice* narrative, a restatement of Carroll's enduring fascination with his bewitching heroine-muse. Backed by a skeleton crew of a band – Stetson on tenor sax, Clausen on unsettling piano, Dawn Harms on violin, and Matt Brubeck on bass – Waits sung a sad lullaby whose intimations of loss and death were all too plain. The closing instrumental "Fawn", with Waits on piano and Carla Kihlstedt on weepy violin, served as a perfect coda to the album.

If the differences between *Alice* and *Blood Money* have been exaggerated by critics, the latter album certainly boasts the greater share of angry, testosterone-fuelled songs. Yet both albums were to an extent bipolar, shifting from rage to contrition. The notion that *Alice* represented Waits' dreamy "feminine" side and *Blood Money* his raging "masculine" side was too glib. "I have no trouble", he pointed out, "jumping from a parlor song to a Nazi carousel" – something that happened several times within the thirteen-song sequence on *Blood Money*. "I run hot and cold," Waits told the *New York Times*. "I like melody and I like dissonance. I guess maybe it's an alcoholic personality. I get mad and I cry." Ten years sober, he was still framing his impulses in the context of addiction. But the same polarities (hard/soft, angry/tender, masculine/feminine) could as easily have been observed in the work of Neil Young, another maverick who'd upped sticks to northern California to rage against the gradual dying of the light.

"Misery Is the River of the World" got things under way on *Blood Money*, setting the harshly anti-humanist tone for Büchner's play. After the twisted roots music on *Bone Machine* and *Mule Variations*, we were back into the curt vile cynicism of *The Black Rider*, complete with percussion and marimbas that dated even further back to the hectoring stomp of "Underground" and "Singapore". The notion of human existence as remorseless and unstoppable was a worldview Waits in any case partly held. Look around you, he might have said: humanity was capable of such rottenness that in the end the only sane response was to surrender to its churning flow.

The misanthropy continued with "Everything Goes to Hell", a jaundiced duet between Marie and the Drum Major set to a jarring time signature and bongo and baritone sax parts that harked back to "Jockey Full of Bourbon". What was the point in being good, the song asked? We were all going to hell anyway.

"Coney Island Baby" was Woyzeck's naive idealization of

Marie as a suburban American princess who took him out to Dreamland – the New York theme park once again standing as a symbol of America's escapism. "It's a circus story, really," Kathleen had said to Waits. "You know, it starts with the Ferris wheel and the whole thing and this gal Marie is a Coney Island baby." When she played Waits a melody she'd found on the piano, he fell in love with it. "I said, 'God, that is just so simple and so beautiful,' and I hung onto it and put it onto a tape recorder and I carried it around." A classic throwback to 1920s Tin Pan Alley, the song was like the missing link between *Mule Variations'* "Black Market Baby" and *Real Gone's* "Dead and Lovely".

"All the World Is Green", one of two Waits tracks Julian Schnabel used in his acclaimed *The Diving Bell and the Butterfly* (2008), was a *thé dansant* piece performed as a duet between Woyzeck and Marie in the play. Colin Stetson's wistfully woody clarinet was the signature instrument on this palm-court reverie about forgiveness.

Picking up from the splenetic mood of "Misery Is the River of the World", "God's Away on Business" was not only a descendant of "Singapore" and "Cemetery Polka" but another instalment in Waits' ongoing iteration of his personal theology. God had been sozzled and wantonly cruel on "Heartattack and Vine", irresponsibly neglectful on "Georgia Lee"; now he was merely out of town like a travelling salesman. Sung by the doctor who performed experiments on Woyzeck, the track was a dwarves' march through WeillWorld – a style that was arguably becoming as predictable as Waits' ballad mode of old.

"Another Man's Vine" was delivered in a voice that – on the chorus, at least – was equal parts Mac Rebennack and "House where Nobody Lives" country-soul. If the piano and horns came from New Orleans, the trademark marimbas added a menacing faux-exotic touch to the arrangement. On its heels, the warped thriller muzak of "Knife Chase" – as sinister as it was suspenseful – sounded like Waits parodying Lalo Schifrin.

"Lullaby" spoke for itself, Waits channelling his own paternal feelings as he sang this tender song performed in *Woyzeck* by Karl, the village idiot who adopts Marie's little boy. "Starving in the Belly of a Whale", sung by the Captain who employs and demeans Woyzeck, was a cross between "God's Away on Business" and *The Black Rider*'s "Just the Right Bullets". Charlie Musselwhite's harmonica gave the track an inflamed bluesiness that was offset by Waits' ticking spaghetti-western guitar.

"The Part You Throw Away", not included in *Woyzeck* itself, was a delicate waltz-time ballad featuring pizzicato strings instead of guitar or piano. Intended as a song of guilt-admission and renunciation (sung by Marie), it was covered by Ute Lemper on her *Punishing Kiss* two years before *Blood Money* came out.* Waits followed it with the short, bittersweet "Woe", a dirgelike ballad sung by Woyzeck as he stares at Marie's lifeless body. "I like beautiful melodies telling you terrible things," Waits said of such songs. "Is it my thorny, dark, oozing side, or is it just the way I see the world?"

"Calliope" was a discordant instrumental played on the old merry-go-round instrument of the same name, accompanied only by Nik Phelps' trumpet and Waits overdubbing himself on a toy piano. It was Greg Cohen who'd found the calliope in question – a fifty-seven-whistle beast built for a circus in 1929 – on a flatbed truck in Iowa. After he called Waits to alert him that it

---

* Along with music by Waits and others of the usual suspects – Kurt Weill, Elvis Costello, Nick Cave – Lemper's album featured a song, "Scope J", by Scott Walker. Interesting, therefore, to note a few parallels between Waits and Walker. Like Waits, Walker had abandoned a generic musical style to embark on a series of radical experiments, his immersion in Jacques Brel paralleling Waits' fascination with the likes of Kurt Weill. Like Waits, he favoured the use of unusual "instruments" – dustbins, cinder blocks, even slabs of meat. And like Waits, he communicated his musical requirements to musicians in bizarre similes and metaphors.

was for sale, his sometime boss sprang for it, no questions asked. "It took four guys to pick it up and put it in the back of an El Camino," Waits said. "It's all hoses and pipes. They're ear-splittingly loud. They suggest you play it with earplugs, but I think, what's the point of that?" Waits claimed that playing the calliope was "probably the most visceral music experience I've ever had". The calliope was also heard on *Blood Money*'s last track, "A Good Man Is Hard to Find", with Waits backed by a blend of horns, harmonium, marimba, and violins. Ara Anderson blew a long Dixieland trumpet solo before Waits resumed Marie's blaring song of unrepentant infidelity.

Performed in *Woyzeck* but not included on *Blood Money* were "Diamond in Your Mind", "Shiny Things", "It's Over", and "It's Just the Way We Are Boys". The first three all found homes – "Diamond" on Solomon Burke's *Don't Give Up on Me*, "Shiny Things" and "It's Over" on *Orphans* – while an early version of "Just the Way We Are" had already featured in the Steppenwolf production of *Frank's Wild Years*. Waits himself recorded "Diamond" live at Healing the Divide, a fundraising show for "peace and reconciliation" staged in New York on 21 September 2003.

With Waits immersed in *Alice* and *Blood Money*, his disowned past came back to haunt him in the form of the Elektra/Rhino compilation *Used Songs, 1973–1980*. "I can't listen to the old stuff," he'd groaned the previous summer. "I've got big ears and I dressed funny. And I have a monochromatic vocal style. I have a hard time listening to my old records, the stuff before my wife."

No doubt this was why Waits repeatedly ignored phone messages from Bones Howe to discuss the mastering and sequencing of the compilation. "There was a track where I thought the bass was a little light, and there was a suggestion I had about the sequence," Howe recalls. "I called him and I could never get to him. A girl said, 'I'm his assistant and you'll have to tell *me* about it.' I said, 'I would really like to talk to Tom about it.' And she

Bones Howe, Montecito, March 2007. (*Art Sperl*)

called me back and said, 'Tom just says to tell me what you wanted to tell him.' So I just said, 'Okay, so that's where we are.' I told her what I thought. She called me back the next day and said Tom agreed with me that there probably should be more bass on that track."

Waits doesn't come out of this looking great. As a mere matter of courtesy, a call back to the man who'd got his career on track in the first place doesn't seem so much to ask. Then again, it's the way the Dylans and Youngs of this world have always operated, and why should Waits be any different? "I'm thinking it's not going to hurt Waits to talk to Bones for half an hour," agrees Michael Hacker, who'd worked with both men on *One from the Heart*. "And yet it's almost part of the toolkit that makes someone like Waits successful. It's almost like you can't leave your past behind unless you cut those people off. I mean, I'm a Dylan freak and *he* certainly cuts people off."

"I think Tom's leery of people that he works with getting too

451

close," says Ralph Carney, himself excommunicated from the Waits inner circle. "That's kind of what happened with *me*. I'm sure if I ran into him he'd be like, 'Hey, Ralphie, how's it goin' . . .' But I'm in a period now where they don't speak to me, even though everyone's like, 'Don't take it personal, man.'" Stephen Hodges, who played behind Waits with Carney on numerous occasions, says this is "maybe not an area I should talk about . . . there's a certain thing going on here with Tom's office, and the deal is that . . . because Ralph's deeply affected by the whole association with Tom and what have you, it's made things difficult between him and the Waits camp".*

Bones Howe, understandably hurt, talks of Waits in the tones of a spurned parent. He reminds me of The Band's "Tears of Rage" – "*Now you throw us all aside and put us all away . . .*" Of all the great musicians Bones has worked with over the years, Waits – with the exception of certain long-gone jazz legends – is the only one he misses speaking to. "I would love to be able to pick up the phone and say, 'Hey man, what's going on? How are your kids?'" Howe says. "We're two complete opposites in a lot of ways but there are parts of us that are very much alike. I wouldn't make another Fifth Dimension record, but I'd make another record with Tom tomorrow. He is a real person and he has good manners. He's a gentleman. That's one of the reasons I miss him."

Howe can only assume that Kathleen Brennan has something to do with the friendship ending; it would hardly be the first time that a relationship or marriage created an unspoken rift. "In a lot of ways Tom is very selfish about his artistry," Howe says. "And I don't know what Kathleen's contributions to those records have really been. I just don't know. She's his wife and the mother of his kids and she's his co-producer and his co-writer." Michael Hacker maintains that "giving Kathleen so much credit is a win-

---

* "And", Hodges added, "in turn that's kind of red-flagged *you* . . ."

win thing for Waits . . . nothing's diminished him and it allows him in a way to deflect certain things. He can be this gracious collaborator but really at the end it's all about Waits."

When the dreaded interview treadmill cranked up again in May 2002, Waits took his usual pains to credit Kathleen while underlining just how averse she was to the whole media circus. "She hates all this," he told one interviewer as he pointed at his minidisc recorder. He had wise counsel for anyone struggling in marriages or relationships. "Everybody wants it to be summer all the time, in relationships and with their career," he said. "And when the weather starts to turn, they think they better get out. So it takes a certain amount of persistence." Recalls Kate St John of the San Francisco rehearsals for *The Black Rider*, "Kathleen was always there and they seemed very happy . . . they were obviously among the chosen few who just *do* meet the right person in their life."

Safeguarding the privacy of family life seemed more important than ever to Waits. He had been quietly appalled by the tele-visual antics of Ozzy Osbourne and family in *The Osbournes*, despite having met and liked the former Black Sabbath singer at their mutual friend Nicolas Cage's house in LA. "I don't think any of us are sick," he said apropos MTV's hit show, "but I think the culture is sick and it gives us the flu." If a man stopped valuing his privacy, Waits said, sooner or later he wouldn't have a life at all.

With Kellesimone in college – and soon to become a painter* – Waits' parental energies were now focused mostly on his sons. With the teenage Casey it was usually a case of drop-offs and pickups, often from shows by hip-hop artists that made Waits feel his age. "As you start getting older, you get out of touch," he admitted. "I'm like a turtleneck sweater. And then your kids kind

---

* An exhibition of Kellesimone's paintings, "Men in Power", was held at San Francisco's Luscious Garage gallery in December 2007.

of enlighten you: 'Dad, have you heard Blackalicious?' I take them to the show but I drop them off. I'm not allowed to go in. It'd be too embarrassing." Waits protested too much: Casey was proud enough of his father to set up an interview with his favourite magazine, *Big Brother Skateboarding*. "We love [Casey]," wrote Russell Bongard. "Without him telling his dad to do this interview we would have never gotten Tom on the phone."

Waits was more comfortable helping out with excursions at Sullivan's elementary school, not least because of the Chevy Suburban he drove. "I'm down with the field trips," he said. "I'm always looking for a nine-passenger opportunity." Once he took Sullivan and assorted classmates to a local guitar factory, only to find that none of the employees recognized him. A few weeks later he drove the kids on another trip, this time to a recycling centre. "We pull up to the dump," he said, "and six guys surround my car – 'Hey! It's Tom Waits!'" Everybody, he remarked forlornly, knew him at the dump.

The longer Waits was a father, the easier he found it to juggle work and domesticity. Where once it was essential to separate the world of "ball games, graduations, and family reunions" from that of Mellotrons and bullhorns, increasingly he saw his life as one seamless thing. "The way you do anything", he liked to say, "is the way you do everything." Now he felt he could "go back and forth between the documentary and the romantic comedy . . ."

"Perhaps the most singular feature about Tom Waits as an artist," Elizabeth Gilbert wrote in a fine *GQ* profile, "is the way he has braided his creative life into his home life with such wit and grace. This whole idea runs contrary to our every stereotype about how geniuses need to work." On the rare occasions when Waits felt conflict between work and home life, the family dog – Bob – became a useful ally. "[He has] a need to mark a territory, and I'm kind of like that," he said. "If I've been gone for three days and I come home, first thing I have to do is take a walk around the house and establish myself again."

Waits was still Mr Cranky when it came to the prying eyes of the outside world. "If people are a little nervous about approaching you at the market, it's good," he maintained. "I'm not Chuckles the Clown or Bozo. I don't cut the ribbon at the opening of markets. Hit your baseball into my yard and you'll never see it again." Quoting Robert De Niro in *Meet the Parents*, Waits said he had a "circle of trust" around him, made up only of close friends and loved ones. Interviewers continued to experience his ire, moreover. When an Australian journalist asked whether basing songs on works by Lewis Carroll and Georg Büchner meant his own "well of characters" was "drying up", Waits let him have it with both barrels. "I beg your pardon, are you trying to insult me?" he snarled down the phone. "Are you saying I'm drying up?" Just because he wasn't living in motels or sleeping in his car anymore, he barked, didn't mean there was "nothing left to write about".

Waits' anger also spilled out when he talked about the music industry. In May 2001 he'd joined forces with Randy Newman and Nancy and Ann Wilson of Heart in filing a $40-million copyright-infringement lawsuit against mp3.com in Los Angeles.* In September 2002, along with his old benefactors Glenn Frey and Don Henley, he would appear at a joint hearing on industry accounting practices, called by members of the California senate judiciary committee and the senate committee on the

---

* That same month found Waits accepting a Founders Award – for being an "extraordinary musical storyteller" – at the eighteenth annual ASCAP Pop Music Awards at LA's Beverly Hilton Hotel. Waits gave a speech and played four songs live, while Keith Richards paid tribute to his friend in a rambling video message. Among the Rolling Stone's more intelligible comments was a story about Waits recommending the purchase of ten thousand worms to aerate his Connecticut lawn.

entertainment industry. "The record companies are like cartels," Waits raged. "It's a nightmare to be trapped in one. I'm on a good label now that's not part of the plantation system. But all the old records I did for Island have been swallowed up and spit out in whatever form they choose." He urged young artists not to sign away their publishing rights as he had done. "Most people are so anxious to record, they'll sign anything," he remarked. "It's like going across the river on the back of an alligator."

Viewing the music industry in the wider context of capitalist entertainment, Waits continued to rail against the use of songs in commercials. He bemoaned the fact that he could no longer hear "Good Vibrations" without thinking of Sunkist orange juice. "In the old days if somebody was doing a commercial, you used to say, 'Oh, gee, too bad, he probably needs the money,'" he said. "But now it's like hawking cigarettes and underwear with rock and roll. While you're dreaming about your connection with that song, why don't you think about soda or candy or something?"* One wonders if Waits ever confronted Keith Richards on this thorny issue. When it came to endorsing products, the Rolling Stones were more shamelessly avaricious than anybody.

Allied to the commercial abuse of music, Waits felt, was a general loss of community in the way music was consumed. Where once blues, country, folk, and gospel had brought people together in shared experience, now music was too "secular and compartmentalized" to provide a genuine connection. "Everyone is really afraid of intimacy," he observed. "Most of our fear really involves fear of each other."

---

* Waits would have been appalled – and Bill Hicks writhing in his grave – at the news in March 2008 that Scottish singer Paolo Nutini had inked a deal to promote sportswear brand Puma by performing his song "New Shoes" across a broad spectrum of TV, mobile, radio, online, and in-store appearances. The deal was set up by a new "brand partnerships division" of Warner Music International. Warners, of course, had been Waits' old home.

As they did for so many artists, the events of 11 September 2001 left Waits shaken and questioning the purpose of what he did. Asked about his worldview post-9/11, he said he felt the planet was "on fire" but added that at least artists were now wide awake. "It's important ... not to go back to sleepwalking in our pajamas, playing golf and contemplating our navels," Waits said. "The rest of the world is tapping us on the shoulder with the oldest conflict of time – the haves and have-nots. It's time for great men to step forward with wisdom and depth and compassion."

Another subject Waits touched on in interviews was acting. With the exception of *Mystery Men*, Waits hadn't appeared in a film for almost a decade. "It's not the life I want to have, wearing someone else's clothes and saying someone else's words," he said brusquely. What thespian inclinations he retained seemed to be fulfilled in his music. "When you sing, you're kind of acting," he said. "The whole act of singing is like a big question you're asking, something you are reaching towards, wondering about or ranting over." It was the sheer vanity of Hollywood actors that riled Waits. A man of rare natural humility in a business rife with narcissistic egomaniacs, he kept a constant check on tendencies to self-aggrandizement. "I try not to let any of it go to my head, but sometimes that's impossible," he said. "I have my own life, and then I do this concentrated stuff of making a record and going on the road and doing interviews."

Released in May 2002, *Alice* and *Blood Money* debuted at 32 and 33 on the *Billboard* chart, each selling 32,000-plus in their first week of release and delivering Waits' highest chart positions to date. He conceded it was "a little bit of a gimmick" to put them out on the same day. "How are they different?" he said. "One's chicken, one's fish." Asked if the albums in any sense rounded off a kind of Robert Wilson trilogy, Waits replied that they could be viewed in those terms. Whether the "gimmick" of the dual release did *Alice* and *Blood Money* any favours was debatable.

While reviewers and fans warmed more to *Alice* than to *Blood Money*, few fell in love with either album in the way they'd fallen for *Mule Variations*.

Within a year, moreover, Waits had swung back towards the more American – bluesier, blacker – feel of *Mule Variations*. Using Larry Taylor, Marc Ribot, Brain, Les Claypool, his son Casey, and former Swedish glam-metal guitarist Harry Cody, Waits set about recording his roughest, most unkempt music to date. "Those last albums were more meticulous," Waits said of *Alice* and *Blood Money*. "There were more ballads on them, and there were strings and all that stuff. You've been kind of staring into the water and now you want to do something that's liberating."

Waits had told me that he wanted to find a way of bringing his hard and soft sides closer to each other – to, in some sense, reconcile rather than dialectically oppose the "grand weepers" and "grim reapers". "I guess I'd like to try and find some way to put those things together instead of end-to-end," he'd said. "Find a way to smash one into the other, or mutate it in some way." He saw the next album as his opportunity to do just that. He also wanted to give voice to a political rage his fans had never heard before, writing three songs with Kathleen ("Hoist that Rag", "Sins of the Father", and "Day after Tomorrow") that directly addressed the malpractices of the Bush administration and the invasion of Iraq. "I'm not a politician," he told me. "I keep my mouth shut because I don't want to put my foot in it. But at a certain point, saying absolutely nothing is a political statement all of its own."

For the new album, Waits decided to forgo any kind of official recording environment, instead using a mobile studio to record in an abandoned schoolhouse in the Chinese immigrant "ghost" town of Locke, located in "the Sacramento delta" a hundred miles east of his home. "We just said the delta," he told me. "Most people assumed it was the Mississippi delta. But see, there's a *Sacramento* delta and that's where we were. The old schoolhouse seemed to help the music somehow, I don't know how." The album would bear the self-consciously bluesy title *Real Gone*.

As blues-rooted as it was, the album also had one foot in the newer African-American art form that was hip hop. "It's the growing edge of the blues," Waits said. "[It's] following in the same tradition and carrying the same rebellious nature." Expanding on the homemade "human beatbox" intro to "Big in Japan", Waits decided to make his own "oral percussion" the rhythmic basis of the new album. Having employed DJ Ill Media on *Mule Variations* – and fallen in love with Missy Elliott and the Wu Tang Clan, to boot – he wanted to incorporate elements of the radical new hip hop that his eldest son loved: San Francisco turntablists and freestylers such as El-P, Sage Francis, and Aesop Rock. "All that stuff gets played around the house because that's what happens when you have kids," Waits said of Casey's tastes. "You stop dominating the turntable. I haven't had that kind of sway around here for years. 'Put on that Leadbelly record one more time, Dad, and I'm going to throw a bottle at your head.'" Kathleen wasn't so sure of the new direction. "I keep wanting to use turntables and stuff but my wife says no," Waits had said in 2002. "She says that's going to be like a ducktail eventually, or a flat-top or mohawk. And I struggle with that. I can't really tell."

Overriding Brennan's misgivings, Waits began recording himself in the bathroom at home, overdubbing percussive sounds and grunted exclamations on his Fostex four-track while the rest of the family slept. "I like to use my voice like a drum, you know," he said. "I counterpoint and all that. And then of course I sub-vocalize, because I'm dyslexic, attention deficit disorder." The "bathroom sessions" left him "sweating, eyes all bugged out, hair sticking up" – and his throat in shreds. He emphasized that these lo-fi recordings weren't loops but oral patterns sustained for

459

upwards of three and a half minutes. "Loops start feeling like wallpaper after a while," he told me. "You know it's coming around again and your mind has no need to probe any further." He compared the crude recordings to the sounds singers make "when you're trying to communicate with a drummer and you don't play the drums".

The bathroom tapes formed the rhythmic ruts for all *Real Gone*'s more raucous selections: "Top of the Hill", "Shake It", "Don't Go into the Barn", "Metropolitan Glide", "Baby Gonna Leave Me", "Clang Boom Steam", and hidden track "Chicka-boom". ("Clang Boom Steam" – originally "clank boom and steam" on *Bone Machine*'s "Such a Scream" – was a virtual ono-matopoeia for Waits' mouthbox sound.) Over the scratchy, dis-torted "beats" of "Top of the Hill" and "Metropolitan Glide", moreover, Casey's turntables could be heard swirling as Larry Taylor anchored the raw sound and Marc Ribot worked his usual jagged magic. "What happened this time was there's one guy in my band who's eighteen and one guy's in his mid-sixties," Waits said. "When everybody gets together you know they're going to learn something. Each wants what the other knows."

The sound of *Real Gone* was echoey and booming. Startling by its total absence was any sign of piano. "I don't know why the piano didn't get used," Waits said. "It just didn't work. I bring hundreds of instruments into the studio, and everybody else who comes in brings a couple of hundred too. You end up with this plethora of instruments that you don't even know where to begin." In fact, there was a decidedly low quota of "exotic" instru-ments on *Real Gone*: only one use of Chamberlin (on "Circus"), and Ribot's cigar-box banjo on "Trampled Rose". After eschew-ing it on *Alice* and *Blood Money*, the guitar had returned with an unholy vengeance. Equally ubiquitous was the percussion: end-less bashings and smashings administered by Brain and/or Waits and son. Here was Waits in his mid-fifties, the mad man of Valley Ford, letting loose in the most unbridled way he'd ever done. "It wasn't really a conscious thing," he said, "but I always figured that you get to be more eccentric as you get older and people have to endure it. 'Old Uncle Al has spittle around his chin, but that's okay, he's old.'"

Real Gone also alluded to the finality of death and loss – of people and places lost to eternity. Death was overtly present on "Don't Go into the Barn", "How's It Gonna End", "Dead and Lovely", and "Green Grass", less overtly on several other tracks. Waits had recently lost both his dear friend Teddy Edwards and *Alice/Blood Money* bassist Matthew Sperry, the latter dead at thirty-four after being hit by a car while cycling in Oakland. "I think there's a pretty heavy emphasis on mortality in whatever you do," he said. "How do you avoid it? We're decomposing as we go. We're the dead on vacation. It's not a theme I need to pursue. It pursues me."

Opening track "Top of the Hill" said, "Welcome to my neck of the woods." It was the sound of a man at once folksy and a bit crusty, doing his oral-beatbox thang out back in the shack. Loops or no loops, the effect was close to trancelike: you either fell into the groove of Waits' mouth percussion or you didn't. (There was a curious synchronicity in the release of Björk's album *Oceania*, on which – in her very different way – the Icelandic siren performed similar trickery.) In Waits' formulation, this was music for dancing like nobody was watching, complete with squiggly turntable scratches and an old kazoo.

"Hoist that Rag", *Real Gone*'s most fearsome song, began with a lurching Afro-Cuban groove, as if some monster had broken into a Havana dance hall and taken over the stage. Ribot, who'd tackled Cuban music with his own occasional outfit Los Cubanos Postizos, twisted and writhed as Waits yelped his song of coded bellicosity, sung as if by a degenerate Donald Rumsfeld. Though "Hoist" consisted of nothing but guitar, bass, and percussion, the brute force of the chorus was a tirade of rage. This was righteous indignation, a magnificently unpatriotic attack on America's stars-and-stripes imperialism. Said Robert Christgau, "I wouldn't put it past [Waits] to actually make some politics out of this life-long dedication of a middle-class teacher's son to the lower reaches – the lower depths . . . to actually politicize a little bit, actually making something out of what I'm sure is a situation that appalls him."

The eight-minute "Sins of the Father", with its fretless banjo and muted rock-steady groove, alluded none too obliquely to George W. Bush and the electoral rigging in his brother Jeb's home state of Florida. Reverbed guitars and banjos vied with bongos-in-the-dirt percussion that recalled "Lowside of the Road". A processional Dylanesque epic with densely allusive verses and a host of quasi-biblical imagery, it told of a wayward son's urge to cleanse the past – to take his inherited sins "down to the pond".

"Shake It" found Waits once again in Stones mode, a Fat Possum version of *Rain Dogs*' "Big Black Mariah". Brash and distempered, the track's telegraphic lyric – the song of a wild jailbird holed up in a motel – read like some cross between Cormac McCarthy and James Ellroy. "Don't Go into the Barn" was more of the same, a splice of "Top of the Hill" and "Murder in the Red Barn". Waits was starting to love barns as much as he loved skies, trees, crows, dogs, monkeys, and roses, but this particular barn was an old slave house where bones and chains were being dug up. Along with Waits' Beefheart snarls, Harry Cody's acoustic guitar gave the track a visceral blues edge.

If "How's It Gonna End" was The Big Death Question, it was also a song about narrative arcs in literature and film. (At the end of the song, an old man slept in the front row of an old movie house.) People – Joel Tornabene, Shane and Bum Mahoney, a girl who drowns in a lake – came to violent ends in this sparse song built around banjo and guitar. Meanwhile, "Metropolitan Glide" was mutant James Brown, a style Waits identified as "cubist funk". A kind of reprise of "Top of the Hill", the song was an instruction manual for a new dance à la Twist or the Mashed Potato – though its immediate inspiration was the Terror Squad's hip-hop track "Lean Back". There was a soul/funk/gospel sample tucked in there – and a passing nod to Beefheart too.

"Dead and Lovely" was another Waits song about a woman gone astray, in this case a nice middle-class girl entangled with a bona fide Bad Guy, a battered trophy wife who'd wound up prematurely deceased. Part-based on Carol Wayne, who – in Waits' words – used to do "goofy dumb blonde stuff" on *The Tonight Show* and later died in mysterious circumstances in Mexico, the song's jaunty rhythm was offset by the lonesome *Twin Peaks* twang of Ribot's guitar.

It's odd in retrospect that it took Tom Waits so long to write a song called "Circus", *Real Gone*'s very own "Ocean Doesn't Want Me" or "What's He Building?". The usual parade of oddities showed up for this track: Horse-Face Ethel and her Marvelous Pigs, Yodeling Elaine, Zuzu Bolin and Mighty Tiny, Molly Hoey with her tattoo gun, one-eyed Myra who trained the ostrich and camels and wore a Roy Orbison T-shirt. You'd think Waits might have outgrown this particular preoccupation. "Everybody wants to run away and join the circus," he said. "That's what a lot of people do in music to some degree. You want something with heightened reality. That's what I wanted to do." Starting life as a song with a hip-hop sample that he'd "looped from the radio", the track, Waits decided, had to be "more pathetic and tawdry". In due course, with Casey on drums, "Circus" turned into spoken word.

A folk song of mythopoeic jealousy, "Trampled Rose" featured Ribot on a boxy banjo that sounded like a dimestore dobro. Like *Alice*'s "No One Knows I'm Gone", "Green Grass" pictured how it would feel to be dead but conscious, addressing those who mourned at the graveside in a whispered sub-baritone. Despite being couched in almost pastoral terms, ultimately its sentiment was that of the late Warren Zevon's heartbreaking "Keep Me in Your Heart".

After that low-key interlude – from "Dead and Lovely" to "Green Grass" – *Real Gone* returned to full-on raucousness with "Baby Gonna Leave Me", a gratuitous splurge of deranged noise. With Waits frothing at the mouth, it was a further footnote to his ongoing love affair with the piratical Keith Richards – except this time with Marc Ribot doing the impersonating. "Clang Boom Steam" was a snatch of Waits in the bathroom that segued straight into "Make it Rain", *Real Gone*'s "Downtown Train". The album's most orthodox track – and a bone thrown to the sales guys at Epitaph – it was a song about a man abandoned by a faithless woman and demanding an apocalyptic deluge to wash away his pain.

The most affecting song on *Real Gone* was saved for last. "Day after Tomorrow" was almost out of place here, so plain and unalloyed was its message, couched in the form of a letter written home from the war front. "The government looks at these eighteen-year-old kids as shell casings, you know," he said, all too aware of his own sons. "Like we're getting low on ammo, send in some more. We're neck deep in the big muddy and the big chief is telling us to push on and offer up our children." The song harked back to Woody Guthrie and early Dylan in its conjuring of a twenty-one-year-old soldier's shell-shocked bewilderment and longing for home. It was interesting that the boy was not from California or the south but from Rockford, Illinois – close to Kathleen's hometown of McHenry. "I saw Tom do the song on *The Daily Show*," says Bones Howe. "It was like going back, just acoustic guitar and bass. Like, 'One more time and we'll have it.' I thought, that's Frank, it's the troubadour, just playing and singing. It was very poignant to me."

Here again Waits worked through some hoary theological dilemmas, asking whose prayers God heeded and whose he refused. Like all great artists, he was forced to confront the concept – the existence or otherwise – of a creator, to address what "God" meant in such a callous universe. For all the evil religion had wrought, Waits saw the value in living by (some of) its principles. His early experience of church was necessarily ingrained in him. Moreover, anyone serious about twelve-step recovery had to acknowledge "God" (or at least a "Higher Power") in some form and could not be entirely atheist/materialist about life. "With the God stuff I don't know," he said. "I don't know what's out there any more than anyone else, 'cause no one's really come back to tell me. I don't know if I'm on a conveyer belt or if I'm on the tongue of a very angry animal about to be snapped back into his mouth. I think everyone believes in something; even people who don't believe in anything believe *that*."

Lest anyone thought Waits might end the album on such a simple, forlorn note as "Day after Tomorrow", hidden track "Chickaboom" was a hectic variation on "Clang Boom Steam", though by this point on the album there was something slightly undignified about a man of Waits' age making such idiotic sounds with his mouth.

Personally I wasn't entirely convinced – or at least entranced – by *Real Gone*. *Mule Variations* had leavened its moments of barking weirdness with plaintive piano ballads. Now here was Waits with an album that featured no piano at all, just a cacophonous brew of human beatbox, threadbare bass, and gnarly guitar. If he was still taking more risks than all the other American "singer-songwriters" of his generation put together, I couldn't help feeling that some of *Real Gone*'s musical modes (the Fat Possum stomp of "Shake It", the Tod Browning galleria that was "Circus", the sepulchral loungecore of "Dead and Lovely") had been done before and better – by *Tom Waits*.

Because the album's main templates ("Temptation", "Such a Scream", "Lowside of the Road") were ultimately more satisfying, hearing them reheated on, say, "Don't Go into the Barn" and "Baby Gonna Leave Me" was oddly disappointing.

Twenty years after *Swordfishtrombones* – and eighteen since Marc Ribot had first worked with him – was Tom Waits finally chasing his own musical tail?

Chapter 8

He's Not There

> *"I'm the albino catfish, you know, in the lake for a long*
> *time. I'm gettin' bigger, and I ain't been caught."*
> (Tom Waits, radio interview with Vicki Kerrigan, *The Deep*
> *End* [Radio National/ Australia], 5 October 2004)

So many desperate and hopeless people are loitering outside the Hammersmith Apollo this Tuesday night – 23 November 2004 – that one feels vaguely ashamed to be in possession of a ticket for Tom Waits' first London concert in seventeen years. Heartless it seems of him to stay away so long – he'd last played London at the very same venue, when it was still hallowed shrine the Hammersmith Odeon – and then limit his appearances to a single date. But such are the whims of this great American entertainer.

Any thoughts of the disappointed outside drop away once

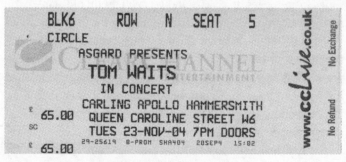

No sleep till Hammersmith, November 2004.

Barking orders or just barking mad? Live at the Apollo, Volume One. (*Jill Furmanovksy*)

Waits takes the stage with Marc Ribot, Larry Taylor, Brain, and his son Casey (who plays congas on the first two songs). Throwing contorted shapes to the crabbed groove of "Hoist that Rag", Waits – part pigeon-toed Lee Evans, part Max Schreck with maracas – is a sight for jaded eyes.

Thunderous with anti-Rumsfeld rage, "Hoist that Rag" is the perfect lapel-grabbing opener. If the set is inevitably heavy on songs from the last five years and (very) light on old staples, the newer material is twistedly thrilling. If only for the reuniting of Waits and Ribot – a James Burton from Planet David Lynch – this 2004 tour has been a triumph. "All right, I know, seventeen years," Waits grunts. "But ya look good . . ." He doesn't look bad himself, and he *sounds* more bone-quakingly bestial than ever. Even the oddly ordinary "Make It Rain" is redeemed by the passionate despair Waits injects into its lyric.

The first real high point of the evening comes paradoxically with the undersold "Sins of the Father". Surrender to the spooky sparseness and loping skank of this veiled assault on Bush and family, and it becomes hypnotic. By contrast, "Eyeball Kid" prompts a rather worn carny routine from Waits as Ribot picks out spiky notes on a fretless banjo. Waits concludes the ritual by playing an atonal flurry of bell-like notes on a keyboard. For the loungecore portion of the show, Waits revives the rabid Sinatra of "Straight to the Top", drunkenly serenading a Vegas moon as Ribot supplies sleazy jazz fills. "God's Away on Business" is pure *cabaret noir.*

Where "Hoist that Rag" was angry and "Sins of the Father" just politically weary, "Day after Tomorrow" is Waits at his most empathically humanist. This callow epistle from Iraq is strummed in straight singer-songwriter mode – "*I still don't know how I'm supposed to feel*" – and sounds chillingly tender.

An upright piano is symbolically wheeled on for the encores. Here at last is the Waits we all secretly want: slurred, mawkish, broken. "Invitation to the Blues" is the only concession to the seventies all night, but it's followed by "Johnsburg, Illinois" and the two great *Mule Variations* odes to home: the front-parlour gospel of "Come On up to the House", the country-soul "House where Nobody Lives".

And then, suddenly, Tom's gone. *Real* gone.

Waits had sold out the Hammersmith Apollo in twenty-nine minutes, with 150,000 people attempting to buy tickets in the space of an hour. With *Real Gone* cracking the *Billboard* Top 30 in America and making the Top 10 in several European charts, he'd kicked off a short tour in Vancouver on 15 October before flying to Europe in mid-November. He was no fonder of touring than he'd ever been. "It doesn't take much to tick me off," he said. "I'm like an old hooker, you know."

Backed by Larry Taylor, Marc Ribot, and Brain – with the nightly cameo from Casey – Waits played sellout shows in

Antwerp, Berlin, Amsterdam, and finally London. The shows were greeted deliriously, with umpteen musical luminaries and assorted celebs – Thom Yorke, Johnny Depp, Jerry Hall, Tim Burton, Fatboy Slim – pulling strings to get into the Hammersmith show.

Waits was now universally acknowledged as an elder statesman of "alternative" rock, a godfather-hero to the likes of Yorke and P. J. Harvey. Fans and admirers the world over paid tribute to Waits in such annual gatherings and symposia as Poughkeepsie's "Waitstock", Denmark's "Straydogs Party", and the "Waiting for Waits" festival in Mallorca. Cabaret performers based entire shows on his repertoire – Robert Berdahl's *Warm Beer, Cold Women*, Stewart D'Arrietta's *Belly of a Drunken Piano* – while countless artists covered his songs. Norah Jones' version of "Long Way Home" – a song Waits and Brennan had written and recorded for Arliss Howard's 2002 film *Big Bad Love* – had swelled their coffers as Rod Stewart had once done.

On other fronts, too, it was business as usual. There was a lawsuit against ad agency McCann Erickson, who'd employed yet another "Waits-alike" singer to record a version of Brahms' "Wiegenlied" in a Scandinavian ad for Opel's new Zafira people-mover. Another suit launched in 2005 – brought by Herb Cohen against the Warner Music Group and alleging that Waits had been shortchanged on the sale of digital downloads – must have been a source of bittersweet irony for Cohen's former client.

There were movie roles that Waits either turned down or was unable to commit to. Robert Altman had wanted him and Lyle Lovett to play singing-cowboy duo Dusty and Lefty in *A Prairie Home Companion*. Rumours circulated that he would appear with Brad Pitt in *The Assassination of Jesse James*. But his feelings about acting hadn't markedly changed since 1999's *Mystery Men*. "I used to have it right there as a clause in my acting contracts:

'Let Waits be Waits,'" he explained. "If they comply with my conditions, I do okay. You might say I'm limited as an actor, and right now I'm not interested in doing any more of it. I don't want to be away from home that much." The excitement Waits had experienced as a movie actor in the late 1980s and early 90s had all but worn off.

In the event, Waits plumped for appearances in three very different films. In Tony Scott's hyper-stylized *Domino*, about the bounty-hunter daughter of actor Laurence Harvey, Waits was "The Wanderer", a gun-toting Seventh-Day Adventist with a bandaged hand who passed through the desert in an old convertible as "Jesus Gonna Be Here" played on the soundtrack. "They won me in a poker game," Waits said of the small role, which had him brandishing a pocket Bible at Keira Knightley and companions and identifying her as "the angel of fire". As he drove them to Las Vegas we again heard him wailing on the soundtrack.

In Goran Dukic's *Wristcutters: A Love Story*, an indie film about the afterlife of suicides, Waits was Ralph Kneller, an "undercover angel" discovered asleep on a deserted highway by the trio of Zia (Patrick Fugit), Mikal (Shannyn Sossamon), and Eugene (Shea Whigham). "I, uh, dozed off," Kneller says upon rising. "I think I slept on my ear wrong. Do I look asymmetrical to you at all?"

In Roberto Benigni's *La Tigre e La Neve* (*The Tiger and the Snow*) – partly set in invaded Iraq – Waits flew to Italy to appear in the film's opening dream scene, performing "You Can Never Hold Back Spring" as Benigni showed up for his wedding in his underwear. "With acting," he said, "I usually get people who want to put me in for a short time. Or they have a really odd part that only has two pages of dialogue, if that. The trouble is that it's really difficult to do a small part in a film, because you have to get up to speed – there are fewer scenes to show the full dimensions of your character, but you still need to accomplish the same thing that someone else has an hour and a half to do . . ."*

The movie cameos were distractions from the real job in hand: an ambitious three-album anthology of "antiques and curios" from the Waits archives, to which he and Kathleen had given the name *Orphans*. The idea dated back at least two years, intended originally for a collection of songs Waits had written for movies. But there were competing claims from an album of Howlin' Wolf covers [*Waits Sings Wolf*] and one he referred to as *Hell Brakes Luce*.

By late 2005, *Orphans* was becoming a reality – a legitimate version of the five-CD bootleg series *Tales from the Underground*, which had brought together a motley assortment of outtakes, miscellanea, and guest appearances, along with performances for Hal Willner ("Heigh Ho", "What Keeps Mankind Alive") and movie soundtracks ("Sea of Love", "Walk Away", "Little Drop of Poison"). Waits described *Orphans* as "songs that fell behind the stove while making dinner", though they included nothing before the mid-1980s. "I'm starting to get more archival as I get older," he said. "It's like, 'Oh, we better hang on to this, honey. We'll need this in our old age.'"

Waits had never been much of a hoarder, and once again he found himself having to acquire DATs of his own work from a dodgy bootlegger. "A plumber! In Russia!" he exclaimed incredulously. "I'm talking to him on the phone in the middle of the night, negotiating a price for my own shit." In addition to such relics as "Poor Little Lamb" and "Take Care of All My Children", Waits wanted to include newer songs he'd recorded with Marc

---

* There was a rather meatier role for Waits when he teamed up with Terry Gilliam again on *The Imaginarium of Doctor Parnassus*. "I am the Devil," he announced. "I don't know why he thought of me. I was raised in the church." Shooting on the film, commencing in London in December 2007, was interrupted a month later by the sudden death of actor Heath Ledger.

Ribot, Brain, and Larry Taylor. These, he explained, were tracks that might have wound up on *Mule Variations* or *Real Gone*. "After we did *Real Gone* we just carried on and wrote a whole bunch of new songs," he said. "You say, you'd better keep going."

The sheer heterogeneity of the material made it difficult to organize. While he saw "no reason you can't do a Sinatra song, then talk about insects, all that stuff on the same record", sequencing upwards of sixty tracks presented problems. In the end it was Brennan who hit on a solution, proposing they divide the songs broadly into rougher, harder-hitting "Brawlers", softer and more sentimental "Bawlers", and "Bastards" that fit neither of those categories. It was the old "grim reapers"/"grand weepers" dialectic, with a new class of song to cover oddities and collaborations. "Orphans are rough and tender tunes," Waits declared in August 2006 as Anti geared up for the release. "Rumbas about mermaids, shuffles about train wrecks, tarantellas about insects, madrigals about drowning. Scared, mean, orphan songs of rapture and melancholy. Songs of dubious origin rescued from cruel fate and now left wanting only to be cared for."

Playing a major part in that care was engineer Karl Derfler, in Waits' words a "battlefield medic" who "did a Lazarus on a number of the songs and recorded all the new material" at Bay View studios in the San Francisco suburb of Richmond. At times the partitioning of the fifty-four tracks eventually selected was as arbitrary as it was expedient. Some of the brawlers bawled and a few of the bastards did both. But then what would one expect in a musical orphanage run by Tom Waits and Kathleen Brennan?

Among the sixteen official "Brawlers" were the *Mule Variations* outtakes ("2:19", "Fish in the Jailhouse", "Buzz Fledderjohn", "Puttin' on the Dog"), a fuzzy cover of the Ramones' "Return of Jackie and Judy" that somehow picked up a Grammy nomination, and a swampy, droning version of Leadbelly's "Ain't Goin' down to the Well" that Waits had recorded for a documentary about protest songs. There was another Stones homage in the grinding bullhorn boogie of "LowDown", and a rare example of Waits attempting rockabilly – a music he'd never especially cared for – in the herky-jerky "Lie to Me". There was a bellyful of hobo wanderlust in "Bottom of the World".

The version of Phil Phillips' 1959 New Orleans classic "Sea of Love" was leaden and unconvincing. "Lucinda" and "All the Time", pained hollers of men driven mad by women, came straight out of *Real Gone*'s "Clang Boom Steam" school. By contrast, "Walk Away" was a bluesy song of redemption, a dry run for "Get Behind the Mule" that came from the soundtrack of Tim Robbins' *Dead Man Walking* (1995). There was a touch of black-face in Waits' treatment of the traditional "Lord, I've Been Changed", originally featured as "I Know I've Been Changed" on John Hammond's *Wicked Grin*. "Rains on Me" was Waits' version of the song he'd co-written on Chuck E. Weiss' *Extremely Cool*, complete with the same namechecks for Messrs Body, Marchese, and Lista.

The track that really jumped out on "Brawlers" was "The Road to Peace", an unprecedented outburst that made *Real Gone*'s "protest" songs look almost evasive. Inspired by a story that appeared in the *New York Times* in June 2003, it was a despairing seven-minute broadside about the relentless and never-ending conflict in the Middle East. "[The] article [was] about a young Palestinian suicide bomber who got on a bus in Jerusalem disguised as an Orthodox Jew," Waits said. "The story seemed to humanize what was going on in a significant way." Backed by Casey on drums and Ribot on glistening vibrato guitar, Waits told the old story of futile eye-for-an-eye revenge, trying hard not to toe the left-liberal line even as he demanded to know why America was arming Israel.

"This song ain't about taking sides," Waits maintained. "It's an indictment of both sides." He acknowledged the futility of what he called "throwing peanuts at a gorilla" but was unrepentant of his need to write the song, which "fell right out of the paper and onto the tape recorder". Long gone was the Waits who, in 1984, had said, "You wouldn't ask Ronald Reagan about Charlie Parker, would you?" Nonetheless, it was strange to hear a man who'd once sung about eggs and sausage now singing about Hamas and Ariel Sharon.

Many of the "Bawlers" on *Orphans* were close in feel to the ballads on *Alice*, with upright piano, banjo, and woodwinds dominant in the sound. "Bend Down the Branches", from the 1998 animated film *Bunny*, was a tender song of resignation to ageing. "You Can Never Hold Back Spring", the song Waits and Brennan wrote for Roberto Benigni, was a sweet statement of the hope that comes with winter's passing. "Shiny Things" was from *Woyzeck*, sung by Karl the Fool, who saw crows as dazzled by glittering objects whereas the only shiny thing *he* wanted was "to be king there in your eyes . . ."

Written for Ed Harris' 2000 biopic of Jackson Pollock, "World Keeps Turning" was reminiscent of "Take It with Me", though its lyric was more ambiguous. The sweetly old-fashioned "Tell It to Me" was a country-folk waltz, a song of tender jealousy with Waits accompanying his own almost bel canto vocal on acoustic guitar, joined halfway through by Bobby Black's divine pedal steel. "The Fall of Troy" was another song from *Dead Man Walking*, the story of two homicidal teenagers in New Orleans that recalled *Mule Variations*' "Pony" and "Georgia Lee". "Jayne's Blue Wish" was a serene fireside ballad written for the Debra Winger vehicle *Big Bad Love* (2002). Another song for *Big Bad Love*, "Long Way Home", was a proclamation of love and fidelity in the face of fate's challenges, with a walking-bass arrangement redolent of Johnny Cash's "I Walk the Line". "When we heard the demos, there were highway sounds on the track," the film's director Arliss Howard recalled of the song. "Then I remembered

475

Kathleen saying that Tom would work in a moving car with a tape recorder. And a tuba."

A couple of the "Bawlers" were closer in spirit to the marching-band feel of "In the Neighborhood". Aptly enough, "Take Care of All My Children" was the oldest orphan of all, dating from Martin Bell's 1984 documentary *Streetwise*. Moreover, it was Bell's 1993 film *American Heart* that had pulled the glorious "Never Let Go" out of Waits and Brennan. Two more songs took us back to Gin Pan Alley. Taken from Teddy Edwards' *Mississippi Lad*, "Little Man" was the saxophonist's own moving message from a father to his son – a song that must have resonated with Waits, who sang it with all the sweet affection he felt for the jazz legend. Sung by Margret in *Woyzeck*, the despondent "It's Over" added harmonica to its late-night mix of piano, tenor sax, and hissing snare shuffle.

A different despondency informed the bellowy version of Leadbelly's "Goodnight Irene", a song of suicidal lovesickness turned into a big folk hit by the Weavers in 1950. Waits felt a special affinity with the blues giant, who'd died a day after he himself was born. "I always felt like I connected with him somehow," he said. "He was going out and I was coming in." Leadbelly was also the inspiration for another "Bawler", the acoustic guitar ballad "Fannin Street". No matter that Waits and Brennan located the latter thoroughfare in Houston rather than Shreveport, Louisiana – the scene of the young Huddie Ledbetter's formative debauches – the song's haunting regret came through beautifully.

The murder ballad "Widow's Grove" was the prettiest song on "Bawlers". A waltz played on accordion and mandolin, the song was originally written as a duet, with the victim speaking as if from the afterworld. "Little Drop of Poison" was a playfully sinister tarantella heard first in Wim Wenders' *The End of Violence* (1997) and then – more profitably – on the soundtrack to *Shrek 2*.

"If I Have to Go" was a piano ballad from Act Two of the stage version of *Frank's Wild Years*, sung by Frank on the park bench in East St Louis as he dreamt of dancing with Willa. "Danny Says" was a *second* Ramones cover, the flipside to "Jackie and Judy" and a tribute to the group's sometime manager Danny Fields. "Down There by the Train" combined two of Waits' favourite genres – gospel songs and train songs. Originally written for John Hammond but never recorded by him, it had subsequently found a home on the first of Johnny Cash's *American Recordings* albums after Waits re-recorded his original demo and sent it to Cash's producer Rick Rubin. Everyone deserved mercy in the eyes of eternity, the song said – even Lincoln's assassin John Wilkes Booth and psycho sniper Charlie Whitman in his Texas tower. "I was like, 'That's it, I'm all done now, Johnny Cash did a song . . . thanks very much,'" Waits said. "That was really flattering, you know."

The last song on the "Bawlers" album made Kathleen Brennan laugh out loud. A version of "Young at Heart", sung most famously by Frank Sinatra in 1954 (and 1963), for Waits it was a virtual manifesto about how to stay fresh and vital when every biological impulse pushed you towards creative senility. Living as she did with Waits' middle-aged grumpiness, Brennan was unconvinced. "My wife just thinks it's hilarious," Waits said. "She says, 'You sound so goddamned depressed singing it . . . I don't believe that bullshit for a minute. Young at heart, my ass!'" She would have been more convinced by "What Keeps Mankind Alive", the start of Waits' long affair with Kurt Weill. Two decades old, Waits' stab at Macheath's song from *The Threepenny Opera* sounded as savagely cynical as the day he'd recorded it for Hal Willner's *Lost in the Stars*; without this performance, no *Black Rider*, no *Blood Money*. That other great Willner track – *Stay Awake*'s "Heigh Ho" – had Waits repurposing the song as a malevolent industrial blues, with the seven dwarves cast as exploited workers grunting to the churning rhythm of a machine going through its motions. So much so, in fact, that Disney freaked out on hearing it, convinced Waits had in some way tampered with the lyrics and made them altogether darker than they were. (He hadn't.) Fortunately for Willner, a threatened lawsuit was dropped.

"Bastards" was otherwise made up of cover versions, spoken-word oddities, and anomalous one-offs. Skip Spence's "Books of Moses" was done as a *Mule Variations* blues, Daniel Johnston's "King Kong" as a post-*Real Gone* exercise in stomping mouth-hop. The furtive, conspiratorial voice of "What's He Building?" reappeared on "Army Ants", a list of facts about creepy-crawlies from an Audubon Society field guide recited to pizzicato strings, and on the Ken Nordine collaboration "First Kiss", about a woman struck by lightning. There was room for a homage to Charles Bukowski, who had died of leukaemia in 1994 and whose late poem "Nirvana" was a favourite of Waits'. "By the time he got to the *Last Night of the Earth* poems [1992]," Waits said of Bukowski, "he's really a wise man and a very thoughtful man [who] was not afraid to be vulnerable. He was turning the ball around in front of him, to let him see as many sides as he could see himself." Waits had seen Bukowski age and mellow, had watched him process his own growing fame after the release of Barbet Schroeder's 1987 film *Barfly*. He'd visited Bukowski in San Pedro to discuss playing Hank Chinaski, and had seen how Linda Lee Bukowski had saved and tamed her wild husband as Kathleen had rescued *him*. Years after first discovering him, he was still following in the tracks of this iconoclastic father figure. "He let you go with him on his journey," Waits said. "[It] was really great for me to have somebody you looked up to take you down the path with him."

"Bastards" also included a nod to Waits' first true literary hero: not one but two versions of a semi-autobiographical song Jack

Kerouac had written and recorded in 1949. "On the Road" was Waits in Beefheart mode, backed by Brain, Les Claypool, and Ralph Carney at Prairie Sun in 1997. The summer of that year found him redoing the song very differently as a piano ballad, "Home I'll Never Be", at a Hal Willner-produced tribute to Allen Ginsberg at UCLA's Wadsworth Theater in Westwood. "I guess Jack was at a party somewhere and snuck off into a closet and started singing into a reel-to-reel tape deck," Waits explained. "Like, '*I left New York in 1949, drove across the country . . .*' I wound up turning it into a song." Kerouac's namecheck for El Cajon, a suburb of San Diego, perhaps brought the lyric close to home for Waits. 1949 was also the year of Waits' birth, "so there were places where I connected with that".

Among the other relics and curios on "Bastards" was "Poor Little Lamb", a sad and fragile song of hobo vulnerability co-written for *Ironweed* with its screenwriter William Kennedy and very much in the John McCormack vein of "Innocent when You Dream". The lyric could almost have been about Rudy the Kraut, with the coyote "waiting out there" to grab him. "It's based on a poem [Kennedy] saw on the side of a bridge when he was a kid," Waits said at the time of the film's release. "It's like those nursery rhymes you may understand one way when you're a kid and another way later on . . ." Also making the cut were two pieces from *Woyzeck*, the gleefully cruel "Children's Story" (aka "Over-turned Pisspot") and the macabre instrumental "Redrum". The first was the tale Margret tells Woyzeck's orphaned son after Karl the Fool sings the "Lullaby" to him, a blackly funny nightmare of disappointment. The second had Charlie Musselwhite blowing alongside Waits' ominous Chamberlin riffs – music for a killing, no less. From *The Black Rider*, meanwhile, came "Altar Boy" – "What Became of Old Father Craft?" redone as a full-on "show tune", with Waits playing the pub-singer Sinatra he'd lampooned on "I'll Take New York".

"Dog Door", Waits' guest turn on Sparklehorse's 2001 album *It's a Wonderful Life*, was blues-funk, as grindingly sexy in its way as "Filipino Box Spring Hog". "I'd done the music already but was having difficulty with the words and melody," recalled Mark Linkous, one of Waits' most intriguing disciples. "It was more like a dirge than a pop song. I called Tom. I said, 'I have this cool-sounding track but I can't finish it. I wonder if you want to take a shot at it?' I sent it to him. He called and said, 'Yeah, come out here. I got something.'" Linkous flew to California and put the finishing touches to a song that was all Waits and wholly untypical of Sparklehorse. "I pay attention to what those guys are doing," Waits said of Linkous and Daniel Johnston. "I respond to it. Something resonates in me with those guys, they're like outsider artists." (He would make a further guest appearance on Sparklehorse's 2006 album *Dreamt for Light Years in the Belly of a Mountain*, playing piano on the song "Morning Hollow".)

Other tracks that might conceivably have worked on either *Mule Variations* or *Real Gone* were "Bone Chain", a harmonica-blasted cross between "Get Behind the Mule" and "Clang Boom Steam", and the crazed "Spidey's Wild Ride". "I had fun doing that song," Waits said of the latter. "Just some singing and some beat-boxing. It's very rudimentary yet at the same time very complete." Waits loved the fact that he could do "hip hop" like this "in the washroom, in the garage, and in the car too . . ."

Did Waits choose to record "Two Sisters", an eighteenth-century Scottish madrigal about homicidal sibling rivalry, because he himself had two female siblings? Either way this was Waits the Pogues fan, singing a hoary ballad of the kind he might have heard in a County Kerry snug as a fiddler sawed in the background. Family certainly played a part in "The Pontiac", an affectionate 1987 impression of Waits' father-in-law as he talked through the various automobiles of his life like they were former wives or old girlfriends. The piece was recorded by Kathleen in – where else – the car.

"Bastards" concluded with a pair of hidden tracks. One was simply Waits the standup comic, introducing "Invitation to the Blues" at a 2005 MusiCares benefit honouring promoter Bill Silva and Waits freak James Hetfield by telling a long story about a type of canine snack made of one hundred per cent bull's penis.* The other was a shaggy-dog leg-puller about a woman asking a man to call her "mom" in a grocery store because she misses her son so much, only for the man to find himself landed with her bill as a result.

When *Orphans* finally appeared in November 2006, packaged as a pocket-size "book" with ninety-four pages of lyrics and pho-tographs – including snaps of Waits with Keith Richards, John Lee Hooker, Nicolas Cage, Fred Gwynne, Larry Taylor, Roberto Benigni, and others – it was hailed as a cross between the Beatles' *Anthology* series and Bob Dylan's *Basement Tapes*. In truth there was so much music on the three CDs that it was hard for any reviewer to get his or her head around it. To my ears, many of the abandoned children gathered on *Orphans* could happily have remained unadopted. For every great track ("What Keeps Mankind Alive", "Little Man", "Widow's Grove", "Take Care of All My Children"), there were at least four that seemed undeserving of retrospective discovery. As for the songs recorded in the after-math of *Real Gone* ("Lucinda", "All the Time", "Bone Chain", "Spidey's Wild Ride", et al.), they confirmed what much of *Real Gone* itself had intimated, which was that Waits was stuck in a kind of self-parodying primitivism.

Nor, apparently, was I entirely alone in my misgivings. Film critic Jonathan Romney had written as early as 1999 that Waits had "simply swapped miniature film noir for scratchy, abstract

---

* Quoth Hetfield in his acceptance speech, "Who needs alcohol and drugs when you have Tom Waits?"

experimental vignettes . . . [his] current roughneck dementia is allowed to exist freely in its own appropriate element: the more savage his new sound is, the less surprising it seems". Writer Ian Penman implicitly concurs. "Personally I still prefer the mid-period Waits," he says. "*Blue Valentine* is my favourite, and I find something just a tad 'off' about most of his subsequent work, especially the stuff that uses the blues for its formal structure. I think there's something of an impersonation going on here that I don't quite buy – or believe. It doesn't *touch* me, ever, the way the mid-period stuff does." I suspect Penman speaks for many closet lovers of the pre-Island Waits.

When *Real Gone* came out, *Harp* interviewer Tom Moon noted that "for much of the last decade there's been a set of recurring complaints about Waits – that he's too obvious about recycling his tricks, that his chronicles of love undone and his almost-romantic odes pondering mortality have become boiler-plate . . . [that] the spectacular, almost shamanic street dramas of *Rain Dogs* and *Frank's Wild Years* have lost a certain animating quality in subsequent iterations."

Moon's perception doesn't quite accord with my own, I have to say. I'd surmise that you could count the negative reviews of Waits' recent albums on two hands. If anything, he's become as much of a sacred cow on the world stage as Bob Dylan. Exactly why and how this has happened is difficult to work out, but it may have something to do with just how intimidating – as well as funny, fascinating, lovable, etc. – he is. More likely, I suspect, it's the result of Waits' standing in the contemporary rock hierarchy, which has everything to do with the assertion of his avant-garde credentials. Certainly Kathleen Brennan has got her wish, which was to change her hubby from jazzbo self-caricature to *sui generis* arthouse eccentric. Arguably, though, Waits has in the process simply dumped one establishment in order to embrace another. As David Smay writes in his excellent study of *Sword-*

fishtrombones, "[his] recent adoption as National-Public-Radio-anointed National Treasure threatens to swaddle him in cultural approval, like spinach".

All this can in a sense be traced back to the part Robert Wilson has played in the second act of Waits' career. In the words of Robert Christgau, Waits has "forged more alliances with the institutionalized avant-garde" than even David Byrne – or, one might add, Lou Reed, another rock star to succumb to Wilson's beguiling, gurulike seductiveness. "A bit like Wilson, Waits has been exquisitely curated," notes David Kamp, *Vanity Fair* contributor and founder of the splendid *Rock Snob's Dictionary*. "He's become an untouchable, and much of that has to do with the way Kathleen has sort of rebranded him." Former *Rolling Stone* staffer Anthony DeCurtis hits the nail on the head when he observes of Waits' recent music that "a lot of critics don't like to admit it, but even experimentalism can become predictable – you start to expect the unexpected".*

Back in England, respected historian Simon Schama declared himself to be a Waits fanatic in a fine piece for the *Guardian* in 2006. While he mostly raved, rightly arguing that there was "something almost Shakespearean about the breadth of Tom Waits' take on modern American life", he also voiced doubts that I and others harboured. "Sometimes [Waits] can push his furious refusal of songster-ingratiation to the edge of self-parody," Schama noted, "so that the primal screams, grunts, howls backed by lid-clanging and stock-banging percussion just collapse into a deep ditch of vocal rage." That got it nicely, I thought. I, for one, did not think my life would be significantly poorer if I never heard "Lucinda" or "Spidey's Wild Ride" (or

---

* That certainly goes for Robert Wilson, who seems increasingly to operate as a super-crony and shameless infiltrator of the moneyed arts world. His *Voom* video portraits of movie stars such as Brad Pitt and Johnny Depp must surely have left a queasy feeling in Waits' stomach.

"Clang Boom Steam" or "Baby Gonna Leave Me") again.

The reader will see from my personal selection of his best tracks (Appendix 1) that I believe Waits made as much great music pre-Brennan/Island Records as he has made since 1982: by no design, the forty songs are split exactly down the middle, with half hailing either from his Asylum albums or from *One from the Heart*. Furthermore, I'm with Ian Penman and others in the contention that nothing post-*OFTH* "touches" or moves me as much as "Tom Traubert's Blues", "Kentucky Avenue", or "Broken Bicycles". Perhaps, as Penman himself wrote me, "I'm just a sad old boho romantic who weeps at the sumptuous strings on 'Somewhere'." Yet whenever I've forced fellow fans into a corner, they've invariably admitted that their favourite Waits music precedes his Brennanite conversion on the road to avant-garde dissonance.

All this would be water off a duck's back to Waits, of course. "I'm just out here trying to build a better mousetrap," he said. "If somebody doesn't like what I do, I really don't care. I'm not chained to public opinion, nor am I swayed by the waves of popular trends." To another interviewer he claimed he didn't follow what his audience wanted to hear: "I just strike out and look behind me and there's a bunch of people following me: 'Go away! Go away!'"

Compiling *Orphans* so energized Waits that he undertook a short summer tour of the US, playing cities he'd rarely if ever visited before. Six of the dates were in the south, the remainder in the Midwest. "I don't know what made me go out," Waits said after the fact. "I really wanted to find out if I like doing this." To his amazement, he liked it a lot. Planning an itinerary that circumvented airports, he travelled from town to town in a bus with a band made up of Casey Waits, the inevitable Larry Taylor, *Woyzeck/Blood Money/Alice* multi-instrumentalist Bent Clausen, and – deputizing for an otherwise engaged Marc Ribot – Roomful of Blues guitarist Duke Robillard. "You see the gig and the town on the way in and the town on the way out," Waits said, "but there's something sort of exciting about that at the same time – the stealth. You come in and sting 'em and go."

Starting with a chaotic evening in Atlanta on 1 August, the shows sold out almost as quickly as Waits' London date had sold out eighteen months earlier. Tour audiences dropped into the palm of Waits' hand from the moment he took the stage. In a more accommodating mood than anyone could have expected, he reached deep into his songbook and pulled out such pre-Island evergreens as "Tom Traubert's Blues", "I Wish I Was in New Orleans", "Invitation to the Blues" (often dedicated to Kathleen), "Christmas Card from a Hooker in Minneapolis", "Whistlin' past the Graveyard", and "Blue Valentines". The lingering influence of Howlin' Wolf was felt not only in a cover of "Who's Been Talkin'" but in arrangements of "'Til the Money Runs Out" and "Heartattack and Vine", the latter including a short snatch of the classic "Spoonful". (Robillard's blues roots may have led Waits to accent this element of his music.) The unusual number of older songs possibly explained Waits' use of a discreet teleprompter for occasional lyrical cues.

Inspired arrangements of Island-era songs (a desperate "Falling Down", a coruscating "Goin' out West", a hauntingly disoriented "Shore Leave", and a wry "Tango 'Til They're Sore" with Waits alone at the piano) fleshed out sets that were otherwise heavy on material from *Mule Variations* (a groovesomely funky "Eyeball Kid"), *The Black Rider* (a bereft "November"), *Blood Money* ("God's Away on Business"), and, of course, *Real Gone*. There were also foretastes of *Orphans* in a revved-up "2:19", a touching "You Can Never Hold Back Spring", and a roaringly sentimental "Bottom of the World". Waits' comic panache was in full flow as he sat at the piano and riffed on such staple subjects as coffee, hotels, and ill-tempered waitresses. Thirty-five years after he'd first hooted at the Troubadour, he remained a brilliantly funny man. An added bonus was having his twenty-one-year-old son in his band. "He's been playing drums since he was eight," said Dad. "He's a big strong guy, taller than me. With families and music, you're usually looking for something that can make you unique, and it can be hard to find that. But he was excellent. It was terrific playing together, as you'd imagine it would be. You learn as much from your kids as they learn from you."

Three further months elapsed before *Orphans: Brawlers, Bawlers & Bastards* showed up in record stores. It retailed in the US at $49.98, and no one at Epitaph expected it to repeat the success of *Real Gone* or its immediate predecessors. In its first week, *Orphans* sold 21,000 copies in the US and made the Top 10 in several European markets. In Britain, however, even the usual rave reviews couldn't push it any higher than No. 49 in its first week, forty places below the chart entry position of *Real Gone*. The promotional grind found Waits in surprisingly good spirits – less churlish, gentler on interviewers. To the surprise of some, he often arrived for his media assignations in a 4x4 Lexus. "I thought, 'Finally he's let go of the pose,'" says Mick Brown, who was interviewing Waits for the fifth time. "But then he very sweetly presented me with a crushed tin can he'd picked up along the road." Brown found Waits "the most genial and personable" he'd ever seen him. Waits also seemed to let his guard down a little, talking openly about his past drug abuse and his father's alcoholism.

Former *Rolling Stone* music editor Mark Kemp was another interviewer struck by Waits' new openness. "One of the more touching parts of my interview with him came when I asked where his Frank character came from," Kemp says. "He actually began to talk about his father before catching himself and moving on to albino moles. When you get a tiny nugget of a man's feeling in a sea of zany metaphors, it's more powerful than an interview filled with personal details." Kemp found even the metaphors illuminating. "I think Waits' bizarre digressions are actually packed with meaning," he says. "If you're willing to follow him and not cut him off before he gets to the end of his strange tales, there's much to glean. Like Jesus, he talks in parables that are very in line with his music and lyrics."

"He kept going off on these long yarn-like tales about strange instruments he'd found over the years," says Tom Moon. "But he also spoke with totally uncorny absolute awe about the late Ray Charles. The thing is, he might like jiving with people and being 'Tom Waits', but at any moment he can shift course and be totally real."

When interviewers asked about his ongoing domestic bliss, Waits said he'd "got the three cherries . . . pulled the handle and all the quarters came out". He even blathered happily about growing his own vegetables – tomatoes, corn, eggplant, squash, beans, and pumpkins – in Valley Ford. "Now when I go away it's a different feeling," he said of home life. "I've got people who care about me waiting at home for me to come back."

On chat shows, meanwhile, Waits assumed the role of affable American eccentric – a distinctive blend of performance art and genuine shyness that achieved its aim of semi-obscuring the man behind the act. His regular appearances on David Letterman found him playing a kind of Kramer – Michael Richards' beloved "hipster doofus" – to his host's Seinfeld. "[My kids] said I made up a war once," he said in an anecdote that might have come straight from that peerless anti-sitcom. "I think I was groping for the real name and, uh, I just substituted it . . . for rhythm, you know?"

"Junkman, crackpot, musical genius." So ran the copy on a cover story on Waits – "the mainstream media's most beloved non-mainstream recording artist" – in *Southwest Airlines Spirit* magazine in March 2007. In Michael O'Brien's sepia photographs for the piece, a huge bullhorn and battered tape recorder were strapped to Waits' back, a manic expression on his face: this was the character who was now becoming fixed in the popular imagination.

Waits continued to make a big deal in interviews about safeguarding his privacy in a celebrity-fixated universe. The public, he said, "want to celebrate you and then they want to kill you . . . And then they want to remember you – even when you're still alive." He was adamant that what people knew about him – or his wife and his family life – was only what he "allowed" them to know. "I'm not one of those people the tabloids chase around," he said. "You have to put off that smell – it's like blood in the water for a shark. And they know it, and they know that you've also agreed. And I'm not one of those. I make stuff up." To *Time Out* he made the point that "we're not sitting in my kitchen with the dog at your feet".*

For actor and novelist Steve Martin, the "concept of privacy" had crystallized one day when a nurse asked him to autograph a print of his erratic heartbeat in hospital. "[Privacy] became something to protect," Martin wrote. "What I was doing, what I was thinking, and who I was seeing, I now kept to myself as a necessary defense against the feeling that I was becoming, like the Weinermobile, a commercial artifact." But Martin was also honest enough to concede something that Waits never does. "Sometimes", he wrote, "a journalist will lean in and say, 'You're very private.' And I mentally respond, 'Someone who's private would not be doing an interview on television.'"

Waits saw celebrity culture as part of a pervasive disease of

---

* I was amused to stumble on this blog entry, posted by a Sonoma County resident after a local musical get-together in November 2007: "After the song was over, all the audience members took turns calling out what personal facts they knew about Waits – that he drives a black Prius, that he visits his local Radio Shack a few times a week, that he lives out near Valley Ford . . . I love how everyone wants so badly to 'know' this man. I am guilty too."

No photographs please: Santa Rosa, April 2002. (*Jurrien Wouterse*)

mediated reality: reality TV, the flood of literary "memoirs". For him these were manifestations of what he called "a deficit of wonder" in the world. "Everything is explained now," he told Tom Moon. "We live in an age when you say casually to somebody 'What's the story on that?' and they can run to the computer and tell you within five seconds. That's fine, but sometimes I'd just as soon continue wondering." Other, younger musicians seemed to be waking up to this "deficit of wonder". "The song is independent of my face and what I look like," said Régine Chassagne of acclaimed Canadian band the Arcade Fire. "I know in pop music people are really used to, like, relating it to the person who made it and what they eat and what they do every day. But to me it's just independent."*

Waits' deepest conviction was that truth itself was overrated. He continued to take his lead from mentors such as Bob Dylan, who'd declared Waits to be one of his "secret heroes", and with whom he occasionally traded tapes of obscure songs. (Waits

---

* In an online interview with himself in May 2008, Waits reiterated that "we are buried beneath the weight of information, which is being confused with knowledge," adding that "quantity is being confused with abundance and wealth with happiness". I think he's right on both counts.

appeared twice on Dylan's acclaimed "Theme Time Radio Hour".) "It was a story, for God's sake, written by somebody who tells stories," Waits said of Dylan's *Chronicles, Volume One*. "No one really knows how much of it was true or not, and no one really should know. It doesn't really matter."*

The flipside of Waits' occasional orneriness was his humility – his willingness to get right-sized about the relationship between Self and Other. Though he was "not embarrassed" to be an entertainer, he was keen not to "overvalue" himself or what he did. "You have to be careful of the ego," he said beautifully. "It'll eat anything." Waits often questioned the value of his art, wondering if plumbers didn't ultimately make a more important contribution to society.

Age has brought Waits wisdom and a growing acceptance of life's tragic absurdity. "Most of the big things I've learned in the last ten years," he said in 2004. "Of course, I've been sober for twelve years." Like any great artist, however, he has one eye fixed on the immortality of his work, acknowledging that "what you really want to do is be valid and vital and in some way, here and after you're gone: to still remain a presence and influence and still be able to sprout and bloom and bear fruit".

Just how "valid and vital" Waits felt when movie star Scarlett Johansson decided to record an album of his songs we do not know. Following up Holly Cole's all-but-forgotten homage *Temptation*, Johansson's *Anywhere I Lay My Head* featured all but unrecognizable versions of "Green Grass", "Fannin Street", and others, recorded in rural Louisiana with TV on the Radio's David

* "The minute you try to grab hold of Dylan, he's no longer where he was," wrote Todd Haynes, director of the 2007 anti-biopic *I'm Not There*. "Dylan's life of change and constant disappearances and constant transformations makes you yearn to hold him and to nail him down. And that's why his fan base is so obsessive, so desirous of finding the truth and the absolutes and the answers to him – things that Dylan will never provide and will only frustrate." The question irresistibly suggests itself: will Waits ever write his own *Chronicles*?

Sitek, Yeah Yeah Yeahs guitarist Nick Zimmer, and (on backing vocals on two tracks) one David Bowie. "It was constantly in the back of my mind", Sitek half-joked, "that if we did something Waits hated he'd come at me with a hammer." The album seemed to cement Waits' status as the coolest old fart in pop culture.

Johansson and Sitek started out in more faithful lo-fi style before filtering the songs through an indie-rock sensibility that's equal parts postpunk-gothic, 4AD dreampop, shoegazing drone, and TV on the Radio epicness. The imprint of Joy Division producer Martin Hannett was all over the album, as was the influence of Suicide ballads like "Cheree" and "Dream Baby Dream". "Falling Down" became a fusion of TVOTR and Sigur Ros, topped off with a mini-homage to the Cocteau Twins. There was even a cheeky drum-machine rendition of *Bone Machine*'s "I Don't Want to Grow Up" that sounded like a Madonna demo from 1982. Johansson's blankly androgynous alto timbre was nothing special but it barely mattered. At moments she was a *Vanity Fair* Nico; at others she sounded like former Moldy Peaches chanteuse Kimya Dawson. In the end *Anywhere I Lay My Head* reminded one of a hundred tribute albums – not least *Step Right Up* – but it was a bravely eccentric selection and a captivating homage to a singular American writer.*

Waits must have been pleased that Johansson recorded only one song – a spectrally lovely version of "I Wish I Was in New Orleans" – from his pre-Brennan period. Recognition of his wife as a collaborator and equal partner was more important than ever to him. While continuing to emphasize that she was "much

---

* A rather more conventional reworking of the Waits songbook – and one tilted slightly more towards his pre-Island oeuvre – was *Grapefruit Moon* by Asbury Park legend Southside Johnny with LaBamba's Big Band. Along with the title track, the 2008 album included "Please Call Me, Baby", "New Coat of Paint", and "Shiver Me Timbers". Waits himself guested on a lusty rendition of "Walk Away".

more adventurous than I am", with "a wilder mind", he said Kathleen was "one of those people that socially is so shy you'll never hear her".

"She's crucial, is she not?" says Sean O'Hagan, who interviewed Waits in 2006. "I wish she'd talk, just once. She's the source of a lot of the Irish stuff that echoes through the later songs, not just the McCormack tracings, but old ballads, stylings, ways of singing."

Johansson's Waits album was evidence of the ever-growing regard in which the crusty Californian was held, and of the sheer timelessness of his appeal. "I love Tom Waits because he's an artist who makes me not afraid to get old," remarked Matt Bellamy, singer and guitarist with UK neo-prog-rockers Muse. "I think it's a rare kind of thing to have that level of wisdom." Another admirer, Mark Everett of Eels, said he hoped to "grow old gracefully like Tom Waits . . . he doesn't have the Mick Jagger problem where it starts to look a little silly after a certain age".

Nor were the plaudits confined to musicians young enough to be his offspring. "I really appreciate him and everything he does and the way he works," avers Ry Cooder, a similarly uncompromising Californian. "He's a fantastic poet and a very high-grade guy, believe me. He's out there and he's one of the last of the best." To guitar god Steve Vai there was "a purity to what [Waits] does that is really unmatched these days".

Though Waits would have appreciated the sentiments, he was not one to rest on his laurels. Looking into the future, he felt as much at the mercy of his audience as he'd done when he first sung on the stage of the Heritage club in 1970. "Nobody knows how long they're going to be able to stay meaningful and continue to work," he said in 2006. "Everybody wonders that. You're at the mercy of your audience in a lot of ways, which is really scary." I have no doubt whatever that if he can resist the impulse to become one of America's sanctioned mavericks, Waits will continue to surprise and delight as he eases into his twilight years. In his sixtieth year on the planet he remains as vital and confounding as any major musician in the culture.

"Do you think it's about creating a mystique?" friends asked when I mentioned the obstacles encountered in writing this book. Generally I said that that was too simplistic, pointing out that Waits had done hundreds if not thousands of interviews over the thirty-five years of his career. I said I thought it was more about impatience with writers stuffing him in a kind of box. He wants to remain uncontained and indefinable. "I don't like to be pinned down," he said in 1992. "I hate direct questions. If we just pick a topic and drift, that's my favorite part."

Waits would surely have agreed with Susan Sontag, in her famous 1964 essay "Against Interpretation", that, "in a culture whose already classical dilemma is the hypertrophy of the intellect at the expense of energy and sensual capability, interpretation is the revenge of the intellect upon art". He might also – like David Smay in his *Swordfishtrombones* study – have invoked Keats' famous concept of "Negative Capability", defined by the poet as "when man is capable of being in uncertainties, Mysteries, doubts without any irritable reaching after fact and reason".

One thing is for sure. For almost all the musicians who've worked with Waits over the years, the experience has virtually been enough to retire on. "My stance is the same as it's always been, which is that I've felt honored and blessed to have played with him," says Stephen Hodges. "As far as artists are concerned, what motherfucking songwriter do I fucking need to play with now?!"

Hodges says he divides the world into people who know about Tom Waits and people who don't. "People ask me who I've played with all the time," he says. "Sometimes I tell them. And if they look at me with a furrowed brow when I say 'Tom Waits,' I say . . . well, actually, I don't say anything. I mean, how the fuck do you explain *Tom Waits*?!"

Coda

Take It with Me When I Go

> *"My deal is, usually [writers] know too much*
> *about you, or they don't know nothing about*
> *you. The nothing is usually fine with me."*
>
> (Tom Waits to Tom Lanham, *Paste*, December 2004)

I left London in a heatwave, pulling out of King's Cross on a packed lunchtime train. Ten hours later I'm standing in the midnight mist of Edinburgh, waiting for Tom Waits at the rear of the city's venerable old Playhouse theatre.

He's just concluded a two-and-a-half-hour show, the second of two nights in bonnie Scotland, and a surprisingly small clutch of admirers hovers beside a pair of tour buses that idle near the theatre's stage door. I am one of their number, feeling more than a little self-conscious as I come to the end of the long Tom Waits journey that is this book. Is this the moment when I finally *do*

Hot ticket, 28 July 2008.

turn into Nick Broomfield – or A. J. Weberman, perhaps? Will I hail Waits out of the misty darkness with the words, "Hey Tom, it's me, the guy who's been rummaging in your (metaphorical) garbage for the last two years"?

It's been a while since I did the stage-door-Johnny thing. Waiting here takes me all the way back to the adolescent desperation of shivering outside Morton's in Berkeley Square, fingers crossed that my then-hero Todd Rundgren might appear for two minutes and deign to sign the cream sleeve of *Faithful*. Surely I'm too old to stand in the spitting Scottish rain at midnight, overhearing the mutterings of young fans brandishing posters for the *Glitter and Doom* tour that winds up in Dublin at the end of the week.

Has Waits already come out? Gone back to his hotel? Is he still in there, and is Kathleen with him? Who's that coming out now? Oh, it's Patrick Warren, the keyboard player introduced by Waits tonight as hailing from this very city. And there's Omar Torrez, the Seattle-based guitarist whose flamenco guitar flourishes were such a highlight of the set. Surely it's only a matter of time before I clap eyes on Waits himself – and even, for the first time, on Kathleen ...

Earlier that evening I stand at the entrance to the Playhouse with a swarming throng of fans whose age range – from eighteen to sixty-five, I'd hazard – speaks volumes for Waits' wide appeal. Few have paid less than £100 for the privilege of being here. Stringent anti-touting measures make the queuing a nightmare but have to be applauded.

The man himself, bowler-hatted and tossing up a small cloud of gold dust, gazes down from the *Glitter and Doom* banner over the foyer. It's an image I first saw back in May, when the first leg of a US tour – starting in Phoenix and winding up in Atlanta – was announced in the form of a press conference staged by Waits himself without a single journalist present.

Glitter and doom: outside the Playhouse. (*Art Sperl*)

Glitter and doom: a typically Waitsian conjunction of showbiz and apocalypse, sparkly artifice and biblical gravitas. "Leona Helmsley's dog made $12 million last year," he noted in an interview he conducted with himself for Anti.com on 20 May. "Dean McLaine, a farmer in Ohio, made $30,000. It's just a gigantic version of the madness that grows in every one of our brains. We are monkeys with money and guns." Waits' disgust at America's values shows no signs of abating. He will not be going gently into that good night.

Waits had begun his last UK tour at this venue back in November 1987. He'd also played the Playhouse in 1981 and 1985. But before these two dates he hadn't performed north of the border for twenty-one years. By 8.30 the mood in the old Victorian theatre – all crimson velvet and vermilion brocade – is growing restless. Mirroring the red interior of the auditorium, the stage setup resembles a dusty antique shop. An ancient marching bass drum sits to the left, while a rack of Waits' beloved bullhorns stands behind a central platform.

It takes a slow handclap to bring the lights down and coax the band on to the stage. Barring Casey Waits, now firmly ensconced in "the family business", the personnel is brand new. Linchpin Larry Taylor has made way for bassist Seth Ford-Young, Marc Ribot for Omar Torrez. Horn man Vincent Henry occasionally doubles as a guitarist. All are adroit, supple players who bring something more intricate and sophisticated to Waits' music than we've heard in recent years. Later in the set, fifteen-year-old Sullivan Waits will supplement the ensemble with a turn on congas and a spot as "assistant" saxophonist/clarinettist.

As it has done every night since Phoenix, the show opens with a medley of "Lucinda" and "Ain't Goin' down to the Well", the two songs sequenced as they are on the first *Orphans* CD. Waits couldn't have begun with a more overt statement of intent: this is not going to be an easy ride through his sentimental back pages. Dredged from deep within, the gargled Waits bark sounds almost monstrous as its owner howls the plaint of William the Pleaser and stamps a booted foot on the riser that supports him, each time bringing up a little cloud of talcum powder. Wearing his bowler hat and accompanying his vocals with pantomime hand gestures that utilize his freakishly long fingers, he could be a demonic Charlie Chaplin. Satanic reds and purples alternate with cooler greens and blues as backdrops to the spectacle.

The set takes a while to ignite. "Rain Dogs" lacks the polka pep of its studio original, and "Falling Down" – with Waits' hoarse bellow masking a lack of genuine tone – fails to convince as the faux-stadium ballad it is. Things gradually improve with *Night on Earth*'s "On the Other Side of the World", aired more than a few times on the European leg of *Glitter and Doom* that started in San Sebastian on 12 July. By the time Waits is through with a crooned "I'll Shoot the Moon" – complete with a kabuki clinch, his giant hands caressing his own back – he has every last man and woman eating out of his palms.

When Omar Torrez brings in the next number, the high-stepping Yiddish rhythm could be any one of a dozen songs from his post-Asylum years. "Christ, which one is it?!" Waits barks as though reading our minds. It's an endearing instant of self-deprecation, followed by "They're all good, you know!" The song turns out to be *Blood Money*'s "God's Away on Business", with Casey on kettledrum sticks and his dad railing against the world like a mad tramp. On its stomping heels, "The Part You Throw Away" is bare and minimal, all plucked pizzicato phrasing and Tom himself on miniature acoustic guitar.

The radical rework of "Eyeball Kid" is the set's glitzy centrepiece, Waits' showbiz parable delivered in a disco-ball bowler hat with the song's blues-funk *Mule Variations* arrangement replaced by an eerie ambient soundtrack akin to *Orphans'* "Army Ants". As a spotlight hits the hat, beams of light stream out to every corner of the theatre, Waits rotating on his riser with an idiot grin plastered across his face. It's pure Robert Wilson, of course. Another mutant-Yiddish classic, "Singapore", picks up from the groove of "God's Away".

Up to this point Waits has barely uttered a word. He only begins to address the audience when he gets behind a piano, as though the very familiarity – the muscle memory – of that perch makes it safe to revert to his comedic self. "We been on the road for a while and it's been fascinating," he remarks before listing examples of entirely fictional local laws he's encountered along the way. (It's schtick he's been doing since the US leg of the tour.) The sight of Waits at the keyboard prompts the more seasoned fans in the Playhouse to beg for older songs. Waits indulges them for a moment before making his boundaries crystal clear. "Okay, those are all requests," he says, "but they're *your* requests."

But then comes the small miracle so many of us are pining for: a "Tom Traubert's Blues" with Waits backed only by Seth Ford-Young, the song raw and ravaged but still, after all these years, delivered with such care, so perfect it is hard to believe it's happening. As it ends a raucous Scots voice screams "Och, ya beauty!!" and we all grin in agreement. A flood of further requests echoes around the auditorium. "You still workin' at the airport?" Waits responds to one particularly persistent disciple, using a line first deployed in the seventies. We don't get "Invitation to the Blues" or "On the Nickel", nor does he play "I Can't Wait to Get off Work" or "Christmas Card from a Hooker in Minneapolis" – all of the above performed at times on the *Glitter and Doom* tour. But we do get "The Briar and the Rose" and then – for the very first time on the tour – "Take It with Me", dedicated to his longtime UK publicist Rob Partridge and sung with such artless tenderness it makes me weep.

The ballad portion of the show concludes with a mass singa-long on "Innocent when You Dream" before the mutant Dixiebilly of "Lie to Me" restarts Waits' uptempo motor, the line "I have no use for the truth!" insistently repeated as Casey thuds out the beat on his tom-toms. Little brother Sullivan, all of fifteen, then joins the troupe for a rousingly ragged version of "Hoist that Rag", smacking the congas as his father howls the splenetic lyric. Superb solos follow from Messrs Warren, Henry, and Torrez.

Waits is back on guitar for "Bottom of the World", its bellowy Celtic feel underscored by Torrez's mandolin, and for "Cold Cold Ground" and "Green Grass". "Way down in the Hole", played on almost every *Glitter and Doom* date, is funkier than I've ever heard it, with electric piano fills straight out of Ray Charles' "What'd I Say". Sullivan plays clarinet alongside Vincent Henry's baritone sax on an aptly funereal "Dirt in the Ground", staying put for "Metropolitan Glide" and the closing "Make It Rain", the latter augmented by a shower of glitter falling over Waits Sr's head. The old stage devices are still the best.

"Jesus Gonna Be Here" is the first of three encores, Vincent Henry blowing two saxes simultaneously à la Roland Kirk/Ralph Carney. When Waits introduces the second as "a little story", somebody shouts "'Step Right Up'!" "Not that one," Waits snaps straight back. It turns out to be a "9th and Hennepin" that's virtually stripped of musical flesh, delivered as spoken-word beneath a flickering naked lightbulb lowered from the rig over Waits' head. "This is about 9th and Hennepin in the *old* days," he informs us. "Anywhere I Lay My Head", a frequent *Glitter and Doom* encore, rounds things off but only leaves the Edinburgh crowd clamouring for more.

As with every show on the two legs of the tour, the Playhouse performance will receive ecstatic reviews and blog posts, numerous voices proclaiming it the greatest gig ever. A five-star *Guardian* review greets me in my hotel the next morning. Apparently I am alone in the world with my churlish misgivings about the set list – and the ultimate worth of songs such as "Lucinda" and "Metropolitan Glide".* But I'll take the memory of "Tom Traubert" and "Take It with Me" to the grave.

The drizzle continues as we wait next to the black tour buses. Hang on a minute, isn't that young puppy Sullivan Waits? And that's definitely big brother Casey, a towel draped round his shoulders as he disappears into the snug recess of the bus closest to us. What would happen if I sidled up to them and asked for a quote about their papa? Bad things, methinks.

---

* Perhaps not entirely alone. Most of the UK broadsheets raved, but in the *Sunday Times* standup comic Stewart Lee was less sure. "The artifice of Waits' act makes it difficult to respond to emotionally," Lee wrote, asking whether Waits – "like the medicine-show shysters of old whose shtick [he] has appropriated" – was "just a master salesman".

Beat the street: desperate fan Natalina Forbovsky peers into the Waits tour bus. (*Art Sperl*)

The dampened fans around me whisper furtively among themselves. He's still in there; he must have gone; he was never here at all. "It's not like there's a lot of us," sighs one disgruntled youth. "You'd think he could just sign a few posters." Yeah, I can really see *that* happening.

Across the street, by the *other* bus, a dreadlocked boy cranes his neck in a flash of recognition. It's clear that he's just spotted our hero on board: seems Waits has been in there all along, yards away from me, coming down from the adrenalizing euphoria of the show. Before I can quite register what's happened, the doors suck shut and the bus pulls away into the damp Edinburgh night.

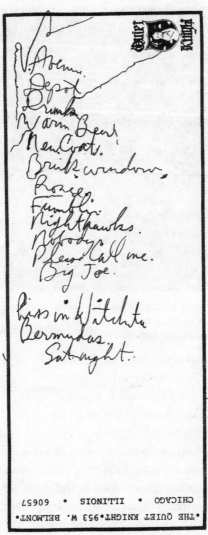

Set list, Quiet Knight, Chicago, December 1975. (*Courtesy of Charlie Thorne*)

Appendix 1

Waits' Greatest Tracks: A Top 40 Countdown

40 Closing Time (*Closing Time*)
39 I Don't Wanna Grow Up (*Bone Machine*)
38 Soldier's Things (*Swordfishtrombones*)
37 Whistle down the Wind (*Bone Machine*)
36 Johnsburg, Illinois (*Swordfishtrombones*)
35 Walking Spanish (*Rain Dogs*)
34 Saving All My Love for You (*Heartattack and Vine*)
33 Jitterbug Boy (*Small Change*)
32 I'm Still Here (*Alice*)
31 Blind Love (*Rain Dogs*)
30 Hold On (*Mule Variations*)
29 $29.00 (*Blue Valentine*)
28 Mr Henry (*Bounced Checks*)
27 What's He Building? (*Mule Variations*)
26 Blue Valentines (*Blue Valentine*)
25 Eggs and Sausage (In a Cadillac with Susan Michelson) (*Nighthawks at the Diner*)
24 On the Nickel (*Heartattack and Vine*)
23 Cemetery Polka (*Rain Dogs*)
22 16 Shells from a Thirty-Ought Six (*Swordfishtrombones*)
21 I Beg Your Pardon (*One from the Heart*)
20 (Looking for) The Heart of Saturday Night (*The Heart of Saturday Night*)

19 Pony (*Mule Variations*)

18 Ruby's Arms (*Heartattack and Vine*)

17 Shore Leave (*Swordfishtrombones*)

16 Christmas Card from a Hooker in Minneapolis (*Blue Valentine*)

15 Lowside of the Road (*Mule Variations*)

14 What Keeps Mankind Alive? (*Orphans*)

13 Potter's Field (*Foreign Affairs*)

12 Temptation (*Frank's Wild Years*)

11 Muriel (*Foreign Affairs*)

10 Such a Scream (*Bone Machine*)

9 Hoist that Rag (*Real Gone*)

8 Burma Shave (*Foreign Affairs*)

7 Ol' '55 (*Closing Time*)

6 Kentucky Avenue (*Blue Valentine*)

5 Heartattack and Vine (*Heartattack and Vine*)

4 Broken Bicycles (*One from the Heart*)

3 Goin' out West (*Bone Machine*)

2 Take It with Me (*Mule Variations*)

1 Tom Traubert's Blues (*Small Change*)

Appendix 2

The Email Trail

From: Jane Rose
Date: Thu, 8 Feb 2007 12:20:42 EST
Subject: Re: Keith Richards
Dear Barney,
Keith has asked me to check with Tom to confirm that this is
authorized before doing any interview. Will get back to you
once I speak to Tom or his representative.
Best regards,
Jane

From: Jane Rose
Date: Thu, 8 Feb 2007 17:47:08 EST
Subject: Re: Jane Rose
Dear Barney,
Keith will not be able to do the interview.
Another time, another situation.
Kind regards,
Jane

*

From: Carter Logan
Subject: Re: Attn Carter or Stacey: Request for interview with Jim
Jarmusch
Date: Tue, 20 Feb 2007 15:40:05

Dear Barney,
Thanks for thinking of Jim for this but he is not interested in participating.
Best wishes,
Carter Logan
Assistant to Jim Jarmusch

*

From: Charles D. De Lisle
Subject: Tom
Date: Wed, 28 Feb 2007 10:46:47
Hi Barney. I'm checking with Tom to see if he gives me the okay to talk with you – not that there's anything to hide.
Charley

Subject: Re: Santa Barbara visit
To: Barney Hoskyns
From: Charles D. De Lisle
Date: Fri, 9 Mar 2007 12:19:19
Hi Barney. I won't be able to meet with you, but best of luck with your book.
Charley

*

From: Mark Rennick
Subject: Re: Tom Waits
Date: Thu, 3 May 2007 19:15:02
Barney
I am under the impression this is an unauthorized biography of Tom. I value my relationship with Tom and respectfully will pass on the interview.
Mark "Mooka" Rennick
Co-Owner/Founder
Prairie Sun Recording

*

From: Joe Gore
Subject: Re: Tom Waits book
Date: Tue, 22 May 2007 10:53:17

Hi Barney – thanks for the note. I certainly know your books and your byline, and I've admired your work.

I'd love to speak to you, as I'm a huge Waits fan myself. But I just checked in with Tom and Kathleen, and they politely asked me not to speak with you. So while I know your book is likely to be a glowing portrait, and my thoughts about working with Tom and Kathleen are equally glowing, I'm regretfully going to have to honor their wishes.

Sorry about that. Good luck. I like your stuff.

Take care,

Joe

*

From: Michael Blair
Subject: Re: Tom Waits book
Date: Wed, 23 May 2007 14:51:40

Hello Barney

What a pleasure to hear from you. I have been a *Mojo* subscriber for years and have certainly read your work when you were there. A fine set of credentials, indeed.

This project sounds good. As a percussionist in particular and musician in general, being able to tackle the Waits songbook has been a journey worth every step. Such theatricality is rare in the world of rock and pop.

I have promised my employers (including Costello and Reed) that I would not speak about their work or anything personal without approval. I found you have interviewed Tom, so I don't see an obstacle. But before we begin, I want an OK from Tom and Kathleen. I'll get back to you as soon as I hear from them.

best

Michael Blair

*

From: Smokey Hormel
Subject: Re: Tom Waits book
Date: Sat, 26 May 2007 21:28:50
Hello Barney,
Sorry for the slow reply. I spent the last week in the California woods, where there is no internet connection. I just received your e-mail. I would love to talk to you about my experience with Tom Waits.
If you are in London, I will be there on June 13th. We can talk then. Let me know if that works. I will bring your contact info with me.
Smokey

From: Smokey Hormel
Subject: Re: Tom Waits book
Date: Wed, 30 May 2007 04:47:26
Hey Barney,
Thanks for the kind words. I am a big fan of yours too. Unfortunately I was contacted by Stuart Ross (Tom's manager), who discouraged me from discussing Tom with you. This is sad to me because I really like your work and I have nothing but positive words about my experiences with Tom. But in this case, I must respect their wishes.
I hope you understand.
sincerely,
Smokey Hormel

*

From: Greg Cohen
Subject: Re: Tom Waits book
Date: Thu, 14 Jun 2007 15:56:03 (PDT)
Hi Barney,
After speaking with Tom . . . I think I had better wait.
Best,
Greg

*

From: Chris Blum
Subject: Re: Tom Waits book
Date: Sat, 16 Jun 2007 12:45:42
Hi Barney,
Unfortunately because this is an unauthorized work I will not
be able to help you. If there are any changes I will certainly get
back to you.
Good Luck with your project.
Chris Blum

*

From: Matt Brubeck
Subject: Re: Tom Waits
Date: Wed, 12 Mar 2008 22:12:24
Hello Barney,
I'd be happy to talk with you if you can provide me with docu-
mentation that Tom Waits has authorized this biography.
Cheers,
Matt B

*

From: Rickie Lee Jones
Subject: Tom Waits
Date: Mon, 8 Sep 2008 11:12:16 EDT
Hi Barney
Good morning from here to there. Waits, hmm, what's to say. I
am waiting for a book about ME.
Let's see if his wife lets him say anything about us, or me . . .
then we'll see.
RLJ

Acknowledgements

Thank you . . .

For making the book happen: Andrew Corbin, late of Broadway Books; Gerry Howard, also of Broadway; Lee Brackstone and Angus Cargill of Faber; my agents Jonny Geller and Sarah Lazin. Thank you, too, to Doug Kean, David Watkins, John Burke, Katie Halleron, and Ian Bahrami.

For answering the questions: Bob Alcivar, Ray Bierl, Chris Blackwell, Paul Body, Mathilde Bondo, Denny Bruce, Ralph Carney, Herb Cohen, Ry Cooder, Sal Crivello, Lou Curtiss, Henry Diltz, Pat DiPuccio, Carey Driscoll, Rick Dubov, Todd Everett, Art Fein, Michael C. Ford, Sadie Frost, David Geffen, Bill Goodwin, Kim Gottlieb, Carlos Guitarlos, Michael Hacker, Herb Hardesty, Martin Henry, Paolo Hewitt, Stephen Hodges, Randy Hoffman, Bones Howe, Jim Hughart, Harvey Kubernik, Bob LaBeau, Gary Leonard, Louie Lista, Robert Marchese, Mary McCaslin, David McGee, Mike Melvoin, Brendan Mullen, Tom Nolan, Ian Penman, Bill Plummer, Suzanne Reed, Elliot Roberts, Hannes Rossacher, Kate St John, Bill Schimmel, Kirk Silsbee, Joe Smith, Ron Stone, Clark Suprynowicz, Jack Tempchin, Bobi Thomas, Fred Toedtman, Danny Trifan, Steve Von Lutes, Jeff Walker, Lenny Waronker, Bob Webb, Chip White, Jerry Yester.

For going way beyond the call of any duty by compiling session details for albums and responding to countless enquiries: Bones Howe and Ralph Carney.

For sharing recollections of their own Waits encounters: Johnny Black, Mick Brown, Richard Cromelin, Karl Dallas, Mick Houghton, Mark Kemp, Gavin Martin, Tom Moon, Sean O'Hagan, Ian Penman, Chris Roberts, Pete Silverton, Adam Sweeting, Joel Selvin, Paul Yamada. Plus thanks to the many other writers whose work I've quoted from.

For providing a home from home: Peter Wilson, Paula Cannon, and Jack and Ella. For being a true friend in LA: Susan Compo. For their help and hospitality in San Diego: George and Beth Varga. And for always being there in Hollyweird: Harvey Kubernik.

For creating and maintaining every Waits fan's dream site and resource: Pieter Hartmans. This book would have been a whole lot trickier without www.tomwaitslibrary.com. Thanks also to the splendid Eyeball Kid blog at www.eyeballkid.blogspot.com.

For invaluable advice and feedback: Martin Colyer.

For sending and lending stuff, and for other incidental kindnesses: Greg Arrufat, Laura Barton, Sylvie Blum, Richard Bosworth, Dale Carter, Sharon Chevin, Richard Cromelin, John D'Agostino, Albert DePetrillo, Hunter Drohojowska-Philp, James Fox, Andy Gershon, Carl Gottlieb, Edward Helmore, Clinton Heylin, Rob Hughes, Jay S. Jacobs, Kari Johnson, Gary Kemp, Howie Klein, Philip McGrade, Jeb Loy Nichols, Tom O'Dell, Rob Partridge, Steven X. Rea, Xan Rufus-Isaacs, Tom Sheehan, Don Snowden, Dave Stewart, Sarah Stitt, Neil Storey, Oscar Thompson, Roy Trakin, John Van Zelm Trubee, Sheila Weller, Paul Yamada.

For occasional sustaining conversation (about Waits, or just about writing): Tom Fry, Martin Colyer, Mark Pringle, Mat Snow, Edward St Aubyn, Christian Preston, James Fox, David Kamp, Jeb Loy Nichols, Tam Hoskyns, Brendan O'Keeffe, Alex

Games, Peter Chapman, and everyone else whose support I've so unforgivably forgotten.

For patience: Tony Keys, Mark Pringle, and all at Rock's Backpages; Michael Bonner, Allan Jones, John Mulvey, and John Robinson at *Uncut*; Caspar Llewellyn-Smith at the *Observer Music Monthly*. And anyone else who had to wait on Waits.

For being the best sons a man could ask for: Jake Hoskyns, Fred Hoskyns, Nat Hoskyns. For accepting me in their lives: George Slater, Freddie Slater.

And for your love, always: Natalie Forbes.

Notes

Where consecutive quotes are taken from the same interview, this is indicated by "*et seq.*"

PROLOGUE

xvii   "What's so bad about being misunderstood?" Bob Dylan, *Radio Times*, 13–19 October 2007

—   "Am I Frank Sinatra or am I Jimi Hendrix?" Waits, author interview, 28 January 1999

—   "I spend my entire time trying to explain", P. J. Harvey to Barney Hoskyns, *Tracks*, Summer 2004

xx   "I'm not sure you can't tell more about *me*", Randy Newman, author interview, 6 November 1995

—   "Most readings of Tom", Pete Silverton, email, 4 June 2008

—   "These American self-created men", Rickie Lee Jones, www.rickielee-jones.com, 2000

xxi   "I don't know anyone on earth that I really consider", Alex Chilton, phone conversation, June 1999

—   Lewis Taylor email, 28 June 2007

xxii   "Tom's a very contradictory character", Jim Jarmusch, Q, 1989

—   "One of Waits' previous biographers": Jay S. Jacobs, email, 27 February 2007

—   "I think I have the right to tell you stuff", Ralph Carney, email, 3 May 2007

xxiii   "I often think of Tom and wish him well", Bob Webb, email, 29 June 2007

—   "It has more to do with the fact", Greg Cohen, email, 25 November 2007

—   "I'm cut off", Bones Howe, author interview, 13 March 2007

xxiv   "I don't think Kathleen is alone in developing their approach", Joel Selvin, email, 27 February 2007

xxv   "You want to make sure", Waits, *The Times* online, 22 October 2004

ACT ONE

CHAPTER 1 SOME WAYS ABOUT ME THAT JUST AREN'T RIGHT

3   "I guess most entertainers", Waits, author interview, 28 January 1999

4   "Everybody in this business called show", Waits in Margaret Moser, *Austin Chronicle*, 10–16 May 2002

—   "I come from a good family and everything", Waits, radio interview, WAMU, Washington, DC, 18 April 1975

—   "I had a pretty normal childhood", Waits in Jim Gerard, *Scene*, 23–29 December 1976

—   "He used to go to our church on occasion", Waits, radio interview with Howard and Roz Larman, KPFK-FM Pasadena, 12 August 1973

5   "Pat Nixon taught at Whittier High", Pat Di Puccio, email, 12 July 2007

—   "Tom grew up very much in the way that I did", Michael C Ford, author interview, 21 March 2007

6   "Waits' regular references to being born in a taxi", e.g. in "Whistlin' past the Graveyard", *Blue Valentine*, 1978

—   "He came west", Waits in Margaret Moser, *Austin Chronicle*, 10–16 May 2002

—   "conceived one night in April 1949", Waits in Bill Milkowski, *Downbeat*, November 1985

7   "He was really a tough one", Waits in Sylvie Simmons, *Mojo*, October 2004

—   "Tom's mom was a very put-together suburban matron", Bill Goodwin, author interview, 19 June 2007

—   "The first time I met Tom's mother", Chip White, author interview, 11 December 2007

—   "On my father's side we had all the psychopaths and alcoholics", Waits, radio interview, WXRT Chicago, 11 July 1986

—   "Tom and his sisters were very independent", Bob LaBeau, author interview, 13 June 2007

8   "About the rest of his childhood he is fairly reticent", Dave Lewis, *Sounds*, 4 August 1979

—   "ate spinach so I could get stronger", Waits in Karen Schoemer, *Newsweek*, 23 April 1999

—   "trick knee", Elizabeth Gilbert, *GQ*, June 2002

—   "What sort of a child was I?" Waits in Pete Silverton, *YOU/Mail on Sunday*, October 1985

— "[grew] up in a drive-in", Waits in Mick Brown, *Word*, December 2006

— "I remember my father", Waits in John Hamblett, *New Musical Express*, 12 May 1979

9 "had an effect on me" *et seq.*, Waits in *Buzz*, May 1993

10 "'Cemetery Polka' was, ah, discussing my family", Waits in Mark Rowland, *Musician*, October 1987

— "We were always waiting for trains to pass", Waits in Mick Brown, *Word*, December 2006

11 "[She] was always like", Waits in Brian Case, *Melody Maker*, 5 May 1979

— "I had a little tree fort and everything", Waits in Jay S. Jacobs, *Wild Years: The Music and Myth of Tom Waits* (Toronto: ECW Press, 2000), p. 22

12 "bees [were] buzzing all around", Waits in Mark Richard, *Spin*, June 1993

— "I made my own shapes out of them", Waits in Tom Lanham, *Paste*, December 2004

— "I juggle with brown", Waits to Elvis Costello, *Option*, February 1989

— "I'd put my hand on a sheet" *et seq.*, Waits in Sean O'Hagan, *Observer*, 29 October 2006

13 "Childhood is very important" *et seq.*, Waits in Gavin Martin, *New Musical Express*, 19 October 1985

— "lovely grief", Geoffrey O'Brien, *Sonata for Jukebox: Pop Music, Memory and the Imagined Life* (New York: Counterpoint, 2004), p. 48

— "He taught me three chords" *et seq.*, Francis Thumm, *Interview*, October 1988

— "the secret knowledge of the chords", Waits in *Buzz*, May 1993

14 "My mom came from a big family", Waits in George Varga, *San Diego Union Tribune*, 3 October 2004

— "had a great low singing voice", Waits in Andrew Dansby, *Houston Chronicle*, 19 November 2006

— "Tom has a background", Francis Thumm in George Varga, *San Diego Union Tribune*, 3 October 2004

— "didn't listen to jitterbug or anything like that", Waits in Kristine McKenna, *New Musical Express*, 1 October 1983

15 "'You ever grow a ducktail'", Waits, radio interview, KCRW-FM, 12 October 1992

— "My dad – I think it was a rebel raising a rebel", Waits in Sylvie Simmons, *Mojo*, October 2004

— "I was real repressed", Waits in Kid Millions, *Rock Bill*, October 1983

16 "a lot of incongruous musical influences", Waits in James Stevenson, *New Yorker*, 27 December 1976

— "an image of me in a dark sport coat", Waits in David McGee, *Rolling Stone*, 27 January 1977

— "I knew what I *didn't* want to do", Waits in Mark Rowland, *Musician*, October 1987

— "There were a lot of preachers", Waits in Gavin Martin, *Uncut*, June 2002

17 "The family kind of hit the wall", Waits in Andrew Dansby, *Houston Chronicle*, 19 November 2006

— "It was an extreme loss of power", Waits in Mick Brown, *Word*, December 2006

— "definitely the upscale area of the whole south county", Carey Driscoll, author interview, 30 May 2007

— "We used to skate down" *et seq.*, Waits in Jonathan Valania, *Magnet*, June–July 1999

18 "The military was the centre of life", Waits, author interview, 28 January 1999

— "at home with these three women", Waits in Patrick Humphries, *Melody Maker*, 14 March 1981

— "When you come from a broken home", Waits, television interview, *Gente de Expressão* (Brazil), 1992

— "God, I loved it", Waits in Mikel Jollett, *SOMA*, July 2002

19 "People have no idea", Todd Everett, author interview, 14 March 2007

— "he used to hear a band playing", George Varga, *San Diego Union Tribune*, 3 October 2004

— "My dad taught Spanish all his life", Waits, author interview, 28 January 1999

20 "If you went to a restaurant in Mexico" *et seq.*, Waits in Sylvie Simmons, *Mojo*, October 2004

— "When I think back on it", Waits in Mick Brown, *Word*, December 2006

— "I was on the back of a motorcycle", Waits in Richard Grant, *Zembla*, 2004

— "You stay as still as a corpse", Francis Thumm, *Interview*, October 1988

21 "She let me squeeze it", Waits in *Buzz*, May 1993

— "probably [hearing] a *ranchera*", Waits in Robert Wilonsky, *Dallas Observer*, 6 May 1999

— "It was something I didn't completely understand", Waits in Pete Silverton, *YOU/Mail on Sunday*, October 1985

— "The first station I got", Waits in Rip Rense, Anti Records promotional interview, reprinted in *Performing Songwriter*, July–August 1999

— "I didn't have a lot of [musical] encouragement", Waits, radio interview, BBC Radio One, 22 October 1983

22   "a predominantly black junior high school", Waits in James Stevenson, *New Yorker*, 27 December 1976

—   "We got in the back of the fence", Waits in Mick Brown, *Sounds*, 12 June 1976

—   "It was like you'd been dosed", Waits in Gavin Martin, *Uncut*, June 2002

—   "surf and soul", Waits in Mikel Jollett, *SOMA*, July 2002

—   "[We were] white kids", Waits in Dan Forte, *Contemporary Keyboard*, April 1977

23   "Here's a guy like Dylan", Waits in Robert Hilburn, *Los Angeles Times*, 6 June 1999

—   "Too many teachers in my family", Waits in Bill Forman, *Music & Sound Output*, October 1987

—   "I wore a tie that cut off the circulation", Waits in Bill Dolan, *Village Noize*, early 1993

—   "kind of an amateur juvenile delinquent", Waits in Bob Claypool, *Houston Post*, 12 December 1976

—   "malicious mischief", Waits in James Stevenson, *New Yorker*, 27 December 1976

—   "enjoyed the thrill of breaking the law", Waits in Pete Silverton, *YOU/Mail on Sunday*, October 1985

24   "and watched my California Scholarship", Waits in Richard Cromelin, *Los Angeles Times*, 14 March 1976

—   "I felt really peculiar", Waits in John Hamblett, *New Musical Express*, 12 May 1979

—   "He managed him for a while", Waits in George Varga, *San Diego Union Tribune*, 3 October 2004

—   "There in the darkness", Waits in Charles Champlin, *Los Angeles Times*, 14 January 1988

25   "Serling had these great eyebrows" *et seq.*, Waits in Tim Perlich, *Now*, 16–22 November 2006

—   "I found [them] when I was a teenager", Waits in Sean O'Hagan, *Observer*, 29 October 2006

26   "We would just see how far we could go", Waits in Jonathan Valania, *Magnet*, June–July 1999

—   "They were singing", Waits, radio interview with Terry Gross, National Public Radio, 21 May 2002

—   "probably the most pivotal religious experience I've had", Waits in Mick Brown, *Word*, December 2006

—   "It was the first time", Waits in Francis Thumm, *Interview*, October 1988

— "I disavow any knowledge of the world of surfing", Waits in Peter O'Brien, *ZigZag*, July 1976

27 "My own background", Waits in Patrick Humphries, *Melody Maker*, 14 March 1981

CHAPTER 2 HOME I'LL NEVER BE

29 "Lou Curtiss is a heroic curmudgeon", Waits in George Varga, *San Diego Union-Tribune*, 23 November 2003

— "He was singing Bob Dylan songs", Lou Curtiss, author interview, 22 March 2007

30 "That guy's got music in him", Bobi Thomas, email conversations, tomwaitslibrary.com, 2006

— "I was never voted", Waits in Bob Claypool, *Houston Post*, 12 December 1976

— "My parents split up", Waits in Clark Peterson, *Creem*, March 1978

— "My brother-in-law", Waits in John Hamblett, *New Musical Express*, 12 May 1979

31 "I don't think he worked there very long", Lou Curtiss, author interview, 22 March 2007

— "He started when he was in high school" *et seq.*, Sal Crivello, author interview, 22 March 2007

32 "I thought high school was a joke", Waits in Rich Wiseman, *Rolling Stone*, 30 January 1975

— "I was wasted all day", Waits in Bob Claypool, *Houston Post*, 12 December 1976

— "Nineteen sixty-three, one a.m.", Waits in *Vanity Fair*, November 2004

— "National City is this Naugahyde town", Waits, radio interview, WAMU, Washington, DC, 18 April 1975

— "Hookers would come in", Waits in Stan Soocher, *Circus Weekly*, 23 January 1979

— "grew up real fast", Waits in *Time*, 28 November 1977

33 "I worked on Saturday nights", Waits, Artist's Choice, HearMusic.com, October 1999

— "a pioneer GM product", Waits, radio interview, WAMU, Washington, DC, 18 April 1975

34 "exhilarating, especially when you set out", Waits in Kristine McKenna, *New Musical Express*, 1 October 1983

— "I wanted to go into the world", Waits, radio interview with Terry Gross, National Public Radio, 21 May 2002

35 "I was a rebel against the rebels" *et seq.*, Waits in Sylvie Simmons, *Mojo*, October 2004

— "slept through the sixties" *et seq.*, Waits, author interview, 28 January 1999

— "the ghost of Jack Kerouac", Waits in Steve Lake, *Melody Maker*, October 1975

— "Kerouac came roaring down", Lester Bangs in Jim DeRogatis, *Let It Blurt: The Life and Times of Lester Bangs* (London: Bloomsbury, 2000), p. 22

— "I guess everybody reads", Waits in Todd Everett, *Los Angeles Free Press*, 17–23 October 1975

36 "just like when you buy a record", Waits, author interview, 28 January 1999

— "Kerouac liked to consider himself", Waits in Rich Wiseman, *Rolling Stone*, 30 January 1975

— "colored section" *et seq.*, Jack Kerouac, *On the Road* (London: Penguin Classics, 2000), pp. 163–4

37 "I enjoy [Kerouac's] impressions", Waits in Kristine McKenna, *New Musical Express*, 1 October 1983

— "ambulance drivers", Waits in James Stevenson, *New Yorker*, 27 December 1976

38 "beat the hell out of putting aluminum siding", Waits in Dan Forte, *Contemporary Keyboard*, April 1977

— "went up for a physical", Waits in Clark Peterson, *Creem*, March 1978

— "had a very low lottery number", Waits in Sylvie Simmons, *Mojo*, October 2004

39 "I think Tom and I", Carey Driscoll, author interview, 30 May 2007

— "He told me he'd been really into it", Jack Tempchin, author interview, 17 March 2007

— "They were real greasy", Bob LaBeau, author interview, 13 June 2007

— "He took it pretty seriously", Ray Bierl, author interview, 30 May 2007

— "I started sitting down", Waits in Lou Curtiss and Stephen Swain, *San Diego's Weekly*, 18–24 July 1974

— "I played and I learned songs", Waits, author interview, 28 January 1999

40 "Monk said", Waits, Artist's Choice, HearMusic.com, October 1999

— "like a couple of old men" *et seq.*, Francis Thumm in George Varga, *San Diego Union Tribune*, 3 October 2004

— "It was a very bohemian area", Randy Hoffman, author interview, 14 June 2007

41 "The Heritage was like a little theater", Jack Tempchin, author interview, 17 March 2007

— "He was doing, I don't know", Waits in Patrick Donovan, *The Age*, 10 May 2002

— "the first real songwriter", Waits, radio interview with Howard and Roz Larman, KPFK-FM Pasadena, 12 August 1973

42 "Tom was a pretty impressive guy", Ray Bierl, author interview, 30 May 2007

43 "Tom was always very friendly", Martin Henry, author interview, 24 June 2007

— "Bill and I were both committed" *et seq.*, Bob Webb, email, 29 June 2007

— "The only thing about the job", Steve Von Lutes, author interview, 19 November 2007

— "The reason I got the job", Waits in Rich Trenbeth, *Rambler*, 30 December 1976

44 "I remember Tom as", Steve Von Lutes, author interview, 19 November 2007

— "I never thought of him as the bouncer", Jack Tempchin, author interview, 17 March 2007

— "I'd bring my books and my coffee", Waits in Mick Brown, *Telegraph* magazine, 11 April 1999

— "I heard about him working as the doorman", Bill Goodwin, author interview, 19 June 2007

— "On slow nights", Ray Bierl, author interview, 30 May 2007

45 "Tom was influenced", Bob Webb, email, 29 June 2007

— "Sometimes it was more fun", Lou Curtiss, author interview, 22 March 2007

— "the 'gravely-voiced' ticket-taker" *et seq.*, Suzanne Reed, email, 1 May 2007

— "We'd have a hamburger", Ray Bierl, author interview, 30 May 2007

— "He was always a late-night guy", Lou Curtiss, author interview, 22 March 2007

46 "It was a cholesterol-loaded place", Steve Von Lutes, author interview, 19 November 2007

— "I remember playing old 78s", Lou Curtiss, author interview, 22 March 2007

— "I started with Bobby Dylan songs", Waits in Lou Curtiss and Stephen Swain, *San Diego's Weekly*, 18–24 July 1974

47 "He did the whole talking thing", Ray Bierl, author interview, 30 May 2007

— "'Big Joe' was one of his set-pieces", Bob Webb, email, 29 June 2007

— "In the beginning Tom was just like the rest of us" *et seq.*, Bobi Thomas, email, 13 June 2007

— "a lot of his stage persona", Ray Bierl, author interview, 30 May 2007

48 "a lot of respect", Bob LaBeau, author interview, 13 June 2007

— "He had a very unusual stage presence" *et seq.*, Martin Henry, author interview, 24 June 2007

— "wasn't really a singer *per se*" *et seq.*, Suzanne Reed, email, 1 May 2007

— "I asked him what kind of stuff" Sal Crivello, author interview, 22 March 2007

— "He had a real nice bluesy sound", Bob LaBeau, author interview, 13 June 2007

— "The first times I saw him play", Lou Curtiss, author interview, 22 March 2007

49 "I don't know if they were really songs", Waits, author interview, 28 January 1999

— "Parodies of country and western", Ray Bierl, author interview, 30 May 2007

— "bluegrassed to death", Waits in Peter O'Brien, *ZigZag*, July 1976

— "Increasingly he performed his own material", Bob Webb, email, 29 June 2007

50 "She lived next door to the Heritage", Bob LaBeau, author interview, 13 June 2007

— "Sherry said, 'Well, that's Tom'", Randy Hoffman, author interview, 14 June 2007

— "I was narrowly interested in traditional music", Bob Webb, email, 29 June 2007

— "I think I made more as a doorman", Waits in Edvins Beitiks, *San Francisco Examiner*, 4 August 1996

— "a couple of months or so" *et seq.*, Bob LaBeau, author interview, 13 June 2007

51 "the single most beautiful love song", Simon Schama, *Guardian*, 9 December 2006

52 "It wasn't until Tom began to write", Bobi Thomas, email, 13 June 2007

— "We all recognized Tom's songwriting genius", Martin Henry, author interview, 24 June 2007

— "Almost all the local musicians" *et seq.*, Bob Webb, email, 29 June 2007

53 "plunking on the old upright", Bobi Thomas, email, 13 June 2007

— "You could tell right off", Ray Bierl, author interview, 30 May 2007

54 "a big thrill for me", Waits in Bret Kofford, *Blues Revue* no. 59, July–August 2000

— "I just hit it off with Tom for a while" *et seq.*, Jack Tempchin, author interview, 17 March 2007

— "A lot of them came down to San Diego" *et seq.*, Ray Bierl, author interview, 30 May 2007

55   "Tom just took the audience", Jack Tempchin, author interview, 17 March 2007

—   "Jack and Tom both had their sights set", Ray Bierl, author interview, 30 May 2007

56   "On the cover it said something", Bob LaBeau, author interview, 13 June 2007

—   "[It] was like a slave market", Waits in Kenny Weissberg, *Colorado Daily*, February 1974

—   "the last resort", Waits in Rich Wiseman, *Rolling Stone*, 30 January 1975

—   "The hoot was the coolest thing", Waits, author interview, 28 January 1999

—   "Clearly his music was wonderful", Martin Henry, author interview, 24 June 2007

57   "The gate at the Heritage", Steve Von Lutes, author interview, 19 November 2007

—   "Mission Beach became a little unseemly", Bob LaBeau, author interview, 13 June 2007

—   "San Diego musicians stay there", Waits in Jeff Walker, *Music World*, June 1973

58   "I was never really part of that coffeehouse scene", Waits, *Swordfishtrombones* promotional interview disc (Island Records), 1983

—   "I think Tom plays down San Diego", Lou Curtiss, author interview, 22 March 2007

—   "I don't want to make this", Waits in George Varga, *San Diego Union Tribune*, 3 October 2004

CHAPTER 3   UNDERSTANDING, SYMPATHY, AND ENCOURAGEMENT

59   "Posterity?" *et seq.*, Herb Cohen, author interview, 8 March 2007

60   "I was on my way to the toilet", Herb Cohen in Stan Soocher, *Circus Weekly*, 23 January 1979

61   "Herb came over to me", Waits in Rich Wiseman, *Rolling Stone*, 30 January 1975

—   "the big jump into showbiz", Waits, radio interview with Howard and Roz Larman, KPFK-FM Pasadena, 12 August 1973

—   "Herbie was a lot scarier" *et seq.*, Jerry Yester, author interview, 8 June 2007

—   "A lot of managers", Henry Diltz, author interview, 19 March 2007

62   "He was like an adventurer soldier of fortune", Joe Smith, author interview, 27 November 2007

—   "a little Jewish man", Frank Zappa in Patrick Humphries, *The Many Lives of Tom Waits* (London: Omnibus, 2007), p. 43

63 "Herb, I have to say", Todd Everett, author interview, 14 March 2007

— "I wasn't a snob or anything", Waits in Dan Forte, *Contemporary Keyboard*, April 1977

— "I wanted a big bruiser", Waits in Jonathan Valania, *Magnet*, June–July 1999

— "Waits knew you needed management", Harvey Kubernik, author interview, 20 March 2007

64 "They gave him a writing contract", Bob LaBeau, author interview, 13 June 2007

— "Newman was always like", Waits, author interview, 28 January 1999

— "writing at gunpoint", Waits, radio interview with Terry Gross, National Public Radio, 21 May 2002

65 "Taylor was immensely popular", Bob Webb, email, 29 June 2007

— "I caught that wave of songwriters", Waits, author interview, 28 January 1999

— "I was very proud when Herb Cohen asked", Bobi Thomas, email, 13 June 2007

— "It was interesting to me", Ray Bierl, author interview, 30 May 2007

— "I felt I'd snuck in the back way", Waits in Patrick Humphries, *Melody Maker*, 14 March 1981

— "He said he was giving it all or nothing", Ray Bierl, author interview, 30 May 2007

66 "as ambitious as hell" *et seq.*, Waits in Richard Cromelin, *Los Angeles Times*, 14 March 1976

— "One thing to learn from Tom", Stephen Hodges, author interview, 20 November 2007

67 "In early 1972, no one was doing stuff like that", Jerry Yester in Jay S. Jacobs, *Wild Years: The Music and Myth of Tom Waits* (Toronto: ECW Press, 2000), p. 42

68 "He showed up at a reading I was doing" *et seq.*, Michael C Ford, author interview, 21 March 2007

69 "Silver Lake was both cheap and bohemian", Jeff Walker, author interview, 15 March 2007

70 "It's a hovel", Waits in Rich Wiseman, *Rolling Stone*, 30 January 1975

— "People rarely understand Los Angeles", Pat DiPuccio, email, 12 July 2007

— "He stayed very tight with his father", Michael C Ford, author interview, 21 March 2007

— "We'd been best friends already for a long time", Bobi Thomas, email, 13 June 2007

71 "The relationship between Tom and Bobi", Bob Webb, email, 29 June 2007

— "Tom would stay up till five or six in the morning" *et seq.*, Bobi Thomas, email, 13 June 2007

72 "He kept everything tightly under his slouch cap" *et seq.*, Bob Webb, email, 29 June 2007

73 "I just thought this was remarkable", Waits in *Bukowski: Born into This* (Magnolia Pictures, 2004)

— "An Alvarado Street bar", Charles Bukowski, "Confessions of a Man Insane Enough to Live with Beasts", *South of No North* (1973)

— "My dad spent a lot of time in the bars" *et seq.*, Waits in *Bukowski: Born into This* (Magnolia Pictures, 2004)

74 "I guess everybody", Waits in Mick Brown, *Word*, December 2006

75 "He was someone that I listened to for several years", Waits, radio interview, WAMU, Washington, DC, 18 April 1975

— "Roger Perry, the hootmaster", Todd Everett, author interview, 14 March 2007

— "I was surprised to see somebody like that", Louie Lista, author interview, 12 March 2007

— "He really created a persona", Bobi Thomas, email, 13 June 2007

76 "Joe was living in California", Jerry Yester, author interview, 8 June 2007

— "a lot of nips on the line", Waits in Jeff Walker, *Music World*, June 1973

— "I would check out the Troubadour" *et seq.*, David Geffen, author interview, 21 March 2007

78 "David said, 'You have to hear this'", Elliot Roberts, author interview, 19 March 2007

— "there were a lot of good writers", Elliot Roberts, author interview, 18 June 1993

— "The first time Elliot heard Waits", David Geffen, author interview, 21 March 2007

— "I think Herbie knew we loved Tom", Elliot Roberts, author interview, 19 March 2007

79 "David Geffen does a lot for his artists", Waits in Jeff Walker, *Music World*, June 1973

— "The criterion at Asylum" *et seq.*, Ron Stone, author interview, 16 March 2007

— "Tom had the soul of a saloon singer", Michael C Ford, author interview, 21 March 2007

80 "I'm very glad I'm a departure for Asylum", Waits in Jeff Walker, *Music World*, June 1973

— "They always try to create scenes", Waits, author interview, 28 January 1999

— "Tom may have interacted with Don Henley", Jack Tempchin, author interview, 17 March 2007

— "It wasn't like I was adopted into a family", Waits, author interview, 3 September 2004

81 "Asylum was an artist-oriented label", Don Henley in Marc Eliot, *To the Limit: The Untold Story of the Eagles* (New York: Little, Brown, 1998), p. 91

— "Tom used to hang around our office", Mark Volman, email conversations, www.tomwaitslibrary.com, May 2006

— "There was a period of about six months" *et seq.*, Jerry Yester, author interview, 8 June 2007

82 "Jerry was a great producer", Waits, author interview, 28 January 1999

83 "We talked together about the instrumentation" *et seq.*, Jerry Yester, author interview, 8 June 2007

84 "It was kind of frightening", Waits in Lou Curtiss and Stephen Swain, *San Diego's Weekly*, 18–24 July 1974

— "Tom was very quiet" *et seq.*, Bill Plummer, author interview, 7 May 2007

— "He was absolutely communicative", Jerry Yester, author interview, 8 June 2007

— "He was just so calm and relaxed", Bill Plummer, author interview, 7 May 2007

86 "That was absolutely the most magical session" *et seq.*, Jerry Yester, author interview, 8 June 2007

87 "We were pulling against each other", Waits in John Platt, *ZigZag*, June 1977

— "There was a place in Burbank", Jerry Yester in Jay S. Jacobs, *Wild Years: The Music and Myth of Tom Waits* (Toronto: ECW Press, 2000), p. 43

— "He liked to buy a six-pack of Coors" *et seq.*, Jerry Yester, author interview, 8 June 2007

— "I think that first album", Jeff Walker, author interview, 15 March 2007

88 "Tom stylized his voice", Jerry Yester, author interview, 8 June 2007

— "Franny said to me", Randy Hoffman, author interview, 14 June 2007

89 "an aura of crushed cigarettes", Stephen Holden, *Rolling Stone*, 26 April 1973

— "He specifically wanted a jazz feel" *et seq.*, Bob Webb, email, 29 June 2007

90 "I was just happy to be", Waits in Adam Sweeting, *Guardian*, 15 September 1992

— "Tom never assumed the mantle of star" *et seq.*, Bob Webb, email, 29 June 2007

91 "just cool as ice", Waits in Lou Curtiss and Stephen Swain, *San Diego's Weekly*, 18–24 July 1974

— "There was quite a hullabaloo" *et seq.*, Bob Webb, email, 29 June 2007

92 "We did matinees at 10 a.m." *et seq.*, Waits in Francis Thumm, *Interview*, October 1988

— "There was a small little postage stamp of a stage", Waits in Lou Curtiss and Stephen Swain, *San Diego's Weekly*, 18–24 July 1974

93 "It was the old case of the one-size-fits-all industry-push", Waits in David McGee, *Rolling Stone*, 27 January 1977

— "It was a way for people from the company", Tom Nolan, author interview, 15 March 2007

— "He was so open", Jeff Walker, author interview, 15 March 2007

95 "Because we were a free magazine", Kim Gottlieb, author interview, 15 March 2007

— "He was looking down", Tom Nolan, author interview, 15 March 2007

— "Mexican-Oriental" *et seq.*, Marv Hohman, *Down Beat*, 17 June 1976.

96 "hurrying for the big-traffic", Jack Kerouac, *Visions of Cody* (London: Flamingo edition, 1992), p. 85

— "We struck on Kerouac's concept", Bob Webb, email, 29 June 2007

97 "Not many people go to downtown LA", Waits, radio interview with Howard and Roz Larman, KPFK-FM Pasadena, 12 August 1973

— "I remember we were both into Kerouac", Jack Tempchin, author interview, 17 March 2007

CHAPTER 4 IN CHARACTER

98 "It was a cramped little store", Carey Driscoll, author interview, 30 May 2007

100 "We went deep into an underground garage", Ken Langford, email conversations, www.tomwaitslibrary.com, 22 July 2004

— "some four thousand stoned and annoyed Zappa fans" *et seq.*, Bob Webb, email, 29 June 2007

— "The tour was not well thought-out", Waits, author interview, 28 January 1999

— "We played two gigs in the Midwest", Bob Webb, email, 29 June 2007

101 "The cats in [Zappa's] band", Waits in Marv Hohman, *Down Beat*, 17 June 1976

— "Frank would just say", Waits, author interview, 28 January 1999

— "Tom Waits slouches on the corner stool", Marco Barla, *LA Free Press*, January 1974

102 "There were no hipster places", Michael Hacker, author interview, 17 March 2007

— "a dedicated Angeleno", Waits, press release, *The Heart of Saturday Night*

— "He evoked those sort of grungy LA intersections", Tom Nolan, author interview, 15 March 2007

— "I try to take myself up on stage", Marco Barla, *LA Free Press*, January 1974

103 "It's hard sometimes to get up", Waits in Lou Curtiss and Stephen Swain, *San Diego's Weekly*, 18–24 July 1974

— "Tom was the world's greatest joke teller", Lou Curtiss, author interview, 22 March 2007

— "recapture the spirit", Ray Bierl, author interview, 30 May 2007

— "He wasn't lazy and he worked", Harvey Kubernik, author interview, 20 March 2007

104 "At this point, to open a show", Waits in Kenny Weissberg, *Colorado Daily*, February 1974

— "bright huge glitter and swarming bums", Jack Kerouac, *Visions of Cody* (London: Flamingo edition, 1992), p. 426

— "I thought he was just some bum folk singer", Chuck E. Weiss, imusic.com, 1999

— "When I arrived at the University of Colorado", Art Fein, "Another Fein Mess", www.sofein.com, March 2003

105 "As far as I'm concerned", Waits in Kenny Weissberg, *Colorado Daily*, February 1974

— "I thought *Closing Time* was a great record", David Geffen, author interview, 21 March 2007

106 "David called me one day", Bones Howe, author interview, 13 March 2007

— "Nobody would even think of sending you", Waits, author interview, 28 January 1999

107 "There were some things Tom wanted to do", Bones Howe, author interview, 13 March 2007

— "You try to distinguish yourself in some way", Waits, author interview, 28 January 1999

— "I'd worked with Bones" *et seq.*, Mike Melvoin, author interview, 20 March 2007

108 "I wasn't quite sure that Tom was even connected" *et seq.*, Jim Hughart, author interview, 15 March 2007

109 "I thought of Tom as a professional poet" *et seq.*, Mike Melvoin, author interview, 20 March 2007

110 "I definitely must have been", Bones Howe, author interview, 13 March 2007

— "There seemed to be a little uneasiness", Jim Hughart, author interview, 15 March 2007

— "Material from one song", Mike Melvoin, author interview, 20 March 2007

111 "Tom just looked at it", Jim Hughart, author interview, 15 March 2007

— "Jim just started playing a modal bass line", Waits, radio interview, WAMU, Washington, DC, 18 April 1975

— "It frees you as a songwriter" *et seq.*, Waits, radio interview with Howard and Roz Larman, KPFK-FM Pasadena, 23 July 1974

112 "some old things that I was writing", Waits in Lou Curtiss and Stephen Swain, *San Diego's Weekly*, 18–24 July 1974

— "'Blue Skies' was very much like a Ray Charles song", Bones Howe, author interview, 13 March 2007

113 "The film came out about 1947" *et seq.*, Waits, radio interview with Howard and Roz Larman, KPFK-FM Pasadena, 23 July 1974

114 "Tom had taken on some of the qualities", Bones Howe, author interview, 13 March 2007

116 "Susan worked at Denny's", Michael C Ford, author interview, 21 March 2007

— "Here's this guy in the hat", Paul Body, author interview, 9 March 2007

— "Waits was an oasis for us", Harvey Kubernik, author interview, 20 March 2007

117 "It was very ill-formed", Waits in Sylvie Simmons, *Mojo*, October 2004

— "a chrome forest", Waits in Russell Bongard, *Skateboarding*, July 2002

— "They figured [Frank] must have *wanted*", Waits, author interview, 28 January 1999

— "Tom used to call me up periodically" *et seq.*, Bob LaBeau, author interview, 13 June 2007

118 "The crowd was most impatient" *et seq.*, Paul Yamada, email, 16 June 2008

— "Frank shows up in my dreams", Waits, author interview, 28 January 1999

119 "Herb Cohen was wise enough", Ron Stone, author interview, 16 March 2007

— "He was so heckled", Michael C Ford, author interview, 21 March 2007

— "I was in a bar one night", Waits, radio interview, WAMU, Washington, DC, 18 April 1975

— "It put Tom on an entirely different level", Louie Lista, author interview, 12 March 2007

120 "David said to me" *et seq.*, Bones Howe, author interview, 13 March 2007

— "I wish he didn't like me", Waits in Fred Dellar, *New Musical Express*, 5 June 1976

— "I found it a lot easier", Mike Melvoin, author interview, 20 March 2007

— "I frankly was not that particularly crazy", Waits, radio interview, WAMU, Washington, DC, 18 April 1975

— "about as exciting as watching paint dry", Waits in Fred Dellar, *New Musical Express*, 5 June 1976

121 "I still remember Tom saying", Jack Tempchin, author interview, 17 March 2007

— "[He's] another one who is embarrassing", Waits in John Platt, *ZigZag*, June 1977

— "I was a young kid", Waits, author interview, 3 September 2004

— "I'd tried to pitch stories", Harvey Kubernik, author interview, 20 March 2007

122 "an evocation of ecstatic", Stephen Holden, *Rolling Stone*, 26 April 1973

— "well on the way to becoming", Michael C Ford, *LA Free Press*, spring 1974

123 "Tom was truly in his element", Danny Trifan, email, 11 October 2007

— "He was singing 'The Heart of Saturday Night'", Bette Midler in Grover Lewis, *New West*, 13 March 1978

— "You need some feathers", quoted in Francis Thumm, *Interview*, October 1988

— "It was okay on the bill with Little Feat", Waits, radio interview with Howard and Roz Larman, KPFK-FM Pasadena, 12 January 1975

— "I thought he was very hip" *et seq.*, Paul Body, author interview, 9 March 2007

124 "My old man likes me a lot", Waits, radio interview, WAMU, Washington, DC, 18 April 1975

— "Doug was smart", Louie Lista, author interview, 12 March 2007

— "The moon beats the hell out of the sun" *et seq.*, Rich Wiseman, *Rolling Stone*, 30 January 1975

125 "Not really", Waits, radio interview, WAMU, Washington, DC, 18 April 1975

— "probably go in the studio some time" *et seq.*, Waits, radio interview with Howard and Roz Larman, KPFK-FM Pasadena, 12 January 1975

— "Chuckie was sort of Tom's road manager" *et seq.*, Paul Body, author interview, 9 March 2007

127 "I think we were all fish out of water" *et seq.*, Louie Lista, author interview, 12 March 2007

— "I just thought Waits was fulla shit", Robert Marchese, author interview, 18 May 2007

— "I'd see Waits with Marchese", Harvey Kubernik, author interview, 20 March 2007

128 "For some odd reason", Robert Marchese, author interview, 18 May 2007

— "I get tired of playing", Waits, radio interview, WAMU Washington, DC, 18 April 1975

129 "Tom never really talked about Herb", Paul Body, author interview, 9 March 2007

— "Herb was a real street guy", Bones Howe, author interview, 13 March 2007

— "Cohen would come and hang out", Louie Lista, author interview, 12 March 2007

— "On one of his albums", Jim Hughart, author interview, 15 March 2007

130 "so it was impossible to intimidate me", Mike Melvoin, author interview, 20 March 2007

— "almost like a big brother" *et seq.*, Bones Howe, author interview, 13 March 2007

131 "I met this very interesting guy" *et seq.*, Bill Goodwin, author interview, 19 June 2007

132 "It was a pretty good-sized room", Jim Hughart in Joseph Scott, *Bassics*, July 2000

133 "You can hear on the record" *et seq.*, Bill Goodwin, author interview, 19 June 2007

134 "I've got a personality that an audience likes", Waits in Betsy Carter with Peter S. Greenberg, *Newsweek*, 14 June 1976

135 "People like Melvoin and Christlieb", Bones Howe, author interview, 13 March 2007

CHAPTER 5 KNEE-DEEP IN GRUNGE

136 "There is a kidney-shaped swimming pool", William S. Burroughs, *Rolling Stone*, 24 January 1980

— "It was black because it was all rusty", Pleasant Gehman, author interview, June 1993

137 "It was like a Motel 6 with shag carpeting", quoted in Jay S. Jacobs, *Wild Years: The Music and Myth of Tom Waits* (Toronto: ECW Press, 2000), p. 45

— "Warren had this thing about the Tropicana", quoted in Crystal Zevon, *I'll Sleep When I'm Dead: The Dirty Life and Times of Warren Zevon* (New York: Ecco, 2007), p. 52

— "The Tropicana was really a businessmen's hotel", Waits, television interview, *Gente de Expressão* (Brazil), 1992

— "If it was your first gig", Todd Everett, author interview, 14 March 2007

— "I was driving from Silver Lake", Waits in Jay S. Jacobs, Popentertainment.com, 1999

138 "Chuckie was doing a lot of drugs then", Robert Marchese, author interview, 18 May 2007

— "I never did any narcotics", Waits in Mick Brown, *Sounds*, 12 June 1976

— "He smoked like a chimney" *et seq.*, Robert Marchese, author interview, 18 May 2007

— "Chuckie was a hanger", Bones Howe, author interview, 13 March 2007

— "When Chuck came into Tom's life", Bobi Thomas, email, 13 June 2007

— "I could never fathom", Mike Melvoin, author interview, 20 March 2007

139 "a lot of faith in me", Waits in Todd Everett, *LA Free Press*, 17–23 October 1975

— "I wasn't surprised by anything Tom did", David Geffen, author interview, 21 March 2007

— "Geffen hated *Nighthawks*", Bill Goodwin, author interview, 19 June 2007

— "I don't know about that", Waits in Nigel Williamson, *Sydney Morning Herald*, 27 April 2002

140 "Tom wanted some musicians" *et seq.*, Bill Goodwin, author interview, 19 June 2007

141 "It was a true nightmare" *et seq.*, David McGee, email, 1 April 2008

142 "Some guy had just shot him", Waits in David Koepp, *Circus*, 22 December 1977

— "I went back to *The Ox-Bow Incident*", Waits in Francis Thumm, *Interview*, October 1988

— "syncopated stutter-step of urban images", Don Ray King, sent as email to "Blue Valentine" (Italian Tom Waits fan club), 2 July 1999

143 "[He's] a real original", Bonnie Raitt in Betsy Carter with Peter S. Greenberg, *Newsweek*, 14 June 1976

144 "When you're on the road doing clubs", Waits in Marv Hohman, *Down Beat*, 17 June 1976

— "I was sick through that whole period", Waits in David McGee, *Rolling Stone*, 27 January 1977

— "He sings everything", Jon Landau, *Rolling Stone*, 18 December 1975

— "Kid Leo really had an interest in Tom", Fred Toedtman, author interview, 29 May 2007

145 "He's great, right?", Waits in Robert Ward, *New Times* magazine, 11 June 1976

— "a real high-voltage bebop trio", Waits in Fred Dellar, *New Musical Express*, 5 June 1976

— "I didn't even know who he was", Chip White, author interview 11 December 2007

— "I got a black bass player", Waits in Rich Trenbeth, *Rambler*, 30 December 1976

146 "Tom had given me a couple of his books", Chip White, author interview, 11 December 2007

— "terrific . . . [it] talks about all the lousy jobs", Waits in Robert Ward, *New Times* magazine, 11 June 1976

147 "He was like a big bear" *et seq.*, Waits in Mikel Jollett, *SOMA*, July 2002

— "Although Waits' integration", Dave Marsh, *Rolling Stone*, 23 October 1975

— "All of a sudden it becomes your image", Waits in Richard Cromelin, *Los Angeles Times*, 14 March 1976

148 "It was like a traveling party" *et seq.*, Chip White, author interview, 11 December 2007

— "Witnessing the big sound" *et seq.*, Hal Willner, from liner notes to *Used Songs 1973–1980* (Rhino, 2001)

— "The eclectic singer/musician", Robert Ward, *New Times* magazine, 11 June 1976

149 "Charlie had been this guy's best friend", Waits in Bob Claypool, *Houston Post*, 12 December 1976

— "Nobody even asked me" *et seq.*, Waits in David McGee, *Rolling Stone*, 27 January 1977

150 "when the moon is high", Waits in Peter O'Brien, *ZigZag*, July 1976

— "a battered Burton's-style suit", Mick Houghton, *Time Out*, June 1976

— "I think he was almost being presented", Mick Houghton, author interview, 17 September 2007

151 "The whole thing is rampant", Waits in Fred Dellar, *New Musical Express*, 5 June 1976

— "beatniks" *et seq.*, Richard Cromelin, *Los Angeles Times*, 14 March 1976

— "Among the English press", Mick Brown, author interview, 16 November 2007

— "Swapping story for story" *et seq.*, Fred Dellar, *New Musical Express*, 5 June 1976

152 "We got in a big fight", Waits in Sean O'Hagan, *Observer*, 29 October 2006

— "two old spade cats" *et seq.*, Waits in Dan Forte, *Contemporary Keyboard*, April 1977

153 "I just don't enjoy talking about it", Waits in Karl Dallas, *Melody Maker*, 5 June 1976

— "He was quite a daunting person", Karl Dallas, author interview, 14 September 2007

— "probably the most delightful" *et seq.*, Mick Brown, *Sounds*, 12 June 1976

155   "Part of the persona", Mick Brown, author interview, 16 November 2007

—   "I grabbed the meat", Waits in Richard Grant, *Zembla*, December 2004

—   "He got pissed off", Chip White, author interview, 11 December 2007

156   "Tom told me one day", Bones Howe, author interview, 13 March 2007

—   "I guess we were both very wild", Mathilde Bondo, author interview, 18 September 2007

157   "nearly died" *et seq.*, David McGee, email, 1 April 2008

—   "They were in two bungalows", Rick Dubov, author interview, 9 March 2007

158   "Tom was a street guy", Henry Diltz, author interview, 19 March 2007

—   "It was like a bungalow", Paul Body, author interview, 9 March 2007

159   "I don't spend evenings around the piano", Waits in Dan Forte, *Contemporary Keyboard*, April 1977

—   "Tom lives . . . sort of knee-deep in grunge", Bette Midler in Grover Lewis, *New West*, 13 March 1978

—   "Though some myths have been perpetrated", Charley De Lisle, *Santa Barbara News and Review*, late 1978

—   "a claw hammer, a small jar of artichoke hearts", Charles Schwab, from liner notes to *Used Songs 1973–1980* (Rhino, 2001)

—   "I remember seeing him", Tom Nolan, author interview, 15 March 2007

—   "I remember him sitting", Michael Hacker, author interview, 17 March 2007

160   "I'd go to Tom's dressing room", Joe Smith, author interview, 27 November 2007

—   "Every wrapper was still in the car", Jerry Yester, author interview, 8 June 2007

—   "He was driven", Paul Body, author interview, 9 March 2007

—   "The image didn't mask the workaholic" *et seq.*, Robert Marchese, author interview, 18 May 2007

161   "You almost have to create situations", Waits in Richard Cromelin, *Los Angeles Times*, 14 March 1976

—   "different criteria for success", Waits in Rich Trenbeth, *Rambler*, 30 December 1976

—   "Bones has a story", Kirk Silsbee, author interview, 20 March 2007

—   "that's how Tom's mind worked" *et seq.*, Bones Howe, author interview, 13 March 2007

162   "There was no actual end", Mike Melvoin, author interview, 20 March 2007

163   "He didn't change that much personally", Jerry Yester, author interview, 8 June 2007

— "Shelly was so outgoing", Jim Hughart, author interview, 15 March 2007

164 "When we went in to assemble" *et seq.*, Bones Howe, author interview, 13 March 2007

— "completely confident in the craft" *et seq.*, Waits in Francis Thumm, *Interview*, October 1988

— "I'd say there's probably more songs", Waits, author interview, 28 January 1999

165 "On one of the tours his voice changed", Paul Body, author interview, 9 March 2007

166 "All that jargon we hear", Waits in David McGee, *Rolling Stone*, 27 January 1977

— "Chuckie was the king of the one-up", Paul Body, author interview, 9 March 2007

168 "I was really starting to believe", Waits in David McGee, *Rolling Stone*, 27 January 1977

170 "purview remains stringently narrow", *Rolling Stone*, 30 December 1976

— "I feel at times I'm residually in jeopardy", Waits in Rich Trenbeth, *Rambler*, 30 December 1976

— "We had a bus together", Ry Cooder, author interview, 22 May 2008

171 "It didn't start till two", Randy Hoffman, author interview, 14 June 2007

— "He came in on a promotional tour", Fred Toedtman, author interview, 29 May 2007

172 "Boy, you're long-winded" *et seq.*, Waits in Jim Gerard, *Scene*, 23–29 December 1976

— "She came down and I set it up", Fred Toedtman, author interview, 29 May 2007

173 "Tom had this thing for Elayne", Robert Marchese, author interview, 18 May 2007

— "ill-lit, vomit-green" *et seq.*, David McGee, *Rolling Stone*, 27 January 1977

CHAPTER 6 REAL ROMANTIC DREAMERS STUCK IN THE WRONG TIME ZONE

174 "$22 a night gets you a room", Mark Williams, *Melody Maker*, 16 December 1978

— "Every day I'd be leaving", Dave Bates, author interview, 7 June 2007

— "nodding acquaintance, literally", Elvis Costello in Patrick Humphries, *The Many Lives of Tom Waits* (London: Omnibus, 2007), p. 178

175 "When I moved into that place", Waits, author interview, 24 April 1985

176 "Of course there was a persona", Tom Nolan, author interview, 15 March 2007

— "If I was going to decide to be a cowboy", Todd Everett, author interview, 14 March 2007

— "I don't normally wear Bermuda shorts", Waits in Marv Hohman, *Down Beat*, 17 June 1976

— "It's usually journalists", Waits in Dan Forte, *Contemporary Keyboard*, April 1977

— "The fact is that everybody", Waits in Mick Brown, *Telegraph* magazine, 11 April 1999

— "I saw Tom on one or two occasions", Jerry Yester, author interview, 8 June 2007

177 "I really became a character", Waits in Dave Zimmer, *BAM*, 26 February 1982

— "The bartenders there were all fucked up", Robert Marchese, author interview, 22 October 2003

— "Things were getting so out of hand" *et seq.*, Louie Lista, author interview, 12 March 2007

178 "They'd taken over the tables", Waits in Jim Jarmusch, *Straight No Chaser*, Spring 1993

— "suspects Weiss and Waits" *et seq.*, Delores Ziebarth, *Rolling Stone*, 14 July 1977

— "[They] threw us into the back", Waits in Jim Jarmusch, *Straight No Chaser*, Spring 1993

— "It dragged on for five years", Waits in Steve Pond, *Rolling Stone*, 1 April 1982

179 "The people were so quiet" *et seq.*, Chip White, author interview, 11 December 2007

— "maniac, misfit unemployed actor", Waits in Clark Peterson, *Creem*, March 1978

180 "The Dead Boys were living there", Chuck E. Weiss in Jay S. Jacobs, Popentertainment.com, 1999

— "It may be revolting", Waits in Clark Peterson, *Creem*, March 1978

— "When people like Crosby", Harvey Kubernik, author interview, 20 March 2007

— "the assholes who live in Resting On My Laurels Canyon" *et seq.*, Waits in Clark Peterson, *Creem*, March 1978

181 "I once asked Waits what touring was like", Harvey Kubernik, author interview, 20 March 2007

— "The whole *band* knew it", Chip White, author interview, 11 December 2007

— "Bones was looking for somebody" *et seq.*, Bob Alcivar, author interview, 14 March 2007

184 "Frank was a bad junkie", Jim Hughart, author interview, 15 March 2007
— "Frank was a pro", Chip White, author interview, 11 December 2007
— "excruciating, like going to the dentist", Waits in Larry Goldstein, *Modern Hi-Fi and Music Sound Trax*, October 1978
— "They were done over two nights", Bones Howe, author interview, 13 March 2007
— "He changed a lot of lyrics", Bob Alcivar, author interview, 14 March 2007
185 "Tom had been dating Bette" *et seq.*, Bones Howe, author interview, 13 March 2007
186 "When you write for a duet", Bob Alcivar, author interview, 14 March 2007
— "She drove me crazy for three months", Bones Howe, author interview, 13 March 2007
— "I actually would prefer", Waits in Colin Irwin, *Melody Maker*, 29 April 1978
187 "[He] had become . . . the great Idiot of us all", Jack Kerouac, *Visions of Cody* (London: Flamingo, 1991), p. 414
— "Tom would often greet you", Michael C Ford, author interview, 21 March 2007
188 "I used Burma Shave as a dream", Waits in Richard Rayner, *Time Out New York*, 3–9 October 1985
— "I was trying to sing", Waits in Larry Goldstein, *Modern Hi-Fi and Music Sound Trax*, October 1978
189 "chief sin [Waits] can't shake", Fred Schruers, *Rolling Stone*, 17 November 1977
— "When Tom came out with a record", Joe Smith, author interview, 27 November 2007
190 "Me and Weiss and Waits", Art Fein, author interview, 16 June 1993
— "Tom was really funnier casually", Rick Dubov, author interview, 9 March 2007
— "Oh you know, they cross their sevens", Waits, TV interview by Mark Volman and Howard Kaylan for *90 Minutes Live*, 6 April 1978
— "I'd rather play a club with vomit all around me", Waits, *Time*, 28 November 1977
— "People would come up and talk", Paul Body, author interview, 9 March 2007
191 "My idea of a good time", Bette Midler in Grover Lewis, *New West*, 13 March 1978
— "the only girl I know", Waits in Richard J. Pietschmann, *Playgirl*, November 1978

— "It was one of the greatest shows", Michael Hacker, author interview, 17 March 2007

— "After ten minutes", Art Fein, Another Fein Mess, www.sofein.com, March 1999

— "a pretty girl with dark brown hair", Louie Lista, author interview, 12 March 2007

— "She was a girl who was", Paul Body, author interview, 9 March 2007

192 "He had a girlfriend in Philadelphia", Chip White, author interview, 11 December 2007

— "I remember Louie Lista telling me", Harvey Kubernik, author interview, 20 March 2007

— "Maybe my family were outlaws" et seq., Rickie Lee Jones, promotional CD accompanying Flying Cowboys (1989)

194 "She didn't appear to be driven", Chuck E. Weiss, unpublished interview with Rob Hughes, 2 February 2007

— "There's nothing guys who are musicians like more", Paul Body, author interview, 9 March 2007

— "It was warm and everyone was sitting out front" et seq., Louie Lista, author interview, 12 March 2007

— "The first time I saw Rickie Lee" et seq., Waits in Timothy White, Rolling Stone, 9 August 1979

— "All the people come out at night", Rickie Lee Jones, in Rob Hughes, Uncut, April 2007

196 "It seems sometimes like we're real romantic dreamers", Rickie Lee Jones in Timothy White, Rolling Stone, 9 August 1979

— "I always tend to become", Rickie Lee Jones in Andy Gill, Independent, 16 January 2004

197 "Rickie Lee arguably cadged her entire characterization", Mike Melvoin, author interview, 20 March 2007

— "We walk around the same streets", Rickie Lee Jones in Timothy White, Rolling Stone, 9 August 1979

— "What's amazing", Chuck E. Weiss, unpublished interview with Rob Hughes, 2 February 2007

— "I'd [. . .] look up at the moon", Rickie Lee Jones, "Furniture For The People" message board, 14 April 2003

198 "very quiet and empty at night" et seq., Rickie Lee Jones in Timothy White, Rolling Stone, 9 August 1979

— "Something happened that was weird", Chip White, author interview, 11 December 2007

— "You always got the feeling", Danny Trifan, email, 11 October 2007. Waits' proclivity for rocking in a chair – usually wrapping his arms round himself as if to protect himself – was also observed in December 1978 by Pete Oppel of the *Dallas Morning News*

199 "Tom may be a bit . . . cranky" *et seq.*, Bart Bull, *New Times*, November 1977

— "There's something about what I'm doing", Waits in David Koepp, *Circus*, 22 December 1977

200 "Once upon a time they'd been black", Waits in Rob Hughes, *Uncut*, April 2007

— "Tom was embarrassed", Chuck E. Weiss, unpublished interview with Rob Hughes, 2 February 2007

— "Tom absolutely despised phonies", Danny Trifan, email, 11 October 2007

— "Maybe Sly saw him at the Troubadour", Bones Howe in Jay S. Jacobs, *Wild Years: The Music and Myth of Tom Waits* (Toronto: ECW Press, 2000), p. 90

201 "Stallone said", Waits in Richard J. Pietschmann, *Playgirl*, November 1978

— "I went and sat in front of a piano", Waits in Peter Guttridge, *City Limits*, 1–7 July 1983

— "We want to say hello to you all", ITV interview by Mark Volman and Howard Kaylan for *90 Minutes Live*, 6 April 1978

202 "Nicky Beat gets up on stage", Paul Body, author interview, 9 March 2007

— "Waits wanted that open-minded punk/new wave audience", Brendan Mullen, email, 22 May 2007

— "a buncha shit", Art Fein, author interview, 16 June 1993

203 "Tom said to me" *et seq.*, Louie Lista, author interview, 12 March 2007

204 "It's about American heroes", Waits in Colin Irwin, *Melody Maker*, 29 April 1978

— "They threw us out", Waits in Richard J. Pietschmann, *Playgirl*, November 1978

205 "never tried anything like this", Waits in John Hamblett, *New Musical Express*, 12 May 1979

— "If I have to write one more song", Waits in Nick Kent, *New Musical Express*, 15 July 1978

— "I think for a while I had a certain romance", Waits, author interview, 24 April 1985

— "I live in a neighborhood", Waits in Charley De Lisle, *Santa Barbara News and Review*, late 1978

— "I'm playing [it] for the first time", Waits in Mikal Gilmore, *Rolling Stone*, 7 September 1978

— "Maybe Tom felt a bit more at ease", Jim Hughart, author interview, 15 March 2007

206 "[I needed] something different", Waits in Charley De Lisle, *Santa Barbara News and Review*, late 1978

— "I think he flew us out to LA", Chip White, author interview, 11 December 2007

— "They're all Negroes", Waits in Charley De Lisle, *Santa Barbara News and Review*, late 1978

207 "I didn't know Tom", Herb Hardesty in Bill Millar, *Melody Maker*, 19 May 1979; also in Millar, *Let the Good Times Rock! A Fan's Notes on Post-War American Roots Music* (York: Music Mentor Books, 2005)

— "a very pleasant human being", Herb Hardesty, author interview, 19 November 2007

— "There's more blood in this record", Waits in Mikal Gilmore, *Rolling Stone*, 7 September 1978

— "stories" *et seq.*, Waits in Stan Soocher, *Circus Weekly*, 23 January 1979

208 "I'm not optimistic about things" *et seq.*, Waits in Greg Linder, *Twin Cities Reader*, 17 November 1978

209 "Tom said, 'I've always wanted'", Bob Alcivar, author interview, 14 March 2007

210 "It still brings tears to my eyes", Bones Howe, author interview, 13 March 2007

— "Once I left town and they'd added strings", Waits, author interview, 28 January 1999

— "I'm really getting a little tired", Waits in Deane Zimmerman, *Hit Parader*, October 1978

CHAPTER 7 READY TO SCREAM

212 "I picked songs that were less dramatic" *et seq.*, Rickie Lee Jones, author interview, 23 October 1991

213 "It's like, 'Isn't there anything else'" *et seq.*, Rickie Lee Jones in Simon Hattenstone, *Guardian*, 18 October 2003

214 "I remember I went to the shoot", Bones Howe, author interview, 13 March 2007

215 "To go on the road for eight months", Waits in Richard J. Pietschmann, *Playgirl*, November 1978

— "Big fat guy", Paul Body, author interview, 9 March 2007

— "Waits auditioned us all at once", Greg Cohen in George Kanzler,

Newark Star Lodger, 22 May 1999

— "We had a good time on the road", Herb Hardesty, author interview, 19 November 2007

216 "It's supposed to be coming out" *et seq.*, Waits in Greg Linder, *Twin Cities Reader*, 17 November 1978

— "I don't like them people" *et seq.*, Waits in Deane Zimmerman, *Hit Parader*, October 1978

217 "Black guy with suspenders", Waits in Jim Jarmusch, *Straight No Chaser*, Spring 1993

— "I'm off the sauce", Waits in Larry Goldstein, *Modern Hi-Fi and Music Sound Trax*, October 1978

218 "This has been one long experiment" *et seq.*, Waits in Pete Oppel, *Dallas Morning News*, 21 January 1979

— "I like it because I'm very accessible", Waits in Stan Soocher, *Circus Weekly*, 23 January 1979

219 "She came in with massive attitude" *et seq.*, Lenny Waronker, author interviews, 20 October 2003 and 19 March 2007

— "I love her madly", Waits in Timothy White, *Rolling Stone*, 9 August 1979

220 "I think she was a lot more special", Rickie Lee Jones in Timothy White, *Musician*, 1984

— "He was always, I thought", Rickie Lee Jones in Mick Brown, *Daily Telegraph*, 26 August 2000

221 "Rickie Lee was fairly wild", Russ Titelman, author interview, 30 June 1993

— "if you talk to magazines" *et seq.*, Rickie Lee Jones in Timothy White, *Rolling Stone*, 9 August 1979

— "I started feeling more insecure", Rickie Lee Jones in Timothy White, *Musician*, 1984

222 "Tom didn't have as much recognition" *et seq.*, Chuck E. Weiss, unpublished Q&A with Rob Hughes, 2 February 2007

— "It affected all three of us", Rickie Lee Jones in Rob Hughes, *Uncut*, April 2007

223 "I'm trying to cut down", Waits in Brian Case, *Melody Maker*, 5 May 1979

— "He came in from Amsterdam", Hannes Rossacher, author interview, 20 May 2008

224 "I've been trying to give up drinking", Waits in John Hamblett, *New Musical Express*, 12 May 1979

— "When you begin, it's a man takes a drink", Waits in Gavin Martin, *Uncut*, June 2002

225 "I'm trying to do an R&B album", Waits in Brian Case, *Melody Maker*, 5 May 1979

— "I think my voice is ready", Waits in John Hamblett, *New Musical Express*, 12 May 1979

— "I was trying to find some new channel", Waits, author interview, 28 January 1999

228 "That's when I said this has gone too far", Waits, author interview, 24 April 1985

— "For all the craziness he projects", Paul Body, author interview, 9 March 2007

— "I found myself in some places", Waits in Sean O'Hagan, *Observer*, 29 October 2006

— "The record company were making such a fuss", Chuck E. Weiss in Rob Hughes, *Uncut*, April 2007

229 "Rickie Lee's heroin problem" Louie Lista, author interview, 12 March 2007

— "The Pigs were a soulful bunch", Stephen Hodges, author interview, 20 November 2007

230 "He hit it off with Jimmy", Carlos Guitarlos, author interview, 23 March 2007

— "It was the whole thing", Stephen Hodges, author interview, 20 November 2007

231 "I think one of the reasons", Robert Marchese, author interview, 18 May 2007

— "I think Tom had his feet on the ground", Rickie Lee Jones in Mick Brown, *Daily Telegraph*, 26 August 2000

— "It's an evil, evil drug", Rickie Lee Jones in Simon Hattenstone, *Guardian*, 18 October 2003

— "explosively passionate and exhilaratingly eccentric", Stephen Holden, *Rolling Stone*, 3 September 1981

232 "The western slopes was a phrase", Rickie Lee Jones in Terry McGaughey, http://jonathan.greer.users.btopenworld.com/interviews/rlj.html, 21 November 2001

— "somewhat worse for wear" *et seq.*, Paolo Hewitt, email, 31 March 2008

— "It got a little too aggravating", Waits, unidentified Canadian interview on www.tomwaitslibrary.com, October 1979

233 "poised on the threshold", Waits, radio interview with Vin Scelsa, WNEW-FM, 31 October 1979

— "Something compels you to be popular", Waits, author interview, 24 April 1985

— "Most of us expect artists", Waits in Mick Brown, *Telegraph* magazine, 11 April 1999

— "As I turn the corner on 30", Waits in Stephen X. Rea, *Ampersand*, September 1980

— "Looking back on those years", David McGee, email, 1 April 2008

234 "For people who are very depressed", Waits, television interview, *Gente de Expressão* (Brazil), 1992

— "I've tried all kinds", Waits in Clark Peterson, *Creem*, March 1978

235 "adopt a bunch of Mexicans" *et seq.*, Waits in Mick Brown, *Word*, December 2006

— "As much as he surrounded himself", Bones Howe, author interview, 13 March 2007

— "Each year they'd resurrect some relic", Paul Body, author interview, 9 March 2007

— "I was moved to participate", Tom Nolan, author interview, 15 March 2007

236 "It was love at first sight", Waits in Clare Barker, *Black + White*, June–July 2002

— "On New Year's morning", Michael Hacker, author interview, 17 March 2007

— "I just needed a new urban landscape", Waits in Stephen X. Rea, *Ampersand*, September 1980

— "a fascinating urban landscape", Waits, radio interview, WPIX-FM, 17 February 1980

237 "The glass . . . [had] some aluminum foil over it", Waits in Robert Hilburn, *Los Angeles Times*, 6 June 1999

— "You're like a wound-up toy car", Waits in Sylvie Simmons, *Mojo*, October 2004

— "to take stock of New York", David McGee, email, 1 April 2008

— "It's a hard city, you know?", Waits, author interview, 24 April 1985

— "I had some plans", Waits in Stephen Peeples, *Heartattack and Vine* promotional pack, 4 September 1980

238 "He liked the relationship", Waits in Dave Zimmer, *BAM*, 26 February 1982

— "I don't know what to do" *et seq.*, David McGee, email, 1 April 2008

239 "step backwards" *et seq.*, Waits, radio interview with Chris Douridas, KCRW-FM, 12 October 1992

— "By the time Francis asked me", Waits, author interview, 28 January 1999

— "prison sentence", Waits in Stephen Peeples, *Heartattack and Vine* promotional pack, 4 September 1980

— "Tom was always just an LA guy", Paul Body, author interview, 9 March 2007

— "One of the things Francis wanted", Bones Howe, author interview, 13 March 2007

CHAPTER 8 LUCKY GUY

241 "distrusted by all the cigar-smoking moguls", Waits in Patrick Humphries, *Melody Maker*, 14 March 1981

242 "The atmosphere at Zoetrope", Michael Hacker, author interview, 17 March 2007

— "I tried to tell a love story", Francis Ford Coppola, DVD Extras interview, *One from the Heart*, 2003

— "Suddenly here was my old street-homey figure", Michael Hacker, author interview, 17 March 2007

243 "I'd never really written in an office before", Waits, radio interview with Chris Douridas, KCRW-FM, 12 October 1992

— "David Niven feel", Waits in Stephen Peeples, *Heartattack and Vine* promotional pack, 4 September 1980

— "I originally told [them]", Francis Ford Coppola, sleevenotes, *One from the Heart: Music from the Motion Picture* (Columbia Legacy), 2004

244 "the most indecisive man", Joe Smith, author interview, 27 November 2007

— "Tom loved Francis", Michael Hacker, author interview, 17 March 2007

— "He certainly keeps my confidence up", Waits, DVD Extras interview, *One from the Heart*, 2003

— "I'd come in at ten o'clock", Bones Howe, author interview, 13 March 2007

— "The Coppola mindset", Bob Alcivar, author interview, 14 March 2007

— "[Richard] would sit in a little room", Waits in Dave Zimmer, *BAM*, 26 February 1982

245 "She was pretty and smart and shy" *et seq.*, Michael Hacker, author interview, 17 March 2007

— "I opened the door and there she was", Waits in Jay S. Jacobs, *Wild Years: The Music and Myth of Tom Waits* (Toronto: ECW Press, 2000), p. 101

— "Tom came in to my office", Bones Howe, author interview, 13 March 2007

246 "We used to play a game", Waits in Gavin Martin, *Uncut*, June 2002

— "We were going into these bars", Waits in Elizabeth Gilbert, *GQ*, June 2002

— "In the beginning", Bones Howe, author interview, 13 March 2007

— "[Kathleen's] most important formative musical experiences", Waits in Sean O'Hagan, *Observer*, 29 October 2006

- — "I think I'm the conservative one", Waits in Clare Barker, *Black + White*, June–July 2002
- 247 "In a good way I'm alive", Waits in Mick Brown, unedited transcript of *Word* interview, December 2006
- — "really the end of a certain long period", Waits in Sylvie Simmons, *Mojo*, October 2004
- — "I got in a humbug" *et seq.*, Waits in Chris Peachment, *Time Out*, 8–14 July 1983
- 248 "I just wanted to stay there", Waits in David McGee, *Record,* November 1983
- — "tried to arrive at some level of personal hygiene", Waits in David McGee, *Rolling Stone*, 27 January 1977
- 249 "I know Tom wanted to change" *et seq.*, Bones Howe, author interview, 13 March 2007
- — "kind of rebelling", Waits, author interview, 28 January 1999
- — "The subject matter I was dealing with" *et seq.*, Waits in David McGee, *Rolling Stone*, 27 January 1977
- 251 "I never thought I would catch myself", Waits in Stephen Peeples, *Heartattack and Vine* promotional pack, 4 September 1980
- 252 "I've done all I can for him", Waits in Bill Flanagan, *Written in My Soul* (London: Omnibus, 1985), p. 390
- — "Overnight, the skid row guy was gone" *et seq.*, Jerry Yester, author interview, 8 June 2007
- — "He wanted it to sound", Jerry Yester, author interview, 8 June 2007
- 254 "the saddest song ever written", sleevenotes, *Step Right Up!* (Manifesto Records, 1995)
- — "woozy, far-out optimism", Stephen Holden, *Rolling Stone*, 5 February, 1981
- 255 "I came right off of the album", Waits in Stephen Peeples, *Heartattack and Vine* promotional pack, 4 September 1980
- — "My wife had fifty bucks", Waits, radio interview with Terry Gross, National Public Radio, 21 May 2002
- — "just the happiest I'd ever seen him", Jerry Yester, author interview, 8 June 2007
- — "dogs, children, blackbirds, and clothesline" *et seq.*, Waits, radio interview with Dave Fanning, RTE-2FM, 8 October 2004
- 256 "Apart from the interview" *et seq.*, Dermot Stokes, *Hot Press*, September 1980
- — "cocktail landscape" *et seq.*, Waits in Dave Zimmer, *BAM*, 26 February 1982

257 "I put on a suit and tie", Waits, *Swordfishtrombones* promotional interview disc, 1983

— "It's mainly for all the churches", Waits, documentary about *One from the Heart*, TF1 (France), 5 January 1982

— "Francis had this mobile home", Bones Howe, author interview, 13 March 2007

258 "The songs were supposed to be a subtext", Waits in Dave Zimmer, *BAM*, 26 February 1982

259 "Tom would come over to the house" *et seq.*, Bob Alcivar, author interview, 14 March 2007

260 "That was where this Bertolt Brecht quality", Bones Howe, author interview, 13 March 2007

— "There were a lot of early contenders" *et seq.*, Bob Alcivar, author interview, 14 March 2007

262 "It was necessary at times", Waits in Dave Zimmer, *BAM*, 26 February 1982

— "He was brittle and unbudging", Ian Penman, email, 21 January 2007

— "but not at gunpoint" *et seq.*, Waits in Ian Penman, *New Musical Express*, 28 March 1981

— "a huge slavering obsessional fan" *et seq.*, Ian Penman, email, 21 January 2007

263 "I've grown a little", Waits in Mick Brown, *Guardian*, March 1981

— "Teddy was very proud", Kirk Silsbee, author interview, 20 March 2007

— "While Tom was gone", Bob Alcivar, author interview, 14 March 2007

264 "[It] was an orphan for a while" *et seq.*, Waits in Dave Zimmer, *BAM*, 26 February 1982

— "I thought she sounded really vulnerable" *et seq.*, Bones Howe in Jay S. Jacobs, *Wild Years: The Music and Myth of Tom Waits* (Toronto: ECW Press, 2000), p. 109

265 "Richard would work up in his studio", Bob Alcivar, author interview, 14 March 2007

— "I thought it was a beautiful-looking movie", DVD Extras interview, *One from the Heart*, 2003

267 "I was listening to a lot of Ellington", Waits, author interview, 24 April 1985

268 "a clue as to where Tom wanted to go" *et seq.*, Bones Howe, author interview, 13 March 2007

269 "Bones is a gentleman", Waits, author interview, 28 January 1999

270 "I said, 'Tom, that's always been your choice'", Bones Howe, author interview, 13 March 2007

— "I just needed to make a clean break", Waits, author interview, 28 January 1999

— "be responsible for all facets" *et seq.*, Waits in Dave Zimmer, *BAM*, 26 February 1982

— "I thought I was a millionaire", Waits, author interview, 28 January 1999

271 "Kathleen told me Herbie had nicked" *et seq.*, Jerry Yester, author interview, 8 June 2007

— "She provided emotional security", Bones Howe, author interview, 13 March 2007

— "Basically, Kathleen saved Tom", Paul Body, author interview, 9 March 2007

— "He cut himself off from his old life", Bones Howe, author interview, 13 March 2007

272 "Everyone was gone except Greg Cohen", Bob Alcivar, author interview, 14 March 2007

— "Kathleen changed his life radically" *et seq.*, Jim Hughart, author interview, 15 March 2007

— "Most of my records were all scratched", Waits in George Varga, *San Diego Union Tribune*, 3 October 2004

ACT TWO

CHAPTER 1 TRYING TO ARRIVE AT SOME TYPE OF CATHARTIC EPIPHANY IN TERMS OF MY BIFOCALS

275 "something you'd want to keep", Waits in Robert Hilburn, *Los Angeles Times*, 6 June 1999

276 "I hatched out of the egg", Waits in Brett Martin, *Time Out New York*, 22–29 April 1999

— "For a long time I heard everything", Waits in Kid Millions, *Rock Bill*, October 1983

— "I found after a while", Waits in Robert Palmer, *New York Times*, 16 November 1993

— "She was the one that started", Waits in Karen Schoemer, *Newsweek*, 23 April 1999

277 "I was such a one-man show", Waits in Sylvie Simmons, *Mojo*, October 2004

— "Once you've heard Beefheart", Waits in Michael Evans, *The Oregonian*, 15 October 1999

— "It was certainly not the first time" *et seq.*, Mike Melvoin, author interview, 20 March 2007

278 "I don't blame Tom for it", Bones Howe, author interview, 13 March 2007

— "You can't really overestimate", Michael Hacker, author interview, 17 March 2007

— "Kathleen was very concerned", Joe Smith, author interview, 27 November 2007

279 "The songs have a relationship", Waits, *Swordfishtrombones* promotional interview disc, 1983

— "I think the whole experience", Waits in David McGee, *Record*, November 1983

— "I could make some very good guesses", Randy Hoffman, author interview, 14 June 2007

280 "Like most innovators", Waits, Artist's Choice, HearMusic.com, October 1999

— "Once upon a time", Waits in George Varga, *San Diego Union Tribune*, 3 October 2004

281 "I remember Tom pounding on my chest", Randy Hoffman, author interview, 14 June 2007

— "suggesting instruments I wouldn't have considered", Waits in Brett Martin, *Time Out New York*, 22–29 April 1999

— "Someone was fixing a mic", Waits in Mikel Jollett, *SOMA*, July 2002

282 "I think they thought I was a drunk", Waits, radio interview with Terry Gross, National Public Radio, 21 May 2002

283 "You have to understand" *et seq.*, Joe Smith, author interview, 27 November 2007

— "It wasn't like I was at a crossroads", Waits in Robert Hilburn, *Los Angeles Times*, 6 June 1999

284 "The idea of [. . .] doing your own record", Waits, radio interview with Terry Gross, National Public Radio, 21 May 2002

— "It was really Kathleen that said", Waits, author interview, 28 January 1999

— "It was like a big old California studio" *et seq.*, Stephen Hodges, author interview, 20 November 2007

285 "really co-produced that record", Waits, author interview, 28 January 1999

— "kind of plumbed more the depths of myself", Waits in George Varga, *San Diego Union Tribune*, 3 October 2004

286 "I broke every stick in my bag", Stephen Hodges, author interview, 20 November 2007

— "I was trying to find music", Waits, author interview, 28 January 1999

287 "He wore two different shoes", Waits, *Swordfishtrombones* promotional interview disc, 1983

— "I guess they're different facets", Waits, author interview, 28 January 1999

288 "[he] looked like he was strangling a goose", Waits in Brian Case, *Melody Maker*, 29 October 1983

— "When my wife heard that", Waits, *Swordfishtrombones* promotional interview disc, 1983

— "I was trying to bring the music outdoors" *et seq.*, Waits in Brian Case, *Melody Maker*, 29 October 1983

289 "I may have been telling some of that story", Waits in Mark Kemp, *Harp*, December 2006

— "Bukowski had a story", Waits in Brian Case, *Melody Maker*, 29 October 1983

— "a little bit of that American dream", Waits, *Swordfishtrombones* promotional interview disc, 1983

290 "Tom called me up", Carlos Guitarlos, author interview, 23 March 2007

— "Sometimes you go to a garage sale", Waits in Brian Case, *Melody Maker*, 29 October 1983

— "That fucking thing is off the hook" *et seq.*, Stephen Hodges, author interview, 20 November 2007

292 "He hated it", Waits in Mark Kemp, *Harp*, December 2006

— "I didn't have enough revenue", Joe Smith, author interview, 27 November 2007

— "They liked dropping my name", Waits in Kristine McKenna, *New Musical Express*, 1 October 1983

— "Amidst all the broken glass", Waits in Gavin Martin, *New Musical Express*, 19 October 1985

293 "I didn't know Tom's albums well" *et seq.*, Chris Blackwell, email, 1 December 2007

— "I'm happier to be on a small label", Waits in Gavin Martin, *New Musical Express*, 19 October 1985

294 "I think I was envious", Elvis Costello in Patrick Humphries, *Small Change: A Life of Tom Waits* (London: Omnibus Press, 1989), p. 165

— "I would rather be a failure on my own terms", Waits in Robert Elms, *The Face*, September 1983

— "I think the main contribution", Stephen Hodges, author interview, 20 November 2007

295 "The music on *Swordfish*", Carlos Guitarlos, author interview, 23 March 2007

— "the uncontrollable urge to play Iowa", Waits in Brian Case, *Melody Maker*, 29 October 1983

— "He said he needed a new image", Michael Andreas Russ in David Smay, *Swordfishtrombones* (New York: Continuum, 2008)

— "It's unbelievable how many people watch them", Waits in Kristine McKenna, *New Musical Express*, 1 October 1983

296 "I think Tom was fascinated", Bones Howe, author interview, 13 March 2007

297 "That was a good moment", Waits in Brian Case, *Melody Maker*, 29 October 1983

— "I had one line", Waits in David Sheff, *Rolling Stone*, October 1988

— "a red convertible going down the Pacific Coast Highway", Waits in Ian Walker, *Observer*, early 1984

— "In a sense I come from a family of runners", Waits in Mick Brown, *Word*, December 2006

298 "A lot of the problems", Waits in Kristine McKenna, *New Musical Express*, 1 October 1983

— "I think you can continue to write", Waits, *Swordfishtrombones* promotional interview disc, 1983

— "You mean like a farming community?," Waits, television interview, *Loose Talk*, 18 October 1983

— "I was in a tuxedo", Waits in David Sheff, *Rolling Stone*, October 1988

— "We used to talk all the time", Waits in Jonathan Valania, *Magnet*, November 2004

299 "I love the way things are", Waits, author interview, 24 April 1985

CHAPTER 2 WRECK COLLECTIONS

300 "This lady came up to me" *et seq.*, Waits, author interview, 24 April 1985

302 "I had one of the last meals with him" *et seq.*, Harvey Kubernik, author interview, 20 March 2007

303 "It was time to get professionally weird", Brendan Mullen, email, 22 May 2007

— "That's what we want here", Waits in Ian Walker, *Observer* magazine, early 1984

— "I was towed three or four times", Waits in Elissa von Poznak, *The Face*, November 1985

— "My wife says, 'Well, you yelled at the guy'", Waits in Kristine McKenna, *Los Angeles Times*, 20 October 1985

304 "There were tiny little rooms", Waits, radio interview, KFOG-FM, 5 October 2005

— "We'd go down there at night" *et seq.*, Tom Waits, author interview, 24 April 1985

— "I guess you could say I rose to the occasion", Waits in Robert Hilburn, *Los Angeles Times*, 6 June 1999

305 "This party was just a great party", John Lurie, interview, Toastmag.com, date unknown

— "I don't really much enjoy that kind of thing", Jim Jarmusch in Bill Forman, *New Musical Express*, 10 January 1987

— "One night Tom sat at the piano", Hal Willner, from liner notes to *Used Songs 1973–1980* (Rhino, 2001)

306 "I remember how excited I felt", Kate St John, author interview, 10 December 2007

— "I didn't really know that much", Waits, author interview, 28 January 1999

307 "take the classic jazz and blues love songs" *et seq.*, Marianne Faithfull with David Dalton, *Faithfull* (London: Penguin, 1995), p. 410

— "I don't write year round", Waits, author interview, 24 April 1985

— "kind of a rough area" *et seq.*, Pete Silverton, *Beat*, March 1986

308 "How that'll integrate itself", Waits, author interview, 24 April 1985

— "Any place you move", Waits, author interview, 28 January 1999

— "You drag these things home", Waits in Elissa von Poznak, *The Face*, November 1985

— "articulate, prose-poetic, boho anecdotes", Chris Roberts, email, 24 March 2008

— "Most of the stories", Waits, *Rain Dogs* promotional interview disc, 1985

309 "people who sleep in doorways", Waits, television interview, CBC Stereo (Canada), late 1985

— "hobos, prostitutes, people in trouble", Waits in Robert Sabbag, *Los Angeles Times*, 22 February 1987

— "try and get rid of this rucksack of bourgeois thinking", Anders Petersen in Sean O'Hagan, *Observer* Review, 1 October 2006

— "me and Liza Minnelli", Waits, radio interview, KCRW-FM, 1987

— "I'd never met Tom before", Ralph Carney, author interview, 3 May 2007

310 "He seemed like the frigging Pope of New York", Stephen Hodges, author interview, 20 November 2007

— "It's more rhythmic", Waits, author interview, 24 April 1985

— "He prepares his guitar with alligator clips", Waits in Bill Forman, *Music & Sound Output*, October 1987

311 "Tom told me he wanted to use instruments", Bill Schimmel, author interview, 12 December 2007

— "I got pushed into a lot of really uncomfortable positions", Stephen Hodges, author interview, 20 November 2007

— "On the last bar of the song", Waits, radio interview with Chris Douridas, KCRW-FM, 31 March 1998

— "I just tried to imagine all these [. . .] guys", Waits, television interview, CBC Stereo, late 1985

— "places that are downbeat", Waits in Gavin Martin, *New Musical Express*, 19 October 1985

312 "There are times when you totally disregard", Waits, author interview, 24 April 1985

— "Never talk about your family", Waits, television interview, CBC Stereo, late 1985

— "*Rain Dogs* wasn't only little mutant ensembles", Stephen Hodges, author interview, 20 November 2007

313 "He was a *huge* fan", Paul Body, author interview, 9 March 2007

— "Somebody said, 'Who do you want'", Waits in Sylvie Simmons, *Mojo*, October 2004

— "entirely shy" *et seq.*, Waits, television interview, CBC Stereo, late 1985

— "You really can't keep up", Waits in Sylvie Simmons, *Mojo*, October 2004

— "You know, you have a little glass of sherry", Waits in Pete Silverton, *YOU/Mail on Sunday*, October 1985

— "bleary-eyed, unshaven", Gavin Martin, *New Musical Express*, 19 October 1985

— "Keith came in on his own", Stephen Hodges, author interview, 20 November 2007

314 "There were two turning points", Steve Jordan, author interview, 10 March 1997

— "Kathleen was there all the time", Stephen Hodges, author interview, 20 November 2007

315 "quite heavily pregnant", Bill Schimmel, author interview, 12 December 2007

— "'Midtown' is . . . kind of what it's like" *et seq.*, Waits, *Rain Dogs* promotional interview disc, 1985

317 "That's kind of a pop song", Waits, television interview, CBC Stereo, late 1985

— "I liked *our* versions of 'Downtown Train'", Stephen Hodges, author interview, 20 November 2007

— "Guys take that real serious", Paul Body, author interview, 9 March 2007

— "gonna work on Maggie's farm no more", Waits in Chris Roberts, *Sounds*, 19 October 1985

— "I like things that are unfinished", Waits in Bill Flanagan, *Written in My Soul* (London: Omnibus, 1990), p. 390

318 "That's when I met all those guys" *et seq.*, Ralph Carney, author interview, 3 May 2007

319 "gets himself whipped up", Waits in Jim Jarmusch, *Straight No Chaser*, Spring 1993

— "On that first tour" *et seq.*, Ralph Carney, author interview, 3 May 2007

— "They're more attuned to the stuff", Waits in Gavin Martin, *New Musical Express*, 19 October 1985

320 "There'd be moments where you weren't ready", Ralph Carney, author interview, 3 May 2007

— "We had band uniforms", Waits on stage in Zwolle, Holland, 7 November 1985

— "That's just sort of what stuck out", Stephen Hodges, author interview, 20 November 2007

— "The first tour was really brilliant", Marc Ribot in Sylvie Simmons, *Mojo*, April 1999

321 "When Tom came out" *et seq.*, Stephen Hodges, author interview, 20 November 2007

— "Tom and I have a kindred aesthetic", Jim Jarmusch in Brian Case, *Time Out*, 11–18 November 1987

323 "faceless nomads" *et seq.*, Waits/Jarmusch in Bill Forman, *Music & Sound Output*, October 1987

— "He didn't like being portrayed", Waits, radio interview with Dierdre O'Donoghue, KCRW-FAM, August 1987

324 "Benigni is filled with hope", Waits in Bill Forman, *New Musical Express*, 10 January 1987

— "[He] worked in a very precise way", Jim Jarmusch, Cannes press conference, DVD Extras, *Down by Law*, 2002

— "Mostly I just tried to relax", Waits in Bill Forman, *Music & Sound Output*, October 1987

— "You feel like a candle" *et seq.*, Waits, taped phone conversation, DVD Extras, *Down by Law*, 2002

325 "somebody who's very tough", Jim Jarmusch in Bill Forman, *New Musical Express*, 10 January 1987

— "[He] said, 'Look, it's not your film'", Jim Jarmusch in Laura Barton, *Guardian*, 9 June 2006

— "Thanks for giving me a chance", Waits, taped phone conversation, DVD Extras, *Down by Law*, 2002

CHAPTER 3 SOMETHING FOR ALL THE FAMILY

326 "story about failed dreams . . ." *et seq.*, Waits, author interview, 24 April 1985

328   "Most people don't want you", Waits in Patrick Goldstein, *Los Angeles Times*, 30 March 1986

—   "We really landed in the right place", Waits, radio interview with Dierdre O'Donoghue, KCRW-FM, 24 August 1987

—   "We had an elaborate rehearsal process" *et seq.*, Bill Schimmel, author interview, 12 December 2007

330   "You have to be a little foolish", Waits, author interview, 28 January 1999

—   "Gary has been great", Waits, radio interview, WXRT-FM Chicago, 11 July 1986

—   "Tom was terrific in it", Bill Goodwin, author interview, 19 June 2007

—   "The play, nearly three hours in length", Moira McCormick, *Rolling Stone*, 28 August 1986

—   "the writing is not sure enough", John Rockwell, *New York Times*, 10 July 1986

331   "I just didn't have the time", Waits in Lynn Van Matre, *Chicago Tribune*, 18 October 1987

—   "Once the play was over", Ralph Carney, author interview, 3 May 2007

—   "In the stage play", Waits, radio interview with Dierdre O'Donoghue, KCRW-FM, 24 August 1987

332   "Tom knew that a record is a record", Bill Schimmel, author interview, 12 December 2007

—   "He'd try things like giving me a marimba", Ralph Carney, author interview, 3 May 2007

—   "You never knew who was playing drums" *et seq.*, Bill Schimmel, author interview, 12 December 2007

333   "[Frank] dreams his way back home", Waits, radio interview with Dierdre O'Donoghue, KCRW-FM, 24 August 1987

334   "It was the right percussive sound", Bill Schimmel, author interview, 12 December 2007

—   "I think it moves along rather well", Waits in Rip Rense, *Frank's Wild Years* tourbook, 1987

—   "get my voice to sound", Waits, radio interview with Dierdre O'Donoghue, KCRW-FM, 24 August 1987

—   "I loved Kirk", Ralph Carney, author interview, 3 May 2007

335   "You always work on your voice", Waits in Mark Rowland, *Musician*, October 1987

—   "That one started out real tame" *et seq.*, Waits in Rip Rense, *Frank's Wild Years* tourbook, 1987

336   "He plugged me into a Leslie Twin-Cat", Bill Schimmel, author interview, 12 December 2007

337   "We wrote that one real fast", Waits in Rip Rense, *Frank's Wild Years* tourbook, 1987

—   "The guy was probably in his late fifties", Ralph Carney, email, 8 January 2008

—   "Waits was definitely anti-jazz", Ralph Carney, author interview, 3 May 2007

—   "It's a secret dream to work the big rooms" *et seq.*, Waits in Rip Rense, *Frank's Wild Years* tourbook, 1987

338   "I'm looking toward that part of music", Waits in Steve Oney, *Playboy*, March 1988

—   "[It's] kind of a gospel number" *et seq.*, Waits in Rip Rense, *Frank's Wild Years* tourbook, 1987

339   "[These] are really songs *about* performance", Barney Hoskyns, *New Musical Express*, August 1987

—   "to write and record and play different characters", Waits in Rip Rense, *Frank's Wild Years* tourbook, 1987

340   "I think he changed the face of photography", Waits in Steve Dollar, *Film Threat*, 1989

—   "He takes a really romantic position", Rudy Wurlitzer in Liz Jobey, *Independent on Sunday*, 29 March 1992

341   "It's an odyssey", Waits in Pete Silverton, *Beat*, March 1986

—   "That guy stole my act!", story from Sue Compo, biographer of Warren Oates

342   "Robert sabotages himself", Rudy Wurlitzer in Liz Jobey, *Independent on Sunday*, 29 March 1992

—   "It's all about [. . .] alcohol, baptism, and redemption", Waits, radio interview with Dierdre O'Donoghue, KCRW-FM, 24 August 1987

—   "a collective soul, anonymous vagabonds", Waits in Patrick Humphries, *The Many Lives of Tom Waits* (London: Omnibus, 2007), p. 191

343   "The character for me was more like a little kid", Waits, television interview, *Rapido* (BBC), 31 October 1988

—   "He looked like any moment he might break", Jack Nicholson in Patrick Humphries, *The Many Lives of Tom Waits* (London, Omnibus, 2007), p. 193

—   "a dark horse", Waits in Charles Champlin, *Los Angeles Times*, 14 January 1988

344   "I have somebody that helps me out", Waits in Bill Forman, *Music & Sound Output*, October 1987

—   "Jack makes you look good", Waits in Charles Champlin, *Los Angeles Times*, 14 January 1988

—   "preparation and commitment and concentration", Waits in Francis Thumm, *Interview*, October 1988

—   "like they build a doll", Waits in Steve Oney, *Playboy*, March 1988

—   "People get frightened" *et seq.*, Waits in Charles Champlin, *Los Angeles Times*, 14 January 1988

345   "forced to drink against my will", Waits, radio interview with Dierdre O'Donoghue, KCRW-FM, 24 August 1987

—   "I think any artist who knows himself", Bill Schimmel, author interview, 12 December 2007

—   "I wasn't well-suited", Waits in Amanda Petrusich, Pitchfork.com, 27 November 2006

—   "I was blurting out obscenities", Waits in Steve Oney, *Playboy*, March 1988

—   "treated better", Waits, *Late Night with David Letterman* (NBC), 5 October 1988

—   "I think Tom had got New York out of his system", Bill Schimmel, author interview, 12 December 2007

346   "I'm more interested in these types of things", Waits in Robert Sabbag, *Los Angeles Times*, 22 February 1987

—   "The music down there was never an event", Waits in Francis Thumm, *Interview*, October 1988

—   "I'm beginning to create a world", Waits in Bill Forman, *Music & Sound Output*, October 1987

347   "Am I still a drunk?", Waits in Sean O'Hagan, *New Musical Express*, 14 November 1987

—   "He'd just moved house", Sean O'Hagan, email, 19 March 2008

—   "a certain gypsy quality" *et seq.*, Waits in Mark Rowland, *Musician*, October 1987

—   "briar patch" *et seq.*, Waits in Robert Sabbag, *Los Angeles Times*, 22 February 1987

—   "I'd get home from the road", Waits, *Big Time* press kit, September 1988

348   "I've been asked all these things before", Waits in Bill Holdship, *Creem*, January 1988

—   "I see the way a lot of people talk", Waits in Robert Sabbag, *Los Angeles Times*, 22 February 1987

—   "Usually you hide what everything represents", Waits in Bill Forman, *Music & Sound Output*, October 1987

—   "Here I have a lot of people", Waits in Bill Holdship, *Creem*, January 1988

349   "very unself-conscious", Waits in Mark Rowland, *Musician*, October 1987

—   "angry" *et seq.*, Waits in Sean O'Hagan, *New Musical Express*, 14 November 1987

— "Keith Richards had an expression for it", Waits in Mark Rowland, *Musician*, October 1987

— "try and do something with a much harder edge", Waits in Bill Forman, *Music & Sound Output*, October 1987

— "I get angry about some of the things I see", Waits in Sean O'Hagan, *New Musical Express*, 14 November 1987

— "a lot of this rap stuff" *et seq.*, Waits in Mikel Jollett, *SOMA*, July 2002

350 "more like dreams themselves", Waits in Steve Pond, *Rolling Stone*, 26 January 1989

— "It was definitely an evening", k.d. lang, author interview, 1 October 1998

— "I'm trying to put together the right way", Waits in Mark Rowland, *Musician*, October 1987

351 "The original stage set" *et seq.*, Chris Blum in *Big Time* press kit, September 1988

352 "We did it in only two nights", Waits in Francis Thumm, *Interview*, October 1988

353 "It's difficult to retain", Waits in Jonh Wilde, *Sounds*, quoted in Patrick Humphries, *The Many Lives of Tom Waits* (London: Omnibus, 2007), p. 200

— "Even when it's great", Waits in Francis Thumm, *Interview*, October 1988

— "the kind of thing I'm working on", Waits in Bill Holdship, *Creem*, January 1988

CHAPTER 4 IN A SUIT WHEN YOU DREAM

355 "I was down on my luck", Waits in Patrick Humphries, *The Many Lives of Tom Waits* (London: Omnibus, 2007), p. 205

— "As Dog travels through the envied and often tempting world", Aisha Film Company, 1981

356 "You know, when a guy is singing", Waits in Mark Rowland, *Musician*, October 1987

— "Songs carry emotional information", Waits, letter, *The Nation*, 19 September 2002

— "another corporate fucking shill", Bill Hicks, *Arizona Bay* (Rykodisc), 1997

357 "go out on the road" *et seq.*, Waits, radio interview, WNEW-FM (New York), October 1988

— "We sawed the floorboards out", Waits, *Mule Variations* promo interview, April 1999

358 "I've known Chuck for about a hundred years", Waits, radio interview, KCRW-FM (Los Angeles), 3 October 1988

— "Movies are done in such small segments", Waits in Patrick Humphries, *The Many Lives of Tom Waits* (London: Omnibus, 2007), p. 189

359 "Waits' advantage is that he's a character actor", Christopher Connelly in Tim Powis, *Graffiti*, 1 December 1988

360 "This is the best summer" *et seq.*, Waits in Francis Thumm, *Interview*, October 1988

— "They've always lived simply" *et seq.*, Chris Blackwell, email, 1 December 2007

— "She's great in emergencies" *et seq.*, Waits in Francis Thumm, *Interview*, October 1988

361 "I feel a little intimidated" *et seq.*, Waits in Tim Powis, *Graffiti*, 1 December 1988

362 "Being awkward and shy", Robert Wilson, *Absolute Wilson* documentary, 2006

363 "almost impossible to describe", *New Yorker*, 27 March 1971

— "It was not coming out of what the popular theatre was", Robert Wilson, *Woyzeck* promotional interview, November 2000

364 "[*Einstein*] was real long", Waits in Francis Thumm, *Interview*, October 1988

— "Tom and I are very different men", Robert Wilson in Robert Palmer, *New York Times*, 16 November 1993

— "When I met him", Waits in Gavin Martin, *Uncut*, June 2002

— "America's greatest minimalist" *et seq.*, Paul Schmidt, television interview, *The Late Show* (BBC), 4 March 1993

— "What I like about Robert", Waits in Francis Thumm, *Interview*, October 1988

365 "I read this strange story in a library" *et seq.*, Robert Wilson and Tom Waits, *Woyzeck* promotional interview, November 2000

— "He was the [Beat writer]", Waits, author interview, 28 January 1999

366 "like the crooked sheriff in a bad town", Waits in Stuart Derdeyn, *The Vancouver Province*, 21 November 2006

— "It was very exciting", Waits, author interview, 28 January 1999

— "When Tom was here in Lawrence", William Burroughs in Robert Palmer, *New York Times*, 16 November 1993

— "piles of material" *et seq.*, Waits in Paul Hodgins, *Orange County Register,* 26 April 2006

— "the rainy streets" *et seq.*, Tom Waits, sleevenotes, *The Black Rider* (Island Records), 1993

367 "Sailors from all over the world", Waits in Robert Palmer, *New York Times*, 16 November 1993

— "For me, in all my years in school", Waits in Tom Lanham, *Paste*, December 2004

— "Somehow he touched me", Robert Wilson, *Woyzeck* promotional interview, November 2000

368 "became a river of words" *et seq.*, Waits, sleevenotes, *The Black Rider* (Island Records), 1993

— "[Greg] uses oboe, bass clarinet", Waits in Francis Thumm, *Interview*, October 1988

369 "We were trying", Waits, sleevenotes, *The Black Rider* (Island Records), 1993

— "I think that was a great test for Tom", Robert Wilson in Peter Laugesen, *Independent*, 19 November 2000

— "fearless, tireless, insane", Waits, sleevenotes, *The Black Rider* (Island Records), 1993

— "It was like, '[Bob's] using these people'", Waits in Robert Palmer, *New York Times*, 16 November 1993

370 "It was all part of inhabiting a persona", Charlie Gillett in John Lewis, *Uncut*, April 2008

— "[Tom] was a friend of [Jeff's]", Terry Gilliam in Phil Stubbs, *Dreams: The Terry Gilliam Fanzine*, December 1997

372 "I told [Francis] I was Renfield", Waits, television interview, Muchmusic (Canada), October 1992

— "a masochist's nirvana" *et seq.*, Waits in Rip Rense, *Image*, 13 December 1992

— "your own dark rooms", Waits in Mark Rowland, *Musician*, October 1987

— "It was great to be in that environment", Keanu Reeves, *Premiere*, February 2005

— "shy and brooding" *et seq.*, Sadie Frost, author interview, 28 February 2008

373 "It was like we hadn't seen each other", Bones Howe, author interview, 13 March 2007

374 "Altman was great to work with", Waits, radio interview with Chris Douridas, KCRW-FM, 12 October 1992

— "Tom is unique", Robert Altman in Mick Brown, *Telegraph* magazine, 11 April 1999

375 "I don't really consider myself", Waits in Robert Palmer, *New York Times*, 16 November 1993

— "I don't know if I really think of myself", Waits, author interview, 28 January 1999

— "I find myself usually having more in common", Waits in Jim Jarmusch, *Straight No Chaser*, Spring 1993

— "Somebody told me acting", Waits, radio interview with Chris Douridas, KCRW-FM, 12 October 1992

CHAPTER 5 BONES, CEMETERIES, AND DIRTY BLOOD

377 "Hey, can I drop you somewhere?", story from *Rolling Stone Raves*, compiled by Anthony Bozza (New York: Rolling Stone/Quill), 1999

378 "It's most disappointing", Rod Stewart in John Smyntek, *Detroit Free Press*, 30 July 1995

— "Tom's brilliant", Rod Stewart in Patrick Humphries, *The Many Lives of Tom Waits* (London: Omnibus, 2007), p. 222

— "I spent it all on candy", Waits in Karen Schoemer, *Newsweek*, 23 April 1999

— "Never get involved in litigation", Waits in Pete Silverton, *Vox*, October 1992

379 "My early records", Waits in Peter Orr, *Reflex*, 6 October 1992

— "We did a little kind of word duet", Waits in Jim Jarmusch, *Straight No Chaser*, Spring 1993

— "[Tom is] America's best lyricist since Johnny Mercer", Teddy Edwards, http://www.tonyspage.com/index.htm

380 "I was over at Bodega Bay", Waits in Tim Perlich, *Now*, 22–28 April 1999

— "It just seemed a good place to go", Waits in Robert Lloyd, *LA Weekly*, 23 April 1999

— "Now I live out", Waits, radio interview with Chris Douridas, KCRW-FM, 12 October 1992

381 "an unplugged appliance" *et seq.*, Waits in Melora Koepke, *Ottawa Xpress*, 7 October 2004

— "Tom lives with his family", Jim Jarmusch, *Straight No Chaser*, Spring 1993

— "Are you a cop?", Waits in Michael Barclay, *Exclaim*, April–May 1999

— "My wife said, 'You drank enough'", Waits in Mick Brown, *Word*, December 2006

382 "Some day you just have to quit", Waits in Michael Fuchs-Gambock, *Rock World*, October 1992

— "I'm in the program", Waits in Sean O'Hagan, *Observer*, 29 October 2006

— "Because I utterly adore my wife and kids", Waits in Michael Fuchs-Gambock, *Rock World*, October 1992

— "no more sombre enemy of good art", Cyril Connolly, *Enemies of Promise* (London: Routledge and Kegan Paul), 1938

— "all the big questions", Waits in Sean O'Hagan, *Observer*, 29 October 2006

— "I never got along with myself" *et seq.*, Waits in Peter Orr, *Reflex*, 6 October 1992

383 "I like things that are kind of falling apart", Waits in Derk Richardson, *PULSE!*, September 1992

384 "There were a couple of things", Ralph Carney, author interview, 3 May 2007

— "It was a fairly egalitarian situation" *et seq.*, Clark Suprynowicz, author interview, 7 February 2008

386 "Blood and death", Waits in Michael Fuchs-Gambock, *Rock World*, October 1992

— "[We] went into a room", Waits in Derk Richardson, *PULSE!*, September 1992

— "I said, 'What about this room'", Waits, radio interview with Chris Douridas, KCRW-FM, 12 October 1992

— "We had airplanes to deal with", Waits in Peter Orr, *Reflex*, 6 October 1992

387 "You can go crazy", Waits in Bill Dolan, *Village Noize*, early 1993

— "I wanted to explore" *et seq.*, Waits in Derk Richardson, *PULSE!*, September 1992

388 "Everybody hates it but me", Waits, television interview, *Gente de Expressão* (Brazil), 1992

— "I thought I was going to be", Ralph Carney, author interview, 3 May 2007

— "I just thought, 'Oh God'", Waits in Mark Rowland, *Musician*, January 1993

— "[Teddy] used to tell girls" *et seq.*, Waits, *Bone Machine* Operator's Manual, 30 November 1992

389 "What I like to try and do", Waits in Derk Richardson, *PULSE!*, September 1992

391 "go back and forth" *et seq.*, Waits in Peter Orr, *Reflex*, 6 October 1992

392 "this golden image", Waits, *Bone Machine* Operator's Manual, 30 November 1992

— "I buy the local papers", Waits, author interview, 28 January 1999

393 "I like that place with my voice" *et seq.*, Waits, *Bone Machine* Operator's Manual, 30 November 1992

394 "Everybody wants to grow up", Waits in Peter Orr, *Reflex*, 6 October 1992

— "put it through a Marshall" *et seq.*, Waits, *Bone Machine* Operator's Manual, 30 November 1992

395 "It wasn't *for* anything", Keith Richards in Ira Robbins, *PULSE!*, November 1992

— "kind of mellow", Waddy Wachtel, email, 10 February 2008

— "You can't drink with [Keith]" *et seq.*, Waits, *Bone Machine* Operator's Manual, 30 November 1992

— "She said it sounds so degrading", Waits, television interview, Telerama (France), 9 September 1992

— "He was staying at a chic hotel", Pete Silverton, email, 4 June 2008

396 "A lot of people seem to have bought one record", Waits in Mark Rowland, *Musician*, January 1993

— "You said this was going to be funny", quoted in Danny Plotnick, *Village Noize*, 1994

398 "Tom had a lot of different horn players", Ralph Carney, author interview, 3 May 2007

— "going out to the meadow" *et seq.*, Jim Jarmusch, *Straight No Chaser*, Spring 1993

402 "[Island] didn't do much with it", Waits in Andrew Dansby, *Rolling Stone*, 4 November 2000

— "I remember I had the same feeling", Kate St John, author interview, 10 December 2007

— "Make hay while the sun shines", Waits in Jim Jarmusch, *Straight No Chaser*, Spring 1993

403 "sighted giant" *et seq.*, Waits, television interview, *The Late Show* (BBC), 4 March 1993

— "I'm still not packed", Waits in Rip Rense, *Image*, 13 December 1992

404 "It was a pretty fraught time for Tom" *et seq.*, Mark Cooper in Paul Gorman, *Mojo*, October 1999

— "We're very different men" *et seq.*, Robert Wilson, television interview, *The Late Show* (BBC), 4 March 1993

— "Once you go down the rabbit hole" *et seq.*, Waits in Rip Rense, *Image*, 13 December 1992

405 "It seemed to me it was kind of a natural connection", Paul Schmidt, *The Late Show* (BBC TV), 4 March 1993

— "Obviously I'm making light of something", Waits in Michael Barclay, *Exclaim*, April–May 1999

— "adult songs for children" *et seq.*, Waits, *Alice* press release (Anti Records), 2002

407 "Not a lot of money", Waits in Margaret Moser, *Austin Chronicle*, 10–16 May 2002

— "Sometimes when I think about touring", Waits in Adam Sweeting, *Guardian*, 15 September 1992

CHAPTER 6 THE CROOKED TREE AND THE STRAIGHT TREE

408 "I got this new hobby" *et seq.*, Waits, author interview, 28 January 1999

410 "but I can tell you I didn't fabricate it", Robert Christgau, email, 1 April 2008

— "It sounds like a loaded question", Waits, author interview, 28 January 1999

411 "toughest thing", Waits in Gil Kaufman and Michael Goldberg, *Addicted to Noise*, April 1999

— "I wanted to pull myself out of the limelight", Waits in Robert Hilburn, *Los Angeles Times*, 6 June 1999

412 "When I was eighteen years old working in a warehouse", Dave Alvin, sleevenotes, *Step Right Up* (Manifesto Records), 1995

— "He sits at the mixing board", Mark Richard, *Spin*, June 1993

— "Hey dad, your pants are halfway down around your knees" *et seq.*, Waits in *Buzz*, May 1993

413 "Although he died before he could hear", Gavin Bryars, www.gavinbryars.com

— "[All] of a sudden this song", Waits, radio interview with Johnnie Walker (BBC Radio 1), 11 September 1993

— "probably one of the most sublime experiences", Waits in David Smay, *Swordfishtrombones* (New York: Continuum, 2008), p. 26

414 "I'm not sure what happened" *et seq.*, Waits, Foreword to Bart Hopkin, *Gravikords, Whirlies & Pyrophones* (Ellipsis Arts, 1996)

416 "Tom was always trying to get me to go into the studio", Chuck E. Weiss in Kevin Matthews, *The Manitoban*, 27 January 1999

— "It was really a labor of love", Waits in Jon Bream, *Minneapolis Star Tribune*, 27 August 1999

417 "[Tom] was really a mentor", Chuck E. Weiss in Marc Weingarten, *Los Angeles Times*, 27 January 2002

— "Tom's contract expired", Chris Blackwell, email, 1 December 2007

— "We're writing it now", Waits, radio interview with Chris Douridas, KCRW-FM, 31 March 1998

418 "Tom's someone I see at the airport", Beck, author interview, 19 January 1997

— "I like him very much", Waits, author interview, 28 January 1999

419 "We call it *surrural*", Waits to Rip Rense, Anti Records promotional interview, reprinted in *Performing Songwriter*, July–August 1999

— "She writes down in journals", Waits, radio interview with Chris Douridas, KCRW-FM, 31 March 1998

— "If it's right for it", Waits in Gil Kaufman and Michael Goldberg, *Addicted to Noise*, April 1999

420 "There's this little room", Smokey Hormel in Karen Schoemer, *Newsweek*, 23 April 1999

— "Nearly all the people that were on *Swordfish*" *et seq.*, Stephen Hodges, author interview, 20 November 2007

421 "We were usually tracking him", Jacquire King in Paul Tingen, Audiomedia.com, February 2000

422 "married a mule", Waits in Rip Rense, Anti Records promotional interview, reprinted in *Performing Songwriter*, July–August 1999

— "There've been plenty of days", Waits in James Sullivan, *San Francisco Chronicle*, 18 April 1999

423 "They're just folks", Waits in Gil Kaufman and Michael Goldberg, *Addicted to Noise*, April 1999

— "this stuff is all over the place", Waits in Brett Martin, *Time Out New York*, 22–29 April 1999

424 "They're really stories", Waits in Jim Jarmusch, *Straight No Chaser*, Spring 1993

— "We seem to be compelled", Waits, author interview, 28 January 1999

425 "the need to stare and ask questions", Mat Fraser, *Guardian*, 15 February 2008

426 "We were always going for a mood", Jacquire King in Paul Tingen, Audiomedia.com, February 2000

— "He's great", Waits in Bret Kofford, *Blues Revue*, July–August 2000

— "Someone might think it's blasphemous", Waits in Rip Rense, Anti Records promotional interview, reprinted in *Performing Songwriter*, July–August 1999

427 "Thanks a lot", Waits in Michael Barclay, *Exclaim*, April–May 1999

— "We checked into a hotel room", Waits in Rip Rense, Anti Records promotional interview, reprinted in *Performing Songwriter*, July–August 1999

— "Maybe I feel more at peace with myself", Waits in Robert Hilburn, *Los Angeles Times*, 6 June 1999

— "back and forth", Waits in David Fricke, *Rolling Stone*, 24 June 1999

— "the grand weeper", James Sullivan, *San Francisco Chronicle*, 18 April 1999

— "two dogs fighting all the time", Waits in Jon Bream, Minneapolis *Star Tribune*, 27 August 1999

429 "I thought it was a really good record", Bones Howe, author interview, 13 March 2007

— "They're pro-artist", Waits in Rip Rense, Anti Records promotional interview, reprinted in *Performing Songwriter*, July–August 1999

— "We'd already started writing", Waits, author interview, 28 January 1999

430 "I don't know why I agreed", Waits in Jonathan Valania, *Magnet*, June–July 1999

— "I get requests", Waits in Jody Denberg, *Mule Conversations* promotional interview, 26 February 1999

431 "Stu told [Tom] I knew vocal exercises", Warren Zevon in Crystal Zevon, *I'll Sleep When I'm Dead: The Dirty Life and Times of Warren Zevon* (New York: Ecco, 2007), pp. 361–2

432 "You use the word 'I'", Waits in Robert Wilonsky, *Dallas Observer*, 6 May 1999

— "I guess it's a question", Waits in Robert Hilburn, *Los Angeles Times*, 6 June 1999

433 "I really want to create a stage environment" *et seq.*, Waits in Jim Jarmusch, *Straight No Chaser*, Spring 1993

— "Everyone was like, 'Let's tour'", Ralph Carney, author interview, 3 May 2007

434 "To the postboomer generation", Karen Schoemer, *Newsweek*, 23 April 1999

— "I always start at the wrong end" *et seq.*, Waits, author interview, 28 January 1999

CHAPTER 7 RUST NEVER SLEEPS

435 "That's not a bad thing to be called", Waits in Bret Kofford, *Blues Revue*, July–August 2000

436 "John's particular dialect", Waits, www.rosebudus.com/hammond/ WickedGrin

— "[Hammond] asked me to produce the record", Waits in Bret Kofford, *Blues Revue*, July–August 2000

— "Tom played guitar a lot better", Stephen Hodges, author interview, 20 November 2007

437 "the most evocative, imagistic" *et seq.*, John Hammond, www.rosebudus.com/hammond/WickedGrin

438 "It's a story that continues to surface", Waits in Edna Gundersen, *USA Today*, 17 June 2002

— "a proletariat story", Waits, promotional video interview for *Woyzeck*, 2000

439 "It's much more contemporary", Robert Wilson in Peter Laugesen, *Independent*, 19 November 2000

— "I must have recognized aspects", Waits in Gavin Martin, *Uncut*, June 2002

— "for a sober person like myself", Waits in Andrew Dansby, *Rolling Stone*, 4 November 2000

— "[It] is not important", Robert Wilson in Peter Laugesen, *Independent*, 19 November 2000

440 "kind of like being an astronaut", Waits in Andrew Dansby, *Rolling Stone*, 4 November 2000

— "You really have to give it away", Waits, promotional video interview for *Woyzeck*, 2000

— "He was really, really interesting", Kate St John, author interview, 10 December 2007

441 "A week before they open", Waits in Edna Gundersen, *USA Today*, 17 June 2002

— "Any regular at Sebastopol's", John Beck, *Press Democrat*, 18 April 1999

442 "We were going to call [it] *Woyzeck*", Waits in Gavin Martin, *Uncut*, June 2002

— "It's like giving away a box of clothes", Waits in James Nicholas Joyce, *Inpress*, 1 May 2002

— "The reason no one does two records", Waits in Terry Gilliam, *Black Book*, June 2002

— "been in the foxhole all day" *et seq.*, Waits in Elizabeth Gilbert, *GQ*, June 2002

443 "If you grow up in the mortuary business", Waits in Nigel Williamson, *Sydney Morning Herald*, 27 April 2002

— "He explained that he needed", Ralph Carney, author interview, 3 May 2007

— "Most of the musicians drove up", Waits in Terry Gilliam, *Black Book*, June 2002

444 "The electric guitar thing", Waits in Ross Fortune, *Time Out*, 24 April 2002

— "I guess *Alice* is probably more metaphysical" *et seq.*, Waits in Terry Gilliam, *Black Book*, June 2002

445 "It's like a private moment", Waits, radio interview with Terry Gross, National Public Radio, 21 May 2002

— "That's the Humpty Dumpty situation", Waits in Carl Wilson, Toronto *Globe and Mail*, 7 May 2002

446 "I'm imagining a whole Victorian atmosphere", Waits in Edna Gundersen, *USA Today*, 17 June 2002

— "always waltzing", Waits, electronic press kit for *Alice/Blood Money* (Anti Records), December 2002

447 "I have no trouble", Waits in Jon Bream, *Minneapolis Star Tribune*, 5 May 2002

— "I run hot and cold", Waits in Jon Pareles, *New York Times*, 5 May 2002

448 "It's a circus story", Waits in Peter Laugesen, promotional interview for *Woyzeck*, November 2000.

449 "I like beautiful melodies", Waits in Rob Brunner, *Entertainment Weekly*, 21 June 2002

450 "It took four guys", Waits in Carl Wilson, *Toronto Globe and Mail*, 7 May 2002

— "probably the most visceral", Waits in Elizabeth Gilbert, *GQ*, June 2002

— "I can't listen to the old stuff", Waits in Bret Kofford, *Blues Revue*, July–August 2000

— "There was a track", Bones Howe, author interview, 13 March 2007

451 "I'm thinking it's not going to hurt Waits", Michael Hacker, author interview, 17 March 2007

— "I think Tom's leery of people", Ralph Carney, author interview, 3 May 2007

452 "maybe not an area", Stephen Hodges, author interview, 20 November 2007

— "I would love to be able" *et seq.*, Bones Howe, author interview, 13 March 2007

— "giving Kathleen so much credit", Michael Hacker, author interview, 17 March 2007

453 "She hates all this", Waits in Gavin Martin, *Uncut*, June 2002

— "Everybody wants it to be summer", Waits in Jon Pareles, *New York Times*, 5 May 2002

— "Kathleen was always there", Kate St John, author interview, 10 December 2007

— "I don't think any of us are sick", Waits in Dan Cohen, *Chico News and Review*, 7 May 2002

— "As you start getting older", Waits, *The Onion*, 29 May 2002

454 "We love [Casey]", Russell Bongard, *Big Brother Skateboarding*, July 2002

— "I'm down with the field trips", Waits in Elizabeth Gilbert, *GQ*, June 2002

— "ball games, graduations" *et seq.*, Waits in Sylvie Simmons, *Mojo*, October 2004

— "Perhaps the most singular feature" *et seq.*, Elizabeth Gilbert, *GQ*, June 2002

455 "If people are a little nervous", Waits, *The Onion*, 29 May 2002

— "well of characters" *et seq.*, Patrick Donovan, *The Age*, 10 May 2002

456 "The record companies are like cartels", Waits in Edna Gundersen, *USA Today*, 16 September 2002

— "In the old days", Waits, *The Onion*, 29 May 2002

— "secular and compartmentalized", Waits in Edna Gundersen, *USA Today*, 17 June 2002

— "Everyone is really afraid", Waits in Dan Cohen, *Chico News and Review*, 7 May 2002

457 "on fire" *et seq.*, Waits in Edna Gundersen, *USA Today*, 17 June 2002

— "It's not the life I want", Waits in Nigel Williamson, *Sydney Morning Herald*, 27 April 2002

— "When you sing", Waits in Gavin Martin, *Uncut*, June 2002

— "I try not to let any of it go to my head", Waits in Carl Wilson, Toronto *Globe and Mail*, 7 May 2002

— "a little bit of a gimmick", Waits in Nigel Williamson, *Sydney Morning Herald*, 27 April 2002

458 "Those last albums were more meticulous", Waits in Richard Cromelin, *Los Angeles Times*, 26 September 2004

— "I guess I'd like to try and find", Waits, author interview, 28 January 1999

— "I'm not a politician" *et seq.*, Waits, author interview, 3 September 2004

459 "It's the growing edge of the blues", Waits in George Varga, *San Diego Union Tribune*, 3 October 2004

— "All that stuff gets played", Waits in Joel Selvin, *San Francisco Chronicle*, 3 October 2004

— "I keep wanting to use turntables", Waits in Ross Fortune, *Time Out*, 24 April 2002

— "I like to use my voice", Waits in James Nicholas Joyce, *Inpress*, 1 May 2002

— "sweating, eyes all bugged out", Waits in Sylvie Simmons, *Mojo*, October 2004

460 "Loops start feeling like wallpaper" *et seq.*, Waits, author interview, 3 September 2004

— "What happened this time", Waits in Tom Moon, *Harp*, November–December 2004

— "I don't know why", Waits, author interview, 3 September 2004

461 "It wasn't really a conscious thing", Waits in Sylvie Simmons, *Mojo*, October 2004

— "I think there's a pretty heavy emphasis", Waits in Vit Wagner, *Toronto Star*, 5 October 2004

462 "I wouldn't put it past [Waits]", Robert Christgau, *Tom Waits under Review, 1983–2006* (Chrome Dreams DVD), 2007

463 "cubist funk" *et seq.*, Waits in Richard Grant, *Telegraph* magazine, 2 October 2004

— "Everybody wants to run away", Waits in Bernard Zuel, *Sydney Morning Herald*, 30 October 2004

— "looped from the radio" *et seq.*, Waits, *Toronto Globe and Mail*, 4 October 2004

464 "The government looks at", Waits in Richard Grant, *Telegraph* magazine, 2 October 2004

— "I saw Tom do the song", Bones Howe, author interview, 13 March 2007

465 "With the God stuff", Waits in Eben Sterling, *Thrasher*, 1 November 2004

CHAPTER 8 HE'S NOT THERE

469 "It doesn't take much", Waits in Jonathan Valania, *Magnet*, November 2004

470 "I used to have it right there", Waits in Richard Grant, *Telegraph* magazine, 2 October 2004

471 "They won me in a poker game", Waits in James Wray, MonstersandCritics.com, 17 December 2004

— "With acting", Waits in Amanda Petrusich, Pitchfork.com, 27 November 2006

472 "I am the Devil", Waits, Anti.com, 20 May 2008

— "songs that fell behind the stove", Waits in Katherine Turman, *Stop Smiling*, 27 October 2006

— "A plumber! In Russia!" *et seq.*, Waits in Mick Brown, *Word*, December 2006

473 "no reason you can't do a Sinatra song", Waits in John Soeder, *Cleveland Plain Dealer*, 19 November 2006

— "Orphans are rough and tender tunes", Waits, *Orphans* press release, 16 August 2006

— "battlefield medic" *et seq.*, Waits, Anti.com, 20 May 2008

474 "[The] article [was] about a young Palestinian", Waits in Tim Perlich, *Now*, 16–22 November 2006

— "This song ain't about taking sides", Waits in Sean O'Hagan, *Observer*, 29 October 2006

475 "fell right out of the paper", Waits in Greg Kot, *Chicago Tribune*, 21 November 2006

— "You wouldn't ask Ronald Reagan", Waits in Ian Walker, *Observer*, early 1984

— "When we heard the demos", Arliss Howard, Anti.com, 20 May 2008

476 "I always felt like I connected with him", Waits, Anti.com, 20 May 2008

477 "I was like, 'That's it'", Waits, radio interview with Terry Gross, National Public Radio, 21 May 2002

— "My wife just thinks it's hilarious", Waits in Mick Brown, *Word*, December 2006

478 "By the time he got to" *et seq.*, Waits in *Bukowski: Born into This* (Magnolia Pictures), 2004

479 "I guess Jack was at a party", Waits in Mick Brown, *Word*, December 2006

— "It's based on a poem", Waits in Charles Champlin, *Los Angeles Times*, 14 January 1988

480 "I'd done the music already", Waits in Alexander Laurence, *Free Williamsburg.com*, February 2002

— "I pay attention", Waits in Sean O'Hagan, *Observer*, 29 October 2006

— "I had fun doing that song", Waits in Tim Perlich, *Now*, 16–22 November 2006

481 "simply swapped miniature film noir", Jonathan Romney, *Guardian*, 30 April 1999

482 "Personally I still prefer", Ian Penman, email, 21 January 2007

— "for much of the last decade", Tom Moon, *Harp*, November–December 2004

483 "[his] recent adoption as NPR-anointed National Treasure", David Smay, *Swordfishtrombones* (New York: Continuum, 2008), p. 8

— "forged more alliances", Robert Christgau, *Village Voice*, 9 July 2002

— "A bit like Wilson", David Kamp, author interview, 25 June 2007

— "a lot of critics don't like to admit it", Anthony DeCurtis in *Tom Waits under Review, 1983–2006* (Chrome Dreams DVD), 2007

— "something almost Shakespearean" *et seq.*, Simon Schama, *Guardian*, 9 December 2006

484 "I'm just a sad old boho romantic", Ian Penman, email, 21 January 2007

— "I'm just out here", Waits in Tim Perlich, *Now*, 16–22 November 2006

— "I just strike out", Waits in Andrew Dansby, *Houston Chronicle*, 19 November 2006

— "I don't know what made me go out" *et seq.*, Waits in Katherine Turman, *Stop Smiling*, 27 October 2006

486 "He's been playing drums", Waits in Amanda Petrusich, Pitchfork.com, 27 November 2006

— "I thought, 'Finally he's let go'", Mick Brown, author interview, 16 November 2007

— "One of the more touching parts" *et seq.*, Mark Kemp, email, 18 March 2008

487 "He kept going off on these long yarn-like tales", Tom Moon, email, 21 March 2008

— "got the three cherries", Waits in Ross Fortune, *Time Out*, 17–24 November 2004

— "Now when I go away", Waits in Mick Brown, *Word*, December 2006

— "[My kids] said I made up a war once", Waits, television interview, *Late Night with David Letterman*, 28 September 2004

488 "want to celebrate you", Waits, *The Times* online, 22 October 2004

— "I'm not one of those people", Waits in Ross Fortune, *Time Out*, 17–24 November 2004

— blog entry at http://juliafrancis.wordpress.com/2007/11/10/house-concert/

— "concept of privacy" *et seq.*, Steve Martin, *Born Standing Up: A Comic's Life* (London: Simon & Schuster, 2007), p. 184

489 "a deficit of wonder", Waits in Tom Moon, *Harp*, November–December 2004

— "The song is independent", Régine Chassagne, *Guardian*, 26 October 2007

— "we are buried beneath the weight of information" Waits, www.antilabelblog.com, 20 May 2008

490 "It was a story", Waits in Bob Mehr, *Memphis Commercial Appeal*, 21 January 2007

— "The minute you try to grab hold", Todd Haynes, Weinstein Company press notes for *I'm Not There*, 2007

— "not embarrassed" *et seq.*, Waits in George Varga, *San Diego Union Tribune*, 3 October 2004

— "Most of the big things", Waits in Jonathan Valania, *Magnet*, November 2004

— "what you really want to do", Waits in Katherine Turman, *Stop Smiling*, 27 October 2006

491 "It was constantly in the back of my mind", David Sitek, press release for Scarlett Johansson's *Anywhere I Lay My Head*, 2008

— "much more adventurous", Waits in Andrew Dansby, *Houston Chronicle*, 19 November 2006

492 "She's crucial, is she not", Sean O'Hagan, email, 19 March 2008

— "I love Tom Waits", Matt Bellamy, *Uncut*, 2007

— "grow old gracefully like Tom Waits", Mark Everett in Patrick Humphries, *The Many Lives of Tom Waits* (London: Omnibus, 2007), p. 306

— "I really appreciate him", Ry Cooder, author interview, 22 May 2008

— "a purity to what [Waits] does", Steve Vai in Ken Capobianco, *Cape Cod Times*, 28 March 2005

— "Nobody knows how long", Waits in Andrew Dansby, *Houston Chronicle*, 19 November 2006

493 "I don't like to be pinned down", Waits in Derk Richardson, *Pulse!*, September 1992

— "in a culture whose already classical dilemma", Susan Sontag, *Against Interpretation* (New York: Delta, 10th edition, 1978)

— "when man is capable", John Keats, letter to George and Thomas Keats, 21 December 1817, in *Letters of John Keats* (London: University of London Press, 1965)

— "My stance is the same", Stephen Hodges, author interview, 20 November 2007

Index